'The implications of Jones's study are wide ranging, shedding light on the vexed issues of the relationship between the City and the domestic economy, on the nature of overseas investment and imperialism, on the nature of British management and on the role of trust and knowledge in economic performance.'

Martin Daunton, Times Higher Education Supplement

'This book is original and subtle . . . It is essential reading for every economic and business historian interested in the history of multinational enterprise, in British economic history, and also in where British business fits in the evolution of the "world economy".'

Mira Wilkins, H-Business

'Jones has written a fine book. Rich in detail, it also uses transaction cost and other theoretical approaches, especially those concerned with business culture, cautiously but effectively. It should be the standard work on its subject for years to come.'

Peter Cain, Economic History Review

'Jones continues to expand the horizon of business and economic history from the "hard" topics of manufacturing and technology to encompass the "softer" service issues of trading, brokering, distribution, knowledge, and managerial culture . . . Utilizing a comparative context and corporate documents, he argues convincingly that British merchant firms were far more successful than previously portrayed. *Merchants to Multinationals* is a clear and coherent analysis of an elusive subject.'

Timothy Whisler, Business History Review

Merchants to Multinationals

British Trading Companies in the Nineteenth and Twentieth Centuries

GEOFFREY JONES

OXFORD

UNIVERSITY PRESS

This book has been printed digitally and produced in a standard specification
in order to ensure its continuing availability

OXFORD
UNIVERSITY PRESS

Great Clarendon Street, Oxford OX2 6DP

Oxford University Press is a department of the University of Oxford.
It furthers the University's objective of excellence in research, scholarship,
and education by publishing worldwide in

Oxford New York

Auckland Bangkok Buenos Aires Cape Town Chennai
Dar es Salaam Delhi Hong Kong Istanbul Karachi Kolkata
Kuala Lumpur Madrid Melbourne Mexico City Mumbai Nairobi
São Paulo Shanghai Taipei Tokyo Toronto

Oxford is a registered trade mark of Oxford University Press
in the UK and in certain other countries

Published in the United States
by Oxford University Press Inc., New York

ISBN 0-19-924999-7

Preface

This study of British trading companies over the last two centuries reflects my long-standing interests in the historical evolution of international business, and especially in the service sector. As in earlier books, I have followed the origins, growth, and performance of a group of firms over a long period of time, attempting to combine a search for systematic influences and trends with an awareness that firms operate in specific conditions of time and place. The result will have too many 'facts' for most theorists, and appear too general and deterministic to most historians, but I remain convinced that longitudinal studies that combine a search for the systematic with a recognition of the complexity of the real world are a promising means to deepen our understanding of the behaviour and performance of firms.

This book draws heavily on confidential business archives of trading companies and banks. I would like to thank the following companies and banks for allowing the use of their archives, either in their own hands or deposited in public institutions: Barclays Bank, Burmah Castrol, Inchcape, James Finlay, Jardine Matheson, John Swire & Sons, Elementis, HSBC, Lloyds Bank, and National Westminster Bank. Unilever provided access to accounting data on the United Africa Company, but was unable to allow access to that firm's archives as they are uncatalogued. However towards the end of this current research I was commissioned to write a history of Unilever between 1965 and 1990, and this permitted some new insights on UAC to be incorporated in this study. This research made great demands on many archivists and others responsible for corporate archives. I would like to thank John Booker, Jessie Campbell, Gill Dewhurst, Edwin Green, Derek Hammond, Martin Henderson, Kate Hutcheson, Sara Kinsey, Fiona MacColl, G. C. Pope, Andrew Riley, and Vanna Skelley. Among others who helped the research through talking about companies or through providing facilities, were Jeremy Brown, the late Sir Colin Campbell, Monica Clough, Duncan Gilmore, Edward Scott, Peter Sutch, Sir Adrian Swire, and Sir John Swire.

Financial support for this research came from the Economic and Social Research Council under grant R000 235612. This made possible the employment of Judith Wale as researcher on the project and the travel to archival collections held in various locations around Britain.

The greatest contribution to the book was made by Judith Wale. She undertook most of the archival research on Harrisons & Crosfield (now Elementis), Antony Gibbs, Balfour Williamson, and John Holt. As a qualified accountant, she also took responsibility for the analysis of accounts and the return on capital employed calculations. She continued to undertake research after her contract ended, and read and commented upon the earlier drafts of this book. This book could not have been written without Judith Wale's outstanding research contribution.

A number of academic colleagues read this manuscript in its penultimate stage and greatly improved it. David Merrett, an outstanding scholar who combines exceptional historical scholarship with a deep understanding of theory, told me what I wanted to say, following a tradition established in two previous books. Mary B. Rose, an expert on family businesses and the textile industry, corrected some of my misapprehensions about the eighteenth and nineteenth centuries, and about much else. Mira Wilkins, the doyen of historians of the multinational enterprise, provided a wonderful set of criticisms and suggestions. Teresa da Silva Lopes not only contributed her knowledge of the port wine industry, but provided valuable criticisms from the perspectives of international business theory. Among the many other scholars who have made valuable contributions to this research, I should especially like to thank Raj Brown, Mark Casson, Jean-François Hennart, Georgine Kryda, Ole Lange, Tom Roehl, Keetie E. Sluyterman, Kenichi Yasumuro, and Mary Yeager. This research has been presented over the last three years at seminars and conferences held in Aarhus, Athens, Budapest, Helsinki, Kobe, Lancaster, Oxford, Oslo, Reading, Terni, Uppsala, Urbana-Champaign, and Utrecht. The comments, criticisms, and patience of participants at these events were greatly appreciated.

Margaret Gallagher played a noteworthy role in getting this book ready for publication, engaging in heroic struggles both with computers and my handwriting. David Musson was the most understanding and supportive of editors at Oxford University Press. Finally I should thank Teresa for many things.

G. J.

Reading
June 1999

Contents

List of Figures

List of Tables

I

Trading Companies in Theory and History

1.1 Issues

The evolution, role, and theory of international business in the service sector remains underdeveloped compared to the attention given to manufacturing. In part this reflects the importance of manufacturing in the world economy after the Second World War, when the first theories to explain the 'multinational enterprise' were developed, and when historians began to search for their origins. In part the focus on manufacturing arises because steel or computers are so much more tangible than services. But at the beginning of the twenty-first century it is services—finance, trade and distribution, communications, and many others—which not only form the largest element of world foreign direct investment, but also the most dynamic.

This book is concerned with the evolution of an important component of international business in services—multinational trading companies. Multinational trading companies can be defined as firms that engage in trade intermediation between countries, and own assets in more than one country. In practice, 'trading companies' are very amorphous and difficult to identify for a number of reasons. They often engage in the provision of financial and transportation services, and it can be purely arbitrary if a firm is classified as a trading company or something else, such as a merchant bank or a shipping company. Moreover, a distinguishing feature of trading companies worldwide is their tendency to diversify from trading into related and unrelated activities. Consequently many 'pure' trading companies became 'hybrid' trading companies over time, and sometimes evolve further into oil, chemical, or other types of firm.[1]

There are further definitional problems arising from the considerable variations of function between trading companies. Trading companies may specialize by product, such as coal, grain, or sugar. Or they may specialize by region, handling multiple products or services but only within one region. General trading companies combine both regional and product-specific features to trade in many products in many regions. Historically, firms have changed function within these categories. Trade intermediation can be conducted through either broking—not assuming the ownership of the

---

[1] Mark Casson, 'The Economic Analysis of Multinational Trading Companies', in Geoffrey Jones (ed.), *The Multinational Traders* (London: Routledge, 1998), 22–47.

product being traded—or through reselling. Further distinctions can be drawn between trading companies which are independent entities, and those which are affiliated with, or part of, manufacturing or resource firms, such as the *maker-shosha* established by Japanese manufacturing multinationals in recent decades.

Though hard to define, multinational trading companies have been and remain significant in international business. Merchant enterprise, trading goods and services between communities, is the oldest form of international business, extending back thousands of years. Between the sixteenth and eighteenth centuries large integrated firms known as 'chartered trading companies' traded between Europe and the rest of the world on the basis of monopoly government contracts. The English and Dutch East India Companies, and the Hudson's Bay Company have been regarded by some as the first 'modern' multinationals.[2] These European chartered trading companies had largely disappeared by the mid-nineteenth century, as government monopolies were dismantled, but much European and Japan trade continued to be intermediated by trading firms. Japanese trading companies —especially the 'general trading companies' or *sogo shosha*—remained very important elements in the Japanese international trade after the Second World War and into the 1990s, when they still handled more than half of Japan's imports.[3] Historically, international trading companies appear less important in the case of the United States, though they certainly existed, and US-based commodity traders such as Cargill have become huge multinational enterprises in recent decades.[4]

The United Kingdom has been an important home to multinational trading companies. Britain's position as the birthplace of the Industrial Revolution led to its becoming the largest foreign trading economy in the nineteenth century. The multinational merchant firms or trading companies which developed from the eighteenth century to handle some of Britain's vast overseas trade, and which served as a model for the first generation of Japanese trading companies, are the central concern of this study. Although less studied than Japanese *sogo shosha*, the British trading companies are interesting for several reasons. Certainly before the interwar years and to some extent much later, they were both important in trade intermediation and as

---

[2] The literature on the chartered trading companies is considerable. For recent debates, see A. M. Carlos and S. Nicholas, ' "Giants of an Earlier Capitalism": The Chartered Trading Companies as Modern Multinationals', *Business History Review*, 62 (1988), 398–419; S. R. H. Jones and S. P. Ville, 'Efficient Transactions or Rent-Seeking Monopolists? The Rationale for Early Chartered Trading Companies', *Journal of Economic History*, 56 (1996), 818–915.

[3] Geoffrey Jones, *The Evolution of International Business* (London: Routledge, 1996), 148–51, 178–80, 181–7; id., 'Multinational Trading Companies in History and Theory', in Jones (ed.), *Multinational Traders*.

[4] Anne C. Perry, *The Evolution of U.S. Trade Intermediaries* (Westport, Conn.: Quorum Books, 1992). Lawrence A. Clayton, *Grace, W. R. Grace & Co.: The Formative Years 1850–1930* (Ottawa, Ill.: Jameson Books, 1985).

conduits for British foreign direct investment (FDI). Conceptually, they are interesting because many firms were organized and managed in different ways from their more-studied manufacturing counterparts. A number of firms also proved extremely long-lasting, and continue in business today. The study of these trading companies can, as a result, provide insights on a form of international business which remains little understood.

This book has three principal aims. The first is to establish the dimensions, functions, and rationale of British-based multinational trading companies over time. Their origins are traced back until the eighteenth and nineteenth centuries, though the bulk of the new research is on the twentieth century.[5] Indeed a central argument is that British trading companies did not cease to develop—or be important—at the time of the First World War, but continued to evolve up to the present day.

The second aim is to examine the business strategies over time of the British trading companies. In particular, it seeks to establish the circumstances under which they engaged in vertical integration and diversification, and the consequences of such strategies. The evolutionary approach taken here enables this 'reinvention' process to be examined in a long-term perspective.

The third aim is to identify the nature of the distinctive competences or capabilities from which British trading companies derived competitive advantages that enabled them to function and, in some cases, survive in a world where their environment underwent massive changes and experienced severe shocks over time. The process of diversification produced complex international businesses. International trading is risky, and the task of managing diversified business activities across borders is complex.

Trading companies have found little place in either theories of the firm and the multinational enterprise, or in the history of international business. The next two sections briefly review relevant concepts in theory and history and the place of trading companies in these literatures. A final section describes the methodology employed in the book.

1.2 Theory

This book will draw on concepts derived from the theory of the firm and of the multinational enterprise, but until recently these theories have had little to say about trading companies. Indeed, their general thrust has been to predict the demise of this type of firm in the twentieth century.

In neo-classical economic theory, trade occupies a central position as a major source of efficiency gains, but trading companies play no role in this story.

---

[5] There are excellent studies of the earlier history of British merchants overseas, especially Stanley Chapman, *Merchant Enterprise in Britain* (Cambridge: Cambridge University Press, 1992); and Charles A. Jones, *International Business in the Nineteenth Century* (Brighton. Wheatsheaf, 1987).

This reflects the general treatment of firms as 'black boxes' and the nature of the assumptions used in the traditional theory. There is no place for trade intermediaries in a world of perfect information and enforcement.

Transactions cost theory has provided a more realistic explanation of the growth of firms. Originating from Coase's pioneering work, as extended by Oliver Williamson and others, transaction cost theory considers firms and markets as representing alternative methods of organizing product markets. This theory suggests that the market is costly and inefficient for undertaking certain transactions, and for that reason firms internalize activities in order to minimize transactions costs. Transactions costs arise from opportunism, frailty of motive, bounded rationality, asset-specificity, uncertainty, frequency of transactions, small numbers, and information impactedness.[6] Transactions cost theory as applied to multinationals proposes that firms expand across borders because the transactions costs incurred in international intermediate product markets can be reduced by internalizing these markets within the firm. This theory predicts that cross-border transactions in intermediate goods, in goods where intangible assets such as patents, brands, and tacit know-how are essential competitive advantages, and in goods that require display and after sales service in foreign markets, will be undertaken through hierarchy rather than market exchange. It follows that merchant intermediaries will over time be displaced as manufacturing firms internalize their activities along production and distribution channels to overcome transactions costs. Principal-agent and contracting theories lend support to such an outcome by suggesting that manufacturing exporters would over time dispense with the services of merchants in foreign markets both because such firms required better information about the needs of customers, and because their 'agents' might behave opportunistically, or fail to invest in transaction-specific assets necessary to protect the firm's reputation.[7]

In the international business literature, the existence of multinational firms is often explained by combining transactions costs with other explanatory variables. An underlying assumption of many theories of the multinational is that a firm requires an 'advantage' in order to compete in an unfamiliar foreign environment, as local firms possess superior information about the

[6] R. H. Coase, 'The Nature of the Firm', *Economica*, 4 (1937), 386–405; Oliver Williamson, *Markets and Hierarchies* (New York: Free Press, 1975); id., 'Transaction cost economics: The Governance of Contractual Relations', *Journal of Law and Economics*, 22 (1979); id., 'The Modern Corporation: Origins, Evolution, Attributes', *Journal of Economic Literature*, 19 (1981); id., *The Economic Institutions of Capitalism* (New York: Free Press, 1985); id., 'Transaction Cost Economics: How it Works; Where it is Headed', *Berkeley CA: Business and Public Policy Working Paper, Haas School of Business, University of California* (Berkeley, Oct. 1997).

[7] J. C. McManus, 'The Theory of the Multinational Firm', in G. Paquet (ed.), *The Multinational Firm and the Nation State* (Don Mills, Ont.: Collier-Macmillan, 1972); Peter J. Buckley and Mark Casson, *The Future of the Multinational Enterprise* (London: Macmillan, 1976); J. F. Hennart, *A Theory of Multinational Enterprise* (Ann Arbor: University of Michigan Press, 1982); id., 'The Transactions Cost Theory of the Multinational Enterprise', in Christos N. Pitelis and Roger Sugden (eds.), *The Nature of the Transnational Firm* (London: Routledge, 1991).

markets, resources, and culture of their country. 'Ownership' advantages can derive from any number of factors, but given the focus on the literature on manufacturing most stress has been placed until recently on superior technology and management structures. 'Ownership' advantages are often joined with 'locational' advantages, which seek to explain why a company should undertake FDI in a foreign country rather than exploit its ownership advantage by exporting. These might include the size and income level of a market, resource endowments, or labour costs, but tariffs and non-tariff barriers to trade are especially important in the case of manufacturing multinationals insofar as that by making exporting difficult companies are encouraged to consider local production.

John H. Dunning's eclectic paradigm provides an organizing framework for the different theoretical approaches. The eclectic paradigm maintains that firms will engage in international production if they possess ownership advantages; if locational advantages make it more profitable to exploit its assets in a particular foreign location rather than at home; and if a firm considers there are advantages in exploiting these advantages themselves—internalization advantages.[8]

The Dunning paradigm has a limited place for multinational trading companies. In his wide-ranging application of his paradigm to the historical evolution of multinationals, Dunning notes the shift over the course of the nineteenth century from the 'age of merchant capitalism' to the new 'era of industrial capitalism', as 'modern multinationals' grew by internalizing their inputs, sales, and production. At least from the 1870s, Dunning suggests, manufacturers were concerned to integrate backwards into resource production and to replace sales agents in foreign markets for transactions cost reasons, or to exploit their ownership advantages. In this context, the changing composition of world production and trade apparently militated against merchant intermediaries, as from the late nineteenth century cross-border trade began to switch from bulk commodities to more complex goods, with manufacturers selling intermediate goods to one another, and their ownership advantages increasingly resting on the possession of intangible assets. Dunning observed the continued existence of trading companies, especially the Japanese firms, but suggested that their primary goal was by then to access raw material supplies.[9]

Although the main thrust of the theoretical literature on international business is to suggest a marginal role for trading companies in the 'era of

---

[8] John H. Dunning, *The Globalization of Business* (London: Routledge, 1993). The eclectic paradigm has been steadily expanded in scope over the decades. For its broadest rendition yet, see John H. Dunning, 'The Eclectic Paradigm as an Envelope for Economic and Business Theories of MNE Activity', *University of Reading, Department of Economics Discussion Papers in International Investment and Management*, vol. ii (1998/99), 1–43.

[9] J. H. Dunning, *Multinational Enterprises and the Global Economy* (Wokingham: Addison-Wesley, 1992), ch. 5.

industrial capitalism', the concepts discussed above can also be used to generate hypotheses to explain their continued existence. For example, multinational trading companies can be seen as possessing ownership advantages, but these are likely to be rather different from those possessed by manufacturing firms. In manufacturing industries, ownership advantages often reside in technologies which are protected by patents, although in industries such as automobiles there were technological advantages that had nothing to do with patents, and other advantages were associated with trade names that designated quality. In services, ownership advantages rest particularly in 'soft' skills, embodied in people rather than in machinery or other physical products. Knowledge, information, and human relationships often provide the ownership advantages of service sector firms.[10] This is likely to be especially true for trading companies. Although when trading companies diversify into natural resource exploitation or manufacturing they develop or acquire 'hard' technologies, in their core trading business the opposite is the case. Their fixed assets such as warehouses or wharves can be important, but in essence trading companies trade with other people's technologies, processes, and brands. They add value to such technologies and brands through their knowledge about markets and relationships and contacts with other firms, suppliers, and consumers.[11]

The importance of knowledge and information in the operations of trading companies points to both transactions and information cost explanations for their existence. As Casson has suggested, significant obstacles to trade arise from lack of trust and lack of information. These costs can be reduced by institutions such as trading companies which specialize in overcoming obstacles to trade on behalf of other people.[12] Information costs arise from the costs of market-making, such as finding a buyer or supplier, or fixing the specifications of intermediating activity.[13] Many of the advantages of trading companies might be explained by reputational and informational asymmetries. Trading companies can be seen as reducing search, negotiation, transaction, and information costs in international trade through their specialist knowledge of markets and business environments.

Moreover trading companies which specialize in particular markets or products might be able to generate efficiency advantages. Information once collected on markets or products can be seen as a quasi-public good within a firm in so far as there is little incremental cost to repeated use. Thus while a manufacturer selling its products to a foreign country collects information solely for the purpose of its own transaction, a trading company can

---

[10] Robert Grosse, 'International Technology Transfer in Services', *Journal of International Business Studies*, 27 (1996), 781–800.

[11] Perry, *Evolution*, 37–9.   [12] Casson, 'Economic Analyis'.

[13] Mark Casson, 'The Organisation and Evolution of the Multinational Enterprise: An Information Cost Approach', *Management International Review*, 39 (1999), 77–121; id., *Information and Organisation: A New Perspective on the Theory of the Firm* (Oxford: Clarendon Press, 1997).

sell information about a market to multiple buyers, thereby spreading the information costs among a larger number of transactions. Insofar as trading companies service multiple buyers and sellers, both marginal and average costs per purchaser of information are likely to be below the cost associated with direct procurement by individual firms. Moreover there will be scale economies in the acquisition of further information about a particular market or product insofar as the incremental costs of learning fall with the accumulation of market or product-specific knowledge. In addition, a broad information base can yield system-related information that cannot be obtained from more narrowly focused knowledge.

As Roehl has hypothesized to explain the existence of Japanese trading companies, the advantages of using a trading company as an intermediary are likely to depend on the characteristics of the product and the volume of trade. Roehl suggests that there are some standardized products and bulk commodities where market exchange is preferable to internalization because a specialized trading intermediary reduces the costs of transacting for both buyers and sellers.[14] Conversely, complexity of specification, difficulty of quality assurance, stability of supply and demand, and a high volume of trade are likely to encourage firms to trade directly without the use of intermediaries such as trading companies.

The above concepts also provide hypotheses about why trading companies might diversify into non-trading activities. Knowledge and know-how about markets can be employed to pursue other profit-making opportunities by exploiting economies of scope. Transactions costs arising from opportunism or information asymmetry can provide incentives for trading firms to integrate backwards or forwards. A distinctive feature of trading companies is that, by removing or reducing the obstacles to trade arising from information asymmetries and opportunism, they ultimately undermine their own business. Trading companies put buyers and sellers into contact, and as a result their business is always threatened by the possibility that their clients will deal directly with each other and save on the commission payments to the trading companies. The bargaining position of a trading company becomes weaker and the value of its information declines as clients become better informed. In order to survive trading companies might seek to pre-empt being excluded from transactions by taking equity stakes in suppliers and customers, or investing in entirely new activities to create new value-added chains.[15]

In summary, although theories of the multinational enterprise, internalization and agent-principal relationships point to the marginalization of trading companies in the twentieth century, they can provide hypotheses

---

[14] Thomas Roehl, 'A Transactions Cost Approach to International Trading Structures: The Case of the Japanese General Trading Companies', *Hitotsubashi Journal of Economics*, 24 (1983), 119–35.

[15] Jean-François Hennart and Georgine M. Kryda, 'Why do Traders Invest in Manufacturing?', in Jones (ed.), *The Multinational Traders*, 214–16.

to explain both their continued existence and their diversification strategies. Such explanations seem likely to reside in the areas of knowledge, information, reputation, and relationships. This book will seek to examine the existence and strategies of the British trading companies in the light of these hypotheses.

1.3 Evolution of International Business

Three decades of research have mapped out the chronology of the growth of international business, but large gaps remain in our knowledge.[16] The term 'multinational enterprise' was coined around 1960, and it was widely believed that the phenomenon itself was largely a post-Second World War one associated with the expansion of large US manufacturing multinationals such as IBM and Ford. International capital movements were known to have been large in the late nineteenth century, but they were believed to have largely taken the form of portfolio investment—not involving managerial control—rather than FDI, an investment in a foreign firm which involves managerial control. However from the 1970s many researchers reconsidered this view, and concluded that around one-third of world investment in 1914 was FDI rather than portfolio. In comparison to the world economy of the time, this made world FDI equal to around 9 per cent of world output in 1913. This proportion declined subsequently, and even in the 1990s FDI only represented around 8.5 per cent of world output.[17]

According to the widely cited Dunning estimates for 1914, the distribution of multinational investment was distinctive. Western Europe was the main home for world FDI, accounting for around 80 per cent of the total stock. The United Kingdom alone accounted for around 45 per cent. The United States held around 14 per cent of the total stock. The United States was also an important host economy—accounting for around 10 per cent of the world stock in 1914—but over one-half of world FDI was located in Latin America and Asia. By sector, at least one-half of world FDI was located in natural resources and almost one-third in services, leaving the remainder in the manufacturing sector.[18]

In essence, this structure remained in place until after the Second World War. Multinational investment continued to grow in the 1920s, with the United States probably becoming the largest home economy in terms of flows of FDI. Hundreds of US manufacturing companies established foreign factories, whilst US utilities invested heavily in Latin America and elsewhere. However it is most unlikely that the stock of US FDI reached that of Britain in the interwar years. According to the Dunning estimates, Britain still

---

[16] The following section draws heavily on Jones, *Evolution*.

[17] United Nations, *World Investment Report: Transnational Corporations, Employment and the Workplace* (New York: UNCTC, 1994), 130.

[18] Dunning, *Multinational Enterprises*, ch. 5.

accounted for 40 per cent of world FDI stock in 1938, and the United States 28 per cent. On the other hand, Germany, which had been a large direct investor before 1914, did not recover from the sequestration of most of its assets after the end of the First World War, and only accounted for a small percentage of the world FDI stock in 1938. Multinational investment as a whole seems to have been stagnant from the 1930s. The onset of the Great Depression, the spread of exchange controls, political instability, and falling commodity prices provided substantial disincentives for new multinational investment, while encouraging firms to join in collusive international cartels as an alternative strategy.

While this overall framework has won wide acceptance, the data supporting it is far from robust. No government before the Second World War made official estimates of the size of FDI except the United States. In other cases, the ratio of direct to portfolio investment has to be estimated from data (also unsatisfactory) for overall foreign investment. Attempts at such disaggregation encounter the particular problem of the institutional diversity of FDI before the Second World War.

When many manufacturing and other companies began making direct investments in foreign countries in the nineteenth century, they were already well-established firms in their own home countries. They had developed managerial and technical competences at home before investing abroad which enabled them to sustain their investments. This pattern was the norm in the case of US firms, but also many European firms. In his studies on the growth of modern industrial enterprises, Alfred D. Chandler Jnr has highlighted the importance of large firms, organization building, and professional management. For Chandler, the firms that became leading participants in the capital-intensive manufacturing industries which developed from the late nineteenth century onwards were those that made a substantial three-pronged investment in production, distribution, and management at a critical early stage, when markets were growing rapidly, and emergent technologies presented opportunities to achieve economies of scale and scope.[19] It was the international growth of such firms that was described by the first theories of the multinational enterprise developed in the 1960s. When business historians began to explain the history of these firms, the eclectic paradigm and transactions costs models were as a result found to be helpful and frequently applied.[20]

[19] A. D. Chandler, Jnr, *Strategy and Structure* (Cambridge, Mass.: MIT Press, 1962), id., *The Visible Hand* (Cambridge, Mass.: Harvard University Press, 1977); id., *Scale and Scope* (Cambridge, Mass.: Harvard University Press, 1990).

[20] S. Nicholas, 'British Multinational Investment before 1939', *Journal of European Economic History*, 11 (1982), 605–30; id., 'Agency Contracts, Institutional Modes, and the Transition to Foreign Direct Investment by British Manufacturing Multinationals before 1939', *Journal of Economic History*, 43 (1983), 675–86; Peter Hertner and Geoffrey Jones (eds.), *Multinationals: Theory and History* (Gower· Aldershot, 1986).

However it is now established that there were other types of firm engaged in international business in the nineteenth century and later. European firms often collaborated with one another abroad through consortium or joint ventures, and it was by no means clear whether a consequent investment fell into the category of portfolio or FDI. More seriously from the point of view of quantitative estimates, much European—and more especially British and Dutch—international business was undertaken by firms floated on the capital markets to undertake business activities exclusively or mainly abroad. Their presence in their home economies was usually no more than a small head office, and typically they specialized in a single commodity, product, or service, usually in a single country or region. Because these firms undertook no prior production in their home economies before investing abroad, early researchers did not identify them as a form of international business, but instead considered them as vehicles for portfolio investment.[21] It was the recognition that such firms exercised management control over their foreign operations and were consequently a form of FDI which led to the upward revision in the size of overall FDI, and made Britain by far the largest home economy. Current estimates of the size of British FDI before the Second World War are based on the issued capital of such specialized overseas firms, a methodology which is open to serious objections.[22]

In the mid-1980s these specialist overseas firms were given a name by Mira Wilkins—'free-standing firms'. She considered them to be 'the most typical mode of British direct investment before 1914'. These firms, the numbers of which she and others observed to run into thousands, were registered in Britain 'to conduct business overseas, much of which, unlike the American model, did not grow out of the domestic operations of existing enterprises that had headquarters in Britain'.[23] Later Wilkins promoted internationally collaborative research which established that this phenomenon was by no means confined to Britain and the Netherlands, though they would appear to have spawned the largest number before 1914.[24] The key importance of the concept, as Wilkins notes in her most recent study, lay 'in its demonstrating that the "classic" American model was not universal; it was not the only form of foreign direct investment'.[25]

---

[21] J. M. Stopford, 'The Origins of British-Based Multinational Manufacturing Enterprises', *Business History Review*, 48 (1974), 303–45.

[22] T. A. B. Corley, 'Britain's Overseas Investments in 1914 Revisited', *Business History*, 36 (1994), 71–88; Mira Wilkins, 'The Free-Standing Company Revisited', in Mira Wilkins and Harm Schröter (eds.), *The Free-Standing Company in the World Economy, 1830–1996* (Oxford: Oxford University Press, 1998), 51 n. 36 for a critical assessment.

[23] Mira Wilkins, 'Defining a Firm: History and Theory', in Hertner and Jones (eds.), *Multinationals*; id., 'The Free-Standing Company, 1870–1914: An Important Type of British Foreign Direct Investment', *Economic History Review*, 41 (1988), 259–85.

[24] Wilkins and Schröter (eds.), *The Free-Standing Company*.

[25] Mira Wilkins, 'The Significance of the Concept and a Future Agenda', in Wilkins and Schröter (eds.), *The Free-Standing Company*.

Wilkins and others have identified trading companies as forming an important element in this pattern of institutional diversity. In their origins as trade intermediaries and in the nature of their competences, they were different from manufacturing companies. They were especially removed from the 'American model' given that US-owned merchant enterprise was much less important than European or Japanese before (and after) the Second World War. British trading companies were also directly involved in 'free-standing' companies. Although much British FDI appeared to take the form of thousands of atomistic firms, many of these firms were linked to wider business networks. Wilkins called these 'clusters' and described how firms were linked in various ways with various degrees of robustness around their original promoters, financial intermediaries, lawyers, accountants, mining engineers, banks, merchants, and trading companies.[26] The process of diversification or 'reinvention' meant that trading companies engaged in FDI not only in trade and distribution facilities in foreign countries, but also in other economic activities. As later chapters will describe, they often did this by promoting 'free-standing' companies.

In her analysis of 'clusters', Wilkins was influenced by the work of Chapman on British merchants before 1914.[27] In a series of studies Chapman showed how British merchants in the nineteenth century evolved into diversified business groups. Chapman termed these as 'investment groups'. He identified thirty leading British-based investment groups active before 1914 divided into regional specialists in Asia, Latin America, Russia, and South Africa. Chapman argued that their main function was financial. 'There can be no serious doubt', he concluded, 'that the investment group was primarily a device to maintain the growth and power of the family (or families) that contributed the particular business.'[28]

This book seeks to build on, and test, the concepts and hypotheses developed by Wilkins and Chapman. It remains quite unknown how many 'clusters' or 'investment groups' existed. Turrell and van Helten have argued, for example, that Chapman's concept lacks clarity as he uses the same term for both merchants and South African mining groups.[29] Certainly the task of identifying 'investment groups' or 'clusters' is not especially easy as they were rather amorphous in character with permeable boundaries, and many of them were to disappear over the course of the twentieth century. Regional specialists are now busy identifying more British 'investment groups' than those found by Chapman.[30]

---

[26] Wilkins, 'The Free-Standing Company'.

[27] Wilkins, 'The Free-Standing Company Revisited', 13–14.

[28] Stanley Chapman, 'British-Based Investment Groups before 1914', *Economic History Review*, 38 (1985), 243; Chapman, *Merchant Enterprise*.

[29] R. Turrell and Jean Jacques van Helten, 'The Investment Group: The Missing Link in British Overseas Expansion before 1914', *Economic History Review*, 40 (1987), 267–74; Stanley Chapman, 'Investment Groups in India and South Africa', *Economic History Review*, 40 (1987), 275–80.

[30] Chapman, *Merchant Enterprise*, 254–6; Charles Jones, 'Institutional Forms of British Foreign Direct Investment in South America', *Business History*, 39 (1997), 21–41.

This literature also poses questions about the competences and capabilities of the trading companies. In her original work on free-standing companies, Wilkins pointed to their lack of managerial hierarchies and suggested that they were fated for extinction over the long term, and indeed suggested that their days were largely over by 1914.[31] This view fitted well with the model proposed by Alfred D. Chandler to explain why Britain fell behind the United States in the development of the new capital-intensive manufacturing industries of the late nineteenth century. Chandler pointed to the growth in the United States of large firms managed by professional managers who were able to invest in mass production and mass marketing, which he termed 'managerial capitalism' and contrasted this with the continued British preference for 'personal capitalism', atomistic firms often owned and managed by families.[32]

Although Chandler was concerned to identify the organizational structures necessary to compete in capital-intensive manufacturing, his critique of British 'personal capitalism' was applied by Chapman in his analysis of the managerial competences of his 'investment groups'. Chapman demonstrated that his 'investment groups' sometimes reached a formidable size —running counter to the Chandlerian view that the problem with British business from the late nineteenth century was its inability to create larger units—but in other respects Chapman supported the Chandlerian critique of 'personal capitalism'. Chapman described the continuation of family influence and the retention of the partnership form which, he argued, often led to 'nepotism' and failure. Chapman's study ended in 1914 with the impression that the British 'investment groups' had lost entrepreneurial drive, and that new opportunities were being lost, though Chapman never lost sight of the diversity of these groups and of their performance.[33]

The issue of the managerial competences of these groups and their subsequent fate remains controversial. If managerial structures and control from Britain were weak or transient, then the classification of free-standing firms and investment groups as FDI is misconceived.[34] In previous studies, the present author has argued that in the case of British overseas banks, which created and managed extensive multinational branch networks in the nineteenth century and later, the lack of US-style managerial structures did not necessarily mean weak or fragile management. British banks made more use of socialization methods rather than bureaucracy to control foreign managers and to reduce agency costs.[35] This seems to have been a feature

---

[31] Wilkins, 'The Free-Standing Company'.   [32] Chandler, *Scale and Scope*.

[33] Chapman, *Merchant Enterprise*, 292, 309.

[34] Mark Casson, 'Institutional Diversity in Overseas Enterprise: Explaining the Free-Standing Company', *Business History*, 36 (1994), 95–108.

[35] Geoffrey Jones, *British Multinational Banking 1830–1990* (Oxford· Clarendon Press, 1993); id., 'British Overseas Banks as Free-Standing Companies, 1830–1996', in Wilkins and Schröter (eds.), *The Free-Standing Company*, 344–60.

of British and other European overseas business in general.[36] In the context of the wider literature on British economic history, the view that merchant enterprise had lost entrepreneurial drive by 1914 certainly looks curious. The widely cited Cain and Hopkins thesis on 'gentlemanly capitalism' emphasizes the dynamic role and continuing influence in Britain of the City of London in particular and services in general. Bankers, merchants, and foreign investment lay at the heart of this story, and continued to do so through the interwar years and beyond.[37] On this view, merchants formed a resilient form of business enterprise in Britain.

By examining in detail the evolving role of trading companies in British foreign direct investment, and their creation of free-standing companies and diversified business groups, this book will provide new empirical information to explore these various suggestions in the literature on the history of international business. In particular it will address how trading companies organized and controlled their international operations, the degree to which family ownership posed a competitive handicap, and whether by 1914 they had indeed lost entrepreneurial dynamism.

1.4 Methodology

This book examines the dimensions and functions, business strategies, and managerial competences of British multinational trading companies over the last two centuries. Although it draws on a great deal of new archival research, the approach is inevitably broad-brush and does not seek to provide a comprehensive history of British merchants overseas in this period, and still less of individual firms. Given the problems of definition already discussed, the inclusion or exclusion of a firm in this study is arbitrary. The term 'trading company' was not in general use in Britain until recently, and contemporaries used a variety of terms, including merchants, agency house, and managing agency. This study will use these terms interchangeably.

A number of criteria have been used to define a 'trading company' for purposes of this study. First, such firms had to be engaged in international trade. Secondly, their business had not to be confined to the export from, or import to, Britain solely from branches located in the United Kingdom, but had to include 'control' of assets in overseas countries. This latter characteristic is especially not clear-cut in the nineteenth century, when although

---

[36] Jones, 'Institutional Forms'; Robert G. Greenhill, 'Investment Group, Free-Standing Company or Multinational? Brazilian Warrant, 1909–52', *Business History*, 37 (1995), 86–111; Geoffrey Jones, 'British Multinationals and British Business since 1850', in Maurice W. Kirby and Mary B. Rose (eds.), *Business Enterprise in Modern Britain from the Eighteenth to the Twentieth Centuries* (London: Routledge, 1994), 188–9; Jones, *Evolution*, 161–2.

[37] P. J. Cain and A. G. Hopkins, *British Imperialism: Innovation and Expansion 1688–1914* (London: Longman, 1993); id., *British Imperialism: Crisis and Deconstruction 1914–1990* (London: Longman, 1993).

some British-based merchant firms undertook FDI by owning, and controlling overseas branches, the more typical pattern was one of interlocking partnerships. Some 'British' firms were legally domiciled in colonies without a base in the United Kingdom at all. These firms were managed and owned by Britons, but not from Britain, although in some cases when partners retired back to Britain from abroad they retained shareholdings and 'influence' of various kinds in their old firms. The process of 'reinvention' raises further definitional problems. A 'trading company' in one generation might be better described as a bank, mining company, or chemicals firm in the next generation, and this raises the problem when a firm should 'exit' from the study. The practice adopted here has been to continue to regard a firm as a trading company until such time as its business portfolio makes this clearly inappropriate.

The firms included in this study are given uneven treatment in terms of the amount of space and attention given to them. This is a consequence of the selective approach taken here. It also reflects the difficulties of research in this area, insofar as the historical records of most firms have disappeared or, for one reason or another, are not available. The generalizations presented here rest on the histories of firms about which information has survived and/or is accessible. Consequently there is a bias also towards large firms which survived rather than the far more numerous population of merchant firms which did not. This survivorship bias means that the firms chosen for attention are not 'representative' in a statistical sense. However these firms are widely dispersed by host region, size, performance, and even survival.

This study offers data on the size and performance of the trading companies in order to provide at least a basic quantitative framework. It is difficult to quantify even the dimensions of British trading companies before 1914—and in many cases later—because of the use of the partnership form, and non-equity modes to control affiliate firms, and sheer data unavailability. Nevertheless an attempt has been made and in this study data on capital employed is calculated for many firms for the benchmark years of 1913, 1938, 1954, 1978, and 1997. The sources for these figures are given in Appendix 3. Capital employed is share capital (ordinary and preference) plus reserves (including profit and loss balance) plus debentures plus any other long-term loans. A more conventional measure of size such as market value of capital cannot be used because so few firms had their shares publicly quoted, at least until the Second World War.

The diversification of trading companies creates problems for the measurement of size. There is a major distinction between the capital employed in the parent company or partnership and the larger amounts of capital controlled by the parent through contracts, interlocks, and equity stakes in affiliate firms. The benchmark tables for 1913 and 1938 are for the size of capital employed for the parent company only. When the partnership form was used, the estimates attempt to add together all the partnerships. For the later benchmark years, the capital employed figures have been taken from the consolidated accounts for the group which UK-based companies were obliged to publish by the 1948 Companies Act. These group accounts included not only all the capital employed in majority-owned subsidiaries, but also a proportion of capital employed for large minority stakes (related to the percentage shareholding in 'associated' companies and joint ventures). They continued however to exclude affiliates in which the parent held only a small equity stake.

An attempt is made to quantify the performance of the firms over time using the standard measure known as return on capital employed (ROCE). Annual post-tax ROCE—profit after tax as a percentage of capital employed —has been calculated for a substantial number of trading companies from 1895 to 1998, and is given in Appendix 1. Before 1895 the near-universal use of the partnership form and the lack of partnership accounts make it not possible to calculate performance using this measure. Following the additional disclosure requirements introduced by the Companies Act in 1948, it is also possible to provide annual pre-tax ROCE. This has been provided for 1948 to 1998 in Appendix 2. The criteria for inclusion in this analysis has been data availability. This biases the sample towards long-lived firms, which can be presumed to have had better ROCE than less 'successful' firms.

ROCE calculations provide a valuable means to compare inter-firm differences in performance over time. They are particularly useful in allowing valid comparisons between firms of different sizes. However they are based on published accounts, at a time when accounting conventions and lack of legislation in Britain before 1948 permitted the existence of undisclosed reserves. In the case of British overseas banks, undisclosed reserves were sometimes substantial, as was the difference between published and 'real' profits.[38] For the trading companies there is a dearth of surviving internal accounts which reveal the internal reserves position. On the other hand, an extensive scrutiny of British company balance sheets before 1924, internal as well as published, demonstrates that not all companies used undisclosed reserves.[39] Over a sufficiently long timespan the main performance trends can be discerned from published accounts and inter-firm differences can be identified.

There are a number of influences on the ROCE calculation. A small capital employed has the effect of exaggerating both good and poor profit performances, and in general makes ROCE figures appear more volatile. Consequently the structure of a firm's business has to be taken into account when noting inter-firm differences. Firms with substantial mining investments have large net assets which dampen ROCE figures. Similarly firms

---

[38] Jones, *British Multinational Banking*, 73–4, 423 ff.

[39] A. J. Arnold, '"Publishing Your Private Affairs to the World": Corporate Financial Disclosures in the U.K. 1900–24', *Accounting, Business and Financial History*, 7 (1997).

with long-term commitments of funds in fixed assets such as offices, ware-houses, and port facilities have the effect of raising the denominator in the ROCE calculation and making the percentage return lower. In general ROCE can be expected to fluctuate substantially for trading companies which usually have large amounts of working capital-stock, trade debtors, and creditors. In summary, while ROCE data might indicate superior manage-ment quality or performance, this is not necessarily so.

The following four chapters analyse the dimensions, functions, and strategies of British trading companies from the late eighteenth century to the end of the 1970s. They will examine and explain the process of 'reinven-tion' and the reasons for the survival of a group of firms long after the 'age of merchant capitalism' had ended. The subsequent five chapters con-sider in more detail their competences in corporate governance, human resources, and relationship building, and their long-lasting investments in natural resources and manufacturing. A final chapter before the conclusion surveys their fate over the last two decades.

2

Foundations

2.1 Introduction

This chapter reviews the emergence of British-owned trading companies in the century before 1870. This was the crucial formative stage of British multinational merchant enterprise. British merchants spread around the ports of the world as trade grew exponentially and the boundaries of the British Empire expanded. From the heterogeneous and changing population of merchant houses, a number of larger and more stable firms had emerged by 1870. These British merchant firms embedded themselves in their host economies at an early stage in their modern economic development, acquiring knowledge and information, which they were able to exploit in many cases for much of the twentieth century.

It was during these decades that the British merchant houses began to diversify, from—in many cases—importing British goods to exporting the 'local' commodities of the countries in which they became established, and then into other services such as shipping agencies, and occasionally into the ownership of plantations and other fixed assets. Indeed the century before 1870 is of great interest because of the fluidity of firm strategies. The distinction between merchanting and banking was, for example, still not rigid, while merchant firms could shift the base of the operations from one continent to another in response to changing opportunities. By 1870 functional and geographical patterns of specialization were already beginning to establish tighter parameters to the extent to which a firm could 'reinvent' itself.

The following section briefly reviews the historical environment which shaped the strategies of the British merchant firms. This is followed, in section 2.3, by an analysis of the origins and growth of British trading companies in their main host regions. Section 2.4 turns to the new generation of companies which emerged during the 1850s and 1860s.

2.2 Britain and the World Economy

The emergence of British-owned multinational trading companies was inextricably related to the expansion of international trade in the nineteenth century, which provided a new scale of opportunities for trade intermediaries. The value of international trade doubled between 1830 and 1850, and may have quadrupled in the following thirty years. In per capita terms, world trade grew at over 50 per cent per decade between 1840 and 1870, far faster than world output per head.[1]

The Industrial Revolution, which had begun in Britain and made that country the world's largest manufacturing country by 1800, was the root cause of the growth of world trade. During the first half of the nineteenth century the Industrial Revolution was diffused to the neighbouring economies of France and Belgium, and thereafter it spread further to Germany and Sweden, and across the Atlantic to the United States. The industrialized areas sought markets for their products and also raw materials for their industries, and foodstuffs for urban populations. These new opportunities for trade were increased by changes in the policy environment. In the early nineteenth century governments imposed numerous obstacles to trade in the form of duties and tariffs. However from the 1840s Britain began to dismantle its protectionism and by 1860 it was more or less a 'free trade' economy. Other nations followed and—temporarily—trade barriers fell.

Britain's position in the international economy at this time was unique. It remained the world's largest manufacturing country until the 1880s, when British output was overtaken by that of the United States. If the whole economy rather than manufacturing alone is considered, as measured by Gross Domestic Product (GDP), Britain was the largest economy in western Europe throughout the nineteenth century, but it was overtaken by the United States around 1850, though even in 1870 there was little difference in the overall size of the two economies.

Britain played a central role in the expansion of world trade. British trade with Europe had expanded considerably in the eighteenth century, and in the same period Britain was a key participant in the growing Atlantic economy, including the slave trade as well as trade in sugar, hardwoods, and other commodities. The next century saw an even faster growth in trade. Britain's total exports grew at nearly 6 per cent per annum between 1831 and 1857, and by 3.5 per cent between 1857 and 1873.[2] In 1840 Britain accounted for around 27 per cent of total world trade. It was almost 26 per cent in 1860, before falling to 19 per cent in 1870.[3] Trade was relatively much more important to Britain than other European economies. Exports comprised over 11 per cent of Britain's gross national product in 1850, compared to the European average of 7.0 per cent respectively.[4] In contrast, international trade was far less important for the economy of the United States in the nineteenth century, whose rapid growth was on the basis of its expanding domestic market.

[1] A. G. Kenwood and A. L. Lougheed, *The Growth of the International Economy 1820–1990* (London: Routledge, 1992), 66–7, 78–9.

[2] Charles Feinstein, 'Exports and British Economic Growth (1850–1914)', in Peter Matthias and John A. Davis (eds.), *The Nature of Industrialisation* (Oxford: Blackwell, 1996), 78.

[3] Peter Davies, 'Nineteenth-Century Ocean Trade and Transport', ibid. 68.

[4] Sidney Pollard, 'British Trade and European Economic Development (1750–1850)', ibid. 36.

Textiles dominated British exports. British exports of cotton goods grew from around 16 per cent of total exports in 1794–6 to almost 48 per cent in 1824–6. They reached 48.5 per cent in 1834–6, before dipping to 34 per cent in 1854–6.[5] Woollen goods accounted for a smaller but still significant share of British exports—around 10 per cent in the first half of the century—and the metal manufacturing industry accounted for most of the remainder. The British textiles and metal manufacturers were heavily export-dependent. The share of exports in the final product value of the cotton industry was 50 per cent throughout the nineteenth century; for the iron products the share was 20–30 per cent in the first half of the century and 40 per cent in the second half.[6] Britain imported few manufactured goods, and the share of manufactured goods in total imports may have been as low as 2 per cent in 1850. At the same date raw materials, dominated by raw cotton, comprised almost two-thirds of British imports, with food products accounting for the remainder.

The British exported their mass-produced, semi-finished goods especially to Europe. Europe took 23 per cent of total British cotton goods exports in 1794–6 rising to 51 per cent in 1824–6. The proportion was 47 per cent in 1834–6, and 29 per cent in 1854–6. The United States was the other main market. The United States and Australia took 72 per cent out of British cotton goods exports in 1794–6: this had fallen to 31 per cent in 1854–6. In contrast developing economies were initially unimportant as a market. The export of cotton piece-goods to India only began in 1814, though by the 1850s India took nearly 20 per cent of British exports of cotton goods. The sources of British imports were rather different. The growth of the raw cotton trade, which was heavily oriented towards the southern United States, meant that the United States became the main source of imports by the middle of the nineteenth century, replacing the West Indies, India, and Brazil as the main sources of supply. From Europe Britain imported grain and timber from the Baltic, tar, hemp, and flax from Russia, and wines and spirits from France, Portugal, and Spain.

The nineteenth century also saw accelerating capital as well as trade flows. British capital exports began in earnest after the end of the Napoleonic Wars, and for the rest of the century Britain was the world's largest capital exporter. London emerged from the wars as the financial centre of the world, displacing Amsterdam. After 1815 capital exports went first to elsewhere in Europe, and then in the 1820s there was a speculative boom in overseas lending to the newly independent Latin American republics. After some major defaults, British capital exports were attracted into the building of railroads in Europe, Canada, and the United States. From the mid-1850s British capital

---

[5] Ralph Davis, *The Industrial Revolution in British Overseas Trade* (Leicester: Leicester University Press, 1979), 15.

[6] C. H. Lee, *The British Economy since 1700* (Cambridge: Cambridge University Press, 1986), 109–10.

exports began to accelerate, as savings accumulated in the British economy as a result of industrialization, and as the demand for capital abroad expanded, especially as a result of railroad building. The late 1850s saw the first large loans to finance Indian railroad construction, but the United States was the main area for investment, until the outbreak of the Civil War (1861–5) followed in 1866 by a major financial crisis in London, which dislocated the capital markets and led to a low level of overseas lending until another boom in the 1870s.

By the mid-1870s British capital holdings abroad amounted to around £1,000 million to £1,200 million, or at least twice as much as the next largest capital exporter, France. British capital exports amounted to around 5 per cent of GDP by this period, which was not insubstantial although considerably smaller than the level seen in the years before 1914. By far the greatest proportion—around 40 per cent—was invested in railroads, sometimes financed directly and sometimes via loans to foreign governments. At mid-century, Europe and the United States received about one-half of British capital exports, but thereafter Europe's share declined rapidly, while countries of recent settlement in the British empire (e.g. Australia and Canada) and Latin America began to grow in importance.[7] The existing patchy evidence would suggest that most of this investment was portfolio in nature, and that the real growth of British FDI took place after 1870. Stone's research in British investment in Latin America estimates that the portfolio share was nearly 80 per cent in 1865, and that it was sometime from the mid-1870s that British FDI began to become relatively more important.[8]

A final aspect of Britain's importance in the world economy was its empire. While the American War of Independence deprived Britain of its colonies in what became the United States, the British retained or established settlements in Canada, the West Indies, Australia, and southern Africa. From the 1750s the East India Company (EIC) had begun to assume governing as well as trading functions in parts of India, beginning a slow process which led, in 1858, to the British government itself assuming control over most of India. During the first half of the nineteenth century the borders of the empire continued to expand, as the British took control and developed key ports on major Asian trade routes, such as Penang (1786), Singapore (1819), and Hong Kong (1842).

Although Britain's importance in world trade and the spread of its empire does not 'explain' the use of merchants as trade intermediaries, it does make clear the scale of the competitive advantage derived by British merchant firms from their home economy which was the world's largest foreign trader and its largest capital exporter. British colonial possessions

---

[7] P. L. Cottrell, *British Overseas Investment in the Nineteenth Century* (London: Macmillan, 1975); Sidney Pollard, 'Capital Exports, 1870–1914: Harmful or Beneficial?', *Economic History Review*, 38 (1985), 489–514; Charles Feinstein, 'Britain's Overseas Investments in 1913', *Economic History Review*, 43 (1990), 280–95.

[8] I. Stone, 'British Direct and Portfolio Investment in Latin America before 1914', *Journal of Economic History*, 37 (1977), 690–722.

were also scattered over much of the world, providing a unique global network of ports and markets for them to conduct business with and in.

2.3 Merchants and Bankers

The origins of Britain's multinational trading companies are to be found in the complex web of merchant enterprise which flourished in the eighteenth and early nineteenth centuries alongside the expansion of British foreign trade. In the wake of the Industrial Revolution, the end of the Napoleonic Wars, and the growth of free trade, a multitude of merchants, both in Britain and resident abroad, were engaged in selling British manufactured goods, primarily textiles, overseas, and importing low-cost raw materials. As the monopoly trading rights held by chartered trading companies were given up, there were spectacular new opportunities for trade by new generations of merchants. Merchants faced literally a world of opportunities, but their world was also a very volatile one. This was partly because of the great risks of overseas trade, and partly because merchants were organized not as modern 'firms' with limited liability, but as either individual proprietorships or partnerships. Generally partnership agreements specified a set length for the agreement—usually three or five years—as well as laying down the terms, such as each partners' share of profits or losses, and the amount each partner could withdraw in a year. When a partner retired or otherwise left a business, the most frequent outcome was that his capital and name were withdrawn from it.

There was a long tradition of mercantile enterprise in Britain. Britain's flourishing trade across the Atlantic in the eighteenth century passed through the intermediation of merchants largely based in London, the country's leading port, and a major international service centre where merchants from many countries settled and conducted business.[9] A noteworthy feature of London at this time was a cluster of large firms with considerable capital—the largest of which included the Bank of England, insurance companies such as London Assurance and the Royal Exchange Assurance, and 'chartered' trading companies led by the East India Company, whose boards or 'courts' of directors were made up of leading merchants and bankers.[10] In the nineteenth century there were still survivors of the earlier age of chartered trading companies. Although the Royal African Company was disbanded in 1712 and the Muscovy Company in 1746, the East India Company retained

[9] Stanley Chapman, *Merchant Enterprise in Britain* (Cambridge: Cambridge University Press, 1992), chs. 2 and 3; J. H. Soltow, 'Scottish Traders in Virginia, 1750–1775', *Economic History Review*, 12 (1959); Jacob M. Price, *Capital and Credit in British Overseas Trade: The View from the Chesapeake, 1700–1776* (Cambridge, Mass.: Harvard University Press, 1980); David Hancock, *Citizens of the World* (Cambridge: Cambridge University Press, 1995).

[10] Barry Supple, *The Royal Exchange Assurance* (Cambridge: Cambridge University Press, 1970), 52–80; K. N. Chaudhuri, *The Trading World of Asia and the English East India Company 1660–1760* (Cambridge: Cambridge University Press, 1978).

a monopoly of Britain trade with India until 1813, and with China until 1834, and was only wound up in 1858. The Hudson's Bay Company, chartered in 1670, proved even more resilient. The firm, controlled from its London headquarters, owned lands and exclusive trading rights over a huge area of Canada, and merged with its non-chartered rival in 1821 to secure a monopoly over the fur trade. It sold its furs in the large London fur warehouse which it owned until 1870. In the late 1850s the firm lost its legal right as a trading monopoly in western Canada, and in 1863 the firm's shares were acquired by a consortium of London merchant bankers who six years later sold much of its western land to the new Dominion of Canada. But the Hudson's Bay Company continued in existence as a British-owned trading company, diversifying into non-fur trade and into retailing.[11]

Merchants formed an essential component of British overseas trade during the Industrial Revolution and subsequently. The cotton textile industry depended on an imported input, and consequently trade and merchants were an essential component of British industrialization. The Lancashire cotton spinning and weaving firms, the great majority of whom were small family firms, used merchants also to sell their products. In the eighteenth and early nineteenth centuries only a few of the larger textile manufacturers combined manufacturing with overseas selling, generally using agents in the American and other markets. A specialized structure emerged with merchant houses based in Liverpool buying raw cotton, wholesale merchants based in London selling textiles to the domestic market, while Manchester was the centre for merchants engaged in the export trade. From the 1790s foreign merchants, especially Germans and later Greeks and others, settled in Manchester, often as agents for continental firms. They brought with them knowledge of the requirements of their home economy, relationships with merchants in that economy, and sometimes links with financiers—also foreign born—in the City of London. These foreign-born merchants dominated the export of cotton textiles to the Continent, and Britain's foreign trade generally, given that in the first half of the nineteenth century over half of British manufactured goods went to continental markets. Sales of British textiles to the American market similarly largely passed through the Manchester merchants, including some agents of American firms with other European countries and the United States in the early nineteenth century, but from the 1830s and 1840s such merchants were often continental Europeans or Americans who opened offices in Britain to buy textiles for their home markets. Germans, including German Jews, were especially prominent in the export of British cotton textiles.[12]

---

[11] Anon., *Hudson's Bay Company: A Brief History* (London: the firm, 1934); Graham D. Taylor and Peter A. Baskerville, *A Concise History of Business in Canada* (Toronto: Oxford University Press, 1994), *passim*.

[12] Stanley Chapman, 'The Commercial Sector', in Mary B. Rose (ed.), *The Lancashire Cotton Industry* (Preston: Lancashire County Books, 1996), 79–82; Chapman, *Merchant Enterprise*, ch. 5.

A number of the foreign merchant houses evolved into 'merchant banks', such as the Rothschilds and Schröders. The general pattern of the transition from merchanting into finance of this group of firms was for trading activities, such as acting as agents for overseas merchants, to lead into banking, as the firms came to collect bills of exchange for customers and deal in foreign exchange. Firms which held a sound reputation developed an 'accepting business' which involved the provision of credits to their merchant customers under which they guaranteed to pay bills of exchange at maturity. This guarantee or 'acceptance' facilitated the discount of the bills, and this mechanism became the major means for financing world trade in the nineteenth century. Merchant banks received a commission for accepting bills which over time replaced trading as their main income source. Their reputations and networks of overseas customers and contacts also led them into the business of 'issuing' on the London market the securities of overseas governments and companies.[13]

The process whereby this group of merchants were 'reinvented' into bankers was long drawn out and firm specific. By 1820 the Rothschilds in London had almost totally specialized in financing trade and loans rather than trading on their account, and can be regarded as a 'merchant bank'. However, over the rest of the nineteenth century the Rothschilds took a wide view of their role as bankers, engaging in commodity dealing, insurance, and taking large equity stakes in such mining firms as De Beers and Rio Tinto.[14] Many of the firms later to become leading London merchant banks were as much embryonic multinational trading companies as banks in this period.[15]

In the case of Barings, while loan issues and other financial activities were extremely important for the firm, during the 1830s and 1840s the 'merchanting' side of the business was renewed. The firm established a Liverpool house in 1832 which became one of the leading cotton importers before 1850. A fleet of cargo ships was briefly acquired for trade with Asia, while trading in commodities such as sugar, tea, coffee, and indigo even led to Barings becoming the owner of plantations, used as security for unpaid debts.[16] A cluster of Anglo-German merchant houses, notably Schröders, Huth and Hambro, also continued to combine merchanting and banking through to the

[13] Stanley Chapman, *The Rise of Merchant Banking* (London: George Allen & Unwin, 1984), 1–15.

[14] Niall Ferguson, *The World's Banker The History of the House of Rothschild* (London: Weidenfeld & Nicolson, 1998), 878–90; Miguel A. López Morell, 'Los Rothschild y Rio Tinto: La influencia del sector financiero en la gran minería (1886–1936)' (University of Seville Tesina, 1996; revised version, 1999).

[15] David Kynaston, *The City of London*, vol. i (London: Chatto & Windus, 1994) provides an excellent study of the world of merchants and bankers in the nineteenth-century City of London.

[16] Ralph W. Hidy, *The House of Baring in American Trade and Finance: English Merchant Bankers at Work, 1763–1861* (Cambridge, Mass.: Harvard University Press, 1949). John Orbell, *Baring Brothers & Co Limited: A History to 1939* (London: the firm, 1985), 30–1; D. M. Williams, 'Liverpool Merchants and the Cotton Trade 1820–1850', in J. R. Harris (ed.), *Liverpool and Merseyside* (London: Frank Cass, 1969), 191, 197.

late nineteenth century. Schröders was organized as interlocked partnerships in London, Hamburg, and—from 1839—Liverpool, and were especially active in trading a wide range of commodities, including Russian grain, American cotton, and Cuban sugar.[17]

A crude distinction between the merchants which eventually evolved into bankers and those that remained merchants and developed into trading companies was ethnic origins. While the great majority of merchant banks originated from emigrant merchants, the trading companies were overwhelmingly British. British merchant enterprise was well established in Europe and elsewhere in the eighteenth century. In the eighteenth century Britain had been Russia's main trading partner. Russian primary commodities such as timber were of great importance for Britain, and a chartered company—the Russia Company—was in existence. British merchant houses were heavily involved in the Russian export trade. During the first half of the nineteenth century their influence waned along with the importance of Britain as a trading partner of Russia, and they never established a strong position in the major Russian export commodity of the nineteenth century, grain, even though Britain was the largest export market for Russian wheat in the early decades. In their place German merchants grew in importance as Germany became Russia's most important trading partner. They often took over established British merchant houses, a trend which seems to have been increased by the Crimean War of the 1850s, when the grain trade was totally disrupted.

However a number of British merchant houses of the eighteenth century continued in business. The Wishaw family began trading in Russia in the late eighteenth century, and became a substantial grain exporter in St Petersburg. Even larger were the Hubbards, which family had also established links with Russia in the late eighteenth century. The Hubbards' business was organized into partnerships in London and St Petersburg, and they were ranked one of the top ten trading houses there between the 1830s and the 1860s. In Russia they offered banking services, and in 1842 diversified into manufacturing when they opened a cotton spinning mill. This was followed by investments in textile weaving and printing.[18]

Among more substantial international traders in Russia in the first half of the nineteenth century were the Rallis. The Ralli family arrived in London in 1818 from Greece. In 1827 the branch was renamed Ralli Brothers and became the headquarters of the Ralli merchant group, which compromised multiple interlocked partnerships. Ralli and other Greek merchants, mostly from the island of Chois, already traded British textiles in the Orient, but by the late 1820s they had also begun exporting to Germany. Ralli Brothers established branches in Manchester and Liverpool as well as London. An

---

[17] Richard Roberts, *Schroders* (London: Macmillan, 1992), 26–80.

[18] Stuart Thompstone, 'British Merchant Houses in Russia before 1914', in L. Edmundson and P. Waldron (eds.), *Economy and Society in Russia and the Soviet Union, 1860–1930* (London: Macmillan, 1992).

extremely large trading business developed with Russia. Ralli opened a branch in the Russian Black Sea port of Odessa in 1827 where it became one of a cluster of Greek merchant houses which were pre-eminent in the Russian grain trade. By the mid-1860s Ralli formed a complex international trading group consisting of at least fifteen interlocked partnerships in Europe, the Middle East, and Asia.[19]

The Choit merchants such as the Rallis largely controlled Liverpool's trade with the eastern Mediterranean by mid-century. They opened up new markets for British textiles in a region where the British mercantile presence was weak. They were characterized by exceptionally close kinship links, which included using family members as their agents in foreign parts to receive and dispatch cargoes, avoiding the cost of using intermediaries. In Russia and the eastern Mediterranean they were able to use the long-established Greek diaspora to access producers of wheat and offer products directly, again avoiding the use of intermediaries.[20]

From the 1860s the Choit merchant network weakened, but Choit firms continued to be important in trading and shipping in Britain. The Rallis withdrew from Russia in response to the decline of Odessa as a grain exporting port and the growing difficulties of the Russian grain trade, and built a new commercial business in India. In 1851 a branch was opened in Calcutta, and from the next decade Ralli Brothers shifted its business to India, where it developed as one of the leading commodity traders.

Portugal saw another cluster of British merchants in the eighteenth century, trading woollen goods and textiles in return for wines. British merchant partnerships were prominent in the export of port wine, a capital-intensive trade because of the need to age the wine before it was sold. The British firms were expelled from Portugal by the French during the Napoleonic Wars, but some re-established themselves subsequently and were joined by other firms. The most important firm from the 1830s was Sandeman, organized as two interlocked partnerships in London and Oporto, the centre of the port trade in Portugal.[21]

While Sandeman remained a port trading company, other British merchant houses in Portugal had more diverse interests. The firm of Hunt, Newman & Roope, founded in Oporto in 1735, was part of a cluster of partnerships in Britain and Newfoundland which was also a substantial trader in fish.[22]

[19] *History and Activities of the Ralli Trading Group* (London: the firm, 1979); Ioanna Pepelasis Minoglou and Helen Louri, 'Diaspora Enterpreneurial Networks in the Black Sea and Greece, 1870–1917', *Journal of European Economic History*, 26 (1997), 69–104; Minoglou, 'The Greek Merchant House of the Russian Black Sea: A Nineteenth-Century Example of a Traders' Coalition', *International Journal of Maritime History*, 10 (1998), 61–104.
[20] Gelina Harlaftis, *A History of Greek-Owned Shipping* (London: Routledge, 1996), 39–69.
[21] Paul Duguid and Teresa da Silva Lopes, 'The Company you Keep: The Port Trade in the Declining Years of the Wine Companies, 1812–1840', in *Os Vinhos Licorosos e a História* (Centro de Estudos de História do Atlântico, 1998), 285–321.
[22] Ibid. 294.

The Grahams, another port exporter, were to acquire much wider interests. The first Graham partnership was founded in 1784 in Glasgow. This firm established a business in Lisbon, Portugal, as a general trading company dealing mainly in cotton textiles. In 1820 another Graham partnership was founded in Oporto which developed a large port wine exporting business having received port in return for a bad debt. W. & J. Graham became one of the leading port exporters.[23] Like Ralli, from mid-century Grahams also sought new opportunities in India. Interlocked partnerships were founded in the major Indian ports, where the firm became one of the largest importers of Lancashire textiles into India. By 1870 the complex web of Graham partnerships can be regarded as a multinational trading company with operations on two continents supervised.

Ralli and Grahams were not the only merchant houses to look beyond Europe as the nineteenth century progressed. British merchants found new markets as they pioneered the trade in manufactured goods to the Southern Hemisphere and Asia. The most typical examples were the numerous individuals who settled in the ports of Latin America, Asia, and elsewhere to serve as the agents of British manufacturers and wholesalers. The merchants often began as 'commission merchants' who dealt directly with manufacturers in Britain. Under these arrangements, the goods were not paid for until the firm had received payments for the goods from their customers. However they also sometimes traded on their own account, which offered the potential of higher profits, in return for greater risks.

The use of merchant intermediaries to sell Lancashire textiles in developing markets is fully understandable in terms of transactions cost theory. The small and specialized Lancashire firms were in no position to sell their products to distant countries about which they had little information. British 'commission merchants' resident in foreign ports provided the essential conduit into such markets. In more developed markets in North America and continental Europe, well-established commercial communities existed alongside a commercial infrastructure of ports and warehousing facilities, so cotton textile sales could be more easily made between merchant intermediaries without foreign direct investment or a physical presence. Cotton textiles lacked technical complexity and were consequently especially suitable for merchant intermediaries, though they were far from homogeneous as their variety was immense.

Once established in the foreign ports, British merchants often became involved in the export of local commodities as well as the import of British goods, and later in other local business activities. The nature of their host was also a decisive influence on this trend. In the developing regions of Latin America and Asia, the lack of infrastructure and of local entrepreneurship meant that British merchants could often not rely upon others to create the

---

[23] Gerald Cobb, *Oporto—Older and Newer* (Chicester: Chicester Press Ltd., 1965), 82.

complementary businesses needed for their trading business. If they wanted shipping or insurance facilities, they had to arrange them. If they wanted better produce to improve trade, they often had to invest in growing it themselves.[24] However the lack of local entrepreneurship was not entirely a negative phenomenon, because it also meant that there were plentiful potentially profitable opportunities if merchants chose to apply their organizational skills and resources to other sectors. From another perspective, local producers of grain, port wine, or other commodities faced high information costs in finding buyers in developed economies and consequently found it preferable to use trading companies as intermediaries. As a result of making such investments, the British merchants began to evolve from trading intermediaries to trade creators.

As hypothesized in Chapter 1, once British merchants were established in a foreign port or region, their local information and knowledge represented indivisible assets that reduced the set-up costs facing new ventures. Backward and forward vertical integration strategies were stimulated by concerns about quality control, and other problems arising from information asymmetry and opportunism. The British merchants, therefore, internalized markets in which transaction costs were perceived as being too high.

Nevertheless investments in fixed assets ran counter in many ways to the core merchant ethos, which was to make profits from the use of other people's capital rather than their own. They made their profits by taking commission and fees for acting as commission agents, or agents for shipping companies and insurance firms. There were always tensions between this ethos and making large capital investments necessary, in some cases, to facilitate trade, or simply to take advantage of opportunities, although there were many historical examples of merchants in all countries making substantial investments as part of diversification strategies.[25]

These processes can be seen in Latin America and Asia. In the early nineteenth century many individual British merchants took up residence in Latin America as the Napoleonic Wars diverted their activities from Europe, while revolution in Latin America removed the restrictions of the old Spanish empire. By the 1820s British commission merchants, of all shapes and sizes, were located in substantial numbers at all the principal centres of international trade in the subcontinent, from Mexico City to Rio to Buenos Aires and Montevideo.[26] In Buenos Aires, numerous British 'import-export' houses were established. They received credit from the mercantile houses of

---

[24] J. S. Fforde, *An International Trade in Managerial Skills* (Oxford: Basil Blackwell, 1957), 115–17.

[25] Hancock, *Citizens*, examines the backward integration of eighteenth-century London merchants into slaving and plantations. Robert F. Dalzell, *Enterprising Elite: The Boston Associates and the World They Made* (Cambridge, Mass.: Harvard University Press, 1987) shows the investments of Boston merchants in cotton manufacturing in the following century.

[26] D. C. M. Platt, *Latin America and British Trade 1806–1914* (London: Adam & Charles Black, 1972), 39–51.

Manchester, Liverpool, and London who acted as agents for British manufacturers, largely of cotton textiles. Sometimes the British merchants in Buenos
Aires also acted as commission merchants for British manufacturers. These
import-export houses also purchased Argentinian produce for export, in which
case they took the risks of the trade. Mercantile houses made their largest
profits when operating on their own account, buying products to send to
the United Kingdom and manufactured goods to sell in Argentina.[27]

A number of these British import-export houses in Buenos Aires were
individual proprietorships, but more usually they were jointly-owned partnerships, sometimes between firms based in the Argentine and in Britain. In
other cases these firms established branches or partnerships elsewhere in
Latin America, especially in neighbouring Uruguay. These cross-border
networks were often fragile and constantly renegotiated. They were also
fluid and ill-defined in terms of 'nationality'.[28] As in other ports around the
world at that time, the merchants engaged in international trade were highly
cosmopolitan in their ethnic origins.[29]

The wide geographical spread of British merchants in Latin America did
not last. By mid-century they had declined in importance or even withdrawn
from Mexico, Central America, and most of the smaller markets elsewhere.[30]
British mercantile enterprise persisted, however, in the River Plate area and
also in Brazil—where (for example) the coffee trading company E. Johnston
& Sons dated from Edward Johnston's arrival in Brazil in 1820. By mid-
century Johnstons was an important shipper of Brazilian coffee, and by the
1870s the firm was the second largest exporter of Brazilian coffee. This
firm sent Brazilian coffee to the United States, then picking up grain and
timber for Liverpool, where manufactured goods were loaded for Brazil.[31]
Among other long-lasting British merchant houses in Brazil were Knowles
& Foster and Wilson, Sons & Co. The former originated as the London
firm of Foster Brothers in 1828 (becoming Knowles & Foster in 1853). It
specialized in trade between Britain, Portugal, and Brazil, and were at
various times appointed bankers to the Portuguese Royal Family and the
Brazilian Emperor.[32] Wilson, Sons & Co. was founded in Bahia, Brazil, in
1837 by the Wilson brothers, who established a London head office in 1845.
The firm concentrated on coal importing and related shipping services, supplying coal to shipping companies from their depots in Brazil.[33]

[27] Vera Blinn Reber, *British Mercantile Houses in Buenos Aires 1810–1880* (Cambridge, Mass.:
Cambridge University Press, 1979), ch. 3.

[28] Ibid. 55–8.

[29] Charles Jones, *International Business in the Nineteenth Century* (Brighton: Wheatsheaf,
1987), ch. 3.

[30] Platt, *Latin America*, 136–72.

[31] Robert Greenhill, 'The Brazilian Coffee Trade', in D. C. M. Platt (ed.), *Business Imperialism 1840–1930* (Oxford: Clarendon Press, 1977), 200.

[32] Anon., *The History of Knowles & Foster* (London: Ted Kavanagh, 1948).

[33] MSS History of Wilson, Sons & Co. July 1975, MS 20203, GHL.

British merchants were also active on the Pacific West Coast of Latin America in the early nineteenth century. Antony Gibbs originated as British merchants exporting to Spain. The London-based partnership of Antony Gibbs & Son was founded in 1808. The firm began trading with Latin America in the early nineteenth century as a result of the disruption of Spanish markets caused by the Napoleonic Wars, and in 1822 a Gibbs partnership was opened in Lima, Peru, followed four years later by the foundation of Houses in Valparaíso and Santiago in Chile. Meanwhile the firm withdrew from Spain, closing their Cádiz branch in 1827 and their Gibraltar branch in 1833. The Gibbs group remained a modest one until 1842 when the Lima branch secured a contract with the Peruvian government to sell guano—which soon became that country's principal earner of foreign exchange—in a substantial number of foreign markets. Gibbs made a loan to the government in advance of sales for every contract, reimbursement coming from the proceeds which they collected abroad. The result was two decades of highly profitable trading, before the guano monopoly was lost in 1861.[34]

Two more important British merchant houses on the Pacific West Coast were founded in this period. Graham Rowe developed out of a partnership established in Lima, Peru in 1822, while Duncan Fox originated as a venture formed in 1843 when a Liverpool merchant sent two of his sons to Chile to develop his trading links. In 1863 the name of Duncan Fox was taken, and soon after a branch was established in Lima.

The pattern of British merchant enterprise in Asia was initially conditioned by the existence of the East India Company (EIC). During the seventeenth and eighteenth centuries the English, Dutch, and other European East India companies had engaged in large-scale trading operations between India and Europe involving the exchange of bullion for spices, silk, and textiles, the latter reflecting India's possession at that time of probably the largest textile industry in the world. During the second half of the eighteenth century British private traders—who had often served with the EIC and who retained close collaborative links with it—developed a large clandestine trade within Asia and between Europe and India, trading in products such as indigo, sugar, cotton, spices, and opium.[35] These merchants, who were clustered in the leading Indian ports of Calcutta, Bombay, and Madras, demonstrated an early tendency to diversify out of trade and to make investments in other activities. By the 1790s British merchant houses in India began investing in indigo plantations, often persuading others to invest in their ventures but retaining the management of them.

---

[34] William M. Mathew, *The House of Gibbs and the Peruvian Guano Monopoly* (London: Royal Historical Society, 1981); id. 'Antony Gibbs & Sons, the Guano Trade and the Peruvian Government, 1842–1861', in Platt (ed.), *Business Imperialism*; W. Maude, *Antony Gibbs & Sons Ltd., Merchants and Bankers, 1808–1958* (London: the firm, 1958).

[35] O. M. Prakash, *European Commercial Enterprise in Pre-Colonial India* (Cambridge: Cambridge University Press, 1998), 286–97.

These 'agency houses' were the origins of the managing agency system which became a prevalent feature of British mercantile enterprise in India, and later elsewhere. In essence, the managing agency system began the process of creating diversified 'business groups' around an original trading enterprise. In its origins, it reflected the circumstances of the Indian economy where opportunities for promoting new commodities or industry coexisted with a lack of formal capital markets to facilitate this process, though it drew on earlier methods of financing and managing subsidiary concerns which were well established in the British mercantile marine in the eighteenth century.

Following the abolition of the EIC's monopoly of the India trade in 1813, the agency houses made further investments in plantations and other activities such as shipowning and mining. However a major commercial crisis in the early 1830s led to the collapse of all the major Calcutta agency houses, but some of the late eighteenth-century agency houses in Bombay and Madras survived. Two of the Madras agency houses, Parry's and Binny's illustrate the process of diversification. The Welsh merchant Thomas Parry and the Scottish merchant John Binny arrived in Madras in 1788 and 1796 respectively, and both developed a trading and private banking business. The EIC set a limit on remittances sent home by its employees, enabling private banks to provide a service in investing this surplus capital. This banking function led Parry's into owning indigo plantations as a result of bad debts, but as early as 1805 the firm had also established a leather tannery. In the 1830s Thomas Parry's successors ventured out further into coffee planting, and acting as agents for a steel company. Binny's growth pattern was not dissimilar, and by mid-century that firm was not only engaged in trading and banking, but also sugar refining, indigo cultivation, and textile production.[36]

The end of the EIC's trading monopoly in 1813 encouraged new British entrants into Indian trade, who were often less anxious to diversify away from trade. Gillanders Arbuthnot, the first of the new generation, originated when John Gladstone, a Liverpool merchant of Scottish origins with large trade, shipping, and plantation interests in the West Indies, decided to diversify into India in 1819 by sending a relative, F. M. Gillanders, to Calcutta. The upshot was the formation of a group of partnerships in Calcutta, Bombay, and Liverpool under the names of Gillanders, Arbuthnot; Ogilvy, Gillanders; and Gladstone & Co. The firm traded in textiles and general goods from Britain and indigo from India, remaining focused on trading until the 1870s.[37]

[36] Hilton Brown, *Parry's of Madras* (Madras: the firm, 1954), 1–76; Stephanie Jones, *Two Centuries of Overseas Trading* (London: Macmillan, 1986), 9–10; Anon., *The House of Binny* (London: the firm, 1969).

[37] Jones, *Two Centuries*, 10–11.

Scottish merchants became especially prominent entrants into Indian—and later other Asian—trade. Scottish pre-eminence may have rested on a more developed education system than in England or on cultural traits, but its initial growth at least was stimulated by Glasgow's initial role as the main British port for exporting textiles.[38] Two Scottish firms which were to assume great prominence in British business in this region were James Finlay and Mackinnon Mackenzie & Co. James Finlay was founded in Glasgow in 1750, and developed a substantial textile import business before, in the early 1800s, establishing three cotton mills in Scotland. The firm exported to continental Europe, opening a German branch in 1800, and soon after US branches were opened in New York, Charleston, and New Orleans to buy and forward raw cotton to Scotland and to sell finished products. Like Gladstone, Finlays responded quickly to the end of the EICs monopoly of trade with India, sending a ship to Bombay in 1816, and forming a Bombay partnership in the following year, although the firm ceased to be partners in 1828. The firm's sales of textiles to Asia were unprofitable, and in 1844 its mills were put up for sale, but no buyers emerged. Instead the production of the mills was switched very successfully to household sheets and towels for the home market. India became a source of supplies for raw cotton, and in 1862 a branch of the firm was opened in Bombay.[39]

Mackinnon Mackenzie & Co. was established in Calcutta in 1847 as a partnership between Scottish merchants from the town of Campbeltown in Kintyre. The firm began with a traditional business importing British textiles and exporting local products such as tea, sugar, and rice. William Mackinnon & Co., a Glasgow partnership, was opened also. Two families, the Mackinnons and the Halls, controlled these partnerships, with William Mackinnon as the key figure before his death in 1893. In retrospect, the most significant innovation of Mackinnon Mackenzie came in 1856 when the firm entered Indian coastal steamshipping by promoting a company to conduct regular sailings between Calcutta and the ports of neighbouring Burma.[40]

The British merchants in Calcutta, Bombay, and Madras spread eastwards and southwards along the Asian trade routes. In the eighteenth century British trade between China and Britain was confined to a single port—Canton—and was conducted by the East India Company on the British side and by an association of Chinese merchants on the Chinese side. This trade was unbalanced as Britain was a large market for Chinese tea, but China

[38] M. Greenberg, *British Trade and the Opening of China 1800–1842* (Cambridge: Cambridge University Press, 1951), 35–40; Chapman, *Merchant Enterprise*, 112; Jones, *International Business*, 51.

[39] J. Brogan, *James Finlay & Co Limited* (Glasgow: Jackson Sons & Co., 1951).

[40] Jones, *Two Centuries*, 12–14; J. Forbes Munro, 'From Regional Trade to Global Shipping: Mackinnon Mackenzie & Co. within the Mackinnon Enterprise Network', in Geoffrey Jones (ed.), *The Multinational Traders* (London: Routledge, 1998).

consumed few British products. This situation changed in the early decades of the nineteenth century when a large export of Indian opium and raw cotton to China developed. In this period private British and Indian merchants seriously breached the EIC's monopoly.

The private British merchants who settled in Canton to conduct this trade were often employed by, or were else former employees of, the East India Company or the agency houses in Calcutta and Bombay. Jardine Matheson, which controlled about half of China's foreign trade by the 1830s, originated in a series of partnerships founded from the 1780s by British merchants resident in Canton. In the 1820s two Scots merchants involved in the trade between Calcutta and Canton, William Jardine and James Matheson, joined these partnerships, and they founded the new firm of Jardine Matheson & Co. in 1832. When the East India Company's China monopoly was abolished in 1834, Jardine Matheson was the first firm to send China tea to London.

During the 1830s the opium trade of Jardine Matheson and the other British merchants in Canton boomed. Jardine Matheson and its principal Canton competitor, Dent's, exercised a virtual monopoly over the price of opium in China. Both firms diversified into related financial and insurance services. Until 1835 they managed alternatively for periods of five years the Canton Insurance Company, formed by British traders in 1805. After 1835 the management remained in Jardines' hands, and Dent's formed its own insurance company six years later. The growth of these firms took place in a highly uncertain and risky economic and political environment. Jardine Matheson's early history featured a 'high frequency of crises', and the firm's attempts to engage in textile and tea trading was far less successful than opium dealing.[41]

A major potential threat arose in 1836 when the Chinese government banned the opium trade, and in 1839 China went to war with Britain in the so-called 'Opium War'. This was a highly dangerous period for the British merchants in Canton who faced first British and then Chinese embargoes on their Canton business, and they responded with a number of strategies including hiding their trade behind 'neutral' flags. James Matheson acted as the Danish consul in Canton and put several Jardine Matheson ships under the Danish flag.[42] The end of the war left the opium trade unhindered, and the Treaty of Nanking in 1842 opened the ports of Amoy, Foochow, Ningpo, and Shanghai to trade, and ceded the island of Hong Kong to Britain. Jardine Matheson and the other British merchant houses had established their headquarters in Hong Kong by 1844, which became the centre for the opium business which flourished during the 1840s and 1850s. Indian opium was sent to Hong Kong, and then shipped to Chinese ports, ships carrying the proceeds back with them.

---

[41] W. E. Cheong, *Mandarins and Merchants* (London: Curzon Press, 1979), 263 and *passim*.
[42] Ole Lange, 'Denmark in China 1839–65: A Pawn in a British Game', *Scandinavian Economic History Review*, 19 (1971), 72–8.

Both Dent's and Jardine Matheson had associated merchant houses in India which supplied information on opium supplies and arranged shipments to the China-based merchants. One of Jardine Matheson's closest Indian associates was Jardine Skinner & Co., originally founded in Bombay in 1825 and reformed in Calcutta in 1844. There was no legal relationship between Jardine Skinner and Jardine Matheson, but both merchant houses used the facilities of the London merchant house of Matheson & Co., founded in 1848 by James Matheson after he left China, and which shared some overlap in shareholding with Jardine Matheson.[43] Both Jardine Matheson and Dent's also had close relations (including shareholdings in) the premier British shipping line in the East, the Peninsular and Oriental Steam Navigation Company (P&O), which from the 1850s established a monopoly over the Bombay-China opium trade which lasted until the early twentieth century.[44]

Although Jardine Matheson and Dent's were by far the largest of the British traders in this period, they coexisted with smaller British trading companies. Gibb, Livingston was founded as a partnership in Canton in 1836 by two former EIC merchants. It established branches elsewhere in China to import British goods and, like the other British merchant houses, soon began acting as agents for insurance and shipping companies. A second partnership, Gilman's, was formed in 1840 from a former employee of Dent's. Both firms were to develop as tea trading companies.[45]

Another cluster of British trading companies developed in South East Asia on the trade route from India to China. British merchants followed the extension of British colonial rule over key ports on the trade route, Penang, Singapore, and Malacca. Singapore, with its fine natural harbour, its location at the southern entrance to the Straits of Malacca which were one of two gateways between the Indian Ocean and the China Sea, and its free port status, was the leading commercial hub of the three 'Straits Settlements', which became a full British colony. It grew as an entrepôt where Western manufactured goods—primarily British cotton textiles—were bought in bulk to be broken down for distribution in the Malayan region and local tropical produce was collected and prepared for shipment to the industrializing countries.

British merchant firms were established quickly in Singapore after 1819. By 1834 at least seventeen British agency houses were founded, of which some—Guthries (1821) and Edward Boustead (1830)—were to become extremely long-lived. As elsewhere, these merchants acted as agents for British

[43] G. C. Allen and Audrey G. Donnithorne, *Western Enterprise in Far Eastern Economic Development* (London: George Allen & Unwin, 1954), chs. 1 and 2; Colin N. Crisswell, *The Taipans. Hong Kong's Merchant Princes* (Hong Kong. Oxford University Press, 1981); chs. 1–4; M. Keswick (ed.), *The Thistle and the Jade* (London: Octopus, 1982).

[44] Freda Harcourt, 'The P&O Company: Flagships of Imperialism', in S. Palmer and G. Williams (eds.), *Chartered and Unchartered Waters* (London· National Maritime Museum, 1981), 14–15.

[45] Jones, *Two Centuries*, 18–19.

manufacturers from which they received credit. The agency houses then broke
down consignments to Asian, primarily Chinese traders, who settled in
Singapore and shaped its character as a primarily Chinese city under British
political rule. Although they usually began as importers, the British agency
houses quickly moved to selling local produce, and a form of barter trade
was conducted whereby Asian traders purchased Western manufactured goods
from the British merchants and in return provided local products such as
spices, sugar, and gin purchased from local cultivators and miners. During
the 1830s and 1840s some agency houses began to make their first investments in the cultivation of sugar, coffee, nutmeg, clove, and other local products in Singapore and on the Malayan peninsular, although the scale of such
diversification was to be dwarfed by developments in the late nineteenth
century.[46] Generally, Singapore's development—and the opportunities for
trade—remained modest until the 1870s when an era of spectacular growth
began.[47]

By 1850 British mercantile enterprise was widespread around the world.
British merchant houses dating from earlier epochs, such as the merchants
in Russia and Portugal, and even the Hudson's Bay Company, coexisted
with embryonic 'merchant banks', which still maintained extensive international trading businesses. New generations of commission merchants had
developed markets for British goods in the developing world, established
themselves at the principal ports, began to develop exports from those ports,
and in some cases—especially in India—made capital investments beyond the
trading sector. Asia was the particular magnet, and had attracted merchants
whose original business had been with the United States, Russia, and other
countries.

2.4 Hubs and Networks

The 1850s and 1860s saw the appearance of a new generation of British
trading companies, as well as the continued evolution of the business of
established firms. In part, these developments represented the continuation
of past trends. Transportation improvements and expansion of European
empires continued to extend the borders of the international economy. In
Asia, Western political influence generally continued to expand. In India,
the last vestiges of the old regime were removed by the abolition of the
EIC in 1857, and the extension of direct British government control over
the whole subcontinent. British influence expanded beyond India's borders

---

[46] G. C. Allen and Audrey G. Donnithorne, *Western Enterprise in Indonesia and Malaya* (London: George Allen & Unwin, 1957), 52–5; S. Cunyngham-Brown, *The Traders* (London:
Newman Neame, 1970), J. H. Drabble and P. J. Drake, 'The British Agency Houses in Malaysia:
Survival in a Changing World', *Journal of Southeast Asian Studies*, 12 (1981), 297–308.
[47] W. G. Huff, *The Economic Growth of Singapore* (Cambridge: Cambridge University Press,
1994), 8.

with the annexation of part of Burma in 1852 and the Bowring Treaty with Thailand in 1855 which opened that country to Western trade. In China, the Treaty of Tienstin signed in 1858 after the Second Anglo-Chinese War opened the great rivers of China to foreign trade. Meanwhile in Japan, the country had been forced to abandon nearly 250 years of seclusion by the arrival of the American Commodore Perry's ships in 1853. On the other side of the Pacific, California was joined to New York by a transcontinental railroad. As countries and regions were opened to the international economy, British merchants followed.

There were also new influences on the pattern strategies of British trading companies. The adoption of limited liability and joint stock legislation in Britain and its empire offered new opportunities for growth without the constraints of the partnership form, though before 1870 few merchant partnerships made much use of the capital markets, preferring to grow largely on the basis of reinvested profits rather than new capital. A stronger influence was in shipping. The mid-nineteenth century saw the spread of the compound marine steam engine, and the worldwide growth of British steamshipping companies. The British accounted for 40 per cent of total world merchant shipping tonnage and 23 per cent of the steam tonnage in 1850. Twenty years later the percentages were 34 per cent and 42 per cent.[48] A cluster of new trading companies were associated with shipping firms, while shipping or shipping agencies became of major importance to the merchant firms.

The role of Liverpool-based merchants and shipowners in the new generation of British traders was striking. During the first half of the nineteenth century London and Glasgow merchants had been especially prominent in the growth of British trading companies abroad, but Liverpool had also served as a third major centre for merchant enterprise. Liverpool replaced London as the nucleus of the raw cotton trade, with the emergence of the United States as an increasingly important source of supplies for the Lancashire cotton textiles industry. By 1850 the port of Liverpool had overtaken not only Glasgow, but also London, in terms of total tonnage.[49] All three towns served as hubs of information, contacts, capital, and personnel which provided a dynamic environment for the emergence of entrepreneurs engaged in international trading. They were places where merchants, shippers, manufacturers, and bankers could interact frequently, developing the kind of high trust atmosphere which facilitated transactions.

In the case of Liverpool, its merchant firms were heavily specialized in the cotton trade in the first half of the nineteenth century. This was mostly undertaken using independent merchant houses in the United States as 'correspondents'. However, some Liverpool-based merchants traded in commodities other than cotton in the first half of the nineteenth century,

---

[48] Davies, 'Ocean Trade and Transport', 66.   [49] Chapman, *Merchant Enterprise*, 82–3.

sometimes establishing partnerships both in Asia and the Americas from the
1820s. The former case included the Gladstone and Gillander families in India.
In the Americas, the firm of Booker Brothers & Co. was established in
Liverpool in 1834 to participate in the rum and sugar trades in British Guyana.
This firm acquired its first ship in 1835 and subsequently purchased sugar
plantations. Duncan Fox, founded in the 1840s, established businesses in Chile
and Peru.[50]

From mid-century a new wave of Liverpool-based merchant firms
expanded abroad. An example was Rathbones, a merchant house dating
from the early eighteenth century which by the early nineteenth century
had become a specialist in the import of American cotton. During the 1840s
this Liverpool partnership, concerned about over-dependence on the cotton
trade, expanded the products in which it dealt and, especially, entered the
trade with China. Early in that decade Rathbones established a partnership
in Canton to sell British manufactured goods exported to it by Rathbones
and to buy tea and silk for export to Britain and the United States. Later
the Canton house was closed and another at Shanghai opened, but this
too was closed in 1852 because of management problems and a reluctance
to become involved with opium trading. Thereafter Rathbones relied on
correspondent relations with independent houses to conduct their China trade.
In contrast, the firm established its own New York agency or branch in
1851, first to assist the cotton trade, and then to import tea and other China
produce. From the 1850s the Rathbones also invested in shipping, joining
with the other Liverpool merchants to found shipping lines to link Britain
with India and Latin America.[51]

At the centre of a major network of Liverpool firms was Alfred Holt
& Company. The Holts were a Liverpool cotton trading family, one of
whose members—Alfred—worked in shipping and over time developed
a compound engine which enabled steamships to run long distances in a
very economical fashion. The Holts ran steamers in the West Indies in the
early 1860s, pulled out because of competition in 1864, and then turned
their attention to a trade which was undeveloped by steamers, that to China,
where the only pre-existing British company was P&O. For this purpose,
the Ocean Steamship Company—or the Blue Funnel Line—was established
in 1865.[52]

In order to exploit the China trade, the appointment of agents was
crucial. In the Far East, the key appointment was the fellow Liverpool-
based merchant house of John Swire & Sons. The founder of the firm had
opened a merchant house in Liverpool in 1816 which imported raw cotton

---

[50] Jones, *International Business*, 147.

[51] Sheila Marriner, *Rathbones of Liverpool 1845–73* (Liverpool: Liverpool University Press,
1961).

[52] Francis E. Hyde and John R. Harris, *Blue Funnel: A History of Alfred Holt and Company
of Liverpool from 1865 to 1914* (Liverpool. Liverpool University Press, 1956).

from New Orleans and exported Lancashire cotton piece-goods. During the 1850s and 1860s his two sons developed new lines of business, visiting the USA and Australia, where a merchant house was briefly established in Melbourne. The Swires were one of the founding shareholders in the Ocean Steamship Company. They were also interested in the China market. They formed a short-lived partnership with a Yorkshire textile manufacturer, R. S. Butterfield, and in 1867 opened the firm of Butterfield & Swire in Shanghai to sell British manufactured goods in China, and to buy teas and silks for export to Britain. Butterfield & Swire were appointed the Far East agents of the Ocean Steamship Company. The Holt agency provided the basis for Butterfield & Swire to rapidly expand their branch network in China.

Within a decade from the mid-1860s Swire's were transformed from British provincial merchants to a multinational trading company with branches in the UK, China, and—from 1873—New York. A major development came in 1872 when Swire's entered the China coastal and river shipping business in direct competition to the established shipping operations of Jardine Matheson and the American firm of Russell and Co. In that year the China Navigation Company was formed to provide steamer services on the Lower Yangtze, and to supply cargoes for Holt's ships. This was a London-registered limited liability company, though its shares were principally held by the Swires, the Holts, and other Liverpool families.[53]

The Holt/Swire network had a third party which was the shipbuilding firm of Scott's, based at Greenock on the Clyde. Alfred Holt ordered his first ship from Scott's in 1857, and a long-term relationship developed between the two firms. Scott's built the first three steamers for the Ocean Steamship Company, and the firm's owner took a large shareholding in the company. Meanwhile in 1874 a member of the Scott family became a partner in Swire's. During the 1870s Swire's purchased ships from Scott's while the Scott family invested in Swire's affiliates. The strong and sustained business links between Swire's, Scott's, and Holts are examined in Chapter 8.

A second key agency for the Holts was Mansfield in Singapore. When the Blue Funnel steamships first reached Singapore, Holt had used an old-established agency house as agents, but this proved unsatisfactory and in 1868 he appointed the Singapore-registered firm of Mansfield & Co., which had originated in 1859 as a ship's chandlery business, as agents. As in the case of Swire's, during the 1870s Mansfields managed a fleet of small steamships carrying regional produce such as rice from Bangkok and sugar and spices from Java and Borneo, where it was transferred to Holt's ocean-going ships.[54]

[53] Sheila Marriner and Francis E. Hyde, *The Senior, John Samuel Swire 1825–1898* (Liverpool: Liverpool University Press, 1967).

[54] Francis E. Hyde, *Far Eastern Trade 1860–1914* (London: Adam & Charles Black, 1973), 89–91; Allen and Donnithorne, *Western Enterprise*, 215.

There was also a strong connection between Holts and the Liverpool merchant firm of Alfred Booth & Co. The origins of this firm lay in a partnership between the Booth family and an American merchant formed to import English sheepskins into the United States. The New York office also acted as an agency for the Holt steamers at that time trading between New York, the West Indies, and Liverpool. The connection with Holts alerted the Booths to the potential of the new compound marine steam engine. The Booths identified the Brazilian trade as the one most suitable, perhaps because Alfred Booth had worked at the New York agency of the Rathbones which was active in that trade, and in 1865 Booths began a steamship service between northern Brazilian ports and Liverpool. As was the norm in that period, the Booths did not 'own' the ships as a company, but held shares in the vessels along with others, including the Holts, and until 1873 Holts' engineers serviced Booths vessels.[55]

The firm of Balfour Williamson also originated from Liverpool in this period, though the three founding partners in 1851 were Scots. The firm was founded to ship British goods to the west coast of South America, to which two of the partners went while one remained in Liverpool. Like the Booths, the partners had strong shipping interests, being shareholders in various ships. A Chilean partnership opened in Valparaíso in 1852. When the partnership was renegotiated in 1863, the Liverpool house took the name Balfour Williamson and the Valparaíso one Williamson Balfour. Following the familiar pattern, the Chilean operation rapidly moved to export local produce as well as to import British goods. In addition, a bad debt in 1869 led to Williamson Balfour taking control of a small flourmill, which was managed until it was sold in 1875, by which time the original debt had been virtually cancelled.

A more radical development followed in 1869 when the firm expanded to San Francisco, when the partnership of Balfour, Guthrie was formed. The state of California was growing rapidly in this period and in 1869 was joined to the East Coast by the first transatlantic railroad. The new operation was focused on the Californian market where it was intended to export Californian grain and other produce and sell imports for the local market, initially chemicals and other products from Britain and coal from Australia.[56]

It was shipping which also provided the key to the rapid growth of Mackinnon Mackenzie to become one of the leading Calcutta agency houses. The granting of government of India mail contracts enabled the venture to expand from coastal shipping and develop liner services all around India, and to Singapore and the Arab Gulf. In 1865 the British India Steam Navigation Company (BI) was formed on the London market with a nominal capital of over £1 million. Mackinnon Mackenzie held the managing agency

[55] A. H. John, *A Liverpool Merchant House* (London: George Allen & Unwin, 1959), chs. 2 and 3.

[56] Wallis Hunt, *Heirs of Great Adventure*, vol. 1: *1851–1901* (London: the firm, 1951), 1–57.

contract for BI. As with Holts, the spread of BI's shipping services meant that reliable agents were required. This was a problem when BI received a mail contract from the government of India to operate a service between India and the Gulf, because there were no suitable merchant houses in that region. The solution was to create them, using another firm within the Mackinnon complex, the London-based partnership of Gray Dawes. This firm was established in 1865 by William Mackinnon to provide business opportunities for his nephew and a colleague, and it acted as the London agents for BI's passenger services. Gray Dawes established a partnership at Bushire, Gray Paul & Co., and one at Basra, Gray Mackenzie & Co., which acted as the agents for BI's services. Once established, they sought to develop a business importing British textiles and exporting any local produce they could find, including opium.[57]

During the 1860s British merchants such as Mackinnon Mackenzie expanded their involvement in the Indian economy. This was a decade of frantic activity in India, with booming tea and cotton prices and new trading opportunities following the opening of the Suez Canal in 1869. The rise in cotton prices reflected the impact of the US Civil War—while in 1860 the United States had supplied four-fifths of the cotton consumed in Britain, by 1864 two-thirds of Britain's supplies came from India. Merchant houses which had earlier established branches in the United States to import cotton now opened branches in India. Meanwhile the large profits that could be made in trade encouraged established firms to diversify. Mackinnon Mackenzie floated tea and jute companies on the Glasgow and London markets, retaining a percentage of the equity and a managing agency contract. The firm also invested in cotton spinning companies before, in 1874, establishing its own cotton spinning company.[58]

The cluster of new managing agencies which were formed in the decade were mostly based in Calcutta. Andrew Yule was established in 1863 in Calcutta by the Yule family, Manchester textile merchants of Scottish descent. The firm initially sold Lancashire textiles in India, and also served as agents for three British insurance companies. Within a few years the firm had also started to take shareholdings in companies involved in the main industries of the Calcutta region, especially jute, tea, and coal.[59] A second firm, Turner Morrison was established in Calcutta in 1864. Morrison was a Liverpool shipowner and the firm developed as important shipping agents, as well as investing in tea. Bird & Company also originated in 1864 on the basis of a handling contract on the East Indian Railway. Balmer Lawrie was established in Calcutta in 1867 as merchants and soon developed a speciality in engineering products, in association with a London partnership.[60]

---

[57] Jones, *Two Centuries*, 53, 81–3.   [58] Munro, 'Mackinnon Mackenzie'.
[59] Andrew Yule & Company, *Andrew Yule & Co. Ltd. 1863–1963* (Edinburgh: T. A. Constable, 1963).
[60] Stephanie Jones, *Merchants of the Raj* (London: Macmillan, 1992), 26–7, 36–7, 42–3.

While the number of British agency houses in Calcutta increased, turning it into the bastion of British business influence which it was to remain until the 1930s and even later, British merchants also expanded eastwards to take advantage of the expansion of British imperial frontiers into Burma. British merchants arrived in Burma soon after the first Anglo-Burmese War in 1826 had led to the extension of British (still EIC) control over a number of territories. Some came from nearby Penang and this was the origin of T. D. Findlay & Son, which by 1850 was organized as two partnerships in Burma and Glasgow, which had teak leases and timber yards and saw mills in the British-occupied port of Moulmein.

The extension of British control over much of Lower Burma following the Second Burmese War in 1852 led to Findlay opening new branches within the annexed area, including Rangoon, and expanding their rice shipping trade. In 1860 in association with the Glasgow shipowning family of Hendersons, a shipping service was started between Glasgow, Liverpool, and the Burmese ports. Five years later a fleet of former British Army steamers was acquired and a Glasgow-registered company, the Irrawaddy Flotilla and Burmese Steam Navigation Company was formed. The registered office was Hendersons in Glasgow while the Burmese management was in the hands of Todd, Findlay & Co. By the mid-1870s the company operated a fleet of modern vessels along 1,000 miles of the Irrawaddy river which linked with the Henderson ocean vessels at Rangoon.[61]

A second Scottish merchant house which was to develop large Burmese operations was Wallace Brothers. The origins of this firm lay in the activities of the six Wallace brothers, originally from Edinburgh, who first arrived in Bombay in the 1840s. A Bombay partnership was formed in 1848 as Wallace & Co. In the mid-1850s one of the Wallaces set up a business in Burma, which began to ship tea to the Bombay house. In 1862 the Wallaces, who had been in partnership with an English merchant both in Bombay and in London, established their own partnership, Wallace Brothers, in London. In the following year the Burmese business was floated as a Bombay public company, The Bombay Burmah Trading Corporation, whose equity was held by Indian merchants in Bombay as well as the Wallace family, but which Wallace & Co. controlled through a managing agreement. By the 1870s the Wallace group consisted of the London firm, whose main function was the provision of finance and charter shipping, the Bombay firm which imported Lancashire textiles and exported Indian produce, and the Bombay Burmah Trading Corporation, which had permits to work teak forests in Burma.[62]

---

[61] A. G. McCrae, *Pioneers in Burma* (Occasional Papers in Economic and Social History No. 2, University of Glasgow, 1986).

[62] A. C. Pointon, *Wallace Brothers* (Oxford: the firm, 1974), 1–25; R. H. Macaulay, *History of the Bombay Burmah Trading Corporation Ltd., 1864–1910* (London: Spottiswoode Ballantyne, 1934), 1–8.

The Borneo Company Limited (BCL) was formed in 1856, to take advantage of opportunities elsewhere in South East Asia. It originated from the establishment of a branch in Singapore by a firm of Glasgow merchants. It became closely linked with the Brooke family which established itself as the rulers of Sarawak in Borneo. The 'White Rajahs', as they were called, ruled Sarawak from the 1840s until 1946, when the British government took over the administration. The venture was given extensive privileges by the White Rajahs, and in order to take advantage of this opportunity, the then most unusual organizational form of a limited liability company was chosen, though in practice all the capital was subscribed by partners and employees of the original Glasgow firm and a close circle of associates, especially R. & J. Henderson, a London and Glasgow merchant house with a merchanting business in Calcutta. The Borneo Company expanded rapidly, developing its trading business in Singapore and opening an office in Bangkok in 1856 immediately after Thailand was opened to trade with the West in that year. Soon afterwards the firm opened jute and sugar mills near Calcutta in India. The Borneo Company's links with Hendersons, its largest single shareholder, were extremely close and initially at least BCL might even be regarded as a subsidiary of that firm.[63]

During the 1850s and 1860s the older established merchant firms also continued to evolve. In the East, Jardine Matheson moved quickly to take advantage of the opening of Japan to trade. In 1858 the firm chartered a ship to take a cargo of sugar to Nagasaki, even before that port had been formally opened to foreign trade, and took a cargo of edible seaweed back to Hong Kong in return. An office of the company was established in Japan at the same time. However the greatest change for Jardine Matheson related to the opium trade. This trade was legalized after the Second Anglo-Chinese War, but it was the arrival of cheaper Chinese-produced opium and the emergence of new competitors selling Indian opium which changed the environment for the Jardine Matheson and Dent's who had formerly dominated Indian opium sales to China. During the 1860s much of the Indian trade was diverted by the Sassoons, Iraqi Jews who had settled in Bombay in the 1820s. David Sassoon & Son purchased unharvested crops directly from Indian producers and were able to undercut the British firms which had obtained supplies from middlemen. Dent's went bankrupt in 1867, while by the early 1870s Jardine Matheson had ceased to be an important opium dealer in either India or China. By then Jardine Matheson had turned from opium to investment in Chinese modernization. In 1865 it formed a company to build a short 12-mile railroad from Shanghai, in 1866 it founded another insurance company the Hongkong Fire Insurance Company, and in 1870 established a silk filiature in Shanghai.[64]

---

[63] H. Longhurst, *The Borneo Story* (London. Newman Neame, 1956); Jones, *Two Centuries*, 19–21.

[64] Crisswell, *The Taipans*; Allen and Donnithorne, *Western Enterprise*, 120, 134–5.

The established British merchant houses in Latin America also continued to evolve. A general trend for all the British merchants was greater involvement in Latin America exporting as local markets continued to fail to live up to expectations in their capacity to absorb imports.[65] Antony Gibbs faced special problems because of the end of the lucrative Peruvian guano monopoly in 1861. The search for alternative sources of income took various directions. The financial side of its business began to grow. The London office made heavy investments in government and railroad bonds, while in South America nitrate became the main replacement for guano. During the 1850s Gibbs became involved in the Peruvian nitrate industry, making advances to producers and selling their products on commission. Gibbs established its own nitrate producing company in Peru in 1865, and four years after became the largest shareholder in a company to exploit Bolivian nitrate fields, holding a contract to manage the company and to serve as their sole agents on the Pacific coast, and in the United States and Europe.[66]

Even by 1870 the distinction between merchants and bankers was an indistinct one. Gibbs spanned both worlds, and was far from alone. The business of all the merchant houses was closely related to banking through their provision of credit to suppliers and customers and their involvement in foreign exchange business, and they often performed banking roles in their host economies. However the general preference of the merchants was not to tie their funds up in banking operations unrelated to their businesses, and consequently they often acted together to found 'overseas banks' to operate in their regions. The subsequent relations between the merchants and the British overseas banks are examined in Chapter 8.

The 1850s and 1860s, therefore, saw both an extension in the geographical frontiers in which the British traders operated, and a deepening of their involvement in some economies. There was an obvious correlation with the growing importance of developing regions as sources of supply of commodities and as markets for manufactured goods. In many developing countries, the lack of modern business institutions and of information about business cultures and markets made it rational to use trading companies to reduce the risks of international trade. These factors also encouraged diversification by the traders. British merchants provided shipping and insurance services, in some cases promoted banks, and on occasion invested in commodities and/or processing. Steamships, especially the perfection of the compound engine, increased the speed and reliability of oceanic transport. Trading and shipping interests, especially from Liverpool, became closely entwined, and some founded their own coastal or river fleets in order to feed into ocean shipping services.

[65] Robert Greenhill, 'Merchants and the Latin American Trades: An Introduction', in Platt (ed.), *Business Imperialism*, 163.

[66] Mathew, *House of Gibbs*; John Mayo, *British Merchants and Chilean Development 1851–1886* (Boulder, Colo.: Westview, 1987), 167–70.

2.5 British Trading Companies, *c.*1870

This chapter has examined the multinational growth of British merchant firms in the century before 1870. British merchants were spread widely around the ports and entrepôts of the developing world by 1870. They sold British goods, especially textiles, and some also exported local products to Britain. The export of local commodities in Latin America and Asia also resulted in substantial 'third country' trade not involving Britain, such as selling Indian opium to China, and Australian coal to California. Most merchants conducted trade intermediation through both broking and reselling. In a world where distances—whether physical, communication, or cultural—remained large and there were high levels of uncertainty about markets, trading company intermediaries reduced transactions and information costs to both buyers and sellers.

The British trading firms were very heterogeneous. There were firms which were heavily specialized in trading in a single commodity, such as coffee, coal, or port, but many merchant houses had taken on a 'hybrid' character by 1870. They acted as insurance and/or shipping agents, while a few had invested or were about to invest in shipping. In Latin America, British merchants were involved in nitrate production and one at least owned a flour mill. In South and South East Asia, agency houses had invested in, or were managing, sugar, tea, and coffee plantations, and teak production in Burma. In many cases, the British merchants had pioneered these industries, creating new trade flows.

British merchants were notably clustered both in their origins and in their destinations into 'hubs'. Table 2.1 identifies some of the 'Glasgow', 'Liverpool', and 'London' merchant houses which have been discussed in this chapter. Although the distinction between 'London', 'Liverpool,' and 'Glasgow' houses is arbitrary—the Borneo Company was registered in London, but heavily Scottish, while Balfour Williamson was founded in Liverpool by Scots—there were real differences in culture and geographical

TABLE 2.1 British trading companies *c.*1870: London, Liverpool, and Glasgow origins

Region	Example
'London'	Antony Gibbs; Knowles & Foster; E. Johnston; Wilson, Sons; Hubbards; Ralli
'Liverpool'	Duncan Fox; Booker Brothers; Rathbones; John Swire & Sons; Alfred Booth; Balfour Williamson
'Glasgow'	Grahams; James Finlay; Jardine Matheson; Jardine Skinner; Mackinnon Mackenzie; Guthries; T. D. Findlay; Wallace Brothers; Borneo Company

orientation. The 'Glasgow' houses were to remain Scottish in their recruitment patterns and 'culture' for many decades. They were also noticeably
oriented towards the Asian region, with the 'English' houses more oriented
towards South America. In terms of their destinations also British merchants
were clustered into hubs such as Bombay, Madras, Calcutta, Singapore, and
Hong Kong in Asia, and Buenos Aires and Valparaiso in Latin America.
These hubs provided concentrations of information, contacts, capital, and
personnel. The externalities of spatially proximate linked activities provided
major locational benefits to the merchant firms.

In organizational terms, the Borneo Company was a rare example of
a firm based in Britain with wholly owned affiliates abroad. In most cases
the 'firm' was a network of partnerships located in different countries.
Sometimes there was a British partnership which effectively 'controlled'
the overseas partnership. In other instances the partnerships resident abroad
were more powerful than the home ones. Some 'British' partnerships were
resident entirely abroad, though when partners from these firms retired
back to Britain they often retained shareholdings and influence in their
old firms.[67] The description of networks of partnerships as multinational
trading companies may seem controversial, but they effectively functioned
as single firms, albeit ones where the internal contractual and institutional
arrangements were periodically renegotiated.

There was nothing inevitable about the growth of British trading companies. This was a period of experiment with modes of operating abroad.
Overseas branches were sometimes opened, and closed again, as firms
reverted to the use of independent agents. Partnership agreements were
periodically renegotiated, often fragmenting established merchant networks.
Even large merchant houses could be overwhelmed by the risks of international trade. Survival required a mixture of skilful judgement, luck, and
the ability to solve the problem of succession in family-based partnerships.
Although there was no common key to success, securing a monopoly over
a valuable commodity often laid the basis for future growth. In the 1840s
and 1850s Jardine Matheson and Antony Gibbs flourished on the basis of
profits from opium and guano.

---

[67] Cunyngham-Brown, *The Traders*, 126.

3

From Trade to Investment

3.1 Introduction

From the 1870s British trading companies intensified their diversification from trade into other activities. By 1914 a number of these firms had become multinational 'business groups' which included trading, financial, natural resources, and manufacturing operations on several continents. The result was a change of function. The trading companies shifted from being the promoters of Britain's foreign trade to being dynamic agents of British FDI.

This was a period of great importance for the British trading companies, when portfolios of businesses were acquired and organizational forms developed which were often to remain in place until the 1960s. After surveying the main trends in the international economy before the First World War, the chapter examines the corporate structures employed by the trading companies and the evolution of 'business groups'. Section 3.4 surveys the diversification strategies pursued in the main host regions, while the following section looks at the growth of British merchants in tropical Africa.

3.2 The First Global Economy

The decades before the First World War saw phenomenal growth in the world economy. Between 1880 and the First World War over 32 million people emigrated from Europe, the majority to the United States, followed—a long way behind—by Argentina, Brazil, Australia, and Canada. Millions of Chinese migrated to South East Asia and California. International trade grew at much higher rates than world output—sometimes growing more than 60 per cent per decade—while international capital flows reached unprecedented proportions after 1870. The flows of people, trade, and capital created a 'global economy' for the first time in history. It was also an environment which offered enormous opportunities to multinational trading companies.

A new wave of imperialism provided further opportunities for the trading companies by extending the borders of Western influence. In Asia, British control was extended over Burma and Malaya, France extended its grip over Indo-China, while the United States took control over the Philippines after a war with Spain in 1898. Especially after the British occupation of Egypt in 1882, European control was extended over almost all of tropical

Africa. The British occupied large areas of West Africa, including the modern states of Nigeria and Ghana (formerly the Gold Coast) and large areas of East Africa, including the modern states of Kenya and Uganda.[1]

The world economy became more complex in this period. In international trade, the earlier pattern of largely disconnected trading arrangements substantially centred on Britain was replaced by a multilateral trading system based on a worldwide pattern of economic specialization. The industrialized countries of western Europe exchanged manufactured goods for the foodstuffs and raw materials produced in most of the rest of the world. In 1913 over 60 per cent of world trade was European, consisting both of intra-European trade and European trade with the rest of the world.[2] In contrast, North America was self-sufficient in most foodstuffs and raw materials.

After 1870 there was a rapid spread of industrialization. At the turn of the century Britain was still one of the world's leading industrial economies, but it had been joined by the United States, Germany, and a number of other European economies. This period saw the new capital-intensive industries of the Second Industrial Revolution, notably chemicals and electrical, develop and spread. The non-industrialized world supplied raw materials and foodstuffs to the industrialized centres and served as their markets. The share of primary products in world trade stayed almost constant between the 1870s and 1914, but there was a shift in its composition. The share of foodstuffs and agricultural raw materials in the total trade declined, while that of minerals increased, reflecting the rapid expansion of metal manufacturing after 1870 and the consequent increase in the demand for ores and concentrates.

There were complexities within this pattern of international specialization. Within Asia, there was a significant development of intra-Asian trade which may have grown faster than Asia's trade with the West. In the 1880s this intra-Asian trade pattern was still dominated by India's export of opium to China, but subsequently trade flows reflected the emergence of a modern cotton spinning industry in India and Japan. Indian cotton goods were exported to South East Asia and Japanese cotton yarn and goods to China, while by 1905 Japan had become the largest single importer of Indian raw cotton. From the 1900s Japan also exported consumer goods to Asian markets, while there were substantial intra-Asian flows of rice. There was no equivalent development of intra-Latin American or African trade.[3]

---

[1] P. J. Cain and A. G. Hopkins, *British Imperialism: Innovation and Expansion 1688–1914* (London: Longman, 1993).

[2] A. G. Kenwood and A. L. Lougheed, *The Growth of the International Economy 1820–1980* (London: Routledge, 1992), 80–1.

[3] Kaoru Sugihara, 'Patterns of Asia's Integration into the World Economy, 1880–1913' (mimeo). The size of intra-Asian trade flows is difficult to estimate because much of the trade passed through Singapore and Hong Kong, which as free ports did not record information on countries of origin or final destination.

Britain itself was no longer the world's largest economy. In 1870 Britain still produced one-third of world manufacturing output, but its share had fallen to one-seventh by 1914. British productivity growth was poor, and the development of new industries such as chemicals and electricals was slow. Britain's rate of export growth declined to 2 per cent between 1873 and 1914, largely as a result of a falling growth rate of textiles which increasingly shifted its exports to Asia. By 1914 as much as two-thirds of the value of British cotton piece-goods exports went to less developed markets.[4] The structure of British exports remained concentrated in the nineteenth-century 'staple' industries. In 1913, textiles and clothing still accounted for over 36 per cent of total British exports, followed by iron and steel and coal with over 10 per cent each.[5] Britain was the most important exporter of manufactured goods to primary producers outside Europe, but its overall share of world manufactured exports fell from just under 38 per cent between 1876–80 to 25 per cent in 1913.[6]

While the productivity performance of the domestic British economy and its export performance suggested that the relative importance of Britain in the world economy was in decline, this was only a partial picture. This was the great era of the spread of 'free-standing firms' and, insofar as they are accepted as a form of direct investment, of the growth of FDI. Britain remained by far the largest capital exporter in 1914, and the largest direct investor. British firms owned and managed plantations, mines, and other resource investments worldwide, as well as manufacturing operations in the developed markets of Europe and the United States. Britain's immense foreign investment stimulated a huge demand for sterling, which became firmly established as the most important international currency and widely used to finance not only British foreign trade but also that of most of the rest of world. World trade was largely financed by short-term credits provided by the London market—the 'bill on London'.

The City of London was the world's premier international financial centre and an enormous agglomeration of financial institutions and markets. It was the largest new issue market in the world and contained numerous specialists on foreign investment. The London money market was large, liquid, and highly internationally oriented. London had a unique role as the international service centre of the emergent global economy, providing information and contacts about investment opportunities worldwide. The City also housed many of the world's organized markets. The Baltic Exchange developed the market for grain and shipping, serving as the place to charter a ship anywhere in the world, while the Metal Exchange was established in 1882 to deal in tin, copper, and lead. London was also

---

[4] William Mass and William Lazonick, 'The British Cotton Industry and International Competitive Advantage: The State of the Debates', *Business History*, 32 (1990).

[5] C. H. Lee, *The British Economy Since 1700* (Cambridge: Cambridge University Press, 1986), 219.

[6] Kenwood and Lougheed, *Growth*, 86.

the world's leading insurance market. British firms were prominent in fire insurance and in marine insurance, where Lloyd's underwriters were especially important. In 1914 around two-thirds of world marine insurance was handled in Britain, mainly in London.[7]

This environment of expanding world trade and investment was ideal for the British trading companies. They had already developed roles beyond servicing the foreign trade of the United Kingdom, so the problematic British export performance was not yet a great handicap, while the commodity booms in rubber, rice, palm oil, and many other products in their host economies offered numerous trade—and investment—opportunities. Meanwhile the growth of Britain's capital markets and capital exports, London's position as the leading international service centre, and the expanding borders of the British Empire, provided the British trading firms with a formidable set of country-specific advantages.

3.3 Traders as Business Groups

The growth of the first global economy provided unprecedented opportunities for merchants. In European countries which, like Britain, possessed substantial colonies, such as France and the Netherlands, trading companies grew rapidly to exploit trade links between the home country and the colonies.[8] Non-colonial countries in Europe saw a similar phenomenon. In Europe, Denmark was the home to a cluster of trading companies engaged in trade with Russia, such as the Siberian Company, and to the East Asiatic Company, founded in 1897 to trade with Asia, especially Thailand. As Japan began its modernization after the Meiji Restoration in 1868, trading companies also emerged to handle much of Japan's foreign trade. In 1876 Japan's first 'general' trading company, Mitsui Bussan, was founded. The rapid growth of British trading companies in these decades, therefore, formed part of a general phenomenon.

In this period merchants diversified extensively into non-trading activities. British trading companies invested extensively in plantations, mines, processing, and other ventures in their host economies. They pursued vertical, horizontal, and unrelated diversification strategies, and in the process became involved in direct investments on a much greater scale than before 1870. Although the scale of the British investments was unique, the trend towards diversification beyond trade was not. Dutch trading companies invested in plantations in the Dutch East Indies. The East Asiatic Company became involved in teak production in Thailand. And during the 1900s Mitsui Bussan invested in cotton textiles and flour milling in China.

[7] Ranald C. Michie, *The City of London* (London: Macmillan, 1992).

[8] Keetie E. Sluyterman, 'Dutch Multinational Trading Companies in the Twentieth Century', in Geoffrey Jones (ed.), *The Multinational Traders* (London: Routledge, 1998), H. Bonin, *C.F.A.O. Cent Ans de Compétition* (Paris: Economica, 1987).

The opportunities for scope economies and the incentive to reduce transactions costs continued to exercise systematic influences on diversification strategies. Like the diversified business groups active in many developing countries today, British merchants had often established extensive 'contacts' with (often colonial) governments and other resource owners which created asymmetries of information and access between them and other foreign firms, and provided considerable potential for scope economies.[9] Time-specific influences explain the pace of diversification seen from the 1870s. The first was the impact of transport and communications improvements. In Asia, a key development was the opening of the Suez Canal in 1869. This suddenly made China more than 3,000 miles closer to Europe. The growth of speedier communications between Asia and Europe resulted in a new range of trading and investment opportunities, such as selling Russian oil to Asian markets.

The spread of steamships was a worldwide phenomenon. From the mid-nineteenth century steamships began to call at the River Plate with increasing frequency. Major port improvements in Buenos Aires, the Brazilian ports, and elsewhere facilitated this improvement in shipping connections.[10] Africa was similarly drawn into the world economy through steamships. In 1852 the first steamship company for trading with West Africa was formed. Consequently the journey from Britain to West Africa was cut from 35 to less than 21 days, and the cost of the journey fell considerably.[11] This provided the basis for the growth of a new generation of British trading companies, active in West Africa. Worldwide, ocean freight rates on long hauls fell from the 1870s until shortly before the First World War, especially because of steamships even though the performance of sailing ships continued to improve.

The impact of the telegraph was perhaps more radical, especially for the business of merchants. The first successful transatlantic cable connection was in 1866. In 1870 London and Bombay were linked by cable. The cable reached Australia in 1872. In 1876 Buenos Aires was connected to the South American submarine telegraph cable. The telegraph offered the prospect of instant communication and of world commodity markets.

The improvements in transport and communications from the 1870s resulted in opportunities and threats for merchants, both of which provided incentives for further diversification. In terms of opportunities, the exploitation of primary commodities in countries located far away from the main

[9] Carl Kock and Mauro F. Guillén, 'Strategy and Structure in Developing Countries: Business Groups as an Evolutionary Response to Opportunities for Unrelated Diversification', *Industrial and Corporate Change*, 10/1 (2001), 77–113.

[10] D. C. M. Platt, *Latin America and British Trade 1806–1914* (London. Adam & Charles Black, 1972).

[11] P. N. Davies, *The Trade Makers: Elder Dempster in West Africa 1852–1972* (London: George Allen & Unwin, 1973).

European markets became far more practical. At the same time new markets were opened by steamships, new ports, railroads, and telegraphs. Latin America was transformed from being a modest market for British textiles into an expanding market not only for textiles, but for British iron and steel, machinery, and coal.[12] However the transport and communication improvements also threatened merchant intermediaries by reducing uncertainty and lowering information costs. The telegraph in particular provided new opportunities for direct communication between suppliers and customers, without the need for middlemen.[13] However some markets were opened more quickly, or were of more interest to, say, European manufacturers, than other countries. Moreover the effects of the telegraph varied commodity by commodity and the bulk of communications continued by sea post until the early twentieth century.

A second major influence on the diversification strategies of the trading companies was the boom in commodity prices. Industrialization in Europe and the United States stimulated a worldwide search for new sources of supply of raw materials and foodstuffs. From the 1870s there was a massive growth in world FDI in mining. As petroleum consumption grew with new uses, the search for oil became worldwide. Oil was the only fuel that could drive the new motor car, while the demand for rubber tyres for cars created an enormous rubber boom in the 1900s. As incomes rose in developed countries, there was a vast increase in demand for products such as tea, coffee, sugar, and tropical fruits which had been luxuries to previous generations. By 1870 the British trading companies were already trading in primary commodities or were at least established in countries which were probably candidates to become major producers. They were consequently well positioned to diversify into production.

A third determinant was the further expansion of imperial frontiers. In Asia, British political influence was extended over the whole of the Malayan peninsular from the 1870s, while the annexation of Upper Burma in 1886 brought the rest of that country under British control. Also during the late nineteenth century large regions of tropical Africa were incorporated in the European, especially British and French, colonial empires during the 'scramble for Africa'. As the imperial frontiers expanded, so the trading companies followed in the wake.

A final determinant of the diversification of the British trading companies in particular was capital availability arising from Britain's booming capital exports from the 1870s. In this period they made much greater use of the British capital markets and the availability of limited liability to raise finance for the new business opportunities which appeared at this time. They functioned in part as venture capitalists identifying opportunities and

---

[12] Platt, *Latin America*, 72–3.

[13] Stanley Chapman, *Merchant Enterprise in Britain* (Cambridge: Cambridge University Press, 1992), 193.

placing potential British investors in touch with them. For the most part this was achieved not by opening up the shareholding of the parent trading company, but by floating separate 'free-standing' firms on the British capital markets, which the merchant houses continued to control through management contracts and other means in the established tradition of 'agency houses'.

The desire to access the capital and information available in London was one reason why from at least mid-century Liverpool-based firms such as Swire's and Harrisons & Crosfield began to shift their head offices to London, although other firms such as Balfour Williamson remained Liverpool-based until the interwar years. The British merchants also sometimes formed locally registered firms, especially in British colonies where the company legislation was modelled on Britain, which mobilized the pools of capital accumulated by resident Europeans in Asia and elsewhere. The colonies also had a fixed exchange rate with Britain which made the operation of a British and colonial share register easier. Conversely, some merchant firms from the colonies relocated to London in order to access the markets for capital and information. David Sassoon moved its head office from Bombay to London in 1872. In 1884 the Australian wool handling and shipping merchant Dalgety, which had been organized as interlocking colonial and London partnerships, incorporated in Britain in order to access the capital required to compete in that trade. Dalgety did not invest in non-trading activities, but it did subsequently diversify on a large scale into selling refrigerated meat and dairy food from New Zealand and Australia to Europe.[14]

The upshot was the creation of diversified 'investment groups', or business groups in the terminology preferred here, around the British merchant houses. The merchant house acted as the 'core firm' within each group, usually responsible through its overseas branches for trading and agency business, while separately quoted or incorporated affiliates—often not wholly owned—were engaged in plantations, mines, processing, and other non-trading operations. Consequently, although reinvested profits continued to be an important source of funds for the British merchant groups, after 1870 they also drew substantially on outside funds to finance expansion into new activities. Partners and directors of the merchant houses did not generally provide large amounts of new capital themselves in this period. The functioning of these business groups is examined in Chapter 6.

The British willingness to use outside capital in affiliate ventures was distinctive. With some exceptions, in other European countries non-trading activities might be separately incorporated but were usually wholly owned. The ability of the British companies to utilize the London capital market and accumulated expatriate savings overseas provided them with funds to

[14] M. J. Daunton, 'Firm and Family in the City of London in the Nineteenth Century: The Case of F. G. Dalgety', *English Historical Review*, 60/11 (1989), 154–77; Wynford Vaughan-Thomas, *Dalgety: The Romance of a Business* (London: Henry Melland, 1984).

expand on a greater scale, though it also created governance structures which were more dependent on contracts and relationships than equity.

Though joint stock companies were used as vehicles for diversification by the British companies, the partnership form remained widely employed by many of the parent merchant firms. By 1914 some of the largest merchant groups continued to employ the partnership form. Even the minority of cases which availed themselves of limited liability generally became private rather than public companies, which enabled family ownership and control and most of the past traditions of the former partnerships to continue with little hindrance. This was not exceptional in the corporate context of Britain of this period—the widespread use of limited companies only got under way in the 1880s, and in 1914 four-fifths of registered joint stock companies were private[15]—but the merchants were certainly among the most reluctant sectors to abandon partnerships and family control.

There were regional differences. The partnership form remained widespread among the British firms specialized in India and in Latin America. In India, exceptions included James Finlay which incorporated as a private limited company in 1909. The leading British traders in Burma also took private limited liability status, Steels in 1890 and Wallace & Co. in 1911. In Latin America, there were a limited number of cases of incorporation. E. Johnston became a private limited company in 1906, and in 1909 a public company, Brazilian Warrant, was formed which took over the business of E. Johnston.[16] In 1914 Alfred Booth converted its partnership into a private limited company.

Family influence often persisted even when firms incorporated. Although Wilson Sons incorporated in 1877, in the mid-1880s there were only ten shareholders, and four members of the Wilson family held 700 of the 1,500 shares.[17] A further 330 shares were held by two members of the Hett family, whose coal importing business on the River Plate and in London Wilsons had just acquired. By 1907, a year before the merger with the Ocean group of coal companies, the number of shareholders had expanded to around sixty and the Wilson family had disappeared from the list, but the Hett and Yarrow families were still prominent.

British merchants active in other host regions appeared more willing to embrace limited liability even if family influence often remained as strong. In South East Asia, the Borneo Company's foundation as a limited liability company in 1856 remained exceptional until the 1900s, when there was a growth of incorporation among the agency houses in Singapore and Malaya.

---

[15] Mary B. Rose, 'The Family Firm in British Business, 1780–1914', in M. W. Kirby and M. B. Rose (eds.), *Business Enterprise in Modern Britain from the Eighteenth to the Twentieth Centuries* (London: Routledge, 1994), 68.

[16] Robert Greenhill, 'Investment Group, Free-Standing Company or Multinational? Brazilian Warrant, 1909–52', *Business History*, 37 (1995), 91.

[17] List of shareholdings in March 1886, Minute book A, MS 20186/1, GHL.

Guthries in 1903, Adamson, Gilfillan in 1904, and Paterson, Simons in 1907 incorporated locally, while Harrisons & Crosfield became a British public company in 1908.[18] The Siam Forest Company, the predecessor to the Anglo-Siam Corporation, was founded as a British public joint stock company in 1897. While there were plenty of partnerships among the smaller British trading companies on the China coast, Dodwells took private limited liability status in 1899 and John Swire & Sons in 1914. Jardine Matheson incorporated as a private company under Hong Kong law in 1906. Among the larger West African trading companies, the African Association was formed as a private limited liability company in 1889, John Holt & Co. took this status in 1897, and Millers formed two private limited companies, Millers Ltd. in 1904 and Miller Brothers (of Liverpool) Limited in 1907. The Niger Company was formed as a public company in 1900.

Table 3.1 provides estimates of the size of the British trading companies before 1914. It shows the wide size dispersion of the British merchant houses at this time, and identifies a cluster of especially large firms with capital near or in excess of £1 million. However there are at least three problems with the data. First, the continued use of the partnership form, and the scarcity of data on private limited companies, means that several figures are estimated, while that for Jardine Matheson is taken from Chapman and is for 'capital' rather than capital employed.[19] It is not possible to derive a con-solidated figure for the Mackinnon/Inchcape group of partnerships at all, though information is provided on its East African and Gulf partnerships. The consolidated size of the Grahams partnerships in Britain, Portugal, and India is similarly unknown. The table also excludes the Indian-based agency houses whose capital was in rupees.

Secondly, there remain acute problems of definition. The distinction between 'merchants' and 'bankers' remained by no means clear-cut. As will be discussed below, Antony Gibbs—included in Table 3.1—continued to span both worlds. It was not an isolated case. By this period Frederick Huth and Co. had a large acceptance business and can be regarded as a 'merchant bank', but it also had an associated house in Manchester and Chile which was a merchant business. Bankers continued to enter merchanting for various reasons and by various routes. In 1876 the long-established London private bankers C. Hoare and Co. acquired the assets of a timber merchant firm who had become indebted to them. As a result, they became the owners of a timber trading company with extensive forests in the British Central American colony of British Honduras, which they only sold in 1942.[20] The exclusion of 'bankers' from Table 3.1 is, therefore, arbitrary.

---

[18] Drabble and Drake, 'British Agency Houses', 308.

[19] Chapman, *Merchant Enterprise*, 254–6.

[20] Kathleen M. Stahl, *The Metropolitan Organisation of British Colonial Trade* (London: Faber and Faber, 1951), 31.

TABLE 3.1 Estimated size of capital employed of selected British trading companies, 1913 (£000s)

Jardine Matheson[a]	2,500
Balfour Williamson	2,000
Wilson, Sons & Co.	1,728
James Finlay	1,500
Antony Gibbs	1,500
Niger Company	1,389
Harrisons & Crosfield	1,226
John Swire & Sons	952
Duncan Fox & Co.	930
John Holt & Co. (Liverpool)	660
Brazilian Warrant	600
Booker Brothers, McConnell & Co.	500
Borneo Co.	425
Dodwell & Co.	225
Guthrie & Co.[a]	163
Smith Mackenzie & Co.	150
Anglo-Siam Corporation	100
Gray Mackenzie & Co.	100

[a] Registration overseas.

Source: Appendix 3.

Thirdly, the 'size' of firms listed in the table needs careful interpretation. On the one hand, capital employed is heavily dependent on the type of business undertaken by a firm. The large size of Wilson, Sons & Co., for example, reflected the capital-intensive nature of its coaling depots, with their coal handling equipment, lighters, ship repair facilities, and other fixed assets. In contrast, Dodwells seems 'small' because its shipping and trading business could be conducted without such large fixed assets. On the other hand, and most seriously, the data in Table 3.1 is for capital employed of the parent firm only. Consequently it does not capture the dimensions of the wider business groups around the core merchant firms.

British trading companies were, and remained, focused on a specific host region, where they acquired and then exploited local knowledge about markets, laws, cultures, and languages and contacts with resource owners. French, Dutch, Danish, and other European trading houses shared this characteristic. Nevertheless during these decades a number of the British merchant houses extended their geographical horizons to take advantage of the emergent 'global economy'. By 1914 a number of embryonic multi-regional business groups had emerged. Table 3.2 lists some of the more extensive cases.

TABLE 3.2 Multi-regional 'business groups' by 1914

Trading company	Major host regions	Outposts
Inchcape/Mackinnon	India; Gulf; East Africa; Australia	
Grahams	India; Portugal	
James Finlay	India; UK	Ceylon; USA; Canada; Russia
Harrisons & Crosfield	Malaya; Dutch East Indies; India	Ceylon; USA; Canada; Australia; New Zealand
Jardine Matheson	China	Japan; USA; South Africa; Peru
Dodwells	China; Canada; USA	Ceylon; Japan
Antony Gibbs	Chile; Australia	Peru; USA
Balfour Williamson	Chile; USA	Peru; Canada
Alfred Booth	Brazil; UK; USA	
Ocean Coal & Wilsons	Brazil; UK	Argentina; North and West Africa

The most extensive multi-regional business group, but also the most diffuse, was the Mackinnon group of interlocked partnerships which continued to grow in complexity following Sir William Mackinnon's return to London from Asia in 1873 through to his death in 1893. His eventual successor was James Lyle Mackay (made the first Lord Inchcape in 1911) who went to Calcutta to work for Mackinnon Mackenzie in 1874, returning to Britain in 1893 as the old generation of Mackinnon and Hall families was dying out. Mackay became a partner in various Mackinnon ventures. William Mackinnon had no son and was succeeded by his nephew, Duncan, whose two sons were killed in the First World War. Over time Mackay's shareholding in the various partnerships grew and, by 1914, the business might be called the 'Inchcape group', even though the Inchcape family did not have a controlling interest in the partnerships until after the Second World War.[21]

The Mackinnon/Inchcape group proliferated by the creation of new partnerships and companies giving its structure a complex appearance. At its heart was a cluster of shipping companies. By the end of the 1880s it owned five steamship companies operating on river, coastal, and oceanic waters, including BI, the Netherlands India SN Co., two Indian-based coastal shipping companies, and the largest coastal shipping firm on the eastern Australian seaboard, formed in 1887. Collectively these companies comprised

[21] Stephanie Jones, *Trade and Shipping: Lord Inchcape 1852–1932* (Manchester: Manchester University Press, 1989).

'almost certainly the largest and most diversified steamshipping complex in existence'.[22] In 1914 Inchcape, who had become chairman of BI in the previous year, merged it with the P&O to become the largest shipping group in the world, dominating the passenger and cargo lines from Britain to Asia and Australia.[23]

Beyond the shipping companies, there was further expansion of the mercantile activities. In 1877 Gray Dawes, which already had related partnerships in the Gulf, founded Smith Mackenzie in Zanzibar, which became the largest British trading company in East Africa by 1914. During the 1870s new partnerships were created by cousins of the Mackinnon family, D. Macneill & Co. in London and Macneill & Co. in Calcutta, which became the major vehicles for investing in tea plantations, as Mackinnon Mackenzie increasingly focused on shipping. Between the various partnerships the group owned tea estates in Bengal and Assam, coal mines in Bengal, and jute and cotton mills in Calcutta. In 1906 Inchcape and his fellow partners in BI acquired the Madras-based company Binny's, which had cotton and woollen mills, and coffee estates as well as a trading business.[24]

Among the other British merchant houses with substantial business in India, at least three can be regarded as 'multi-regional' by 1914. Grahams and Finlays remained Glasgow-based firms. The Grahams consisted of multiple interlocked partnerships which combined a large trading business in India with a diversified business in Portugal. In that country, Grahams diversified from port into manufacturing, acquiring a printing factory in 1875, a spinning and weaving mill in 1888, and a paper mill in 1899. James Finlay diversified extensively in India after 1870, initially using the profits from its Scottish cotton mills. It began manufacturing jute in 1873, and cotton textiles in the 1900s. Its largest diversification was into tea plantations, of which by 1900 it controlled a very large acreage in India. Finlays in turn established distribution, packaging, and warehousing facilities in Britain, the United States, Canada, and Russia.

Harrisons & Crosfield was founded as a Liverpool-based partnership engaged in tea trading, buying tea in India and China and selling it in Britain and elsewhere. From the 1890s, when the first overseas branch was opened in Colombo, and 1910, a network of offices were opened in India, Malaya, the Dutch East Indies, the United States, Canada, Australia, and New Zealand. These branches were usually established to trade in tea, but soon acquired a wider range of import and export trade, as well as acting as agents for insurance and shipping companies. The tea trading interests led to the

---

[22] J. Forbes Munro, 'Scottish Overseas Enterprise and the Lure of London: The Mackinnon Shipping Group, 1847–1893', *Scottish Economic and Social History*, 8 (1988), 75; id., '"The Gilt of Illusion"· The Mackinnon Group's Entry into Queensland Shipping, 1880–1895', *International Journal of Maritime History*, 3 (1991), 1–37.

[23] Stephanie Jones, *Two Centuries of Overseas Trading* (London. Macmillan, 1986), 56.

[24] Ibid.

purchase of tea estates in Ceylon beginning in 1899, followed by further estates in south India, and the development of distribution facilities in tea consuming countries. In 1903 the firm floated its first Malayan rubber company, while 1906 saw its first such investment in the Dutch East Indies, where it was also involved in tea and tobacco. By 1914 the firm held shares and management contracts in around forty rubber plantation companies.[25]

On the China coast, Jardine Matheson and Dodwells both evolved as multiregional groups. The former was based on the partnerships of Matheson & Co. and Jardine Matheson, which had overlapping but not identical shareholders and partners. Hugh Matheson was the senior partner of Matheson & Co. between 1848 and his death in 1898. William Keswick, a relative of the Jardine family and the first of five generations of Keswicks in Jardine Matheson, went to China in 1855 after a period with Matheson & Co., and by 1874 was 'taipan' or the senior manager. In 1886 he settled permanently in London and, responsible only to the senior partner in the firm—Sir Robert Jardine—he took complete charge of the management of Jardine Matheson, serving as its Managing Director following its incorporation in 1906 until his death in 1912. In that year the Matheson family interest in Matheson & Co. was bought out and the two firms thereafter had identical shareholders.

Though Jardine Matheson and Matheson & Co. were intimately related they can also be seen as representing two sides of the group. Between the 1860s and 1914 Jardine Matheson was transformed from being an opium trading company with some general trading, shipping, and financial activities into a diversified conglomerate with branches all over China, as well as in Japan and New York. Matheson & Co. grew over the same period as a London merchant house acting as agents for both Jardine Matheson and Jardine Skinner in Calcutta, but it also served as an international venture capitalist, with a special interest in mining. In the last three decades of the century Matheson's invested in copper mining in Spain and California, banking in Iran, and gold mining in South Africa.[26] In the late nineteenth century Keswick also invested in an oil company in Peru. This experience, as well as unsatisfactory involvement in various Russian mining ventures in the 1900s, seems to have dented the enthusiasm for such investments. 'Past experience', a director of Matheson's wrote to Jardines' taipan in Hong Kong in 1915 'has taught us that it is wiser to leave mines alone'.[27]

[25] R. A. Brown, *Capital and Entrepreneurship in Southeast Asia* (London: Macmillan, 1994), 57–8. Harrisons & Crosfield, *One Hundred Years as East India Merchants: Harrisons & Crosfield 1844–1943* (London: the firm, 1944); G. C. Allen and A. G. Donnithorne, *Western Enterprise in Indonesia and Malaya* (London: George Allen & Unwin, 1957), 56–7.

[26] Charles E. Harvey, *The Rio Tinto Company* (Penzance: Alison Hodge, 1981), esp. 5–11, 188; Mira Wilkins, *The History of Foreign Investment in the United States to 1914* (Cambridge, Mass.: Harvard University Press, 1989), 267, 769 n. 22. Geoffrey Jones, *Banking and Empire in Iran* (Cambridge: Cambridge University Press, 1986), 11–12; Chapman, *Merchant Enterprise*, 247.

[27] C. H. Ross to David Landale, 10 June 1915, S/O Letters London to Hong Kong 1915, JMA, CUL.

On a smaller scale, Dodwells also became a multi-regional business. Dodwell & Co. was founded as a British company in 1899, but the firm's origins were in a trading and shipping agency firm originally formed in Shanghai in 1858, and reconstructed as Adamson Bell & Co. in 1867. George Benjamin Dodwell was recruited as a shipping clerk, and in the 1880s he was active in developing shipping links between the Far East and the Pacific coast of Canada and the United States. The great coup came in 1887 when Dodwell secured the agency for chartering and managing ships on behalf of the Canadian Pacific Railway between Hong Kong and Vancouver, Canada. A few years later Dodwell's firm got into serious financial problems and, in a second coup, Dodwell and a colleague formed a partnership which took over most of Adamson Bell's agencies and business on the day of its collapse in 1891. This partnership was reconstructed as a London-based firm in 1899.

Dodwells developed as a trading firm with branches in China, Japan, Sri Lanka, the Pacific coast of Canada and the United States, and, from 1912, New York. Shipping agency and tea trading were major concerns. Having lost the Canadian Pacific contract in 1892, Dodwells secured another trans-Pacific contract with an American railroad company, and by the turn of the century could claim to be the largest shipping firm on the Pacific coast. Dodwells were large exporters of China and Japanese teas, which they sold especially to Britain, the United States, and from 1901, to Russia. When demand began to shift towards Indian teas, Dodwells opened a branch in Colombo in Ceylon (Sri Lanka) in 1897 to purchase and sell Ceylon teas. However branches initially opened for shipping agency or tea trading often developed other activities. The Vancouver branch invested in salmon canneries, developing a business exporting canned salmon to Britain and elsewhere. In the United States, the Tacoma and Seattle branches helped develop a local flour milling industry. The Colombo branch diversified from tea trading to the export of coconuts. It established a desiccating mill in 1910, and acquired a number of tea and coconut plantations.[28]

Both Antony Gibbs and Balfour Williamson expanded into multi-regional business groups. Gibbs became a large-scale nitrates producer first in Peru and then in Chile, when the main nitrate fields were transferred to that country following the war of 1879–82. By the 1880s nearly half of Chilean nitrate mines were British owned, and Gibbs was among the largest of those nitrate producers.[29] Although Chilean nitrates were the core of the business, it was also involved in copper production in the 1880s and 1900s, and in 1912 acquired a British investment house active in the south of Chile which included a flour milling business. A calculation of Gibbs' share of Chilean

[28] Edmund Warde, *The House of Dodwell. A Century of Achievement 1858–1958* (London: the firm, 1958); Jones, *Two Centuries*, 160–82.

[29] Robert Greenhill, 'The Nitrate and Iodine Trades 1880–1914', in D. C. M. Platt (ed.), *Business Imperialism 1840–1930* (Oxford: Clarendon Press, 1977), 231–65.

exports estimated that it accounted for 27 per cent in 1870, 10 per cent in 1890, and 4 per cent in 1907. Its share of Chilean exports to Britain was 32 per cent, 23 per cent, and 15 per cent in the same years.[30]

Gibbs' business horizons widened in this period. In 1881 Antony Gibbs in London took over the fading associate house of Gibbs Bright & Co., based in Liverpool and Bristol, which in turn had an operation in the West Indies and a partnership in Australia. The Caribbean business was rapidly abandoned, but Gibbs Bright & Co.—which had large offices in Melbourne and Sydney as well as branches in Perth, Adelaide, and Brisbane—developed a business in importing as well as acting as shipping agent for lines working between Australia and the Far East, and established a company for coastal shipping between Australian ports. In 1885 they acquired a wool shipping firm in Newcastle, New South Wales, and became substantial wool shippers as a result. The firm also made substantial investments in Australian sheep and cattle ranching, a mining company, and a wire netting manufacturer.[31] In 1913 Gibbs also opened a small New York office, initially to promote nitrate sales and South American produce generally in the United States, and to facilitate imports into Chile from the United States. In London, Antony Gibbs functioned as a merchant bank, becoming a major acceptance house, though its volume of acceptances remained below that of the market leaders. From the late 1880s Gibbs also started a securities issuing business and became active in the issue of foreign loans on the London market, primarily to Central and South American countries.[32]

Balfour Williamson also greatly expanded its geographical horizons from the 1870s. Like Gibbs, it built an extensive business in Chile and Peru. In Chile Balfour Williamson took a number of equity stakes in nitrate, railroad, and water companies, and a coastal shipping company. From the late 1880s it owned a company which smelted silver, lead, and copper. A branch expansion programme between 1880 and 1914 extended the firm's operations from Valparaíso to many inland towns. In 1892 the firm also began flour milling on a large scale by building a mill. They also had a mill in Peru, and in 1913 these were combined into the British-registered Santa Rosa Milling Company. In Peru, Balfour Williamson was closely associated with the firm of Milne & Co., although they did not enter a formal partnership until 1912. Milne made investments in flour and rice mills, and in 1901 joined in a syndicate to prospect for oil at Lobitos, Peru. In 1905 Milne's syndicate found oil, and in 1908 Balfour Williamson supervised the public flotation in Britain of Lobitos Oilfields.[33]

---

[30] Manuel A. Fernández, 'Merchants and Bankers: British Direct and Portfolio Investment in Chile during the Nineteenth Century', *Ibero Amerikanisches Archiv* (1993), 362–3. Antony Gibbs & Sons, *Merchants and Bankers 1808–1958* (London: the firm, 1958).

[31] Antony Gibbs & Sons, *Merchants and Bankers*, 107–13.

[32] Stanley Chapman, *The Rise of Merchant Banking* (London: George Allen & Unwin, 1984), 121, 209.

[33] Platt, *Latin America*, 138.

Balfour Williamson also invested on a large scale in North America. By 1914 it had accumulated a portfolio of businesses in California, Oregon, and British Columbia through the Balfour Guthrie partnership. During the 1870s its main business in California was the export of wheat, to which the firm rapidly added ancillary services such as marine insurance and the building of a warehouse in San Francisco to clean, store, and load the commodity. Subsequently the firm invested in lumber, coal mining, and salmon fishing in California and Oregon. In 1889 it built a wharf and storage depot in Portland, Oregon, together with a network of forty country warehouses in that state's wheat districts. By the early 1900s the firm had eighty grain warehouses and elevators in the wheat producing areas of the Pacific coast, and in 1910 purchased a flour mill in Portland (Crown Mills). Among the other investments in this region, the Pacific Loan and Investment Company was formed in 1878 to undertake mortgage loans and land investments, and from the 1880s Balfour Guthrie made investments in potential fruit growing land, and this led to investment in fruit and vineyard properties, and in packing and drying fruit. Most spectacularly, Balfour Williamson formed California Oilfields Limited in 1901, which found oil in the following year, becoming the first successful British investment in American oil before its sale in 1913.[34]

On a smaller scale, Alfred Booth & Co. evolved as a multi-regional group. The firm continued to trade in sheepskins, but made a radical diversification into leather. In 1877 the firm acquired an interest in a New York firm of tanners and dressers, which owed money to Booths for deerskins and goatskins, and by 1886 Booths had purchased this factory outright. Between the mid-1880s and 1914 the firm developed a vertically integrated business in the manufacture of 'kid leather' following the invention of a new method of tanning leather by chemical means. It owned tanneries in Britain and the United States, where the business was placed under the control of the US-registered Surpass Leather Company, owned by Booths, in 1906. Initially using goatskins from Brazil, Booths expanded its sources of supply first to India and then to China. Parallel with the expansion of their leather interests, the Booths formed the Booth Steamship Company in 1881, whose shipping activities flourished alongside the boom in Brazilian natural rubber exports before the First World War. Booths invested in port services and river transport facilities in Brazil, and in the 1900s undertook the building of harbour facilities up country (at Manáos).[35]

A final case of a 'Latin American' specialist becoming a multi-regional group was Wilson, Sons & Co. Having concentrated on coal importing and shipping in Brazil before the late 1860s, Wilsons subsequently diversified into

[34] Wallis Hunt, *Heirs of Great Adventure 1901–1955* (London: the firm, 1960), *passim*; Morton Rothstein, 'A British Firm on the American West Coast, 1869–1914', *Business History Review*, 37 (1963), 392–425; Wilkins, *Foreign Investment in the United States to 1914*, 284–91.
[35] A. H. John, *A Liverpool Merchant House* (London: George Allen & Unwin, 1959), 71–106.

contracting. It became involved in arranging contracts for infrastructure projects in Brazil, especially railroads and dockyards. By the early 1880s these contracting projects had resulted in losses,[36] and the firm refocused on coal imports and related shipping services, which were developed further to include stevedoring, lighterage, towage, and ship repair and related engineering work. The decision to concentrate on coal imports led to expansion to the River Plate, where an office was opened in Buenos Aires in 1888, and by the 1900s Argentina had become the firm's largest market.[37] Wilsons also expanded its coal depots beyond the East Coast of South America. By the early 1890s it had a coal depot in St Vincent, while later a depot in the Canaries was established. It acquired coal depots in Tunisia in 1902 and Senegal in 1903, and in Egypt soon afterwards. Finally, and unusually, in 1908 Wilsons merged with its long-term supplier of Welsh steam coal to form a holding company, Ocean Coal & Wilsons.

The growth of British merchant groups across different regions was a striking development after 1870, especially as many firms continued to be family owned or use the partnership form. No single model emerges of such groups. The Mackinnon/Inchcape complex was primarily a shipping group spread over Asia and Australia with a trading business in the Gulf, India, and Africa as well as plantations in India. The Jardine Matheson group combined a diversified services and manufacturing business in the Far East with a worldwide venture capital business. Gibbs and Balfour Williamson had diversified mining and trading investments in China and Peru, to which Gibbs added trading in Australia and London merchant banking, while Balfour Williamson undertook trading, flour milling, real estate, and financial services in North America.

3.4 Business Strategies

Between 1870 and 1914 the pace of diversification intensified in many regions as British merchant houses became direct investors on a large scale in Asia and the Americas. They exploited their knowledge and 'contacts' to diversify into new profitable opportunities, often in the process overcoming the mercantile suspicion of fixed investments. Diversification can be readily understood in these years as a result of systematic factors, but at the level of individual firms it was often a more chaotic or 'entrepreneurial' process, as merchants responded to 'unexpected' opportunities, or as the assets seized from bad debts were used to build new business streams.

There were, as usual, distinct regional differences. By the late nineteenth century the remaining British merchant houses in Russia had only a marginal role in Russian foreign trade, the survivors diversifying into manufacturing

---

[36] Wilson, Sons & Co. directors report 1883, Minute book A, MS 20186/1, GHL.
[37] Wilson, Sons & Co. annual accounts, 1904, Minute book C, MS 20186/3, GHL.

or finance. Of the leading British merchant groups, both the Whishaws and the Hubbards experienced major financial crises in the late nineteenth and early twentieth centuries. The latter combined their textile manufacturing operations into a 'free-standing' company, the Anglo-Russian Cotton Company in 1897. They also held large timber concessions, but succession problems and the requirement to provide funds for the large Hubbard family seem to have led to under-investment in the business and repeated financial problems.[38] The London-based Ralli Brothers had entirely withdrawn from the Russian grain trade by this period, although a Ralli partnership in Russia had large farming investments in the south of the country.[39]

British merchant enterprise in Latin America had settled into clear patterns by this period. It was firmly concentrated in a few subregions—the River Plate, Brazil, and the West Coast—with almost nothing elsewhere, including Central America, Columbia, and Venezuela. In these places, business was concentrated in the hands of a small number of large firms or groups, while most of the numerous import-export houses seen earlier in the century had become extinct. Charles Jones identifies fourteen British business groups —or 'mercantile investment groups' in his terminology—active in Latin America by 1914.[40]

There was a distinction between British merchants operating on the East Coast and those on the West Coast. Before 1914 Argentina was the most dynamic economy in Latin America, and by far the most important host country for total British foreign investment and FDI. In 1913 it accounted for almost one-half of British FDI in the whole of Latin America. Argentina displaced Brazil as Britain's most important market in Latin America towards the end of the century, while Britain was also a major export market for Argentina's principal exports of wool, grain, and meat. However, British merchant houses formed only a part—and not the most important part— of the constellation of British business active on the River Plate.

Argentina was one of the countries where the opportunities for British merchants to act as trade intermediaries declined in the late nineteenth century alongside transport and communication improvements. Steamships and the telegraph put pressure on the traditional roles of British merchants as intermediaries. Argentina's wheat was increasingly handled by major foreign grain firms that bought locally and supplied European millers directly. The leading wool firms in Belgium, France, and Britain sent out

[38] Stuart Thompstone, 'British Merchant Houses in Russia before 1914', in Linda Edmondson and Peter Waldron (eds.), *Economy and Society in Russia and the Soviet Union, 1860–1930* (London: Macmillan, 1992), 123–4; Natalia Gurushina, 'Free-Standing Companies in Tsarist Russia', in Mira Wilkins and Harm Schröter (eds.), *The Free-Standing Company in the World Economy 1830–1996* (Oxford: Oxford University Press, 1998), 173–80.
[39] Ioanna Pepelasis Minoglou, 'The Greek Merchant House of the Russian Black Sea: A Nineteenth Century Example of a Traders' Coalition', *International Journal of Maritime History*, 10 (1998), 96.
[40] Jones, 'Institutional Forms', 30.

their own representatives to the Argentine to purchase wool directly. Conversely, British-owned railroads and utility companies in the region set up their own buying agencies overseas. A further source of pressure came from foreign merchants, who were able to supply new products not manufactured in Britain. By the early twentieth century, as a result, British trading companies were reduced to a limited role in the River Plate area. They were not important in the major exports of wool, grain, and meat, nor had they invested in railroads or utilities. Nor had the surviving firms looked to other countries for new growth opportunities, except in neighbouring Montevideo in Uruguay. The remaining British trading companies tended to become specialized importers, in particular of machinery, capital goods, and branded consumer products.[41]

Despite this general trend, a number of British merchant groups remained active in the River Plate. These included Drabble Brothers, which had investments in land, sheep-farming, and meat-freezing plants; the Morrison family, in land, utilities, transport, and financial services; the Nield family, in trading and insurance agencies, and footwear, cement, and paint factories; and a group around the Gunther family, Belgian merchants resident in London, with substantial investments in meat extracts, controlling the Liebig's Extract of Meat Company, and involved in establishing the Forestal Land, Timber and Railway Company in 1906, designed to exploit 'quebracho', a tree whose extracts were used for the tanning of heavy leather.[42]

The British merchants in Brazil also generally remained specialists focused on that country rather than seeking to diversify elsewhere. The Ashworth family had three mills in Brazil manufacturing shoes, woollens, and cotton, as well as one in Lancashire. Knowles & Foster invested in banking, brewing, sugar, and—especially—milling.[43] Booths followed its trade up country by building harbour facilities. During the 1900s the coffee traders E. Johnston responded to the growth of competition in the coffee trade and to price falls by investing in a range of services to supply to the Brazilian coffee trade, such as storage, credit, a warehouse and warrant system, facilities for future trading, and transport. In 1909 the firm also established a coffee marketing company in Britain, which developed its own blend of pure roasted

[41] Colin Lewis, 'British Business in the Argentine' (mimeo); R. Greenhill and R. Miller, 'British Trading Companies in South America after 1914', in Jones (ed.), *Multinational Traders*.

[42] Jones, 'Institutional Forms'; M. Cowen, 'Capital, Nation and Commodities: The Case of the Forestal Land, Timber and Railway Company in Argentina and Africa, 1900–1945', in J. J. van Helten and Y. Cassis (eds.), *Capitalism in a Mature Economy* (Aldershot: Edward Elgar, 1990).

[43] Jones 'Institutional Forms'; R. Graham, 'A British Industry in Brazil: Rio Flour Mills, 1886–1920', *Business History*, 8 (1966); Anon., *The History of Knowles & Foster 1828–1948* (London: Ted Kavanagh, 1948); Robert Greenhill and Rory Miller, 'Merchants, Industrialists, and the Origins of British Multinational Enterprise in Latin America, 1870–1950' (mimeo, 1996).

coffee under its own brand name, though it made little progress in that tea drinking market.[44] Wilson, Sons & Co. also sought initially to diversify inside Brazil, but after the failure of its contracting ventures, pursued its coal and shipping business elsewhere.

The British trading companies on the Pacific West Coast had different characteristics from those on the East Coast. The West Coast markets were less exposed to European manufacturers seeking direct representation, and this enabled the British merchant firms to retain more of their share of the trade.[45] Perhaps because their local markets were much smaller, these firms also took on a much wider range of activities, both geographically and functionally.

While the investments of Gibbs and Balfour Williamson in mining, oil, flour milling, and other activities were especially extensive, at least three other British merchant houses on the West Coast also diversified. During the early 1890s Duncan Fox purchased a railway in southern Chile, built a pier and warehouses, and then built a flour mill on the site. During the 1900s it invested in a copper company and acquired a nitrate company in 1905. The largest venture, however, was the creation of a 5 million acre sheep farm in the extreme south of Chile. Like Balfour Williamson, Duncan Fox also expanded inland in Chile from the mid-1880s, opening a series of branches in the country.[46] Graham Rowe specialized in sugar production and marketing in Peru and Chile, but also invested in banks and also in railroad construction in Chile.[47]

The merchant firm of W. and J. Lockett, which also developed a substantial business in Chile and Peru, demonstrates the complexities of the diversification process during these decades. The Lockett partnership originated in Liverpool in the late 1830s, specializing in wine importing, but also trading more widely. They owned their own sailing ships, which carried textiles to Asia, Latin America, and elsewhere, and brought back timber, tea, and sugar in return. Locketts acted as the British agents for a Scottish sugar planter in Peru, who became progressively indebted to them from the 1870s until, in 1900, the sugar estates were put into a new Liverpool-registered company—the British Sugar Company—in which the Locketts and the family of the now deceased planter held the equity. In the previous year the Locketts opened their first branch in Peru, which became the agents for the sugar company, and subsequently developed a general trading business. By 1911 the Locketts had acquired all the equity of the British Sugar Company.

In Chile, the Locketts made substantial investments in alliance with a British entrepreneur, 'Colonel' North, who built a large nitrates group during the

---

[44] Greenhill, 'Investment Group', 88–93.   [45] Platt, *Latin America*, 150.

[46] Fernández, 'Merchants and Bankers', 356, 360; Rory Miller, *Britain and Latin America in the 19th and 20th Centuries* (London: Longman, 1993), 101.

[47] Mayo, *British Merchants*, 220–1.

1880s. North and the Locketts—who were joined by marriage when a Lockett married North's only daughter—floated the Liverpool Nitrate Company in 1883, followed by a cluster of other nitrate companies. During the remainder of the decade North and the Locketts promoted other companies involved in Chilean railroad and water utilities, and also a bank in 1888 which was to become one of the largest British overseas banks in South America. North and the Locketts also made a series of unsuccessful mining investments outside the region, and also acquired collieries in South Wales in 1889, Locketts developing a business selling coal to Liverpool shipping companies and to Chile. Following North's death in 1896, Locketts acquired the trading firm he had owned in Chile, and developed a merchanting business. The upshot was that over the last decades of the century, a Liverpool wine importing and shipping company was transformed into general traders in Chile and Peru, and the owners of nitrates, sugar, and utility businesses in those countries.[48]

Sugar and rum remained of central interest to the merchant houses in the British West Indian colonies. From the late nineteenth century, British merchant groups began to acquire ownership of sugar plantations on a larger scale, replacing the traditional planter class. This trend was stimulated by the result of the growth of competition in the world sugar industry, which led to many planters becoming indebted. The merchants moved into sugar production to stabilize their sources of supply, and several large groups emerged. Booker Brothers amalgamated in 1900 with the London-based John McConnell and Co. to form Bookers Brothers, McConnell which acquired large sugar estates in British Guiana, where it was the largest owner of property by the 1920s. A second British merchant firm, Henckell Du Buisson and Co., also acquired sugar estates and sugar factories, especially in Trinidad, from the late nineteenth century.[49]

In India, the British agency houses continued to extend their activities in the period before 1914. Calcutta and its surrounding region of Bengal remained the centre of the activity of the British-managed agency houses. Although almost all these firms continued to import Lancashire cotton textiles, many firms also took advantage of the new opportunities for commodity exports after the opening of the Suez Canal in 1869 to participate in the procurement and processing of India's primary commodities. By 1914 their extensive fixed investments made them a very 'hybrid' form of trading company: indeed, they might be better regarded as diversified quasi-conglomerates.

---

[48] Richard Cyril Lockett, *Memoirs of the Family of Lockett* (London: private circulation, 1939), 99–122; Bill Albert, *An Essay on the Peruvian Sugar Industry 1880–1920 and the Letters of Ronald Gordon, Administrator of the British Sugar Company in Canate, 1914–1920* (Norwich: School of Social Studies, University of East Anglia, 1976), 225a–241a: David Joslin, *A Century of Banking in Latin America* (London: Oxford University Press, 1963), 174–97.

[49] Stahl, *Metropolitan Organisation*, 40–6; R. W. Beachy, *The British West Indian Sugar Industry in the Late Nineteenth Century* (Cambridge: Cambridge University Press, 1957).

This period saw extensive investments into jute, coal, and tea in particular. The British traders pioneered jute milling in Calcutta and dominated the industry down to 1914.[50] They also invested strongly in the coal industry, located largely in Bengal, which expanded rapidly from the late nineteenth century to supply the needs of the railroads. They were also dominant in the major tea growing regions of Eastern India, where the industry was established in the second half of the nineteenth century.[51] A small group of large British agency houses held especially prominent positions in these three industries. An analysis of Indian-registered (i.e. rupee) companies in 1911 showed that seven agency houses controlled 55 per cent of the jute companies, 61 per cent of the tea companies, and 46 per cent of the coal companies. With exceptions such as Finlays, the agency houses were mostly headquartered in India, while their management and (usually) family shareholding was British, their links to the British economy were otherwise fragile. Their managements often regarded themselves as less an extension of British business than as autonomous, Indian-based, firms.[52]

The diversification strategies of the agency houses in Calcutta to some extent reflected the seasonality of many Indian industries. Tea, jute, sugar, cotton were all seasonal crops which meant that the provision of short-term finance—one of the most important functions of the agency houses—could move from one industry to another over the course of the year. The peak demand for tea crop finance in north India, for example, occurred in June–July, whereas the demand for jute finance was at its height in October. As the finished products were sold, loans were repaid and the funds could be reallocated to another industry.[53]

Virtually all of the British agency houses diversified from trade into other activities in this period, with Ralli Brothers as the main exception with its continued focus on trading in wheat and cotton. However each agency house had a distinctive portfolio of investments and tended to specialize in particular areas, and there were also considerable differences in their performances. A crude measure of the size of these business groups—the total paid-up rupee capital of the companies under their management—suggests a wide size dispersion in 1914. Bird and Andrew Yule were the largest groups, with Duncan, Jardine Skinner, Gillanders Arbuthnot, and Heilgers about half their size, and then another group of substantially

---

[50] B. R. Tomlinson, 'British Business in India, 1860–1970', in R. P. T. Davenport-Hines and Geoffrey Jones (eds.), *British Business in Asia since 1860* (Cambridge: Cambridge University Press, 1989), 87. Gordon T. Stewart, *Jute and Empire* (Manchester: Manchester University Press, 1998), ch. 2.

[51] Bishnupriya Gupta, 'Collusion in the Indian Tea Industry in the Great Depression: An Analysis of Panel Data', *Explorations in Economic History*, 34 (1997), 159.

[52] A. K. Bagchi, *Private Investment in India 1900–1939* (Cambridge: Cambridge University Press, 1972), 176–7; Stewart, *Jute and Empire*, 167–8.

[53] Geoffrey Tyson, *Managing Agency: A System of Business Organisation* (Calcutta: Houghty Printing Co., c.1960), 10–11.

smaller firms including Begg Dunlop, Octavius Steel, and Balmer Lawrie. With the exception of Bombay-based Killick, Nixon, the Bombay- and Madras-based firms fell into this smaller category also.[54]

Andrew Yule & Co. emerged as the most diversified of the Calcutta agency houses. By the early 1900s this firm managed four jute mills, one cotton mill, fifteen tea companies, four coal companies, two flour mills, a small railroad company, an oil and navigation company.[55] Bird & Co. managed a substantial number of coal and jute companies, but no tea companies. Duncan Bros., Octavius Steel & Co., Williamson, Major & Co., and Davenport and Co. managed a large number of tea companies but few if any coal and jute companies. Gillanders Arbuthnot, the oldest of the agency houses, showed a different pattern again. After sharply focusing on trading until 1870, from the late nineteenth century the firm invested in various mining ventures in coal, diamonds, tin, copper, gold, and oil, and also opened branches in other parts of India.[56]

The new entrants to the Calcutta agency houses included Shaw Wallace. This had begun as a firm in Calcutta in 1868, but was restructured as the London firm of R. G. Shaw and its Calcutta partnership of Shaw Wallace in 1886. The firm initially was involved in importing Lancashire cotton goods and in tea trading and subsequently the management of tea companies, but it also developed a strong expertise in mining. By 1911 the firm managed eleven Indian-registered coal companies, making it jointly the biggest 'coal' group along with Andrew Yule and Bird.[57] The acquisition of another Calcutta firm in 1891 brought with it the selling agency in India of the Burmah Oil Company. The view of competitors was that the Burmah Oil agency had become 'the great mainstay' of the firm by this period.[58]

The Bombay-based trading companies, such as Greaves Cotton and— the largest—Killick, Nixon also diversified. Killick, Nixon developed and managed light railways—which mostly served plantations—all over India. This firm also acted as the managing agents for a coastal steamer company founded in Bombay in 1906.[59] These firms also invested in the cotton textile industry, based in Bombay, though Indian entrepreneurs took the lead in this industry.[60]

India provided evidence of the risks of diversification. The Madras-based firm of Binny's launched two cotton mill companies in 1876 and 1881, and

[54] Rajat K. Ray, *Industrialisation in India* (Delhi: Oxford University Press, 1979), 260–1.

[55] Andrew Yule & Co., *Andrew Yule & Co. Ltd. 1863–1963* (Edinburgh: T. & A. Constable, 1963); Stephanie Jones, *Merchants of the Raj* (London: Macmillan, 1992), 23–5.

[56] Chapman, *Merchant Enterprise*, 118–19; Bagchi, *Private Investment*, 177, 179.

[57] Sir Harry Townend, *A History of Shaw Wallace & Co. and Shaw Wallace & Co. Ltd.* (Calcutta: the firm, 1965); Charles Jones, *International Business in the Nineteenth Century* (Brighton: Wheatsheaf, 1987), 150–1.

[58] Kleinwort Information Book, Guildhall Library 22025/I, report on Shaw Wallace by McLeod Russel & Co., 4 Mar. 1908: report by Cox McEwen, 8 June 1909.

[59] Bagchi, *Private Investment*, 181, 263 n. 7.

[60] Ibid. 229–37; Ray, *Industrialisation in India*, 24–6, 31–3.

cotton textiles manufacture developed as one of Binny's core businesses. From
the mid-1880s Binny's diversified further into the ownership of tramways,
coffee plantations, and many other activities, which proved hard to manage.
A coal company promoted in 1892 went into liquidation, and investments
in ice and salt also failed. Another company founded in the same year which
owned a sugar refinery and a rum distillery became heavily loss-making
and loaded with debt, and in 1902 was taken over by Binny's Madras competitors, Parry's.[61] In its weakened position, Binny's was overwhelmed in
1906 when the collapse of the agency house and private banking firm of
Arbuthnot—which had a large business in Madras as well as London—caused
a crisis of confidence for the other two Madras firms with private banking
businesses, Binny's and Parry's. Binny's went into liquidation and was purchased on the cheap for £50,000 by James Mackay, thereby becoming part
of the nascent Inchcape 'group'. The firm was restructured as the British-
based Binny & Co., with its London office in the same building as BI. Under
Mackay's control, Binny took over the BI agency at Madras and acquired
a flotilla of small boats to provide port services, while remaining large
textile manufacturers and owners and traders of coffee plantations.[62]

In Burma, the most diversified of the British trading companies, Todd,
Findlay & Company, was also almost destroyed by a major banking crisis
in Scotland when the City of Glasgow Bank failed in 1878. The Findlay
partners held shares in this bank which had unlimited liability, and as a
result they lost all their assets in Burma including the Irrawaddy Flotilla
Company. The firm was revived in the 1880s on a more modest scale as
T. D. Findlay & Son, concentrating on extracting, milling, and shipping
teak and rice.[63]

The extension of British rule over the remainder of the country with
the annexation of Upper Burma in 1886 and the abolition of Burmese
rule extended the opportunities for British trading companies in Burma.
Wallace Brothers' Bombay Burmah Trading Corporation extended its
teak operations, the largest in Burma. In 1885 Wallace Brothers also established a British company, the Arracan Company, to engage in rice trading.
The Burmese businesses formed only a part of the Wallace portfolio. In 1886
the firm rationalized its Bombay organization by giving Wallace & Co. the
exclusive responsibility to manage Bombay Burmah, while forming the
Bombay Company to take care of other interests. Initially this firm's main
business was the import of Lancashire textiles and the export of raw
cotton, but in 1901 it invested in a Bombay cotton textile company. Wallace
Brothers also tried but failed to build a presence in the oil industry, but

[61] Hilton Brown, *Parry's of Madras* (Madras: the company, 1954), 162–5.
[62] Jones, *Two Centuries*, 48–52; Percival Griffiths, *A History of the Inchcape Group* (London:
the firm, 1977), 42–9; Ray, *Industrialisation*, 264–5.
[63] A. G. McCrae, *Pioneers in Burma* (Occasional Papers in Economic and Social History
No. 2, University of Glasgow, 1986).

succeeded in acquiring plantations, establishing a rubber plantation company in the Dutch East Indies in 1906 and one in Malaya in the same year, and acquiring Indian tea estates just before 1914. Like Antony Gibbs, Wallace Brothers also developed a London merchant banking business and it was one of the founding members of the Accepting Houses Committee in 1914.[64]

From the late nineteenth century Steel Brothers became the second major British trading company in Burma. While Wallace Brothers dominated teak, Steel Brothers emerged as the major presence in the rice trade. William Strang Steel was a Glasgow merchant who, after working with British merchant houses in the Dutch East Indies and Burma, founded his own firm in Rangoon in 1870. Three years later Strang himself moved to London and founded Steel Brothers, which took control of W. Strang Steel & Company in Burma. There was a close association with James Finlay which took some of Steel's shares.

Steels focused on the rice trade and built their first rice mill in 1871, and this was greatly enlarged in 1895 to become the biggest rice-milling unit in Burma. Rice cultivation expanded rapidly as the Suez Canal opened new markets for the product. Steels integrated forwards, participating in 1906 in the formation of a British company which owned rice mills in Germany. Within Burma, Steels expanded horizontally. In the late nineteenth century the firm exported teak, and then in 1900 it purchased from another British company teak forests and elephants herds. In 1908 they also founded a successful oil company.[65]

The British trading companies in South East Asia went through a period of great expansion from the 1870s. The two key factors behind this growth was the opening of the Suez Canal and the rapid increase in the world demand for the primary commodities produced in the region. The port of Singapore was the shipping hub of the region and boomed. Its trade increased more than sixfold between 1871 and 1902, and the city's population doubled in the last two decades of the century. By 1914 Singapore was the seventh busiest port in the world in terms of shipping tonnage handled.[66]

Through to the end of the century the British agency houses in Singapore and Malaya were primarily concerned with trade, and acting as shipping and insurance agencies. They played almost no role in the initial development of the rubber plantations in Malaya by individual British planters. Thereafter, led by Guthries, the agency houses entered the industry on a large scale as the advent of motor vehicles caused a surge in demand for rubber and the price of the commodity rose rapidly. Individual planters had insufficient resources to increase their output and the 'agency houses' replaced them from the mid-1900s. They would promote new joint stock

[64] A. C. Pointon, *Wallace Brothers* (Oxford: the firm, 1974), 31–53; Chapman, *Rise*, 55.

[65] H. E. W. Braund, *Calling to Mind* (Oxford: Pergamon Press, 1975); 'Steel Brothers: Brief Histories', MS 29557, GHL.

[66] Huff, *Economic Growth*.

companies in London to acquire the estates of proprietary planters, retaining a share of the equity and, especially, a management contract. By 1914
Guthries, Harrisons & Crosfield, Edward Boustead, and a number of other
agency houses controlled large 'networks' of rubber companies.[67]

In this period there were new entrants to ranks of the agency houses.
Boustead Brothers, unrelated to the older agency house of Edward Boustead,
had grown tea on plantations in Ceylon, where it also ran tramways and
electricity generation in the 1890s. Having introduced rubber growing on
the tea plantations, the firm invested in Malaya, floating its first Malayan
plantation company in 1909.[68] Sime Darby originated as European planters
and subsequently went into merchanting. The firm was founded in 1902
by the merger of two groups of proprietary estates in Malacca. Sime Darby
opened an office in Singapore a decade later. The firm was the only British
agency house with an overseas Chinese interest right from the beginning.
It was involved with, and supported by, Malaccan Chinese entrepreneurs.[69]

Shipping remained of vital concern to mercantile activity in Singapore and
Malaya. Holts' Ocean Steam Ship Company, working in close partnership
with Mansfields, became involved in the expanding trades of the region—
tobacco and rice—and developed new regional routes linking Singapore with
neighbouring countries. In 1882 Holts and Mansfields began a steamship
line to carry rice and later passengers between Singapore and Bangkok,
although the two firms did not always act so closely. In 1891 Holts did not
join with Mansfields and a group of Chinese merchants which founded the
Straits Steamship Company in Singapore to carry local produce between
Singapore and west coast Malayan ports. In 1903, when Mansfields' senior
partner retired, Ocean took the opportunity to acquire control of its
former agent. A new company, W. Mansfield and Co., was incorporated
in Liverpool with Ocean controlling a majority of the shares.[70]

British trading companies were also active elsewhere in South East Asia.
The Borneo Company, initially traders in Sarawak and Singapore and
jute millers in India, 'reinvented' itself several times. After the Treaty of
Chiengmai in 1883, which extended extraterritoriality, the way was opened
for this and Western firms to cut trees rather than buy them from indigenous foresters in northern Thailand. The Borneo Company diversified into
teak production, using its close 'contacts' with the Thai royal family, and
becoming the second largest teak producer after the Bombay Burmah Trading

    [67] S. Cunyingham-Brown, *The Traders* (London: Newman Neame, 1970).
    [68] D. J. M. Tate, *The RGA History of the Plantation Industry in the Malay Peninsula* (Kuala
Lumpur: Oxford University Press, 1996), 241.
    [69] Allen and Donnithorne, *Western Enterprise in Indonesia and Malaya*, 56–7; Tate, *RGA History*,
244.
    [70] Hyde, *Far Eastern Trade, 1860–1914*, 89–93; Gordon Boyce, *Information, Mediation and
Institutional Development* (Manchester: Manchester University Press, 1995), 65; Malcolm
Falkus, *The Blue Funnel Legend* (London: Macmillan, 1990), 40–4, 71–9.

Corporation. In Sarawak, the firm obtained the right to work gold mines in 1879, bought out the pre-existing Chinese mines, and by 1885 had established a virtual monopoly over the industry. Up to 1914 Thai teak and Sarawak gold were the mainstay of the firm's profitability, though the Borneo Company also began several new initiatives, including the manufacture of bricks in Singapore in 1899 and a tea plantation in the Dutch East Indies.[71]

The third largest teak producer in Thailand was another British trading company, the Anglo-Siam Corporation, which originated from British merchants in Bombay searching for a supply of teak at lower prices than those on offer from the Bombay Burmah Trading Corporation. Having secured a lease in a teak forest, the Siam Forest Co. was founded in 1884 in Bombay. Three years later this was reconstructed as a London registered firm. The firm was initially entirely concerned with the Thai teak industry, but in 1908 it acquired the general trading business of a British merchant in Bangkok which provided new business as agents for mines, insurance companies, and banks.[72]

On the China coast, Chinese governments prohibited foreign ownership of land or factories until 1895 so the pattern of diversification was different again, focused on the colony of Hong Kong, and later on Chinese ports. The 1870s saw the British trading companies in East Asia make capital investments on a much larger scale than seen earlier. Jardine Matheson established a silk filature in Shanghai, and a sugar refinery and ice factory in Hong Kong. In 1881 Jardines merged its various coastal and river shipping operations into a single company, the Indo-China Steam Navigation Company, and subsequently made large investments in Hong Kong's docklands with the formation of the Hong Kong and Kowloon Wharf and Godown Company in 1886. In 1895 a cotton mill was built in Shanghai, and two years later a textile spinning and weaving factory began in Hong Kong. In 1898 the British and China Corporation was founded jointly with the Hongkong Bank to build railroads in China.[73]

After the failure of Dent's in 1867, Jardine Matheson's great regional competitor was Swire's. However the two firms developed different business profiles. By 1890 Swire's had ceased to export Lancashire textiles to China, and in 1893 it stopped exporting tea to Britain, although exports to Australia continued for seven more years. By the early 1900s Swire's had withdrawn from trading per se. In contrast it continued to make heavy investments in shipping. Swire's continued to open branches at ports in China, Japan, and even Vladivostock in Russia to provide agency services for the Ocean Steamship Company. Swire's China Navigation Company grew in

---

[71] Griffiths, *History*, 134–8; Jones, *Two Centuries*, 196–205.
[72] Jones, *Two Centuries*, 206–14.
[73] Maggie Keswick (ed.), *The Thistle and the Jade* (London: Octopus, 1982); Chapman, *Merchant Enterprise*, 237–41.

the late nineteenth century as one of the leading shipping companies in the Far East. In China the firm expanded from its initial business of running steamers up the Yangtze river to the coastal trade, which by the 1890s had become the main source of revenue. The growth of the China Navigation Company was achieved by breaking into the rates agreements of the pre-existing companies, and then organizing stronger cartel arrangements with Swire's inside them. By the late 1890s China Navigation had a fleet of forty-seven ships, considerably larger than Jardines' Indo-China, and was declaring dividends of 20 per cent per annum, although in the 1900s Japanese and other competition ended the period of great prosperity. In this decade further shipping-related investments were made, notably the building of a large dockyard and a firm to provide lighter services for China Navigation.

The second initiative of Swire's was sugar refining. In 1881 the Taikoo Sugar Refinery Co. was established in Hong Kong to compete with the Jardine Matheson sugar refinery, which at that time had a monopoly of the refined sugar market in China and Japan. Holts took a shareholding in the firm. Taikoo Sugar refined raw sugar from Java and the Philippines, and sold it in China and Japan. As in shipping, Swire's venture was able to overcome initially strong competition from Jardines, though Japanese competition in the 1900s presented more challenges.[74]

The smaller trading companies on the China coast undertook a narrower range of activities. Dodwells concentrated on trading and shipping agency business in China. Gilmans recovered from near bankruptcy in the 1870s by becoming the agent for an Australian sandalwood company and was thus able to supply the huge demand for sandalwood for use as joss sticks. Gibb Livingston diversified from tea trading into owning and chartering ships, and developed a large marine insurance business. Another firm, Caldbeck's, originated in Shanghai in 1864, and spread along the China coast in subsequent decades, opening a London office in 1882. This firm specialized in trading in wines and spirits.[75]

Most of the larger British traders on the China Coast established branches in Japan when that country opened its doors to foreign enterprise. Chinese merchants initially dominated Japan's export business, but British merchants such as Jardine Matheson were also important for a time until Japanese-owned firms supplanted them.[76] Among the British merchant

---

[74] S. Marriner and F. E. Hyde, *The Senior, John Samuel Swire, 1825–98* (Liverpool. University of Liverpool Press, 1967); S. Sugiyama, 'A British Trading Firm in the Far East: John Swire & Sons, 1867–1914', in S. Yonekawa and H. Yoshihara (eds.), *Business History of General Trading Companies* (Tokyo: University of Tokyo Press, 1987); Hyde, *Far Eastern Trade*, 26–36, 89–105.

[75] Jones, *Two Centuries*, 186–8; Griffiths, *History*, 141–2, 147–9.

[76] R. P. T. Davenport-Hines and Geoffrey Jones, 'British Business in Japan since 1868', in R. P. T. Davenport-Hines and Geoffrey Jones (eds.), *British Business in Asia since 1860* (Cambridge: Cambridge University Press, 1989), 221–2.

firms which specialized in Japan was M. Samuel & Co. This London firm initially traded in shell-boxes and other goods from the East, but in 1878 expanded by opening a partnership—Samuel Samuel—in Japan. This firm developed a substantial business importing British machinery into Japan and exporting Japanese products, including rice, sea-shells and other ornaments, and also Japanese coal, used for steamships. In London it maintained a small workshop which manufactured shell-boxes from the sea-shells imported from the East.[77]

As explained in more detail in Chapter 10, M. Samuel & Co. became a radical example of 'reinvention' following its entry into the oil business. The firm distributed Russian oil in Asian markets, acquired its own oil tankers, and then found its own supply of crude oil in the Dutch East Indies in 1898. A new 'free-standing' company, the Shell Transport and Trading Co., was floated in London in the previous year which acquired the oilfield, tanker fleet, and distribution operations. However M. Samuel & Co. lacked the organizational capabilities required by the nascent oil company, and in 1907 it was effectively acquired by its Dutch competitor, the Royal Dutch Petroleum Co. Under the merger arrangements, the new 'Shell group' was organized as two 'holding companies' with the Dutch/British shareholding fixed in a 60/40 ratio. The firm of M. Samuel & Co. itself continued in existence as a merchant bank.

Although the Far East saw British and other merchants competing fiercely with one another, it was also the place where British firms began to form collusive agreements. From the 1870s British shipping companies began to combine to set uniform rates on shipping lines, notably in the 'liner' trade, which consisted of general-purpose ships carrying small consignments sailing on fixed rates to scheduled timetables. This contrasted with 'tramp' steamers which were slower and went from port to port in search of cargoes which would fill an entire ship full of cheap bulky goods such as coal or grain. The liner trade was vulnerable to rate-cutting as part empty ships could carry additional freight at low marginal costs, and because some freight could be carried by both liners and tramps, and this led to a drive to regulate competition. At the same time the fact that British ship lines were pre-eminent and that so much trade passed through Britain or the British Empire facilitated the reaching of collusive agreements.

The origins of the system lay with Swire's and the China Conference of 1879. During the 1870s John Swire was involved in attempts to regulate competition on the Yangtze river following the foundation of the China Navigation Company in 1872. Later in the decade the growth of competition to Holt's Blue Funnel Line from new competitors convinced Swire of the need for regulation. The China Conferences, whose original signatories were five British lines and one French line, had John Swire as its chairman

[77] Robert Henriques, *Marcus Samuel* (London. Barrie and Rockliff, 1960), 48–50, 59–65.

until 1882 and the Holt brothers, after initial scepticism, became converted
to the idea. Subsequently the 'conference' system spread and by 1909 there
were at least sixty-four formal conferences in existence.[78]

The importance of shipping agency work for many British trading
companies meant that they were active participants in the conference system and it had direct implications for them. A vivid example came from
the extension of the conference system to the Straits. After a number of
failed attempts, the Straits Homeward Conference was founded in 1897. Holts
and the other shipowners in the Conference became a monopoly seller of
shipping services from Singapore to Britain and Europe. In 1905 a similar
conference was formed for liner traffic from Singapore to the east coast
of the United States. A unique feature of the Singapore Conference was
a 'secret' rebate made by the shipowners to a group of trading companies
to buy their agreement to a conference system, which was additional to a
10 per cent rebate to all Singapore shippers adhering to the conference. Five
merchant houses shared the secret rebate—Boustead; Adamson, Gilfillan;
Paterson, Simons; the Borneo Company; and the German merchants Behn,
Meyer. These five firms were able to get a very large share of exports
of tropical produce from Singapore as a result of this system, and was one
reason why other firms such as Guthries diversified into the management
of rubber plantations. In 1911 a public outcry in Singapore led to the end
of the 'secret rebate', but by then the position of the conference merchants
in the export trade was so strong that the same firms continued to retain
a very prominent position.[79]

The trend towards collusion extended beyond oceanic shipping. By the
1880s Swire's, Jardines, and other firms were joined in 'pooling agreements'
on the Yangtze river.[80] In other aspects of their business in China too,
competition was often followed by collusion, even as natural suspicions,
distrust, and disagreements persisted. In other regions, collusive agreements
on various matters had become quite widespread by 1914, even though they
were often unstable and constantly renegotiated.

In general, and with regional exceptions, the British trading companies
appear as dynamic entrepreneurial firms in these years. Misjudgement or
bad luck brought some large groups to the edge of bankruptcy. Family businesses sometimes crumbled, if succession problems were not resolved or
family shareholders drained firms of profits. This seems to have been the
fate of the Rathbones, whose business was 'allowed to run down' in the
late nineteenth century because of rigidity and because the partners became
preoccupied with politics and philanthropy.[81] Its shipping interests were sold
in 1889. By 1912, when the business was reconstructed after a series of losses,

---

[78] Falkus, *Blue Funnel*, 117–35.   [79] Ibid. 127–30; Huff, *Economic Growth*, 127–30.
[80] Hyde, *Far Eastern Trade*, 102–5.
[81] Sheila Marriner, *Rathbones of Liverpool 1845–73* (Liverpool: Liverpool University Press,
1961), 131–2.

merchanting had been abandoned in favour of finance and investment.[82]
Marcus Samuel & Co. lost control of Shell Transport for broadly the same
reasons. However the ability of the British trading companies as a whole
to invest in long-lasting assets, which they managed across borders and added
value, was the more striking.

The diversification strategies of the trading firms had made them substantial direct investors by 1914. They were extensively involved in the
provision of trade-related services in shipping, insurance, and finance. They
had also in some regions integrated backwards on a large scale into mines
and plantations. British merchants were less active in manufacturing and
processing, though some substantial investments existed in textile manufacture. There was a conspicuous lack of investment in their own home
economy. Dutch trading companies were also specialized in overseas markets, but it was not the universal pattern.[83] By 1914 Denmark's East Asiatic
Company had integrated forwards into processing and refining in Denmark
the vegetable fats, soap, and foodstuffs it imported from the East on its own
ships, which returned to Asia loaded with products including cement produced in East Asiatic's own plants.[84] Swedish trading companies similarly
integrated backwards into production in Sweden.[85]

3.5 New Frontiers: Africa

During the late nineteenth century large regions of tropical Africa were
incorporated into the international economy and trading companies were
an important part of this story in West and East Africa, though the
spread of British business interests northwards from southern Africa was
spearheaded by mining groups, notably the British South Africa Co.
and De Beers. Business strategies and structures had some characteristics
familiar from elsewhere, though with distinctive region-specific features
reflecting the continent's late incorporation into the world economy and
its position at the centre of European imperial rivalry at the end of the nineteenth century. Africa became a new 'frontier' for British merchants, where
high information costs and uncertainty provided a new range of opportunities for intermediaries.

A general trend in all African regions was a shift in corporate structures
used by merchants from individual partnerships to larger companies. This
trend was found in other regions also, but Africa did see a distinctive variant

[82] Lucie Nottingham, *Rathbone Brothers: From Merchant to Banker 1742–1992* (London: the firm, 1992).

[83] Sluyterman, 'Dutch Multinational Trading Companies'.

[84] Ole Lange, *Den hvide elefant: H. N. Andersens eventyr og ØK 1852–1914* (Copenhagen: Gyldendal, 1986).

[85] Hans de Geer, 'Trading Companies in Twentieth-Century Sweden', in Jones (ed.), *Multinational Traders*.

with a brief revival of chartered trading companies. Elsewhere, the British government progressively abandoned the granting of royal charters for private companies. However a number of factors including imperial rivalry led in the 1880s to the resurrection of granting royal charters to three firms in Africa; the Royal Niger Company in 1886, the Imperial British East Africa Company in 1888, and the British South Africa Company in 1889.[86]

British merchants had long experience with West Africa as it was the region where tens of thousands of Africans were exported as slaves to the Americas. By the mid-eighteenth century British merchants dominated the carriage of slaves to the Caribbean and North America. However in 1807 trading in slaves was made illegal for British subjects. Trading continued in other commercial activities, notably in palm oil, which was used as an industrial lubricant and to make candles and soap. However the scale of this trade was limited because British merchants were confined to the coast, both because of African opposition to their penetration inland and because of acute physical and health problems in travelling to the interior.

The advent of steamships in the early 1850s led to a doubling of the tonnage of British shipping to West Africa more than every decade between 1854 and 1904. The most important company was the Liverpool shipping firm of Elder Dempster & Co.—controlled by the mid-1880s by Alfred Jones— which acted as shipping agent for the African Steam Ship Co. from 1869, and subsequently purchased most of the shares of the two principal British shipping lines to West Africa. Jones eliminated other competition in the West African trade and in 1895 formalized his collaboration with the rival German shipping line by setting up the West African Lines shipping conference.

Elder Dempster remained a shipping rather than a trading company, though the distinction is not clear-cut. Jones purchased or set up coastal and river boat firms, port and cold storage facilities, and hotels in West Africa, and in 1894 established a bank, the Bank of British West Africa, which had the privilege of being the sole supplier of new silver coins. Elder Dempster also partly owned a banana trading company, though this was sold to the US firm United Fruit in 1910.[87]

Elder Dempster's customers in West Africa were the trading companies, of whom a number of large companies had emerged as a result of amalgamation by the turn of the century. The Niger Company originated in 1879 by an amalgamation of four British merchant firms trading on the Niger. Against the background of imperial rivalries when the 'scramble for Africa' began in 1884, the British government gave the firm a Royal Charter in 1886

[86] A. G. Hopkins, 'Imperial Business in Africa. Part 2: Interpretations', *Journal of African History*, 17 (1976), 267–90; Scott R. Pearson, 'The Economic Imperialism of the Royal Niger Company', *Food Research Institute Studies in Agricultural Economics, Trade, and Development*, 10/1 (1971), 70.

[87] Davies, *The Trade Makers*; id., 'The Impact of the Expatriate Shipping Lines on the Economic Development of British West Africa', *Business History*, 1 (1977), 3–17.

and it became the Royal Niger Company. The company's administrative rights were over an area of the Niger Delta which was claimed by Britain, and although its charter attempted to limit its monopoly, its administrative powers enabled it to secure a de facto commercial monopoly.[88]

When the Royal Charter terminated in 1900, the Niger Company was the largest firm in Nigeria and it flourished with the loss of its administrative responsibilities. The company's business consisted of buying local produce—led by palm oil and palm kernels, but also tin, groundnuts, hide, rubber, ivory, and other products—and importing whatever the market wanted, beginning with gin and guns and later textiles and many types of consumer goods. This business was conducted from a large number—42 in 1900 increasing to 154 in 1920—of trading 'stations' in the country, though these were often mobile shelters which moved with the markets they served. As the production of export crops remained in the hands of peasant cultivators, the Niger Company's diversification was mainly horizontal—along the coast but in activities related to importing and exporting—rather than vertical.[89] However the Niger Company did promote some 'free-standing' tin companies, while its trade in groundnuts led to it taking shares in a Belgian nutcracking firm with which it had a contract, and which established a British company.[90]

The chief competitor of the Niger Company was formed in 1902 when the firms of F. & A. Swanzy and Miller Brothers came together. The Swanzys were Irish merchants who had traded in West Africa since the late eighteenth century. The Millers were Glasgow merchants who originally traded with the West Indies, but in 1868 turned their attention to West Africa. During the 1890s Millers grew rapidly by exporting cocoa. Swanzy's made a speciality of trade between the United States and the Gold Coast, using sailing ships to carry palm oil, rubber, monkeys, and parrots to the United States and carrying back rum, tobacco, patent medicines, and sewing machines. The trade in rum was so substantial that they financed an American firm to produce it on a larger scale. However Swanzy's made heavy losses after becoming involved in gold mining, and in 1902 had to turn for help to Millers, their chief competitor in the Gold Coast, which took them over, and thereafter they acted as a unified group, though keeping separate identities.[91]

The Liverpool-based African Association was founded in 1889 by nine British firms whose business lay in the delta of the Niger—a region known as the 'Oil Rivers'. At mid-century the British palm oil trade was dominated by a small group of merchant houses—all but one based in Liverpool—which followed the pattern of the West African slave trade in being both traders

---

[88] Pearson, 'Economic Imperialism'.   [89] Hopkins, 'Imperial Business', 277.
[90] Colin Newbury, 'Trade and Technology in West Africa: The Case of the Niger Company, 1900–1920', *Journal of African History*, 19 (1978), 551–75; Frederick Pedler, *The Lion and the Unicorn in Africa* (London: Heinemann, 1974), 164–71.
[91] Pedler, *Lion*, 99–111.

and shippers. The control of shipping enabled the merchants to keep new competitors out of the trade. In 1850 the biggest eight Liverpool firms provided over 60 per cent of Britain's palm oil imports.

Subsequently the advent of steamships opened up the palm-oil trade to new competitors who could charter space in one of the steamers. The traditional uses of palm oil were also challenged by petroleum, by the development of gas and electric lighting, and by its replacement by zinc chloride in the tin plate industry. All these changes led to a large fall in prices, only partly compensated by a new market for the palm kernel in the production of margarine and cattle fodder. In these circumstances, some of the older traders went out of business, while others shifted from palm oil trading to general trading. Many firms cut costs by using steamers instead of their own ships. These commercial pressures led to a growing number of mergers and the abandonment of the partnership form in favour of joint stock companies which were better able to provide new capital. In 1889 the nine largest British firms in the delta merged to form the African Association, which dominated the palm oil trade through to 1914.[92] After a period of intense competition with other companies, in 1899 the African Association, the Niger Company, Millers, and a smaller company formed the 'Niger Pool' under which the contracting parties agreed to pool profits, which were to be divided in specified proportions, and to avoid competition in each other's markets.[93]

Among the other Liverpool-based trading companies active in West Africa was another firm, John Holt & Co. This venture grew out of a store established on Fernando Po in the 1860s by John Holt. In 1869 the firm opened 'factories' in the Cameroons and began trading in rubber, wood, ivory, and palm oil, being one of the new entrants into the business at that time. Holt was involved at one time as chairman of the African Association, but a conflict led to his withdrawal and the continued development of John Holt & Co. as an independent entity which by the 1900s was established in Nigeria and other West African colonies including the Cameroons, Guinea, Gabon, Fernando Po, and Dahomey, though not the Gold Coast until the 1930s. The firm exported palm oil and kernels and other local produce, and imported a range of general merchandise. Most strikingly in 1907 the firm purchased its own steamship and by 1914 John Holt had three steamships carrying about half its cargoes, the remainder carried by conference vessels. In 1914 the firm declined an offer from Elder Dempster to buy these ships.[94]

---

[92] Martin Lynn, *Commerce and Economic Change in West Africa* (Cambridge: Cambridge University Press, 1997), chs. 4 and 6; id., 'From Sail to Steam: The Impact of the Steamship Services on the British Palm Oil Trade with West Africa, 1850–1890', *Journal of African History*, 30 (1989), 222–45.

[93] Pedler, *Lion*, 263–8.

[94] C. Gertzel, 'John Holt: A British Merchant in West Africa in the Age of Imperialism' (unpublished Oxford D. Phil, 1959); Davies, *Trade Makers*, 173–8.

There was one major outlier among the British investors in West African trading before 1914. This was the large British soap manufacturer Lever Brothers, the predecessor to Unilever. During the 1900s Lever Brothers began to integrate backwards in search of reliable sources of raw materials. In 1911 the firm secured a very large concession in the Belgian Congo to grow oil palms. In British West Africa, such backward integration was not possible, and instead Lever began to acquire trading companies. In 1910 it bought W. B. MacIver and Company, a Liverpool firm trading in Nigeria, mainly in timber. This firm was then used to expand into the palm oil trade, other acquisitions were made, and by 1920 Lever Brothers had overtaken the Niger Company, the African Association, and Miller Brothers to become the largest palm oil trader.[95]

In East Africa, the origins of the British trading companies and their subsequent evolution was considerably different. Commercial expansion was conditioned by the opening of the Suez Council, which increased competition among shipping companies in the Indian Ocean. This greatly increased the significance of Africa's East Coast, and British trading interests in India turned their attention to the region.

This was the case with the most important of the British trading companies, Smith Mackenzie, which was another part of the Mackinnon complex. This London partnership was formed in 1877 and included partners of Gray Dawes, but it grew from the agency of the BI established in Zanzibar earlier in 1872 following the opening of a regular steamer service from Aden and Bombay to Zanzibar. At the end of the 1880s Mackinnon became involved in the project to found a chartered trading company, the Imperial British East Africa Company, he and his associates taking half of the equity in the venture designed to open up the East African hinterland. Mackinnon failed to secure the large government subsidies for ships and railroad promotion that he had hoped to secure for the chartered company, which surrendered its charter in 1897. The failure of the Imperial British East African Company left Smith Mackenzie as again the main vehicle for the Mackinnon group. The firm expanded in the mainland, at Mombassa and later other ports. It acted as agents for petroleum firms, insurance companies, and for manufacturers in Europe. In Zanzibar Smith Mackenzie invested in coffee and rubber plantations, apparently unsuccessfully.[96]

Although Smith Mackenzie was the largest of the British traders in East Africa, there were other companies, several of which were outgrowths of firms active in Asia. David Sassoon invested in Zanzibar and later on the mainland also, conducting the same kind of business as Smith Mackenzie

---

[95] Pedler, *Lion*, 172–7; Charles Wilson, *The History of Unilever* (London: Cassell, 1954), i. 159–87.

[96] J. Forbes Munro, 'British Rubber Companies in East Africa before the First World War', *Journal of African History*, 24 (1983), 369–79; Jones, *Two Centuries*, 111–34; Griffiths, *History*, 55–64.

in trading and shipping agency work, although over time developing a speciality in 'native' produce, especially hides and skins. In 1915 this business was reorganized into a private London-registered company, the African Mercantile Co.[97] After 1910 two British agency houses in Malaya, Boustead and Row, White acted as agents and secretaries to a number of companies formed to develop rubber plantations in the region.[98]

By 1914 tropical Africa had become an important host region for British mercantile enterprise. In West Africa, the process of 'reinvention' was very evident. Slave traders became palm oil traders who became general traders. Traders and shippers were initially one and then became specialists as elsewhere. Business strategies were region-specific. In West Africa, the British trading companies diversified horizontally, leaving agriculture in the hands of peasant proprietors. In East Africa, British mercantile enterprise was largely an outgrowth of firms active in India.

3.6 British Trading Companies c.1914

The decades before 1914 appear as ones of continued growth for the British trading companies. Although the new era of 'industrial capitalism' had dawned, to revert to Dunning's terminology, merchant capitalism remained alive and entrepreneurial. Although British merchants had declined in importance in countries such as Argentina and Russia, their activities had grown in Asia and Africa. They continued to specialize in host regions where they held or were developing competitive advantages, but a number had also extended the boundaries of their operations in this period to become at least embryonic multi-regional business groups. Transport and communication improvements had reduced uncertainties in trade and lowered transaction and information costs, but not to such an extent as to leave no opportunities for trading companies. The merchants had continued to build on knowledge and contacts within host economies to extend their range of business, and they followed the products in which they had expertise into new countries. In some commodities they had internalized the flow of commodities from production to distribution.

The British experience had many commonalities with that of other European countries in this period, though unlike some there was little interest in investing in Britain itself, while the British merchants had a distinctive preference for employing other people's money to expand their business, even while preserving the ownership of the core merchant firm to a tight circle of, often family, shareholders.

The fortunes of individual firms fluctuated considerably with movements in commodity prices and as a consequence of misjudgements and, occasionally,

---

[97] Stahl, *Metropolitan Organisation*, 213–14.
[98] Munro, 'British Rubber Companies in East Africa', 379.

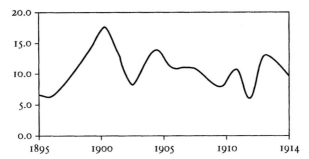

FIG. 3.1 Average post-tax ROCE of British trading companies, 1895–1914

defalcations. It remains difficult to provide quantitative evidence on the performance of the merchant firms in this period, but Appendix 1 assembles data on the post-tax return on net capital employed (ROCE) for eight companies which had taken limited liability status by 1914. The fluctuations in the annual average rates for all firms combined are shown in Figure 3.1—though they only represent the performance of a handful of firms in the early years—while Table 3.3 provides averages for time periods between 1895 and 1914 together with a calculation of the standard deviation of the annual figures as an indication of volatility.

The companies in Table 3.3 include a good spread of firms in terms of capital employed, but they exclude partnerships and only three can be regarded as 'family firms', while five out of eight firms had a substantial proportion of their assets in Asia. Despite such caveats about the representativeness of the sample, the overall picture that emerges is of considerable prosperity. A calculation of *pre-tax* ROCE for four British industrial sectors—brewing, commercial and industrial, iron, coal and steel, and shipping—between 1899 and 1914 indicates that the post-tax ROCE of the trading companies was often higher.[99] Among the trading companies there were noticeable differences in volatility, with Dodwells especially volatile, partly—but not only—because of a heavy loss in 1911 as a result of speculative trading in Ceylon.

The considerable inter-firm differences in performance provide some insights into the relative profitability of different activities in this period. The firms that invested in the production of commodities such as rubber, teak, gold, and tea performed better than the ones that were principally

[99] A. J. Arnold, 'Profitability and Capital Accumulation in British Industry during the Transwar Period, 1913–1924', *Economic History Review* (1999), 60. As well as being pre-tax, Arnold's figures are calculated on a different basis from the data presented here, including the use of profit before interest as the numerator for ROCE, though for these firms the differences are not wide. The ROCE of the large Liverpool shipping company Harrisons was higher than that of virtually all these companies in this period. See Francis Hyde, *Shipping Enterprise and Management 1830–1939: Harrisons of Liverpool* (Liverpool: Liverpool University Press, 1967), 114.

TABLE 3.3 Average post-tax return on net capital employed of selected British trading companies, 1895–1914 (%)

	Borneo Company	Swire's	Dodwells	H&C	Finlays	Brazilian Warrant	Wilson, Sons	Niger Co.	Average
1895–1900	9.4	8.7	10.0				10.0	10.0	9.5
1901–1908	18.0	5.4	(1.3)				12.5	9.5	11.1
1909–1914	14.9	7.2		15.0	11.3[a]	10.8[b]	13.1	8.0	9.8
Std[c]	5.1	4.5	14.4	5.5	2.3	3.4	4.9	4.3	—

[a] 1910, 1911, 1913, and 1914 only.
[b] 1910–1914 only.
[c] Standard deviation is calculated on the annual figures given in Appendix 1. It only applies for the years for which data exists.

engaged in trading, shipping, and agency business, though Wilsons demonstrated that supplying coal to the world's ships could be profitable also. Indeed, in a period of rapid growth in world trade and capital flows, rising commodity prices, and still expanding imperial frontiers, there were profitable opportunities in many activities and regions, and if there were often high risks, there could also sometimes be high rewards.

4

Trading in Crisis

4.1 Introduction

The First World War ended the golden age of dynamic growth for British trading companies. Two major trade depressions, one soon after the end of the war and the second in the early 1930s, the secular decline in primary commodity prices, the growth of trade barriers and exchange controls, competition from US, Japanese, and other firms, and the weakening trade performance of their British home economy were some of the problems faced by the trading companies in this period.

This chapter examines the changed environment faced by the trading companies and assesses their response. In terms of corporate organization, there was remarkably little change, with family influences persisting in many cases. The momentum to create multi-regional business groups slackened, though a major shift in ownership patterns occurred with Unilever's acquisition of most British trading interests in West Africa. There were incremental rather than radical changes to corporate strategies. The process of 'reinvention' did not end in 1914 but continued into this era. Trading companies in all regions continued to develop new businesses, while abandoning older ones. However the British firms needed to change a lot, in the light of their changing environment, so an underlying question is whether their strategies changed sufficiently, or whether they 'missed opportunities'.

4.2 The World Economy in Crisis

The First World War halted the growth of the global economy which had developed before 1914. An economic environment which was highly favourable to multinational trading economies was replaced by one which was highly unfavourable. The end of the war was followed by a deep depression in 1920. A period of recovery was followed by the Great Depression beginning in 1929. By the early 1930s the global economy had been shattered and replaced by one of trading blocs, exchange controls, and protectionism. Barriers to flows of trade and capital became all-prevalent.

The collapse of world trade presented the most obvious challenge to firms whose core business was international trade. While before 1914 world trade grew much faster than world output, in the interwar years this position was reversed. The rate of growth of total trade per decade declined from an average of almost 40 per cent between 1881 and 1913 to 14 per cent between 1913 and 1937. After the First World War protectionism continued to spread, including within the British Empire to India and Australia, and to Latin America, as these countries sought to develop their own manufacturing industries. In the wake of the Great Depression protectionism reached new heights. In 1932 Britain abandoned free trade and by the end of the 1930s close to half the world's trade was restricted by tariffs.

There were special problems for primary producers. During the 1920s rising output of many products led to weakening prices, especially for raw materials and certain foodstuffs, such as sugar and wheat. A further problem was the development of new sources of supply. Africa emerged as a major supplier of tropical foodstuffs, especially cocoa and oilseeds and fats. This led to the advent of commodity control schemes as in sugar and producers of products such as rubber, coffee, sugar, petroleum, and tin tried to establish collaborative arrangements to restrict output and/or control prices. In the early 1930s the prices of Brazilian and East African coffee, Argentinian and Australian wool, Chilean nitrates, West African cocoa and palm oil, and other primary products all tumbled. Against this background, governments supported international commodity agreements, which came in the 1930s to cover most of the world's primary products. There were distinct differences within the general category of primary products. The trade in minerals such as petroleum, copper, bauxite, and iron ore—products in which the British trading companies were little involved—grew rapidly in the interwar years. The trade in certain tropical foodstuffs such as cocoa, coffee, and bananas also increased substantially. However the trade in non-tropical foodstuffs, especially cereals, stagnated while a group of agricultural raw materials including cotton, silk, and hides and skins experienced falling trade volumes.[1]

At the end of the 1930s well over one-half of world trade was still European, and the export trade of developed countries continued to be dominated by manufacturers while their import trade consisted of primary goods. However the interwar years did see a fall in Europe's share of world export trade in manufactures from over four-fifths of total trade in 1913 to two-thirds in 1937. This reflected the growing importance of the United States, and also the continued industrialization of Japan. By the early 1930s the volume of Japanese textile exports had overtaken those of Lancashire. A number of other developing countries, especially India and the larger Latin American republics, underwent considerable industrialization in this period.

Before 1914 the British trading companies had become at least as important as mobilizers of international capital flows as of trade flows, but the interwar years also saw a marked deterioration in the conditions for such activity. The international monetary system was severely disrupted by

---

[1] A. G. Kenwood and A. L. Lougheed, *The Growth of the International Economy 1820–1990* (London: Routledge, 1992), 212–17.

wartime inflation and the suspension of the gold standard. Although many countries returned to the gold standard in the mid-1920s, capital flows were often speculative and short term. Certainly in the case of the United States, which had become the chief international creditor, portfolio lending grew faster than FDI.[2] International lending collapsed in the 1930s. Britain was forced off the gold standard in 1931 followed by the United States two years later. Regional currency blocs developed—a US dollar area including Latin America, a sterling bloc covering most of the British Empire, etc.— supported by extensive exchange controls. Cross-border capital flows fell sharply, and were often confined within currency blocs.

Much remains unclear about the fate of FDI in this era. As suggested in Chapter 1, world FDI seems to have continued to grow in the 1920s, with the United States probably becoming the largest home economy in terms of flows, but Britain remains the largest in terms of stock. During the following decade exchange controls and political risk encouraged firms in many industries to enter international cartels rather than risk capital through FDI, though multinational investment continued in a number of industries such as automobiles and branded foodstuffs, and also in the international petroleum industry. From the late 1920s, new FDI in many primary commodities afflicted by excess capacity and falling prices was rarely an attractive proposition.[3]

If the world economic environment in general became difficult for trading companies, the home economy of the British trading companies was also less favourable than before 1914. The British economy as a whole experienced the frequent fluctuations and the heavy unemployment which characterized the world economy as a whole. During the 1920s its economic growth was rather slower than many other industrialized economies, but it suffered less in the Great Depression, and in the 1930s its growth was rather better, based on non-export sectors such as building, electricity, and a number of industries such as automobiles and electricals.

However Britain's role in the world economy was more problematic for its trading companies. The British Empire remained intact politically, but Britain's economic performance deteriorated. Britain's share of exports of world manufactured goods continued to fall, from 25 per cent in 1913 to 19 per cent in 1937. During the interwar years British exports never regained their 1913 level. A key problem was the declining demand for its main export industries of textiles, coal, and engineering products. There was an overall decline in world trade in such 'staples' even before the Great Depression. There were special problems in textiles, once a major source of business for British merchants. There was a marked decline in international trade in textiles—the overall volume of world exports of cotton goods fell 40 per cent

[2] Geoffrey Jones, *The Evolution of International Business* (London: Routledge, 1996), 40.
[3] Ibid. 43, 109–12.

between 1913 and 1936—while within this context the Lancashire industry seriously lost international competitiveness. In 1913 it supplied two-thirds of the world trade in cotton cloth: by 1938 the figure was down to 25 per cent. Lancashire exports to India and also Latin America fell massively, in part because of tariffs and import substitution, while in China and later elsewhere they were decimated by Japanese competition.[4]

Britain's export performance was poor in the regions in which its trading companies were concentrated. In India, Britain had accounted for 80 per cent of total imports of manufactured goods in 1913. The proportion fell to 53 per cent in 1929 and 40 per cent in 1937. Japan's share grew from 1 per cent in 1913 to 29 per cent in 1937.[5] The British trading position also deteriorated sharply in the major Latin America markets of Argentina, Brazil, and Chile. Having fallen sharply during the First World War, British exports recovered in the 1920s, but by 1929 British exports to Latin America were only 80 per cent of their 1913 level. There was a collapse in trade during the early 1930s, and British exports to the subcontinent never regained more than two-thirds of their 1929 value in any year in that decade. They also became highly concentrated on Argentina, which in 1938 accounted for 52 per cent of all Britain's sales to Latin America. In contrast, by 1938 the value of British exports to Brazil was only a quarter of their 1913 level.[6]

Britain lost its position as the world's largest capital exporter during the First World War to the United States, while the City of London lost its pre-eminence as the world's largest international financial centre as New York and Paris grew in importance. During the First World War Britain sold off assets and accumulated debts, with the result that Britain's overseas assets fell by £2.4 billion between 1913 and 1924. British capital exports resumed in the 1920s, but collapsed with the onset of the Great Depression. In 1931 strict exchange controls were adopted which severely restricted access to the London capital market for foreign (i.e. non-empire) borrowers.[7] British exchange controls meant that forming new free-standing companies to operate outside the empire was not possible—even if conditions had made it an attractive proposition, though continued investment could be made from reinvested earnings.

---

[4] Mary B. Rose (ed.), *International Competition and Strategic Response in The Textiles Industry Since 1870* (London: Frank Cass, 1991); id., *Firms, Networks and Business Values: The British and American Cotton Industries since 1750* (Cambridge: Cambridge University Press, forthcoming); Marguerite Dupree, 'Foreign Competition in the Interwar Period', in Mary B. Rose (ed.), *The Lancashire Cotton Industry* (Preston: Lancashire County Books, 1996).

[5] B. R. Tomlinson, 'Imperial Power and Foreign Trade: Britain and India (1900–1970)', in Peter Mathias and John A. Davis (eds.), *International Trade and British Economic Growth* (Oxford: Blackwell, 1996), 151.

[6] Rory Miller, 'British Trade with Latin America (1870–1950)', ibid. 130–2.

[7] P. J. Cain and A. G. Hopkins, *British Imperialism: Crisis and Deconstruction 1914–1990* (London: Longman, 1993), 87.

4.3 Structures and Performance

The three decades after 1914 proved ones of acute difficulty for the British trading companies. A number of large firms collapsed or came near to collapse, while the financial performance of virtually all firms deteriorated sharply. This section reviews the pressures on the trading companies, their financial performance, and changes in corporate structures.

A number of factors in the external environment of this period put acute pressures on the British trading companies. The first was the severity of the economic downturns after the First World War and after 1929. Of the two, the impact of the post-war crisis seems to have been most severe, especially because of the suddenness of the crisis after the good years of the First World War. However many firms had ample reserves as a result of their former profitability and it was in the 1930s that shareholders —especially ordinary shareholders—experienced the full brunt of the crisis. A cluster of firms were unable to pay dividends to their ordinary shareholders.

The second adverse influence on the trading companies was the interwar commodity price crisis. Gibbs was devastated by the collapse in nitrate prices after the First World War, while the trading companies in West Africa were hit by a fall of almost 60 per cent in cocoa prices between 1927 and 1929.[8] Brazilian Warrant's fortunes were linked to coffee prices, which fell in the early 1920s and then tumbled after 1929.[9] The Borneo Company was undermined by falling teak prices after 1929, and as a Thai producer it was especially hit by the introduction of Imperial Preference in favour of teak from India and Burma.[10] Insofar as many trading companies were also major importers into their host economies, the decline in incomes as a result of falling commodity prices had a very adverse effect on their business. In many cases the suddenness of external shocks left them with large stocks of unwanted merchandise.

Thirdly, the competitive environment of the trading companies was changed by new entrants. In Latin America, the British trading companies faced increased competition from German and US firms. In China, Japanese trading and shipping companies caused difficulties in all sectors of the business of Jardine Matheson and Swire's, as well as for the smaller companies such as Dodwells. 'At the root of everybody's troubles', Stanley Dodwell wrote in May 1934, 'is the Japanese competition which will always be with us becoming more fierce and wider spread every year.'[11]

---

[8] D. K. Fieldhouse, *Merchant Capital and Economic Decolonization* (Oxford: Clarendon Press, 1994), 88.

[9] Robert G. Greenhill, 'Investment Group, Free-Standing Company or Multinational? Brazilian Warrant 1909–52', *Business History*, 37 (1995).

[10] H. Longhurst, *The Borneo Story* (London: Newman Neame, 1956), 77.

[11] Stanley Dodwell to George Dodwell, 16 May 1934, Dodwell Archives, GHL MS 27512.

The business of the trading companies began to be seriously affected by the internalization strategies of British manufacturing and resources firms which sought to dispense with the services of the merchants. The entry of Lever Brothers into West Africa and its acquisition of trading companies was an exceptional case, but Levers was not the only firm to engage in backward integration. Tate & Lyle, the largest British sugar refining firm, began to acquire West Indian sugar plantations in 1936, providing a new competitor for the British trading companies in that region.[12] More generally, in India and the larger Latin American states, a number of British manufacturers established factories or at least distribution facilities prompted by growing tariff barriers.[13] British oil companies also established their own distribution facilities in this period, dispensing with the services of the merchants who had served as their agents.

A fourth problem for the British trading companies was that, within the overall context of stagnating international trade, British export performance —especially cotton textiles—was especially weak. Although the firms had long since performed tasks other than selling British exports, the declining competitiveness of British goods, the growth of competition and import substitution in the interwar years adversely affected what in most instances had remained a profitable part of their business before 1914.

The British firms in Asia were especially badly affected by the decline in British piece-goods exports. In the 1920s Ralli headed the list of British importers of textiles into India, followed by Grahams, James Finlay, the Bombay Co., and Forbes, Forbes, Campbell.[14] These firms suffered badly when the post-war recession left them with huge stocks, and thereafter this aspect of their business was in progressive decline. From the mid-1920s at least the internal correspondence of firms on the issue reflected a sense of the inevitable demise of Lancashire textiles in the Indian market.[15] Nationalist resentment at British rule heightened the pressures on British imports, because from the 1920s there were 'boycotts' of British textiles, a movement which reached its peak in 1930. There 'appear(ed) little likelihood of Manchester regaining a very much larger share of the Indian markets', a report to the chairman of Ralli concluded in 1939.[16] By that year Lancashire's exports to India were only 6 per cent of the level in 1913.[17] However the difficulties of the British importers in India—and other markets also—were in fact not as

[12] Phillipe Chalmin, *The Making of a Sugar Giant. Tate and Lyle 1858–1989* (Chur: Harwood, 1990).

[13] Geoffrey Jones (ed.), *British Multinationals: Origins, Management and Performance* (Aldershot: Gower, 1986).

[14] Memo by Judd Gorden & Co., 16 Oct. 1930, HO/GM/Bea.22, Lloyds TSB Group Archives.

[15] Memorandum by G. W. Chambers enclosed in London to Madras, 8 Nov. 1928, MS 27159/6, GHL.

[16] Report to the chairman of Ralli Brothers Limited, 12 Apr. 1939, MS 23834, GHL.

[17] B. Chatterji, *Trade, Tariffs and Empire: Lancashire and British Policy in India, 1919–1939* (Oxford: Oxford University Press, 1992).

straightforward as simply the decline in the competitiveness of Lancashire textiles. In India, the indigenous trading groups who had traditionally worked as middlemen for British firms sought more independent roles, while British textile firms began to bypass the British merchant houses to deal directly with Indian merchants.[18]

A number of merchant houses collapsed altogether in the face of these conditions. The two periods of greatest danger were after the end of the First World War and the early 1930s. The first period saw the elimination of all the British merchant houses in Russia: the Hubbards estimated the value of their lost cotton textile manufacturing assets in Russia at £2.5 million.[19] In the early 1920s Federick Huth, which like Gibbs combined a merchant banking business in London with a trading business in Chile and elsewhere in Latin America, was overwhelmed by debts. Huths was rescued by the Bank of England, merged with another firm, and the merchant and banking business separated, and slowly liquidated, the whole process lasting until the 1940s.[20]

On a larger scale, the early 1920s saw the end of Grahams. This group of interlocked merchant partnerships based in Glasgow, India, and Portugal was badly hit by the recession of 1920 and 1921, and they were overwhelmed when the London partnership embarked on a variety of speculative schemes, including investments in a film company in California and a scheme to import US cars into Britain and India. This had been financed by bank debt and in 1924 its principal creditor, Lloyds Bank, began a long reconstruction of the Grahams group. In 1924 a new firm, Grahams Trading Company, was established to run the main Indian and Portuguese businesses. The port business of W. & J. Graham was not involved in the collapse and remained a partnership, albeit with family links to the other parts of the Graham business in Portugal. Grahams Trading continued to rank as one of the largest importers of Lancashire textiles into India in the 1920s, but in its weakened state it could not continue as an independent entity.[21] In 1930 the Portuguese business of Grahams was placed into a separate company, and in 1931 the Indian business was sold to Turner Morrison, the Calcutta managing agency which had formerly specialized in shipping agency business.[22]

The Great Depression saw further casualties. In 1930 the Ashworth group, which had substantial manufacturing interests in Brazil, collapsed. In the following year Graham Rowe also collapsed. This firm had large sugar

[18] M. Misra, Entrepreneurial Decline and the End of Empire (Oxford D. Phil., 1994), 88–9.

[19] Stuart Thompstone, 'British Merchant Houses in Russia before 1914', in L. Edmondson and P. Waldron (eds.), *Economy and Society in Russia and the Soviet Union, 1860–1930* (London: Macmillan 1992), 124.

[20] R. S. Sayers, *The Bank of England 1891–1944*, vol. i (Cambridge: Cambridge University Press, 1976), 268–71.

[21] File on Grahams 1929/30 HO/GM/Bea.22, Lloyds TSB Group Archives.

[22] Grahams Board Minutes, 2 Nov. 1930, MS 22465, GHL.

estates in Peru, and seems to have made losses in the post-war crisis in the early 1920s, though it was still regarded by their bankers as a 'very respectable, old established and well managed concern' in 1922.[23] They subsequently developed a large business distributing imported US cars, and also invested in various manufacturing businesses in Chile making, amongst other things, soft drinks and perfumes. Following the collapse in 1931, the firm was reconstructed by its British bankers (see Chapter 8).

The most spectacular problems came in West Africa. During the First World War Lever Brothers continued to acquire further trading companies culminating in 1920 with the purchase of the Niger Company for £8 million.[24] Soon afterwards it was discovered that the firm was £2 million in debt to its bankers and, in addition, commodity prices collapsed. In the ensuing crisis Lever Brothers was forced by the Niger Company's bankers to issue debenture stock to be held by the banks as collateral security for their loans.[25] After the Niger Company was taken over by Lever, it made losses for five years before a small profit was made in 1925, and it was only in 1929 that it paid its first dividend after its acquisition. Meanwhile the large-scale entry of Lever Brothers into West Africa stimulated a merger between the African Association and Millers which became the African & Eastern Trade Corporation in 1919.[26] This venture also made a huge loss of £1.8 million in 1921, but then recovered. Between 1920 and 1928 it made a net post-tax profit of over £2 million, whereas the Niger Company made a net loss of over £1.6 million.

At the end of the 1920s the West African trading companies again went into crisis. The African & Eastern's finances deteriorated in 1929 and prompted a merger with the Niger Company. The outcome was the formation of the United Africa Company, initially owned 50/50 by the shareholders of the African & Eastern and Lever Brothers. Subsequently, the merger of Lever Brothers and Margarine Union of the Netherlands to create Unilever shifted the balance of the stockholding by bringing five small Dutch-owned trading companies into the UAC, while a major financial crisis in 1931/2 resulted in UAC's rescue by Unilever. As shown in Chapter 8, Unilever was eventually obliged by UAC's banks to write down the firm's capital by a half in 1932 to £7.5 million, and to recapitalize the firm with an additional £3.5 million of working capital, a procedure which left Unilever with 80 per cent of the equity.[27] UAC and its predecessors, therefore, survived through the willingness of the shareholders of Lever and subsequently Unilever to subsidize their business. The problems of the West African trading companies were particularly striking as they enjoyed

---

[23] London to Valparaíso, 2 Aug. 1922, London & River Plate Bank Archives, D 55/6, UCL.
[24] C. Wilson, *The History of Unilever*, vol. 1 (London: Cassel & Co., 1954), 234–40, 250–3; F. Pedler, *The Lion and the Unicorn in Africa* (London: Heinemann, 1974), 172–84.
[25] Wilson, *History*, 257–8.   [26] Pedler, *Lion*, 225–38.
[27] Fieldhouse, *Merchant Capital*, 9–18.

considerable fiscal privileges from the colonial governments. In Nigeria, there
was no company tax until 1938, and they were also entitled to representation on the executive and legislative councils of Nigeria.[28]

These failures or near failures were the tip of an iceberg in which most
British merchant firms experienced great financial problems. On the China
coast, political and economic chaos and Japanese competition caused deep
problems for all the British trading companies. Dodwells could only pay
its shareholders one dividend between 1926 and 1936, and wrote down its
capital in that year.[29] After making large profits during the war, Jardine
Matheson experienced large losses in 1921, through trading in produce and
silk.[30] From the mid-1920s losses on sugar and shipping began to mount.
The Indo-China shipping company made losses every year between 1922
and 1936 except in 1928, accumulating a total loss of £1.8 million.[31] Jardine
Matheson as a whole was loss-making by 1930 and remained so before returning to profitability in 1936.[32] By 1939 the firm felt 'no longer . . . ashamed'
of [its] balance sheet, but overall the firm was unable to pay any dividends
between 1927 and 1940.[33] From the outbreak of the Sino-Japanese War in
1937, Jardines, Swire's, and other British firms operated in a battle zone,
and by 1945 virtually all their assets in China and Hong Kong had been
destroyed.

In South East Asia, the Borneo Company made losses in both the early
1920s and the early 1930s. It had to transfer all its secret reserves to support
its published balance sheet in 1931, and was unable to pay dividends on its
ordinary shares between 1931 and 1940.[34] Guthries made losses in 1920 and
1922, recovered in the late 1920s, made losses in 1931 and 1932, and was
making larger profits by the mid-1930s. Anglo-Siam had a profitable 1920s
—its dividend to shareholders seldom fell below 30 per cent throughout
the decade, earning it many favourable comparisons with the Borneo
Company from the financial press.[35] In the early 1930s its profits fell away,
but it does not seem to have made a loss.[36]

[28] Robert L. Tignor, *Capitalism and Nationalism at the End of the Empire* (Princeton: Princeton
University Press, 1998), 200.
[29] Edmund Warde, *The House of Dodwell* (London: the firm, 1958), 127. The writing down
of the capital in 1936 should not be seen as an emergency measure, but rather as an attempt
to bring the balance sheet more in line with reality and to wipe out accumulated losses.
[30] D. Beith to D. G. M. Bernard, 29 Mar. 1935, S/O Shanghai to London 1935, JMA, CUL.
[31] Hong Kong to D. G. M. Bernard, 8 Feb. 1938, S/O Hong Kong to London, 1938, JMA,
CUL.
[32] Robert Blake, *Jardine Matheson. Traders of the Far East* (London: Weidenfeld & Nicolson),
chapter 15 provides annual profit figures which show losses in 1920/1, in 1925/6 and 1926/7, in
1930/1, and between 1932/3 and 1934/5. There is no figure for 1929/30 but the correspondence
files in JMA indicate a loss.
[33] J. H. Keswick to D. Beith, 6 Feb. 1940, S/O Shanghai to London 1940; J. H. Keswick
to D. Paterson, 2 Apr. 1940, S/O Shanghai to Hong Kong, Jan.–June 1940, JMA, CUL.
[34] Board Minutes, 5 Aug. 1931, 23 Sept. 1931, BCL Archives, MS 27178/19, GHL.
[35] File of newspaper cuttings, Anglo-Thai archives, MS 27011, GHL.
[36] Board Minutes of Anglo-Thai, MS 27008/8, GHL.

In South Asia, Finlays made major losses in the post-war slump. Its four large Indian tea companies lost £458,000 in 1920 and its Indian piece-goods business lost over £160,000 in 1921. The post-war crisis was especially acute in India because of a sudden depreciation in the rupee/sterling exchange rate. Birds lost over £1.25 million when its post-war expansion plans were caught by the slump, and made further losses in 1931 and 1932.[37] In Madras, Parry's was caught by the collapse of the rupee with large orders for Lancashire piece-goods financed by a bank loan.[38] During the 1930s Wallace Brothers passed through a major financial crisis also. The profits of the Bombay Company collapsed and it made losses in 1934 and 1936, the Bombay Burmah Trading Corporation earned only 'small' dividends between 1932 and 1937, and Wallace Brothers itself was caught in 1931 with too many investments in depreciating securities.[39] Ralli Brothers avoided a major crisis in the 1930s, but its profitability dropped away and for most of the 1930s it was unable to pay dividends on its ordinary shares.[40]

The surviving evidence on the British firms in Latin America points to similar trends. Balfour Williamson's partnerships made substantial profits during the First World War, but in 1920 the firm made losses of £600,000 on trading in nitrate, wool, and cotton, plus unspecified bad debts. A recovery by 1923 was hit by losses in the following year of around £700,000 through a defalcation. In 1930 the firm's income plunged again. The capital of the US and Chilean subsidiaries—Balfour, Guthrie, and Williamson Balfour —was reconstructed in 1935. Balfour Williamson was unable to pay any dividends between 1930 and 1946.[41]

Gibbs made extremely large losses on its core nitrate business in the early 1920s as the artificial substitutes developed during the First World War undermined Chilean production.[42] Gibbs & Co., the Chilean partnership, made large profits on nitrate sales during the period 1915 to 1919, which turned to losses in 1920 and an over £500,000 loss in 1921, and by 1922 the London partnership had lent Gibbs & Co. over £1 million.[43] By 1928 accumulated losses in Chile had increased and the partners' capital in Chile was negative.[44] The Australian partnership, Gibbs Bright, was profitable during the war and seems to have remained so during the early 1920s. In 1923 the £62,000 profit represented a return on capital employed of 12.9 per cent, though it could hardly offset the scale of the losses made in Chile.

---

[37] B. R. Tomlinson, 'Colonial Firms and the Decline of Colonialism in Eastern India 1914–1947', *Modern Asian Studies*, 15 (1981), 465; Misra, 'Entrepreneurial Decline', 26, 52–4.
[38] Hilton Brown, *Parry's of Madras* (Madras: the firm, 1954), 258, 335.
[39] A. C. Pointon, *Wallace Brothers* (Oxford: the firm, 1974), 68–70.
[40] Report to the Chairman of Ralli Brothers Limited, 12 Apr. 1939, MS 23834, GHL.
[41] Wallis Hunt, *Heirs of Great Adventure*, vol. II (London: the firm, 1960), 142–239.
[42] Antony Gibbs & Sons, *Merchants and Bankers 1808–1958* (London: the firm, 1958), 47–8.
[43] Telegram from D. Blair, 4 Aug. 1922; H. C. Gibbs to D. Blair, 14 Sept. 1922; Journal entries, Antony Gibbs Archives, MS 11115/3, GHL.
[44] Lord Hunsdon to D. Blair, 10 Sept. 1928, MS 11115/3, GHL.

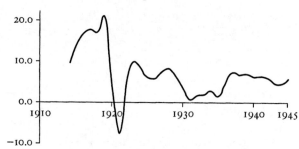

Fig. 4.1 Average post-tax ROCE of British trading companies, 1914–1945

Thereafter, and in contrast to the general pattern, the performance of Gibbs Bright deteriorated to the end of the decade, partly because of losses incurred during the process of diversification into the timber industry.[45] The New York branch/partnership of Gibbs made an average overall profit for the whole 1920 to 1938 period of only a little over $16,000, but this concealed an erratic pattern with a large profit in 1920, dropping away to losses in 1926–7, 1929–34, and 1938.[46]

In contrast to the problems of Gibbs and Balfour Williamson, and the collapse of Graham Rowe, W. and J. Lockett extracted itself from Chile and Peru on favourable terms. During the First World War their Peruvian sugar estates were profitable, and subsequently they sold them to local capitalists, putting the British Sugar Company into liquidation in 1922. In 1928, shortly before the virtual collapse of the Chilean nitrates industry, they also sold their trading and nitrate business in Chile to a local entrepreneur. Locketts reverted to its traditional wine importing and other largely British-based activities.[47]

The data on post-tax ROCE in Appendix 1 provides a more systematic view of performance. Figure 4.1 illustrates the trend in the annual average rates for all firms combined, while Table 4.1 gives averages for time periods between 1914 and 1945 and a calculation of the standard deviation of the annual figures.

The financial difficulties of these decades emerge clearly from the graph and the table. While the First World War was a highly profitable era, especially towards the end, this was followed by a sharp decline in profitability during the post-war recession, and another serious downturn from

---

[45] Ibid., Private Letter Books from London to Australian branches 1919–30, MS 11110/7–12, GHL.

[46] New York's profit was $368,000 in 1920, $79,000 in 1921, $5,000 in 1923. It made a large loss of $138,000 in 1930, Antony Gibbs & Co. Inc., Accounts 1913–38, Antony Gibbs Archives, MS 11109, GHL.

[47] Richard Cyril Lockett, *Memoirs of the Family of Lockett* (London. private circulation, 1939), 116, 123–4.

TABLE 4.1 Average post-tax return on net capital employed of selected British trading companies, 1914–1945 (%)

	Borneo Company	Swire's	Dodwells	H&C	Finlays	Brazilian Warrant	Wilson, Sons	Booker McConnell	Niger Company/ UAC	Average
1914–1919	19.7	19.9	20.3	11.5	17.2	8.1	21.1	—	8.4[d]	15.9
1920–1929	3.8	13.5	(8.6)	10.0	11.1[b]	5.2	7.0	4.5[c]	—	5.7
1930–1939	1.4	4.9	(2.0)	9.4	4.9	2.0	3.2	5.8	4.7	3.8
1940–1945	0.8[a]	2.0	2.6	9.6	4.6	6.7	5.8	6.8	12.4	5.7
Std[e]1914–1945	8.3	9.0	15.5	2.3	5.5	4.3	7.6	6.6	—	
Std[e]1920–1939	4.2	7.4	14.6	2.2	3.6	4.6	4.0	5.6	6.3[f]	

[a] Data for 1945 missing.
[b] Data for 1921 and 1922 missing. These seem to have been years of heavy losses.
[c] Data for 1920 missing.
[d] Niger Company data for 1919 missing.
[e] Standard deviation is calculated on the annual figures in Appendix 1. It only applies for the years for which data exists.
[f] 1930–1939 only.

1930.[48] Overall ROCE emerges as consistently lower after 1920 than before 1914, and much lower in the 1930s. With the exception of Harrisons & Crosfield, financial performance was also more volatile than before 1914. There were noticeably wide inter-firm differences in performance. Dodwells was especially weak after 1920, as was the Borneo Company. Harrisons & Crosfield, on the other hand, maintained a persistently high and stable ROCE throughout the period.

The financial pressures of the interwar years did not lead to radical changes in corporate structures. Despite the problems caused by the death or retirement of partners, the partnership form continued to be used in some of the largest groups, including Antony Gibbs and the Inchcape family.[49] Nonetheless, there was a continued shift towards incorporation, mostly in the form of private limited companies. Among the Latin American groups, Duncan Fox converted from a partnership to a private limited company in 1928, and in 1930 the three interlinked partnerships of Balfour Williamson incorporated. The British-based Balfour Williamson became the sole owner of the ordinary shares in the two overseas companies, Williamson Balfour & Co. in Chile and Balfour Guthrie & Co. in the United States. Among the large West Indian sugar traders, Henckell DuBuisson incorporated as a private company in 1920, while Booker Brothers, McConnell, which became a private company in 1908, converted to a public company in 1927. A number of Inchcape affiliates also incorporated as private companies. These included Smith Mackenzie, which incorporated in East Africa, and Gray Mackenzie which incorporated in London, both in 1936.

The partnership form remained strong among the British traders active in India,[50] but there were exceptions. Finlays converted from a private to a public company in 1924, and Ralli Brothers incorporated as a private company in 1931. Parry & Co. incorporated in Madras in 1928. An exceptional case was Andrew Yule, which incorporated in Calcutta in 1919. This firm was acquired by the US banking group J. P. Morgan and its British merchant banking affiliate Morgan Grenfell. Lord Catto was sent to run the firm, and during the 1920s the London branch was renamed Yule, Catto & Co. The Morgan interests sold their shares again in the early 1930s, but strong connections continued between the firms.[51]

---

[48] It is not possible to make valid comparisons with Arnold's data for pre-tax ROCE for 1914–23 since tax payments and refunds were substantial in this period. A comparison with Arnold's calculation of post-tax return on equity has more validity. For 1914–19, post-tax ROCE for the industrial sectors selected by Arnold was 13.6 per cent.

[49] Percival Griffiths, *A History of the Inchcape Group* (London: the firm, 1977), 116–17; Stephanie Jones, *Trade and Shipping: Lord Inchcape 1852–1932* (Manchester: Manchester University Press, 1989), 150–4, 203–4.

[50] Misra, 'Entrepreneurial Decline', 23.

[51] Sir Humphrey Baskerville Mynors, *Thomas Sivewright Catto* (Edinburgh: T. & A. Constable, 1962); Kathleen Burk, *Morgan Grenfell 1838–1988* (Oxford: Oxford University Press, 1989), 81–3.

In most cases incorporation did little to change the pattern of owner-ship and control by a small group of shareholders, usually but not always families. Firms such as Harrisons & Crosfield and the Borneo Company, which were genuinely managerial enterprises, remained exceptional, and even their shares were closely held. Although founded as a public company, it was only in 1922 that the Borneo Company sought a quotation on the London Stock Exchange. The stockholding structure of Steel Brothers was a variant of this pattern. The controlling ordinary stock, with two exceptions, could only be held by active executives of the company usually after fifteen years' or more service. On retirement, they had to sell their holdings. The two exceptions were descendants of the founding Steel family and James Finlay & Co.[52]

Incorporation was usually designed to perpetrate family control rather than end it. For example, Duncan Fox's decision to incorporate in 1928 followed the recent death of two partners and the retirement of a third. This did not cause an immediate crisis as the partnership agreement provided for repay-ments of capital over a period of years, but the opportunity was taken to bring new money into the business through incorporation. The capital of all partners was transferred to the new company. There were only seven shareholders in the new company. Of the ordinary share capital of £700,000, F. H. Fox—the former Senior Partner—held £315,000 and his brother a further £100,000.[53] Even the creation of a public company did not signal the end of family influence. At James Finlay, the Muir family retained firm control until the early 1950s, and effectively the firm functioned as a family business regardless of its legal status.

Jardine Matheson and Swire's exemplified the continuing family influence in the major trading companies. John Swire & Sons remained a private limited company owned by the Swire and Scott families throughout the interwar years. Jardine Matheson's shares were closely held by the Jardine and Keswick families and a small group of former senior managers. The share capital had a complicated structure with five different categories of shares comprising different voting rights, but in 1936 Sir John Buchanan-Jardine's shares controlled 73.9 per cent of the total votes, or just short of the absolute control which required three-quarters of the total vote.[54]

The 1920s were a period of rapid growth in concentration levels in the domestic British economy, largely as a result of a great merger wave. However, there was no strong parallel trend among the trading companies, with the conspicuous exception of West Africa. There was some consolida-tion in India. In 1917 Bird & Co. merged with F. W. Heilger to create

[52] H. E. W. Braund, *Calling to Mind* (Oxford: Pergamon Press, 1975), 113–14.

[53] Head Office Midland Bank, Lancashire Section, General Managers' Diaries of Interviews 1928, 21 Feb. 1928, Acc 30/122, HSBC Group Archives.

[54] Hong Kong to D. G. M. Bernard, 13 Oct. 1936, P&C London, Hong Kong, Shanghai 1935–7, JMA, CUL.

a large Calcutta managing agency with over 100,000 employees and large investments in jute, coal, and paper manufacturing.[55] Some acquisitions were made of financially distressed companies. An example was the acquisition by Blyth, Greene, Jourdain in 1935 of a Malayan agency house—Harper, Gilfillan, whose parent firm had run into financial difficulties. Blyth, Greene, Jourdain owned a partnership in Mauritius primarily engaged in sugar trading.[56] In a number of other cases larger companies acquired smaller expatriate firms. In the West Indies, Booker Brothers, McConnell merged with Curtis, Campbell & Co., an old-established family partnership with sugar estates in British Guinea, in 1939.[57] On a smaller scale, in 1920 the Borneo Company acquired the Penang-based expatriate firm of Allen Dennys & Co., which held agencies for insurance and whisky companies, and earned substantial commission on rubber sales.[58] There was one failed attempt at consolidation in the Gulf. In 1920 Gray Mackenzie merged its business with Lynch Brothers, a London merchant partnership with shipping and agency business in the Gulf, to create the Mesopotamia Persia Corporation (or Mespers), but the two parties separated again in 1936.[59]

It was West Africa where the most radical concentration occurred. By the early 1930s most of the British trading companies in that region had been absorbed into the newly created UAC. This firm was no longer 'British' but Anglo-Dutch, though it was London-based and its management remained overwhelmingly British. During the 1930s UAC absorbed a number of other small West African merchant houses of various nationalities. These included the Manchester-based G. B. Ollivant, which was acquired in 1932. This merchant house remained an autonomous firm based in Manchester. It was not until 1945 that UAC's ownership was made public and not until 1980 that Ollivants were fully integrated into UAC.[60] The upshot was that by the end of the 1930s John Holt & Co. was the main surviving independent British trading company in West Africa.

Table 4.2 shows the rankings of British trading companies by size of capital employed at the end of the 1930s.

There were some obvious differences between the earlier ranking for 1913. In 1938 UAC was three times larger than James Finlay, the next largest firm for which data is available. However both the Inchcape family interests and Jardine Matheson are likely to have been larger than Finlays given their considerable fixed capital investments, but it is impossible to give a reasonable estimate of their size. Finlays and Harrisons & Crosfield had both grown

[55] Tomlinson, 'Colonial Firms', 465.

[56] Augustus Muir, *Blyth, Greene, Jourdain & Co. Ltd. 1810–1960* (London: the firm, 1961), 38–41.

[57] Kathleen M. Stahl, *The Metropolitan Organisation of British Colonial Trade* (London: Faber and Faber, 1951), 44.

[58] Report on the Affairs of Messrs Allen Dennys & Co. 31 Oct. 1919, MS 27361, GHL.

[59] Griffiths, *History*, 75–6; Stephanie Jones, *Two Centuries of Overseas Trading* (London: Macmillan, 1986), 102–4.

[60] Fieldhouse, *Merchant Capital*, 19–20.

TABLE 4.2 Net capital employed of selected
British trading companies, 1938 (£000s)

United Africa Company	13,549
James Finlay & Co.	4,513
Harrisons & Crosfield	3,117
Wilson, Sons & Co.	2,132
Antony Gibbs & Sons	2,000
Balfour Williamson & Co.	2,000
John Swire & Sons	1,469
Duncan Fox & Co.	1,300
Booker Brothers, McConnell & Co.	1,195
Borneo Co.	1,134
John Holt & Co. (Liverpool)	1,000
Anglo-Siam Corporation	800
Brazilian Warrant	758
Guthrie & Co.	618
Smith Mackenzie & Co.	271
Dodwell & Co.	217
Gray Mackenzie & Co.	160

Source. Appendix 3.

quite substantially since 1913. Booker Brothers, McConnell had also doubled in size since 1913. This firm was unique among the firms in Table 4.1 for improving its post-tax ROCE in the 1930s. In contrast, Dodwells was smaller in 1938 than it had been in 1913.

The weakened financial performance of many of the trading companies and the continued preference of many firms for private companies and partnerships suggested that firms would face a financial constraint on their strategies in the interwar years. The large number of private companies and partnerships implied a continued unwillingness to seek outside capital for the core trading firm. Even the public companies preferred to rely on reinvested earnings rather than raise new funds from the capital market. Harrisons & Crosfield, the best performing firm in Table 4.1, did not go to the capital market after 1920 and for the remainder of the period before 1945. The many other companies which experienced serious periods of loss-making were hardly in a position to finance expensive diversifications. During the 1920s new ventures could still be financed by the flotation of 'free-standing' companies in the established tradition of 'business groups', but by the 1930s exchange controls and the international environment greatly restricted this option also.

In summary, the two interwar recessions, the collapse of many commodity prices, the entry of new competitors and the declining competitiveness of British exports took a heavy toll on the British merchant groups. While the

First World War offered them a final surge of profitability, the subsequent decades were ones of weakened financial performance, sometimes dramatically so. Apart from the exceptional consolidation of West African trading companies into the Unilever-owned UAC, corporate structures remained broadly in their pre-1914 pattern.

4.4 Strategies

Before 1914 the trading companies had grown and diversified—becoming 'hybrids'—in response to a number of factors including the boom in commodity prices, capital availability, and the expansion of imperial frontiers. They responded to both opportunities and threats, seeking new opportunities when former activities became unviable, and responding in various ways when their roles as trade intermediaries were challenged. In the process they developed knowledge about and contacts in their particular areas of enterprise, proved responsive to opportunities to develop new lines of activity, and were creative in forming diversified 'business groups'. The globalization of the world economy had stimulated the growth of multi-regional business groups.

The interwar years presented a wholly new environment. Most commodity prices were falling. Britain's position as the leading capital exporter ceased and, by the 1930s, exchange controls were in place. Imperial frontiers had ceased to expand. The global economy was replaced by one of increasing barriers to flows of trade, capital, and people. Insofar as the traders faced a combination of threats and opportunities, it was the threats that seemed to stand out after the First World War.

The strategies pursued by Japanese trading companies indicated possible responses to the new circumstances of the interwar years. The Japanese companies also experienced major difficulties in the 1920s and one *sogo shosha*, Suzuki Shoten, went bankrupt in 1927. The other *sogo shosha* responded in a number of ways to the changed conditions. During the 1920s Mitsui Bussan invested in manufacturing companies in Japan to prevent them from developing their own distribution facilities. During the 1930s the *sogo shosha*, helped by the expansion of Japan's exports in this decade, expanded the range of commodities in which they traded, and opened up new markets in Latin America, the Middle East, and the Soviet Union. They developed 'global sales networks' in this era.[61] The Japanese companies, therefore, followed strategies to spread risks and/or search out new opportunities by diversifying geographically, and to develop greater linkages with their home economy, in part to secure their traditional trade intermediation role as well as to identify new opportunities.

---

[61] N. Kawabe, 'Overseas Activities and their Organisation', in S. Yonekawa (ed.), *General Trading Companies* (Tokyo: United Nations University Press, 1990), 174.

The multi-regional business groups which had developed before 1914 had the potential to develop as 'global sales networks', but in practice the momentum towards a global strategy weakened in these decades. Among the groups which retained the partnership form, the Grahams never recovered from their collapse in the early 1920s, and by the following decade they were left with some Portuguese assets only. During the 1920s the Inchcape group showed signs of continuing to evolve as a coherent multi-regional business group. There was an attempt to develop more synergies inside the group with, as Chapter 6 will show, the foundation of a 'group bank'. However the resources of the group were directed to support the troubled shipping companies, especially P&O, whose profitability fell with the growth of competition to British shipping, whose competitiveness was undermined by the continued support for collusive conferences, the rigid division between tramps and liners, and limited technical change, including an aversion to oil-fired ships.[62] After Inchcape's death in 1932 in his eightieth year, the Inchcape group seemed to have lost continuity of strategy, with successive heads of the family businesses dying within a few years of each other, in 1939 and 1944 respectively.[63]

Balfour Williamson initially expanded the range of its interests. The firm, partly under the prompting of the British government, anxious to counter German commercial influence, opened branches in Bolivia, Ecuador, and Columbia. In the latter two countries they were the only British merchants active in the country. In Ecuador, the firm continued its long tradition in natural resource exploration when its affiliate, Lobitos Oilfields established a new company, Anglo-Ecuadorian Oilfields Ltd., to explore for oil. The investment in Bolivia, whose economy was based on tin, was related to the wartime purchase of a tin smelting company in Britain, formerly owned by the Metallgesellschaft. In 1920 Balfour Williamson also took a 25 per cent holding in a new firm, Metal Traders Ltd., designed to trade in non-ferrous metals, ores, and minerals. A final diversification involved the purchase of a number of small merchant firms in West Africa in 1918.[64]

The financial crises of the early 1920s and again in 1930, as well as management problems, halted and then reversed Balfour Williamson's expansion as a diversified business group. The West African venture proved 'an unmitigated and irredeemable failure', and the business was abandoned.[65] The firm divested from its Californian mortgage business in 1922 and 1923.[66] The primary strategic aim became to increase liquidity which was interpreted as reducing its fixed investments, especially those of Balfour Guthrie in the United States. Between 1942 and 1946 there were large realizations on the

[62] Jones, *Trade and Shipping*, esp. pp. 122–50; Christopher J. Napier, 'Allies or Subsidiaries? Inter-Company Relations in the P&O Group, 1914–39', *Business History*, 39 (1997).
[63] Jones, *Two Centuries*, 242.   [64] Hunt, *Heirs*, ii. 108–27.   [65] Ibid. 155–6.
[66] Ibid. 132–3.

Pacific coast, including holdings connected with fruit, hotels, wharves, and grain warehouses. Elsewhere, Balfour Williamson sold most of its Metal Traders shares in 1933 and in the early 1940s sold its shareholding in its tin mining company in Bolivia.[67] By the mid-1940s Balfour Williamson had become much more focused on trading in Latin America, though it retained the management of large flour milling operations in Chile and Peru, and the oil companies in Peru and Ecuador.

Antony Gibbs remained a more diversified business group, resembling in some respects contemporary Japanese *zaibatsu*.[68] The firm's extensive business continued to span South America, Australia, and New York together with its financial activities in London. In South America, Gibbs established a new affiliate in Peru, where it had ceased operations in 1880, in 1930 in search of wool for the emerging Chilean textile industry. In 1944 a Brazilian affiliate was also founded.[69] In Australia in the 1920s Gibbs Bright diversified into timber sales, a strategy which led the firm into purchasing shares in forest-owning and timber manufacturing companies.

Gibbs' branches traded in numerous commodities. New York sold Australian exports, Melbourne imported sugar from Mauritius and sacks from Calcutta, Sydney imported tractors, and Adelaide held a large dried fruit sales agency. The Australian business also controlled through agency agreements and small shareholdings a number of public companies which owned lead and silver mines and associated smelting works, and also manufactured cement and fertilizers. Gibbs also continued to expand its range of financial services. Long involved in the provision of insurance for nitrate sales, Gibbs expanded its insurance business during the 1930s using its nitrate connections—producing fire insurance for fertilizer factories in the United States—and in 1937 established an Underwriting Agency at Lloyd's. At the end of the 1930s Gibbs were planning to extend their insurance business to South Africa before the outbreak of war halted new developments.[70]

However Gibbs' strategies in the interwar years were financially constrained. It was handicapped by the serious losses from the collapse of the Chilean nitrate business. The collapse of nitrate prices also devastated the firm's trading business in Chile and led, in 1934, to a merger of Gibbs' trading operations with Balfour Williamson into the jointly owned Gibbs Williamson & Co. Ltd. These problems and the continued adherence to the partnership form made Gibbs reluctant to undertake fixed investments, leading to

[67] Hunt, *Heirs*, ii. 211–44.
[68] Shin'ichi Yonekawa, 'General Trading Companies in a Comparative Context', in S. Yonekawa (ed.), *General Trading Companies* (Tokyo: United Nations University Press, 1990), 15. *Zaibatsu* were family-owned business conglomerates which were influential elements of the Japanese business system before 1945. They were dissolved during the Allied occupation after the Second World War.
[69] Antony Gibbs & Son, *Merchants and Bankers 1808–1958* (London: the firm, 1958), ch. 9.
[70] Ibid. 71–5.

missed opportunities in the Chilean copper trade.[71] The diversifications which were made often did not turn out well. The Australian timber ventures contributed to the deteriorating profitability of the Australian partnership by the end of the 1920s.[72]

The Jardine Matheson 'group' narrowed its geographical horizons in the interwar years. Jardine Matheson continued to diversify in China, making a large investment in the 1920s in the export of dried eggs, and in the 1930s in brewing. It also established an engineering affiliate in the 1920s and in the following decade the firm developed an extensive business selling armaments in China.[73] However outside China Jardine Matheson reduced its activities rather than extended them. The firm's New York branch, established to sell China tea and silk, expanded greatly in the First World War, but then made heavy losses as it engaged in a variety of speculative business such as the sale of dogskins, designed to generate sufficient income to meet overheads.[74] In 1931 the branch was closed and thereafter Jardines' New York business was handled by Balfour Guthrie.

The major change compared with the pre-First World War period was that Matheson & Co. no longer functioned as a worldwide venture capitalist. Matheson's performed in London a variety of banking and merchanting services for Jardines and became closely involved with the dried egg business, but it did not scan the world for investment opportunities. The main exception was the use of Matheson & Co. to undertake a number of small investments in East Africa after 1936. The firm seems to have originally envisaged a small East African version of the British & Chinese Corporation, in alliance with the National Bank of India and the merchant bankers Samuel Montague, designed to exploit agricultural opportunities.[75] Over the next few years it invested in sisal estates in Tanganyika, though the original intention had been to use Jardine Matheson as the main corporate vehicle.[76] By 1945, when Matheson's sold their shareholding in the firm which was renamed Bovill, Matheson & Co., the venture was among the largest sisal producers in East Africa and had a large estate agency business including many different crops.[77]

[71] R. Greenhill and R. Miller, 'British Trading Companies in South America after 1914', in Geoffrey Jones (ed.), *The Multinational Traders* (London: Routledge, 1998), 114.

[72] Private Letter Books from London to Australian branches 1919–30, Antony Gibbs Archives, MS 11110/7–12, GHL.

[73] D. G. M. Bernard to D. Beith, 10 Aug. 1933, S/O Letters between London, Shanghai, and Hong Kong, July–Dec. 1933, JMA, CUL. J. S. Swire to Warren Swire, 23 Feb. 1935, Swire ADD 16, Swire Archives, SOAS.

[74] D. G. M. Bernard to J. J. Paterson, 6 May 1931, S/O London to Hong Kong, Jan.–June 1931, JMA, CUL.

[75] D. G. M. Bernard to J. J. Paterson, 1 July 1936, S/O London to Hong Kong 1936, JMA, CUL.

[76] John Keswick to D. G. M. Bernard, 19 Dec. 1938, S/O London to Hong Kong, 1939, JMA, CUL.

[77] Stahl, *Metropolitan Organisation*, 259–60.

Dodwells, another of the pre-1914 multi-regional groups, remained widely spread in the interwar years with branches in China, Japan, Ceylon, the United States, and Canada, but the firm followed Jardine Matheson in becoming much more focused on China. Shipping agencies, tea trading, and general trading remained at the core of its business. After the First World War Dodwells attempted to extend its operations further, opening new branches in Cuba and Buenos Aires, but by 1923 both had been closed after making losses.[78] Thereafter Dodwells was afflicted by losses from ill-advised speculations such as in cement for a Miami building firm in the 1920s, by irregularities in the trade in Chinese dogskins, and from losses in China. The general thrust of Dodwells' strategy was a greater focus on Asia apart from shipping offices. Dodwells had sold its canned salmon and flour milling business in Canada and the United States, and withdrew from general trading from its US branches in the early 1930s.[79] Conversely new business in the distribution of branded alcohol products and automobiles in Hong Kong were developed, though initially with few profits.

The two groups with substantial assets in Brazil, Ocean Coal & Wilsons and Alfred Booth, evolved in different ways in the interwar period. In the case of the former company, the response to the interwar recession in shipping was to deepen its involvement in its Latin American host economies by developing a general trading business in Brazil and the River Plate area.[80] During the 1920s Wilsons actively sought the selling agencies of as many British manufacturers as possible, though by the 1930s it ran into severe difficulties in importing British goods, especially into Brazil, through exchange restrictions, currency depreciation and tariffs, while it and other British firms were further hit by a trading agreement between Brazil and Germany in 1935. In 1939 Wilsons also began exporting Brazilian and Argentinian local produce.[81]

In contrast, Alfred Booth evolved further from merchanting to manufacturing and contracting. Its business in skin trading—one of the depressed agricultural raw materials of the interwar years—largely became concentrated on supplying the needs of its leather products factories in the United States and Britain, which were at the centre of its interwar business. The firm continued its shipping business but cargoes from Brazil fell in volume. The purchase of the firm of J. G. White & Co. in 1917, a British firm specializing in the management of public utilities in Latin America and contracting work, proved unsuccessful because of the problems of Latin American economies, and in 1929 it was resold to its founder. However an

---

[78] Warde, *House of Dodwell*, 116.
[79] Notes on Profit and Loss Accounts, Dodwell Archives, MS 27501, GHL.
[80] Chairman's statements on 1946 Annual Report of Ocean Coal & Wilson Ltd., MS 20196, GHL.
[81] Ibid. Board and General Minute Book 1920–40, MS 20186/6–8, Wilson, Sons Archives, GHL.

acquisition of a firm of building contractors in Britain in 1919 launched Booths into a booming business, and it became particularly active in building construction on behalf of local government.[82]

Harrisons & Crosfield, like Jardine Matheson, Dodwells, and Wilsons, deepened its involvement in its main host region rather than diversifying further, investing in logging in Sabah in the interwar years (Chapter 9). Its 'outpost' investments evolved in a more modest fashion. Its Canadian branches, first opened in 1904, initially imported tea which was sold to local wholesalers, and exported a range of Canadian products such as nails and newsprint. When the export business floundered in the post-First World War slump, the Canadian company responded by developing a more general import business, especially in industrial raw materials. By the late 1920s the Canadian affiliate began importing steel products from Europe. Protectionism and growing political uncertainties led to the decision to broaden the base of the business by diversification into chemical distribution. This was achieved by acquisition of small Canadian chemicals distribution companies in the mid-1930s. These investments were to lay the basis for the firm's post-war growth in chemicals.

James Finlay continued up to the 1930s to search for new opportunities outside its core host region of India. The firm tried unsuccessfully to expand in South Africa. Before 1914 Finlays had a shareholding in two firms active in South Africa, Webster, Steel in London and Steel, Murray in Natal. In 1914 the South African government involved Steel, Murray in a project to develop the sugar lands of Zululand and a new company, St Lucia Sugar Co., was formed. A sugar refinery was built. However the area was subject to flooding, and in 1915 the factory and much of the cultivated cane land was duly flooded. In 1923 the St Lucia company was wound up.[83] In 1931 Steel, Murray itself was wound up, and Finlays reverted to the use of independent agents in South Africa to sell its wool sacks from Calcutta and Scottish cotton goods. However the British-based Webster, Steel continued in business related to South Africa.[84] More successfully, in 1926 Finlays purchased land in Kenya and began to develop tea plantations. Its Anglo-American Direct Tea Trading Company also opened new distribution branches in the United States, and in 1927 opened an office in Taiwan to secure supplies of 'green' tea. These developments are reviewed in Chapter 9.

In the 1930s UAC and Unilever appeared to resemble a Japanese 'business combine' far more than Antony Gibbs or any other of the pre-1914 multi-regional groups. Unilever was among the largest European manufacturing multinationals. Its margarine and soap factories spanned Europe, the United States, Asia, Latin America, and Australia, but it also owned numerous other

---

[82] A. H. John, A *Liverpool Merchant House* (London: George Allen & Unwin, 1959), 107–51.

[83] Annual Reports of St Lucia Sugar Co. 1914–23, UGD 91/362.

[84] Brogan, *James Finlay*, 77–9; J. F. Muir to Mr Gatheral, 22 Sept. 1945, UGD 91/413/1.

activities from retail fish and grocery shops to whaling fleets. In Africa,
its HCB subsidiary (Huileries du Congo Belge) owned large concessions
for palm oil cultivation in the Belgian Congo, which Unilever began to
develop as plantations from the late 1930s.[85] UAC itself was a giant general
trading company primarily engaged in importing all types of goods into
West Africa and exporting local produce. In the 1940s it imported 300 main
classes of goods, with 4,000 types of articles and up to 50,000 particular
lines. While these goods were normally sold at the wholesale level, it also
owned retail stores. UAC were also major exporters of West African produce, principally palm oil, cocoa, and groundnuts. UAC also operated a
river transport system in Nigeria and had an ocean-going shipping fleet
which by 1939 owned fourteen cargo ships and two palm oil tankers. UAC
also inherited from the African & Eastern Trade Corporation and retained
a diverse collection of small trading firms in Morocco, the Mediterranean,
Turkey, the Middle East, and East Africa.[86]

In practice, UAC was not integrated into Unilever. From its formation
until the mid-1980s UAC operated as a virtually independent company with
minimum control by Unilever. This partly reflected developments in the 1920s
when, following the commodity price crash, Levers' original vertical integration strategy was abandoned. African produce bought by the Niger Company
was sold on the open market, while Lever Brothers' products imported into
West Africa by the Niger Company were bought at 'arms length' from Levers.
When Unilever was formed in 1929, its trading and manufacturing interests
in Africa were separated administratively and this remained the case until
1987. UAC retained its own, autonomous board, and in the early 1930s
an 'arms-length' arrangement was reached between UAC and Unilever.
Under the terms of this agreement, UAC had some priority as a supplier
of Unilever raw materials, but not a monopoly—Unilever was treated as a
most favoured customer of UAC, which had to offer oilseeds and palm oil to
Levers at prices no higher than to any other buyer. Unilever would not buy
or sell produce in West Africa except through UAC, nor buy West African
produce from any other supplier without giving UAC first option. There
were no special arrangements in merchandise business. UAC could sell
products from other manufacturers in competition with those of Unilever,
while Unilever was not restricted to selling its products through UAC.[87]

The lack of integration of UAC into Unilever was curious, but not
exceptional, and it fitted into a more general pattern in British business. There
are clear parallels with overseas banking. During the interwar years two
of Britain's five largest domestic banks invested in a number of overseas
banks. Barclays acquired three overseas banks active in the West Indies and

[85] Wilson, *History of Unilever*, 301–72; D. K. Fieldhouse, *Unilever Overseas* (London: Croom
Helm, 1978), 497–529.
[86] Fieldhouse, *Merchant Capital, passim*   [87] Ibid. 3–9.

West Africa, Egypt, and South Africa to create a multi-regional banking group, Barclays DCO, formed in 1925. This functioned as a wholly autonomous unit to its British parent. Lloyds Bank also took large stockholdings in the Bank of London & South America, as well as a bank with branches in India and Egypt, and also made small investments in other overseas banks. These interests were neither merged into a coherent group nor integrated with the British parent but left to function as autonomous overseas banks, the only exception being the Indian branches which were absorbed into an 'overseas' department of Lloyds.[88]

The interwar years, therefore, did not see a fundamental reorientation in the strategies of British mercantile groups, but many firms continued to seek profitable opportunities. Firms responded to the declining competitiveness of British staple exports in a number of ways. A number of British trading companies in India sought to sustain their piece-goods business by changing their distribution arrangements. By the late 1920s Ralli, Shaw Wallace, and the Bombay Company were among the firms conducting their piece-goods business through Marwari dealers to whom they extended long lines of credit, though other firms such as Binny's and Gillanders considered Indian traders too 'speculative' to do business with them.[89]

Another strategy for British merchants was to sell Japanese textile goods. Ralli established a 65 per cent owned Japanese firm—Showa Menka KK—to sell Indian cotton to Japan. When an Indo-Japanese Trade Agreement came into force regulating by quota the import of Japanese piece-goods into India in terms of exports of Indian cotton to Japan, Ralli built up a Japanese piece-goods business by purchasing a quota sufficient to balance the Indian cotton exports. In 1938 it imported £500,000 worth of Japanese piece-goods compared to Ralli's turnover of £1.25 million of Lancashire piece-goods.[90] Similarly, when Smith Mackenzie's cotton piece-goods business was threatened by the entry of Japanese goods into the East African market, from the late 1920s, the firm responded by acquiring the sole East African agency for two large Japanese manufacturers.[91]

There was also the option of shifting the types of British imports handled. There was a widespread assumption, even by contemporaries, that the changing structure of British exports was away from staples towards more complex goods requiring after sales servicing.[92] However the more dynamic British firms, at least, foresaw the possibilities of upgrading their imports rather than simply losing the market. Thus Swire's advised Holts in 1934,

---

[88] Geoffrey Jones, *British Multinational Banking 1830–1990* (Oxford: Clarendon Press, 1993), 138–57.

[89] Memo on Piecegoods and Yarns. Present general position in Madras, May 1927, MS 27163/2, GHL; Misra, 'Entrepreneurial Decline', 88.

[90] Report to the Chairman of Ralli Brothers Limited, 12 Apr. 1939, MS 23834, GHL.

[91] Stahl, *Metropolitan Organisation*, 212.

[92] Political and Economic Planning, *Report on International Trade*, May 1937, 132.

as far as she is able China intends to become a manufacturer, first for her own needs and ultimately for export. This development may take two or three decades during which—if Britain is to increase her trade to China—we must go all out in equipping Chinese industry and participating therein. When China becomes a successful industrial country we shall reap our future reward in her higher standard of life, and our increased sales to her of our quality goods.[93]

British trading companies began to handle more complex products than textiles in the interwar years. Although internalization theory might imply that manufacturers of branded or more technologically complex products would undertake their own distribution, and certainly that trend was observable in the interwar years,[94] a number of factors worked in favour of the continued use of merchant intermediaries in the countries where the British trading companies were active. The markets for such products in most developing economies were small, and such relatively low volume and frequency of trade provided no strong internalization incentive in many cases. Moreover the trading companies continued to possess information about market access in their host economies even if they lacked technical knowledge. Consequently, as economies developed and consumption patterns changed, the trading companies built on their experience of merchanting and distribution by handling different types of product.

Agency agreements with British (and other) manufacturers, provided one means for the trading companies to acquire technical knowledge about products, because frequently the home manufacturer provided specialist staff as part of the contract. By the 1930s Indian managing agencies such as Gillanders and Birds made a 'substantial' share of their profits from such agencies. Gillanders for example, had a selling agency agreement with Nobel's Explosives and later ICI. However there was a tendency for firms like ICI to demand greater technical expertise from its agents, while the possibility that the manufacturer would eventually choose to internalize its distribution hung over such arrangements.[95] Indeed, the more successful the trading companies were in developing markets, the greater were the risks that their services might be replaced.

British merchants developed extensive business in branded products such as alcohol, which sold to local elites and expatriates. In the early 1920s branded alcohol sales was one of the areas into which Wilson, Sons moved as it sought to reduce its dependence on coal sales. In 1922 it signed a five-year agreement with the Scottish firm John Walker & Son for the sale of their whisky in five Brazilian states, and in the Canary and Cape Verde

[93] Butterfield & Swire to R. D. Holt, 2 Feb. 1934, Swire Archives, JSSXI/I/8, SOAS.
[94] S. Nicholas, 'Agency Contracts, Institutional Modes, and the Transition to Foreign Direct Investment by British Manufacturing Multinationals before 1939', *Journal of Economic History*, 43 (1983), 675–86.
[95] Misra, 'Entrepreneurial Decline', 96–101.

islands.[96] Surprisingly in view of its Islamic host region, liquor sales became an important of Gray Mackenzie's business in the Gulf sheikhdoms, where British officials issued permits to avoid Muslims getting the products.[97] The importance of alcohol sales created a dilemma for Dodwells—which acquired the wines and spirits business of a British firm in Hong Kong in the mid-1920s—because of the consequences of alcohol consumption on its staff. 'Everybody drinks too much gin and whisky', Stanley Dodwell reported from China, 'but cut that out and what becomes of our one really profitable department? It's all a vicious circle.'[98]

British merchants also became involved in motor distribution. Market access was again important in this activity. Motor distribution required showrooms and on-site servicing staff, and it was rational for motor companies to use trading companies in markets where sales volumes were low. The British merchants distributed both British and US vehicles. Dodwells acquired the agency for Morris Motors in 1929, and following the acquisition of the Chrysler agency for their Dodge cars and trucks in 1937 this business grew rapidly, and a separate Hong Kong registered subsidiary, Dodwell Motors, was formed.[99] In South East Asia, the Borneo Company began importing and selling cars into Singapore and Malaya in the early 1920s, and a subsidiary—Borneo Motors Ltd.—was formed in 1924 as a Singapore private company and two years later a public company. This affiliate had a difficult start and paid no dividends between 1929 and 1933, but a sustained recovery began from the mid-1930s. By that time it was selling a range of both UK and US makes, especially Austin and General Motors. The motor distribution business of both the Borneo Company and Dodwells contributed to the financial recovery of these firms in the late 1930s. In West Africa, the African & Eastern Trade Corporation and its predecessors took the lead in motor distribution, representing first Ford and later General Motors. The Niger Company established a motor distribution business in 1926 representing Austin, and Morris and Brockway trucks of the USA.[100] UAC continued as major motor importers, concentrating on Vauxhall and Bedford (owned by General Motors) in West Africa and holding the Austin agency in East Africa.[101]

Not all companies found motor distribution a viable strategy. In Malaya and Singapore Guthries tried to develop the business after 1926, but failed to get a General Motors agency and developed a motley business for Renault and smaller British producers, Lea Francis and Daimler cars and

[96] Board and General Minute Book, 1920–7, Minutes 4 Mar. 1920 and 27 Nov. 1922, MS 20186/5, Wilson, Sons Archives, GHL.

[97] Undated History of Gray MacKenzie Co. Ltd., c.1970, Gray MacKenzie Archives, MS 27734A, GHL.

[98] Stanley Dodwell to George Dodwell, 16 May 1934, Dodwell Archives, MS 27512, GHL.

[99] Warde, *House of Dodwell*, 65.   [100] Pedler, *Lion*, 252–6.

[101] Fieldhouse, *Merchant Capital*, 399.

Rudge-Whitworth motorcycles. In 1929 Guthries motor department was closed.[102] In Latin America, the British trading companies were active as the importers of US cars and trucks, but in the larger markets such as Argentina and Brazil the US firms rapidly established their own distribution and assembly plants. Even the smaller markets were vulnerable. In the early 1920s Gibbs had a contract to distribute Ford vehicles in Chile. The value of Ford shipments reached $459,000 in 1923, but the termination of the contract led to a reduction in the value of shipments to $57,000 in the following year.[103] Balfour Williamson's vehicle distribution in Chile also led to heavy losses at the end of the First World War.[104] Graham Rowe's large business importing US cars into Chile and Peru, using hire purchase to boost sales, contributed to the firm's collapse in 1931.[105]

An alternative or supplementary strategy to importing different categories of goods was to become further embedded in their host economies by continuing to exploit their knowledge of markets and marketing channels. For example, firms responded to the growth of local industries by distributing their products. From the 1930s, Gibbs seized the opportunity provided by Chilean import substitution of gaining new agencies for the distribution of locally manufactured goods. Some were sales agencies for Chilean-owned firms, but others, especially those which originated as subsidiaries of British manufacturing concerns, involved also the purchase of equity and membership on the board. As part of this strategy, Gibbs acquired a stake in Graham Agencies, which was formed in the mid-1930s following the bankruptcy of Graham Rowe.[106]

However the possibilities for seizing new business opportunities in many host economies were rather limited in the interwar years. The falling prices of many commodities and the problem of excess capacity made large-scale new investments in commodity production unlikely. There were more potential opportunities in manufacturing, but British traders in Latin America and India were on the whole reluctant to make further investments. In South East Asia, there was some import substitution industrialization in the interwar years, especially in Singapore, but the British agency houses appear conspicuous by their lack of participation in interwar industrialization.[107] Guthries considered local manufacturing on several occasions, but did not act.[108] The

---

[102] Import Department (Singapore) to London, 21 Jan. 1929, G/COR/11; London to Singapore, 24 Mar. 1927, London to Singapore, 7 Apr. 1927, G/COR/18; Sir John Hay to Singapore, 8 Dec. 1927, G/MIS/9, Guthrie Archives, SOAS.

[103] Report to AG&S London, 1924, Antony Gibbs Archives, MS 11109, GHL.

[104] Lord Forres to Williamson Balfour & Co., 25 Oct. 1920, Sir Archibald Williamson's Private Letter Books No. 6, Box 11, Balfour Williamson Archives, UCL.

[105] Greenhill and Miller, 'British Trading Companies'; BOLSA Archives, B10/4, UCL.

[106] Valparaíso to London, 16 Feb. 1932, BOLSA Archives, B10/4, UCL.

[107] W. G. Huff, *The Economic Growth of Singapore* (Cambridge: Cambridge University Press, 1994).

[108] J. H. Drabble and P. J. Drake, 'The British Agency Houses in Malaysia: Survival in a Changing World', *Journal of Southeast Asian Studies*, 12 (1981), 311.

financial difficulties of the interwar years exercised a major constraint on further fixed investments, though, conversely, the sustained profitability of Harrisons & Crosfield—and at least some of the other agency houses—may have served as a disincentive for them to venture beyond their traditional areas of trade, shipping, and primary commodity production.

The large British companies in China made some manufacturing investments. While Jardine Matheson invested in engineering, the processing of dried eggs, and brewing—though closing down its loss-making sugar refining company in 1929—Swire's strategy was distinctly more evolutionary, with considerable synergies between different parts of the group. The sugar produced by Taikoo Sugar, for example, made up a large percentage of the China Navigation Company's northbound cargo from Hong Kong. In 1934 Swire's established a paint company in Shanghai, in a joint venture with a British paint manufacturer, which became China Navigation's principal supplier of paint.[109] The British merchants faced a very immediate threat to their established businesses from the Japanese, and this may have stimulated a more active search for new opportunities than elsewhere.

In Africa, British trading companies made few investments in manufacturing before the Second World War, although Lever Brothers were the pioneers of modern industrial manufacturing in West Africa. Levers' acquisition of W. MacIver in 1910 brought with it sawmills on which Levers set up kernel-crushing mills. It became apparent that crushing palm kernels near to where they were grown rather than in Europe was uneconomic, but this led to the construction of a soap factory on the same premises in Apapa, Nigeria. The West African Soap Company (WASCO) was managed by the Niger Company, which also established a tannery in Nigeria. Neither venture was successful in the 1920s, and in 1929 WASCO was detached from the newly formed UAC and placed under the direct control of Unilever. In the 1930s UAC owned a small number of minor industrial ventures, including a soap factory in the Belgian Congo, a sawmill and a bacon and ham factory in Lagos, and in 1938 it established a shirt manufacturing plant in Nigeria, followed by a similar venture in Ghana in the following year.[110] John Holt & Co. also had a minimal presence in West African manufacturing before 1940. In the 1920s the firm was in negotiation with the colonial government about a scheme to establish palm oil factories, but Holts decided against involvement in 1928.[111] In the 1930s Holts helped the Liverpool soap manufacturer Bibbys to penetrate the Nigerian market in competition to WASCO.[112]

---

[109] Swire Group, *180 Years* (Hong Kong: the firm, 1996).
[110] Fieldhouse, *Merchant Capital*, 300.
[111] Ibadan to H. J. Rawlings, 19 Dec. 1924, Liverpool to Supervising Agent, Lagos, 2 Jan. 1928, Holt Papers, File 216, MSS Afr. s825, Rhodes House, Oxford.
[112] Fieldhouse, *Unilever Overseas*, 348.

The reluctance of British merchants to 'reinvent' themselves as manufacturers can be explained in several ways and is discussed further in Chapter 10.
A lack of technical skills was a constraint, and this was exaggerated by
conservative risk assessment. Perhaps most significantly of all, the weak
financial performance of many firms and the instability of earnings in the
interwar period resulted in an emphasis on increasing liquidity rather than
making large new fixed investments. This was especially so as the former
strategy of placing new ventures in 'free-standing' companies was made
much more difficult by the decline in British capital exports and exchange
control restrictions.

The trading companies which were exporters of commodities responded
in a number of ways to the decline and instability of primary prices. In some
cases they withdrew from commodities whose business prospects were poor.
In Latin America, Gibbs withdrew from nitrates during the 1920s when it
became evident that the artificial substitutes developed during the First World
War would continue to undersell Chilean production. Similarly the Latin
American houses retreated from cocoa and to some extent from sugar.[113]
Elsewhere some companies withdrew from the export of local 'produce' to
focus on imports or other activities. This was the case of Smith Mackenzie
in East Africa, which had formerly had a large business in cotton, sisal,
and coffee. However its Sassoon-owned competitor, the African Mercantile
Company, stayed in the business, buying 'native' produce such as groundnuts,
coffee, and hides and skins, and exporting it.[114] Some companies invested
in commodities with better growth prospects. In South East Asia, Guthries
was among the pioneers of the commercial planting of palm oil in the 1920s.
Brazilian Warrant developed backward linkages into coffee plantations and
estate management—by the middle of the 1920s it controlled three major
coffee estates in Brazil—while investing in marketing and brand naming
Brazilian coffee in Britain.[115]

Given their large involvement in the trading and production of commodities, it is not surprising that British merchants were active participants
in interwar commodity cartels. These arrangements were supported and often
enforced by British and other colonial governments. In West Africa, UAC
and Holts were at the heart of the web of buying pools for products which
dominated the region's trade. UAC held a special position in most West
African products. It bought 69 per cent of all Nigerian palm oil in 1930, was
the sole owner of bulk palm oil installations on the coast, and had Unilever
as a guaranteed market for part of its products. In cocoa, UAC and its affiliates
bought 45 per cent of Gold Coast cocoa in 1937, although in that product
it competed with UK chocolate manufacturers led by Cadbury's. Initially

---

[113] Greenhill and Miller, 'British Trading Companies', 210.
[114] Stahl, *Metropolitan Organisation*, 212–14.   [115] Greenhill, 'Investment Group'.

opposed to such pools, in 1937 Cadbury's joined UAC in a cocoa pool in the wake of a dramatic fall in cocoa prices.[116]

In virtually every commodity they traded in British firms sought collaborative arrangements with other firms. Ralli Brothers, one of the largest commodity traders in India in the 1930s, had a range of collusive agreements with other firms. In groundnuts Ralli's largest competitor was Louis Dreyfus, the French commodity dealer, with whom by 1939 'satisfactory arrangements have been made on a basis of mutual advantage in the buying markets'.[117] During the 1930s Jardine Matheson was engaged in constant negotiations between Chinese frozen, dry, and shell egg exporters to stabilize prices and establish quotas.[118] In the coal business, Wilsons negotiated an extensive range of collusive agreements with other British coal merchandising firms in the interwar years, designed to share markets and to reduce overhead costs, particularly for coal handling facilities. In 1930 Wilsons and other British firms pooled their coal, shipping, and other agency business in Las Palmas, enabling a significant reduction in the numbers employed on the island.[119]

In terms of geographical expansion, imperial frontiers were no longer expanding by the interwar years, nor were most companies able let alone willing to venture far into virgin territories, especially after the post-First World War recession. East Africa was a partial exception. UAC inherited from African & Eastern a small trading firm in Kenya, and in 1937 it purchased another expatriate British merchant firm in Kenya, specializing in the import and supply of farm equipment on the basis of an agency agreement with the US tractor firm Caterpillar.[120] During the interwar years Finlays, Jardine Matheson, and David Sassoon were among the 'Asian' trading companies which made investments in the region. Dalgety made a rare investment outside Australasia in the 1920s when it acquired a Kenyan firm, and by the 1930s had developed a loss-making business handling and financing the growing of coffee and sisal.[121]

Another entrant to East African trading was Mitchell Cotts and Co. This firm began as a shipping and coaling business in South Africa, which became a British registered private company—the City of London and Colonial Trust Ltd.—in 1919 and a public company in 1936. The firm's main business was as coaling contracting and shipping agents in East, South, and North Africa. The firm opened in East Africa in the mid-1920s, and as

[116] Fieldhouse, *Merchant Capital*, 146–75.

[117] Report to the Chairman of Ralli Brothers Limited, 12 Apr. 1939, MS 23834, GHL.

[118] D. G. M. Bernard to J. J. Paterson, 1 Jan. 1931, P&C Letters London, Hong Kong, and Shanghai 1935–7; D. G. M. Bernard to W. J. Keswick, 12 Mar. 1937, S/O London to Shanghai, JMA, CUL.

[119] Board and General Minute Book, 1920–40, MS 20186/6–8, Wilson, Sons Archives, GHL.

[120] Fieldhouse, *Merchant Capital*, 22.

[121] Stahl, *Metropolitan Organisation*, 228–9; Simon Ville, *The Rural Entrepreneurs* (Cambridge: Cambridge University Press, 2000), 46.

well as coaling and shipping agency work became extensively involved in
imports and exports, largely on a commission basis as bulk distributors. In
addition the firm established a sisal estate in East Africa. In effect, Mitchell
Cotts by the end of the 1930s had become a 'hybrid' trading company.[122]
The same can be said about Gellatly's, a shipping and shipping agency firm,
which developed a large trading business in the Sudan in the 1920s, as well
as in Saudi Arabia, where the firm transported pilgrims and later provided
banking facilities.[123]

Underlying the corporate strategies of this era were sometimes striking
differences in risk assessments. In India, the British managing agencies Birds
and Gillanders are cast by Misra as rigidly conservative. They were hostile
to import substitution industries and slow to consider the possibilities of
collaborating with Indian business groups, such as the Marwaris.[124] In contrast, the British firms on the China coast, operating by the 1930s in a war
zone, and threatened by both Chinese nationalism and Japanese competition, were more flexible in their outlook. During the 1930s Swire's sought
an accommodation between its shipping interests and the Chinese, and was
ready 'to move with the times as we have done many times before, and
hail down the British flag and hoist the Chinese flag'.[125] In 1940, when Jardines
was considering selling its brewing venture in China to the Japanese, the
Shanghai *taipan* or chief manager reflected on the firm's philosophy. 'We may
temporarily lose face in selling; it may be interpreted as a Jardine failure.
. . . It is always preferable to lose face rather than money'.[126]

In summary, it is evident that the British trading companies continued
to evolve after 1914. In the face of the declining competitiveness of British
manufactured exports and declining prices for commodity exports, they
undertook new activities, disposed of others, and invested in new countries.
However, the entrepreneurial dynamism which had characterized many
companies before 1914 looked decidedly weaker subsequently, and especially
after the post-First World War depression. The evolution of multi-regional
business groups lost momentum in most cases. The new products that
the firms developed—frozen eggs, Borneo timber, East African sisal—were
not the great revenue earners of earlier generations, such as opium and
nitrates. Given the nature of the international economy, the most profitable opportunities were probably in import substitution manufacturing, in
which few firms made substantial investments.

---

[122] Stahl, *Metropolitan Organisation*, 214–17. The name became Mitchell Cotts in 1932.
[123] George Blake, *Gellatly's 1862–1962* (London: Blackies & Son, 1962).
[124] Misra, 'Entrepreneurial Decline', 66.
[125] Minute of meeting with J. V. Soong, 9 May 1935, JSSI 3/6, SOAS.
[126] W. J. Keswick to D. Beith, 2 Apr. 1940, S/O Shanghai to London 1940, JMA, CUL.
Taipan, which means 'great-manager' or 'the main plank in the root' in Chinese, was the name
used to describe the heads of merchant houses ('*hongs*') on the China coast. In modern terminology he was the chief executive officer.

4.5 British Trading Companies *c.*1945

In some respects the most noteworthy feature of the list of British trading companies in 1945 was that it so closely resembled that of 1914. The merchant firms had survived recessions, the collapse of primary prices, and import substitution with only a limited number of fatalities. They had flourished during the First World War, though less so during the Second, when the British firms in East and South East Asia had their assets first taken by the Japanese and later badly damaged or destroyed by warfare. By 1945 Swire's and Jardine Matheson in particular had had their considerable fixed assets in China and Hong Kong, including large parts of their shipping fleets, destroyed.

The British trading companies had remained impressive forms of international business in the interwar years. On the China coast, in South East Asia, in West Africa, and in Chile and Peru, they were giants of modern business enterprise. British merchant enterprise expanded in East Africa, which saw 'new' trading companies such as Mitchell Cotts expand. The pace of diversification slowed in the interwar years, though it did not stop. Firms with investments in commodities diversified into distribution and branding. The selling of imported textiles was supplemented and often replaced by the distribution of more complex types of product. There were modest new investments in manufacturing in some regions. In retrospect, a loss of entrepreneurial vigour might be discerned, both in seeking new opportunities and in the declining momentum to build 'global' trading groups, but given the scale of the external shocks, it is perhaps the survival of the trading companies that is the more noteworthy.

The survival of the British merchant groups in this period indicated that their organizational structures and management systems—which changed little from those prevailing before 1914—were robust. However there were also other elements in their survival. Family and other shareholders sustained companies paying low or no dividends, while Unilever's shareholders underwrote British trading interests in West Africa. Many of the firms had all or most of their business within the sheltered confines of the British Empire. They sometimes still benefited from fiscal and other privileges from colonial governments, while collusive cartels were permitted and usually supported.

5

Concentration and Diversification

5.1 Introduction

The post-war world economy offered a much improved environment for multinational trading companies as tariff barriers fell and world trade boomed. However it was not an environment which was especially favourable to the British-based firms. The fast trade and economic growth was largely concentrated in developed economies, while their business was heavily concentrated in the developing world. In these regions economic performance was weaker, and economic nationalism grew. Decolonization resulted in growing political risks. Finally, their home economy missed the 'economic miracle' seen elsewhere in western Europe in the 1950s and 1960s, and its relative importance in the world economy was much reduced.

This chapter examines the considerable changes in organization and strategy in the three post-war decades. The partnership form gave way to incorporation. From the late 1950s a process of concentration reduced the number of British multinational trading companies, some of which were also taken over by other British firms or by interests in their host regions. There were major changes in strategies also. There was a strong shift towards trading in more specialized products, such as automobiles, and more involvement in manufacturing and a number of services.

5.2 Economic Miracles and Decolonization

Despite the massive devastation caused by the Second World War, there was no repeat of the post-war depression and instability seen after the First World War. By the late 1940s the western European economies, assisted by the United States which had emerged from the war in a uniquely powerful position in the world economy, had begun to recover and growth had resumed. During the following two decades the western European economies grew rapidly, often in excess of 6 per cent per annum, and from the late 1950s Japan underwent even faster rates of economic growth. These high per capita growth rates were sustained until the oil price rises of 1973 pushed the industrial world into a major recession. A second oil price rise in 1979–80 largely accounted for another major recession in the early 1980s.

In striking contrast to the interwar years, world trade boomed. In part this reflected falling trade barriers. Under the auspices of the General Agreement on Tariffs and Trade signed in 1947, tariffs were reduced, mostly for manufactured goods, while the formation of the European Economic Community sharply reduced trade barriers between its six original members. This trade growth was heavily concentrated between developed market economies, including Japan.

In the developing world trade growth was less significant. The Communist countries, including China after 1949, had little participation in the international economy. Many developing countries sought to reduce their exposure to international trade by import substitution policies. The exception was a handful of East and South East Asian economies—Hong Kong, Singapore, South Korea, and Taiwan—which began to expand their exports from the 1960s, and were subsequently to become the NICs. The terms of trade shifted against primary producers, and the trade of many developing countries in commodities such as crude rubber, nitrates, jutes, and hides and skins went into decline as the result of the development of synthetic products. The emergence of synthetic products, together with anti-trust pressures and the end of colonialism, undermined most of the interwar commodity cartels, though governments did intervene extensively in the marketing of many products, with the widespread adoption of state control of produce marketing.

From the 1950s there was a recovery in the growth of world FDI. Between 1945 and the mid-1960s the United States accounted for 85 per cent of all new FDI flows. World FDI was radically redistributed from the developing world to developed countries. By 1980 almost two-thirds of world FDI was located in Western Europe, the United States, and Canada. This reflected the new emphasis in multinational investment in market-oriented activities, especially manufacturing, largely located in developed countries. Conversely there was a sharp relative decline in FDI in natural resources, especially during the 1970s as many developing country governments nationalized foreign firms in these industries. Though FDI boomed, even in 1980 its relative importance in the world economy remained lower than in 1914. This reflected the exclusion of multinationals from the Communist world and their relative insignificance in major developing countries such as India by that date.[1]

The end of European imperialism radically changed the political economy of the world. In 1947 India, Pakistan, Ceylon, and Burma became independent of Britain. Ten years later Malaya and the Gold Coast (Ghana) became independent. Nigeria and Kenya followed in 1960 and 1963, and most of the West Indies in the early 1960s. In Africa, only southern Rhodesia (Zimbabwe) remained a formal British colony until 1975—though ruled by its rebellious white colonists—while Hong Kong lingered as a colony until 1997. In the post-colonial period, governments were anxious to establish their national identities, and this often involved seeking to limit foreign investment in

[1] Geoffrey Jones, *The Evolution of International Business* (London: Routledge, 1996), 46–52.

their economies, especially over sensitive resources and utilities. Generally developing governments in this era intervened extensively in their economies through planning, import controls, and exchange controls.

Britain's relative importance in the world economy shrank in this period. The country did not experience fast trade growth in the 1950s and 1960s. Its trade performance was poor with the result that, while in 1950 it still accounted for 25 per cent of world exports of manufactured goods, by 1970 the figure had reached 8 per cent. The nature of British trade changed also. Its exports shifted further from low-technology products such as textiles to chemicals and electrical goods, and in turn this affected the geographical direction of British trade. By 1971 45 per cent of Britain's exports went to elsewhere in Europe. Britain's declining competitiveness also undermined the use of its currency as a reserve currency. Sterling was devalued against the US dollar in 1949 and again in 1967. However, during the 1950s around one-half of all world trade remained denominated in sterling. The second devaluation ended sterling's role as the second reserve currency after the dollar, and by 1970 only 20 per cent of world trade was denominated in sterling.

However Britain remained strongly integrated into the international economy. At the end of the 1950s the role of London as an international financial centre was renewed following the advent of the Euro-currency market and its location in London. Britain also remained the world's second largest direct investor after the United States. Its stock of outward FDI was relatively much more important compared to its GDP compared to other large European economies and the United States. British international business also shifted its geographical focus. From the 1960s British multinationals also progressively relocated from the developing world and the Commonwealth to elsewhere in Europe and, especially, the United States. By 1981 the United States alone accounted for over a quarter of British outward FDI.[2]

5.3 Structures and Performance

In the post-war decades the British business system was transformed. Merger waves, peaking in the 1960s, transformed an economy of small atomistic firms into Europe's most concentrated 'big business' economy. In the process family influence or personal capitalism was largely swept away also.[3] The radical changes in the corporate structures of British trading companies broadly followed this trend. There was a general move to public companies and

---

[2] Geoffrey Jones, 'British Multinationals and British Business since 1850', in M. W. Kirby and M. B. Rose (eds.), *Business Enterprise in Modern Britain* (London: Routledge, 1994), 190–201.
[3] Geoffrey Jones, 'Great Britain: Big Business, Management, and Competitiveness in Twentieth Century Britain', in A. D. Chandler, Jnr, Franco Amatori, and Takashi Hikino (eds.), *Big Business and the Wealth of Nations* (Cambridge: Cambridge University Press, 1997), 112–22.

TABLE 5.1 Net capital employed of selected British
trading companies, 1954 (£000s)

UAC	39,403
Ralli Brothers	9,377
Booker Brothers, McConnell	8,614
Harrisons & Crosfield	6,541
James Finlay	6,050
Jardine Matheson	5,993[a]
John Holt & Co. (Liverpool)	5,512
Borneo Co.	4,140
Duncan Fox	2,314
Wilson, Sons	2,256
Guthries	2,200[b]
Anglo-Thai	2,158
Balfour Williamson	1,705
John Swire & Sons	1,698
Dodwell & Co.	1,053
Gray Mackenzie	600

[a] 1957 figure. HK$94,937 million converted to sterling.
[b] 19 million Straits dollars converted to sterling.

Source: Appendix 3.

a greater willingness to access the capital markets for funds, even by firms whose ultimate parent company remained family controlled.

The changing corporate structure of British trading companies can be seen in Tables 5.1 and 5.2, which rank companies for which such data is known by size of capital employed.

In 1954 the names and rankings of firms had strong similarities to those in 1938. UAC continued to tower over other firms in terms of capital employed, though its status as a wholly owned subsidiary of Unilever needs to be borne in mind. After the Companies Act of 1948 compelled privately owned companies, such as UAC, to disclose financial information, there were a number of asset transfers between UAC and its parent, especially designed to reduce the apparent profitability of UAC in West Africa. There were major transfers of assets in both 1948 and 1961.[4] The other large firms included in the top five of known companies were Ralli Brothers, which had converted from a private to a public company in 1941, Harrisons & Crosfield, James Finlay, and Booker McConnell, which had increased its relative size considerably between 1938 and 1954. The Latin American-based companies had become relatively less important, though Duncan Fox had surpassed Wilson Sons and Balfour Williamson in terms of size.

[4] D. K. Fieldhouse, *Merchant Capital and Economic Decolonization* (Oxford: Clarendon Press, 1994), 63–5.

TABLE 5.2 Net capital employed of selected
British trading companies, 1978 (£000s)

Lonrho	497,080
UAC	450,000
Jardine Matheson	292,755[a]
Swire 'group'	265,763[b]
Inchcape	252,606
Guthrie Corporation	224,118
Harrisons & Crosfield	171,109
Booker McConnell	93,018
James Finlay	71,972
Steel Brothers Holdings	46,948
Yule Catto	15,532
Antony Gibbs	14,664
Blyth, Greene, Jourdain	11,934[c]
Boustead	11,059
Ocean Wilsons	10,992

[a] HK$2,869 million converted to sterling.
[b] The capital employed of John Swire & Sons
in 1978 was £145,329 million. Its large quoted affiliate
Swire Pacific which had a capital employed of £174,542
million was not consolidated. John Swire owned 31 per
cent of the equity, and the 31 per cent of net capital
employed—£54,108 million—was in John Swire's
balance sheet. The residual has been added here to get a
'group' picture.
[c] 1979.

Source: Appendix 3.

By 1978 the corporate landscape looked very different. The five largest
firms included two which had not been in existence in 1954: Inchcape, a
consolidation of the Inchcape family interests dating from 1958, and
Lonrho, which had grown rapidly after 1961 from its origins as a mining
company in Rhodesia (Zimbabwe). The African-centred Lonrho and UAC
were the largest trading companies. They were followed by a cluster of firms
whose main business lay in East and South East Asia: Jardine Matheson,
Swire's, Inchcape, Guthries, and Harrisons & Crosfield. Among the many
missing names were most of the great British merchant groups once active
in South America, though Antony Gibbs and Ocean Wilsons still lingered
at the bottom of the ranking.

Table 5.3 identifies three different fates of the British trading companies which either disappeared altogether or else passed out of British
ownership between the 1950s and the 1970s. First, there was a process of
consolidation which saw many trading companies merged into larger

TABLE 5.3 The fate of British trading companies, c.1950–c.1980

(a) Acquired by other UK trading companies

Acquirer	Firm acquired (and date)
Inchcape	Binny (1958), Gray Mackenzie (1960), AUSN (1960) Smith, Mackenzie (1964), Borneo Company (1967), Gibb Livingston (1967), Gilman (1969), Dodwell (1973), Anglo-Thai (1975), part of Balfour Williamson (1981)
Lonrho	John Holt (1969), part of Balfour Williamson (1975)
Borneo Company	Gibb Livingston (1964)
Anglo Thai	Caldbeck Macgregor (1967)
Ralli	Naumann Gapp (1970), Maclaine Watson (1970), Duncan Fox (1971)
John Swire & Sons	James Finlay (29%, 1976), Blyth, Greene, Jourdain (30% 1976, 1979)

(b) Acquired by other UK firms

Acquirer	Firm acquired (and date)	Ultimate fate
Bank of London & South America	Balfour Williamson (1960)	Sold to Dalgety (1966), Lonrho (1975), Inchcape (1981)
Hongkong Bank	Antony Gibbs (1972)[a]	Non-financial assets sold
Standard Chartered	Wallace Brothers (1977)	Non-financial assets sold
British & Commonwealth	Steel Brothers (40%, 1969)	Trading interests sold 1980s
Bowater[b]	Ralli (1972)	Sold to Cargill (1981)

[a] Full ownership 1980.
[b] Renamed Rexan 1995.

(c) Acquired by host country interests

Decade	Firm acquired (and date)
1950s	Brazilian Warrant (1951), Octavius Steel (1958) Turner Morrison (c.1959)
1960s	Duncan Brothers (1960), Birds (1965), Gillanders Arbuthnot (1969), Andrew Yule (1969)
1970s	Jardine Henderson (1971), Shaw Wallace (1976) Sime Darby (1976), Guthries (1981)

trading firms. A number of acquirers were themselves subsequently acquired. The growth of Inchcape was the most striking example. In 1948, when the third earl became the 'Senior', the family interests continued to consist of a considerable number of partnerships, with their assets heavily concentrated in India. The growth of taxation in India and increased death duties in Britain prompted a reorganization of Inchcape interests. In 1949 a 48 per cent holding in Macneill and Barry, which acted as managing agents for jute mills, tea estates, and Indian river steamers, was sold to the Tata business group in India, providing the resources to fund subsequent reorganization. The Mackinnon Mackenzie companies were sold to the P&O group, reducing Inchcape's involvement in shipping agency business. Meanwhile, shareholdings in firms such as Binny's which were intended to be retained were increased. Finally in 1958 Inchcape & Co. was floated on the London Stock Exchange as a holding company with seventeen subsidiaries, their assets mainly based in Britain and India, and active in merchandising, marine services, insurance, and tea estates. Initially only 25 per cent of the equity was held by the general public, and the family influence remained strong.

After the formation of Inchcape, the company began acquiring full ownership of partly owned affiliates such as Gray Mackenzie and Smith Mackenzie, while expanding by acquisition, especially in the British Commonwealth and the Middle East. In 1967 the Borneo Company was acquired, which gave Inchcape a large business in South East Asia and representation in Hong Kong, where the Borneo Company had acquired Gibb Livingston three years previously. It also brought into the group its first major involvement in motor distribution.

During the late 1960s and 1970s Inchcape progressively divested from India while acquiring firms active elsewhere in Asia and other regions. In 1969 Inchcape acquired Gilmans, which had a substantial trading, shipping, and insurance business in Hong Kong. In 1973 Dodwells—which remained controlled by a small group of the Dodwell family and company employees —was acquired, followed in 1975 by the Anglo-Thai Corporation, which had itself acquired the Hong Kong-based wines and spirits trader Caldbeck, Macgregor & Co. in 1967, as well as motor distributors in Britain. Beyond the Asia/Pacific region, in the late 1960s Inchcape failed to buy John Holt & Co. (Liverpool), but did acquire a smaller trading company in Nigeria and a British-based distributor of cars in Britain and Nigeria. In 1981 Inchcape expanded into Latin America with the purchase of nineteen companies belonging to the former Balfour Williamson group in Chile, Peru, Ecuador, and Columbia.

The Inchcape group was effectively 'reinvented'. In 1958 38 per cent of Inchcape's net assets were in India and Pakistan, 12 per cent each in the Middle East and East Africa, and most of the remainder were allocated to Britain. By 1976 only 2 per cent of the firm's assets were in India, with 6 and 4 per cent in East Africa and the Middle East respectively. In contrast, 34 per cent were in South East Asia, 23 per cent in Hong Kong, and 7 per cent were in Australia. A business based on shipping agencies, trading, tea plantations, and Indian textile manufacture had become a highly diversified multinational trading company with a large international automobile distribution business.[5] The firm was in effect a British style *sogo shosha*.

A number of other British trading companies were acquired by Lonrho. Lonrho was incorporated in Britain in 1909 as the London & Rhodesian Mining & Land Co. Ltd., but until 1961 its activities were confined to mining, ranching, and real estate in the (then) British colony of Rhodesia. In the late 1950s the firm lost the contract to manage two mines, which had formed an important part of its business, and in 1961 Roland W. ('Tiny') Rowland joined the board, becoming joint managing director and acquiring 27 per cent of the issued share capital. Thereafter Lonrho began a period of rapid growth and diversification in Central, East, and South Africa through acquisition. In West Africa, Lonrho acquired John Holt and 80 per cent of Ashanti Goldfields Corporation, the owner of rich gold mines in Ghana, in 1969. In the mid-1970s part of the assets of Balfour Williamson were acquired, and the firm also made manufacturing and other investments in Britain.

By 1980 Lonrho was a large regional trading company active primarily in Africa and the United Kingdom. Its large size reflected in part its rapid growth through acquisition, and in part its considerable portfolio of capital-intensive mining operations, which generated nearly 37 per cent of profits in that year, even though comprising less than 5 per cent of Lonrho's turnover. Lonrho was a public company, but in the mid-1970s Rowland held around 17 per cent of the issued share capital which, because of an absence of large institutional investors and thousands of small private shareholders, enabled him to exercise virtual personal control over the firm.[6]

Among the other trading companies which acquired other firms were the very different cases of Ralli and John Swire. The former in the 1950s still had a board composed of Rallis and other ethnic Greeks. It was a large commodity trader with the majority of its business connected with South Asia, though it had a number of other businesses, including a sisal plantation in East Africa and a small banking business.[7] In 1959 Ralli was acquired by a company controlled by Sir Isaac Wolfson, who had diversified interests including a large retail business in the UK, and subsequently the firm expanded rapidly. Its capital employed was almost £20 million at the end of the 1960s, making it around two-thirds of the size of UAC and Inchcape.

---

[5] Stephanie Jones, *Two Centuries of Overseas Trading* (London: Macmillan, 1986), 241–84; Sir Percival Griffiths, *The History of the Inchcape Group* (London: the firm, 1977).
[6] S. Cronjé, M. Ling, and G. Cronjé, *Lonrho. Portrait of a Multinational* (London: Penguin, 1976); *Lonrho Ltd : Investigation under the Companies Act 1948, Report by DTI Inspectors* (London: HMSO, 1976); Lonrho Annual Reports.
[7] *Ralli Brothers Ltd.* (London: the firm, n.d.).

In 1969 Ralli's future was transformed when Wolfson sold his shareholding to Slater Walker, a rapidly growing group noted for financial manœuvring. Ralli's bank, which was licensed, was renamed Slater Walker Ltd. and used as the group's entry into banking, later making large losses in the early 1970s. Ralli's trading business was merged with a leading manufacturer of hand-made carpets—Oriental Carpet Manufacturers—whose shares Slater Walker had purchased, and the resulting creation—Ralli International—was floated as a public company in 1969. There was no strategic logic to a merger of a commodity trader with a carpet manufacturer, but Slater Walker was primarily concerned with profits from share transactions. Ralli followed the Slater Walker pattern of acquisitions, buying Naumann Gapp—coffee merchants in the UK, Kenya, and Brazil—and Maclaine Watson—rubber and metal merchants in the UK and Singapore—in 1970, and Duncan Fox in 1971. Duncan Fox had become a public company in 1955, but Fox family members still sat on the board through the 1960s, and the firm continued to have substantial trading and other interests in Chile and Peru.

Two other old-established British trading companies came under the control of John Swire & Sons in the 1970s. In 1976 Swire's took a 30 per cent shareholding in Blyth, Greene, Jourdain, a Mauritius-centred firm whose business included the Malaysian company Sharikat Harper Gilfillan. In 1979 full ownership was acquired. In 1976 Swire's also acquired 29 per cent of the stock of James Finlay. Through to the early 1950s Finlays remained substantially owned by the Muir family, but the deaths of several Muirs around that time led to the shares becoming more widely dispersed. By the early 1970s Slater Walker had acquired almost 23 per cent of James Finlay's equity, but the subsequent collapse of that firm led first to speculation that Lonrho would buy Finlays, and then to the intervention by Swire's, who were seeking a 'hedge' against political risk in Hong Kong and who sought at that time to be represented in India.[8]

A second group of British trading companies were acquired by non-trading company firms, in most cases leading over time to the liquidation or sale of their businesses. Balfour Williamson had, during the interwar years, withdrawn from many of its fixed investments to concentrate on trading, and this policy was maintained after the war. However there were some new developments, including a joint venture with Jardine Matheson to market tea in the United States, and the acquisition by 1950 of a controlling interest in a Bradford firm of wool merchants and manufacturers.[9] During the 1950s Balfour Williamson also opened new subsidiaries in Australia, New Zealand, and Africa, but in 1960 the Bank of London and South America (BOLSA) acquired Balfour Williamson.

[8] Interview with Sir Colin Campbell, 16 Apr. 1996; Interview with Sir John and Sir Adrian Swire, 30 July 1996.
[9] Wallis Hunt, *Heirs of Great Adventure*, vol. ii (London: the firm, 1960), 236–41.

During the 1940s and 1950s BOLSA had declined alongside other British business interests in Latin America, but the bank was revitalized at the end of the decade becoming a pioneer of the new Eurodollar markets. BOLSA's strategy of diversification out of Latin American retail banking into wider financial and commercial activities made Balfour Williamson attractive.[10] Balfour Williamson retained an independent identity within the bank, but its new owner did not provide a basis for growth. In 1966 the Balfour Guthrie business in Canada and the United States was sold to Dalgety. The firm's trading and industrial assets in Chile and Peru were run down, and in 1973 BOLSA itself was merged into Lloyds Bank International, wholly owned by the British domestic bank.[11] In 1975 a large part of Balfour Williamson was sold to Lonrho.[12] The sale excluded the trading companies in Chile and Peru, including Milne & Co., which were sold to Inchcape six years later.

In 1948 Antony Gibbs had finally abandoned the partnership form to become a private limited company, but it remained wholly owned by the Gibbs family and continued as a diversified merchant and banking operation. Although it divested from Chilean flour milling, Gibbs retained an extensive merchanting and agency business in Chile, where it had substantial stockholdings in manufacturing companies, and it also had small businesses in Bolivia and Peru. During the 1960s the Australian business of Gibbs Bright with its extensive timber interests grew in importance, and Gibbs also retained a New York office. The firm also opened insurance companies in southern Africa in the 1950s.[13]

The Gibbs family finally sold their stockholding in 1972 and the firm went public. The Hongkong Bank, anxious to acquire a merchant banking presence in London without any 'Jewish' connection—due to its extensive retail banking interests in the Middle East—acquired 20 per cent of Gibbs. Gibbs offered an avenue for the bank into Latin America and Australia, and into insurance and commodity dealing and broking, but Gibbs performed poorly through the 1970s, and finally in 1980 the whole capital was acquired.[14] The Gibbs name was dropped and its residual mercantile business sold.

Wallace Brothers was the third large trading group to be acquired by a bank. Like Gibbs, the Wallace family retained control of this private company until the 1970s. Wallace lost its once extensive teak business in Burma and Thailand in the decade after 1945, and during the 1960s its Indian trading and plantations business was also liquidated. However there were new investments in timber in the British colony of North Borneo (Sabah)

---

[10] H. A. Holley, 'Bolsa under Sir George Bolton', in Richard Fry (ed.), *A Banker's World* (London: Hutchinson, 1970), 214–16; Geoffrey Jones, *British Multinational Banking 1830–1990* (Oxford: Clarendon Press, 1993), 264–6.

[11] Jones, *British Multinational Banking*, 266–8.   [12] Cronjé *et al.*, *Lonhro*, 103.

[13] Antony Gibbs & Sons, *Merchants and Bankers 1808–1958* (London. the firm, 1958), 68, 75–7.

[14] F. H. H. King, *The History of the Hongkong and Shanghai Banking Corporation*, vol. iv (Cambridge: Cambridge University Press, 1991), 714–16, 869–70; Jones, *British Multinational Banking*, 343.

and even East Africa in the 1950s, and in the following decade there was a rapid expansion in its British banking business. This got into difficulties, and in 1976 the Bank of England asked Standard Chartered, a large British overseas bank, to rescue it. Wallace Brothers was acquired in the following year and most of its business subsequently disposed of.[15]

Steel Brothers and Ralli were acquired not by banks, but other types of British enterprise. In 1969 Steel Brothers' distinctive shareholding structure was reorganized with all the equity made publicly available. The British & Commonwealth Shipping Company took a 40 per cent stake in the firm. This firm, formed in 1955 by a merger of the Clan and Castle shipping lines, and owned largely by the Cayzer family, had diversified shipping, transport, and industrial interests. Steel Brothers was retained through the 1970s as an independent entity with trading, construction, and foodstuffs interests and a capital employed of £47 million in 1978. In 1984 it was fully absorbed into British & Commonwealth, which after the sale of the family shareholding in 1986, divested from shipping and grew rapidly as a financial services firm until it went bankrupt in 1990.[16]

Ralli's independent existence also ended in the 1970s. After the firm's rapid growth under Slater Walker, in 1972 Slater Walker arranged a merger between Ralli and Bowater, Britain's largest paper manufacturer and tenth largest industrial company, in which Slater Walker held 12 per cent of the ordinary capital.[17] After the acquisition of Ralli, the Bowater Corporation combined extensive paper manufacturing operations in the UK and North America with Ralli's international commodity trading and handmade carpet businesses. In 1972 paper, pulp, and packaging contributed 37 per cent of Bowater's sales, and international trading 52 per cent.[18] During the 1970s there was further expansion in cotton trading, and expansion in trading elsewhere, including the purchase of an Ethiopian produce exporter, but the former Duncan Fox business in Chile and Peru was sold. In 1981 Bowater sold the Ralli business to Cargill of the United States.

A third fate for British trading companies was acquisition by host country interests. In Latin America, Brazilian Warrant faced competition from US and German firms in the Brazilian coffee trade, while exchange controls hindered the repatriation of dividends, even though the British devaluation in 1949 sharply increased Brazilian earnings, which were linked to dollars. The firm's coffee trading and estates business made it of interest to Brazilians and in 1951 its shares were acquired by a Brazilian group.[19]

[15] A. C. Pointon, *Wallace Brothers* (Oxford: the firm, 1974), 79–101; Jones, *British Multinational Banking*, 340.

[16] H. E. W. Braund, *Calling to Mind* (Oxford: Pergamon Press, 1975), 115–16; *The Economist*, 1 Aug. 1987, 9 June 1990.

[17] *History and Activities of the Ralli Trading Group* (London: the firm, 1979); Charles Raw, *A Financial Phenomenon* (New York: Harper & Row, 1977), 248–66.

[18] W. J. Reader, *Bowater: A History* (Cambridge: Cambridge University Press, 1982).

[19] Robert G. Greenhill, 'Investment Group, Free-Standing Company or Multinational? Brazilian Warrant, 1909–52', *Business History*, 37 (1995), 104–5.

The 1970s saw most of the remaining assets of the British traders in Chile and Peru either liquidated or passing into local ownership.

In South Asia, virtually all the assets of the British managing agencies were transferred into Indian ownership between the late 1950s and the late 1970s. After Indian Independence the British managing agencies were badly affected both by increases in taxation and changes in the nature of taxation. In 1948 new legislation made companies with less than 51 per cent of their shares in public hands liable to pay Indian tax at individual rates—which were far higher than corporate taxes. This led to a number of firms, such as Gillanders and Birds, converting to public companies in order to enable them to repatriate enough capital to Britain to pay out retiring partners, while still managing to retain control of the new public companies. The continued growth of powerful Indian business houses, especially Marwaris in the Calcutta region, provided new challenges. During the 1950s they lost many agencies of firms they 'managed', but in which they held only small equity stakes, as a result of these firms being acquired by Indians. At this stage only a number of managing agencies themselves were localized. Marwaris bought into the equity of Octavius Steel and Duncan Brothers and controlled both of them by the end of the decade, while the Turner family sold its shareholding in Turner Morrison—weakened by the decline of Calcutta as a port in the 1950s—to Indians.[20]

Over the next fifteen years the major British managing agencies passed into Indian hands. Bird/Heilgers remained owned by Edward Benthall until his death in 1962, when his shares passed to a family trust, who sold out to one of the Indian directors on the board in 1965. The Indian devaluation in 1966 increased the pressures on the remaining British firms, increasing the costs (in local currency) of British expatriates while reducing the sterling value of dividends. In 1969 the Gladstone family sold most of their 60 per cent shareholding in Gillanders Arbuthnot to Indian interests, although the family retained some shares until 1988. In the same year the London-based Yule Catto sold its 24 per cent shareholding in Andrew Yule to the Indian government. Jardine Henderson, created in 1946 by a merger of Jardine Skinner and George Henderson, remained controlled by the Jardine and Steuart families but the Mehta family—which had controlled George Henderson—also held about 40 per cent of the shares, and the death of members of the British families in the early 1970s led to the transfer of a majority of shares into Indian hands.[21]

It was only from the mid-1970s that there was transfer of control of the British agency houses in South East Asia into local hands. There was some restructuring after Malaysian independence in 1957, in part designed to attract British shareholders. In 1958 Sime Darby Holdings Ltd. was incorporated in London, but with the Head Office remaining in Singapore. In 1961 Guthries

[20] Stephanie Jones, *Merchants of the Raj* (London: Macmillan, 1992), 135–205.
[21] Ibid. 221–307.

also split its trading and estate management businesses and registered the latter as a private company in Britain. This began a process of consolidation within the Guthrie group of plantations culminating in 1965 with the formation of the Guthrie Corporation Ltd., a publicly quoted company, which owned plantations as well as joint managing them.[22]

During the 1970s the Malaysian government adopted a strategy to bring the country's tin and rubber industries under local control, using state-owned companies, and several of the British agency houses were acquired by Malaysian interests. The first company to be affected was Sime Darby, which included within its orbit the Indian managing agency of Shaw Wallace. Sime Darby, Shaw Wallace, and the London firm of R. G. Shaw had long-standing interlocking shareholdings, with R. G. Shaw holding 40 per cent of Sime Darby and Shaw Wallace's shares, while Sime Darby held a substantial shareholding in R. G. Shaw. In 1971 Sime Darby made a reverse takeover of R. G. Shaw, acquiring control and with it 40 per cent of Shaw Wallace.[23] Sime Darby had always had a local Chinese connection and from the 1960s many of its shares had also shifted into local hands so that by the mid-1970s only 10 per cent of its shareholders were domiciled in Britain, compared to 40 per cent in Singapore, 36 per cent in Malaysia, and 6 per cent in Hong Kong. In 1976 a Malaysian government company acquired a 9 per cent shareholding in the firm, and used their influence to remove the British directors from the board. In 1980 legal domicile was moved to Malaysia. In 1981 Guthries was acquired by the same means, and in 1989 it was listed on the Malaysian stock market as a public company.[24]

By the end of the 1970s, therefore, a small number of British trading firms remained as independent survivors. These included Lonrho and Inchcape, and Unilever's subsidiary UAC. UAC remained wholly owned but virtually autonomous within Unilever. In 1959 its London head office moved into a separate building to that of its parent, and it was hardly integrated at all within Unilever. A far-reaching report by McKinsey on Unilever's organization in 1972 omitted any mention of UAC. Nevertheless it formed a major contributor to Unilever's revenues and, sometimes, profits. During the 1960s UAC produced around 15 per cent of Unilever's total turnover, and around 9 per cent in 1978, while in the 1970s it contributed up to one-third of Unilever's profits, in some years making large cash transfers to its parent, exceeding £40 million in 1975 and again in 1979.

[22] J. H. Drabble and P. J. Drake, 'The British Agency Houses in Malaysia: Survival in a Changing World', *Journal of Southeast Asia Studies*, 12 (1981); Lim Mah Hui, *Ownership and Control of the One Hundred Largest Corporations in Malaysia* (Kuala Lumpur: Oxford University Press, 1981), 97–8.

[23] Stephanie Jones, *Merchants*, 277–80.

[24] Jean-Jacques van Helten and Geoffrey Jones, 'British Business in Malaysia and Singapore Since the 1870s', in R. P. T. Davenport-Hines and Geoffrey Jones (eds.), *British Business in Asia since 1860* (Cambridge: Cambridge University Press, 1989), 184–6; J. Thomas Lindblad, *Foreign Investment in Southeast Asia in the Twentieth Century* (London: Macmillan, 1998), 109.

Jardine Matheson and Swire's recovered from the devastation of their business caused by the Pacific War and the Communist Revolution in China in 1949 and re-emerged as major business groups in Hong Kong and the Pacific. Both firms remained family controlled. After the war Sir John Jardine owned around a 75 per cent share of Jardine Matheson, but he lost his substantial Shanghai assets following the Communist Revolution in China and by 1961, when Jardine Matheson became a public company, he had sold all his shares in the firm. This ended the involvement of the Jardine family in the company, but the Keswick family retained a substantial shareholding. Throughout the period John Swire & Sons remained a private limited company owned by the Swire and Scott families, though in 1974 there was a major reorganization when the majority of the Far Eastern businesses were placed in a publicly quoted holding company, Swire Pacific, in which John Swire & Sons initially held 27 per cent of the equity. Both firms remained heavily dependent on Hong Kong, but also diversified extensively both geographically and functionally. Swire's built a major regional airline and expanded into Australia, while Jardine Matheson also expanded into Australia and South East Asia, and in the 1970s into Africa and the Middle East.

Among the once-extensive British agency houses and managing agents in South East and South Asia there were a number of 'survivors' by the end of the 1970s. The largest were Guthries, which was about to lose its independence, and Harrisons & Crosfield, which combined its still-extensive plantation business with timber, engineering, and chemicals businesses on five continents by 1978.[25] On a smaller scale, Boustead also remained an independent firm with Malaysian plantations and a metal trading and broking and engineering business in South East Asia, Australia, and Britain. Yule Catto, still owned by the Catto family, had been created in 1974 from a merger between the former firm of that name and Catto interests in Malaysia. It combined Malaysian plantation interests with trading and the ownership of marinas in Britain.[26]

Beyond Asia, Booker McConnell (as the firm was known from 1968) also remained a substantial trading company at the end of the 1970s. In the late 1940s this firm remained focused on the colony of British Guiana, where nearly half of its profit was earned, and the production and sale of sugar was its major concern. Over the next two decades—the firm expanded through acquisitions into other parts of the Caribbean, Africa, Britain, and Canada, in tropical agriculture, wholesale, and retail food distribution, alcohol production and marketing, shipping, and engineering. This wider business which was to lead the firm's evolution into a food and agribusiness

---

[25] Geoffrey Jones and Judith Wale, 'Diversification Strategies of British Trading Companies: Harrisons & Crosfield *c*.1900–*c*.1980', *Business History*, 41 (1999).

[26] Annual Reports, Boustead and Yule Catto.

firm enabled Booker McConnell to survive the nationalization of its business in Guyana (formerly British Guiana) in 1976.[27]

In Latin America, Wilson, Sons & Co. continued in independent existence in this period. During the late 1940s this group's British coal mining interests—owned by the Ocean Coal Company—were nationalized, though it retained a role as a large general coal trader, handling imports of coal into Britain in odd years of shortage and, more importantly, procuring coal from a variety of suppliers in order to meet the needs of their subsidiary importing companies in Spain and Italy. In 1955 the former holding company was reorganized and a new public company, Ocean Wilsons (Holdings) formed, which acquired all the assets of Wilsons, Sons & Co. In 1960 the main Brazilian operations were placed in the locally registered Wilson, Sons SA, whose head office was transferred to Rio de Janeiro in 1971. Many of the non-Brazilian investments were sold and Wilsons refocused on shipping and towage business in Brazil. Ocean Wilsons also developed as a kind of investment trust. By 1980 it combined its still large holding in the Brazilian-registered Wilson business with an investment portfolio in British listed companies.[28]

A number of general factors explain the survival of some firms and the merger or disappearance of others in this era. The 'fate' of firms was in part correlated with their main host regions. The British traders were heavily embedded in these countries, where their contacts and knowledge were major sources of their competitive advantage, and they owned large fixed assets. This became a source of competitive disadvantage if, as happened after 1945, some host regions became hostile to foreign firms or imposed penal rates of taxation. This happened to the British firms in South Asia and Latin America—and more especially for a period at least the southern cone countries of Chile and Peru. East and South East Asia and West Africa—at least through to the 1970s—offered much greater prospects. Hong Kong from the 1950s, which combined fast economic growth with low taxes and a British legal system, offered especially favourable conditions.

However managerial discretion meant that the 'fate' of firms was not wholly dependent on their host economies. Swire's and Jardines survived the loss of their Chinese investments in 1949. Inchcape and Booker McConnell both successfully escaped from 'difficult' host countries to more attractive areas. And while overall political and economic conditions in Africa deteriorated from the perspective of Western firms from the 1960s, Lonrho developed as a large 'hybrid' trading company in this period. Conversely, British mercantile interests in Chile were wound down during the 1970s despite the

---

[27] Annual Reports, Booker Brothers, McConnell and Booker McConnell Ltd. 1945–80; M. H. Caine, 'John Middleton Campbell', in D. J. Jeremy (ed.), *Dictionary of Business Biography*, vol. i (London: Butterworths, 1984).
[28] Annual Reports, Ocean Wilsons (Holdings) Ltd., 1955–80.

fact that the Pinochet coup in 1973 made it again a profitable and hospitable environment for foreign firms.

The 'fate' of the firms was also related to the stability of their shareholding structure. In a considerable number of cases, the decision by family shareholders to sell their shareholding was the catalyst which ended the independent existence and/or British ownership of firms. These decades saw many founding family shareholders sell out—such as the Muirs, the Foxes, the Gibbs, and the Holts, who remained in control of John Holt until 1966 even though the firm went public in 1950. The problem was that for a number of reasons many firms were not well equipped to retain their independence once the family shareholding had gone. This was partly because of the risky nature both of international trading and investments in developing countries. In some cases it was because good franchises were not well managed. Coincidently, the development of a more fluid market for corporate control in Britain from the 1950s meant that the vulnerability of firms to takeover was much greater. At the same time, powerful business groups in many host economies were better able to value the worth of British trading company assets in their countries than the London capital market. The firms which survived in British hands were ones that possessed 'stable' shareholding structures. UAC as a wholly owned subsidiary of Unilever was not vulnerable to takeover. Lonrho was a 'quasi-family firm' through the large shareholding of Rowland. The Inchcape family managed the transition to a public company in such a way and at sufficient size that it did not fall victim to takeover bidders.

The quantity and determination of a firm's leadership was another influence, if one hard to quantify. The experience of the British trading companies in this period would lend support to the view about the beneficial impact of 'traumatic experiences' on firms.[29] The war and the subsequent Communist Revolution in China deprived Jardine Matheson and Swire's of most of their core business, but the effect appears to have been to instil a determination to survive. The British agency houses in South East Asia went through a similar wartime 'shock' only to recover and expand in the post-war decades. In contrast, the steady incremental decline of business faced by the British merchants in India and Latin America appears to have instilled a feeling of the inevitable about their ultimate demise.

The fate of firms also reflected their financial performance. Tables 5.4 and 5.5 provide summaries of the post-tax and pre-tax ROCE data in Appendices 1 and 2.

Table 5.4 shows that on average the financial performance of the selected trading companies was far better than in the interwar years, and volatility on the whole lower, although the high growth decades of the 1950s and 1960s did not see post-tax ROCE return to the pre-1914 levels. The 1970s saw

---

[29] Interview with Sir John and Sir Adrian Swire, 30 July 1996.

TABLE 5.4 Average post-tax return on net capital employed of selected British trading companies, 1946–1979

	Borneo Company	Anglo-Thai	Dodwells	Gray Mackenzie	Smith Mackenzie	Inchcape	H&C	Finlays	Swire's
1946–1951	12.5	15.1[b]	13 4	8.0	12 3	—	13 7	6.6	2 1
1952–1959	10 2	8 6	6.1	12.0	9.0		9.2	4.4	9.6
1960–1969	8 4[a]	9.9	13.3	—	7 4[c]	7.4	10 9	5.3	8 7[f]
1970–1979	—	16 7[c]	11.4[d]	—	—	11.4	16.6	7.4	10.7
Std°1946–1951	8.9	3.1	6 6	6.4	4 3		8.6	2.4	1 4
Std°1952–1959	8.4	6 0	5 7	4 8	3.3		4 6	1 6	10.2
Std°1960–1969	1.3	1 7	5 6		2 3	1.1	3.6	1 4	3 3
Std°1970–1979	—		3.9	6.9		2.7	5.5	4.3	3.2

[a] 1960–1967 only.　[g] 1957–1959 only.　[m] 1952–1954 only
[b] 1948–1951 only.　[h] 1966–1969 only.　[n] 1946–1949 only
[c] 1970–1975 only.　[i] 1961–1969 only.　[o] Standard deviation is calculated on
[d] 1970–1973 only　[j] 1973–1979 only　　the annual figures in Appendix 1
[e] 1960–1964 only.　[k] 1954–1959 only.
[f] 1965 and 1966 missing.　[l] 1970–1975 only.

TABLE 5.5 Average pre-tax return on net capital employed of selected British trading companies, 1948–1979

	Borneo Company	Anglo-Thai	Dodwells	Gray Mackenzie	Smith Mackenzie	Inchcape	H&C	Finlays	Swire's	Jardine Matheson
1948–51	33 5	32 7	36.4	20.1	24 1	—	23 1	10.5	3 4	—
1952–59	21.2	16.8	15.9	22 5	—	—	20.6	9 5	10 3	9.8[l]
1960–69	14 9[i]	17 6	27.7	—	11.7[d]	10.9	19.3	10 2	10.6[e]	15.8
1970–79	—	29.0[b]	20 4[c]	—	—	20 3	28.3	15.6	16 1	19.7

[i] 1960–1967 only.　[f] 1957–1959 only.　[l] 1970–1975 only.
[b] 1970–1975 only　[g] 1966–1969 only.　[k] 1954–1959 only.
[c] 1970–1973 only　[h] 1970–1973 only.　[m] 1952–1954, 1959 only
[d] 1960–1964 only　[i] 1950 and 1951 only.　[n] 1948–1949 only
[c] 1965 and 1966 missing.　[j] 1961–1969 only

significant higher ROCE, though this reflected in part the consequences of the continued use of the historic cost convention in British company accounts at a time of high inflation, which reached an annual rate of almost 25 per cent in the United Kingdom by the mid-1970s. Because profits were earned in current prices while assets, much of the expenditure on which had been incurred years previously, were stated at original cost, nominal profits increased rapidly but the denominator in the ROCE calculation did not increase proportionately.

Although the relationship between 'fate' and financial performance is not clear-cut from these figures, it is possible to observe some general patterns. Among the major survivors, Harrisons & Crosfield always performed higher than the overall average, Swire's was higher than the average after 1952, Jardine Matheson after 1960, and Booker McConnell except in the 1960s.

Jardine Matheson	Guthries	UAC	John Holt	Lonrho	Booker McConnell	Antony Gibbs	Duncan Fox	Balfour Williamson	Wilson, Sons	Brazilian Warrant	Average
		10.0	7.8		9 9			4.2	6 1	13 7ⁿ	9 6
7.3ᵍ		6.9	5.5		9 4		7 3ᵏ	6 7	(4 5)ᵐ		7.6
10 8	11 6ʰ	3 3	4.5	5 2ⁱ	7 4		6.1	4.1			7.7
10.9	6.4	11.7		9.4	12.8	2.0ʲ	2.0	6.9ˡ	15.9		10 2
		3 4	0.5		2.8			2 7	0 9	14.3	—
1 0		1 2	3 4		1 2		2 0	1 4	8 1		—
2.5	2.4	1.7	5.1	1.7	1.4		1.7	3.4			—
2 7	4.2	5 5		2.9	4.9	2.9	12.6	4 6	5.3		—

Guthries	UAC	John Holt	Lonrho	Booker McConnell	Duncan Fox	Balfour Williamson	Wilson, Sons	Brazilian Warrant	Average
—	14.3	8.2ⁱ	—	20.0	—	8.9	14.6	34 0ⁿ	20 8
—	10 1	8 7	—	22.1	16.3ᵏ	11.1	(1.3)ᵐ	—	14.7
21.8ᵍ	6.2	8 7	13.2ʲ	14.9	11.9	8.5	9.0	—	13 5
11.4	10.4ʰ		17.0	22 8	4.5	13 4ˡ	26 0	—	18.3

UAC's performance deteriorated sharply to reach a nadir in the 1960s, but in the 1970s it became highly profitable. Balfour Williamson, Duncan Fox, and Guthries had weak financial performances in the period before they were absorbed by other firms or by foreign investors. However success was no guarantor of independence. Borneo Company, Anglo-Thai, and Dodwells were notably profitable prior to their acquisition by Inchcape, indicating that company's judicious choice of takeover targets. However, the high ROCE figure for Dodwells may have continued to reflect in part its small capital employed, and Anglo-Thai also had relatively small net assets compared to the breadth of its activities. The Borneo Company achieved a high ROCE with a larger capital, with an especially impressive performance during the Korean War period of the early 1950s. In contrast, Lonrho's fast growth was not matched by an especially impressive financial performance, though its

TABLE 5.6 Comparison of pre-tax returns on net capital employed of selected
trading companies and all UK quoted companies

	1948–64 average (%)	1964–71 average (%)
Harrisons & Crosfield	20.5	20.8
Guthries	—	21.1
Finlays	10.0	9.6
Borneo Company	22.5	—
Anglo-Thai	20.3	20.0
Dodwells	23.7	29.5
Gray Mackenzie	21.4	—
Inchcape	—	11.4
John Swire & Sons	8.7	11.1
Balfour Williamson	9.5	10.9
Duncan Fox	14.2	8.0
Wilson, Sons	—	8.6
UAC	10.9	7.3
John Holt	8.1	9.7
Lonrho	—	13.9
Booker McConnell	20.4	12.7
Jardine Matheson	—	18.6
Average	15.9	14.2
Average all quoted	17.9	17.5

Source: Data on ROCE for all quoted UK companies derived from Royal Commission on
the Distribution of Income and Wealth, report 2: *Income from Companies and its Distribution*
(HMSO, 1976) (Cmnd. 6172), 166 (Table Q1).

ROCE figures reflected in part the distinctive business portfolio of Lonrho,
whose extensive investment in mining gave it large assets which reduced
the ROCE calculation compared to other firms.

Table 5.6 puts the performance of the trading companies in a comparative perspective. The availability of data on pre-tax ROCE for all UK quoted
companies permits the trading companies to be compared more systematic-
ally to the population of UK firms as a whole. The table shows the companies which were absorbed into Inchcape (Borneo Company, Anglo-Thai,
Dodwells, and Gray Mackenzie), Booker McConnell, and Harrisons &
Crosfield performing significantly better than the UK average, and most of
the remainder much less, between 1948 and 1964. For the 1964–71 period,
only Dodwells spectacularly outperformed the UK average, but Guthries,
Harrisons & Crosfield, Anglo-Thai, and Jardine Matheson were also above
it. But these were difficult years for the otherwise above-average performing Booker McConnell, while the dire performance of UAC in this period
is also noteworthy.

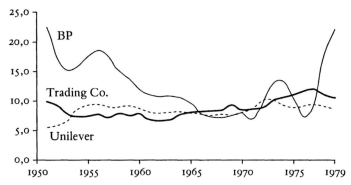

FIG. 5.1 Post-tax ROCE of trading companies, BP, and Unilever, 1950–1979 (three year moving averages)

Another comparison is provided in Figure 5.1, which compares the post-tax ROCE of BP, the oil company, and Unilever, part of whose profits came from UAC, with the average for all trading companies in the sample. Although crude, the graph suggests that from the late 1960s in particular the performance of the trading companies compared reasonably with these large multinationals. Indeed during the 1970s Inchcape, Harrisons & Crosfield, Swire's, Jardine Matheson, UAC, Booker McConnell all had a higher ROCE than Unilever, and sometimes than BP apart from during the two oil crises of that decade.

5.4 Strategies

The recovery of world trade from the 1950s presented new opportunities for trading firms. In post-war Japan, trading companies became central actors in the 'miracle' economy, as the *sogo shosha* of the former *zaibatsu* were reborn after being dismantled by the Allied occupation, and a new generation of *sogo shosha* emerged from the ranks of specialist trading companies of the pre-war era. They were, along with a 'main' bank, at the core of Japan's six large horizontal business groups, or *kigyo shudan*. These *kigyo shudan* consisted of considerable numbers of firms in many industries joined by webs of cross-shareholdings. The *sogo shosha* functioned as the trading arms of these groups, and had a special role in handling the exports of smaller manufacturers, to whom they also provided credit. This trade and financial intermediation role was an important element of Japan's industrial policy and fully supported by the government. Within this context, the *sogo shosha* occupied a leading position in Japan's foreign trade in the post-war era, and also undertook substantial direct investment in resources and manu-facturing outside Japan.[30]

[30] M. Y. Yoshino and B. L. Thomas, *The Invisible Link: Japan's Sogo Shosha and the Organ-isation of Trade* (Cambridge, Mass.: MIT Press, 1986).

European-based trading companies also continued to develop. A number of long-established Swiss trading companies such as André, Diethelem, and Volkart expanded rapidly, especially into commodity trading. André, which became one of the world's largest grain traders, made large-scale investments in Argentina and Brazil. A new generation of Swiss trading companies, notably Marc Rich which was founded in 1974, rapidly grew to become large-scale multinational commodity traders. From the 1950s the US grain traders such as Cargill and Continental also expanded internationally on a large scale, taking advantage of trading opportunities with the Soviet Union and diversifying from grain into other commodities.[31]

The British trading companies appeared not well positioned to take advantage of the post-war economy. The declining competitiveness of British exports, and their shift to developed markets where the traders were not represented, offered them limited opportunities for growth. Indeed, and in contrast to the nineteenth-century situation, their main businesses were increasingly located on the margins of Britain's trade and investment flows. While many Japanese firms in the post-war period utilized trading companies because of the continuing informational and cultural gaps between Japan and the West, British trading companies had no realistic role as intermediaries for British trade with Western Europe or the United States, where their knowledge and contacts were less than most British manufacturers. A further problem was that the informational value of their once-important London bases was in marked decline. London underwent a sharp decline as a centre for international commodity trading.[32] In their traditional host economies the trading companies became agents for foreign firms, but as British firms they at least in theory lacked the specialist 'insider' knowledge and contacts with such firms that they had once held with the British textile industry. The trade in commodities was changed by state control of produce marketing, and they faced new competition from commodity producers who wanted to sell directly or enter long-term supply contracts to overseas customers, and from state marketing boards. The end of most commodity cartels and decolonization removed important cushions which had supported their operations in earlier decades.

The most obvious strategy was to further embed themselves in their host economies, many of which from the 1950s adopted import substitution policies. They continued to possess considerable knowledge and informational advantages in these countries. However political developments also constrained this option. In many developing and post-colonial countries governments intervened more in economies, taxation levels were increased,

---

[31] Sébastian Guex, 'The Development of Swiss Trading Companies in the Twentieth Century', in Geoffrey Jones (ed.), *The Multinational Traders* (London: Routledge, 1998); Wayne G. Broehl, Jnr., *Cargill: Going Global* (Hanover, NJ: University Press of New England, 1998).
[32] Ranald C. Michie, *The City of London* (London: Macmillan, 1992), 55–6.

controls on foreign firms introduced, and—in some cases—nationalization of foreign assets occurred. Under these circumstances, many trading firms sought to reposition themselves, sometimes seeking to transfer the skills learnt in their host economies to other developing economies, and later to politically safer developed markets, sometimes engaging in wholly unrelated diversification.

The post-war period saw a number of British firms obliged to withdraw completely from their long-established host regions. The most spectacular instance was China, where Jardine Matheson, Swire's, and a number of other British firms effectively lost all their assets following the Communist Revolution.[33] Wallace Brothers and Steels had their teak forests in Burma nationalized after that country's independence in 1948. Steels persisted in Burma with a trading, shipping, and insurance business, and also acquired and managed hotels, but in 1963 all its business in Burma was nationalized.[34] Thirteen years later Booker McConnell's assets were nationalized in Guyana, ending the firm's association over more than 150 years.

The withdrawal of the British companies from India happened more incrementally. Despite substantial increases in taxation after Independence, the managing agencies initially remained committed to staying in business in India.[35] However their traditional organization came under attack when new legislation was introduced in 1956 which limited the number of managed companies per managing agency to ten after 1960.[36] In 1967 the Indian government abolished the managing agency system altogether. By the late 1960s the government had introduced tight exchange control regulations especially for firms with a foreign shareholding of 40 per cent or over, making it difficult either to repatriate profits or to expand operations. The upshot was a progressive decline in all foreign-owned business in India.

The British shareholders in Indian managing agencies generally sold their shares to Indians, while firms with interests elsewhere—such as Inchcape or Yule Catto—progressively divested from India. James Finlay also took this route. In 1964 a joint venture was formed with the Tata group to develop tea packaging in India. The firm's senior management became extremely pessimistic about the penal rates of taxation and the general business climate in India, and during the 1970s had decided to withdraw from the country.[37] In 1976 Finlays sold all its plantations to the Tata-Finlay joint venture. Initially it retained a 20 per cent shareholding, but this was sold

[33] Jürgen Osterhammel, 'British Business in China, 1860s–1950s', in Davenport-Hines and Jones (eds.), *British Business in Asia*.

[34] Pointon, *Wallace Brothers*, 79; Braund, *Calling to Mind*, 55, 79.

[35] M. Misra, 'Entrepreneurial Decline and the End of Empire' (Oxford D. Phil, 1994).

[36] Geoffrey Tyson, *Managing Agency: A System of Business Organisation* (Calcutta: Houghty Printing, 1960), 16–19.

[37] Interview with Sir Colin Campbell, 16 Apr. 1996.

in 1981. This ended the firm's involvement in India, although it retained tea plantations in Bangladesh and a small trading and agency business in Pakistan and Sri Lanka.[38]

However in the immediate post-war decades some developing countries still seemed attractive investment propositions. Sometimes firms spilled over into neighbouring countries. In Latin America, Duncan Fox moved beyond Chile and Peru to establish an affiliate in Argentina in 1947.[39] Wilsons, which had twenty-two branches in Brazil, Argentina, and Uruguay, opened a branch in Columbia in 1946 and in Venezuela in 1948. However it proved hard to sustain such new ventures. By 1953 Wilsons had withdrawn from Venezuela, as well as closing down most of its business in Argentina and southern Brazil.[40] Duncan Fox liquidated its Argentinian business in 1965. Gibbs ended its modest involvement in Argentina in the 1950s on their withdrawal from a mining concern which was effectively bankrupt. More sustained was the post-war expansion of Booker Brothers, McConnell from British Guiana to other parts of the Caribbean, beginning with Trinidad and later Jamaica, and other islands.[41]

The same pattern of regional expansion was evident in Asia. Wallace Brothers responded to the loss of its Burmese teak forests by a large-scale move into timber exploitation in North Borneo in 1949.[42] In the late 1940s the Anglo-Thai Corporation expanded its investments in India and Malaysia, and in 1965 established a branch in Hong Kong. In 1954 Jardine Matheson began to extend its business to South East Asia when it purchased a share in the Singapore agency house Henry Waugh & Co. Soon after the end of the war Dodwells opened a branch in Manila in the Philippines, though it was unsuccessful and closed in 1960.[43]

There was a renewed interest in multi-regional investment. During the 1950s East and southern Africa, still under British colonial rule, was a major centre of attraction for British trading companies. It received investment from British traders active elsewhere in Africa, including John Holt, which established South African companies in 1947, though these were wound up in 1962. British merchants from Asia and Latin America were also attracted to Africa. Guthries purchased an agricultural and building equipment supply firm in southern Rhodesia (later Zimbabwe) in 1951.[44] Dodwells opened an East African company in 1951 to import office equipment and other

[38] Annual Reports, James Finlay, 1963–82.
[39] Minutes of Gibbs & Co., 3 June 1947, MS 16870, GHL.
[40] Annual Reports, Ocean Coal & Wilsons Ltd., MS 20196/7, GHL.
[41] Annual Reports, Booker Brothers, McConnell 1945–70.
[42] Pointon, *Wallace Brothers*, 83.
[43] Percival Griffiths, *A History of the Inchcape Group* (London: the firm, 1977), 160; Minutes of Conference Meetings of directors, 10–28 Oct. 1954 and Board Minute 20 Dec. 1960, Dodwell Archives, MS 27498/6 and MS 27498/7, GHL.
[44] S. Cunyngham-Brown, *The Traders* (London: Newman Neame, 1971), 308.

consumer goods, and after making heavy losses diversified into retail stores.[45] Wallace Brothers and Steels both made trading and other investments in East Africa from the 1950s.[46] In 1951 James Finlay, which already owned tea plantations in East Africa, opened an office in Kenya for trading and purchased a shareholding (which became full ownership in 1968) in a leading import agency. In 1959 a brush manufacturer and a forwarding and warehousing business were acquired.[47] Gibbs and Balfour Williamson also invested in the region in the 1950s,[48] and on a large scale Booker Brothers, McConnell built up a trading business in northern Rhodesia (Zambia) in the late 1940s. By the mid-1950s it had retail operations in that country and neighbouring Nyasaland (Malawi), and later developed management and consultancy services in Kenya and Tanzania.[49]

As governments intervened more in commodity and marketing, the role of the British firms as exporters of local 'produce' declined sharply and in many cases disappeared. In West Africa, UAC's business had revolved around the import of thousands of commodities in return for exports of cocoa, groundnuts, and palm products. At the end of the 1940s UAC accounted for 43 per cent of all non-mineral Nigerian exports, and 34 per cent of all commercial imports. However, the creation of state marketing boards for produce in the late 1940s reduced the speculative—and profitable—aspect of the business by setting a minimum buying price for each product in advance for a whole season. By 1961 UAC had abandoned the business.[50] During the 1950s, Holts also experienced problems with the declining profitability of its West African produce buying business.[51] However, during the early 1960s Holts persisted in the business after UAC's withdrawal, and even secured a new appointment as managing agents for the West Cameroon Produce Marketing Co. However, by the mid-1960s they too had withdrawn from produce.

Beyond West Africa there were different patterns for different regions and products. The British traders in Latin America had little business in exporting local produce, though Gibbs in the 1950s exported wool from Peru and a variety of Chilean produce such as beans and prunes, though by the early 1960s this business had shrunk in importance.[52] However, Booker McConnell's Guyana estates remained major sugar producers—producing

---

[45] Griffiths, *Inchcape Group*, 160, Board Minutes 24 Sept. 1957 and 26 Apr. 1958, Dodwell Archives, MS 27498/7, GHL.

[46] Pointon, *Wallace Brothers*, 88–9; Braund, *Calling to Mind*, 57, 91–3.

[47] 'The Group in East Africa', Finlays House Magazine, Spring 1970, UGD 91/377.

[48] Antony Gibbs, *Merchants and Bankers*, 68, 76.

[49] Annual Reports, Booker Brothers, McConnell, 1945–70.

[50] Fieldhouse, *Merchant Capital*, 425–48.

[51] e.g. Correspondence on palm oil and palm kernels 1948–55, John Holt & Co. (Liverpool) Ltd., Archives, MSS Afr. S825, file 86, Rhodes House, Oxford.

[52] Memoranda of discussions on Chile and Peru, 1960–2, Antony Gibbs Archives, MS 16878, GHL.

an annual average of 268,000 tons of sugar in the second half of the 1960s
—and sugar trading remained an important part of that firm's business until
the nationalization of its estates. The British trading companies in Asia
remained large-scale traders in tea, rubber, palm oil, timber, and other
tropical products throughout the period, though the end of the collusive
commodity control schemes of the interwar years made the markets for some
products, like tea, much more unstable.

Among the trading companies, Ralli remained distinctive for its focus on
commodity trading, even if some diversification into owning plantations
and other activities made it also a 'hybrid' firm. During the 1960s the firm
established itself as the leading cotton trading company in the world. Ralli
acquired cotton and cotton broking firms in Liverpool in the early 1960s,
and by the end of the decade the firm had cotton trading subsidiaries
in Uganda, Kenya, Tanzania, Sudan, Nigeria, the Netherlands, Germany,
and France, and buying and selling agents in almost every producing and
consuming country in the world. During the 1970s US and Hong Kong
subsidiaries were founded to expand the cotton trading business. Ralli also
dealt in jute, industrial metals, sugar, cocoa, and grains.[53]

The example of Ralli raises the issue why no British merchant firm emerged
as a large-scale commodity trading company on the scale of the US or Swiss
firms. Ralli itself, but also other firms such as Gibbs, had considerable
expertise in commodity trading, but were probably handicapped by London's
post-war decline in international commodity trading. Many British merchant
houses were too embedded in their host economies, owning or managing
substantial fixed assets. They had evolved out of the trading business mentality necessary to build a commodity trading business. Finally the ownership of many firms was a constraint. Although family ownership was
frequent in the largest of trading companies—Cargill remained and remains
a private company owned by the Cargill and MacMillan families—many of
the British families owning the Latin American and Indian firms in particular lacked both the resources and the mentality to become large commodity
traders. Flotation on the British capital markets provided an even less supportive context. Ralli's encounter with Slater Walker, its merger with the
carpet manufacturer, and its subsequent sale to Bowater and finally to
Cargill put an end to a firm which in the 1960s had the potential to grow
as a major British-based international commodity trader.

In the post-war period British merchants continued to sell British goods
in overseas markets. According to one estimate, 'merchants' still handled one-
third of British exports in 1950. However, as many British manufacturers
integrated forwards themselves, and British trade shifted to Europe, this
business became much less important. By 1965 'merchants' only accounted
for 15 per cent of British exports.[54]

---

[53] *History and Activities of the Ralli Trading Group*   [54] Ibid. 49.

During the 1950s and 1960s the trading companies withdrew from selling British 'staples' and concentrated on goods which involved technical expertise and, especially, those which often involved agency agreements with manufacturers. Swire's was one firm which re-entered trading at that time. In 1946 it founded a joint venture, Swire & Maclaine, which became the basis of an extensive international trading business based on marketing franchises. Companies increasingly sold non-British goods and acted for non-British manufacturers. The British merchants became increasingly 'semi-detached' from the United Kingdom, providing a major contrast with their Japanese counterparts.

The West African case was again striking. In the 1940s UAC continued to import tens of thousands of different articles which were sold through UAC stores which stocked almost every commodity. By the early 1960s the company had withdrawn from such 'general trading' partly because of the growth of strong local competition, and partly because rising incomes caused a declining demand for 'staples' and an increased demand for more sophisticated products. The firm's residual trading activities were concentrated in five divisions concerned with cars, chemist shops, cold storage and refrigerated foodstuffs, hardware, and textiles. In addition, most of the firm's retail and wholesale stores had been sold off.[55] John Holt paralleled UAC's strategies. During the 1950s the firm reduced the number of retail outlets in its main market, Nigeria, and concentrated resources into wholesale outlets.[56] There were similar developments elsewhere.[57]

General trading was replaced by a number of strategies. Firms specialized in products where they held expertise. In Brazil, Wilsons by the late 1950s had substantially reduced its once-extensive trading business and refocused on its traditional role as shipping agents, stevedoring, and repair workshops, while their trading was limited to the specialist area of agricultural supplies.[58] The British traders also searched for more attractive goods to sell, increasingly not from the United Kingdom. By 1961 the Borneo Company's agency agreements for South East Asia included many US, Australian, and European firms.[59] In West Africa, Holts in the 1950s purchased cheap cloth from Japan to sell in place of Lancashire textiles. This firm also purchased a large equity share in a tobacco manufacturing company in Kentucky in 1953 in an attempt to improve the quality of its supplies to West Africa.

In general, firms sought to focus on products to which they could add value by after sales service and marketing. Traditionally the trading companies

---

[55] Fieldhouse, *Merchant Capital*, 410–25.
[56] Annual Reports, John Holt & Co. (Liverpool) Ltd., 1950–60.
[57] Borneo Company (Sarawak) to Managing Director, London, 9 Aug. 1956, Borneo Company Archives, MS 27297, GHL.
[58] Ocean Wilsons (Holdings) Ltd., Annual Reports, 1960–80.
[59] List of agency agreements held at 31 Dec. 1961, Borneo Company Archives, MS 27232A, GHL.

had offered their 'Principals' access to markets. Increasingly, 'Principals' sought more if they were to continue to use their services. The traders had also to add value. On the other hand, there remained potential for trade intermediaries in such products in some markets of Asia, Latin America, and Africa, either because volumes remained insufficiently low to encourage internalization by manufacturers, or between the 'psychic distance' in terms of culture, language, and business systems because those countries and Western manufacturers remained sufficiently large to discourage direct investment.[60] Information asymmetries persisted in many developing countries which provided a continuing role for the trading companies. Information and transaction costs became particularly high in post-colonial Africa, providing opportunities for a firm such as Lonrho to grow rapidly.

Motor distribution grew in importance. This was a particular achievement given the decline of the British-owned companies in this industry over these decades. Motor distribution was a capital-intensive business as the merchants purchased motors and then sold them, and they had to invest in showrooms and service facilities. There was also a constant risk that once a market was established, the services of the trader would not be required. Their distribution contracts with manufacturers were often cancellable at any moment. However motor manufacturers continued to face high information costs in many developing markets, and market access continued to be a major asset which the merchant firms could offer. The need to invest in showrooms and services facilities provided a disincentive for manufacturers to integrate forward into distribution unless volumes reached a high level. As a result, the British traders were able to develop strong relationships with the leading US manufacturers Ford and General Motors, and from the mid-1960s Inchcape began to evolve as one of Toyota's largest distributors.

In South East Asia, the Borneo Company distributed Austin and General Motors vehicles, and in 1957 held 22 and 40 per cent respectively of the Singapore and Malayan passenger and commercial vehicles markets, despite a loss of market share through a reluctance to introduce Asian capital and directorships.[61] In 1967, when the Borneo Company merged with Inchcape, motor distribution accounted for 40 per cent of the firm's net profit.[62] Dodwells and Anglo-Thai also built significant motor distribution businesses in Hong Kong and Thailand respectively. In Thailand, Anglo-Thai distributed Ford and other vehicles in the post-war period, and in the 1970s acquired

[60] For the concept of 'psychic distance', see (for example) Jan Johanson and Jan-Erik Vahlne, 'The Internationalization Process of the Firm: A Model of Knowledge and Development and Increasing Foreign Market Commitments', *Journal of International Business Studies*, 8 (1977), 23–32; id., 'The Mechanism of Internationalisation', *International Marketing Review*, 7 (1990).

[61] N. J. White, *Business, Government and the End of Empire* (Kuala Lumpur: Oxford University Press, 1996), 243–5.

[62] Annual Report, Borneo Company, 1967.

Ford dealerships in Britain. In 1975 motor vehicles represented 27 per cent of Anglo-Thai's turnover and 18 per cent of pre-tax profits.[63] Inchcape's acquisition of these and other firms, created a substantial multi-regional motor distributor and this activity contributed 40 per cent of Inchcape's total profits in 1980.[64]

The British traders in Africa were also active in motor distribution. In the late 1950s UAC was the largest importer and part-assembler of motor vehicles in Nigeria.[65] In 1957 Holts entered motor distribution when it purchased a British firm, Bartholomew (London) Ltd., engaged in motor distribution and related engineering in West Africa. Holts invested further capital in the business, which distributed Ford cars, and in 1961 also acquired a firm of Ford dealers in the Kent region of the UK.[66] During the 1970s Lonrho also acquired a series of motor distributors and distributed British, US, Japanese, German, and French motor vehicles in Nigeria, Malawi, Zambia, Kenya, and Zimbabwe, as well as the UK. The firm's chief executive claimed his firm was 'probably Africa's largest and most widespread motor distributor'.[67] In the main Latin American markets the major motor distributors had their own distribution arrangements, but Balfour Williamson's Milne & Co. built a large business in Peru post-war in Ford dealerships. In the 1960s Milne's had four dealerships and were the largest sales group in Peru, with around one-third of all the Ford sales. In 1959 Milne also bought a Ford dealership in Ecuador.[68] This business passed to Inchcape in 1981.

In a few cases host government pressure and competitor strategies led firms from motor distribution to local assembly. UAC established an assembly plant in Nigeria in 1958 and by the mid-1960s was making bus bodies. However UAC's partner, General Motors, had little interest in designing cars or trucks specifically for the African market, and several attempts to develop a car assembly plant in Nigeria floundered. By the 1970s German, French, and Japanese firms were assembling in the country.[69] John Holt seems to have been rather more successful than UAC. Despite severe losses in the Nigerian civil war, Holts persisted with its distribution business in Nigeria and by 1970 had a commercial vehicle assembly plant in operation. Under Lonrho ownership, Holts began assembly of motorcycles in Nigeria.[70] In Thailand, Thai government pressure and large fiscal and import duty concessions prompted Anglo-Thai to build a Bangkok assembly plant for

---

[63] Annual Report, Anglo-Thai Corporation, 1975.

[64] Annual Report, Inchcape plc, 1980. The proportion fluctuated considerably. It was 26 per cent in 1978 and 14 per cent in 1982. Jones, *Two Centuries*, 262.

[65] Fieldhouse, *Merchant Capital*, 533.

[66] Annual Reports, John Holt & Co. (Liverpool) Ltd., 1958–70.

[67] Annual Report, Lonhro, 1979.

[68] John Bingham Powell, 'History of the Milne Group of Companies' (Aug. 1987), Burmah Castrol Archives.

[69] Fieldhouse, *Merchant Capital*, 533–7.

[70] Annual Reports, John Holt & Co. (Liverpool) Ltd., 1960–70.

Ford vehicles in 1960. The venture was almost 100 per cent owned by Anglo-Thai but received Ford technical and personnel assistance.[71] At the end of the 1960s, however, Ford became dissatisfied with its 3.5 per cent share of the Thai passenger car market and decided to build a much larger plant with a substantial local content of materials. In 1970 Anglo-Thai sold its Thai assembly plant to Ford.[72]

Although motor distribution developed as a major dimension of the post-war business of several companies, others remained aloof. In Hong Kong, it was not until the 1970s that Jardine Matheson acquired a majority share-holding in the firm of Zung Fu, which since 1954 had had a relationship with the German luxury car manufacturer Mercedes-Benz. As Hong Kong incomes rose, this became a lucrative franchise, because margins were high in luxury cars.[73] Jardines also exploited the relationship elsewhere, acquiring the Mercedes-Benz franchise for Hawaii in 1979.

In Chile, it was not cars but sales of electrical and military equipment which Gibbs tried to promote in the 1950s and 1960s. In 1946 Gibbs secured an agency agreement with the British armaments manufacturer Vickers which covered the supply of military equipment to the Chilean army, navy, and air force, and of civilian aircraft to the national airline. This relationship continued through the 1960s. Gibbs also acted for other British defence contractors and for non-British firms, selling German machine guns to the Chilean army in 1966. This business involved extensive contacts with the Chilean government and involvement in the financing of the deals.[74] AEI and Hawker Siddeley were among the other large British electrical and defence firms with whom Gibbs were involved. Sales of aircrafts and ships were especially lucrative as they resulted in substantial sterling commissions on the initial sale, and commission on the sale of spares extending over sub-sequent years. In 1966 Gibbs secured two contracts with Hawker Siddeley as a supplier: one for eight aircraft for the Chilean airline and the other for twenty-one ex-RAF reconditioned aircraft for the airforce. Gibbs expected to receive over £320,000 in commission in total and the signing of the deal led to Gibbs in London congratulating their Chilean affiliates on their 'anno mirabilis' (sic).[75]

As discussed in more detail in Chapter 10, British trading companies remained cautious about investing in manufacturing. In India and Latin America, there were relatively few new initiatives in manufacturing, though some substantial industrial holdings were retained into the 1960s and even

[71] Anglo-Thai Board Minutes, 4 Mar. 1959, 8 July 1959, 10 Feb. 1960, 24 May 1960, 13 July 1960, Anglo-Thai Archives, MS 27008/12, GHL.
[72] Anglo-Thai Board Minutes, 30 Apr. 1969, 18 Nov. 1969, 22 Nov. 1970, Anglo-Thai Archives, MS 27068/13, GHL.
[73] Interview with Jeremy Brown, 21 Jan. 1999.
[74] T. Gibbons to D. C. Campbell, 12 Feb. 1963, MS 16876/8; T. Beven to A. D. Gibbs, 9 Aug. 1966, MS 16876/9, Antony Gibbs Archives, GHL.
[75] Ibid., A. D. Gibbs to T. Beven, 3 Nov. 1966, MS 16876/9.

later, and a few firms did make new investments. In East Asia, the British trading companies lost their long-established manufacturing operations in China, and did not become very active in Hong Kong's industrialization. In Malaysia and Singapore, it was not until the 1970s that the British agency houses became extensively involved in local manufacturing. In Africa, the British merchant firms were initially more active. African markets were not sufficiently attractive or familiar for many manufacturers to consider investments on their own, and the 'contacts' of the trading companies remained important assets. During the 1960s UAC as well as Holts made quite substantial investments in West Africa, especially in brewing and textiles, but by the 1970s growing political risks and the civil war in Nigeria had largely ended such investment. In East and Central Africa, Lonrho also made quite large investments in brewing, textiles, and bottling, though again with declining momentum by the 1970s.

For many firms, distribution, transportation, and other services were more congenial activities than manufacturing. Often companies had long been engaged in wholesaling of various types and also retailing activities such as the provision of cold stores. After 1945 a number of trading companies, both British and French, expanded their retailing interests, especially in Africa.[76] UAC had divested from its extensive general merchandising stores by the early 1960s, but in 1948 opened its first European-style departmental store in Lagos, Nigeria. This was a 'Kingsway store' and other such stores followed.[77] John Holt's investment in West African retailing also changed from general 'shops'—sold by the early 1960s—to more specialist retailing. In 1960 it acquired the West African Drug Co., a British firm which operated chemists stores in Nigeria, Ghana, and Sierra Leone. Branches in the latter two countries were later closed, but by the late 1960s the Nigerian business was profitable.[78] Holts also invested in wine retailing in Britain. In 1951 'shopkeeping' became one of Booker McConnell's four main divisions—along with sugar, rum, and shipping—and the firm built retail chains not only in Guyana and Trinidad, but also Zambia and Malawi.[79]

In Asia, the main company to develop retailing was Dodwells, but its initial involvement also began in Africa. The firm's East African branches had been established in 1951 for importing office equipment and other consumer merchandise, but when this business did not flourish in the face of import restrictions, Dodwells began opening retail stores, after initially rejecting the idea as being 'outside the Company's scope of activities'.[80] A subsidiary—Deacons—was established which obtained the franchise to sell Marks & Spencer 'St Michael' brand merchandise. The venture was closed

---

[76] Stanley C. Hollander, *Multinational Retailing* (East Lansing: Michigan State University, 1970), 33–41.

[77] Fieldhouse, *Merchant Capital*, 412–13.   [78] Annual Reports, John Holt, 1960–70.

[79] Hollander, *Multinational Retailing*, 131–2.

[80] Board Minutes, 24 Sept. 1957, Dodwell Archives, MS 27498/7, GHL.

in Tanzania because of political difficulties, but in 1966 the first branch was opened in Hong Kong, again to sell Marks & Spencer's goods as well as locally made clothes. A successful retailing business developed.[81]

There were also noteworthy developments in the companies' involvement in transportation services. Among the trading companies which were also shipowners, in 1946 Alfred Booth sold its shipping company with its long-established liner shipping services between northern Brazil, Britain, and the United States.[82] Booker McConnell, however, retained its Booker Line fleet serving Britain and Guyana. During the 1960s it introduced bulk carriers and acquired a fleet of trawlers for shrimping and fishing operations in the Eastern Caribbean. It was not until 1983 that Booker disposed of its ships.[83]

UAC and John Holt both also persisted with their own shipping lines, though both put them into separate companies—the Palm Line and Guinea Gulf Line—at the end of the 1940s, in response to various changes, including the creation of marketing boards which meant that control of home-bound cargoes largely passed out of company control. These shipping lines joined the West African shipping conferences. In 1964, as shipping volumes between the UK and West Africa fell and competition from locally based and other non-conference firms increased, Holts sold Guinea Gulf to the Nigerian state shipping company, though it continued to invest in its river fleet in Nigeria and in port services, though this business was disrupted by the Nigerian civil war. The Palm Line was poorly performing in the 1960s, but then profits soared with the Nigerian oil boom of the 1970s. The collapse of this boom led to large-scale losses and by 1986 UAC had sold all its ships.[84] UAC's once extensive coast and river transport fleet was sold in 1970, after heavy losses during the civil war period.[85]

In the Far East, both Jardine Matheson and—especially—Swire's remained major shipowners in this period. The former's Indo-China Steam Navigation Company maintained liner and tramp services and owned twenty-nine ships by 1979. Swire's China Navigation Company retained and developed extensive operations in the Asia-Pacific area, and in 1979 shipowning and operating contributed around one-third of John Swire's turnover and profits.

Many more firms remained involved in shipping agency work and provision of port facilities. Although Inchcape greatly reduced its shipping agency work, and the unsuccessful outcome of a merger proposal with the P&O Group in 1972 meant that the group's exposure to shipping remained modest compared to the past, Inchcape's affiliates continued to provide marine services of various kinds, including shipping agencies but also other activities. In the Gulf, for example, the building of ports meant that Gray

[81] Griffiths, *Inchcape Group*, 160.
[82] A. H. John, *A Liverpool Merchant House* (London: George Allen & Unwin, 1959), 157–8.
[83] Annual Reports, Booker McConnell, 1950–84.
[84] Fieldhouse, *Merchant Capital*, 184–94.   [85] Ibid. 194–203.

Mackenzie's traditional lightering business was not needed, but through the 1950s and 1960s the firm developed an extensive business in specialized craft working and servicing of offshore oil rigs. In 1972 Gray Mackenzie took over the operation of Dubai's new port.[86] Among the firms with continuing investment in ports and related facilities was Ocean Wilsons, which owned port, warehouse, and tug facilities in Brazil through the period. In 1978 Ocean Wilsons took a 35 per cent stake in a joint venture with Inchcape to provide services for the offshore oil industry in Brazil by the provision and operation of oilfield supply bases and ancillary services.[87]

During the interwar years trading companies had begun to act as airline agencies as the British government's airline, Imperial Airways, expanded its route network outside Europe. In the post-war period this became a very much more important business for many firms. This represented a positive response on the part of the trading companies to the challenge of the sharp decline from the 1950s of the long-distance transport of people by sea. Harrisons & Crosfield and Wilsons in Brazil were among the companies which acquired agencies for airlines, but it was the Hong Kong-centred firms that appeared especially aware of the potential of the industry. In November 1942, in the midst of the Pacific War, the chairman of Dodwells explained to his board during a discussion on the future of his company that the firm: 'should make every endeavour to obtain agencies for air transport. Commercial flying must, in the nature of things, make tremendous strides in the near future and it was incumbent on us to be in at the start.'[88]

Dodwells' two larger competitors went further and acquired their own airlines. After the end of the war Jardines established Hong Kong Airways in association with the successor to Imperial Airways, BOAC. This venture did not prosper and Jardines withdrew from it, and it was subsequently acquired by Cathay Pacific Airways. This airline had been started in 1946 by an American and an Australian, but in 1948 Swire's took a controlling stake in it. The airline was initially loss-making, but Swire's persisted and various companies also invested in the venture in 1952, including the Borneo Company and P&O, which took a 31 per cent shareholding. Although Swire's overall business strategy was in some respects cautious and incremental, the creation and expansion of Cathay Pacific—as well as some of the firm's shipping investments—involved very real and bold risks. By the 1960s Cathay Pacific had become a leading regional airline. In 1962 it acquired its first jet and in the early 1970s the introduction of wide-bodied aircraft enabled the company to establish routes to Australia and the Gulf, and in 1980 Cathay began flying from Hong Kong to London.[89]

    [86] Gray Mackenzie & Co. Ltd., undated (*c.*1970), Gray Mackenzie Archives, MS 27734A, GHL.
    [87] Annual Report, Ocean Wilson (Holdings) Ltd., 1978.
    [88] Board Meeting, 17 Nov. 1942, Dodwell Archives, MS 27498/5, GHL.
    [89] Gavin Young, *Beyond Lion Rock* (London: Hutchinson, 1988), *passim*; Sir John Swire to the author, 24 May 1999.

It was also in Hong Kong that British firms made large and profitable investments in real estate. Real estate was a traditional area for investment by trading companies everywhere, often stemming from their possession of wharves and warehouses at ports. Jardine Matheson controlled two long-established wharf and warehouse companies owning harbour property in Hong Kong and Shanghai, the Hongkong & Kowloon Wharf & Godown Company and the Shanghai & Hongkew Wharf Co. The latter owned 3,000 feet of the most valuable wharf frontage on the Shanghai side of the river, which was lost in 1949. Jardines also had a shareholding and a close relationship with the Hong Kong Land Investment Company, the owner of substantial real estate. In 1958 Jardines established a civil engineering affiliate—Gammon—which in the early 1970s expanded into building contracting and undertook a series of landmark developments in the colony, by then undergoing a huge property boom.

Swire's also became substantive owners of Hong Kong real estate. In the early 1970s Taikoo Dockyard was closed, as it was too small to handle containerized shipping, and in 1972 the sugar refinery was also closed in order to concentrate on specialized sugar products and packaging. This released a large area of land in the Quarry Bay area of Hong Kong. Instead of selling the land—the strategy followed by Swire's old allies the Holts for their Hong Kong property—Swire's decided to develop it themselves.[90] In 1972 they established Swire Properties and three years later began the development of one of Hong Kong's first major private housing estates—Taikoo Shing, eventually completed in 1986. By the 1980s Swire's were one of Hong Kong's largest property companies.

By the 1960s the enthusiasm for new investments in many developing countries had dissipated, in part because many of the earlier investments had not proved sustainable. The managements of many firms became increasingly concerned about political risks, as well as the problems of high taxes and exchange controls found in many countries, especially in South Asia and Latin America. British firms often felt their positions were particularly unfavourable, insofar as local firms often found ways to circumvent regulations or taxes, while they were either unable or unwilling to act in a similar fashion.[91]

Gibbs had a definite policy not to increase investment in Chile by the 1960s at the latest but instead to focus on countries where they could be more sure of receiving a worthwhile return in sterling, such as Australia.[92] The companies active in South East and East Asia also became preoccupied with political risk and concerned to diversify into developed countries. By 1953 the Borneo Company's strategy was already 'to reduce rather than increase

[90] Interview at Swire House, 28 Jan. 1999.
[91] Interview with Sir Colin Campbell, 16 Apr. 1996.
[92] H. K. Goschen to T. Gibbons, 21 June 1963, Antony Gibbs Archives, MS 16876/8, GHL.

its commitments in the East' and to reinvest 'in other safer territories'.[93] In 1959 Anglo-Thai's board resolved to make no more major investments in South East Asia, but to 'look to other countries within the Commonwealth for an expansion of its interests'. Dodwells considered the position of Hong Kong 'fraught with uncertainty' in 1954,[94] and a decade later the firm remained thoroughly alarmed by prospects in Hong Kong and Asia.[95]

For the British companies in Hong Kong, the 'Cultural Revolution' and the 1967 riots in the colony had a large psychological impact. Swire's sought to diversify out of Hong Kong while attempting to avoid the impression that they were leaving. The firm's investments in Australian cold storage and transport were expanded, and in the mid-1970s partial control was taken in James Finlay and Blythe, Greene, Jourdain, the latter in order to access the Malaysian market.[96] In the same decade, Jardine Matheson acquired trading interests in the Philippines, Hawaii, South Africa, and the Middle East, and formed a joint venture merchant bank with Robert Fleming, a family-owned firm with long-standing connections to the Keswicks.[97]

The strategy of many firms increasingly focused on 'safer' developed markets, initially in the Commonwealth, including Britain. Between 1946 and the late 1950s several British trading companies established or acquired small manufacturing operations in Canada, while Booker Brothers, McConnell invested in automobile spares and accessory wholesaling in 1954, Finlays in jute trading, and Wallace Brothers in real estate in 1958. In Australia during the 1950s, Dodwells, Guthries, and Balfour Williamson, the Borneo Company, Wallace Brothers, and Duncan Fox were among the firms which opened trading and other businesses. Swire's, which had had Australian interests in the nineteenth century, returned to the country in 1952 when the China Navigation Company began a service between Brisbane and Papua New Guinea, motivated by a search for a home for some of the ships displaced after their trade to and from China was stopped.[98] In the same year an investment was made in a small haulage company, followed in 1956 by the acquisition of a freezer trucking company, and in 1970 by the acquisition of a cold store company. On the other hand Dalgety, alarmed by the effects of a massive drought on the Australian wool industry, began a large-scale diversification into agricultural and food businesses in Britain, Canada, and the United States.

[93] Board Minutes, 24 Feb. 1953, Borneo Company Archives, MS 27178/24, GHL; White, *Business*, 237.
[94] Minutes of Conference Meetings of Directors, 18–28 Oct. 1954, Dodwell Archives, MS 27498/6, GHL.
[95] Board Minutes, 26 Jan. 1965, Dodwell Archives, MS 27498/7, GHL.
[96] Interview at Swire House, 28 Jan. 1999.
[97] Interview with Jeremy Brown, 21 Jan. 1999.
[98] Memorandum by Edward Scott, 7 May 1999.

During the late 1940s there were also modest investments in manufacturing and other activities in Britain. In 1949 Steels began insurance broking in London, and by the 1960s had diversified into life assurance and property development. By the 1960s there was growing interest in investment in Britain. While growing political risks in developing countries were a major factor, changes in UK tax laws also had an influence. In particular under the 1965 Finance Act the nature of corporation tax discriminated against firms with large overseas incomes who needed British profits to provide taxable allowances to offset overseas earnings. In 1964 Anglo-Thai's board heard of the 'need for the Corporation to look for additional sources of trading income and the advantages to be derived from UK taxed income'.[99] In the following year it tried to buy two Ford dealerships in the UK, but Ford objected to the control of two proximate dealerships by the same firm.[100] Consequently it was not until 1973 that the firm acquired a British Ford dealership, followed by a second firm in 1975 which included an industrial engine operation.[101] Among the other companies, Guthries began acquiring firms in Britain in various areas of rubber and carpet manufacture.

Harrisons & Crosfield was particularly active in building up business activities in Britain. The firm expanded into chemicals, especially from the late 1960s. By 1972 British industrial interests accounted for 24 per cent of total pre-tax profits, and two-thirds of these profits were from chemicals.[102] From 1960 Harrisons & Crosfield's joint venture affiliate, British Borneo Timber (renamed Sabah Timber in 1963) also began to invest in timber and general building merchandising in Britain in response to concerns about the viability of the large logging concessions held in Sabah. Before learning at the end of the 1960s that the concession would end in 1982, Sabah Timber began acquiring a number of small timber merchandising firms in Britain.[103]

Some firms tried their luck with multiple investments in Britain. During the 1960s John Holt (Liverpool) developed an insurance broking business, acquired a Ford automobile dealer, and expanded on a large scale into wines and spirits. In 1960 Holts purchased two French vineyards and a shipper and blender of Alsace and Bordeaux wines, and in the following year began buying small retail 'off-licences', mainly in the north of England. Later in the 1960s Holts established a factory in Liverpool which fermented 'British wines' from imported grape juice. By 1969 the firm had almost 80 retail wine outlets in Britain, and wines and spirits accounted for 25 per cent of group turnover. In 1967 Holts entered a joint venture in coin-operated

[99] Board Minutes, 4 Nov. 1964, Anglo-Thai Archives, MS 27008/13, GHL.
[100] Board Minutes, 22 Sept. 1965, 10 Nov. 1965, 18 Jan. 1966, ibid., MS 27008/13, GHL.
[101] Griffiths, *Inchcape Group*, 194–5.
[102] Company Position, 1973, Harrisons & Crosfield Archives, GHL.
[103] Report by Cazenove & Co. on Harrisons & Crosfield, Mar. 1984; Jones and Wale, 'Diversification Strategies'; G. Nickalls (ed.) *Great Enterprise: A History of Harrisons & Crosfield* (London: the firm, 1990).

launderettes and dry cleaning shops in Britain and by 1970 had forty-four such outlets.[104] James Finlay was another diversified investor. In 1965 it turned one of its Scottish textile mills into a malt whisky distillery, which it operated until 1972, closing the remaining mill in the previous year. In 1971 Finlays made its first investment in North Sea oil exploration, followed by a series of acquisitions in this sector, including in 1974 control of a Scottish oilfield supply and engineering services firm.[105]

The accelerating pace of investments in the UK peaked in the 1970s. Booker McConnell began buying engineering and food distribution companies in Britain from the late 1960s.[106] Inchcape focused on motor distribution in Britain, buying BEWAC, a firm which distributed in Nigeria and Britain in 1970, followed by a large distributor of British Leyland cars, Mann Egerton in 1973. The Anglo-Thai acquisition in 1975 bought further motor distributorships, and in 1978 the firm holding the exclusive Toyota distributorship in Britain was acquired.[107] Lonrho also invested in British motor distribution, buying in 1975 the sole British distributor of Volkswagen and Audi vehicles. By 1979 its British interests—which generated 62 per cent of total turnover but 42 per cent of pre-tax profit—included engineering and textile manufacturers, property and finance companies, printers and publishers, newspapers such as the *Glasgow Herald*, hotels and a Scottish whisky distiller, plus the former Holts wine and spirits business.[108]

During the 1960s UAC began to consider 'redeployment' of some of its capital and skills outside Africa. Initially UAC was concerned to find employment for its large staff of expatriate managers, but later risk avoidance became a more central issue, as Zaire and Nigeria fell into civil wars and other countries such as Ghana went bankrupt. The company made a number of modest investments in Europe, which mostly 'ended in more or less complete failure'.[109] The exception was the acquisition in 1969 of one of the two British dealerships for Caterpillar tractors—with whom UAC had had a long prior relationship in Africa.[110] In 1971 UAC adopted a more active policy of diversification designed 'to secure more balanced geographical distribution of Group operations by reducing our dependence on Africa'.[111] Unilever was anxious to develop new markets outside Europe at that time, but despite its urging, UAC focused on Europe and especially Britain and France.

UAC's 'redeployment' strategy was misconceived both in design and in execution. While geographical diversification made sense for independent trading companies, it made much less sense viewed as a part of Unilever, which had worldwide interests. The whole process also proceeded erratically. Following the 1973 oil prices rises, the economies of Nigeria and the Gulf

---

[104] Annual Reports, John Holt & Co. (Liverpool) Ltd., 1960–70.
[105] Annual Reports, James Finlay plc, 1965–80.
[106] Annual Reports, Booker McConnell, 1968–80.   [107] Jones, *Two Centuries*, 277–82.
[108] Annual Reports, Lonrho Ltd., 1970–9.   [109] Fieldhouse, *Merchant Capital*, 680.
[110] Ibid. 707–10.   [111] Ibid. 719–20.

boomed, and UAC was preoccupied with servicing its business in those countries. Acquisitions in Europe slowed. In the mid-1970s UAC's financial performance was outstanding. The collapse of the oil business in 1976 led to renewed European acquisitions, but then the second oil price boom at the end of the 1970s pushed many of the acquired firms into difficulty. UAC's diversification was also undertaken in a highly decentralized fashion, as it was its twenty-four divisions rather than the corporate centre that searched for and made acquisitions. The upshot was a considerable number of acquisitions of small firms engaged in multiple activities in Britain and elsewhere, including automobile body building and services, builders' merchants, pharmaceutical companies, and office equipment manufacturers. UAC experienced acute problems in absorbing numerous small companies.[112]

UAC was not alone in the poor performance of many of its investments. Harrisons & Crosfield succeeded in establishing a successful chemicals and timber business, Booker McConnell built an engineering and, especially, food distribution business in Britain, while Inchcape built a motor distribution operation in Britain. But the list of failed or unsuccessful diversifications was also long. Duncan Fox's fate was sealed by its failed geographical diversification strategy. The growing losses of its British metal printing and light engineering subsidiary contributed to the firm's heavy loss in 1971 and subsequent acquisition by Ralli.[113] Duncan Fox's Australian subsidiary also failed and was closed in 1973. The failure of UAC's 'redeployment' helped seal its fate also. In many cases, there was a serious misjudgement about the transferability of skills and knowledge which were in reality region-specific.

Through to the 1960s the search for new investment opportunities in the 'developed' Commonwealth—including Britain—was in line with the general pattern of post-1945 British FDI. The United States was *terra incognita* for most British firms and it was not surprising that the traders largely avoided it. There was some divestment. Alfred Booth sold its leather manufacturing business in the United States in 1942, and Finlays sold its tea distribution business in 1944. During the mid-1950s, Wilsons sold its New York subsidiaries which had once purchased merchandise for its South American business. Duncan Fox, Antony Gibbs, and Balfour Williamson retained US affiliates to service their Latin American business. Duncan Fox's New York affiliate was modest and not very profitable, and was eventually sold in 1971. Antony Gibbs' New York operation was larger and important for the finance of its Chilean business, though in the early 1960s part of the equity was sold.[114] During the 1950s Balfour Guthrie remained a substantial if slowly growing business, now based in New York and focused largely on trading, but this was closed in 1965.

[112] Fieldhouse, *Merchant Capital*, 716–62.
[113] Annual Reports, Duncan Fox, 1959–71.
[114] Correspondence between New York and Chile, 1960s, Antony Gibbs Archives, MS 16878/8 and MS 16881/17, GHL.

Among the few new entrants to the United States was John Holt, which founded a US affiliate to engage in trading, but it remained an inconsequential concern.[115] Harrisons & Crosfield also expanded its operations in the United States, which before the war were confined to the partly owned tea distribution business of Irwins-Harrisons-Whitney Inc. In 1945 the firm founded H&C (America) Inc. which imported a variety of products before concentrating on chemicals distribution in the late 1950s.[116] Harrisons & Crosfield's US interests remained at this modest level until the end of the 1970s, when the minority shareholders in Irwins-Harrisons-Whitney Inc. were bought out and a chrome chemicals manufacturer in Texas was acquired.[117]

It was only in the 1970s that the trading companies began to make their first US acquisitions. UAC began in 1977 to search for a US acquisition in medical diagnostic equipment, but never found one.[118] Among other British traders, Guthries purchased the US company which had imported its rubber in 1972, and after 1974 began buying small US manufacturing companies.[119] In 1974 Inchcape purchased a Californian-based international trading company, though the Californian office was subsequently closed. Other firms edged towards the United States as the decade progressed. In 1973 Jardine Matheson acquired a Hawaii-based trading company, while at the end of the decade Swire's invested in bottling and Booker McConnell in engineering companies. In 1979 Finlays opened an office in Houston, Texas, the start of a disastrous period of investment in Texan oil, Californian fruit farming, and other ventures.

The search for 'safe' investments in the developed world was not unique to British trading companies. All of the European trading companies whose traditional host regions became or looked risky searched for new opportunities, and 'coming home' was an obvious option. Dutch trading companies, whose extensive assets in Indonesia were nationalized in 1957, invested in manufacturing in the Netherlands during the 1960s. Hagemeyer, for example, invested in leatherware, kitchenware, cosmetics, and electrical manufacture in this period. Like many British trading companies, this strategy proved unsuccessful and had to be reversed from the 1970s.[120] In this comparative context, some British firms were notably more successful than the Dutch in 'evolving' into manufacturers or distributors in developed markets.

During the 1960s a number of firms also began to return to their historic origins as 'bankers' as well as merchants. Antony Gibbs, Wallace Brothers, and Matheson & Co. had always functioned as merchant banks, albeit on

---

[115] Annual Reports, John Holt & Co. (Liverpool), 1947–65.
[116] The H&C Organization in the USA, Dec. 1961, Harrisons & Crosfield Archives, GHL.
[117] Annual Reports, Harrisons & Crosfield, 1945–80.
[118] Fieldhouse, *Merchant Capital*, 711–13, 754–8, 747.
[119] Annual Reports, Guthrie Corporation, 1972–80.
[120] Keetie E. Sluyterman, 'Dutch Multinational Trading Companies in the Twentieth Century', in Jones (ed.), *Multinational Traders*, 93–5.

a small scale, but from the 1960s they and other firms expanded this side of their business in response to London's growth as an international financial centre, sometimes with fatal consequences. In the late 1960s Wallace Brothers became one of the fringe or 'secondary' banks which grew rapidly taking advantage of developments in the wholesale markets to engage in lending on property in particular at a time when Britain's clearing banks had their lending closely regulated by the government. Wallace's was submerged by the 'secondary banking crisis' which developed as the British property boom collapsed in 1973 and lost its independence three years later.[121] Finlays established an insurance broking subsidiary in 1965, but closed it in 1973 and opened a bank, which in turn was closed two decades later. Also in 1965 John Holt established a finance company in a joint venture with the merchant bank Hill Samuel designed to provide export finance, not only for African trade but also elsewhere. This was taken over by Lonrho in 1970, who bought out Hill Samuel, and turned the venture into a central purchasing, confirming, credit finance, and insurance company for the group.

Financial services proved to be another area where firms misjudged their competences. The business was risky and new entrants were obliged to take especially large risks to acquire market share. These risks were well understood by the cautious Swire's, who declined to become involved in financial services except insurance through a long-standing aversion to 'making money out of money'.[122] However their long-standing 'hands off' policy to affiliates meant that they permitted Finlays to lose considerable sums in this area. The best opportunities lay not in London, but in the host regions where the traders possessed the local knowledge and contacts which could facilitate safe lending. It was for that reason that Jardine Matheson's joint venture with Robert Fleming was able to become a considerable success.

Although in retrospect the changing strategies of the British traders can be understood and explained in terms of systematic factors, there was little strategy formulation in most firms, except in the bureaucratic UAC. There was a strong ethos in many companies that they were 'merchant adventurers', who could turn their skills to anything if it was a good deal.[123] As a result, business strategies were often opportunistic. Swire's, for example, were approached by Finlays to acquire a shareholding, and by Coca-Cola to become a bottler in Hong Kong and the United States.[124] In the 1970s Jardine Matheson were approached by firms in South Africa and the Middle East to invest in them, and responded because they seemed like profitable opportunities.[125]

---

[121] Pointon, *Wallace Brothers*, 97–9; Margaret Reid, *The Secondary Banking Crisis 1973–5* (London: Macmillan, 1982), 145–6.
[122] Interview with Sir John and Sir Adrian Swire, 30 July 1996.
[123] Interview with Sir Colin Campbell, 16 Apr. 1996.
[124] Interview at Swire House, 28 Jan. 1999.
[125] Interview with Jeremy Brown, 21 Jan. 1999.

The British firms often used their 'core' activities to fund diversification strategies. Harrisons & Crosfields used its profits from rubber plantations and logging to fund its growth in chemicals and timber merchants.[126] Swire's after the 1967 riots in Hong Kong continued to plough back profits into their Hong Kong ventures, but used the funds sent back to John Swire & Sons in London to expand outside Hong Kong, rather than to distribute as dividends.[127] UAC used its high profits from Nigeria to pay for its 'redeployment' strategies. James Finlay set aside profits from its tea business in the 1970s to fund its acquisitions in the United States.[128]

The difference between 'successful' and 'unsuccessful' diversification strategies was not in the degree of 'opportunism', but whether the firms had the competences to manage the opportunities that presented themselves. UAC or, on a smaller scale, Duncan Fox had no competence to manage the British manufacturing companies in which they invested, and could add no value to them. In general, it was firms that sought to expand incrementally, building on either regional or product-specific skills, which seem to have had the most successful outcomes. After the Second World War both Swire's and Harrisons & Crosfield provide major examples. Swire's expanded incrementally within the general areas of distribution and transport, moving from shipping to airlines, from sugar refining to bottling, and using the disused land from its dockyards and sugar refinery to enter real estate. The same incremental pattern can be observed in Harrisons & Crosfield, as it moved from chemicals distribution to manufacture and from logging to timber merchandising.

Overall, the post-Second World War decades saw the British traders continuing to 'reinvent' themselves. The handling of commodity exports of their host regions declined in importance or disappeared altogether, while firms refocused on importing more specialized products to which they could add value. Providing mere access to overseas markets was no longer a sufficient competitive advantage. The British merchant houses in the Far East and South East Asia rose from the ashes of the wartime destruction of their assets and built vibrant new businesses, becoming large-scale automobile distributors and even the owner of a major airline. However, the British trading companies in India and Latin America were notably unsuccessful in finding new strategies to fit changing circumstances. Many of the attempts by firms to invest in developed countries appear misconceived, either because firms lacked the capabilities or because the strategies employed were faulty. In some cases the opportunity cost of attempting to build a presence in Britain or elsewhere was the neglect of potential opportunities in host developing countries.

---

[126] Jones and Wale, 'Diversification Strategies'.
[127] Interview at Swire House, 28 Jan. 1999.
[128] Interview with Sir Colin Campbell, 16 Apr. 1996.

5.5 British Trading Companies *c.*1979

British trading companies remained large multinational firms at the end of the 1970s. Four firms were ranked among the largest 100 UK industrial companies in terms of turnover: Inchcape (19th), Lonrho (30th), Booker McConnell (64th), and Harrisons & Crosfield (91st).[129] John Swire & Sons was only ranked 461, but this excluded the unconsolidated Swire Pacific. Jardine Matheson, registered in Hong Kong, and UAC, wholly owned by Unilever, were also excluded. These three firms would otherwise also have been ranked among the largest 100 British firms in terms of turnover. As employers, some firms were also very significant. In 1979, Lonrho's worldwide employment was 140,000, UAC's 71,000, and Jardine Matheson's 50,000. Among the smaller firms Booker McConnell employed 18,560 persons worldwide and Boustead 4,000.

British trading companies did not occupy the equivalent position in the British economy as their counterparts in Japan. There was no British equivalent of Japan's *kigyo shudan* to give the trading firms a strategic position within a wider business group. However the larger British companies such as Inchcape and Harrisons & Crosfield can be regarded as 'general trading companies' by this date. Their businesses were spread widely, including Britain, and they had diversified activities. Inchcape operated in forty-four countries and marketed the products of 2,750 manufacturers. Apart from general merchandising, its activities included shipping, travel agents, port operators, timber sawmillers, tea producers, commodity dealing, and local manufacturing, though 40 per cent of its profits were derived from automobile distribution, and 60 per cent came from Hong Kong, Malaysia, and Singapore. Harrisons & Crosfield retained its large plantation business in South East Asia, alongside its general trading, chemicals, and timber business. In the 1970s the firm had eighty branches in twenty countries, including thirty in Asia, fourteen in Canada and the United States, and smaller numbers in Australia and Africa.

In a different category, but also very substantial enterprises, were the group of diversified regional trading companies. These included UAC and Lonrho, both of which counted among tropical Africa's largest business enterprises. Both firms had also invested elsewhere, with UAC in particular having trading business in the Gulf and the south Pacific, and operating in a total of thirty-nine countries. Swire's and Jardine Matheson were major Asia/ Pacific multinationals.

The thirty years after the end of the Second World War had shown the continued resilience of British merchant enterprise. Although British trading firms had almost disappeared from South Asia and Latin America, they had survived and 'reinvented' themselves in South East and East Asia

---

[129] *The Times 1000, 1979–1980.*

and in Africa, where they continued to benefit from informational asymmetries and to take advantage of their accumulated knowledge and contacts. Evidently the British trading companies in these decades did not match the pre-eminence of the *sogo shosha*. Nor did they evolve into large-scale commodity trading companies. The potential for evolution in this direction was constrained by the ownership of the firms, and by the fact that many of them had evolved too far beyond pure trading. The following chapters now turn to a closer examination of the managerial competences and organizational structures of the British trading companies between the late nineteenth century and the 1970s.

6

Business Groups

6.1 Introduction

The previous four chapters have examined the evolution of British trading companies over time, and explained their continued existence in terms of information, reputation, and contacts. Attention now turns to the systems of corporate governance, human resource management, and relationship building utilized by the British trading firms to derive competitive advantages. Chapters 9 and 10 examine how merchants managed long-lasting investments in natural resources and manufacturing.

Resource-based theories of the firm provide insights to understand the 'competences' of the trading companies. This literature builds on the basic premises that firms differ in their 'resources' and that these differences are relatively stable. These 'resources', variously known as 'competences' or 'capabilities', are accumulated over time and are embedded in a firm's routines and cultures.[1] The 'core competence' of a firm has been defined as 'the collective learning of the organisation, especially how to co-ordinate diverse production skills and integrate multiple streams of technology'.[2] This approach involves taking a more holistic analysis of a firm's resources, which consist not only of discrete resources, but also how the whole organization interacts.

Within this general framework, Kay identifies three 'distinctive capabilities' of firms which can contribute to competitive advantages. These are innovation, reputation, and 'architecture', defined as the 'network of relational contracts within, or around, the firm'. Kay distinguishes between three types of architecture: internal architecture (relationships with and among a firm's employees); external architecture (relationships with suppliers or customers); and networks (relations among a group of firms engaged in related activities). From this perspective, a firm's ability to build and sustain long-term relationships provides a critical source of competitive advantage.[3] Kay's principle concern is to identify those intangibles that give a particular firm

---

[1] This literature can be traced back to Edith T. Penrose, *The Theory of the Growth of the Firm* (Oxford: Oxford University Press, 1959). Seminal studies include Birger Wernerfelt, 'A Resource-Based View of the Firm', *Strategic Management Journal*, 5 (1984), 171–80 and Richard R. Nelson 'Why do Firms Differ, and How Does it Matter', *Strategic Management Journal*, 14 (1991), 61–74.

[2] C. K. Prahalad and Gary Hamel, 'The Core Competence of the Corporation', *Harvard Business Review*, 66 (1990).

[3] John Kay, *Foundations of Corporate Success* (Oxford: Oxford University Press, 1993).

a competitive advantage rather than to explain the competences of an entire species of firms such as trading companies. Nevertheless these concepts, notably that of architecture, provide tools and hypotheses to explore this wider issue.

A starting point is the organization of the diversified business built up by the trading companies. When British trading companies diversified they faced the challenge of how to organize increasingly complex businesses. In the late nineteenth-century United States, firms grew in size, and the manufacture of different products in different countries was undertaken within the boundaries of a firm. To handle diversity, a new type of organizational form—the multi-divisional structure (M-form)—appeared in the interwar years, which separated planning and coordination from operating divisions. The M-form has become widely accepted as the most appropriate organization form to manage such diversified firms.[4]

The British trading companies organized their diversified operations in different ways. Not only was there little attempt at divisionalization at least until the 1960s, but often full internalization was avoided. Instead, as in many developing countries and Japan, 'business groups' emerged consisting of constellations of firms linked by various forms of 'binding' including ownership relations, interlocking directorships, contacts, and ethnic ties.[5] The existence of business groups in developing countries has often been explained in terms of rent-seeking behaviour, a view reinforced by the Asian financial crises of the late 1990s. If any capability was identified, it was one of financial intermediation in conditions of capital market imperfection, but more recently important capabilities related to local knowledge and 'contacts' have also been stressed.[6] This debate finds strong resonances in interpretations of the 'clusters' or 'investment groups' around the British trading companies, which have been seen either as fragile forms of governance unable to sustain complex enterprises over the long term, or as rent-seekers serving the interests of the controlling family.[7]

This book casts the business groups around the British trading companies in a more dynamic light than as mere rent-seekers, showing that they had a wider range of functions related to imperfections in capital, labour, and product markets and to the need for property rights enforcement. They possessed competences which sustained long-lasting and relatively successful

[4] A. D. Chandler, Jnr, *Strategy and Structure* (Cambridge, Mass.; MIT Press, 1962); Oliver M. Williamson, *Markets and Hierarchies* (New York: Free Press, 1975).

[5] Mark Granovetter, 'Coase Revisited: Business Groups in the Modern Economy', *Industrial and Corporate Change*, 4 (1995), 93–150.

[6] Carl Kock and Mauro F. Guillén, 'Strategy and Structure in Developing Countries: Business Groups as an Evolutionary Response to Opportunities for Unrelated Diversification', Paper presented at Annual Conference of Academy of International Business, Vienna, 1998.

[7] Mira Wilkins, 'The Free-Standing Company, 1870–1914: An Important Type of British Foreign Direct Investment', *Economic History Review*, 41 (1988), 259–85; Stanley Chapman, *Merchant Enterprise in Britain* (Cambridge: Cambridge University Press, 1992); id., 'British-Based Investment Groups before 1914', *Economic History Review*, 38 (1985), 230–51.

international businesses and which gave them genuine efficiency-enhancing roles. This chapter examines the organizational characteristics of the business groups while Chapter 7 considers their management structures and systems.

6.2 A Typology of Business Groups

As British trading companies diversified over the course of the nineteenth century and especially after 1870, they organized their activities in a number of ways. Table 6.1 offers a typology identifying three organizational forms.

Three organizational patterns were employed between the 1870s and the 1970s. In the 'unitary' business groups activities were wholly owned, although this did not mean that they were integrated in the sense of a 'modern' corporation. The second, 'network', form consisted of a core trading company with multiple wholly owned branches surrounded by a cluster of partly owned firms linked not only by equity, but also debt, management, cross-directorships, and trading relationships. A variant of the type, called a 'loose network' here, had no corporate 'core' beyond family shareholdings.

The choice of organizational form was determined in part by the business portfolios of companies. Trading operations and acting as agents for shipping, insurance, and manufacturing firms were generally internalized. These activities required either a large knowledge base on the part of firms, or the maintenance of a sound reputation among actual or potential clients. Within 'network'-type business groups, these activities were the responsibilities of wholly owned branches. Trading companies whose business consisted primarily of trading and shipping agency and other agency work were mostly organized on a unitary basis.

In contrast, 'network'-type business groups were those that had diversified into plantations, mines, processing, and in some cases the ownership of shipping companies. Merchants made their profits from commissions on trade and agency business. As a result, they sought access to trade flows and information, and to prevent being denied access by being bypassed by parties they had brought together. Outright ownership of mines and plantations

TABLE 6.1 Typology of the business groups around British trading companies, *c.*1870s–*c.*1970s

	Organizational Form	Examples
A	Unitary	UAC; Booker Brothers, McConnell; Dodwells; Wilson, Sons
B	Network	Swire's; Jardine Matheson; James Finlay; Harrisons & Crosfield; Balfour Williamson
C	Loose Network	Grahams; Inchcape family

was, as a result, unnecessary. These 'network' groups therefore, placed their activities into separate partly owned firms, through which sufficient access was secured by non-equity modes.

If ownership of non-'core' activities could be shared, there were other advantages. It limited the risks of the parent trading companies, while enabling outside capital to be bought into ventures. This permitted the use of other people's money to undertake entrepreneurial investments designed to generate new sources of income for them through commission and fees. The trading companies were fully cognizant of this aspect of their strategy. 'As regards palm oil', the managing director of Guthries observed to the principal shareholder in the firm in 1928, 'we cannot afford to lock up our own capital in that direction, as one unit alone necessitates the provision of a very large sum. Through our associated companies, however, we are practically the pioneers of Malaya of the cultivation of this product on a large scale. . . . As agents for these companies we hope to benefit from this new venture.'[8] 'The policy of building up our business with other people's money', Jardine Matheson's manager in East Africa reported in 1937, 'is being rigorously pursued.'[9]

The prevailing conditions in nineteenth-century capital markets made the strategy of sharing ownership in affiliate firms very feasible. European expatriates and sometimes local people in host regions, or potential investors on the British stock exchanges, were faced by numerous opportunities to invest in plantations, mines, utilities, and virtually anything else as the nineteenth century progressed. They had, however, little information on whether such ventures were well managed or even honest. Many resource and commodity investments carried inherent risks, which the state of company law did little to modify. Companies operated in a veil of secrecy, even from their shareholders. In Britain, the Companies Acts of 1856 and 1862, which laid down the lines of modern corporate law, were extremely liberal and 'the most permissive in Europe'.[10] Public limited companies had no statutory obligations in revealing information, although a 'model' article of association stated that a printed copy of a balance sheet laid before an annual general meeting of shareholders should be sent in advance by post to each shareholder. British private limited companies, which were not even recognized until the Companies Act of 1907, did not have to reveal any information. It was not until the Companies Act of 1929 that it was stipulated in the case of British public companies that balance sheets should be sent to all shareholders prior to the annual general meeting, and not until 1948 that it stipulated that the profit and loss account also had to be circulated. The association of a reputable trading company with a new company

[8] John Hay to Lady Anderson, 8 June 1928, Guthrie Archives, G/MIS/9, SOAS.
[9] East African Report No. 6, 22 Sept. 1937, S/O London to Hong Kong 1937, JMA, CUL.
[10] P. L. Cottrell, *Industrial Finance* (London: Methuen, 1980), 52.

provided an assurance to investors of honest and competent management. Thus the merchants' desire to use other people's money was married to the desire of individual investors to reduce the risks of their portfolio.[11]

The other major influence on choice of organizational structure was the preference of the owners of the firm. A number of the family-owned businesses were especially concerned not to permit 'outsiders' access to their affairs. Dodwells' tea trading and shipping agency business was conducted by branches, but it also organized its salmon canneries, flour mills, and plantations in this way. Antony Gibbs also preferred to control most of its business through its interlocking partnerships, except its operations in Australia, where a number of partly owned ventures owning ranches, mines, and a wire netting manufacturer were limited companies.

In West Africa the British companies were largely concerned with trading and related activities which they conducted through their wholly owned branches. Only the rather modest ventures beyond this core business were placed in separate limited companies. This was the case of the tin mining companies promoted by the Niger Company. This firm also established a separate French subsidiary, Compagnie du Niger Français, in 1913 to operate in French West Africa. The general preference of these firms was for full control. When John Holt established its own steamship line, it was fully internalized within the firm rather than placed in affiliated firms as in the case of Swire's and Jardine Matheson.

After 1914 the West African trading firms continued to favour a more unitary approach. During the 1920s the diversification strategies of African & Eastern and, to a lesser extent, the Niger Company bequeathed the United Africa Company on its formation a considerable collection of subsidiary firms, mostly related to trade in West Africa, but also in East Africa, the Mediterranean, the Middle East, and Singapore, plus some small industrial firms in Britain. Although many of these were retained by UAC, they were organized as wholly owned subsidiaries. This reflected the overall Unilever policy to wholly own all its businesses.[12] In this respect UAC did not employ a 'network' form of organization. On the other hand it was not a single integrated business either, as UAC's London headquarters presided over a complex of semi-autonomous (if wholly owned) enterprises, often using their original names such as G. B. Ollivant, and registered in Britain, France, or Belgium.[13] Ollivants continued through the 1960s and 1970s to function almost independently of UAC, and competed directly with UAC in some of its trading business.[14]

[11] Jean-François Hennart, 'Transaction Cost Theory and the Free-Standing Firm', in Mira Wilkins and Harm Schröter (eds.), *The Free-Standing Company in the World Economy 1830–1996* (Oxford: Oxford University Press, 1998), 71–2.
[12] D. K. Fieldhouse, *Merchant Capital and Economic Decolonization* (Oxford: Clarendon Press, 1994), 622–3.
[13] Ibid. 26–30.   [14] Ibid. 157–9.

Among the other trading companies, Booker Brothers, McConnell also employed a hierarchical structure. Its trading, plantation, shipping, and other businesses were in the hands of wholly owned subsidiaries. The exceptions were a number of companies in Africa and in the West Indies—such as two small retail businesses in Trinidad—where former proprietors of acquired firms had retained a shareholding. In 1951, the lowest share of the equity held in any affiliate was 60 per cent.[15]

During the post-war decades the unitary forms of business group came under two kinds of pressure. The first was that firms which wished to diversify into manufacturing in particular needed joint ventures to access technical expertise. UAC began to move beyond full ownership of its businesses after the Second World War as the firm used joint ventures to develop non-trading interests in West Africa. An early and important example was the creation of Nigerian Breweries Ltd. in 1946, a Nigerian registered company in which UAC and Heineken jointly owned 33.3 per cent of the equity. In the same year UAC formed a joint venture with the British construction firm Taylor Woodrow.[16] At about the same time Holts also began to enter modest joint ventures; one of the earliest was with another British construction company, Richard Costain.

Secondly, in the immediate post-colonial period, as many governments sought to curtail or limit foreign investments in their economies, they encouraged local participation in shareholdings, and in some cases obliged it. Consequently the trading companies came under considerable pressure in many host economies to form locally registered companies with local equity participation. During the 1960s the newly independent African states began to urge or pressure foreign companies to take a local shareholding. Booker McConnell's retailing business in Africa was 'localized' in this fashion in this decade. In 1968 the firm sold half the equity of its Zambian stores to the government in return for a 49 per cent interest and a management contract in the new corporation which acquired them and a number of other retail stores.[17]

In West Africa, the wholly owned structure of UAC was eventually broken up by host government pressure for localization. During and after the 1950s, UAC turned some of its overseas branches into locally registered companies, but these remained 100 per cent owned. However in the early 1960s the firm began to come under pressure for localization of the equity, initially in Ghana, the first country in Black Africa to become independent. UAC began to consider selling equity of Ghanaian subsidiaries in the early 1960s in order to improve its public image, and eventually in 1967 it sold

[15] Annual Report 1951, Booker Brothers, McConnell, 'family tree'.

[16] Fieldhouse, *Merchant Capital*, 384–7.

[17] Stanley C. Hollander, *Multinational Retailing* (East Lansing: Michigan State University, 1970), 131–2.

II per cent of the equity of its Kingsway stores. Government pressure in-tensified subsequently and by 1976 most UAC businesses in Ghana had a local participation of 40 per cent, leaving UAC in management control.[18]

However, it was Nigeria where the biggest change to UAC's organ-ization occurred. Nigeria was the UAC's largest single host economy. The pressure for localization was delayed until 1970 by the civil war, but thereafter government pressure increased and in 1974 40 per cent of UAC's business in Nigeria was sold to the public. The price was set by the government and considerably undervalued the company, while half of the proceeds had to be reinvested in Nigeria. Further government legislation in 1977 reduced the UAC shareholding in UAC (Nigeria) to 40 per cent.[19] This dilution of ownership changed the nature of UAC's organization. In 1973 the company was renamed UAC International (UACI). This presided over a substantial number of separate companies, only some of which were wholly owned.[20] These 'localizations' had considerable consequences. The most obvious was the reduction in the flow of profits and dividends to the parent company, but for a firm such as Unilever there was even greater con-cern about the moral hazard and reputational implications of losing control of their affiliates to local managements whose standards of ethical conduct were not those prevailing in Europe.

While some of the largest trading companies preferred full ownership of their business groups, most of the 'hybrid' trading companies used network forms of organization. By 1870 use of 'networks' of partly owned affiliates was well established, especially in the Indian managing agencies, but not well developed. However, over the following decades, large and complex business groups organized as networks developed as the trading companies diversified their activities and took full advantage of the capital availability in Britain by floating new 'free-standing' companies on the British or colonial capital markets. Both trading companies which retained the partnership form and those that had incorporated adopted this organizational form.

The scale and complexity of the business groups organized around trading companies varied considerably by 1914. Table 6.2 shows the organization of John Swire & Sons around 1914.

The headquarters of John Swire & Sons was in London after 1870. The head office provided agency services for its affiliated firms and for Alfred Holt's Ocean Steamship Company. Among other tasks, London recruited the expatriate staff for the Far East and the affiliated companies, and handled contracts for the building of new vessels for its fleets. In the East the firm operated under the name of Butterfield & Swire—in practice they were one firm—which was jointly headquartered in Hong Kong and Shanghai. Butterfield & Swire had a network of wholly owned branches in China and two in Japan.

[18] Fieldhouse, *Merchant Capital*, 37–8.   [19] Ibid. 662–74.   [20] Ibid. 52–78.

TABLE 6.2 John Swire & Son 'group', *c*.1914

Wholly owned branches	Date opened	Principal activities in addition to imports, shipping, and insurance agencies
United Kingdom		
London	1870[a]	Head office of John Swire & Sons; management services for affiliated companies; London agency of Ocean Steamship Company
China		
Shanghai	1867	Head office for Butterfield & Swire
Hong Kong	1870	Head office for Butterfield & Swire
Foochow	1872	
Swatow	1882	
Kiukiang	1886	
Tientsin	1886	
Hankow	1887	
Canton	1892	
Amoy	1896	
Tsingtao	1890s	
Japan		
Yokohama	1867	
Kobe	1888	

Principal affiliates	Date started/ acquired	% equity held	Place of registration	Principal activity
China Navigation Co.	1872	'Largest stake'	London	Shipping; 50 per cent of Tientsin Lighter; 33 per cent of Luen Steamship Co.
Taikoo Sugar Refining Co.	1881	?17%	London	Sugar refining
Tientsin Lighter Co.	1904	50% CNC	London	Lighter services
Taikoo Dockyard and Engineering Co.	1908	Majority	London	Dockyards

[a] Established in Liverpool 1832, head office moved to London in 1870.

Source: Swire Archives, SOAS; S. Sugiyama, 'A British Trading Firm in the Far East: John Swire & Sons, 1867–1914', in S. Yonekawa and H. Yoshihara (eds.), *Business History of General Trading Companies* (Tokyo: University of Tokyo Press, 1987).

John Swire & Sons held shareholdings in all its affiliated firms. The China Navigation Company was established with most of the initial capital put up by the Swires and their close associates, and in 1911 the firm 'and [its] retired partners' still held 'the largest stake in the Company'.[21] The Taikoo Sugar Refinery was also established in the same fashion, but more capital may have been sold to outsiders over time. In 1934, the firm held a 17 per cent stake.[22] The Taikoo Dockyard and Engineering Company was majority owned. When the company was founded, John Swire & Son received a large percentage of the shares and debentures as a consideration for the expenditure it had incurred in setting up the Hong Kong shipyard earlier in the 1900s, but thereafter outside capital was also attracted. The Tientsin Lighter Company was a joint venture between Swire's and Alfred Holt designed to serve the China Navigation Company, and it was jointly owned by the two firms. The equity relationship formed an important component of the 'binding' between Swire's and its affiliates, but as important were the agency agreements, cross-directorships, and flows of funds between the parent and the affiliate.

A second example of a network form of a business group before 1914 can be provided by Harrisons & Crosfield. This firm had a different business profile from Swire's and this was reflected in the different organizational structure shown in Table 6.3.

As in the case of Swire's, the London head office presided over a network of wholly owned branches and affiliated companies. The branches traded in teas and later other commodities, acted as agents for shipping and insurance companies, and provided plantation management services. The firm's diversification into tea plantations in Ceylon and later India after 1899, and rubber plantations in Malaya from 1903, was made by establishing separate plantation companies. Although Harrisons & Crosfield's interests spanned a number of countries, the affiliates specialized in one country. For example, the Lunuva (Ceylon) Tea & Rubber Estates Ltd., established in 1908, owned tea and rubber plantations in Ceylon. Harrisons & Crosfield's share of the equity of these companies in 1914 varied from under 1 per cent to over two-thirds. Shareholdings were held by the firm itself, or through the Rubber Plantations Investment Trust, which Harrisons & Crosfield controlled through a large but not majority shareholding.[23] The plantation companies were formed and floated on the London market, but another component of the 'group', Irwin-Harrisons & Crosfield Inc., was registered in the USA. This was formed in 1914 by a merger of the firm's New York tea importing affiliate, Harrisons & Crosfield Inc., and A. P. Irwin & Co. of Philadelphia. Harrisons & Crosfield held 20 per cent of the shares—and half the seats on the board—while over two-thirds of the capital was taken by the Irwin family.

[21] J. D. Scott to J. Bruce Ismay, 29 May 1911, Swire Archives, JSSI/1/15, SOAS.

[22] John Swire & Sons to V. Grayburn, 9 Nov. 1934, Swire Archives, JSSI/4/13, SOAS.

[23] R. A. Brown, *Capital and Entrepreneurship in South-east Asia* (London: Macmillan, 1994), 57–8.

TABLE 6.3 Harrisons & Crosfield 'group', *c.*1914

Wholly owned branches	Date opened	Principal activities in addition to import, shipping, and insurance agencies
United Kingdom		
London	*c.*1845[a]	Head office: secretarial services to plantation companies
South East Asia		
Kuala Lumpur, Malaya[b]	1907	Rubber export, plantation management
Medan, Sumatra, Dutch East Indies[b]	1910	Rubber export, plantation management, engineering workshops
Batavia, Java, Dutch East Indies[b]	1911	Tea and rubber export, plantation management
South Asia		
Colombo, Ceylon[b]	1895	Tea and rubber export, plantation management
Calcutta, India[b]	1900	Tea export, plantation management
Quilon, India[b]	1912	Tea and rubber export, plantation management, engineering workshops
Elsewhere		
New York, USA	1904	Tea import and distribution
Montreal, Canada[b]	1905	Tea and rubber import, chemicals distribution
Melbourne, Australia	1910	Tea and rubber import, general distribution
Wellington, New Zealand	1910	Tea and rubber import, general distribution

Principal affiliates	Date started	% of equity held	Place of registration	Principal activities
*c.*40 plantation companies	1903–14	<1%–70%	London[c]	Rubber and tea plantations
Rubber Plantations Investment Trust Ltd.	1908	?30–50%	London	Holding shares in plantation companies
Irwin-Harrisons & Crosfield Inc.	1914	?20%	New York	US tea trading

[a] The first office was opened in Liverpool in 1844, but the partnership early established a second office in the City of London, which soon became the centre of the firm's operations.
[b] In these countries Harrisons & Crosfield had branch offices in a number of locations in addition to the main offices listed here.
[c] In the case of several companies with plantations in Java, the London-registered company was merely a holding company for a wholly owned and locally registered operating company.

Sources: One Hundred Years as East India Merchants: Harrisons & Crosfield 1844–1943 (London: the firm, 1944); annual reports and board minutes of individual plantation companies; Harrisons & Crosfield lists of shareholdings in 'secretarial' companies; all in Harrisons & Crosfield Archives, Guildhall Library, London.

TABLE 6.4 Balfour Williamson 'group', *c.*1914

Wholly owned branches and partnerships	Date opened	Principal activities
United Kingdom		
Balfour Williamson		
London	1899	Head office from 1909; secretarial services; share underwriting
Liverpool	1851	
Chile		
Williamson Balfour		
Valparaíso	1852	Selling and managing agents
Concepción	1889	
Valdivia	1903	
Santiago	1904	
Williamson & Co.	1911	Nitrate, grain milling, investments
Peru		
Milne & Co.		
Lima	1912	Oil company agents
United States		
Balfour Guthrie		
San Francisco	1869	Selling and managing agents; agricultural land
Portland, Oregon	1876	
Tacoma, Washington State	1888	
New York	1889	
Los Angeles, California	1895	
Canada		
Vancouver	1911	Trading in fish oil, newsprint, and wood pulp

Principal affiliates	Date started	% equity held	Place of registration	Principal activities
Pacific Loan and Investment Co.	1878	? Majority	UK	Mortgage loans; farms and ranches in California
Balfour Guthrie Investment Co.	1889	? Majority	USA	Investment company
*c.*5 wharf and warehouse companies	1880–1900		USA	Grain storage and handling facilities in California and Oregon
W. F. Stevenson & Co.	1904	25%	Philippines	Trading

TABLE 6.4 (*cont'd*)

Principal affiliates	Date started	% equity held	Place of registration	Principal activities
Lobitos Oilfields	1908	Minority	UK	Peruvian oil production/oil tankers
Sociedad Comercial Harrington Morrison & Co.	1910	75%	Chile	Trading in north Chile
West Coast Oil Fuel Co.	1911	30%	USA	Chilean oil storage 70% Standard Oil
Olympic Portland Cement	1911	?1%	UK	Cement plant, Washington State
Crown Mills Corporation	1911	100%	US	Flour mills, Portland, Oregon
Santa Rosa Milling Co.	1913	45%	UK	Flour mills in Chile and Peru
Sociedad Molinero de Osorno	1913	100%	Chile	Flour mill in Southern Chile

Source: Balfour Williamson Archives, UCL; Wallis Hunt, *Heirs of Great Adventure*, vols. i and ii (London: the firm, 1951 and 1960).

Contracts and cross-directorships bound the group together. Harrisons & Crosfield acted as secretaries and/or agents to almost all the plantation companies in which it held equity shares. In most cases, it acquired those functions at the company's formation. The secretarial function was performed in Britain and included the provision of management support to the board of an individual plantation company. The overseas branches performed the agency function which involved the management of the business on the spot, and the collecting and transmitting to individual company boards in Britain all relevant information to assist decision-making. Each agency agreement would put one or two of Harrisons & Crosfield's own directors on the plantation company's board.

Balfour Williamson provides a third variant example of a 'business group' on the eve of the First World War. Unlike the other two examples, this firm retained the partnership form in 1914, and was also distinguished by the diversity of its geographical and business interests along the Pacific coast of the Americas, which apart from cereal and grain trading, included substantial financial services, oil production and transport, flour milling, and cement production. Table 6.4 describes the main components of the group in 1914.

At the heart of the group were a number of interlinked partnerships. Balfour Williamson's head office was in Liverpool until 1909 and thereafter in London. The two other core partnerships were Williamson Balfour & Co. in Chile and Balfour Guthrie & Co. in the United States. From 1912, there was a fourth main element in the group in the form of an equal shares partnership in Peru between Balfour Williamson and the Milne family, with whom Balfour Williamson had long connections. A fifth partnership, Williamson and Company, was formed in 1911 under Chilean law which took over the nitrate and grain business, milling agencies, and other business from Williamson Balfour, apparently as a device to avoid British income tax.[24] The partnerships in the United States and Chile each operated from a number of branch offices which were wholly owned and an integral part of the partnership. The affiliated companies of the group were owned with varying proportions of equity, some were UK and others foreign registered, and some were private and others public companies.

Contracts and cross-directorships were again used to bind the group together. The first chairman of Olympic Portland Cement was a Williamson; another Williamson was chairman of Sociedad Comercial Harrington, Morrison & Co. The senior partner of Balfour Williamson, Lord Forres, also served as chairman of many of the largest affiliates. Balfour Guthrie, Williamson Balfour, and Milne & Co. also acted as selling agents and managers for affiliated concerns. Balfour Guthrie's Seattle office, for example, were managing agents of Olympic Portland Cement. They negotiated all the factory construction contracts and supervised them, and then undertook the entire business management of the cement plant. In the case of Lobitos Oilfields, Milne & Co. managed the Peruvian oilfields and were selling agents in Peru, while Williamson Balfour acted as selling agents in Chile.

This organizational pattern of core partnerships/branches and affiliated limited companies was widespread in 1914. However there were many firm-specific variations in shareholding proportions and the nature of linkages between groups. Moreover, there were not entirely consistent patterns in the use of different modes. The Borneo Company, for example, used its wholly owned branches to own and manage not only its trading and agency business but also its large Thai teak business, though its Indian jute mill, Singapore brickworks and Dutch East Indies tea plantation were owned in 1914 by Indian, Singapore, and British-registered companies respectively.[25]

For the most part the basic organizational pattern of the network form of business groups as they had developed by the early twentieth century remained in place until at least the 1960s. The creation of new affiliate firms to undertake non-trading activities continued, and in the 1920s a new

[24] Hunt, *Heirs*, ii. 85.
[25] Geoffrey Jones and Judith Wale, 'Merchants as Business Groups: British Trading Companies in Asia before 1945', *Business History Review*, 72 (1998), 367–408.

generation of partly owned 'free-standing' companies was floated on the British capital market. Harrisons & Crosfield, for example, continued to expand its rubber plantation interests using this mode. In the mid-1920s it floated a new plantation company, Allied Sumatra Plantations Ltd., and in 1921 it also consolidated a number of tea and rubber plantations in southern India into one company, Malayalam Plantations. These new companies were linked by agency and secretarial agreements which were virtually identical to those made before 1914.

After 1929, British exchange controls on investments outside the sterling Area as well as the perceived risks of international investment effectively ended the flotation of new firms on the British capital markets. However well before then the trading companies had begun to make more use of locally registered firms or other types of institutional arrangement. The growing burden of British taxation on companies whose profits were earned largely abroad during and after the First World War was initially an important consideration, and this led to the registration of several 'affiliated' firms being shifted. In 1915, Jardine Matheson's Indo-China Steam Navigation Company shifted its head office from London to Hong Kong. This had the effect of making the company only liable for tax on profit remitted to and distributed from London. Shareholders on the London register still had tax deducted from their dividends, but those on the Hong Kong register and resident there—which included Jardine Matheson itself—escaped it.[26] In 1921 James Finlays' Champdany Jute Co., founded as a Glasgow company in 1873, shifted registration to India. Finlays believed that they would save £30,000 that year in income tax by such a move.[27] During the interwar years locally registered firms were used often to locate new activities. For example, the motor distribution companies established by the Borneo Company and Dodwells respectively in the 1920s and 1930s were locally registered.

A number of the larger network-forms of business group consisted only of locally registered affiliates in the interwar years. This was the case of Duncan Fox. Duncan Fox had branches in Chile and Peru which directly owned facilities such as warehouses. It also controlled through partial ownership, agency agreements, and cross-directorships six locally registered affiliates. Three of these were registered in Peru: La Fábrica Aceite San Jacinto, which owned two cotton seed crushing mills; Fábrica Tejidos La Unión, which owned a cotton ring spinning and weaving mill; and Cía Agricola San Antonio, which owned a cotton estate. Three more affiliates were Chilean: Cía Refinería de Vina del Mar, which owned a sugar refinery, Cía Molinera El Globo, a flour milling company, and Sociedad Explotodora de Tierra del Fuego. This sheep farming concern in the extreme south of

[26] C. H. Ross to D. Landale, 8 Oct. 1915, 29 Oct. 1915, 12 Nov. 1915, S/O London to Hong Kong Sept. 1915–Mar. 1916, JMA, CUL.

[27] Finlays Calcutta to J. Kay Muir, 12 Jan. 1921, Finlays Archives, UGD 91/279; James Finlay to Shareholders of Champdany Jute Co., 2 Sept. 1921, UGD 91/447/6/2.

Chile was Duncan Fox's largest affiliate. In the mid-1930s it had about 1.3 million sheep, grazing on 2.5 million acres of its own land in Chile, plus leased land from the Chilean government and a small amount of land in Argentina which was also owned.[28]

There were also other alternatives, including the use of joint ventures. Before 1914, British trading companies had seldom used the joint venture form. A partial exception had been Jardine Matheson's joint venture with the Hongkong Bank, the British and Chinese Corporation, formed in 1898, but even in that case at least 70 per cent of the subscribed capital was placed outside the promoting companies and their networks of associations.[29] In the interwar years, a number of genuine joint ventures were created. A major example was Harrisons & Crosfield's joint venture in logging in North Borneo with the British North Borneo Co. formed in 1920. Harrisons & Crosfield initially owned around 42 per cent of the equity of the British Borneo Timber Co. Ltd., but was responsible for the development of the firm, both as regards technical expertise in developing logging and sawmilling and as regards creating markets for the various hardwoods.[30]

Tables 6.5 and 6.6 show the organizational pattern of two business groups arranged around trading companies at the end of the 1930s. They show a structure very similar to that prevailing in 1914.

James Finlay was presided over by its Glasgow head office which maintained wholly owned branches in London and South Asia. The Scottish textile mills were also wholly owned by the firm. However the firms' tea plantations, jute and cotton mills, and sugar refining businesses were in separate companies, as were its warehousing, packaging, and blending and chocolate manufacturing businesses in Britain. A number of the affiliates had their own wholly owned overseas offices, and the major tea plantation companies held equity in each other. The Finlay branches performed the usual secretarial and managing agency functions for the affiliated firms in India, but not in East Africa—where no branch was established—nor for the Anglo-American Direct Tea Trading Co.'s tea distribution in Canada and the United States.

Jardine Matheson's organization was a little different. The head office and place of registration was in Hong Kong, and formally Jardine Matheson owned and controlled Matheson & Co. in London, though in practice, ultimate control lay with the proprietors in Scotland. Jardine Matheson in 1938 had a dozen or so wholly owned branches in China and one in Japan, the branch in New York having been closed in 1931. Its affiliated companies, for most of which it acted as agents and secretaries, were mainly registered

[28] Midland Bank General Managers Diaries of Interviews, Lancashire Section, 4 May 1934, Acc 30/126, HSBC Group Archives.

[29] F. H. H. King, *History of the Hongkong Bank*, vol. ii (Cambridge: Cambridge University Press, 1988), 295–7.

[30] Records of British Borneo Timber Co., Harrisons & Crosfield Archives, GHL.

TABLE 6.5 James Finlay 'group', *c.*1938

Wholly owned branches	Date opened	Principal activities in addition to import, shipping, and insurance (including Lloyd's) agencies
United Kingdom		
Glasgow	1765	Head office: secretarial services to plantation and other companies
Catrine and Deanston	1801/6	Textile mills
London	1871	Secretarial services to plantation companies
South Asia		
Bombay, India	1862	Textile mill management
Calcutta, India	1870	Jute mill management
Karachi, India	1890	Cotton ginning management
Chittagong, India	1901	
Vizagapatam, India	1932	Manganese ore exports
Colombo, Ceylon	1893	Plantation management; warehouses

TABLE 6.5 (cont'd)

Principal affiliates	Date started/ acquired	% of equity held	Place of registration	Principal activities
Golabarry Co.	1872	95	India	Calcutta jute milling
Champdany Jute Co.	1873	95	India	Calcutta jute milling
Consolidated Tea and Lands Co.	1896	?30[a]	Glasgow	Indian tea plantations
Amalgamated Tea Estates Co.	1896	?30[a]	Glasgow	Indian tea plantations
Kanan Devan Hills Produce Co.	1897	?30[a]	Glasgow	Indian tea plantations; rice milling
Anglo-American Direct Tea Trading Co.	1898	?30[a]	Glasgow	Indian tea plantations; tea distribution in Canada and USA; office in Taiwan
Swan Mill	1908	?30	India	Bombay textile mills
Finlay Mills	1908	?30	India	Bombay textile mills
United Provinces Sugar Co.	1912	?30	India	Sugar refining in United Provinces
Belsund Sugar Co.	1932	100	India	Sugar refining in Bihar
African Highlands Produce Co.	1926	100	Glasgow	East African tea plantations
P. R. Buchanan & Co.	1894	?30	London	Agents for Indian tea plantations; tea warehousing in UK; selling agents for coffee, cocoa, and other products
George Payne & Co.	c.1900	?30	London	Packing and blending of tea, coffee, and cocoa in UK; chocolate manufacture in UK; offices in Colombo (Ceylon), Calcutta (India), Durban (South Africa)

[a] The tea companies also held cross-shareholdings in one another.

Source: J. Brogan, James Finlay & Co Limited (Glasgow: Jackson Sons & Co., 1951); James Finlay Archives, University of Glasgow.

TABLE 6.6 Jardine Matheson 'group', *c.*1938

Wholly owned branches	Date opened	Principal activities
United Kingdom		
Matheson & Co.	1848	Banking, insurance, secretarial services, tea and egg imports
China Coast		
Jardine Matheson		
Canton	1832/43	
Hong Kong	1844	Head office
Shanghai	1844	
Foochow	1854	
Peking	1861	
Swatow	1861	
Tientsin	1861	
Hankow	1860s	
Chung King	1860s	
Tsingtao	1860s	
Taipei	1860s	
Japan		
Kobe	1890s	

TABLE 6.6 (*cont'd*)

Principal affiliates	Date started/ acquired	% of equity held	Place of registration	Principal activities
Canton Insurance Office	1836	?	Hong Kong	Marine, fire, accident insurance
Hong Kong Fire Insurance	1868	?	Hong Kong	Marine, fire, accident insurance
Shanghai & Hongkew Wharf	1875	?	Hong Kong	Shanghai wharves and warehouses
Hong Kong & Kowloon Wharf & Godown	1886	7	Hong Kong	Hong Kong wharves and warehouses
Indo-China Steam Navigation Co.	1881	?	UK	Ocean shipping
Hong Kong Land Company	1889	?	Hong Kong	Hong Kong real estate
Lombard Insurance Co.	1895	100	UK	Formerly reinsurance; mostly investments
Ewo Yuen Press Packing Co.	1919	100	Hong Kong	Packing in Shanghai
Ewo Cold Storage Co.	1920	100	Hong Kong	Manufacture and export of dried eggs, Shanghai
Ewo Cotton Mills Ltd.	1921	12	Hong Kong	Shanghai cotton mills
Jardine Engineering Corporation	1923	100	Hong Kong	Engineering agencies in China
Ewo Breweries	1936	100	Hong Kong	Shanghai beer brewing
Various East African companies	1936	?	East Africa	Plantations; mines in East Africa

Sources. Jardine Matheson Archives, CUL; Edward Le Fevour, *Western Enterprise in Late Ch'ing China,* (Cambridge, Mass.: East Asian Research Center, 1968)

TABLE 6.7 The 'real' size of Harrisons & Crosfield and Guthries, 1922 and 1932
(£ million)

	Harrisons & Crosfield		Guthries	
	Capital employed	'Real' capital employed	Capital employed	'Real' capital employed
1922	2.5	10.8	0.2	5.1
1932	2.8	16.3	0.4	9.7

Source: Geoffrey Jones and Judith Wale, 'Diversification Strategies of British Trading Companies: Harrisons & Crosfield *c.*1900–*c.*1980', *Business History*, 41 (Apr. 1999), 72.

in Hong Kong. Before 1914 they generally took the form of public limited companies in which only a share of the equity was held. This category included the Ewo Cotton Mills Ltd., formed in 1921 by a merger of Jardine's Ewo Cotton & Spinning Co. with two newly acquired Shanghai mills. However the new investments made in the interwar years remained wholly owned private companies. Jardines were interested in floating such companies, but their poor profitability in the interwar years did not provide suitable circumstances.[31]

It is difficult to establish the contours and size of the 'network' business groups before the Second World War. The net capital employed of parent trading companies only partially captures the dimensions of business groups with many partly owned affiliates. Table 6.7 estimates the 'real' size of the Harrisons & Crosfield and Guthries business groups, including the net assets of the many plantation companies which the firms controlled.

The table shows the 'real size' of the two business groups was much larger than for the parent company alone. This was particularly the case for Guthries. A comparison can be made with the British overseas banks active in Asia in the same period. In 1922 the net capital employed of the Hongkong Bank was £9.5 million, that of Chartered Bank £6.8 million, and of Mercantile Bank of India £2.3 million. Ten years later the respective figures were £8.4 million, £6 million, and £2.1 million. While the capital employed figures of the primarily 'unitary' organizations such as UAC, Booker Brothers, McConnell, and Dodwells can be taken as a reasonable proxy for the size of their whole operations, this is not the case for many other firms employing network forms.

A complication is that the boundaries of these business groups were permeable in a number of respects. As new activities were spun off into separate companies, there was an ongoing process of new firm creation.

[31] J. J. Paterson to D. G. M. Bernard, 10 Dec. 1936, S/O Hong Kong to London, 1936, JMA, CUL.

Moreover the boundaries of groups were blurred in other respects. In the case of Jardine Matheson, the affiliates listed in Table 6.6 were 'bound' to the parent firm through ties of equity, contracts, and cross-directorships, which enabled it to exercise 'control'. However Jardine Matheson also had a looser but long-term relationship with Jardine Skinner in Calcutta which involved none of these linkages, though Matheson & Co. acted as agents in London for both firms. The relationship between Jardine Matheson and Jardine Skinner seemed distant by the 1930s,[32] but earlier Jardine Skinner might plausibly have been included within the Jardine Matheson 'group'.

During the 1950s the organizational structures of the 'network' business groups remained in place, but from the 1960s there were considerable pressures for change. In some countries, the managing agency system came to be regarded as politically unacceptable. It was made illegal in India in 1967. At the same time its original rationale disappeared. Improvements in corporate reporting and the emergence of organized capital markets in many countries meant that investors no longer needed the brand of a British trading company to guarantee that their savings would be 'safe'. Indeed, complex groups with cross-shareholdings and internal transfers of commission and fees within the group were no longer attractive. The trading companies themselves had in the past reduced their risks by using other people's money, but this strategy emerged as a potential threat to their control as shareholders changed from being atomistic individuals to institutional investors (in Britain) or powerful business elites (in Asia and elsewhere). The Marwari assault on the Calcutta managing agencies from the 1940s was an early sign of this latter trend.

From the 1960s there was a general trend either to take full ownership of affiliates or—as in the case of most of the Indian managing agencies—sell out altogether. An early consolidator was Guthrie Corporation, which not only managed but owned the plantations. During the early 1970s it continued to control most of its affiliates with minority equity stakes,[33] but in the mid-1970s a major reorganization resulted in most partly owned firms either becoming wholly owned subsidiaries or being sold, as in the case of the Indian plantation companies sold to Tata-Finlay. The result was almost all of Finlays' business was controlled by wholly-owned companies, with a few exceptions such as the 20 per cent stake in Tata-Finlay, disposed of a few years later.[34]

Harrisons & Crosfield began to reorganize its 'network' structure a few years after Finlays. This firm had developed an especially complex pattern of cross-shareholdings. It actually owned itself none of the issued capital

---

[32] B. D. F. Beith to W. J. Keswick, 10 Jan. 1940, S/O London to Shanghai 1940, JMA, CUL.

[33] Annual Report, James Finlay Ltd., 1970.

[34] Annual Report, James Finlay Ltd., 1976.

of Harrisons Malaysian Estates, its largest plantation affiliate formed in 1976 by a merger of its three largest plantations companies, though other affiliated firms were investors in the plantation company. A strategic part within the group was played by Harcros, the investment trust which had been known as the Rubber Plantations Investment Trust Ltd. until the 1960s, which was managed and controlled by Harrisons & Crosfield's directors, but the firm's share of Harcros's ordinary capital was small.[35]

Between 1978 and 1981 this network structure was swept away, prompted by a takeover bid for one of its plantation companies which made apparent the firm's vulnerability, especially if it lost control of Harcros.[36] Harrisons & Crosfield purchased the outstanding equity of its major plantation affiliates —becoming for the first time an owner rather than a manager and selling agent.[37] In 1978 Harrisons & Crosfield also acquired the 40.9 per cent of the Sabah Timber Co. (formerly the British Borneo Timber Co. until 1963) which it did not own. Ironically, government pressures for 'localization' rapidly ended the brief moment of internalization. In 1982 the majority of the equity of Harrisons Malaysian Estates was sold to a state-owned company, Harrisons & Crosfield retaining a 30.3 per cent interest in the successor company. In the same year the firm was obliged to sell 34 per cent of its equity in its Indian plantations company to Indian nationals, reducing its shareholding to 40 per cent. In 1989 the remaining shareholding in the Malaysian company was sold.

In the 1980s it was only the Hong Kong-centred British trading firms which retained the network form of organization. The large conglomerates owned by overseas Chinese also often operated through partly owned affiliates, perhaps because it permitted faster growth and a higher level of risk-taking. The British firms in Hong Kong continued to be sheltered from governmental pressures for 'localization', and it was not until 1979 that one of the large British 'hongs' in the colony—Hutchinson Whampoa—was 'captured' by a local Chinese businessman.

Both Jardine Matheson and Swire's retained a 'network' form of organization. The former was attacked on several occasions. In 1980 Hong Kong entrepreneurs bought into and took control of one of Jardines' associated property companies, the Hong Kong and Kowloon Wharf and Godown Company. Jardines however increased its shareholding in the second major local company, Hongkong Land Company, and secured 40 per cent of the equity. In 1981 Hongkong Land took a 40 per cent stake in Jardine Matheson.[38]

[35] Guy Nickalls (ed.), *Great Enterprise* (London: the firm, 1990), 205–7; Geoffrey Jones and Judith Wale, 'Diversification Strategies of British Trading Companies: Harrisons & Crosfield c.1900–c.1980', *Business History*, 41 (1999).
[36] *The Times*, 13 Dec. 1977.
[37] Chairman's statement, Harrisons & Crosfield Annual Report, 1978.
[38] M. Keswick (ed.) *The Thistle and the Jade* (London: Octopus, 1982), 234–5.

Swire's undertook a limited consolidation. In 1974 Swire's placed most of its Hong Kong affiliates into the partly owned but publicly quoted holding company, Swire Pacific, which in turn held equity in the principal Hong Kong affiliates, including Cathay Pacific and Swire Properties.[39] At that time John Swire & Sons directly held 50 per cent of the China Navigation Company, the major shipping subsidiary which was British-registered, and in 1976 the firm acquired the remaining 50 per cent of the equity. Most of the other affiliates remained partly owned, different classes of shareholding meaning that full control remained in the hands of John Swire & Sons, itself still wholly owned by the founding families.

Finally, a variant of the 'network' form of organization employed by British trading companies can be termed the 'loose network'. In the first part of the nineteenth century merchant firms typically took the form of interlocked but independent partnerships lacking an overall 'corporate centre' or parent, but this form tended to evolve into the 'network' form with a parent merchant firm (or partnership) bounded to affiliates. However in some instances 'loose networks' persisted. The Graham 'group's' network of interlocked partnerships was not consolidated until the 1920s, and then as a result of the group's bankruptcy and reconstruction.

A more durable instance of the 'loose network' organization was the large cluster of companies in which the Inchcape family held shares. This lacked a 'parent' trading company and was dependent on Inchcape family shareholdings to provide some coherence. During the 1920s the Inchcape group appeared to be evolving into a 'network' form of business group with relationships other than family shareholdings to bind different parts. There was an attempt to develop more synergies inside the group. For example, the different companies made diverse insurance arrangements, and attempts were made to encourage firms to use the Inchcape-controlled Gray Dawes as brokers.[40] In 1920 Inchcape established a bank, the P&O Banking Corporation, to develop the private banking business of the P&O Steam Navigation Company.[41]

The coordination of business services within the Inchcape network proved difficult to achieve. The P&O Bank was unable to attract the custom of many Inchcape companies, which stayed loyal to their old bankers, leading the bank to seek more risky business, which in turn caused bad debts. In 1927 Inchcape sold three-quarters of the shares in the bank to the Chartered Bank, and some years later it was totally absorbed by the latter, having never established a viable business.[42] The allocation of resources within the 'group' was distorted by Lord Inchcape's determination to support his financially

[39] Annual Report, John Swire & Sons, 1974.
[40] Memorandum for Lord Inchcape, 8 Nov. 1923, Gray Dawes Archives, MS 27605, GHL.
[41] Geoffrey Jones, *British Multinational Banking 1830–1990* (Oxford: Clarendon Press, 1993), 158.
[42] Ibid. 159.

troubled shipping companies, while Inchcape himself was too immersed in details and too involved with past tradition and practices to develop a coherent business group further.

After Lord Inchcape's death in 1932, the group persisted through the 1930s as a large but amorphous collection of trading and shipping companies especially focused on India, but extending to the Gulf, East Africa, and Australia. It was not until the third earl became the 'Senior' in the firm in 1948 that the consolidation and reconstruction of this structure began, culminating in the formation of Inchcape & Co., a public limited company in 1958.

In summary, as British trading companies diversified from the 1870s they organized their business groups using different degrees of ownership. In some firms there was a strong preference for full ownership, though this did not translate into an 'integrated' enterprise. However many of the British trading companies organized non-trading activities as partly owned affiliates bound by non-equity modes. The change in capital market and political circumstances from the 1950s prompted many of the companies to seek full ownership of their businesses, though host government policies in many developing countries subsequently 'fragmented' such groups again.

6.3 The Functioning of 'Network' Groups

This section examines in more detail how the business groups which employed network forms of organization functioned over time. It is this type of business group which has been most discussed in the literature, and whose alleged rent-seeking and weak organizational capabilities have been the object of debate. The section examines in turn the means by which the different parts of each group were linked: management contracts, equity, debt, cross-directorships, and repeated trading transactions.

Management contracts provided pivotal elements of the business groups. 'Managing agency' and 'secretarial' agreements between the trading company and the affiliate firms were set for a number of years, which could be as short as one year or as long as twenty, but once the contractual relationship started it was very unusual for agreements not to be renewed. They formed the most important 'permanent' binding within the network.

The income earned by trading companies under agency and secretarial agreements for their services provided a valuable source of income as in most cases it was not linked to profits or dividends. Under the terms of most agreements, the agent earned commission on sales turnover or—in the case of plantations—planted acreage. Secretarial and agency fees were fixed amounts which did not vary either with profitability or turnover. This was an especially favourable arrangement for the trading companies at times of external shocks, such as the interwar falls in commodity prices. Typically trading companies received multiple sources of income from management contracts. At each stage of the production and associated activity of a typical commodity, for example, the trading company would derive its own income. This included not only buying imports for and selling outputs by plantations, but also commission on both shipping and insurance. Commission earned on insurance could often be considerable. Each plantation company, for example, needed fire insurance for its products and premises, as well as marine insurance for its products. A further source of commission was often earned from guaranteeing bank loans to affiliated companies.

Though consistent financial information on sources of income is hard to identify for most firms, the importance of commissions and fees from affiliated firms is evident. Companies which became involved in high value activities such as oil could earn especially substantial sums from an agency contract. This seems to have been the case for Balfour Williamson and its relationship with Lobitos Oil.[43] In India, Shaw Wallace held for thirty-six years until 1928 the Indian selling agency for Burmah Oil, and this seems to have been also especially lucrative.[44] The trading companies in South East Asia which managed substantial numbers of plantation and other companies were noteworthy beneficiaries of the system, earning much of their income from commission and fees.[45]

Management contracts were often very durable. Harrisons & Crosfield were appointed agents and secretaries of the British Borneo Timber Co. on its formation in 1920. The firm's shareholding in the venture fluctuated— falling from 42 per cent in 1920 to 32 per cent in 1948, then rising to 57 per cent in 1973 and becoming wholly owned six years later—but the agency agreements persisted until forest concessions in Sabah came to an end in 1982. The 1920 agency agreement for British Borneo Timber gave Harrisons & Crosfield a higher than normal selling commission: it was 2.5 per cent on gross proceeds, instead of the usual 1.5 per cent.[46] However the firm derived multiple sources of income from the association. While London earned secretarial fees and also commission from sales of timber to European and US buyers, and Harrisons & Crosfield in Borneo earned management commission, the firm also earned almost about as much profit from the supply of 'indirect' services such as shipping, insurance, and stevedorage.[47] New agency agreements were drawn up in the post-war period, and different parts of

---

[43] Rory Miller, 'Small Business in the Peruvian Oil Industry: Lobitos Oilfields Limited before 1934', *Business History Review*, 56 (1982), 413–14; John Bingham Powell, 'History of the Milne Group of Companies', Burmah Castrol Archives.

[44] Memo on Piece Goods and Yarns, May 1927, Binny Archives, MS 27163/2, GHL; Sir Harry Townend, *A History of Shaw Wallace & Co. and Shaw Wallace & Co. Ltd.* (Calcutta: the firm, 1965); T. A. B. Corley, *A History of the Burmah Oil Company 1886–1924* (London: Heinemann, 1983).

[45] Harrisons & Crosfield ledgers, Harrisons & Crosfield Archives, GHL; Guthrie Archives, G/MIS/9, SOAS.

[46] 1920 Agency Agreement, British Borneo Timber Co. files, Harrisons & Crosfield Archives, GHL.

[47] Ibid., file of company's dealings with the British Borneo Timber Co.

the Harrisons & Crosfield group earned profits from business with the British Borneo.[48] During the early 1960s some sales in the United States, for example, were handled by Harrisons & Crosfield (America) Inc., which received a 2.5 per cent selling commission in return for sharing some risk.[49]

The long-standing nature of the management contracts can also be illustrated in the case of Balfour Williamson and the Santa Rosa Milling Co. Williamson Balfour in Chile and Milne & Co. in Peru were already the managing agents of the two pre-existing flour milling companies whose merger in 1913 formed the Santa Rosa Milling Co. These arrangements continued as the new company evolved. From 1916 Santa Rosa had a controlling interest in the Cía Molinera San Cristóbal, which owned one flour mill in Santiago—purchased on its behalf by Williamson Balfour—and acquired a second one in San Fernando in the following year. In 1925 Santa Rosa gained a second mill in southern Chile through acquiring the entire share capital of the Sociedad Molinero Osorno from Williamson Balfour which had established that concern in 1913. In all these cases Williamson Balfour acted as managing, buying, and selling agents.

In addition to the commission earned by Milne & Co. and Williamson Balfour from Santa Rosa business, Balfour Williamson also performed secretarial services for Santa Rosa's London board. Balfour Williamson were only formally appointed as company secretaries in 1942, and prior to that a company secretary channelled the correspondence of the agents to the board. However in practice Balfour Williamson provided all the administrative support and Santa Rosa paid an annual fee—£1,000 from 1925—to cover the secretary's salary and office rent and charges. After 1942 Balfour Williamson performed the secretarial function in London directly, and one or two of its representatives attended each board meeting of Santa Rosa. This function involved among other things the recruitment of mill managers and their assistants, who then worked under the instructions of Williamson Balfour when they went to Latin America.

Although once again the exact sums involved cannot be established, the surviving correspondence of Balfour Williamson's senior partner, Lord Forres, in the 1920s certainly supports the view that commission from Santa Rosa and their affiliates was very important for the firm.[50] 'If it were not for our agency business (commissions)', Forres wrote in 1930, 'it is difficult to see how we could make ends meet'[51]—though the fall in flour selling prices and lower flour output with the onset of the Depression rather diminished his confidence in the business before his death in the following year.[52]

---

[48] Ibid., Directors File, 1958–67.   [49] Ibid., Company Board Minutes.

[50] Lord Forres to Jack Henderson, 9 June 1927, Sir Archibald Williamson's Private Letter Books, No. 9 (box 13), Balfour Williamson Archives, UCL.

[51] Ibid., Lord Forres to Jack Henderson, 7 Aug. 1930, Lord Forres Letter Books, No. 10 (box 13).

[52] Ibid., Lord Forres to Fred Milne, 6 Aug. 1931, Lord Forres Letter Books, No. 11 (box 14).

The problems of the 1930s subsequently caused a rearrangement of the agency arrangements in Peru. In Peru, where competition due to over-production was especially severe, Santa Rosa merged its milling interests in 1934 with those of the powerful Argentinian wheat trader Bunge & Born to make a 50/50 joint venture. Though it was Santa Rosa's Callao mill which was selected for retention and Bunge & Born's mill that was closed, it was Bunge & Born that became managing partners and wheat buying agents, with Milne & Co. retaining only the selling agency for flour. In 1951 Santa Rosa withdrew entirely from Peru, selling its shareholding to Bunge & Born.

In Chile Balfour Williamson's agency continued in the post-1945 period. In 1947 Santa Rosa ceased to operate mills directly and became purely a holding company, following the formation of a Chilean company to run the Concepción mill, the Cía Molinera Santa Rosa Chile SA. Santa Rosa there-fore controlled three companies: Cía Molinera Santa Rosa, Cía Molinera San Cristóbal, and Sociedad Molinera de Osorno. Williamson Balfour acted as agents for all these firms and to some extent provided a unified structure which was managed initially in all locations. The agreements signed in 1954, 1956, and 1965 with these firms were all to run for twenty years.

The 1956 agreement with Cía San Cristóbal—which can serve as an example—noted that the existing agreement had already run for thirty-six years, and was thus being renewed for twenty years, with further twenty-year renewals (subject to three years' notice) anticipated. Williamson Balfour was given the exclusive agency for both purchases and sales and were thus to receive commission on the totals of purchases and sales, even if some arrangements were made—with Williamson Balfour's consent—directly with suppliers or customers. In return Williamson Balfour undertook not to sell products of third parties similar to those of San Cristóbal mills. Rules of commission were specified, though they could be altered by mutual agree-ment.[53] Balfour Williamson's withdrawal from Chile in 1967 ended this and other agreements.

There were considerable potential conflicts of interest between the trad-ing companies and the companies they managed, and more especially the outside shareholders of these companies. This tension became especially apparent when the trading companies continued to receive fees and com-mission payments when affiliate companies made losses. There were also underlying conflicts in the incentives of the system. Commission incomes based on sales provided incentives to promote growth through retained earn-ings, and thus to suppress the distribution of profits to the shareholders of affiliated firms. There were a number of vocal conflicts on this matter, especially before 1914. Jardine Matheson's management of the Indo-China Steam Navigation Company received considerable criticism from its share-holders in the late 1900s.[54] There was also a celebrated Scottish court case

[53] Santa Rosa Archives, box 6, UCL.
[54] Correspondence in S/O London to Hong Kong, July 1908 to June 1910, JMA, CUL.

in the 1890s between James Finlay and the shareholders in the Champdany Jute Company.[55]

Yet, given the widespread use of management contracts and the potential for conflicts of interest, it is surprising how few legal cases occurred. It would seem that the trading companies seldom sought to pursue their interests to such an extent that outside shareholders were blatantly disadvantaged. In part this was because the merchant houses were themselves shareholders, so dividends were also of a concern to them. But the boards of affiliate companies retained some autonomy and legal responsibilities to all their shareholders. Typically they would negotiate the level of agency and secretarial fees, authorize capital expenditure recommended by the agents, and request and receive information on production and sales. The trading companies also sought to encourage confidence in their integrity by postponing, reducing, or forgoing commissions when corporate performance was very bad.[56] Given that the creation of new affiliates continued at least up to the 1920s, maintaining a reputation for honesty and good management was essential for raising further outside capital. When shareholders became restive, the trading companies often attempted to calm matters behind the scenes.[57]

The shareholdings of many companies were also closely held, often by people linked in social or familial networks, and for the most part these people were not ones to complain or even to sell their shares to secure a higher return. In many cases, especially before the Second World War, the market for shares in such firms were very illiquid, and quite often Articles of Association laid down the conditions under which shares could be traded. For example, when a member of the Holt family approached Swire's in November 1931 about selling some stock in the China Navigation Company, he received the disheartening news that, although others had been trying to sell, the last actual sale had been in the previous March. Moreover there were strict rules about the sale of shares in the firm:

unless you dispose of it privately to another stockholder you have got to circularise it round the stockholders with your minimum price; but, if that does not succeed and you can produce a non-stockholder as purchaser, we [i.e. Swires] shall not raise any difficulty, always provided that he is not connected with the BI [i.e. British India Steam Navigation Company] or any of the China Coast lines and cannot make use of any knowledge acquired as a stockholder to our disadvantage.[58]

---

[55] This is discussed in detail in Ross E. Stewart, 'Scottish Company Accounting, 1870–1920: Selected Case Studies of Accounting in its Historical Context' (unpublished Ph.D. thesis, University of Glasgow, 1986), 327–50, Alistair Smith, 'The Champdany Jute Company Ltd., 1873–1921' (unpublished final year undergraduate dissertation, Department of Economic History, University of Glasgow, Oct. 1988); and Jones and Wale, 'Merchants as Business Groups', 396–9.

[56] Champdany Board Minutes, 1899–1914, Finlays Archives, UGD 91/178/5.

[57] D. G. M. Bernard to J. J. Paterson, 13 Nov. 1930, S/O London to Hong Kong, July 1930–Dec. 1930, JMA, CUL.

[58] G. W. Swire to Lawrence D. Holt, 11 Nov. 1931, Swire Archives, JSSI/4/12, SOAS.

The 'passive' shareholder voice helps to explain the kind of 'moral' responsibility often expressed by the trading companies in their internal correspondence for the shareholders of companies they managed. Thus Jardine Skinner's Senior Partner in London advised Calcutta in 1911 concerning the shareholders of the mill companies managed by the firms that it was 'not in the spirit of antagonism that the shareholders should be dealt with, but as friends and practically partners'.[59] The 'moral' or legal responsibilities of the agent to the shareholders were frequently referred to by Lord Forres in the case of the Santa Rosa Milling Co.[60] In 1916 he expressed his philosophy about the agents' duties to a Williamson Balfour partner in Valparaíso: 'When the interest of the firm and the company conflict, the interests of the milling company must not be subordinated to those of the firm in connection with trading transactions.'[61]

Lord Forres' concern for shareholder rights was not unrelated to his own personal shareholding in most of the companies managed by the group. He was a living embodiment of the conflicts of interest within the system. When the Santa Rosa Milling Co. was formed in 1914, the Williamson family took 22.9 per cent of the shares and Lord Forres himself 9.4 per cent.[62] He also became chairman in 1921. He was also a substantial shareholder in and chairman of Lobitos Oil, as well as the group's other spin-off oil company, Anglo-Ecuadorian Oil Company. In his various positions he was acutely sensitive of the numerous conflicts of interest within the group. For example, Balfour Williamson's New York branch in the 1920s received export commissions for sales of oil produced by Lobitos and Anglo-Ecuadorian, but they also made a charge to each firm for the cables dispatched on behalf of each, which produced a considerable profit for the New York office. Forres advised the New York manager that it was 'not the intention that a profit on cables should be made out of these companies' which might lead 'a shareholder (to) make trouble with the board'.[63]

The 'moral' responsibilities of the parent trading companies to outside shareholders in affiliate firms was, at least before the Second World War, interpreted in a paternalistic fashion. They were asked to take their agents on trust and were rarely provided with much information, unless they held major blocks of shares. An internal memorandum in Binny's in 1930 described one person as 'quite a good type of Shareholder, not likely to give trouble'.[64] The balance sheets of many affiliates were not even made

[59] W. A. Barkier to Horne, 11 Apr. 1911, Jardine Skinner Archives, in-letters, General Books from Senior Partner London, CUL.

[60] Lord Forres to Harry Williamson, 11 Sept. 1909, Sir Archibald Williamson's Private Letter Books No. 1 (box 9), Balfour Williamson Archives, UCL.

[61] Ibid., Lord Forres to Hope Simpson, 22 Febr. 1916, No. 4 (box 10); Lord Forres to Jack Henderson, 1 Oct. 1923, No. 7 (box 12).

[62] Santa Rosa Milling Co. Minute Book No. 1, Santa Rosa Archives, box 1, UCL.

[63] Lord Forres to B. D. Blyth, 10 May 1928, Balfour Williamson-Balfour Guthrie: Sir Archibald Williamson's Private Letter Books, No. 9 (box 13), UCL.

[64] Memorandum by Binny & Co., 25 Feb. 1930, Binny Archives, MS 27163/4, GHL.

available to shareholders. When Swire's approached the National Provincial Bank about overdraft facilities for the China Navigation Company in 1923, they sent a balance sheet but asked to keep it confidential, as 'even of the Stockholders only a few of the more important ones see as detailed a Balance Sheet as this'.[65]

The equity relationships between trading companies and their affiliates varied widely within and between business groups. The percentage of equity held often reflected the level of public subscriptions when these shares were initially offered for sale, but there was often a minimum level of shareholding needed to maintain an agency agreement. The trading companies derived dividends from their shareholdings, but these were seldom as significant a source of income as commission and fees. A key reason for holding equity in affiliates was to retain the all-important managing agency business. Jardine Matheson, for example, held equity in public companies such as 'the Indo China SN Co., China Sugar Refinery etc where it [was] necessary to hold shares to protect our position as Managers'.[66] Jardines in the 1920s experienced several attempts to 'take the management of the [China Sugar Refinery] Company away from [them]' and had 'to buy a sufficient number of shares to protect [their] position'.[67] However the firm's share portfolio remained rather lacking in rationality, consisting—Henry Keswick complained in 1940 —of excessive amounts of shares in some firms (such as Ewo Breweries) and other shareholdings 'acquired for no particular reason and retained because they have become difficult to dispose of'.[68] Usually firms could rely on a circle of friendly shareholders as well as their direct holdings, though the growth of powerful local business houses from the 1940s made the strategy of maintaining 'control' through the votes of allies increasingly hazardous.

The percentage of equity held in a particular affiliate often fluctuated. Trading companies bought and sold stock in response to stock market conditions as well as their own financial circumstances. In the 1930s, for example, the Borneo Company sold shares in a number of affiliates if it could get a good price for them.[69] Plans were advanced to sell part of the equity in the firm's Singapore brickworks and Borneo Motors, their motor distribution branch, shortly before the outbreak of the Pacific War.[70] Buying and selling stock in affiliate firms provided opportunities for 'insider dealing'

[65] J. S. Swire to National Provincial & Union Bank, 9 Feb. 1923, JSSI/4/10, Swire Archives, SOAS.

[66] David Landale to John Johnstone, 9 Sept. 1920, S/O London to Hong Kong, Jan.–Dec. 1920, JMA, CUL.

[67] L. N. Leefe to D. G. M. Bernard, 19 Mar. 1926, S/O London to Hong Kong, 19 Mar. 1926, JMA, CUL.

[68] W. J. Keswick to J. J. Paterson, 15 Mar. 1940, S/O Shanghai to Hong Kong, Jan.–June 1940, JMA, CUL.

[69] Borneo Company Board Minutes, 7 Mar. 1934, 9 May 1934, 30 May 1934, 1 Aug. 1934, 2 July 1935, 22 Apr. 1936, Borneo Company Archives MS 27178/20, GHL.

[70] Ibid., Board Minute 10 Apr. 1940, MS 27178/21.

and in fact this activity was regarded as a legitimate source of profit. The practice was probably most widespread before 1914, but lingered longer in Asia, though by the end of the interwar years it also seems to have been on the wane there. In 1940 Keswick in Shanghai predicted that Jardines' trading in shares would become less than previously as 'share speculation as a means of earning revenue will become no more a part of our business than it would be in a similar concern at home'.[71]

Debt was often more important than equity within business groups. The parent trading companies served as in-house banks which sometimes made substantial loans to affiliates. They also guaranteed loans from commercial banks to affiliates. In several cases it has been shown that before 1914 debt was used as much as or more than equity to finance operations within the group.[72] The interest from advances to affiliate companies was often an important source of income for the trading companies. This was the case for Swire's before 1914.[73] However, these advances could also become illiquid if the financial performance of a venture faltered. This happened to Swire's Taikoo Sugar Refining Company after 1914. The venture lost almost £1 million in 1921, and after further losses reserves had been nearly wiped out by 1928 with no significant recovery until the mid-1930s. In this situation, Swire's had to provide substantial amounts of working capital in the 1920s and, in 1930, made a £245,000 loan to the company, which remained outstanding through the 1930s.[74]

Swire's was far from alone in providing credit to affiliates in the 1930s. The Borneo Company lent considerable sums to its Borneo Motors affiliate in the early 1930s, especially before a large overdraft was arranged in the early 1930s.[75] Jardine Matheson lent heavily to affiliates such as the Jardine Engineering Corporation and especially the Indo-China Steam Navigation Company. By June 1930 the latter's overdraft reached 2,268,000 Hong Kong dollars.[76] It also made large loans in the 1930s to the London distributors of its dried and frozen eggs, the firm of Goldrei Foucard.[77]

---

[71] W. J. Keswick to J. J. Paterson, 15 Mar. 1940, S/O Shanghai to Hong Kong, Jan.–June 1940, JMA, CUL.

[72] Jones and Wale, 'Merchants as Business Groups', 388 for Finlays. The case of the Hubbards in Russia is examined in Natalia Gurushina, 'British Free-Standing Companies in Tsarist Russia', in Wilkins and Schröter (eds.), *The Free-Standing Company*, 174–80.

[73] S. Sugiyama, 'A British Trading Firm in the Far East: John Swire & Sons, 1867–1914', in S. Yonekawa and H. Yoshihara (eds.), *Business History of General Trading Companies* (Tokyo: Tokyo University Press, 1987).

[74] File JSSV 4/4–5, Swire Archives, SOAS.

[75] Borneo Company Board Meeting, 4 Dec. 1929, 10 Oct. 1934, 12 June 1935, MS 27178/19 and MS 22178/20, Borneo Company Archives, GHL.

[76] J. J. Paterson to D. G. M. Bernard, 12 June 1931, S/O Letters London to Hong Kong Jan.–June 1931, JMA, CUL.

[77] D. G. M. Bernard to J. J. Paterson, 20 Oct. 1930, P&C Letters from London to Hong Kong Aug. 1929–Dec. 1930, D. Beith to D. G. M. Bernard, 3 Nov. 1933, S/O Letters London/Shanghai/Hong Kong, July–Dec. 1933, JMA, CUL. J. J. Paterson to W. J. Keswick, 16 Aug. 1939, S/O London to Shanghai, JMA, CUL.

Not surprisingly, the Balfour Williamson group's relationship with the Chilean and Peruvian milling companies included debt. Before the formation of the Santa Rosa Milling Co. Williamson Balfour acted as bankers for the mills, lending working capital required, and thereby earning significant interest as an additional source of income from the mills. The rate of interest charged to the mills was another cause of concern for Lord Forres. The Concepción mill had been set up explicitly on the assumption that 'it would be a good thing to let the company have no working capital and borrow all it required from us', but as the mill grew in size the burden of providing working capital grew alongside the interest charges, which by 1912 threatened 'to see the bulk of the profits absorbed in payment of interest'.[78]

Williamson Balfour were appointed sole bankers of the Santa Rosa Milling Co. in 1914. They were authorized to lend up to £100,000 to the company on current account in addition to the £200,000 raised from a public issue of debentures two months after the formation of the Santa Rosa. A further £50,000 could be made available at an interest rate 1 per cent higher. This limit was to include sums which Williamson Balfour borrowed from local banks in local currency for the use of the mills. Williamson Balfour derived income from this by charging 1 per cent more interest to Santa Rosa than the rate at which it borrowed from banks to Chile.

The amounts of lending varied greatly. For a brief period in 1915 Williamson Balfour exceptionally owed money to Santa Rosa. Forres was quick to check that only 2 per cent interest was allowed on credit balances rather than 6 per cent as then charged on debit balances, in order to ensure that Williamson Balfour's interests were being protected.[79] More typically, Santa Rosa required large sums of working capital which reached during and immediately after the First World War over £150,000. In 1920, for example, Williamson Balfour in Valparaíso was authorized by the Santa Rosa board to draw on the London & River Plate Bank in the name of Santa Rosa up to £200,000 for three months against wheat purchases for Concepción and Callao mills. Balfour Williamson guaranteed to that bank the due payment of the drafts at maturity, and in return for its guarantee received 0.25 per cent on the actual amount of acceptances.[80]

In the 1920s, the first moves were made to set up credit facilities with local banks for Santa Rosa in its own right as a borrower, though even then guarantees to banks by Williamson Balfour seem to have been required.[81] The growing financial problems of the Balfour Williamson partnership lay behind this move as they were increasingly unable and unwilling to provide large sums for working capital, especially in the circumstances of the

[78] Lord Forres to Harry Williamson, 5 June 1912, Sir Archibald Williamson's Private Letter Books, No. 1 (box 9), Balfour Williamson Archives, UCL.
[79] Ibid., Lord Forres to Hope Simpson, 10 Nov. 1915, No. 4 (Box 10).
[80] Santa Rosa Milling Co. Minute Book No. 1, Santa Rosa Archives, box 1, UCL.
[81] Santa Rosa Milling Co. Minute Books Nos. 1 and 2, Santa Rosa Archives, box 1, UCL.

depreciating Chilean currency. However the role of Balfour Williamson as bankers to affiliate firms certainly did not cease, though from the 1930s they were not providers of large sums of credit. Through the 1950s Balfour Williamson was one of the two bankers for Lobitos Oilfields, which sometimes placed quite large sums on deposit with them, and Balfour Williamson also provided investment advice for the oil company.[82]

The affiliate firms in a business group were typically linked to the parent trading company by cross-directorships. Directorships were regarded as an important means of securing the all-important managing agency contracts, of securing new contracts, and of providing information about companies. As Harrisons & Crosfield spawned plantation companies before 1914, its directors took directorships on their boards. As a result, most Harrisons & Crosfield directors in 1914 held directorships on multiple plantation companies. In the interwar years each plantation company in the Harrisons & Crosfield business group had a board of directors of whom the greater proportion were also members of the Harrisons & Crosfield board or had served as senior Harrisons & Crosfield managers in the East. These appointments were made without regard to the size of the shareholding in the affiliate. In the case of locally registered companies, senior managers at the overseas branches of the trading companies would typically provide several of the directors.

Cross-directorships were also a prominent feature of the Balfour Williamson group. Four of the first six directors of Santa Rosa Milling were partners in Balfour Williamson or Milne & Co. Lord Forres—then Sir Archibald Williamson—was its first chairman. Cross-directorships persisted through the post-1945 period. The chairman of Santa Rosa in the mid-1950s and from 1962 onwards was J. S. Dent, a grandson of Stephen Williamson, who had been promoted from member of staff to director of Balfour Williamson in 1946. The chairman of Santa Rosa up to 1962 was W. H. Williamson, a partner in Williamson Balfour since 1938. Through the post-war period all the directors of the two companies operating Concepción and Osorno mills were nominees of Williamson Balfour, while a majority of the Cía San Cristóbal board were from Williamson Balfour. Though directors of the Concepción and Osorno companies received no remuneration, the amount of directors' fees at San Cristóbal was significant and provided a source of income for Williamson Balfour, since those who were directors of both companies handed over their fees to Williamson Balfour.

Contemporaries were well aware of the conflicts of interest involved in cross-directorships. Within the interwar Guthrie group, Sir John Hay—Guthries' managing director—was a director and often the chairman of a large number of rubber and palm oil estate companies for which Guthries

---

[82] Lobitos Oilfields Board Minutes 1946–55, Nos. 14–16, Burmah Oil Archives.

held the managing agency. Hay on several occasions recorded his discomfort at the ambiguity of his situation. In 1936, after a three-month tour of the firm's Asian business, he noted that:

> two managers of our palm oil estates begged to be excused from dealing with Guthrie & Co. because they were uniformly inefficient and quite frequently discourteous. I had to use my influence as chairman of those two companies to maintain the connection with Guthrie & Co. In doing so I was left with the uncomfortable feeling that perhaps I was not dealing quite honestly with the shareholders of those two companies.[83]

The trading companies over time evolved a number of practices to make the conflict of interest less blatant. Following the firm's conflict with the disgruntled shareholders of the Champdany Jute Co., Finlay directors on Champdany's board always abstained from voting on issues relating to the firm's agency and commission payments.[84] This also became standard practice at Harrisons & Crosfield and other firms.[85]

A final binding between the different constituents of business groups was provided by trading transactions. Swire ships carried Swire sugar to its markets, and Swire paint was used to maintain its vessels. Jardines' ships were an important source of profits for its wharf company in Hong Kong.[86] Tea produced on Finlay plantations passed through wholly owned Finlay branches which sold and moved the produce which was warehoused, packed, blended, and distributed through Finlay affiliates in consuming countries. Servicing their own affiliates provided a large part of the shipping and insurance agency work of many firms.

It is difficult to reach an overall assessment of the costs and benefits, and the winners and losers, from these networks. In the literature on the host regions where the managing agency system was most developed, South and South East Asia, their complexity and the multiple conflicts of interest have been emphasized.[87] In a classic study of the Malayan rubber industry Bauer drew attention to the small size and large number of companies in the industry. Although this reflected the conditions under which the industry initially developed, it multiplied the secretarial and director's fees earned by the agency houses and provided them with little incentive to amalgamate small units. Moreover Bauer criticized the practice of taking shares in other plantation companies within the group which he regarded as 'hardly in the best interests of the rubber companies. Tropical agriculture

---

[83] Sir John Hay's memorandum, 5 May 1936, on James Robertson's memorandum of 24 Apr. 1936, G/MIS/9, Guthrie Archives, SOAS.

[84] Champdany Board Minutes, 1899–1914, Finlays Archives, UGD 91/178/5

[85] Board Minutes of plantation companies, Harrisons & Crosfield Archives, GHL.

[86] D. G. M. Bernard to J. J. Paterson, 29 Aug. 1930, P&C Letters from London to Hong Kong Aug. 1929–Dec. 1930, JMA, CUL.

[87] For example, J. H. Drabble and P. J. Drake, 'The British Agency House in Malaysia: Survival in a Changing World', *Journal of Southeast Asian Studies*, 12 (1981), 308–9.

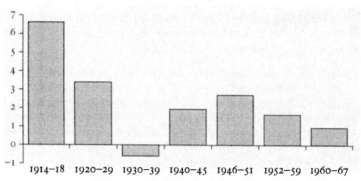

FIG. 6.1 Average post-tax return on net capital employed of Santa Rosa Milling Co., 1914–1967 (%)

Source: Santa Rosa Milling Co. Ltd. annual reports, Santa Rosa Archives, box 4, UCL. The 1919 accounts are missing.

is a risky business, and to invest the surplus funds of a rubber company in other plantation ventures (usually rubber companies) seems difficult to justify.'[88] Later studies also suggested that the British agency houses had a vested interest in maintaining the multiplicity of rubber companies and avoiding the rationalization of the industry.[89]

The management costs of the system were often substantial, and may have fallen heavily on outside shareholders in affiliate firms. If the case of the Malayan rubber industry is taken again, while Harrisons & Crosfield was notable for its relatively high ROCE in the interwar years, the same was not true of the rubber companies, which it managed. In 1922 the average ROCE for the 34 out of 38 Harrisons & Crosfield managed rubber companies for which data are available was −1.5 per cent. For 1932 the average of all 43 managed companies was the same. In contrast, Harrisons & Crosfield's ROCE was almost 6 per cent in 1922 and 6.4 per cent in 1932. In the latter year most plantations had virtually ceased rubber tapping and their workforce had been laid off. However the companies had to continue to pay Harrisons & Crosfield lump sum secretarial fees and agency fees per planted acre, and concessions on fee levels were limited.

In the case of the Santa Rosa Milling Co., Figure 6.1 demonstrates that management by a trading company was no guarantor of a good performance. Santa Rosa's post-tax ROCE in most periods was well below that of the average British trading companies, and poor from the 1930s onwards. The company was unable to pay an ordinary dividend in 1928, 1930, and between 1932 and 1948. Although Balfour Williamson's ROCE is not known, it is evident that Santa Rosa provided multiple sources of income for its 'parent'.

[88] P. T. Bauer, *The Rubber Industry* (London: Longmans, 1948), 10–12.
[89] John H. Drabble, *Malayan Rubber· The Interwar Years* (London: Macmillan, 1991), 57, 82.

Such evidence is suggestive—though no more—that the conflicts of interest within the business groups sometimes worked to the benefits of the shareholders in the parent trading company. Yet the evidence elsewhere in this chapter suggests that rent-seeking behaviour was constrained by the need to maintain reputation and by contemporary views of legitimate ethical behaviour. The worst defects of the 'managing agency' system may have been seen in India and elsewhere when it was imitated by business elites less constrained by ethical standards.[90]

Moreover the business group system added value rather than merely transferring it from one group of shareholders to another. Although the costs of agency agreements and the fees of directors seem high for affiliate firms, services were rendered in return. The trading companies not only 'managed' companies, but enabled them to benefit from being a part of a much wider group. This affected everything from expatriate staff recruitment to the international marketing of products. A contemporary study of the British managing agencies in interwar India observed that they achieved economies in both buying and selling through acting on behalf of a large group of companies.[91]

Moreover business groups provided a mechanism for spreading information and knowledge between firms. This can be illustrated in the case of the rubber plantations in interwar Malaya. Harrisons & Crosfield, for example, provided specialist technical services for its affiliated plantation companies in Malaya. In 1925 it purchased the Prang Besar Estate which had been created in 1921 as a new estate in Malaya designed to produce high-yielding rubber trees. The techniques developed at Prang Besar were diffused to the other rubber companies within the group and led to productivity improvements. Guthries established its own research station in 1934 and subsequently made large advances in bud-grafting and selective breeding. Systematic replanting on a large scale by high-yielding bud-grafted trees took place on all the main Guthrie estates in this decade.[92]

The network-style business groups built around British trading companies were complex and contained multiple conflicts of interest. Within this context, the organization of the business groups can be seen as generally working to the benefit of the parent trading company and its shareholders. However rent-seeking behaviour was constrained and real managerial, financial, and other services were provided in return for commissions and fees.

[90] J. S. Fforde, *An International Trade in Managerial Skills* (Oxford. Basil Blackwell, 1957), 122–4.
[91] P. S. Lokanathani, *Industrial Organisation in India* (London: George Allen & Unwin, 1935), 286–9.
[92] D. J. M. Tate, *The RGA History of the Plantation Industry in the Malay Peninsula* (Kuala Lumpur: Oxford University Press, 1996), 416–21.

6.4 Business Groups: An Assessment

The British trading companies built extensive and complex business groups in response to their strategies of diversification. The activities and purposes of these business groups extended beyond the financial, and are consequently greatly underestimated by the term 'investment group'. The business groups are better regarded as diversified business organizations employing a variety of institutional and contractual modes and inside which there existed flows of managerial, financial, and trading information and relationships.

These business groups were robust forms of business organization. They lasted over long time periods, survived external shocks, and evolved in function. In the conditions of the booming world economy before 1914, business groups provided a means for merchants to exploit the numerous opportunities available by using other people's money to create new trading opportunities. Then and afterwards they provided a mechanism for information gathering, interpretation, and dissemination between collections of firms. In the interwar years the structure enhanced the ability of the parent trading companies to withstand external stocks. This may have been at the expense of outside shareholders in affiliate firms, although affiliates were also supported by credit from their parents. In general, reputation was an important asset for the trading companies which constrained extreme rent-seeking behaviour. In the depressed economic environment of the interwar years, the business group structure may have worked more towards survival than innovation. In the post-war period, the dynamic economic conditions seen in East Asia from the 1950s provided the basis for the renewal and dynamic growth of 'network' forms of business organization, though in the less dynamic environments of Latin America and South Asia network forms may have hindered innovation.

It is tempting to compare the business groups around the British trading companies with other forms of business enterprise. They differed in most respects from the large managerial enterprises which developed in the United States in the late nineteenth century, though a number of the groups grew to a large scale. There are rather more parallels with the continental European 'universal banks' which flourished between the mid-nineteenth century and the 1930s. Like the universal banks, the trading companies functioned as venture capitalists which identified profitable opportunities and exploited them. They resembled the universal banks both in their combination of financial and entrepreneurial roles, and in their ongoing managerial involvement in the enterprises they promoted. Their managerial competences will be examined further in the next chapter.

7

Governance and Human Resources

7.1 Introduction

The management of multinational trading companies controlling diversified business groups was a risky and complex business. They often operated in the nineteenth century at the boundaries of the international economy and at the frontiers of European empires. Like all multinational firms of the period, they faced the problem of controlling and monitoring businesses in distant locations at a time when transport and communications were slow and unreliable. Over the course of the century this situation improved as steamships speeded up transport by sea and the telegraph provided a far faster —if expensive—means of communication.[1] However these developments lowered rather than abolished the management costs faced by these firms. International trading was an especially risky business, involving political, exchange rate, and commodity price risks. Moreover as the traders evolved into hybrid trading companies and business groups, so they faced the serious challenges of managing a diversified portfolio with assets spread internationally. This chapter examines the management competences of the trading companies, and how they changed over time.

7.2 Structures and Systems

Although there were strong firm-specific differences, the management structures established by the trading companies by the late nineteenth century largely remained in place until the 1970s. The robustness and longevity of many, if not all, the trading companies suggests that these structures were quite effective, though in this context the environment in which the firms developed has to be taken into consideration. The trading companies established themselves in many markets in the nineteenth century at a time when local organizational or technological capabilities were very low. Consequently their required level of managerial competence to survive and flourish was not necessarily very large. Once established, they enjoyed first-mover advantages and enjoyed strong franchises which were not easily challenged. Moreover, the trading companies grew and diversified in the late nineteenth century and continued to operate in many instances even

---

[1] Geoffrey Jones, *The Evolution of International Business* (London: Routledge, 1996), 28–9, 41.

in the 1950s, in a colonial or 'semi-colonial' context which considerably lessened the risks they faced operating abroad. The cartelization of shipping services, and many commodities, had the same effect.

At the apex of the management structures of the trading companies was the board of directors or, in some cases, the dominant shareholding family. Decision-making was heavily concentrated at this level, even as the traders diversified into multiple activities. In companies which took British limited liability status the heart of the management was the board of directors sitting in London, or sometimes Liverpool or Glasgow. These boards were usually rather small, but made executive decisions at their (often) weekly meetings. Boards made overall strategic decisions, but also concerned themselves with a multitude of other issues from the selection of staff and their monitoring—including giving permission for them to marry—through to approving small items of expenditure. This structure was far removed from the separation of strategic and operating decisions found in M-form firms.

Directors were a very important part of the management system. In many cases they had served with their companies for long periods and accumulated considerable region-specific experience. They were the physical embodiment of the local knowledge, information, and relationship building which gave the firms their advantages. Collectively they held formidable tacit knowledge about products and regions, and had extensive personal contacts with the directors of other firms and government officials. They were also important means of controlling partly owned affiliates, for main board directors also typically held seats on the boards of affiliate firms.

The evolution of a board's role can be examined in the case of Harrisons & Crosfield. In the initial stage of the firm's diversification from tea trader to manager of rubber and tea plantations, the key figure was Arthur Lampard, appointed as director in 1894. He was largely responsible for the establishment of overseas branches and the development of rubber plantations in Malaya. Lampard took a very direct and personal interest in all aspects of the firm's business, issuing detailed instructions on a wide range of matters through until his death in 1916.[2]

As Harrisons & Crosfield diversified, the accumulation of information and decision-making at board level became extensive. Consequently in an administrative reorganization implemented immediately after the end of the First World War, each director was given a specific aspect of operations to be in charge of, and three advisory committees of directors were formed to cover plantations, trading, and general administration.[3] Directors had

---

[2] Harrisons & Crosfield, *One Hundred Years as East India Merchants: Harrisons & Crosfield 1844–1943* (London: the firm, 1944), 20–9; Arthur Lampard's Correspondence, Harrisons & Crosfield Archives, GHL.

[3] Report of the Organization Committee, 18 July 1919, Harrisons & Crosfield Archives, GHL.

usually acquired specialist knowledge about particular products during their service abroad, so that at any given time Harrisons & Crosfield's London board included experts in rubber, tea, timber, and other products.

After Lampard's death, the Harrisons & Crosfield's board functioned as a collective team without a particularly strong entrepreneurial figure standing out, though continuing to exercise a strong centralized executive decision-making role. The same collective phenomenon is evident elsewhere, but in the interwar years certain dominant personalities continued to be present. Sir John Hay, the general manager and later chairman of Guthries, was one such figure in the interwar years, exercising a strong personal influence on all aspects of his firm's business.[4]

UAC shared the characteristics of a high degree of centralization of decision-making at board level. Between 1930 and 1945 UAC was effectively run by its three managing directors rather than the board as a whole. They exercised tight and continual control over all the company's affairs, from the price to be paid for produce to salaries, and exercised a particularly tight control over spending. As with most other trading companies, even small items of expenditure had to be approved in advance by head office. This principle that UAC head office controlled its overseas operations very tightly prevailed through until the 1980s.[5] UAC's centralization stood in marked contrast to that of its parent Unilever, which traditionally allowed its national affiliates great autonomy.

In the firms that retained the partnership form, centralized decision-making from the British head office was less apparent, although usually the London-based partnership had the largest voice in decision-making. Antony Gibbs provides an example. From the early twentieth century this was organized as four partnerships in Britain, Chile, Australia, and the United States. Valparaíso, and Santiago after 1945, was the residence of the Chilean partnership, and New York that of the American. The Australian partnership of Gibbs, Bright & Company was based in Melbourne while there was also an important office in Sydney. Unlike some firms—such as Balfour Williamson where one person could be simultaneously a partner in London or South America—partners in Gibbs was only partners in one location, though Gibbs family members were partners in London, Chile, and New York.

Within this structure, the London-based partnership had a central coordinating role. As in the case of other companies, the importance of London as a market for commodities such as nitrate and wool reinforced the importance of the London office and meant that it was natural for London to sell goods on behalf of the Australian and Chilean partnerships. In the case of Gibbs in particular, the role of the City of London in international finance

---

[4] D. J. M. Tate, *The RGA History of the Plantation Industry in the Malay Peninsula* (Kuala Lumpur: Oxford University Press, 1996), 316, 319 n 22.

[5] D. K. Fieldhouse, *Merchant Capital and Economic Decolonization* (Oxford: Clarendon Press, 1994), 24–6.

further reinforced the power of the London partnership, given that its short-term financing of the other partnerships was frequent and substantial. However, there were differences in the relative importance of London versus the other partnerships. Certainly in the early twentieth century the Chilean business was closely controlled, and this remained so after the transformation of the Chilean branch into a partnership.[6] The Australian partnership acted more independently than the Chilean one, and the New York one even more independently, especially before the appointment of a Gibbs family member as a director in the late 1920s. However, the preservation of the resemblance of independence was very important because if the overseas partnerships had been seen to have been controlled from Britain they would have been subject to British income tax.

Before their incorporation in 1929–30, the three partnerships of Balfour Williamson in Liverpool (or London after 1909), Williamson Balfour in Chile, and Balfour Guthrie in the United States were also closely linked. In this case, Balfour Williamson's partners were mostly resident in Britain, but one was always resident in Chile and one in San Francisco, while only some of the partners of the other two partnerships were resident overseas, and there was always some from each overseas firm working in Britain. The US-resident partners were on the whole given more scope for independent decision-making than the Chile-resident ones, but in the case of this group particularly strong individuals took a prominent role in decision-making: Stephen Williamson to 1901 and his eldest son—Lord Forres—over the succeeding thirty years.

As in the case of Gibbs, the desire to escape liability to British income tax led to a heavy emphasis on formal independence between the partnerships. The 1920s partnership agreements for Balfour Guthrie stated that 'the complete and exclusive control and management of the business of the firm and the right to sign the firm name belonged to the partners permanently resident in San Francisco, Portland, Seattle, and to such other partners as may become active partners'.[7] Most of the partners at that stage, including Lord Forres, were in fact resident in Britain. Despite such formal structures, during the 1920s the London partners persistently sought to increase their degree of control over both Balfour Guthrie and the New York partnership, which had become a separate partnership in 1918, again largely so that it would escape British income tax. The US branches of the firm had a persistent tendency to become entangled in illiquid investments, especially in property. The London partners had a direct and personal influence in such matters because their agreed shares in the profits of Balfour Guthrie and of the New York partnership were so substantial.

---

[6] Lord Cullen to David Blair, 4 Nov. 1926, MS 11115/3, Antony Gibbs Archives, GHL.
[7] Partnership agreement for 1 Jan. 1924 to 31 Dec. 1925, Partnership Agreements BW box 1, Balfour Williamson Archives, UCL.

The cases of some of the firms registered abroad was different again. Jardine Matheson's head office was in Hong Kong, and it owned and controlled the London firm of Matheson & Co. The desire to avoid British income tax meant that formally control and much else lay on the China coast. 'When in China I held strongly to the opinion that it was better for profits to be made by Jardine Matheson & Co. than by Mathesons', a former *taipan* and then a director of Mathesons noted in 1930, 'as it was largely the same pocket, and in the former case not subject to taxation'.[8] In practice the family shareholders in Scotland were not only the ultimate arbiters on policy, but also on matters such as staff recruitment. The annual accounts were closely scrutinized at meetings at Castlemilk, the Scottish home of the Jardine family, and strategy decided. The actual decision-making structure was almost the opposite to that on paper. The same director of Matheson & Co. explained the relations of the London office to Jardine Matheson in the East in 1930. 'Briefly, it is that the Proprietors, through this office, indicate how they wish the firm's business to be conducted, and your people in the East do the conducting of it.'[9]

In the case of Guthrie & Co. the firm was Singapore registered, though by the 1920s one of the directors was based in the London office. After the death of Sir John Anderson in 1924, his widow Lady Anderson owned most of the company. However, John Hay became General Manager in London in the following year, at the same time purchasing one-sixth of the business. Lady Anderson would receive the annual accounts, and Hay would duly translate the views of 'the Proprietors' to the Singapore management.[10] Hay in fact, rather than the Andersons, dominated Guthrie until his death in the 1960s, even though in 1950 he sold back his shareholding to the family.[11]

The size of the head office staffs supporting directors varied enormously. UAC had a large London head office staff of 800 in the 1920s, divided into specialized departments such as capital expenditure, produce-purchasing, accounts, and property. They were physically located on the second and third floors of Unilever's London headquarters, Unilever House, until 1959, when they moved over the Thames to their own building.[12] The head office continued physically separated from Unilever until both UAC and its building were closed down by Unilever in 1987–8.

The large head office staff reflected the centralized control exercised over UAC's business by London, and also the fact that UAC performed core value-adding activities in London. Before the 1960s in particular the London

[8] D. G. M. Bernard to D. Paterson, 1 May 1930, P&C Letters from London to Hong Kong Aug. 1929–Dec. 1930, JMA, CUL.
[9] Ibid., D. G. M. Bernard to J. J. Paterson, 12 June 1930.
[10] J. G. Hay to Guthries Singapore, 2 July 1925, G/MIS/9, Guthrie Archives, SOAS.
[11] S. Cunyngham-Brown, *The Traders* (London: Newman Neame, 1970), 249–51.
[12] Fieldhouse, *Merchant Capital*, 23–6.

head office staff were extensively engaged in selling the commodities produced in West Africa and buying the goods consumed there, and even afterwards they retained a role in providing services for UAC's diversified operations.[13] By the 1980s, however, UAC's large head office was becoming increasingly anomalous. UAC also inherited from the Niger Company a French subsidiary, whose headquarters were initially in Liverpool but then transferred to Paris. From the mid-1930s this emerged as the focus of UAC's business with French Africa, although it was not until 1959 that all UAC companies operating in francophone Africa were placed under a single company, Niger France, with its own chairman and board of directors.[14]

Harrisons & Crosfield also had a large bureaucracy in its London head office, which in 1952 employed over 300 persons.[15] As in the case of UAC, the staff were divided into departments such as secretarial, finance and accounts, shipping and estates. The considerable administrative work generated by the numerous plantation companies under its control helps to explain the relatively large size of Harrisons & Crosfield's head office. Another firm with a substantial corporate headquarters was Ralli, which like UAC undertook considerable commodity trading in London. Ralli had a total employment in its British offices of just under 300 in the 1930s.[16]

In contrast, the London head office of many companies was much smaller. Steels' head office in London had a staff of about eighty in the interwar years, of whom about a quarter were juniors awaiting transfer to serve in Burma or India.[17] Despite the scale and spread of its business, Finlays' Glasgow head office was also small in the late nineteenth century, and only had a total staff of 65 in 1950.[18] Knowles & Foster, whose activities included a large flour milling business in Brazil, had twenty-one staff in London in 1896, and seventy in 1948.[19]

A potential disadvantage of boards consisting of directors who had spent their entire careers overseas with the company was that their knowledge might become out of date. Indeed this became a serious problem after 1945, when the directors of many firms active in India and Latin America seemed unable to adjust to the new political circumstances in those regions, and instead either resented them or felt threatened by them. An important means of keeping directors informed of current situations was the regular visits to them especially during the cold winter months in Europe. By the interwar years transportation and communication improvements had made 'directors tours' a regular feature of most companies. In 1923 Wilsons' chairman, after

---

[13] Fieldhouse, *Merchant Capital*, 769–72.   [14] Ibid. 23–4.

[15] List of London head office staff in 1952, Harrisons & Crosfield Archives, GHL.

[16] Report to the Chairman of Ralli Brothers Limited, 12 Apr. 1939, Ralli Archives, MS 23834, GHL.

[17] H. E. W. Braund, *Calling to Mind* (Oxford: Pergamon Press, 1975), 21–2.

[18] J. Brogan, *James Finlay & Co. Limited* (Glasgow: Jackson Sons & Co., 1951), 255–62.

[19] *The History of Knowles & Foster 1828–1948* (London: Ted Kavanagh, 1948), 90.

visiting South America, persuaded fellow directors to agree that a director should visit the overseas branches at least once every two years.[20] At Harrisons & Crosfield directors spent months overseas at a time, inspecting operations in detail and reporting to their colleagues with recommendations for improving the management of operations or expanding communications with London. As most directors had spent their entire careers with the company overseas before becoming directors, they acquired an in-depth knowledge of particular countries and products. At Swire's, there was another system in place in the interwar years whereby a director spent one year in Asia, the directors alternating this role. At Dodwells, the scale of their problems in China in the early 1930s led the firm's chairman, Stanley Dodwell, to relocate in person from London to Hong Kong in 1932.[21] Directors were not the only members of head offices to travel to the overseas branches. In the interwar years Harrisons & Crosfield had two branch-travelling inspectors charged with visiting every branch and affiliate and company one a year.

The 'knowledge' of directors usually combined two elements—products and locations—which raised the question whether board members took product or territorial responsibilities. In practice directors usually took responsibility for both products and countries, though the balance differed between firms, and from the 1960s the advice of management consultants such as McKinseys was always to move towards a system based on functional responsibilities. In UAC from the 1960s directors had both product and territorial responsibility, but the former was more important and controlled substantial resources. This was why UAC's diversification was conducted by product divisions, often with little regard to synergies between different divisions in the same area. At Jardine Matheson in this period, the board only met quarterly but the ten or so executive directors met every week in Hong Kong, with each director in charge of an 'area', either geographical or functional. In Jardine Matheson, region rather than product was on the whole more important, though a report by the management consultants McKinsey in 1978 recommended the firm to move towards a more functional system.[22]

The branch systems of the trading companies were organized without recourse to complex layers of managerial hierarchies. Often there was a 'chief' overseas branch, which served as a regional headquarters which supervised the branch network. Swire's various branches—operated under the name of Butterfield & Swire—had a joint headquarters in Hong Kong and Shanghai before the Second World War. All correspondence to London from the East was conducted through the two head offices, and they divided

[20] Minute 17 July 1923, Minute Book F (4 Mar. 1920–26 July 1927), MS 20186/6, Wilson, Sons Archives, GHL.
[21] Stanley Dodwell to George Dodwell, 8 Feb. 1931, MS 27512 Dodwell Archives, GHL.
[22] Interview with Jeremy Brown, 21 Jan. 1999.

responsibility for the branches and also the affiliated firms. Hong Kong supervised Butterfield & Swire and China Navigation branches and agencies on the South China coast and in South East Asia, and the management of the dockyard and refinery in Hong Kong, and it was the senior Blue Funnel agency in the East, dealing directly with the shipping firm of Holts in Liverpool. Shanghai controlled Butterfield & Swire and China Navigation branches in Shanghai, along the Yangtze river and in coastal parts north of Ningpo, and the management of the Tientsin Lighter Co.

UAC, which had the most complex bureaucracy, had a system of regional general managers. All communications to and from the head offices in London and Paris passed through the general managers, who had considerable authority except in areas such as capital expenditure and the quantity and price of produce bought. Beneath the general manager there were regional, branch, and district managers. This structure remained in place until the 1960s.[23]

The trading companies developed extensive bureaucratic rules, regulations, and routines to formalize flows of information and decision-making. Information flows between traders and head offices were considerable, both as regards the number of communications by telegraph, letter, and reports and as regards the detail of reporting. Overseas traders reported at regular intervals to their head offices, providing detailed financial information and analysis of all aspects of the business.

In Harrisons & Crosfield by the interwar years reporting flows and obligations were clearly codified. The overseas branches which acted as managing agents for plantations sent reports to London, usually monthly, on plantation performance. Routine correspondence between the branches and the plantation companies was not required to be sent to London, but 'important' or strategic issues were always referred to head office. Letters on the general working of plantation companies were sent to the estates office in head office, where Harrisons & Crosfield had different 'estates secretaries' dealing with each country in which the firm managed estates. At the overseas branches, the branch manager communicated constantly with the plantation managers, who were advised of important communications from head office and allowed to express opinions on proposals. Consequently final decisions made in London rested on consultations among various layers of management. Typically, branches also appointed 'visiting agents' who visited plantations and drew up reports on them following periodic visits.[24]

Harrisons & Crosfield developed standardized management information reporting systems. Every year the branches produced for each plantation

[23] Fieldhouse, *Merchant Capital*, 26–41.
[24] *One Hundred Years*, 53; correspondence files held at Harrisons & Crosfield head office; Report of the Organization Committee, 18 July 1919; Report of the Advisory Committee on the Organization of the Estates Department, *c.*1920; Board Minute, July 1913, Pataling Rubber Estates Ltd., Harrisons & Crosfield Archives, GHL.

company a standard data sheet which was submitted to the individual company board of directors. This contained eighteen sets of data, all but three of which covered the two preceding years as well as the current one. Besides basic information on profits and dividends it included selling prices achieved and costs of production; the breakdown of rubber sales into different grades; production and cost estimates for the following year; and information on productivity improvements, and the physical condition of the rubber estates, such as yield per acre. The standard sheets also recorded the Harrisons & Crosfield shareholding in the plantation companies.[25]

Although the nature of the reporting systems differed between companies, the other trading companies with large plantation interests also had standard reporting systems in place by the interwar years. Finlays, for example, had extremely detailed standardized procedures for the compilation of financial and other information on the tea estates under its control.[26] As in the case of Harrisons & Crosfield, this information flowed through the different levels of the business group—the overseas branches as managing agents; the 'visiting agents' which they used to monitor the tea estates; the Glasgow head office as the secretaries of the individual tea companies; and finally the board of directors of the tea companies.[27]

The efficiency of such management information systems rested on the reliability of the data recorded. There were potential problems in this respect because of the ways the business groups functioned. For example the payment of commission to staff—discussed below—provided an incentive to distort data. The monitoring of data by several layers of the bureaucracy also had the potential to make managers distort information to avoid adverse criticism. Consequently firms such as Finlays stressed in their internal communications the need for accurate information, and to assure managers that severe sanctions would not be applied if (for example) budgets were exceeded, provided satisfactory explanations were given.[28]

Trading companies operating extensive international trading operations and managing plantation—or other—enterprises needed extensive and accurate management information in order to function. However, two other factors encouraged firms to develop elaborate management information systems. The first was the importance of commission in the employment contracts of managers. The use of commission meant that accounting practices within organizations had to be detailed and transparent.[29] Given that trade moved between different branches of trading companies, the proper calculation

---

[25] Harrisons & Crosfield 'secretarial' companies: file of company results submitted to the board, 1940–54, Harrisons & Crosfield Archives, GHL.

[26] Mr Jamieson's Notes on Tea Estate Accounts, Jan. 1936, Finlays Archives, UGD91/117/II.

[27] Ibid.   [28] Ibid.

[29] Ross E. Stewart, 'Scottish Company Accounting, 1870–1920: Selected Case Studies of Accounting in its Historical Context' (unpublished Ph.D. Thesis, University of Glasgow, 1986), 186–217. This is examined further below. For the case of Swire's, see G. W. Swire to Colin and John, 6 Oct. 1941, 28 Oct. 1941, Swire Archives, MS Swire ADD 18, SOAS.

of commission also meant that accurate financial accounts had to be kept so as to identify which branch had the rights to particular business and commission. In 1920 Harrisons & Crosfield issued detailed rules on inter-branch trading, establishing the procedures to be followed, and basis of commission to be charged, in all possible circumstances that could arise between an 'exporting' branch and an 'importing' branch. The stated intention of the regulations was to allocate profits fairly between branches while encouraging different parts of the organization to work together rather than to compete.[30]

A second factor which compelled the development of extensive management information systems was the inclusion within the network form of business group of partly owned affiliate companies with outside shareholders. This became an important issue when administrative or other services were shared between companies, which meant that the value of such services needed to be costed and allocated to individual companies.

Finlays encountered this problem in its tea estates in Travancore in south India. In the mid-1930s there were forty-two tea estates all in land leased to the Kanan Devan Company—one of the four big Finlays-affiliated tea companies—from the local government. Kanan Devan controlled most of the tea estates, but three belonged to the Anglo-American Direct Tea Trading Co.—another large Finlays affiliate—while nine others were not affiliated to Finlays in any way, except that they were sub-tenants of Kanan Devan and, in two cases, Kanan Devan sold them rice and transported their goods and tea. Kanan Devan operated a variety of central services for its estates, but these were also used by the Anglo-American estates. Consequently Finlays developed elaborate accounting procedures for allocating costs between the two different companies.[31]

The management structures described above remained in place until the 1960s, and in some instances later. Managerial competences were tacit and evolutionary, built up by years of service in overseas branches before someone became a director. Centralized decision-making rested on extensive rules and routines for information gathering and dissemination, supported by programmes of directors' visits, visiting agents, and so on designed to provide up-to-date knowledge of conditions.

From the 1960s the management structures employed by the trading companies began to change. This reflected the changing nature of their business. Tacit and evolutionary competences declined in value as firms sought to enter new markets and undertake new types of business. Simultaneously the environment faced by the trading companies became more competitive and more hostile, as cartels were dismantled and colonies became independent.

[30] Harrisons & Crosfield regulations in regard to inter-branch trading adopted by the Board on 6 Jan. 1920, Harrisons & Crosfield Archives, GHL.

[31] Mr Jamieson's Notes on Tea Estate Accounts, Jan. 1936, Finlays Archives, UGD 91/117/II.

This was a period of great organizational change for British companies as a whole, as partly in response to changing competitive pressures, and partly under the influence of American management models transferred by management consultants, there were extensive mergers, the elimination of much family influence, and the adoption of M-form structures of organization albeit somewhat adopted to British management style.[32]

UAC was among the first of the trading companies to move towards divisionalization, stimulated by the great changes in its business from the late 1950s as it pulled out of produce and general trading into more specialized trading activities. Between 1958 and 1963 UAC created new functional companies to run the more dynamic and specialized parts of the business, such as motor distribution and brewing. However, the reorganization was far from complete because of the complexity of the historical inheritance, and parts of the business—such as the Ollivant trading company—remained outside the structure and diversified into activities run by UAC functional companies. In 1973 a more comprehensive divisionalization of the company was implemented when nine divisions were created, each responsible for all activities overseas and in Europe. Each division had a chairman and was responsible to the managing directors on the UAC board.[33]

UAC's path to divisionalization was generally followed by the other trading companies over the 1960s and 1970s. UAC's West African competitor, John Holt & Co. adopted a divisional form in 1958 with four divisions, but like UAC the structure was slow to develop and settle down. Diversification was so rapid that as early as 1962 the existing divisions were replaced by four new ones, each with a managing director. These were West African trade, wines and spirits, shipping, and group services. Nine 'business areas' reported to the four divisions. In 1966 the number of divisions was reduced to three, and this structure was retained following Holts' acquisition by Lonrho. During the 1960s Booker McConnell also began to reorganize on a divisional basis. By the end of that decade its international business was organized into a form of divisional structure, with divisions for shops, wholesale distribution; light industries; tropical agriculture; engineering; printing; rum and produce; shipping; and books. A decade later, after further changes to the business, Bookers had been fully organized on a divisional basis with eight divisions: food distribution; fluid engineering; general engineering; overseas trading; alcohol; shipping; agriculture; authors and services.

---

[32] Derek F. Channon, *The Strategy and Structure of British Enterprise* (London: Macmillan, 1973); Bruce Kogut and David Parkinson, 'The Diffusion of American Organising Principles to Europe', in Bruce Kogut (ed.), *Country Competitiveness* (New York: Oxford University Press, 1993), 179–202, Geoffrey Jones, 'Great Britain: Big Business, Management, and Competitiveness in Twentieth-Century Britain', in A. D. Chandler, Franco Amatori, and Takashi Hikino (eds.), *Big Business and the Wealth of Nations* (Cambridge: Cambridge University Press, 1997), 128–30.
[33] Fieldhouse, *Merchant Capital*, 52–63.

By the end of the 1970s the management structures of the trading companies looked much more like the US model than twenty years previously. Divisionalization was commonplace. For reasons discussed earlier, the British firms had a long tradition of generating management information, and as new management systems were adopted there was a growing reliance on financial controls to monitor the affiliates. At Jardine Matheson, tight financial controls were always a feature of the organization, but one of the major recommendations of the McKinsey report on the firm in 1978 was to tighten up their financial reporting systems further. Jardine affiliates were obliged to send monthly reports to the corporate centre and similar tight financial reporting was found elsewhere.[34]

7.3 Human Resources

The staff of the trading companies consisted of several distinct elements. In almost all cases through to the 1970s there was a basic division between the 'home' staff in Britain and the expatriate or overseas staff, who generally served their entire careers abroad. The overseas staff were usually themselves divided into those working for the parent trading company and those working for affiliate firms. Until the post-Second World War this staff, which performed managerial and technical tasks, was almost exclusively European. They were supported by locally recruited clerical and other workers. In the case of companies which managed plantations, mines, and other labour-intensive operations, the total numbers employed rose to substantial amounts.

From its creation through to the 1980s UAC was probably the largest employer of European staff and among the largest total employer of all the trading companies. In the late 1930s, after a period of substantial job cuts, UAC employed around 1,000 expatriate staff.[35] In the mid-1960s the firm still employed over 1,000 expatriates in its overseas branches, though the number then fell sharply with the 'localization' of managers to reach around 300 in the mid-1970s. This expatriate staff managed large numbers of employees in West Africa and other regions where UAC operated. The total numbers employed by the firm at the end of the 1970s was in excess of 70,000 persons.

Table 7.1 gives a breakdown of staff numbers at the Calcutta branch of another large employer, James Finlay, in 1945. In addition to the staff shown in the table, Finlays employed workers in western India, including its cotton mill operations, in Ceylon, in its Kenyan plantations, and in Scotland, resulting in a total workforce approaching 160,000 and an expatriate management

[34] Interview with Jeremy Brown, 21 Jan. 1999; interview with Sir Colin Campbell, 16 Apr. 1996.

[35] Fieldhouse, *Merchant Capital*, 28.

TABLE 7.1 Employment at Calcutta Branch of
James Finlay, 1945

	European	Total
Branch	33	540
Jute mills	21	6,421
Sugar mills	13	2,337
Tea estates	287	129,962
Total	354	139,260

Source: Calcutta to Glasgow, 17 Sept. 1945, UGD
91/413/1.

cadre of around 450 in the late 1940s. In the interwar years Steels and its affiliates employed over 250 expatriate managers and around 50,000 people in general.[36] In China, Jardine Matheson operations employed around 113,000 in 1930.[37] In 1937 the firm's expatriate management staff in the East was 117, though this figure excluded expatriate managers in its affiliate firms.[38] The expatriate staff of Swire's was around the same size—140 in 1933. In addition, Swire's employed 434 Europeans in the China Navigation Company, 58 in Taikoo Dockyard, and 25 in the Taikoo Sugar Refinery, making an over-all total of 657.[39] Harrisons & Crosfield had 104 expatriate management staff in the East in 1924 and 196 in 1951. In the latter year it also employed 195 staff in the United States and Canada.[40]

The trading companies gave considerable attention to the selection of their future expatriate managers, especially those to be employed by the 'core' trading firm, whose reputation and performance rested crucially on their probity and ability. They were often recruited in Britain as the result of personal recommendation or acquaintance with directors. 'In the past', a Jardine Matheson manager noted in 1933, '"friends and relations" of the Firm or nominees of retired partners have been our chief source of supply'.[41] They were often personally interviewed by directors. At Finlays, potential employees were extensively questioned on their family backgrounds, their family's position in society, and the occupations of their relatives.[42] The general profile of a recruit was of a respectable, privately educated young man preferably with some sporting achievements at school. Often such men

[36] Steel Brothers: Brief Histories, *c.*1970, Steel Brothers Archives, MS 29557, GHL.

[37] M. Keswick (ed.), *The Thistle and the Jade* (London: Octopus, 1982), 260.

[38] D. Beith to D. G. M. Bernard, 15 Aug. 1933, S/O London, Shanghai, Hong Kong, July–Dec. 1933, JMA, CUL.

[39] J. K. Swire to C. G. Heywood, 8 June 1934, JSSI/4/13, Swire Archives, SOAS.

[40] Staff Lists, Harrisons & Crosfield Archives, GHL.

[41] D. Beith to D. G. M. Bernard, 15 Aug. 1933, S/O London, Shanghai, Hong Kong, July–Dec. 1933, JMA, CUL.

[42] Stewart, 'Scottish Company Accounting'.

had had a few years' experience working in a domestic merchant or shipping office. This approach fitted the general British preference for 'character' and social skills as the main qualification for management.[43]

There were ethnic biases in recruitment practices. Finlays, the Borneo Company, and Jardine Matheson were among the firms which recruited a high proportion of their staff from Scotland. Even the Liverpool-based Balfour Williamson in the nineteenth century 'refused to send any but Scottish recruits to the foreign Houses'.[44] Ralli was distinct in its employment of Greeks as managers. The firm employed some 150 Greeks in India in the interwar years, with only a handful of ethnic British as managers.[45]

British business as a whole was suspicious of the employment of university graduates until well into the post-Second World War period. During the interwar years a number of the larger British manufacturing companies, such as Lever Brothers and its successor Unilever, had begun to recruit graduates as trainee managers,[46] but they remained the exception rather than the rule. British overseas banks considered employing graduates in the interwar years, but rarely did so, and this remained the case until the 1960s.[47] It is therefore striking that the trading companies were among the first British enterprises to begin recruiting from universities. Before the First World War the trading companies also rarely considered such a source of recruitment. After receiving an approach from Oxford University in 1912, Jardine Skinner's Senior Partner firmly declared 'that the class of men available from such a source would not be suitable'.[48] However, sentiment began to shift during the First World War. By the end of the war Harrisons & Crosfield was actively recruiting graduates.[49]

During the interwar years the employment of graduates increased. Swire's appear to have been particularly active in this regard. J. K. Swire, the grandson of the firm's founder, John Samuel Swire, and the firm's chairman between 1946 and 1966, was educated at Eton and Oxford, and became a director of the firm 'with special responsibilities for Overseas Staff' in 1919 aged 26. He developed the idea of hand-picking undergraduate recruits from the universities specifically for service in the Far East. Swire was especially concerned to recruit 'the very best', who 'must be good linguists and thoroughly understand the Chinese'.[50] By the 1930s members of the Swire

---

[43] Shirley Keeble, *The Ability to Manage* (Manchester: Manchester University Press, 1992).

[44] Wallis Hunt, *Heirs of Great Adventure*, ii: *1901–1951* (London: the firm, 1960), 50.

[45] Note by Leoni M. Calvocaressi on the House of Ralli Brothers, Dec. 1952, Ralli Brothers Archives, MS 23836, GHL.

[46] Charles Wilson, *Unilever 1945–1965* (London: Cassell, 1968), 48–9.

[47] Geoffrey Jones, *British Multinational Banking 1830–1990* (Oxford: Clarendon Press, 1993), 171–2, 281–2.

[48] W. A. Barkier to Gresson, 3 Jan. 1912, in-letters from Senior Partner 1911, No. 17, Jardine Skinner Archives, CUL.

[49] Report of the Organization Committee, 18 July 1919, Harrisons & Crosfield Archives, GHL.

[50] Gavin Young, *Beyond Lion Rock* (London: Hutchinson, 1988), 93–5.

family were on both the Cambridge and Oxford Universities Appointments Boards, and their new recruits were largely from both universities, plus a tiny handful from Edinburgh.[51] In 1939 the firm described its Far Eastern expatriate staff as 'recruited largely from the Universities'.[52]

Jardine Matheson's conversion to graduates appears to have been in the 1930s, though by the 1920s the sons of several senior managers who had gone to Oxford or Cambridge were joining the firm as juniors.[53] By 1933 the firm's *taipan* in Shanghai was alarmed by a shortage of 'good younger men coming on' and suggested a change of recruitment strategy: 'perhaps we should try to obtain the very best from institutions such as the Appointment Boards of the Universities . . . Brains, school and/or University record of work, reliability of character and health might be substituted for friendship in qualifying for selection.'[54] By that year Jardines was recruiting staff from the Oxford and Cambridge Appointments Boards.[55] However, senior figures such as W. J. Keswick in the company retained more mixed feelings than at Swire's, even though the Swire example impressed them. 'I do not want the Eton/Cambridge type, of which . . . we will have enough', Keswick wrote in 1936:

With of course all due deference to the 'east coast of England', I do feel that men from north of the border are the most suitable for our routine business and heads of Department. I am very keen on keeping the Scottish entity of the Firm. If you can find someone with Scottish University education, so much the better.

If we take on any more University men I think they should be from the Appointments Boards and should have obtained first class degrees. It is interesting to note that both Masson and Lock, No 1 in Hong Kong and No 2 in Shanghai of Taikoo respectively, are men with 'double first'. I know the 'double first' minds do not generally make good business minds, but so far we have not set our standard very high.

I hope I have not conveyed that I have swung against the University man. This is not so; I merely consider that he must be aided and abetted by the solid, plodding type from Scotland.[56]

By the 1930s it would seem that many of the British trading companies elsewhere in Asia were recruiting some graduates. Finlays appointed a number of graduates, especially from Glasgow University. Shaw Wallace in the 1930s recruited mostly from the Cambridge University Appointments Board, 'who seemed to specialise in men suitable for work in the

[51] London Staff Ledger, JSSI/5/I, Swire Archives, SOAS.
[52] Ibid., JSS to Staff Manager, Imperial Airways, 19 Jan. 1919, JSSI/4/16.
[53] D. Landale to D. G. M. Bernard, 11 Feb. 1926, S/O London to Hong Kong, 1926, JMA, CUL.
[54] Ibid., D. Beith to D. G. M. Bernard, 15 Aug. 1933, S/O London, Shanghai, Hong Kong, July–Dec. 1933.
[55] Ibid., D. G. M. Bernard to D. Beith, 29 Dec. 1933, S/O London to Shanghai, Jan.–June 1934.
[56] Ibid., W. J. Keswick to D. G. M. Bernard, 20 Nov. 1936, S/O Shanghai to London, 1936.

East'.[57] The London office of Binny's described as 'just the type of young Assistant . . . you want' a young man who had just graduated in law from Cambridge who 'got his Blue for Rugby Football in his first year at Cambridge, and for the last three years has been a Scottish International player'.[58] The staff of Wallace Brothers' Bombay Burmah Trading Corporation in the 1930s was described by someone working for their competitor Steels as 'recruited mainly from the Universities, with the accent perhaps more heavily on the athletic than the academic qualifications'.[59] The preference for sporting talents reflected the fact that the traders were looking for a particular type of character who would take risks, albeit in a team context, and Japanese trading companies also sought to recruit staff with a combination of academic attainment and sporting ability. However the progress of graduates in the British companies was by no means continuous or as prevalent as in Japan. Harrisons & Crosfield, an early pioneer in their employment, over time shifted towards recruiting people with special technical skills, especially accounting and engineering.[60]

In West Africa, the predecessor firms to UAC rarely if ever employed graduates, but there was a shift in policy under UAC's first chairman, Sir Robert Waley Cohen. Cohen was a former executive of Shell and an enthusiast for the recruitment of graduates in firms, becoming a member of the Cambridge University Appointments Board. At a time when UAC was cutting its staff, Waley Cohen recruited a number of Oxford and Cambridge graduates as future managers. Although Waley Cohen was forced to resign in 1931, and the new recruits 'did not have an easy time in winning acceptance', the policy of graduate recruitment was retained by UAC.[61]

Certainly the trading companies as a whole did not confine entry to their management cadre to graduates until well into the 1960s. Harrisons & Crosfield's job advertisements in that decade—which always mentioned the firm as a 'well-known British merchant company' or 'a prominent British commercial firm operating in the Far East'—usually specified a school leaving certificate ('A' level, obtained at age 18) and then an accounting or sometimes an engineering qualification. One such advertisement in the *Daily Telegraph*—a right-wing British 'establishment' newspaper—for 1962 sought 'a well-educated young man aged 22–26' for 'one of its offices in south India':

---

[57] Sir Harry Townend, *A History of Shaw Wallace & Co. and Shaw Wallace & Co. Ltd.* (Calcutta: the firm, 1965), 177.

[58] London to Madras, 25 June 1935, Binny Archives MS 27159/8, GHL.

[59] 'But the Melody Lingers on'. A Personal Story by Harold Braund, Steel Brothers Archives, MS 29556, GHL.

[60] See, for example, the descriptions of the long-standing existing organization in: Memorandum on Colombo branch administration, 1959, files of Harrisons Lister Engineering Ltd., Harrisons & Crosfield Archives, GHL.

[61] Frederick Pedler, *The Lion and the Unicorn in Africa* (London: Heinemann, 1974), 307–8; Fieldhouse, *Merchant Capital*, 97–8.

He should be single, should hold at least one 'A' level pass in the G.C.E. and should have the ability and energy to take up a position of responsibility in the trading or shipping sides of the Company's business after a period of training.

Another advert in 1965 sought a Tea Trainee,

18–21 single. Previous experience in Tea Trade not essential—one 'A' level pass in G.C.E. minimum. After London training, take up appointment in Company's Eastern Service as a Tea Buying Assistant.[62]

By the interwar years, if not earlier, the trading companies began to seek also men with specific training. Firms that traded in commodities such as tea had for a long time recruited staff with knowledge of the product, and were very aware of having—for example—a good 'tea man'. In Jardine Matheson, when W. J. Keswick heard that their chief 'tea man' was looking for a successor, he returned to a favourite theme. 'I stress the importance of ability and knowledge of tea rather than a sufficiency of "Eton and Oxford"'.[63] In the interwar years other types of prior training also began to be valued. Staff with accountancy experience and qualifications began to be sought. The growing importance of sales agencies for engineering and other more technical products required also the recruitment of staff with some technical knowledge of the products they were selling. 'In view of the increase of our engineering Agencies', Binny's in Madras told their London office in 1934, they wanted someone with 'some engineering training. What we have in view is a man with practical experience in Engineering salesmanship who would be able to go out on tour and would have sufficient technical knowledge to demonstrate the advantages of our productions to would-be clients and their engineers.'[64]

Strong firm-specific differences persisted in recruitment patterns during the post-Second World War period, though all the British trading companies continued to emphasize the importance of 'character'. At Jardine Matheson in the 1960s and 1970s, the firm sought generalists with leadership ability for its 'House' staff. As a trading firm, there was an interest in 'entrepreneurial types' able to take risk, and a cautious attitude towards recruiting very good 'academic' types, who often left the firm after a period of years.[65] Although Swire's recruited staff from similar educational and social backgrounds as Jardine Matheson, the nature of the firm's business made it less interested in risk-taking 'trader' personalities, although its transport and distribution businesses were themselves 'risky' and required individuals able to take such risks. Swire's sought a 'mix' of recruits, both in terms of social background and personality types. The firm liked characters lacking

[62] Harrisons & Crosfield recruitment advertisement, Harrisons & Crosfield Archives, GHL.
[63] W. J. Keswick to D. G. M. Bernard, 16 Jan. 1936, S/O Shanghai to London 1936, JMA, CUL.
[64] Madras to London, 8 Feb. 1934, Binny Archives, MS 27160/18, GHL.
[65] Interview with Jeremy Brown, 21 Jan. 1999.

in self-importance, reflecting the 'low profile' corporate culture of that group.[66] At both firms recruitment was regarded as a most important matter. Sir John Swire, the firm's chairman between 1966 and 1987, personally conducted forty-five-minute interviews with applicants.

Staff recruited for the affiliate firms often had more specialist qualifications than the generalists recruited to the House staff, though not all firms followed this model. At Swire's all the core 'House' staff which provided the senior management of affiliates such as Swire Pacific were employed by John Swire & Sons, providing an important element of control over those affiliates. In many cases, however, staff had different terms and conditions from those of the core trading company and were engaged to work solely for those enterprises. Finlays, like all the British firms in India, recruited from the Dundee jute industry to staff its jute factories.[67] Other men were recruited to serve as tea planters on the Finlay estates. Sometimes staff for the affiliates were recruited by the parent trading company, and sometimes by the company itself. The boards of Harrisons & Crosfield plantation affiliates appointed estate managers, though in some cases the directors merely confirmed appointments arranged by officials of the local Harrisons & Crosfield branch.[68] In the case of Antony Gibbs, the directors of affiliates appointed staff. However since parent trading companies usually had directors on the boards of affiliates it is evident that no clear distinction can be made.

Although the trading company and affiliate staffs were often separated, it would seem that one of the benefits of the business group system may have been that affiliates could attract better managers because they were part of a bigger group rather than 'free-standing' companies working in far away places. In this sense, the trading company's reputation served not only to reassure and attract potential investors, but also potential managers. However the different terms and conditions inside business groups also caused problems. This was one of the difficulties faced by Swire's in the late 1920s when its crews on the China Navigation fleet went on strike. Interviews with the strikers established that

the C.N.Co is never talked of or known . . . as the C.N.Co, but is always spoken of as the 'B&S' ships—they regard themselves as Taikoo and . . . do not see why their treatment should be different from that accorded to their opposite numbers . . . It comes out again and again in these conversations how Taikoo is looked upon as all one show: the whole outfit, to them, is 'Taikoo'.[69]

[66] Interview at Swire House, 28 Jan. 1999.

[67] Gordon T. Stewart, *Jute and Empire* (Manchester: Manchester University Press, 1998), 18–19.

[68] Board Minutes of British Borneo Timber, Bajoe Kidoel Rubber, and Lunuva (Ceylon) Tea & Rubber Estates, Harrisons & Crosfield Archives, GHL.

[69] H. W. Robertson to John Swire, 30 Dec. 1927, Swire Archives, Swire ADD 15, SOAS.

Warren Swire considered the seamen 'hopelessly muddle-headed' and unable to 'grasp the single fact that J.S. & Son, C.N.Co, T.S.R. and T.D. & E. Co are entirely different and distinct concerns, owned by different people and with different conditions of service'.[70]

On joining a trading company or an affiliate, there was an expectation of 'lifetime employment', or—more specifically—twenty-five or thirty years' service in Asia, Africa, or Latin America followed by early retirement in a man's early fifties. However there was absolutely no legal entitlement to such lifetime employment. Managers were usually appointed on three- to five-year contracts which were not renewed automatically. Ralli's expatriate managers in India in the interwar years were employed on an annual basis as 'a means of inducing efficiency'.[71] Contracts specified salary—which usually had small increments from one year to the next—and entitlements to travelling expenses for him and his family, accommodation, and leave.[72] In the case of the West African trader John Holt, its 'agents'—as they called them—were allocated to specific African 'stations' in their two- or three-year contracts, but they could change location when or if their contract was renewed.[73] At Finlays, at least before the First World War, as each contract neared expiry, there would be a negotiation about terms and conditions of the next one, if one was to be offered.[74] Staff were removed or their contracts not renewed in serious cases of misjudgement or inefficiency. In addition, the early 1930s saw substantial staff reductions made in companies such as UAC on general grounds of economy. During these years the difficult economic environment was often used to remove sub-optimal staff. 'The first step', Guthries' Singapore manager was told in 1931, 'is to reduce the staff by weeding out the inefficient or doubtfully efficient'.[75]

After recruitment, staff were typically given on-the-job training and familiarized with the firm's business in London, Liverpool, or Glasgow before transfer to Asia, Africa, or Latin America. Swire's explained their system in 1933:

Before proceeding to join our Far Eastern staff, candidates spend from 6 to 18 months on probation in this office. During this time they are expected to go in for either the Junior Certificate in Book-keeping & Accountancy of the London Chamber of Commerce or the Intermediate Certificate of the Institute of Chartered Shipbrokers. In addition, we attach considerable importance to their obtaining a certain elementary knowledge of the Chinese language, manners, customs and country.[76]

[70] Ibid., G. W. Swire to S. A. Townley, 30 July 1928, JSSI/1/4/11.
[71] Report to the Chairman of Ralli Brothers Limited, 12 Apr. 1939, Ralli Brothers Archives, MS 23834, GHL.
[72] There is a description of a Swire employment contract in G. W. Swire to H. A. McPherson, 20 Oct. 1931, Swire Archives, JSSI/4/12, SOAS.
[73] Records of John Holt & Co. (Liverpool) Ltd., 1900–12, 380 HOL 1/5/1–3, Liverpool Record Office.
[74] Correspondence in Finlays Archives, UGD 91/447/2/I.
[75] Sir John Hay to James Robertson, 4 June 1931, G/MIS/9, Guthrie Archives, SOAS.
[76] J. S. Swire to A. R. Malcolm, 31 Mar. 1933, Swire Archives, JSSI/4/13, SOAS.

The Chinese language and cross-cultural training was provided by London University's School of Oriental and African Studies, which the Swire men attended three hours a week after work for two hours of Chinese plus a one-hour lecture on Chinese culture and history. The Swire emphasis on formal qualifications and instruction was unusual, but the initial training in London was the norm. At Dodwells, the policy in the interwar years was 'of engaging public school boys and training them for three years in the London Office', but the introduction of compulsory military service after the Second World War resulted in a reduction of the time spent in London to three months, followed by further training overseas.[77] Training was not always especially systematic. A junior recruited to Steels in the 1930s spent two years in the Rice Department in London, but was then posted to Burmese oilfields.[78]

In Asia at least, the British trading companies also placed considerable emphasis on acquiring some knowledge of local languages. Swire's was distinctive in its strong emphasis on learning Chinese in the interwar years, but other firms also considered language skills to be important. As early as 1907 Anglo-Thai specified that new staff had to acquire a knowledge of Thai before being given salary increments.[79] By the interwar years junior recruits to Steels had to study Burmese at the School of Oriental and African Studies, but more seriously once in Burma or India staff were not allowed to own a car or join a club until they passed examinations in Burmese and Urdu.[80] Harrisons & Crosfield and Finlays were among other companies which had incentives and expectations for managers to learn —in those cases—Malay and Tamil in the interwar years. Beyond Asia, the staff sent out to Latin America had of necessity to learn Spanish and/or Portuguese. Even the British traders in West Africa were early converts to the idea that their staff needed to know foreign languages. In 1906 John Holt offered to pay the fees of any of its clerks who undertook to learn French, German, or Spanish out of office hours.[81]

There is some evidence that the actual language attainments of trading company staff, certainly with the 'difficult' Asian languages, may have been modest in many cases before the Second World War. Not infrequently employment contracts specified that staff had to learn local languages but they were not taken too rigorously. The end of colonialism and the growth of nationalism in the 1950s and 1960s changed attitudes. 'In view of the prominence this subject was receiving at the present time', the Board of

[77] Board Minutes, 17 Oct. 1950, Dodwell Archives, MS 27498/6, GHL.
[78] 'But the Melody Lingers on'. A Personal Story by Harold Braund, Steel Brothers Archives, MS 29556, GHL.
[79] Board Minutes, 24 Apr. 1907, Anglo-Thai Archives, MS 27008/1, GHL.
[80] Braund, *Calling to Mind*, 22–3.
[81] Board Minutes (draft), 4 Dec. 1906, 380 HOL 1/5/3, John Holt & Co. (Liverpool) Ltd. Archives, Liverpool Record Office.

Borneo Motors resolved in 1960, 'to call the attention of all staff to Clause 7 of their Service Agreement which required that staff attain proficiency in (Malay)'.[82] In 1959 the Assam Company—the large British tea plantation company in India subsequently acquired by Inchcape—introduced a bonus for staff passing oral and written examinations in Assamese, 'in view of the fact that Assamese would in due course become the official State language'.[83] Despite the loss of its business in China, Swire's continued to stress Chinese language knowledge for the staff recruited to the 'core' trading company. By the 1990s the small number of new British expatriates recruited to that firm were all graduates in Chinese.

On transfer to overseas branches, there was considerable emphasis on socialization, with unmarried juniors living and dining together in the larger branches. This was typical of British overseas business and its effect was to build bonds of friendship and trust within the managerial cadre. On-the-job training and job rotation also continued as juniors spent their first years in the organization, often moving between branches. As a result, they developed over time both considerable knowledge of the products and services provided by their firms, and tacit knowledge of the organization for which they worked, and trust in their fellow employees. The firm provided an all-embracing environment for its staff, from awarding them permission to marry and—often—screening potential spouses, to acting as banker for their private funds. Thus Duncan Fox in the 1930s held the current accounts of many of their directors and staff, who were said to look on the firm 'as their bank'.[84]

Although rules and procedures were explicitly codified in the trading companies, and staff were monitored closely, considerable effort was made also to set standards of morality for staff. This was most important for companies which needed reputations for fair dealing and for being trustworthy. In addition, one of the greatest threats to a trading company was from unauthorized speculative dealing by their staff. There was a real problem in this respect given the nature of the business of the trading companies. A trading company was very different from, say, a mass production-type automobile firm, where tasks could be routinized and closely monitored. Trading involved numerous non-routine transactions, and it involved entrepreneurial decision-making. Although the trading companies were in one sense highly centralized, in another they relied on individual judgements of their staff. This raised acute potential problems of opportunism.

Apart from regular monitoring, the best defence against speculative and unauthorized dealing lay in developing a strong corporate culture. 'We intend

---

[82] Borneo Motors Board Minute, 3 Feb. 1960, Borneo Company Archives, MS 27189, GHL.

[83] Minute Book of Assam Company, 22 Sept. 1959, Assam Company Archives, MS 9924/20, GHL.

[84] General Managers Diaries of Interviews, Midland Bank Head Office, Lancashire Section, 28 Apr. 1932, Acc 30/126, HSBC Group Archives.

to adhere to what has been the rule of our Firm in the past', Finlays' Calcutta branch affirmed in 1910, 'and to go in as little as possible for business of a speculative nature. We prefer to do a small business on safe lines rather than a large one on speculative lines.'[85] The same sentiments permeated the corporate culture of Ralli, whose founder laid down as basic rules that 'no partner and no employee is permitted to lead a life unduly luxurious or extravagant; no one may embark in any sort of speculation'.[86] In the early 1950s a writer on Ralli stressed the firm's strong emphasis on avoiding speculation, and its two main principles of 'a small profit on a big turnover' and 'proverbial honesty'.[87] Ritual denunciations of speculation permeated the correspondence of most companies, more especially when staff guessed wrongly about the movement of a price or currency, and made heavy losses.

Although this combination of monitoring, socialization, and 'moral' corporate cultures seems to have worked quite effectively in British merchant houses, there were certainly some serious cases of defalcations and unauthorized speculations. Dodwells, for example, seems to have been afflicted by this problem. The firm made a huge loss in 1911 as a result of its Colombo manager speculating on his own account, and then using the firm's money to meet his commitments. Further losses followed in the early 1930s through another scandal.[88] Balfour Williamson lost a large amount of money in its London office in the 1920s when the need for internal auditing procedures seems to have been ignored.[89]

Almost all the British trading companies which established New York offices in the late nineteenth century and the 1920s ran into serious problems preventing their staff from engaging in 'speculative' activities. The dynamic business culture of New York seemed to override the more staid and risk-averse cultures of the British firms, often causing them losses in the process. A particular problem was that British firms—uncharacteristically—usually employed 'locals' in senior positions in their management posts, adding to the problems of controlling them, especially by socialization strategies.

Balfour Williamson was one of the trading companies which indeed experienced considerable problems with its New York office's 'speculative' activities in the 1920s. During this decade the office began speculating in pepper, rice, and Chinese rugs, the latter ending up with the firm holding large stocks until the late 1920s. Later they became involved in Chilean

[85] James Finlay Calcutta to James Finlay Bombay, 11 Feb. 1910, Finlays Archives, UGD 91/447/6/1.

[86] J. Gennadius, *Stephen A. Ralli: A Bibliographical Memoir* (London: privately printed, 1902), 23.

[87] Note by Leoni M. Calvocaressi on The House of Ralli Brothers, Dec. 1952, Ralli Archives, MS 23836, GHL.

[88] Stephanie Jones, *Two Centuries of Overseas Trading* (London: Macmillan, 1986), 182–3.

[89] Hunt, *Heirs*, ii. 149–50; Robert Greenhill and Rory Miller, 'British Trading Companies in South America after 1914', in Geoffrey Jones (ed.), *The Multinational Traders* (London: Routledge, 1998), 115.

walnuts and trading on the Calcutta market.[90] Gibbs, which established a New York office in 1913 with a US citizen as manager, ran into the same experiences as Balfour Williamson, with the office speculating in produce by buying up considerable quantities at favourable prices without having identified a market, and ending up with excessive stocks. Ill-advised speculations included one into Cuban sugar bags. Only after a member of the Gibbs family became a resident director in New York later in the 1920s was speculative activity controlled.[91] Jardine Matheson had the same fate in New York. The firm repeatedly sought to constrain the 'speculative' instincts of its New York office—as it 'invariably lost money in the States when we went in for large speculations'[92]—but to little avail. The office continued to make substantial losses through 'risky' trading.[93] Following heavy losses in dogskin trading, the New York office was closed in the early 1930s, and Jardines' business passed to Balfour Williamson.

Although corporate culture and socialization formed an important element of the human resource management of the trading companies, their staff were motivated and incentivized by remuneration packages. An important element of the employment contracts of expatriate managers was their entitlement to commission, and in some cases there were also profit-sharing schemes. By the late nineteenth century many managers were paid by a combination of a fixed salary and a commission on profits, as well as sometimes receiving bonuses, though some staff were paid entirely by a fixed amount, while others were paid solely on commission with a guaranteed minimum. A study of 620 employment contracts offered by Finlays before 1914 showed growing numbers of overseas employees receiving commission, the basis of which was more tightly defined over time. In the late nineteenth century commission was paid on sales figures at overseas branches or on the basis of cash remitted to the head office. Subsequently tighter definitions of 'profits' were employed with specific provisions about what items should be charged to the profit and loss account before commission was paid.[94]

Virtually all the companies paid at least some of their expatriate managers commission before the 1950s. Directors, managers, accountants, and so on all received commission payments, though the basis for the calculation differed greatly inside firms and business groups, and between them. The year 1926 saw the introduction of a formal system for the payment of commission to the European staff of Guthries: one-sixth of profits were set aside for this purpose. Directors, however, were treated differently from other

[90] Lord Forres to Alexander Torrance, 25 June 1923, No. 7, Box 12; Lord Forres to B. D. Blyth and P. M. Nicholson, 14 Jan. 1927, Lord Forres to B. D. Blyth, 19 Jan. 1927, Balfour Williamson Archives, UCL, No. 9, box 13.

[91] MS 11109; MS 11112/2, Antony Gibbs Archives, GHL.

[92] David Landale to Johnstone, 23 Nov. 1922, C/O London to Hong Kong, Jan./Sept. 1922, JMA, UCL.

[93] Ibid., G. W. Sheppard to David Landale, 25 Apr. 1927, S/O London to Hong Kong 1927.

[94] Stewart, 'Scottish Company Accounting', 186–217.

staff.[95] In the multi-firm business groups, staff received commission from different sources.[96] The amounts of commission payments were agreed in each employment contract, and terms were modified along with circumstances.[97] Companies rarely acknowledged any automatic right to commission, and sometimes awarded it on an annual basis.[98] However in the 1930s UAC seems to have introduced a standard commission distributed annually on the basis of 15 per cent of UAC's total net profits.[99] Commission payments continued into the post-Second World War period. They remained widespread within the Harrisons & Crosfield group, for example, even for its business in Britain.[100]

In addition to the payment of commission, the traders sought to use remuneration of various kinds to attract and retain good staff. Alfred Booth in the late nineteenth century had 'a belief that high wages and salaries, with permanency of tenure, in return for loyalty and efficiency, was in the long run the only satisfactory method of employment'.[101] An internal committee at Harrisons & Crosfield in 1919 declared that company policy should be to pay salaries rather higher than the average ruling for similar positions in similar business and to expect services above the usual average.[102]

More innovative was the introduction of profit-sharing schemes by a number of companies. Booths introduced a profit-sharing scheme in the 1870s.[103] Swire's had a profit-sharing scheme in the interwar years, though only for the staff of Butterfield & Swire and not the affiliate firms. Steels adopted a distinctive shareholding structure after it became a limited company in 1890 whereby its controlling ordinary shares could only be held by fifty or so senior managers of the company, who became entitled to buy the shares after fifteen or more years' service. On retirement, these shareholders had to sell their shares at a price certified by the company's auditors each year on the basis of a specified formula.[104]

By the 1960s some trading companies seem to have experienced problems recruiting British staff of the calibre required. From the interwar years

[95] Directors' Minutes, Guthrie Archive, G/MIN/1, SOAS.

[96] See for example Board Minutes, 29 Oct. 1930, Borneo Company Archives, MS 27178/19, GHL.

[97] See the examples of contracts for John Holt & Co. (Liverpool) Ltd. between 1900 and 1907 in 380 HOL 1/5/1–3, Liverpool Record Office.

[98] Board Minutes, 10 Mar. 1932 (Minute Book No. 2), Pataling Rubber Estates Ltd., Harrisons & Crosfield Archives, GHL.

[99] Fieldhouse, *Merchant Capital*, 28.

[100] Agendas and resolutions file, 1930–57, Wilkinson Rubber Linatex Ltd., Harrisons & Crosfield Archives, GHL. For the Borneo Company, see Board Minutes, 20 Sept. 1950, Borneo Company Archives, MS 27178/23, GHL.

[101] A. H. John, *A Liverpool Merchant House* (London: George Allen & Unwin, 1959), 161–2.

[102] Report of the Organization Committee, 18 July 1919, Harrisons & Crosfield Archives, GHL.

[103] John, *Liverpool Merchant House*, 164–5.   [104] Braund, *Calling to Mind*, 113–14.

depreciation of local currencies, exchange controls, growing economic and political nationalism, and deteriorating career prospects through the localization of management posts combined to reduce the appeal of employment with British trading companies. After 1945, the general decline of British commercial interests in Latin America and perhaps the less-than-dynamic image of firms such as Gibbs and Balfour Williamson resulted in the British firms having problems recruiting and retaining expatriate staff.[105] One solution was to employ ethnic Britishers in the Latin America branches, as countries such as Chile and Argentina had a substantial British emigrant community. Although reluctant to take this step before the Second World War, subsequently Antony Gibbs—for example—did employ considerable numbers of Anglo-Chileans in its Chilean offices in the 1950s.[106] However by this period Anglo communities in Latin America were diminishing and not being renewed by new emigrants.[107]

After the Second World War British trading companies in Asia and Africa experienced the same problems. Events in the post-war years combined several vivid demonstrations of the effects of developing country nationalism on expatriate careers. The nationalization of BP's vast oil operation in Iran in 1951, for example, led to the redundancy of nearly 1,700 British expatriate managers, who could not be redeployed in the firm's much smaller operation in other countries.[108] Not surprisingly, it became harder for companies whose business resided in 'risky' countries to recruit young Britishers to work for them, as the prospect of a full career ending with a pension seemed to recede. The British trading companies in India were afflicted by this problem. 'Our European staff is dwindling', a manager of Binny's reported in 1961, 'and will undoubtedly dwindle still further'.[109] Five years later Anglo-Thai found, in the context of 'Malayanization' of its business in Malaysia, that 'uncertainties regarding continued employment after 1970 was causing some concern among the younger members of the staff'.[110] In this situation it was hard to recruit good quality staff, and in turn this became a constraint on the options of the firms to pursue new lines of business. From the 1950s UAC was experiencing similar problems. A report in 1963 on UAC's management over the next twenty-five years identified a problem of morale among managers arising from 'doubt as to the future of the Company in Africa'.[111]

[105] Greenhill and Miller, 'British Trading Companies', 118; Goschen to A. N. Beven, 19 Feb. 1965, Antony Gibbs Archives, MS 16876/9, GHL.

[106] MS 16869/1, Antony Gibbs Archives, GHL.

[107] Rory Miller, 'British Free-Standing Companies on the West Coast of South America', in Mira Wilkins and Harm Schröter (eds.), *The Free-Standing Company in the World Economy 1830–1996* (Oxford: Oxford University Press, 1998), 242.

[108] James Bamberg, *British Petroleum and the Political Economy of International Oil 1950–1975* (Cambridge: Cambridge University Press, 1999).

[109] Hunter to R. E. Castell, 5 June 1961, Binny Archives, MS 27164, GHL.

[110] Board Minutes, 15 Sept. 1966, Anglo-Thai Archives, MS 27008/13.

[111] Report on The United Africa Company Group Management 1963–1985, 31 Jan. 1964, Unilever Historical Archives, 45/1, Box 6.

In UAC's case, the considerable size of its head office and expatriate bureaucracy made the employment consequences of 'localization' acute. It would appear that a strong motive for the firm's diversification from the 1960s was to provide continued employment for its existing staff. An obvious solution to the problem of 'surplus' staff would have been to transfer them to the wider Unilever organization, but this was not seriously considered given the very different types of job undertaken within the two entities. The 1963 report concluded that 'the chances for UAC Overseas Management staff being redeployed within the Unilever Overseas Companies are at present, negligible'.[112] The alternative solution was therefore favoured of diversifying out of Africa into new ventures which—as a key paper in 1960 argued, 'should . . . be capable of being reasonably manned by people withdrawn from the African territory and not basically involve employment of new staff'.[113] Although there were other reasons for UAC's diversification strategies and other factors in its ultimate failure, the assumption that its managers possessed skills which were easily transferable from Africa to running businesses in Europe and elsewhere turned out to be thoroughly misconceived.[114]

It is difficult to escape the conclusion that the diversification strategies of all the traders from the 1960s were constrained by the managerial resources available to them. The strengths of the management system rested in site-specific learning and in recruitment patterns and socialization routines which produced able and reliable managers capable of running trading companies and related businesses. However these skills and competences were not generally, or at least immediately, transferable to other regions or technically complex industries. In fact, they were even of diminishing value—or at least in need of upgrading—in traditional host regions. As their governments and business elites became more exposed to international experience and opportunities so 'local' knowledge also diminished in value.

Yet expatriate staff remained of central importance to the trading companies at the end of the 1970s. They continued to be distinctive from the staff of, say, large manufacturing multinationals. They were usually appointed to managerial posts early in their careers rather than working their way up managerial hierarchies. This made UAC staff, for example, different from those of its Unilever parent. At Swire's there was—and into the 1990s there remained—a strong emphasis on giving young managers an experience of 'running something' at an early stage of their careers. A young manager might initially serve with Cathay Pacific, then be transferred to run a small trading business, and then return to Cathay Pacific after having acquired management experience.[115]

---

[112] Report on The United Africa Company Group Management 1963–1985, 31 Jan. 1964, Unilever Historical Archives, 45/1, Box 6.

[113] Fieldhouse, *Merchant Capital*, 680–2.   [114] Ibid. 761.

[115] Interview at Swire House, 28 Jan. 1999.

These staff remained imbued with strong and distinctive firm cultures. In family-owned firms such as Swire's and Jardine Matheson, the family provided an important element of this culture, providing continuity in an otherwise changing business. Cultures reflected origins, geographical locations, and the policies of past leaders. Thus Jardine Matheson's 'culture' was said to be outward looking and entrepreneurial, reflecting its base of operations in Hong Kong, with a strong Scottish connection. Swires emphasized modesty and a low profile, with a stress on the importance of its staff.[116]

7.4 Local Staff

While the recruitment and motivation of expatriate managers was a central human resources issue for the trading companies, locally recruited staff were always essential to the operations of the traders, not only as clerks and plantation workers, but also as intermediaries with local business cultures. They were often essential to accessing marketing and distribution channels in host economies.

The most well-known intermediary figure was the 'comprador' in Chinese-speaking cultures. Compradors were the Chinese managers of foreign firms in China. As the manager of the Chinese staff, they were held liable for all conduct on the part of their staff. They were essential for operating in nineteenth-century China, and the British traders all relied heavily on their compradors. These compradors were in turn also often independent businessmen on their own account. Jardines' compradors in the late nineteenth and early twentieth centuries were also investors in, and directors of, banks, industrial companies, and other enterprises.[117]

During the interwar years the trading companies in China began to reconsider the use of compradors. Swire's was at the forefront of the move from compradors to incorporating Chinese within the mainstream management system. There were a number of factors leading Swire's in this direction. In part there was a recognition that China was in the throes of modernization and the old system was no longer appropriate. During the 1920s the comprador system was attacked by Chinese nationalists. In part it was a question of economy, as Chinese were cheaper than expatriates. 'There are very few junior jobs of a routine nature', a Swire partner noted in 1925, 'which cannot be done as well, if not better, by good Chinese or by women clerks'.[118] Above all, there was the characteristic Swire emphasis on recruiting high-quality staff. The same partner stressed that 'native staff must be paid well' and that 'in our service we ought to have the best and that

[116] Ibid., interview with Jeremy Brown, 21 Jan. 1999.   [117] Keswick, *Thistle*, 85–101.
[118] Colin C. Scott to J. K. Swire, 22 May 1925, Swire Archives, Swire ADD 15, SOAS.

means disregarding the market rate'.[119] The need to recruit well-educated and well-connected Chinese into Swire management became a regular theme of correspondence within the company.[120]

An analysis of the role of the Swire's comprador at Nanking in 1930 showed the advantages of the system. The comprador secured considerable business for the China Navigation Co. for a commission of 5 per cent on net 'Chinese freight'. He arranged sugar sales to local and up-country dealers for a commission of 1.5 per cent. Dealers paid the comprador ten days after delivery was completed by crediting his account at Chinese banks, which meant that for these ten days the comprador bore the financial risk of the transaction. He also secured insurance business through Chinese brokers, who paid their premium on the last day of each month. If a broker failed the comprador had to make good any amount due to Swire's. Other functions included guaranteeing Butterfield & Swire's Chinese staff and recruiting coolies to act as stevedores. However the costs of the system were substantial. Though the Nanking comprador claimed he was losing money working for Swire's, the firm was dubious and certainly felt he had got away with big sums in the past.

Swire's problem was that 'the man, not the system, plays an essential part in our business'. Though Swire's could function without a comprador, it could not function without a Chinese 'manager' who would act as 'some form of transformer and buffer between the foreign Staff and the Chinese Staff and business world generally'. Swire's analysis of the real value-added of the Nanking comprador demonstrated the need for such a 'transformer':

The *Compradore* makes compassionate allowances to our staff when their parents die, if the Hong Kong *Compradore's* business friend comes to Nanking, he takes him out to Sun Yat Sen's tomb, if a sugar dealer's son dies he sends a scroll to the funeral, if a big shipper's nephew is married he sends a present, if the manager of a piece goods hong insured with us wants to get to Shanghai the *Compradore* pays his passage. He greases the palms that need greasing, he gives a few dollars to the police, the postman and the telephone man, he supports local charities, he gives tips where it is wise to give them. It may seem unnecessary but it is the Chinese way of doing things and it is all for Taikoo's good and it helps to get and retain clients.

The *Compradore* has undoubtedly insured the China Navigation Co getting certain shipments by means we cannot recognise. . . . Our competitors are not so scrupulous about these things. We may not like it or generally admit it but it has happened and whilst Chinese do business it will go on happening.

The *Compradore* passes our ideas, wishes, sympathy, anger and commands, as necessary, in an Oriental manner to the Chinese concerned and, whilst the Agent is a foreigner, a transformer of this nature will always be to a greater or lesser degree essential.[121]

[119] Colin C. Scott to J. K. Swire, 15 May 1925, Swire Archives, Swire ADD 15, SOAS.
[120] Ibid., G. W. Swire to J. Swire, 31 May 1931; G. W. Swire to G. J. Swire, 3 Mar. 1930; Young, *Beyond Lion Rock*, 94.
[121] J. K. Swire to N. Brown, 23 Mar. 1930, Swire Archives, Swire ADD 15, SOAS.

During the 1930s Swire's modified the comprador system to become a Chinese manager system, but with the recognition that such managers had to be the essential cross-cultural 'transformers'. There were in fact strong continuities between the contracts of the comprador and the Chinese managers of the 1930s and 1940s, though with changes of emphasis. For example, while compradors had to make full compensation to Swire's if their customers did not fulfil their obligations, the Chinese manager's responsibility was only 'to mediate whole-heartedly', while Swire's would assist the Chinese manager to claim money owed to them by law 'or other means'. There was also a change in the situation regarding employees. While under the comprador system all Chinese employees were employed and controlled by the comprador, under the new system they were employed by Swire's. However the Chinese manager was still responsible for the conduct of the employees, for under the terms of the contract if 'any action' of employees 'inflicted damages' on Swire's, the Chinese manager 'would be contingently liable and would have to make compensation without delay'. As with the expatriate managers, the Chinese managers were paid partly by salary and partly by commission.[122]

The transformation of compradors to managers was followed by the other firms, and the status of Chinese employees in Hong Kong rose steadily in the post-war period. In 1950 the comprador was formally abolished in Jardine Matheson, and in 1961 the first ethnic Chinese was appointed to the main board of that company. In South East Asia, the transition from comprador to Chinese manager seems to have taken rather longer, but as in China there was a strong continuity in the people holding the posts regardless of their description. Harrisons & Crosfield's Singapore office still employed a Chinese comprador through the 1950s and 1960s, and the same Chinese family provided the comprador or manager's post at Singapore for sixty years until 1979.[123]

Although the comprador system was confined to Chinese-speaking business cultures, and such intermediaries hold an especially important position in Chinese business culture[124] elsewhere in Asia, Africa, and Latin America 'local' staff performed key functions including serving as cross-cultural 'transformers' in the nineteenth century and later. However they had no opportunity to go beyond a certain point in the staff hierarchy. In UAC in the 1930s, for example, there were a considerable number of Africans in charge of district branches by the 1930s, but that was as far as they could rise until the 1950s. By 1939 there were thirty-nine African managers on the trading side of the business in British West Africa, as compared with 435 Europeans.[125]

---

[122] Zhang Zhongli, Chen Zengnian, and Yao Xinrong, *The Swire Group in Old China* (Shanghai: Shanghai People's Publishing House, 1995), 237–40, 329–32. The description of the manager's contract is from an actual contract drafted in Mar. 1947.

[123] Guy Nickalls (ed.), *Great Enterprise* (London: the firm, 1990), 166–7.

[124] Albert Feuerwerker, 'Doing Business in China over Three Centuries', *Chinese Studies in History*, 31 (1998), 16–34.

[125] Fieldhouse, *Merchant Capital*, 28 n. 61, 375.

In India, on the other hand, the 1930s saw the beginning of appointments of Indians to the managerial staff, both for reasons of economy and because of needing to respond to national feelings. Early in the decade Andrew Yule, Bird & Co., Mackinnon Mackenzie, and other Calcutta agency houses began, in the words of Binny's London office, 'to make some concessions to Indian national sentiment in this direction'.[126] Other companies such as Shaw Wallace and Binny's itself began appointing Indians to managerial grades immediately following Indian independence in 1947.[127]

After the end of the Second World War the 'localization' of managerial staff became more pressing, both because of the cost of expatriates and because of political circumstances. In 1948 UAC identified a major problem in the relations between its European and African staff, and considered new policies to reduce the discriminating salaries and conditions between European and Africans, and to Africanize the management. However UAC's progress was not especially fast. Between 1946 and 1957 the number of African managers in British West Africa rose from 119 to 304, but the number of European managers increased from 547 to 1,463 over the same period.[128]

Subsequently, however, the Africanization of UAC's managerial staff accelerated, beginning with Ghana. By 1962 the first Ghanaian was appointed UAC general manager for that country. Schools were opened in Nigeria, Ghana, and East Africa to provide training for Africans to join UACs technical staff.[129] During the 1960s the introduction of work permits and quotas in many African countries led to growing Africanization of the managements in most of the English-speaking countries, though less so in francophone Africa. By 1975 the chairmen of the main UAC company in four African countries were Africans, with many directorships and senior appointments held by Africans, half of them in Nigeria and the remainder in another twenty-six countries. By this period the number of European expatriate managers had fallen to 330. In Nigeria 10 per cent of UAC managers were European expatriates, though in francophone Africa the figure was still 68 per cent and in the Gulf 80 per cent. From the early 1960s around 100 Africans a year were sent to Britain on management courses and for technical and specialized training.[130]

Elsewhere, in Latin America and in Asia the same combination of pressures obliged the localization of managerial staff. As early as 1945 a director of Harrisons & Crosfield (Malaya) and various plantation companies within that business group openly advocated 'the gradual promotion of Asiatic

[126] London to Madras, 5 Aug. 1937, Binny Archives MS 27159/9, GHL.
[127] Ibid., Hunter to R. E. Castell, 5 June 1961, MS 27164, GHL.
[128] Fieldhouse, *Merchant Capital*, 339–41, 375–7.   [129] Ibid. 379–81.
[130] Supplement on UAC International, Unilever Reports and Accounts 1975.

supervisors to the highest ranks of management'.[131] In practice, innate conservatism and the problems of incorporating foreigners into the very British cultures of the firms resulted in slow progress among the British traders in South East Asia, who responded grudgingly to the pressures for localization.[132] Some firms experimented with bringing local staff to work in Britain for a period to expose them to their corporate cultures, but this often did not work, in part because such staff resented transfers away from their home. There was a trade-off between reducing staff costs by employing more local staff, and increasing the risks of moral hazard by relying on local managers not schooled in the cultures of the merchant houses.[133]

By the 1960s political circumstances as well as the cost of expatriates were such that the more pressing problem faced by many companies, especially in faster growing South East Asian countries, was to attract sufficient good-quality local candidates for managerial posts. Whatever the reason, localization of staff at Harrisons & Crosfield and Guthries proceeded rather slowly until the 1970s. Even at the end of that decade Harrisons & Crosfield had almost no local directors on the boards of its major Malaysian rubber company affiliates.[134]

Over time the balance of power between the British trading companies and their local staff changed in most regions, as the companies became ever more anxious to find good staff who would promote their interests. Gray Mackenzie, Inchcape's trading and shipping company in the Gulf, already faced that situation in the 1960s, finding itself needing 'local' staff to build up its business while unable to find such staff because of the 'reluctance of young educated Arabs, most of whom were very wealthy anyway, to undertake regular work'.[135] This was a general problem for British firms in the Gulf by this period.[136]

From the 1970s at the latest most British traders recognized that for a combination of reasons, from cost to political expediency, their local staff needed to be incorporated into senior management of their affiliate firms, though inclusion in the core 'House' staff came later. Historically, however, the operations of the trading companies had always rested heavily on their ability to recruit and retain local staff to serve as 'transformers'.

---

[131] H. B. Egmont-Hake, *The New Malaya and You* (London: Lindsay Drummond, 1945), 101.

[132] Chairman's statement to Harrisons & Crosfield AGM, Dec. 1956.

[133] Interview with Sir Colin Campbell, 16 Apr. 1996.

[134] J. H. Drabble and P. J. Drake, 'The British Agency Houses in Malaysia: Survival in a Changing World', *Journal of Southeast Asia Studies*, 12 (1981), 321–2; Nicholas J. White, *Business, Government, and the End of Empire. Malaya, 1942–1953* (Kuala Lumpur: Oxford University Press, 1996), 243–5; Lim Mah Hui, *Ownership and Control of the One Hundred Largest Corporations in Malaysia* (Kuala Lumpur: Oxford University Press, 1981), 107.

[135] Gray Mackenzie & Co., Meeting held on 15 Dec. 1964, Gray Mackenzie Archives, MS 27699, GHL.

[136] Geoffrey Jones, *Banking and Oil* (Cambridge: Cambridge University Press, 1987), 122–3.

7.5 Competences

The management systems employed by British trading companies between the late nineteenth century and the 1970s differed considerably from those employed in the United States. Strategy and operating decisions were centralized on boards of directors. Ownership was not separated from control in many cases. Professional managers were hired, but they never had MBAs and the emphasis was on on-the-job and site-specific learning. They were motivated until the post-war period by old merchant devices such as payment of commission and they were controlled in part by strong and 'moral' corporate cultures.

This management system generated competences which help to explain how the trading companies functioned. Managers and directors who spent their entire careers abroad acquired a formidable level of tacit knowledge about their chosen region, which was often reinforced by requirements to learn local languages. They had the contacts that helped the business to survive and identify new opportunities. Information systems were also well developed. Systems and routines seem to have achieved in many cases an appropriate balance in a trading firm between close control of risks and enabling staff to take legitimate risks. Like all British companies of the time, the trading companies stressed 'character' and social background in selecting their managers, but at least some of them were ahead of their British peers in searching for managers from universities. Meanwhile the 'business group' system meant that affiliate firms could attract better staff than real 'free-standing' firms.

This management system, developed at a time when many host economies were either colonies or in a semi-colonial status, worked well in its time and its place. British expatriate managers took their places amidst other elements of colonial society. This management system permitted the trading companies to diversify as large 'business groups' before the First World War, but once in place it was more effective at survival than innovation and in dealing with incremental change rather than radical restructuring. It was not a system that would have sustained a modern industrial enterprise in, say, motor manufacture, and it ran into difficulties when some trading companies attempted to restructure their businesses as industrial enterprises from the 1960s. It was probably an obstacle to such restructuring, but the transformations achieved by some firms demonstrated continuing reserves of flexibility. Indeed, the continued ability of some of the British trading companies to evolve provided a testimony to the adaptability of their management systems.

8

External Relationships

8.1 Introduction

This chapter examines the external architecture of the British trading companies. Their relations with banks, shipping and insurance companies, and manufacturers were crucial elements in their business. These relationships were often sustained over long periods, and often relied as much on trust as on contracts.

8.2 Trading Companies and Banks

The relationship between trading companies and banks was both multi-faceted and highly significant for both parties. As noted earlier, in their origins merchants and bankers were virtually indistinguishable, and it was only slowly over the course of the nineteenth century that a clearer separation occurred. In several cases, such as Antony Gibbs, Wallace Brothers, and Mathesons, merchant banking remained part of the business portfolio. Matheson & Co. regarded its legal status in a pragmatic fashion. 'The whole question of whether the profit or loss on the sale of investments can be taken into consideration for Income Tax is a very complicated one and depends on whether a Firm poses as Merchants or Bankers', Matheson's wrote to Jardine Matheson in Hong Kong in 1926. 'At present we pose as Bankers because by doing so we get better treated in the matter of interest earned, but if we happen to make a large profit on an Investment it might pay us to call ourselves Merchants.'[1]

In their overseas branches, the trading companies often served as quasi-banks by providing credit, taking deposits, and dealing in foreign exchange. However by mid-century the desire for liquidity encouraged merchants to promote banks to operate in their regions. A number of merchant houses often collaborated to promote such banks, not least because such an institution's viability rested on the willingness of a range of firms to use its facilities. In 1865, to give one important example, the Hongkong Bank was founded by a group of merchants in Hong Kong wanting a local bank to finance regional trade. The founding committee included representatives from five British trading firms, led by Dent's and including Gilmans and the Borneo

---

[1] D. Landale to D. G. M. Bernard, 24 June 1926, S/O London to Hong Kong 1926, JMA, CUL.

Company. There were also German and American merchants, and three Bombay trading houses, including David Sassoon. The founder was the future chairman of the P&O Steam Navigation Company. Jardine Matheson stood aloof from the new bank, not only because of the leading role of Dent's but also because of the prominent position of the Sassoons, its leading competitor in the opium trade. It was only in 1877 that a member of Jardine Matheson joined the board of the Hongkong Bank. Merchants were similarly prominent also in the foundation in the 1860s of the first British overseas banks to operate in South America, the London and River Plate Bank, and the London and Brazilian Bank.[2]

Although most trading companies had divorced themselves from commercial banking by the late nineteenth century, a number of firms did promote their own banks, but never with any great success. In the 1890s, the Elder Dempster Steam-Ship Line, which by then virtually monopolized the ocean-going traffic to West Africa, set up the Bank of British West Africa (BBWA), which was granted by the colonial government a monopoly of the provision of silver coinage to the British territories in the region. However the competitor trading companies greatly disliked the power of the BBWA/Elder Dempster group and promoted a rival bank, the Bank of Nigeria in 1899. This bank was taken over by BBWA in 1912, but Elder Dempster's competitors continued to suspect BBWA, and subsequently welcomed and supported another bank, the Colonial Bank (subsequently acquired by Barclays) when it entered West Africa during the First World War. Generally the overseas banks and the trading companies in West Africa came to coexist, with the traders performing many banking functions, but looking to the banks for advances or overdraft facilities.[3] The other attempts by British-based trading companies to promote overseas banks were also not very successful. In 1909 E. D. Sassoon, the Anglo-Persian Jewish trading house, promoted the Eastern Bank as a new Eastern Exchange Bank, but although this established branches in Asia and the Middle East and retained its independence until 1957, it never grew to any great size.[4] More surprising was the failure of the P&O Banking Corporation, given the scope of Inchcape family interests in the 1920s.

Even if most traders separated themselves from banking, they continued often to perform a 'quasi-banking' role in their host regions. In many regions

---

[2] F. H. H. King, *The Hongkong Bank in Late Imperial China 1864–1902* (Cambridge: Cambridge University Press, 1987), 47–62, 335; David Joslin, *A Century of Banking in Latin America* (London: Oxford University Press, 1963), 28 ff.; Charles Jones, 'Commercial Banks and Mortgage Companies', in D. C. M. Platt (ed.), *Business Imperialism, 1840–1930. An Enquiry Based on British Experience in Latin America* (Oxford: Clarendon Press, 1977), 17–52; id., 'Institutional Forms of British Foreign Direct Investment in South America', *Business History*, 39 (1997), 31.
[3] Geoffrey Jones, *British Multinational Banking 1830–1990* (Oxford: Clarendon Press, 1993), 76; Richard Fry, *Bankers in West Africa* (London: Hutchinson Benham, 1976), 106.
[4] Jones, *British Multinational Banking*, 77–8.

the provision of short-term credit was an essential part of their business. In West Africa, UAC extended credit for both its importing and exporting. UAC sold its imports to African traders on credit, while it also provided credit to produce buying agents when they went to the villages to buy commodities. Through to the 1950s UAC and Holts functioned effectively as retail banks in West Africa, and were more important in this business than the overseas banks in the region, which lent relatively little to indigenous Africans until after the Second World War.[5] Among other examples, Gibbs functioned as a de facto commercial bank in the late nineteenth century, and perhaps later, and took sufficient equity in the local Banco de Valparaíso to make one of their partners president of the bank.[6] In a number of underdeveloped regions the trading companies continued to serve as de facto banks up to the 1930s and beyond. This was the case of Sarawak, where the Borneo Company functioned as the sole bank until after the Second World War. In Saudi Arabia, where Gellatly's had established a business based on the transport of pilgrims in the 1920s, the British company performed a range of banking functions in the interwar years, including lending to the government.[7]

As the customers of banks, the trading companies sought credit and foreign exchange facilities to finance their foreign trade business, and to finance seasonal fluctuations in the growing of commodities. They also needed banks to place deposits. Sometimes they required facilities to develop a new line of business, or to build ships. Given the nature of the British banking system, there was never any expectation that banks would be a source of funds for capital investment, except to the indirect extent that provision of short-term loans improved the cash flow of the trading companies and thus perhaps allowed them to undertake capital investment more easily than if the banks had not financed their sales and purchases of goods.

Conversely, British trading companies were valuable customers to banks because of the range of services which they used, each of which provided an additional source of commission income for the bank. As well as foreign currency and other routine transactions, banks welcomed one-off services provided the risk was acceptable; for example, giving guarantees that their clients' bills would be honoured at maturity. Trading companies were also substantial organizations which generated both a high volume of transactions and individually large transactions. Thus even a small percentage commission could accumulate to a significant sum in absolute terms. Moreover, the 'business group' system meant that a trading company account could translate in practice into multiple accounts from affiliate firms.

---

[5] D. K. Fieldhouse, *Merchant Capital and Economic Decolonization* (Oxford: Clarendon Press, 1994), 103, 107–8, 111–23; Jones, *British Multinational Banking*, 303.

[6] Manuel A. Fernández, 'Merchant and Bankers: British Direct and Portfolio Investment in Chile during the Nineteenth Century', *Ibero-Amerikanisches Archiv* (1983).

[7] George Blake, *Gellatly's 1862–1962* (London: Blackies & Son, 1962); Geoffrey Jones, *Banking and Oil* (Cambridge: Cambridge University Press, 1987).

TABLE 8.1 Trading companies and their 'main' banks, c.1890–1960

Trading company	UK clearing Bank	UK overseas Bank
Jardine Matheson	Commercial Bank of Scotland	Hongkong Bank
John Swire & Sons	National Provincial	Hongkong Bank
Dodwells	Barclays	Hongkong Bank
Harrisons & Crosfield	Barclays	Various
Guthries		Mercantile Bank of India
Borneo Company	Bank of England	Chartered Bank
James Finlay	Royal Bank of Scotland	National Bank of India
John Holt & Co. (Liverpool) Ltd.	District	Bank of British West Africa
Gray Mackenzie	Barclays	
Balfour Williamson	Martins	Bank of London and South America
Duncan Fox	Midland	Bank of London and South America

Perhaps because of the value to both sides of the relationship, the relationships between the British trading companies and British banks were long term and supportive, in contrast to the familiar characterization of British banking relationships as short-term and arm's length. In most cases trading companies had a relationship with a 'main' British clearing bank for its British operations (and for British registered affiliates), while the overseas branches of the firms banked with British overseas banks. Table 8.1 identifies some of the long-term banking relationships of the trading companies between the late nineteenth century and the 1960s.

Many of these relationships were forged in the nineteenth century. The choice of overseas bank reflected the main focus of the firm's business, given that the British overseas banks were as region-specific as the trading companies. The Hongkong Bank was the leading bank in the colony, and so the obvious bank for the trading companies whose main business was located there, although in practice relationships developed slowly between it and the trading companies. As noted above, it was only in 1877 that a member of Jardine Matheson's joined the board. Jardine's presence on the board antagonized its competitor Swire's, which would not even borrow from the bank in the 1890s, and it was not until 1914 that a representative of Swire's joined the bank's board, and he became its chairman in 1921.[8] In other instances relationships were forged in the early days of each institution. The Chartered Bank of India, Australia & China, formed in 1853,

[8] King, *Hongkong Bank*, 54–148; id., *The Hongkong Bank in the Period of Imperialism and War, 1895–1918* (Cambridge: Cambridge University Press, 1988), 20–1.

initially used the Borneo Company as its agents in Batavia in the Dutch East Indies until opening its own branch in 1863.[9]

In Latin America, the trading companies initially used a number of different banks. For example, Duncan Fox's chief relationship was with the London and River Plate Bank before its merger in 1923 to form the Bank of London and South America. By 1936 all British banking interests had been concentrated in the Bank of London and South America, which all the traders used as their local banker, though rarely exclusively. Certainly Antony Gibbs after 1945 used the British bank extensively for credit facilities at its Latin American branches, but it also used the Royal Bank of Canada and leading local banks such as the Banco de Chile. In the West Indies, the British companies such as Booker Brothers, McConnell and Henckell, Du Buisson used the Colonial Bank and its successor Barclays Bank (DCO).

The choice of clearing bank typically reflected the regional 'hub' from which a merchant house had emerged. Thus the 'Scottish' trading companies used Scottish banks. The Liverpool origins of several of the companies was reflected in their banks. John Holt used the District Bank, a bank headquartered in nearby Manchester. Duncan Fox were long-standing customers of the North & South Wales Bank, which was taken over by the Midland Bank in 1908, and which had its head office in Liverpool. W. and J. Lockett were similarly customers of the North & South Wales Bank who subsequently moved to the Midland Bank. Balfour Williamson's bank was initially the Bank of Liverpool, which merged with Martins Bank in 1918. Religious networks could also be important. Harrisons & Crosfield had a very long-term relationship with Barclays Bank which may have originated in Quaker networks, as the original Harrisons & Crosfield partners were Quakers, as were Barclays. In some instances, the London office of an overseas bank also provided facilities to the British office of the merchant company. This was the case of Guthries, which received considerable facilities from the Mercantile Bank of India.

Banking relationships formed in the late nineteenth century were strong and persistent, surviving mergers between banks to last over decades. Swire's were customers of the Union of London & Smiths Bank, and then followed its former bank when it merged with National Provincial Bank in 1918. Balfour Williamson followed the Bank of Liverpool when it merged with Martins in 1918, so that in 1959 Martins could describe Balfour Williamson as valuable customers who had 'banked with us for over a century'.[10] As trading companies diversified, they often used 'their' bank as banker to affiliate firms. For example Barclays were normally appointed bankers when Harrisons & Crosfield established a new company, and became its

---

[9] Compton Mackenzie, *Realms of Silver* (London: Routledge & Kegan Paul, 1954), 119.
[10] Martins Bank Daily Standing Committee, 25 Sept. 1959, Acc 80/604, Barclays Bank Archives.

secretaries and agents, although when it acquired companies it tended to leave established banking relationships in place.

It was a rare event for 'main' bank accounts to be transferred to another bank, at least until the post-Second World War period. It seems to have caused internal dissension within John Holt when, in 1957, the major portion of its banking business was transferred to Martins Bank, even though Holts' chairman had been a director of Martins since 1950.[11] However trading relationships were not exclusive, and in the Far East especially trading companies would often spread their various requirements over a number of banks, generating competition between the banks. Harrisons & Crosfield, for example, used both Hongkong Bank and Mercantile Bank, sometimes at different branches and sometimes—as in the case of Singapore—at the same one. James Finlay had intimate relations with the National Bank of India, but the firm's Bombay business had an account with Chartered Bank, while it had accounts with Mercantile Bank of India at several Indian branches and in Colombo in Sri Lanka.[12]

Banks could not assume that they could keep even long-established banking connections. Hongkong Bank, for example, held the account of the Taikoo Sugar Refinery. In 1914 John Swire & Sons, the parent company, gave a guarantee for advances to the refinery of up to $1.5 million, which was not released until 1931. In 1925, at a time when the refinery was making large losses, the bank wanted to increase the amount of the guarantee, but decided not to raise the issue as it feared that if it 'showed any signs of uneasiness, they might suggest a competitor relieved us of a share of the liability'.[13] On the other hand, companies that found themselves heavily indebted to one bank found their freedom to use other banks constrained. Thus in the early 1930s, when Dodwells were heavily indebted to Hongkong Bank, they were told in no uncertain terms to stop financing some of their business through the Mercantile Bank.[14]

In general the trading companies faced far from competitive banking markets in the interwar years. By this period British overseas banks—and their domestic counterparts—had extensive collusive agreements covering both price and non-price competition, and including agreements not to 'poach' the customers of banks. Competition continued, especially for premium business, but it was highly constrained, and this situation continued in the 1950s and 1960s.[15] A distinction can be made between domestic and overseas banks in this respect. The British domestic banking market was highly collusive until the 1960s, so there was not much competition for the head office accounts of the trading companies. However, overseas British

[11] Board Minutes of District Bank, 9 July 1957, 11033, NatWest Group Archives.
[12] Mercantile Bank Information Card MBH 649, HSBC Group Archives.
[13] London to Hong Kong, 9 June 1925, 8 Sept. 1925, GHO 10.2, HSBC Group Archives.
[14] Hong Kong to London, 4 May 1932, GHO 11.3, HSBC Group Archives.
[15] Jones, *British Multinational Banking*, 201–5, 290.

banks did compete, sometimes strongly, for the foreign exchange business of the traders.

The close relationships between trading companies and their 'main' banks were over time cemented by cross-directorships. Hongkong Bank's board came to include directors of the main trading companies in the colony. A partner or director of James Finlay was always on the board of the National Bank of India after 1895. During the 1880s the Mercantile Bank appointed to its board a representative of Guthries and a member of the Yule family, cementing what proved to be a long-term relationship with Guthries, Andrew Yule, and Yule, Catto.[16] Chartered Bank's board was largely dominated by merchants from the beginning. In the 1880s representatives of Jardine Matheson and Jardine Skinner joined it. By the interwar years it included directors or former directors from Borneo Company, Swire's, Boustead, and Wallace Brothers. After the Second World War a member of Steel Brothers became a director.[17]

Cross-directorships were much rarer between the traders and the domestic banks. A notable exception was the relationship between Duncan Fox and Midland Bank. Frederick Hynde Fox, the largest shareholder in Duncan Fox, was a director of North & South Wales Bank prior to its merger with Midland Bank in 1908, and thereafter he served as a Midland Bank director until his death in 1939. Informal contacts over Duncan Fox's affairs were thereby eased. At the end of Midland board meetings Fox frequently made a point of speaking with a general manager.[18] Moreover a Midland Bank director, Sir Thomas Royden, also became a director of, and substantial shareholder in, Duncan Fox from 1928. During the 1930s he would leave the room while Midland Bank's Liverpool committee discussed Duncan Fox's overdraft, emphasizing to a general manager at one meeting in 1932 that he wanted the bank to treat Duncan Fox as it did any other account.[19]

Reinforced by common backgrounds of social class and outlook, the relations between the trading companies and the banks were noteworthy for their flexible and informal nature. On occasion banks relied on trust rather than formal guarantees, aware that insistence on standard procedures involving a director's guarantee for loans or other matters might antagonize trading company directors, who sometimes refused to give a guarantee in principle, not just on particular occasions.[20] Sometimes banks were able to obtain informal undertakings—for example, to issue debentures if the bank so requested, so that there was some tangible expression of a company's

---

[16] Stuart Muirhead, *Crisis Banking in the East* (Aldershot: Scolar Press, 1996), 171, 173, 235.

[17] Mackenzie, *Realms*, 15–16, 155–6, 271, 311.

[18] General Manager's Diaries of Interviews, Midland Bank Head Office, Lancashire Section, Acc 30/118–136, HSBC Group Archives.

[19] Ibid., 15 Jan 1932, Acc 30/126, HSBC Group Archives.

[20] Some directors of Swire's in the 1920s, for example, refused as private individuals (as opposed to officials of a company) to give a formal guarantee to the Hongkong Bank. GHO 10.7, HSBC Group Archives.

intention to strengthen the bank's ability to trust. The risk assessment of banks rested heavily on senior bank managers' opinions of the managerial competences of directors and partners of the trading company, together with the degree of trust which they felt they could place in their business leaders.

Relationships between bankers and merchants were rarely wholly relaxed either. In the interwar years there were regular disputes about the interest charged by the Hongkong Bank on its credit facilities to Swire's.[21] And the private opinion of Swire's of the Hongkong Bank in this period was not especially favourable: through to the 1930s they regarded it as engaged in 'Exchange manipulation' rather than 'true Banking'.[22] There was a noticeably acerbic relationship between Stanley Dodwell and its main banker, Hongkong Bank. There was a long-running dispute between Dodwell and the bank over prices quoted and commission rates charged for purchases of foreign exchange.[23] The bank's Hong Kong manager described Dodwell as a 'confirmed grouser' in 1932,[24] while another manager referred to him as 'surprisingly stupid'.[25] On the other hand personal friction never translated into a serious deterioration in the relationship, and the firm received considerable overdraft facilities during its difficulties in the early 1930s. Dodwells were, the Hongkong Bank's London manager observed in 1931, 'one of the very few old established firms left, have always been fairly close constituents of ours, and I think we might do all we reasonably can to assist them. . . . We can always feel assured that we are dealing with honest straightforward people, which goes a long way towards minimising any risk.'[26] Jardine Matheson had an especially close relationship with the Hongkong Bank, to whom in the 1930s it gave 'first offer of all our business' in Hong Kong, but even that firm's management felt it to be 'very healthy' when the Mercantile Bank offered competitive rates for business.[27]

The routine banking facilities required by the trading companies involved short-term credit and exchange facilities. This credit was provided by overdrafts the size of which fluctuated greatly with movements in trade and the stage of a commodity's production cycle. Overdrafts had to be renewed on a regular basis, with borrowing limits set only for a year at most at a time, but they were typically though not automatically 'rolled over' by domestic and overseas banks, and thus acquired a position rather different from mere

---

[21] Messrs J. S. Swire to G. Warren Swire, 9 Mar. 1934, Swire ADD 16, Swire Archives, SOAS.

[22] Ibid., Colin Scott to J. Swire & Sons, 19 Jan. 1937, Swire ADD 17.

[23] London to Hong Kong, 15 Dec. 1931, GHO 10.12; London to Hong Kong, 8 June 1932, GHO 10.13, HSBC Group Archives.

[24] Ibid., Hong Kong to London, 10 Sept. 1932, GHO 11.4.

[25] Ibid., Hong Kong to London, 20 Feb. 1934, GHO 11.5.

[26] Ibid., London to Hong Kong 10 July 1931, GHO 10.10.

[27] W. Keswick to D. Landale, 19 May 1939, S/O Shanghai to Hong Kong 1939, JMA, CUL.

short-term finance. For example, when Gibbs sought the renewal for a year of its large overdraft limit at the Valparaíso branch of the Bank of London & South America, the London head office of the bank advised that 'loans for a period of one year are not be encouraged', but in view 'of the value of the connection', they were approved.[28] Similar sentiments and a similar outcome can be found in numerous instances.

The 'rolling-over' of overdrafts meant that ostensibly short-term credit facilities could be utilized to finance long-term business strategies. When Swire's wanted to expand its sugar marketing operations into the interior of China in 1918, it sought substantial overdraft facilities from the Hongkong Bank, which the bank saw no difficulty in providing, both then and 'in the future'.[29] National Provincial Bank and its predecessor provided finance before the First World War and in the interwar years when Swire's China Navigation Co. wanted to build new tonnage.[30] However bank credit was not generally intended for, or used as, capital for major capital projects, which needed to be financed either out of retained profits or out of a new issue of shares or debentures.

The trading companies, as valued customers, were allowed to borrow on easier terms than many of the customers of the banks. A great deal of lending was 'unsecured'.[31] This was partly because of the 'trust' nature of the relationship between traders and bankers, but also because in several instances trading companies declined to provide guarantees. For example, in 1926, the Bank of London & South America's overdraft to Gibbs & Co. in Valparaíso, Santiago, and Antofagasta exceeded both its agreed limits— 1.785 million pesos against limits totalling 1.6 million—and the bank's own rules concerning the amount that should be lent to a single firm. Gibbs & Co. were asked for guarantees, but sent the reply that 'it would not suit them', but Gibbs were prepared to compromise by restricting their use of credit facilities to 1.2 million pesos at their three branches.[32] Often the mixture of 'secured' and 'unsecured' lending fluctuated over time, and was a matter of negotiation. Thus the chairman and managing director of the Midland Bank had a discussion with Duncan Fox's chairman in 1933 about his firm's overdraft limit,

---

[28] London to Valparaíso, 4 July 1924, BOLSA Archives, D55/1–15, UCL.

[29] Messrs J. S. Swire to N. J. Stabb, 12 July 1918; Hongkong Bank to Messrs J. S. Swire, 20 Sept. 1918, Swire Archives, JSSI/4/9, SOAS.

[30] General purposes committee of National Provincial Bank, 16 Feb. 1931, 31 Aug. 1931, NW13016, NatWest Archives; John Swire to Union of London's Smiths Bank Ltd., 19 June 1913, JSSI/4/8; John Swire to National Provincial and Union Bank, 19 Feb. 1923, JSSI/4/10; China Navigation Co. to National Provincial Bank, 9 Feb. 1931, JSSI/4/12, Swire Archives, SOAS.

[31] For the case of Barclays (DCO) lending to trading companies such as Booker Brothers, McConnell in the West Indies, see Kathleen E. A. Monteith, 'Barclays Bank (DCO) in the West Indies, 1926–1962' (unpublished Ph.D., University of Reading, 1997).

[32] Valparaíso to London, 15 July 1926, BOLSA Archives, B11/4, UCL.

We told him that in view of the present position in South America we felt that if we continued the Duncan Fox limit of £350,000 it would be necessary to make some provision on our doubtful sheets. This would mean we could not continue to give the good reports to enquirers that we had been in the habit of giving. In order to obviate this position and to enable us to submit the renewal application to the board, we suggested to Fox that the limit should be reduced to say £200,000 and he and his associates should give us their personal guarantee. On £200,000 we should feel safe with a guarantee for £40,000.[33]

In some instances technically 'unsecured' lending was secured 'informally'. For example, National Provincial Bank's overdraft lending to both John Swire & Sons and the China Navigation Company was officially regarded as unsecured in the interwar years, but in practice 'informal' arrangements were made. In the case of the China Navigation Company, there was an unregistered resolution to issue up to £250,000 debentures to the bank if it so requested.[34] The bank's lending to the China Navigation Company during the 1950s and 1960s remained on this 'informally' secured basis. Generally, through the late 1940s and 1950s many banks continued to provide unsecured lending to the traders. For example, Mercantile Bank of India provided both secured and unsecured overdrafts for Anglo-Thai's Indian and Thai branches in this period.[35]

Lending to affiliates within business groups was often 'guaranteed' in some fashion by the parent trading company. National Provincial Bank's lending to the Taikoo Dockyard & Engineering Co. was supported by an 'informal' letter of guarantee by Swire's for the whole limit, while bills, though accepted by the dockyard company, were discounted by the bank to a John Swire & Sons account.[36] On the other hand, affiliates could also provide security for the parent company. In the interwar years Duncan Fox's at times substantial borrowing from the Midland Bank was on the basis of the security of its shares in its affiliates, all of which were domiciled in Chile or Peru. The largest affiliate, the sheep farming concern Explotodora was very profitable in the mid-1930s and had a deposit varying between £400,000 and £450,000 at the Midland Bank in 1936.[37] Not surprisingly, Midland Bank was concerned to monitor the progress of their affiliates, and sought access to their accounts, both in sterling and in local currency, so as to be better able to assess their 'true' position undistorted by exchange rate effects.[38]

---

[33] Midland Bank Head Office, Lancashire Section, General Managers' Diaries of Interviews 25 Aug. 1933, Acc 30/127, HSBC Group Archives.

[34] General purposes committee of National Provincial Bank, minutes on John Swire & Sons Ltd. and China Navigation Co. Ltd., 1926–65, ref. 12998–13041, NatWest Group Archives.

[35] Mercantile Bank Information Card, MBH 637, and Limit Letters, MBH 2750, 2753, and 2767, HSBC Group Archives.

[36] 13016, NatWest Group Archives.

[37] General Manager's Diaries of Interviews, Midland Bank Head Office, Lancashire Section, 7 July 1936, Acc 30/130, HSBC Group Archives.

[38] Ibid., 25 Aug. 1933, Acc 30/127.

The Midland Bank's relationship with Duncan Fox was especially close. When the firm converted from a partnership to a limited company in 1928, Midland Bank provided funds to assist the formation of the new company, including lending over £100,000 to F. H. Fox (the largest shareholder) to fund a cash injection into the new firm.[39] Duncan Fox also used Midland Bank as a source of advice. In 1931 the bank discouraged Duncan Fox from undertaking a proposal to work with a small oil company to finance the storage of oil in tanks.[40] Three years later when Duncan Fox incurred a bad debt in Bolivia for which there was a prospect of receiving compensation in tin, the company sought the advice of Midland Bank's general manager regarding both the market prospects of tin and the behaviour of the Bolivian government.[41]

Bank lending played an important but not critical—except in special circumstances—role in the business of trading companies. To the extent that trading companies merely acted as agents and operated on a commission basis, as opposed to taking ownership of the goods passing through their hands, their requirements for short-term borrowing over the working capital cycle were much reduced. However bank credit allowed trading companies to take the risk of acting as merchants in a larger number of cases, since they could see that funds were available, and to grow more rapidly in the volume of trade they handled. In the interwar years, the trading companies had no great demand for funds to expand, either from banks or from new issues of equity, as their main emphasis was on survival, while in the post-war decade profits were frequently at a high level, with operations generating cash inflows at a rate sufficiently above working capital needs to allow significant capital investment. Overall from the First World War until the 1960s the trading companies relied on ploughing back profits rather than issuing new capital, and the main purpose of bank lending—except in crisis conditions—was to finance the movement of trade and the growing of crops.

During the interwar years, however, the banks showed a willingness to support trading companies or their affiliates that experienced serious financial crises, subject to their general concern to avoid making loans which had little or no prospect of repayment. Given that the trading companies were valued customers, with a long-term relationship between banks and the companies, and that even the loss of one large client could destroy economies of scale in operations at certain branches, banks were prepared to be flexible to avoid liquidations.

A number of companies received support from their banks. Chartered Bank provided substantial overdrafts in London, Malaya, and Thailand in the early 1930s to support the Borneo Company, which at that time could

[39] Ibid., 4 Oct. 1928, Acc 30/122.   [40] Ibid., 21 May 1931, Acc 30/125.
[41] Ibid., 27 Feb. 1934, Acc 30/128.

not pay its dividends.[42] The Hongkong Bank was a strong supporter of Dodwells and Jardine Matheson in this period also. The latter firm's engineering affiliate was in such debt to the bank by 1931 that Jardine Matheson recognized that its fate 'more or less repose(d) with the bank'.[43]

There were a number of occasions, again in the interwar years, when banks intervened directly in the affairs of their clients. The most important case was during the financial crises of the UAC immediately after its formation. UAC had substantial lending from a number of British clearing banks (including Lloyds, Martins, Westminster, and the Commercial Bank of Scotland) and merchant banks (including Lazards and Rothschilds). In early 1931 these banks became so concerned about their lending that they collectively, through Rothschilds, insisted on UAC agreeing to a series of conditions, including provision of full information about its business, before continuing financial support. The banks also seem to have insisted that Unilever, at that stage only a part-owner of UAC, should be a party to the agreement.

By October 1931 the banks had again become alarmed about UAC following a radical writing down of its assets. The Westminster Bank, acting for all the banks, made the continuation of their lending dependent on the recapitalization of UAC with an additional £3.5 million of working capital. UAC's debt to the banks at that time stood at over £3.8 million. This was the crucial intervention because, as the shareholders of the African & Eastern Trade Corporation could not find their share of this sum, Unilever had to do so, becoming the owner of 80 per cent of UAC in the process.[44]

The banks also became involved in a number of reconstructions or liquidations of trading companies which collapsed. In the early 1920s the most serious case concerned the Grahams partnerships. After the war Grahams had used credit from the London private bank of Cox & Co. to diversify into speculative ventures. In 1923, when Lloyds Bank rescued and took over Cox's at the instigation of the Bank of England,[45] Cox's was owed over £1 million by Grahams. Grahams also owed £266,000 to the Royal Bank of Scotland, £81,000 to the Union Bank of Scotland, £329,000 to the US banks Citibank and the International Banking Corporation, and 'a very considerable amount' to the London and Brazilian Bank, just about to be merged into the Lloyds-controlled Bank of London and South America. Grahams were, as a report in 1924 put it, 'hopelessly insolvent'.[46]

Lloyds Bank undertook a reconstruction of Grahams. A new firm—Grahams Trading Company—was established in 1924 to run the core Indian

---

[42] Board Minutes, Borneo Company Archives, MS 27178/20, GHL.

[43] B. D. F. Beith to D. G. M. Bernard, 13 Aug. 1931, P&C Letters, London, Hong Kong, and Shanghai, 1935–7, JMA, CUL; Hong Kong to London, various 1931, GHO 11.3, HSBC Group Archives.

[44] Fieldhouse, *Merchant Capital*, 89–92.

[45] Jones, *British Multinational Banking*, 239–40.

[46] Memorandum on Grahams & Co., 7 July 1924, Lloyds TSB Group Archives, A56c/176.

and Portuguese business, while the residual assets of dubious value were placed in a separate company to be liquidated over time. Lloyds put a director on the board and provided substantial unsecured credit—amounting to at least £250,000 between 1925 and 1927—and a considerable amount of management time was spent on reorganizing the firm, a task made no easier by the continuing influence of the family in the form of 'the warring and clashing interests of the three rival Graham families'.[47]

By 1929 Lloyds Bank's patience had worn thin and it imposed a reorganization scheme on Grahams, including the resignation of three family members from the board.[48] Lloyds orchestrated the creation of a separate company for the Portuguese business in 1930, and then in 1931 declined to provide further credit except on security.[49] This effectively finished off the firm and it was sold to Turner Morrison later in the year.

In 1931 Martins and the Bank of London and South America were involved in the collapse of Graham Rowe & Co. By the beginning of that year Graham Rowe owed 500,000 pesos to the Bank of London and South America and £280,000 to Martins Bank. In September the former bank's London office heard that an auditor's report on the firm's Peru operations would prove very unfavourable, and by November the firm had at least partly ceased trading.[50]

Martins Bank took the lead in a reconstruction scheme involving the liquidation of the firm's Chilean business and the formation of a new company which would act as agents and distributors for the Chilean subsidiaries in which Rowes had an interest. The scheme involved Gibbs & Co. and represented a partial merger of Gibbs' trading operations also. The new company, to be named Graham Agencies Ltd., was intended to trade only in locally manufactured goods—often made by subsidiaries of foreign multinationals such as Dunlop and Martini—which it was hoped would make it commercially viable. The initial plan was for the 2 million pesos capital of the new company to be subscribed by Martins Bank, two former partners of Graham Rowe and Gibbs & Co., but the latter depended on a 1 million peso loan from the Bank of London and South America, which was vetoed by that bank's London management.[51] Eventually the company went ahead with an issued capital of 1.5 million pesos, of which 100,000 each was taken up by Martins Bank and the Banco de Chile. Gibbs found sufficient borrowed funds to take a substantial shareholding in the early 1930s. Eventually Graham Agencies became profitable and a market in its shares developed in Chile, enabling Gibbs to dispose of virtually all its shares in the early 1950s.[52]

---

[47] Ibid., B. C. Reade to Montague Norman, 28 Jan. 1931, HO/GM/Bea.25.
[48] Board Minutes, 21 May 1929, Grahams Trading Company Archives, MS 22465, GHL.
[49] Ibid., 13 Feb. 1931.
[50] London to Valparaíso, 15 Sep. 1931, D55/15, BOLSA Archives, UCL.
[51] Ibid., London to Valparaíso, 17 Dec. 1931, B22/11.
[52] Antony Gibbs Archives, MS 16869/1-2, GHL.

Martins Bank spent the remainder of the 1930s and early 1940s trying to liquidate the former Graham Rowe assets it had inherited. It appointed a representative who moved between Santiago and Lima. In Santiago Martins became the owners of a warehouse and a garage, and had shares in other companies. In Peru, its assets including shares in a substantial cotton estate, which led the bank into involvement in estate management. It was not until 1944 that these shares were finally sold and the bank's involvement in Peru finally ended.[53]

During the early post-war decades the pattern of relationships between the trading companies remained close and very similar to that prevailing in the interwar years. There were no serious crises or failures on the scale of UAC, Grahams, or Graham Rowe, and instead the period was generally one of growth and of expanded use of banking facilities by the traders. As the trading companies opened branches in new regions, so they turned naturally to the British overseas banks for advice and credit.[54] In Hong Kong the Hongkong Bank played an especially active role in the colony's recovery and growth, which included extensive and flexible lending to the trading companies such as Jardine Matheson and Swire's.[55] Hongkong Bank had in its past shown a willingness to take shares in trading company ventures, notably in the British and Chinese Corporation joint venture with Jardine Matheson, and in the 1960s it resumed this tradition by acquiring 30 per cent of the shares in Swire's airline, Cathay Pacific.[56]

Long-established banking relationships remained firm despite the mergers and consolidations of these decades. The long connection between Chartered Bank and the Inchcape family—three generations of whom sat on that bank's board—continued despite Inchcape's conversion to a public company and Chartered's merger with Standard Bank of South Africa to form Standard Chartered in 1970. In 1979 Standard Chartered's lending to Inchcape—whose chairman was still Lord Inchcape, also a director of the bank—totalled £144 million, or nearly 3 per cent of Standard Chartered's total advances.[57]

From the 1960s the weakening position of the British trading companies in Latin America and parts of Asia produced a curious reversal of the relative positions of banks and merchants of a century ago. While the merchants had been instrumental in establishing overseas banks in the nineteenth century, during this period banks acquired Balfour Williamson, Antony Gibbs,

[53] Martins Bank Daily Standing Committee, 1933–45, Acc 80/579–588, Barclays Bank Archives.

[54] Board Minutes, 29 May 1956, Dodwell Archives, MS 27498/7, GHL. Dodwells opened an account with the National Bank of India for its East African business.

[55] F. H. H. King, *The Hongkong Bank in the Period of Development and Nationalism, 1941–1984* (Cambridge: Cambridge University Press, 1991), 349–63; Gavin Young, *Beyond Lion Rock* (London: Hutchinson, 1988), 101.

[56] Young, *Beyond Lion Rock*, 226.

[57] Standard Chartered's Commercial Banking Operations around the World, Corporate Strategy Conference, 1979, Standard Chartered Archives.

and Wallace Brothers. This attempt to reintegrate merchants and bankers was unsuccessful. Balfour Williamson's merchanting business in Latin America wilted under Bolsa's ownership. 'To all intents and purposes Williamson Balfour ceased to exist when Balfours were taken over by the Bank of London & South America,' a Gibbs director noted in 1965. 'While they may be first class bankers, the general impression here is that as merchandising traders Williamson Balfour are losing ground'.[58] The same fate awaited the merchant business of Gibbs and Wallace Brothers. Conversely, most attempts of the merchants to expand their financial activities from the 1960s ended in disappointment.

Finance was at the heart of the business of trading companies, and it is not surprising that their relationship with banks was important. In the nineteenth century bankers and merchants had initially been virtually the same, but many if not all merchants had subsequently encouraged the formation of separate British overseas banks to serve their regions over the course of the century. In the late nineteenth century and for much of the twentieth century the trading companies developed close relations with British commercial banks, both domestic and overseas. These relationships were characterized by their long-term, but non-exclusive nature, and by the importance of them both to the routine business of the trading companies, and at times of crisis and of rapid growth. The relationships with banks provided an important element of the external architecture of the trading firms. During the 1960s and 1970s banking rather than merchanting became the focus of attention. Banks acquired trading companies, while traders attempted to develop the financial side of their businesses, but for the most part there were few successful outcomes from this era.

8.3 Agencies

An important part of the business of the trading companies was acting as agents for 'principals'. Initially the most important agencies held were for shipping and insurance companies, and the sale of shipping and insurance services was often a lucrative part of the business of many of the trading companies in the nineteenth century. After 1945 airline agencies also became important. As the twentieth century progressed, the holding of agencies for manufacturing companies became progressively more important also. As in the case of banks, many of these agency relationships proved long-term and durable, surviving external shocks and changed market conditions.

The relationship between Swire's, Alfred Holt, and the shipbuilding firm of Scott's was a striking example of a business network linked by 'reciprocal investment, shared information and common standards of

---

[58] A. D. Gibbs to Beven, 29 Oct. 1965, Antony Gibbs Archives, MS 16876/9, GHL.

business conduct'.[59] As explained in Chapter 2, the origins of this network lay in the 1850s and 1860s when the Swire, Scott, and Holt families became involved in a web of interconnected business interests. The Scott's began building ships for Holts in 1857, and in 1866 built the three steamships for the new Ocean Steamship Co. which demonstrated the superiority of steam over sail on long haul routes. Swire's and Scott's took shareholdings in the Ocean Steamship Co., and Swire's became their Far East agents in 1867. During the 1870s a member of the Scott family became a partner of Swire's, and the family invested in the China Navigation Company. Also included in this network were the Singapore-based firm of Mansfields, appointed Ocean's agent in 1868, and acquired by that firm in 1903.

The relationship between the Swire's, Holts, and Scott's was characterized by 'mutual growth and active cooperation'.[60] The relationship developed in dynamic ways with frequent interactions strengthening the level of trust between the different parties. By the late 1870s Swire's was concerned that Holts' ships were losing competitiveness compared to newer vessels employed by new competitors. Both Scott's and Swire's attempted to help Holts. Scott's encouraged Holts to commission larger vessels with higher boiler pressures, and operating speeds. Swire's tried to protect Holts' position by forming the first China conference in 1879, the forerunner of the collusive agreements which were to become such a feature of the world shipping industry. However the Holts remained committed to obsolete ships and to staying out of cartels until the end of the 1880s, when a new generation of the Holt family began to assume positions of authority.

The routine shipping agency work for Alfred Holt was an important source of income for Swire's. The firm had wide discretion in booking cargo and in return earned substantial fees and commission, which however were regularly renegotiated. An agreement signed in 1927 stipulated that Swire's would receive in return for managing Holts' business in Hong Kong and for acting as its agents in London an annual Hong Kong management fee of £8,000, an annual allowance of £10,000, and a commission of 91 pence per ton in London on imported cargo.[61] The Butterfield & Swire branches in Hong Kong and Shanghai had separate 'Blue Funnel' departments to handle the agency work, and a heavy emphasis was given to flows of information between the four firms.[62] When the Swire's managers in the East responsible for Holts' work came back to Britain on leave, they were dispatched to Holts' office in Liverpool for debriefing.[63]

[59] Gordon Boyce, *Information, Mediation and Institutional Development* (Manchester: Manchester University Press, 1995), 65.
[60] Francis E. Hyde, *Blue Funnel: A History of Alfred Holt and Company of Liverpool from 1865 to 1914* (Liverpool: Liverpool University Press, 1956), 34; Boyce, *Information*, 65.
[61] J. Swire & Sons to Alfred Holt & Co., 10 Jan. 1927, Swire Archives, JSSI/4/11, SOAS.
[62] Ibid., Butterfield & Swire to J. S. Nuttall, 10 Oct. 1913, JSSI/1/15.
[63] Ibid., J. Swire & Sons to Alfred Holt & Co., 14 June 1933, JSSXI/I/8.

The third leg of the network, Scott's, built ships for both Holts' and Swire's China Navigation. Between 1868 and 1920 Scott's built 57 ships for Holts and 81 ships for Swire's. These contracts produced 16 per cent and 40 per cent respectively of Scott's net profits in this period. After the First World War the Swire and Holts connection remained crucial for Scott's. Ocean Steamship grew in this period through the acquisition of competitors such as Elder Dempster.[64] During the interwar years 44 per cent of all Scott's contracts came from the two firms, and between 1946 to 1969 Holts and Swire's represented 24 per cent of the tonnage built for the firm. Scott's built its last ship for Swire's in 1969, and for Holts in 1980. Between 1868 and 1969 Swire's and Holts together provided order for 196 ships or 42 per cent of the total built by Scott's.[65]

The relationship between the firms was cemented by ties of equity and directorships. The partners, and later directors, of John Swire & Sons were largely drawn from the Swire and Scott families. J. H. Scott served as senior partner following John Samuel Swire's death in 1898 until his own death in 1912. His elder son became a partner in Swire's in 1910 and was chairman of Scott's from 1939 to 1950. Another son spent his career with Swire's, becoming a director in 1931 and deputy chairman 1961–6, and was also a director of Scott's from 1951 until 1972. The Scott's, Swire's, and Holts also remained linked in shareholding. Between 1917 and 1953 Holts held one-third of the shares in Scott's, and this passed to the Swire's, who held that share until 1977 when shipbuilding was nationalized by the British government.

The network also collaborated in new ventures. Holts and Scott's encouraged Swire's to establish a shipbuilding and repair subsidiary in Hong Kong to compete with Jardine's dockyard and to service the China Navigation fleet. John Samuel Swire opposed the idea, but following his death the firms went ahead with the building of the Taikoo Dockyard. Members of Scott's directed the construction of the new dockyard, and then served as technical advisers through the interwar years and beyond into the post-war period. After the shipbuilding facility was ready, Scott's designed ships for construction in Hong Kong, supplied machinery, and recruited and trained staff for the dockyard until well into the post-Second World War period.[66]

Although the Swire–Scott–Holt network was notable both for its duration and its multifaceted nature, it was by no means unique. Another notable example was the relationship between James Finlay and the Clan Line. In 1878 Sir John Muir invested in a new shipping line being established in Glasgow by Charles Cayzer, a former employee of the British India Steam

[64] Malcolm Falkus, *The Blue Funnel Legend* (Basingstoke: Macmillan, 1990).
[65] A. Slaven, 'A Mersey-Clyde Connection: The Holts, Swire's and Scott's 1858–1980' (unpublished paper).
[66] Slaven, 'Mersey-Clyde Connection'.

Navigation Co. Cayzer and Muir entered into an agreement to build two ships, which became the nucleus of the Clan Line, which was essentially a cargo carrier with some passenger accommodation. Muir arranged that Finlays should hold all the Clan Line agencies east of the Suez Canal and that his teas should be carried at favourable rates. Later the Clan Line also took the 'gunny' produced by the Finlay jute mills for export.[67]

In the case of Finlays and the Clan Line, the trader-shipping company relationship was unstable. Muir was an aggressive entrepreneur who sought to acquire control of the Clan Line in the late nineteenth century. These attempts were ultimately unsuccessful and in 1898 Muir's shareholding was sold.[68] However the agency relationship continued. When the Clan Line expanded into the South African trade in 1882 to transport the expanding gold production, Finlays opened a private company—Steel Murray & Co.—in Durban to act as the Clan Line agent.[69] By the time of the First World War Clan Line owned fifty-six ships, and Finlays represented the shipping company at its major South Asian branches at Bombay, Calcutta, and Colombo. When Finlays entered East Africa in the interwar years, its teas were exported using Clan Line vessels. Although the Clan Line was merged into the British & Commonwealth Shipping Company in 1955, the relationship with Finlays continued. In 1967 Finlays office in Calcutta were still managing twenty Clan Line ships and their Pakistan offices another fourteen.[70]

A shipping–trading relationship where cross-shareholding was essential was the Mackinnon/Inchcape group. From the 1860s the British India Steam Navigation Co., the Indian managing agency of Mackinnon Mackenzie and the London-based board of Gray Dawes were connected by equity, family, and director ties. This cluster spawned other partnerships, such as Gray Paul & Co. and Gray Mackenzie in the Gulf, and Smith Mackenzie in East Africa, a major part of whose business was to act as agents for the British India Steam Navigation Co.

The amalgamation of the British India and the P&O in 1914 increased the shipping agency work of Gray Dawes, which moved its office into the P&O office in London in 1917. During the 1920s a substantial element of the earnings of Mackinnon Mackenzie in Calcutta were earned from commissions from the P&O. One estimate is that Mackinnon Mackenzie earned over £1.4 million from P&O commission payments between 1922 and 1931. On the other hand in the late 1920s Mackinnon Mackenzie and other Inchcape agencies gave substantial rebates to P&O in order to enable

[67] Monica Clough, 'Muir Family'. Unpublished draft for *New Dictionary of National Biography*; J. Brogan, *James Finlay & Co Ltd.* (Glasgow: Jackson Son & Co., 1951), 87, 92; Boyce, *Information*, 90–1.
[68] Clough, 'Muir Family'.   [69] Brogan, *James Finlay*, 78.
[70] 'Clan Line', *Finlays House Magazine* (Summer 1967); 'British and Commonwealth Shipping Co. Ltd.', *Finlays House Magazine* (Summer 1967).

that firm to show higher profits.[71] The close relationship between the shipping companies and the three trading company agents within the Inchcape group continued until the reorganization of Inchcape interests in the 1950s. In 1957 Mackinnon Mackenzie and the shipping business managed by Gray Dawes were sold to the P&O Group.

Although the examples of long-term relationships between trading and shipping companies were impressive, a number of caveats need to be made. First, the trading companies as shipping agents seldom exclusively served one company. For example, Gray Mackenzie were the agents for British India in the Gulf, but they were also agents for the Ellerman Bucknell Line. Secondly, it is certainly not true that all shipping agency relations were long term and amicable. There was competition between trading firms for shipping agency business, and shipping companies shifted agencies if they could get better terms. This happened in the interwar years and even more so in the post-war period. The Borneo Company's Singapore manager's report to his London management in 1955 illustrated the way firms changed their agents,

Blue Funnel will drop Bousteads as Port Swettenham Agents for their F.E.F.C. services, and will appoint Guthries instead. Bousteads will become full Agents for Clan Line, with outwards and homewards. Previously they were Agents homewards only. It is believed that Guthries have achieved this thanks to their increasing cargo command, particularly in Latex.[72]

Agency agreements with insurance companies were also important parts of the business of many trading companies. When British insurance companies sought to expand their business abroad, they used specialist insurance brokers in developed and larger markets, particularly in Europe, but in developing countries they employed British trading companies.[73] In general, the relationships between traders and insurance companies were more contractual than with the shipping companies. Insurance companies were often not very impressed by the efforts of their agents, and would write on occasion stressing the need for more activity on their part.[74]

Equity and board links were slow to develop between the trading and insurance companies. By the time of the First World War Lord Inchcape was an investor in, and director of, the Atlas Assurance Company, and pressure was exercised on Binny's and other Inchcape affiliates to transfer their

[71] Christopher J. Napier, 'Allies or Subsidiaries? Inter-Company Relations in the P&O Group, 1914–39', *Business History*, 39 (1997); Stephanie Jones, *Trade and Shipping. Lord Inchcape 1852–1932* (Manchester: Manchester University Press, 1989), 153.

[72] Manager Singapore to Manager London, 12 Apr. 1955, Borneo Company Archives, MS 27259/1, GHL.

[73] Oliver M. Westall, *The Provincial Insurance Company 1903–38* (Manchester: Manchester University Press, 1992), 305.

[74] London & Lancashire Insurance Company to J. Swire & Sons, 24 Mar. 1936, Swire Archives, JSSI/4/14, SOAS.

business to Atlas.[75] Binny's remained Atlas's agents until 1958, when the insurance company opened its own branch in Madras.[76] Swire's had a long-term agency relationship with the Royal Exchange and the London & Lancashire insurance companies, but it was not until 1937 that the former company suggested John Swire might like to become a director 'to cement the connection'.[77]

Selling agency agreements with manufacturers were on an even more contractual basis than with insurance companies. Shipping companies had a vested interest in a long-term relationship with a trading company which handled, for example, substantial flows of trade in commodities. Equally trading companies which managed plantations, or shipping companies, or cotton textile factories, had substantial insurance requirements on their own account, which meant that a long-term relationship with one or more of them was attractive. Manufacturers, on the other hand, simply required a trading firm which would sell their products effectively, and not destroy the value of their brands by incompetent marketing or after sales service. For the most part, they tended to use the trading companies in new or smaller markets which did not merit their own distribution facilities. It was a distinctive feature of the relationship that if the trading company successfully developed a market for a product, its services were likely to be disposed of by the manufacturer who would seek to internalize the business itself.

The importance of selling agencies, which normally gave traders the exclusive right to sell a product in a particular area, grew over time in the business of the trading companies. In the nineteenth century many companies were heavily engaged in selling piece-goods on their own account. Over time this business declined, the composition of imports of the trading companies changed, and more of the business was undertaken on a commission agency basis. By the interwar years trading companies had selling agency agreements with many British, and some foreign, manufacturers of branded consumer goods, chemicals, and machinery. In the 1930s Jardine Matheson's agencies included Seagram's Rye Whisky, White Horse Whisky, Fry's Chocolate, Sharps Toffee, Pears Soap, Remington Typewriters, and Nobel's Explosives.[78] Similarly among the thousands of articles imported into West Africa by UAC in the 1930s and 1940s, there were agency agreements with manufacturers of branded consumer goods, electrical goods, bicycles, and automobiles.[79]

In the post-war period the British trading companies held an increasing number of agency agreements with foreign firms. In 1961 the Borneo

---

[75] Mackinnon Mackenzie Binny's Madras, 11 Sept. 1916, Binny's Archives, MS 27160/5; GHL.
[76] Ibid., Memo on Binny's & Co., c.1959, MS 27167.
[77] J. Swire to C. C. Scott, 19 Feb. 1937, Swire ADD 17, Swire Archives, SOAS.
[78] Arthur Piercy, history of Import Department, 7 Feb. 1939, in W. Keswick to J. J. Paterson, 10 Feb. 1939, S/O Shanghai to Hong Kong 1939, JMA, CUL.
[79] Fieldhouse, *Merchant Capital*, 103.

Company had agency agreements with 208 companies for its branches in South East Asia, of which over forty firms were non-British. These included US firms such as Campbell (soup), Kodak (film), GE (electrical equipment), Norton (grinding wheels), and Sprayway (aerosol), as well as companies from Australia, Belgium, France, Canada, Germany, Netherlands, India, Norway, and Switzerland.[80]

In Latin America too, US and continental European firms featured among the agencies held by the British trading companies. In Chile, Gibbs had agency agreements with German and Swiss armaments manufacturers, while in Peru Milne & Co. held important agencies in the 1950s and 1960s which included Goodrich (tyres) and Ford (automobile dealerships). A new post-war development was also selling agencies for state-owned firms. During the 1950s and 1960s Gibbs in Chile earned substantial commission from its agency agreement for distribution of sugar on behalf of the state-controlled firm Iansa.[81] Gibbs & Co. directors developed networks involving Chilean officials in order to ensure that they were well placed to win the business of such firms.[82]

Agency agreements, although always signed for a limited period of years, were in practice held by the same firm over long periods. An example of an extremely long-term relationship was that between Dodwells and Underwood Typewriter, one of the largest US typewriter and office equipment manufacturers. In 1900 Dodwells obtained the agency for Underwoods throughout China and Japan on the basis of the personal friendship of A. J. H. Cahill, joint founder of Dodwells, and John T. Underwood. The relationship continued on the basis of trust alone with no written agreement and this remained the case as late as 1957, when Underwoods merged with National Cash and was subsequently sold to Olivetti.[83] Dodwells itself retained business machines as one of its most important activities through to the firm's acquisition by Inchcape and subsequently.[84]

In the interwar years and later many British merchant houses were rather passive about the agencies they held. A report on the Borneo Company's business in the mid-1950s noted that though the firm held many agencies at its Sarawak branch, 'the goods represented by these agencies (were) mainly sold if a customer happens to ask for them'.[85] It seems likely that

[80] Agency Agreements 1961, Borneo Company Archives, MS 27232A, GHL.

[81] Antony Gibbs Archives, MS 16881/8, GHL. John Bingham Powell, 'History of the Milne Group of Companies', Aug. 1987, Burmah Castrol Archives.

[82] Antony Gibbs Archives, MS 16276/9, GHL.

[83] Edmund Warde, *The House of Dodwell: A Century of Achievement 1858–1958* (London: the firm, 1958), 18; Dodwell Board Minutes, 26 Mar. 1957, 22 Oct. 1959, Dodwell Archives, MS 27498/7, GHL.

[84] Dodwell in Japan, c.1977, Dodwell Archives, MS 27518, GHL.

[85] Report on the Activities and Resources of Borneo Company Ltd., 15 Feb. 1955, Borneo Company Archives, MS 27180, GHL.

this situation was far from untypical. The markets concerned were often marginal to the manufacturers, who were consequently not very energetic in encouraging the merchants to be more energetic. The web of collusive agreements between the merchant firms also did not provide a context for aggressive marketing.

This passive stance came under pressure from the 1950s. The British traders began losing agencies to other firms through what the Borneo Company's management regarded disdainfully as 'agency pinching'. In Thailand by 1956 this prompted the British firms to consider retaliating by adopting a '"do as you would be done by" policy . . . so long as it is applied with discretion'.[86] As more manufacturers sought to integrate forwards into Asian and other developing markets, the British traders sought to retain their roles by adding value through providing after-sales facilities, local advertising, and so on. As discussed in Chapter 5, motor distribution was one of the activities which the British traders were able to develop a continuing role in the markets of Asia, Africa, and Latin America.

There were even examples of 'adding value' in post-war Latin America, where the British trading companies rarely presented a dynamic profile. In Peru, Milne & Co. held the sales agency for the US agricultural machinery firm John Deere throughout the interwar years, but the business involved little more than selling mule-drawn ploughs and harrows to cotton farms, while the sale of tractors was dominated by Ford and International Harvester. After the end of the war, the agency became much more active selling John Deere tractors and other more advanced farm machinery. Milne & Co. built a special plant in Lima for service and sale of spare parts plus a showroom. In the provinces, showrooms were set up with resident and mobile mechanics who went out to service tractors on the farms.[87]

In Chile, Gibbs was not in the forefront of 'adding value' and it lost a number of important sales agencies from discontented manufacturers. In 1961, for example, the British textile machinery manufacturer Platts cancelled its agency agreement with Gibbs which it had held since 1936.[88] However Gibbs had a technical department in Chile with technical expertise and by the mid-1960s Gibbs was involved in a number of new technologies including a chemical process for sulphur pelleting.[89]

In general, from the 1950s the function of selling agent for manufacturers changed from wholesale distribution to marketing. As volumes increased in a market, manufacturers showed a greater proclivity to replace British mer-

[86] Report on the Activities and Resources of Borneo Company Ltd., London to Singapore, 31 Dec. 1956, Borneo Company Archives, MS 27180, GHL.

[87] John Bingham Powell, 'History of the Milne Group of Companies', Aug. 1987, Burmah Castrol Archives.

[88] Directors' Minutes for Gibbs y Cía, 30 Nov. 1961, Antony Gibbs Archives, MS 16869/3, GHL.

[89] Ibid., MS 16876/8, GHL.

chants with their own operations. However in many developing countries in Asia, the Middle East, Africa, and parts of Latin America, there continued to be a role for trade intermediaries. This was partly because volumes were too small to encourage forward integration by manufacturers. It was also because information costs remained substantial, though they changed in their nature. While communication improvements resulted in much greater accessibility of information about foreign markets, persistent cross-national differences in business cultures, institutional arrangements, and contract enforcement meant that the local knowledge and contacts of the trading companies remained important assets.

8.4 External Architecture

The trading companies operated within an environment of external relationships with other firms. Relationships with banks were important for the routine business of the merchant firms, and also at times of crisis and of rapid expansion. There were sustained relationships with shipping and insurance companies. Agency agreements with manufacturers were more contractual, and the merchant intermediaries more regularly faced the risks of being squeezed out of the business. This part of their business was constantly under threat. However even some relationships with manufacturers proved very long term.

It is important not to romanticize the nature of these networks. They were at times as much collusive as dynamic, and they were sustained in part because of the depressed economic conditions of the interwar years. However their long-term nature is not simply explained by collusion, and the effects were not simply collusive. An especially noteworthy feature of external architecture of the traders was that it was often trust rather than contract based. In many relationships, parties could have acted opportunistically, but in practice the advantages derived from the ongoing relationship were greater than the expected gains from such opportunistic behaviour.

9

Natural Resources

9.1 Introduction

This chapter discusses the role of British trading companies in the exploitation of natural resources. As the British merchants first established themselves in overseas countries to sell British goods, they rapidly also began to sell the products of their host economies, which were primarily agricultural commodities and minerals. Initially in India, and later elsewhere, some firms also diversified backwards from trade into local production. By 1914 they had become owners of large tropical plantations, timber, and farmlands, while a number of firms had also invested in minerals, gold, and petroleum. Many of these investments, especially in plantations and timber, remained important features of the business portfolios of the trading companies through to the 1960s.

The investments of the trading companies in natural resource exploitation were part of a major flow of funds into this sector which intensified in the late nineteenth century. Industrialization created a huge demand for minerals such as copper and tin and foodstuffs for expanding urban populations. There was extensive foreign direct investment aimed at locating new sources of supply. The trading companies became major participants in these trade flows, but in their capacity as direct investors they also created new sources of supply as well as just trading in commodities.

The chapter begins with a survey of trading company investments in the resource sector. This is followed by case studies of investments in tea and tropical timber, and in oil. In the former commodities British merchant firms made large and sustained investments, and these case studies demonstrate their roles as managers of extensive resource enterprises. In the case of oil, several firms were entrepreneurial pioneers of the industry in the nineteenth century, but only in a few cases were investments sustained.

9.2 Traders as Producers

During the eighteenth and the first half of the nineteenth century British merchants were major traders in commodities but only rarely invested in their growing or exploitation. They traded in everything from guano to opium, though more 'routine' articles such as coffee, tea, sugar, and grain predominated. A rare exception was in India, where as early as the 1790s British agency houses began to invest in indigo plantations, mainly in

TABLE 9.1 Principal investments in natural resource exploitation by British trading companies before 1914

Resource	Country
Indigo	India
Rubber	Malaya, Dutch East Indies
Tea	India, Ceylon
Coffee	India, Malaya, Dutch East Indies
Sugar cane	West Indies, Brazil, Peru
Teak	Thailand, Burma
Farms	USA (West Coast), Chile
Nitrates	Chile
Coal	India, UK
Tin	Nigeria
Gold	Sarawak
Oil	USA (California), Peru, Burma, Borneo

Bengal, where the extension of the political rule of the East India Company coincided with a boom in the export demand for the commodity, used as a dyeing agent for textiles. The collapse of the Calcutta agency houses in the 1830s caused a major hiatus in this first wave of plantation ownership, though the Madras agency houses maintained their indigo plantations and also invested in coffee growing.[1]

During the last third of the century the trading companies began to invest on a much larger scale in the ownership of renewable resources. Table 9.1 summarizes the main products and countries involved before the First World War.

There were a number of systematic influences which led the trading companies into commodity production and mining. In the majority of cases they began as traders in the commodity. Backward vertical integration can be explained by transaction cost factors arising from problems of asset specificity, uncertainty, and opportunism. In natural resources, as in other activities, their branches and contacts in host economies also provided a source of information about profitable opportunities, and given the booming world trade in commodities prior to the First World War, there were incentives to diversify into production. Certainly in the case of plantation agriculture, initial development was often in the hands of expatriate planters who lacked the capital to invest in the machinery, marketing, and processing facilities needed in many sectors. Among other ownership advantages, the greater financial capabilities of the trading companies, and their ability

[1] Dharma Kumar (ed.), *The Cambridge Economic History of India* (Cambridge: Cambridge University Press, 1983), 315–18; Hilton Brown, *Parry's of Madras* (Madras: the firm, 1954), 63, 80, 100, 121, 128, 185.

to access plentiful funds by 'floating' new joint stock companies in the context of business groups, led the merchants in many cases to buy out or otherwise displace the planters.

However there were distinctive patterns in the particular commodities in which the traders became involved in production. The trading companies became extensively involved in tea and rubber production, but far less in coffee, and with almost no investment in tropical fruit or wine. Minerals such as copper and bauxite received almost no investment, while the trading companies made only modest investments in tin mining. There was an early and strong interest in petroleum, but here the merchants could not as a whole command the resources required to sustain their investments.

There was no single explanation for these patterns. In the Portuguese port wine industry, the existence between the middle of the eighteenth century and the 1860s of a quasi-regulator of production and quality—the Companhia Geral de Agricultura das Vinhas do Alto Douro—reduced the transaction costs of procurement and helps explain why no British merchant house integrated backwards into wine production for export.[2] The frequency and volume of transactions were important also in explaining why investments in tea and sugar were greater than in coffee. The British began drinking tea around the middle of the seventeenth century, and although coffee initially remained the favourite beverage for another half a century, by the eighteenth century tea had replaced it. During the nineteenth century British per capita consumption of tea rose from 1.2 pounds per annum in the 1830s to just over 6 pounds in 1900, and 9 pounds in the interwar years, by which period Britain alone consumed over 50 per cent of world tea output.[3] Similarly, Britain was a huge market for sugar as the British had one of the highest rates of sugar consumption per head in the nineteenth century. Much of this sugar consumption was used to sweeten tea, as well as other beverages.[4]

In the nineteenth century the extensive British trade in tea—examined in more detail in section 9.3 below—was centred on China and India. Trading and—in India—growing tea was a very important business for British merchants. In contrast, few British merchants in Asia invested in coffee growing on a large scale, although Harrisons & Crosfield had coffee estates in Java until the 1980s, while Binny's had a number of coffee estates in Mysore, which were eventually liquidated in 1936.[5] British merchants

---

[2] Paul Duguid and Teresa da Silva Lopes, 'Ambiguous Company: Institutions and Organisations in the Port Wine Trade, 1814–1854', *Scandinavian Economic History Review*, 47 (1999).

[3] V. D. Wickizer, *Coffee, Tea and Cocoa* (Stanford, Calif: Stanford University Press, 1951), ch. 7; Guitam K. Sarkar, *The World Tea Economy* (Delhi: Oxford University Press, 1972), ch. 1.

[4] Philippe Chalmin, *The Making of a Sugar Giant: Tate and Lyle 1859–1989* (Chur: Harwood, 1990), 12–14.

[5] Memo on Binny & Co. (Madras) Ltd., c.1959, Binny Archives, MS 27167, GHL.

such as Johnstons and Naumann Gapp were significant in the processing and export of Brazilian coffee—which accounted for 75 per cent of world production in 1900—at the end of the century British firms only handled around 20 per cent of Brazilian coffee, and German and American houses were more important. However there was no investment in coffee estates until the turn of the century, perhaps because market incentives were weak. Per capita consumption of coffee was actually falling in Britain, while British consumers preferred the mild coffee produced in India or Jamaica to Brazilian coffee.[6]

British trading companies also invested in sugar cane plantations, mainly in British Guiana and Trinidad, two West Indian colonies acquired by Britain after the Napoleonic Wars. During the first half of the nineteenth century sugar production in British Guiana expanded rapidly under the control of an expatriate planter class. Subsequently, however, the capital requirements of the industry increased with technological innovations in milling and manufacture which increased the optimum size of plantations—at a time of declining prices caused by the rapid growth of competition from beet sugar produced in Europe, the United States, and China. Merchants supplied the funds and ended up acquiring the plantations. Booker Brothers, McConnell came to dominate the colony's industry, accounting for 70 per cent of total sugar output by the late 1940s, and vertically integrating the industry by owning the cane fields and factories, supplying machinery, and transporting and marketing the sugar. A similar process occurred in Trinidad and some other West Indian islands, where Henckell Du Buisson among other merchants acquired estates.[7] Beyond the West Indies, Knowles & Foster, Locketts, Milne & Co., and Graham Rowe were among the firms which invested in sugar cane production and milling in Brazil and Peru, while in Mauritius, Blyth, Greene, Jourdain shipped sugar and provided credit to the planters, but did not make direct investments in sugar cane estates until after the Second World War.[8]

The substantial investment in West Indian sugar contrasted with a lack of investment in tropical fruits such as bananas. The production and marketing of Caribbean bananas became concentrated in the hands of two US-owned firms, United Fruit and Standard Fruit, which began as traders in bananas and evolved as integrated multinationals owning huge areas of plantations, shipping, and distribution facilities. Transactions cost considerations, especially the need to ensure adequate supplies and maintain quality control because of the problem of perishability, explain the degree of vertical

[6] Robert Greenhill, 'The Brazilian Coffee Trade', in D. C. M. Platt (ed.), *Business Imperialism 1840–1930* (Oxford: Oxford University Press, 1977), 198–230.

[7] J. H. Galloway, *The Sugar Cane Industry* (Cambridge: Cambridge University Press, 1989), 173–80; Kathleen M. Stahl, *The Metropolitan Organisation of British Colonial Trade* (London: Faber & Faber, 1951), 36–46.

[8] Augustus Muir, *Blyth, Greene, Jourdain & Co. Ltd 1810–1960* (London: the firm, 1961).

integration in the industry, but not the reason why British merchants did not seek to become involved in it.[9]

In fact there was initial British investment in Caribbean bananas by the Liverpool shipping firm of Elder Dempster & Co. As described in Chapter 3, this dynamic shipping company all but dominated shipping between West Africa and Britain, and established an extensive trading and transport infrastructure on the West African coast in the late nineteenth century. Elder Dempster established a coal bunkering depot for its ships on the Canary Islands and to fill unoccupied space on vessels that called for fuel the firm pioneered the export of bananas to Liverpool. This led to the formation in 1901 of a joint venture called Elders & Fyffes with a firm of London fruit merchants.

Elders & Fyffes was a shipping and marketing firm. A shipping line was operated, equipped with special refrigerating machinery and subsidized by the British and colonial governments, to carry bananas bought in Jamaica for their sale in Britain. However Elders & Fyffes did not invest in banana production in Jamaica, which was dominated by United Fruit, and when a hurricane devastated the crop in 1903, the British firm had to seek assistance from the US company. In return for a purchase contract guaranteeing supplies of bananas, United Fruit acquired 45 per cent of the shares and subsequently took full control in 1910. Elders & Fyffes retained its identify—even establishing its own banana plantations in the Canary Islands—but was in reality the European affiliate of United Fruit.[10] The American acquisition of Elders & Fyffes, therefore, pre-empted the development of what might have become a British-owned banana trading company with integrated producing and shipping interests.

The other plantation crop in which British trading companies became extensively involved before 1914 was rubber in South East Asia. Through to the end of the nineteenth century the British agency houses took little part in the initial development of the rubber plantations in Malaya. Following the transfer of rubber seeds from Brazil to Singapore, individual British planters began to establish rubber estates, in many instances in response to the destruction of the coffee crop by pest. Guthries, which already had spice and coffee plantations, took a pioneering step in this direction in 1895 when it laid out an experimental rubber plantation. During the 1900s, as the price of rubber rose, alongside the development of the motor car, individual planters had insufficient resources to increase their output, the British traders acquired estates in Malaya and the Dutch East Indies and formed companies. By 1914

    [9] Robert Read, 'The Growth and Structure of Multinationals in the Banana Trade', in Mark Casson (ed.) *The Growth of International Business* (London: George Allen & Unwin, 1983), 180–213.
    [10] P. N. Davies, *The Trade Makers: Elder Dempster in West Africa 1852–1972* (London: George Allen & Unwin, 1973); P. N. Davies, *Fyffes and the Banana* (London: Athlone, 1990); Read, 'Growth and Structure'.

large areas of the south and west of the Malayan peninsula had been turned into rubber tree plantations managed by the leading British agency houses. Malayan rubber exports reached 30,000 tons in 1913 and 200,000 in 1919, by which time rubber had replaced tin as the country's largest export.[11]

Teak was the final tropical commodity in which British traders made large investments in Burma and Thailand. British and other European traders were buying Burmese teak as early as the seventeenth century, but it was with the extension of British rule over Burma progressively from the 1820s that British merchants and others secured leases and began exploiting it themselves, consolidating their position as British political control grew over the country. A small group of firms, led by the Bombay Burmah Trading Corporation, dominated the teak business.[12] In neighbouring Thailand, British merchants also attempted to secure control over the teak forests, but it was only after the extension of extraterritoriality to the north that the central government could grant leases, and this opened the way for Western firms to cut logs themselves instead of buying them from native foresters. The British firms introduced the methods already developed in Burma to directly manage the forests.[13] The British share of Thai teak output peaked at 88 per cent in 1906.[14]

The teak industry in South East Asia was noteworthy for the extent of vertical integration. The British firms leased the forests, cut the trees, transported the logs by elephants and river craft to their sawmills, and exported the logs. The conditions of the industry help to explain this integration. It featured high degrees of asset-specificity—herds of elephants and sawmills —and the need for heavy capital investment. Teak trees chosen for felling were 'girdled', and thereafter the trees had to stand for at least three years so that they dried out and seasoned sufficiently to become floatable. They were then dragged by elephants or buffalo to a river. During the annual rainy season single logs were then floated down the rapids to collecting points in calmer waters, and then bound into rafts to be floated down to sawmills in Bangkok. However the rains were unpredictable so teak supplies could

[11] G. C. Allen and A. G. Donnithorne, *Western Enterprise in Indonesia and Malaya* (London: George Allen & Unwin, 1957), 106–20; P. T. Bauer; *The Rubber Industry* (London: Longmans, 1948); J. H. Drabble, *Rubber in Malaya 1876–1922: The Genesis of the Industry* (Kuala Lumpur: Oxford University Press, 1973); D. J. M. Tate, *The RGA History of the Plantation Industry in the Malaya Peninsula* (Kuala Lumpur: Oxford University Press, 1996); J. H. Drabble and P. J. Drake, 'The British Agency Houses in Malaysia: Survival in a Changing World', *Journal of Southeast Asian Studies*, 12 (1981).

[12] R. H. Macaulay, *History of the Bombay Burmah Trading Corporation Ltd., 1864–1910* (London: Spottiswoode Ballantyre, 1934); A. C. Pointon, *Wallace Brothers* (Oxford: the firm, 1974); A. G. McCrae, *Pioneers in Burma*, Occasional Papers in Economic and Social History, No. 2, 1986).

[13] Malcolm Falkus, 'Early British Business in Thailand', in R. P. T. Davenport-Hines and Geoffrey Jones (eds.), *British Business in Asia since 1860* (Cambridge: Cambridge University Press, 1989), 134–46; Macaulay, *History*, 51–78.

[14] R. A. Brown, *Capital and Entrepreneurship in Southeast Asia* (London: Macmillan, 1994), 74.

fluctuate sharply, locking up large amounts of capital for several years. The high asset-specificity of felled trees, herds of elephants, and sawmills encouraged internalization.[15] The high-risk element of the teak industry may have given the trading companies with their diversified portfolios advantages over more specialist firms.

In the exploitation of plantation commodities and/or tropical products such as teak, the relative importance of the British merchants in the industry as a whole varied enormously. British trading companies were the foremost investors in the Burmese and Thai teak industries. There were other producers, such as small-scale local or overseas Chinese firms or—in the case of Thailand—the Danish-owned East Asiatic Company—but the British firms were paramount.[16] The British agency houses controlled large numbers of 'free-standing' firms active in the South East Asian rubber and South Asian tea plantations, though other types of firm were also found, including British and US rubber manufacturers. A peasant smallholder sector also grew in Malaya, although it was not until the 1920s that its output became significant.[17] In India, there were specialist tea producers not linked to agency houses, and in Ceylon British tea distributors and blenders such as Lipton —subsequently acquired by Unilever—and Brooke Bond purchased estates.[18] In the sugar cane industry, Booker Brothers, McConnell emerged as the largest sugar plantation owner in British Guinea, but elsewhere in the British islands sugar was owned by a complex mix of different types of firm, local and British owned, even before the large-scale investments of the British sugar refiner Tate & Lyle in the 1930s.

On the Pacific West Coast of the United States and Chile the British trading companies became large-scale owners of farmlands. In the former, Balfour Williamson was one of the first movers in the region's large-scale wheat and, subsequently, fruit exports. In the case of fruit, during the 1880s the firm sought to integrate backwards into owning their own fruit lands in order to guarantee supplies. The firm acquired a number of fruit farms and vineyards in California, and established a packing company to dry and pack its own fruit. The firm also invested in orange-growing in California and in the Fresno raisin trade, where the firm had its own business and acted as agents for the much larger Californian Fruit Canners' Association.[19]

In Latin America, Balfour Williamson, Gibbs, and Duncan Fox were major wheat exporters from Chile, and had large investments in flour milling, but they also invested in land. Balfour Williamson developed farms on Easter

[15] Falkus, 'Early British Business', 145–6; Geoffrey Jones and Judith Wale, 'Merchants as Business Groups: British Trading Companies in Asia before 1945', *Business History Review*, 72 (1998).

[16] Falkus, 'Early British Business', 143.

[17] Keetie E. Sluyterman, 'Dutch Multinational Trading Companies in the Twentieth Century', in Geoffrey Jones (ed.), *The Multinational Traders* (London: Routledge, 1998), 89; Allen and Donnithorne, *Western Enterprise in Indonesia and Malaya*, 114–15.

[18] Stahl, *Metropolitan Organisation*, 167–9.

[19] Wallis Hunt, *Heirs of Great Adventure*, ii (London: the firm, 1960), 25–7.

Island, while Antony Gibbs undertook cattle-rearing and wine-growing on the Wellington Islands.[20] Duncan Fox's sheep farming business in Chile was probably the largest farming investment in the region. Elsewhere in Latin America, some of the British merchant groups on the River Plate invested in land, but specialist types of British firms became more pre-eminent in the huge Argentinian meat export business, such as the Vestey family, which owned extensive farms and ranches in Argentina (and else-where), a large fleet of refrigerated ships, and—by the 1920s—a network of butchers' shops in Britain.[21] From the mid-1900s US meat packing firms such as Swift established a dominant position in the Argentinian trade, though they did not integrate backwards into the ownership of land.[22]

There were other agricultural commodities in which British trading com-panies were extremely important as traders and processors, but which they did not enter the direct exploitation themselves, often employing contrac-tual means to control supplies from individual producers. In Burma, Steel Brothers handled half the total rice crop in the 1930s and were counted among the leading millers and shippers of rice in the world, but the production of rice was left to the peasantry and control was exercised over the industry from the milling stage. The British merchants controlled very large mills in Rangoon, and established a strong—and collusive—position in Burma, while elsewhere in South East Asia it was overseas Chinese who predomin-ated in the industry.[23]

During the late nineteenth century there was a huge boom in FDI in the non-renewable resources of mining and petroleum. Britain became the world centre of the international mining industry, spawning large numbers of 'free-standing' companies.[24] However, despite their presence in some major mining regions, trading company investments in mining proved muted before 1914. A major exception was the pre-eminent role of British merchants, espe-cially Antony Gibbs and, on a lesser scale, Locketts, in Chilean nitrates.[25] Gibbs were also involved in copper mining in Chile between the 1880s and

[20] Ibid. 159–61; Robert Greenhill, 'Merchants and the Latin American Trades: An Intro-duction', in D. C. M. Platt (ed.), *Business Imperialism 1840–1930* (Oxford: Clarendon Press, 1977), 172.

[21] Richard Perren, 'William Vestey and Sir Edmund Hoyle Vestey', in D. J. Jeremy (ed.), *Dictionary of Business Biography*, vol. v (London: Butterworths, 1986), 618–21.

[22] Mira Wilkins, *The Emergence of Multinational Enterprise* (Cambridge, Mass.: Harvard University Press, 1970), 189–90; Charles Jones, 'Institutional Forms of British Foreign Direct Investment in South America', *Business History*, 39 (1997); Robert Greenhill and Rory Miller, 'British Trading Companies in South America after 1914', in Geoffrey Jones (ed.), *The Multinational Traders* (London: Routledge, 1998), 110–11.

[23] McCrae, *Pioneers in Burma*; H. E. W. Braund, *Calling to Mind* (Oxford: Pergamon, 1975); Brown, *Capital*, 126–7.

[24] Charles Harvey and Jon Press, 'The City and International Mining, 1870–1914', *Business History*, 32 (1990).

[25] Robert Greenhill, 'The Nitrate and Iodine Trades 1880–1914', in Platt (ed.), *Business Imperialism*, 231–83; Antony Gibbs & Sons, *Merchants and Bankers* (London: the firm, 1958), chs. 2 and 3.

the 1900s, and Duncan Fox and Balfour Williamson also had modest investments in mining and smelting silver, lead, and copper in Chile.

Apart from nitrates, the other large mining investments by British merchants before 1914 were in the Indian coal industry. During the 'boom' of the 1860s the Calcutta agency houses such as Andrew Yule began to float coal companies whose managing agencies they retained. The Indian coal industry was located largely in Bengal and expanded rapidly to supply the needs of the expanding Indian railroad system. Prior to 1914 the British agency houses controlled all the large coal mining companies with up-to-date mechanical equipment, and coal ranked with tea and jute as the three 'core' activities of the British merchant houses in Calcutta. Their diversified business portfolios which included the management of jute mills, and shipping companies provided markets for their coal, while their contracts with the British railroad authorities also worked in their favour, probably to the detriment of the large number of Indian-owned collieries of small size.[26]

On a far more modest scale, the coal industry was an exceptional instance when trading companies undertook vertical integration into mining in Britain. W. and J. Lockett controlled a south Wales coal company for several decades after 1889 before selling its shares.[27] A more substantial case was that of Wilson, Sons the coal trader. Wilsons' main suppliers of coal came from south Wales, and its shipments of coal from south Wales to its various depots grew from 64 to over 1,400 thousand tons between 1877 and 1907.[28] In Wales it developed a long-term relationship with a colliery company, the Ocean Coal Company, which supplied high-grade steam coal. The nature of the coal business encouraged a closer relationship between Wilsons and its main coal supplier. Wilsons were primarily merchants taking ownership of the coal which they delivered and hence assuming the risk. They signed long-term supply contracts with customers which made them vulnerable both to changes in freight rates and to fluctuations in the purchase price of coal in Britain. A closer relationship between the trading company and the south Wales coal company was one response to this latter problem. At the same time, the Ocean Coal Company sought more guaranteed export outlets for its colliery production rather than selling on the open market. This latter consideration led to Ocean acquiring control of Wilson, Sons in 1907 and the formation of a holding company, Ocean Coal & Wilson, Sons Ltd.[29] However Ocean Coal could not supply all Wilsons' requirements at peak years and in 1911, for example, the firm 'had to buy considerable quantities of coal in the market'.[30]

[26] Rajat K. Ray, *Industrialisation in India* (Delhi: Oxford University Press, 1979), 115–25.
[27] Richard Cyril Lockett, *Memoirs of the Family of Lockett* (London: private circulation, 1939), 115–16.
[28] Wilsons Minute Books 1877–1907, Wilson, Sons Archives MS 20186/1–3, GHL.
[29] Ibid , Chairman's statements to AGM of Ocean Coal & Wilsons Ltd., 1952, MS 20197.
[30] Ibid., Chairman's statement Mar. 1911, Minute Book D, 8 Jan. 1907–6 Feb. 1911, MS 20186/4.

In South East Asia, the Borneo Company's investment in gold mining in Sarawak was one of the few mining investments by agency houses. The firm replaced the pre-existing immigrant Chinese gold mining community by the 1880s and, employing a new method of extracting the gold from ore, developed a large gold mining industry which formed a major component of the firm's profits until the early 1920s. The Borneo Company also mined diamonds, antimony, silver, copper, and other minerals in the region, but the twin pillars of the company were gold and Thai teak in this period. In 1921, however, the principal gold mine flooded after a period of heavy rains and the company ceased production, surrendering its exploitation rights, having not invested in development expenditure in surrounding areas.[31]

Elsewhere in the region, a striking feature of the tin industry of Malaya was the limited investment by the agency houses. Malayan tin production grew very rapidly from the 1870s, following the extension of British political control over the Perak region, but in 1913 three-quarters of production was by Chinese. British mining companies began to increase in importance in the 1900s with the introduction of a more capital-intensive mining technology, dredging. British free-standing companies—sometimes clustered around specialist mining groups—were the main corporate vehicle, and investments by the British agency houses were very modest.[32] Their lack of investment was probably related to a perceived lack of technological expertise and an unwillingness to commit substantial capital to a risky industry with poor collateral at a time when the profits from plantation rubber were substantial. In West Africa, the Niger Company made modest investments in tin mining in the 1900s before focusing on the transport and sale of ores.[33]

The remaining industry in which the trading companies invested was oil. In late nineteenth-century Asia, California, and Peru, British trading companies became involved in the marketing and production of oil, although by 1914 most of the larger operations had been transferred to the control of large specialist oil companies. This process is examined in section 9.4 below.

The interwar years offered poor prospects for new investments in most natural resources. From the 1920s, and especially during the 1930s, problems of excess capacity and declining demand from the industrialized countries caused the prices of many products to fall. Not surprisingly, especially in view of the deteriorating profitability of most of the firms, the main emphasis was on consolidation of existing interests or their incremental growth rather than new ventures. Harrisons & Crosfield, for example, consolidated its various tea and rubber plantations in south India, and continued to expand its rubber investments in South East Asia until the end of the 1920s, but

---

[31] Stephanie Jones, *Two Centuries of Overseas Trading* (London: Macmillan, 1986), 196–201; 'A report on the Closing Down of the "Tai Parit" mine at Bau in 1921', by T. C. Martine, Aug. 1939, Borneo Company Archives, MS 27288, GHL.

[32] Stahl, *Metropolitan Organisation*, 114–16.

[33] Frederick Pedler, *The Lion and the Unicorn in Africa* (London: Heinemann, 1974), 170.

not so much in Malaya and Java as had occurred in the decade before 1914, but more in Sumatra, where a new plantation company, Allied Sumatra Plantations, was formed in 1925.

In some instances there were divestments from commodities whose future seemed bleak, as in the case of Gibbs and Locketts from Chilean nitrates. Some British firms clung to their investments even when their prospects were poor. This was the case of the Calcutta managing agencies Gillanders and Birds, which continued to expand their interests in the coal industry even though its prices weakened greatly from the mid-1920s. This strategy seems to have arisen from a misplaced optimism about the export prospects of Indian coal combined with a preference for security offered by long-term supply contracts for the Indian railroads.[34]

The British trading companies were enthusiastic promoters of commodity cartels designed to support prices and restrict output. In tea and rubber these were especially successful. In the latter industry, the British agency houses in Malaya were closely involved in the complex negotiations to 'restrict' rubber production. The chairman of Guthries was the architect of the International Rubber Restriction Agreement in 1934 between the British, Dutch, French, and Thai governments—responsible for territories which produced 98 per cent of the world's rubber exports—which allocated quotas and 'stabilized' the industry, as well as favouring estate producers in Malaya over smallholders.[35] In other commodities such as teak, commodity control schemes were absent or unsuccessful. In the latter industry, the British producers in Thailand also found themselves outside the tariff preferences within the British Empire.

There were also strategies to enhance the value-added nature of commodities, through improving yields—as in the case of the rubber plantation industry—and through vertical integration and branding strategies. Steels in 1915 acquired a shareholding in a London rice milling company which in 1928 became wholly owned as Carbutt & Co. (1928). A second rice mill in Hull was acquired soon afterwards.[36] In Brazil, Brazilian Warrant integrated backwards from coffee trading into coffee plantations, estate management, and marketing in Britain.[37]

A handful of investments in new minerals and commodities occurred, in Asia, and mostly to reduce the risks of over-exposure to one commodity. In India, in 1919 Wallace Brothers invested in, and acquired control of, one of the largest producers of mica from mines in Bihar.[38] Harrisons &

---

[34] Maria Misra, 'Entrepreneurial Decline and the End of Empire', (Oxford D. Phil., 1994) 70–6.
[35] Allen and Donnithorne, *Western Enterprise*, 120–6; Tate, *RGA History*, chs. 25–7; John H. Drabble, *Malayan Rubber: The Interwar Years* (London: Macmillan, 1991).
[36] Braund, *Calling to Mind*, 40–4.
[37] Robert G. Greenhill, 'Investment Group, Free-Standing Company or Multinational? Brazilian Warrant, 1909–52', *Business History*, 37 (1995); Greenhill and Miller, 'British Trading Companies', 111.
[38] Pointon, *Wallace Brothers*, 62.

Crosfield invested in logging in Borneo in the 1920s. Guthries was among the pioneers of palm oil in Malaya. The commercial planting of oil palm as a sole crop did not start in the Malaya peninsula until 1917, with the Franco-Belgium-owned Hallet group as the pioneer. In 1924 Guthries began to invest in palm oil in order to reduce its reliance on rubber.[39] By 1931 Guthries accounted for one-third of the total area planted with oil palm in Malaya, making it the second largest producer after Hallet. Guthries set up research facilities on its oil palm estates and, after 1945, was responsible for introducing into Malaya a new type of oil palm developed in the Belgian Congo. In 1932 Guthries also established storage and pumping installations at Singapore Harbour which enabled the shipment of palm oil in bulk, and whose facilities were available to the many small-scale Malayan producers.[40]

Palm oil was also the focus of UAC's investment in plantations in the 1930s. Plantation agriculture was rare in West Africa, and on its formation in 1929 UAC inherited from its predecessor companies only a handful of small rubber, oil palm, and banana plantations in the region. In 1930 UAC also received a new lease from the colonial government in Nigeria to develop palm oil plantations, designed to have a demonstration effect on the African peasantry, whose traditional production methods were rendered uneconomic by the plantations of the Dutch East Indies and Malaya. During the 1930s UAC developed palm oil in West Africa and had a number of rubber and banana estates, but none of these ventures were large, however, or comparable to the scale seen in South East Asia.[41] By contrast, UAC's parent Unilever owned through its Belgian-registered affiliate—Huileries du Congo Belge—huge land concessions in the Belgian Congo on which it developed oil palm plantations in the 1930s. By the 1950s this venture was to account for over 9 per cent of world trade in palm oil, but it was kept wholly separate from UAC.[42]

From the 1950s the ownership of natural resources in developing countries by foreign companies began progressively to decline as host governments sought to increase national ownership and control over natural resources. By the mid-1970s the nationalization of large-scale mining and petroleum ventures was virtually complete throughout the developing world, and foreign-owned plantations had also become a rarity.[43] The upshot was that by this

[39] Sir John Hay to Lady Anderson, 8 June 1928, Guthrie Archives, G/MIS/9, SOAS.

[40] Tate, *RGA History*, 458–63.

[41] D. K. Fieldhouse, *Merchant Capital and Economic Decolonization* (Oxford: Clarendon Press, 1994), 204–9.

[42] D. K. Fieldhouse, *Unilever Overseas* (London: Croom Helm, 1978), ch. 9.

[43] M. L. Williams, 'The Extent and Significance of the Nationalizations of foreign-owned assets in developing countries, 1956–1972', *Oxford Economic Papers*, 27 (1975); S. J. Kobrin, 'Expropriation as an Attempt to Control Foreign Firms in LDCs: Trends from 1969 to 1979', *International Studies Quarterly*, 18 (1984); E. Graham and I. Floering, *The Modern Plantation in the Third World* (London: Croom Helm, 1984); Charles R. Kennedy, 'Relations between Transnational Corporations and Governments in Host Countries: A Look to the Future', *Transnational Corporations*, 1 (1992).

period the control of the exploitation of most resources by multinationals was weakened or eliminated, though such firms continued in many cases to exercise a great influence through their long-term contracts with producers and by their control over transportation, processing, and marketing.[44]

The British trading companies were fully exposed to this general trend. In former colonies they had often been closely integrated into colonial society and were especially vivid symbols of past British hegemony. The result was the political risks of controlling mines and plantations grew substantially. At the same time the economic risks of commodities increased also as the interwar commodity control schemes, which had often benefited them, were unwound after the war. The International Rubber Restriction Agreement ended in 1944 and subsequently the rapid rise of the US synthetic rubber industry created entirely new and competitive conditions. It was not until the International Natural Rubber Agreement in 1979 that a renewed attempt was made by producing and consuming countries to control price.[45]

The substantial investments made by British merchants in the resources of South Asia meant that they were soon affected by the changing political environment, as the successor states to the British Raj were among the earliest and most active ex-colonies to adopt policies against foreign ownership of resources. The British firms in Burma had their teak forests nationalized soon after that country's independence in 1948. This left substantial investments in Thai teak—described within the Borneo Company as late as 1955 as 'our most valuable asset'[46]—but by the 1960s their involvement had effectively ended.

In India, the most substantial trading company investments remained in coal and tea. During the 1950s the Indian coal industry boomed, with a large export business, and the companies managed by the British agency houses were profitable. Andrew Yule, which had one of the largest stakes in the coal industry invested in new collieries and modernized old ones in this period, benefiting from World Bank loans to buy coal mining equipment.[47] However the nationalization in 1970 of the Indian coal industry ended the role of the British firms, and most of the tea plantations were sold to local interests over the following decade.

During the late 1960s and 1970s sugar plantation and related interests in the West Indies were nationalized. In Jamaica there was widespread resentment at the foreign dominance of the sugar industry, which was the country's largest employer. In 1970 Booker McConnell were obliged to sell half of their 49 per cent shareholding of a large sugar factory on their plantation

---

[44] Geoffrey Jones, *The Evolution of International Business* (London: Routledge, 1996), 91–8.

[45] Tate, *RGA History*, ch. 39.

[46] Comments on Wells Report, 26 Apr. 1955, Borneo Company Archives, MS 27181, GHL.

[47] Andrew Yule & Company, *Andrew Yule & Co. Ltd. 1863–1963* (Edinburgh; T. & A. Constable, 1963), 20–1; S. Jones, *Merchants of the Raj* (London: Macmillan, 1992), 146–54.

to the government, and British sugar investments were transferred to the government by the mid-1970s.[48] Booker McConnell continued to dominate the Guyanese sugar industry. Bookers Sugar Estates in Guyana produced an annual average of 268,000 tons of sugar between 1965 and 1970. It undertook extensive research on sugar growing, and was the basis for the Booker's diversified business in Guyana, which included general trading, department stores, stockfeed manufacturing, dairy farming, beef production, a lime plantation, shrimp freezing, advertising agencies, alcohol distilling and shipping, and insurance agencies. However in 1976 the sugar plantations and all the other businesses were nationalized.[49]

In South East Asia, it was not until the late 1970s and early 1980s that the extensive rubber and oil palm plantations of the agency houses were transferred into local ownership. Malaya remained the world's largest producer of rubber in the post-war period and the British agency houses were the leading forces in the industry. This prominence aroused hostility, and during the early 1950s the plantations became the target of armed attacks by Communist insurgents during the so-called 'Emergency'. However a more fundamental threat came from the continued growth of synthetic rubber. In 1962 total world production of synthetic rubber overtook that of natural rubber for the first time.

The British agency houses responded to this latter problem quite effectively. Guthries pioneered the replanting of rubber trees in the interwar years, and subsequently this became an important strategy adopted by other firms to raise productivity and reduce prices. The rising costs of replanting encouraged amalgamations between estates, and the agency houses over time created larger groups with central factories to cater for dedicated processing and administrative services. The overall result was to further strengthen the position of the British agency houses. Guthries and Harrisons & Crosfield, the two leading firms, were active in research and in 1964 Guthries invented crumb or block rubber which enabled rubber of higher and more consistent quality to be sold.[50]

Between the 1950s and the 1980s oil palm cultivation in Malaya also expanded dramatically. By 1985 the area under oil palm in the Peninsula was only one-fifth below that for rubber. Pioneered by Guthries along with Socfin and the East Asiatic Company, its cultivation was taken up by other agency houses from the late 1940s, attracted by high prices in world markets which made it seem an attractive alternative to rubber. After its initial hostility to oil palm cultivation, Harrisons & Crosfield also invested in the industry. In 1955 Harrisons & Crosfield set up its own oil palm research centre and in 1960 one of the most important Malayan companies managed by Harrisons & Crosfield, Pataling Rubber Estates, purchased an existing

[48] Chalmin, *Making of a Sugar Giant*, 504–10.
[49] Annual Reports, Booker McConnell, 1960–76.   [50] Tate, *RGA History*, chs. 35–9.

company with a substantial acreage in order to implement plans for extensive oil palm development.[51]

Another new entrant to Malayan oil palm plantations was the United Africa Company through its plantation affiliate Pamol. In 1947 UAC, seeking to expand its plantation interests to the higher productivity South East Asian region, purchased an estate in Johore and by 1960 the firm had 11,400 acres planted. In 1955, however, control over UAC's plantation interests was transferred to its Unilever parent.[52] Research at Pamol in the 1970s was to make a major contribution to increasing the yields of Malayan oil palm by establishing that insects were the main agent for oil palm pollination and that West African insects were more effective than their South East Asian counterparts. Subsequently in 1980 Pamol successfully transferred the more efficient West African insects onto its Malaysian oil palm estates.[53]

The position of the British agency houses in the Malaysian plantation industry was extremely strong. In the 1950s about 70 per cent of the total planted rubber acreage was in the hands of the British agency houses. Harrisons & Crosfield controlled 63 companies with a total rubber acreage of 226,074 acres—the largest amount. The other large agency houses included Boustead (47 companies with 169,555 acres), Guthries (21 companies with 156,306 acres), Sime Darby (32 companies with 109,901 acres), and Harper Gilfillan (25 companies with 92,145 acres). Though there were certainly competitive rivalries between the firms, interlocking directorships also linked rubber companies that were managed by different agency houses.[54]

During the 1970s the position of the British agency houses in the Malaysian plantation industry was finally overturned. The introduction of the New Economic Policy in 1971 spelled the beginning of the end, as state-owned companies were used as a vehicle to acquire and 'localize' agency houses such as Sime Darby and Guthries. Boustead, Yule Catto, and Harrisons & Crosfield survived as firms, but in the 1980s their Malaysian plantations were sold to local interests. Plantations were Harrisons & Crosfield's largest operating division in 1979 and the one making the largest contribution to group profits in 1980. However by 1982 the firm's equity in Harrisons Malaysian Estates—Malaysia's largest plantation company—had fallen to 30 per cent, and the residual shareholding was sold altogether in 1989. Harrisons & Crosfield however retained full control of London Sumatra Plantations in Indonesia until it was sold in 1994.

The British trading companies were active in oil palm exploitation beyond Asia in the post-war period. In 1967, for example, Harrisons &

[51] Annual Reports of Pataling Rubber Estates Ltd., Harrisons & Crosfield Archives, GHL; Tate, *RGA History*, 579–84.
[52] Fieldhouse, *Merchant Capital*, 220–1.   [53] Tate, *RGA History*, 584.
[54] J. J. Puthucheary, *Ownership and Control in the Malayan Economy* (Singapore: Eastern Universities Press, 1960), 23–59.

Crosfield invested in Papua New Guinea in a joint venture with the government—at that time still the Australian government acting as trustees for the United Nations—to develop oil palm plantations in virgin jungle. Harrisons & Crosfield transferred technical personnel from its operations in South East Asia, and established research facilities while the government built all the necessary residential facilities. This venture was successful, and by 1985 Papua New Guinea's palm oil production had risen from nil to the fourth place in the world.[55] Harrisons & Crosfield only divested from its plantations in 1996.

There were also new plantation investments in Africa. By the mid-1940s UAC was anxious to expand its oil palm plantations in Nigeria which were increasingly profitable, but the colonial government was hostile to further plantation development, while after 1949 the introduction of marketing boards made the profitability of palm products uncertain. A search for other plantation opportunities led UAC in the late 1940s both to Malaya and into proposing a project to produce groundnut plantations in East Africa. By 1948 the latter venture had lost £35 million in public funds and subsequently came to be regarded as 'perhaps the most ill-conceived and in the event disastrous large-scale attempt at economic development in modern colonial history'.[56] The transfer of UAC's plantations to the control of Unilever effectively ended the firm's role in Africa in this respect.

Apart from the groundnuts venture, British trading companies continued to develop plantations successfully in East and Central Africa. Finlays expanded its tea plantations in Kenya, which have been retained until the present day, and in 1956 opened a tea plantation company in the British colony of southern Rhodesia, disposed of in 1976. Wallace Brothers purchased ranching and plantation interests in Kenya, Tanganyika, Uganda, and Zanzibar between 1950 and 1954. Wallace Brothers, like Finlays, was able to build on expertise from its pre-existing Indian tea plantations.[57] However the most substantial new entrant into African agriculture was Lonrho, which from the late 1960s acquired tea estates and sugar plantations in Malawi, sugar plantations in South Africa, Swaziland, and Mauritius, and livestock and crop farming estates in Zambia and Kenya.

The nationalization or loss of plantation interests in the 1970s did not always lead to a total cessation of involvement with the sector. A number of the British trading companies in the post-war period developed consultancy services in 'tropical agriculture' on a large scale, including assignments in countries where the trading company did not own plantations, but could instead apply their knowledge to a particular crop. This was the case of Booker McConnell, which by the late 1960s had a full-scale agricultural consultancy business selected—for example—by the World Bank to undertake studies of the Indonesian sugar industry. This activity survived the loss of the Guyana plantations and in the late 1970s and early 1980s, Booker McConnell was active in sugar consultancy in the West Indies and Africa, as well as undertaking the management of a rice project in Belize and soil surveys in the Middle East. In 1980 this consultancy service was merged into the US firm specializing in genetic research in poultry, Ibec, owned largely by the Rockefeller family, and by 1983 Bookers held 80 per cent of the equity.

In the case of non-renewable resources, by the time of the Second World War trading company investments were already modest, and most of the remainder were sold in the subsequent decades. The only firm to make substantial new investments in mining in developing countries in this period was Lonrho. This was a special case, both because of the firm's pre-1961 origins as a mining company in Rhodesia, and its chief executive's Rowland's past experience in mining, and because the firm's close political relationships with certain African governments placed it in a favoured position to continue to own mining investments despite the general trend to nationalize such investments. Before 1965 the firm was already one of Rhodesia's gold producers. Subsequently it diversified in southern Africa into copper, coal, and platinum mining. In 1969 the acquisition of 80 per cent of the equity of the Ashanti Goldfields Corporation, the owner of large gold mines in Ghana, gave the firm extensive mining interests in West Africa also. By 1979 mining and refining generated almost 40 per cent of Lonrho's profits, and through the 1980s coal, gold, and platinum mining and refining were the core areas of profitability of the group, despite its highly diversified business.[58] In a sense, Lonrho always remained more of a mining than a trading company, as was ultimately acknowledged at the end of the 1990s when the firm divested its non-mining interests to focus entirely on mining.

In the manufacturing sector, British trading companies switched their attention to developed countries from the 1950s, hoping to find new growth opportunities in politically secure environments. There was little scope for investing in natural resources in developed countries, but a handful of such investments were made. Jardine Matheson's acquisition of the Hawaii-based trading company Theo. H. Davies in the 1970s brought with it two large sugar plantations on the Island of Hawaii. On the whole, there were few opportunities for resource investments in developed countries, and the traders had even fewer capabilities to exploit what opportunities did exist.

9.3 Tea and Tropical Hardwoods

This section examines at a more firm-specific level investments in tea and tropical hardwoods. The former industry saw British merchants establish

---

[58] Annual Reports, Lonrho plc, 1970–90.

strong positions as plantation owners before the First World War, while the second industry especially flourished after 1945. In both cases, extensive vertically integrated international businesses were built by British trading firms.

The British trading companies became involved in all aspects of the tea trade, from the ownership of plantations through to distribution in the major consumer markets in the developed countries. In the nineteenth century British merchants were extensively involved in the export of Chinese tea, including its sale to Britain and elsewhere. Foreigners were legally prohibited from owning land outside the Treaty Ports so these firms were unable to integrate backwards to establish tea plantations. Moreover the great distance of the tea-growing regions from the Treaty Ports, as well as the fact that the export market never formed a large part of total production, meant that the British merchants could exercise no strong influence on the production methods of the Chinese tea industry.

The normal practice, therefore, was for the foreign merchant to buy the tea from Chinese dealers at the ports. Thereafter foreign merchants, Russian as well as British, dominated the export and transport of Chinese tea until it was sold on the London and other tea markets.[59] However in the 1850s and 1860s Jardine Matheson, Dent's, and other Western merchant houses did in some cases seek to influence marketing channels in the interior of China. In Fujian province, these firms used their compradors to engage in 'up-country' purchases, establishing warehouses in tea-growing regions and sending buyers out to markets in the countryside. By the late 1860s, however, Chinese merchants had taken over these commercial channels.[60]

The export of Chinese tea was a major concern of the British traders on the China coast. A. J. H. Carlill, the twin founder of Dodwells in 1891 with Stanley Dodwell, was the firm's tea specialist, and tea and shipping agencies were the twin pillars of the firm's growth. Subsequently firms such as Dodwells experienced difficulties as the British market shifted towards drinking Indian black teas rather than Chinese teas.[61] However other markets continued to be supplied. Between 1901 and 1917 Dodwells exclusively supplied the Moscow firm of W. Wissotzky & Co.—allegedly the largest tea firm in the world—with China teas. In the United States, Dodwells sold through agents until in 1912 it opened its own New York branch, but heavy losses were made in the 1920s when the branch underestimated the declining popularity of Chinese teas and ended up with large unwanted stocks.[62] This left North Africa as Dodwells' primary market for China teas in the 1930s.

---

[59] Allen and Donnithorne, *Western Enterprise*, 52–5.
[60] Robert Gardella, *Harvesting Mountains Fujian and the China Tea Trade, 1757–1937* (Berkeley and Los Angeles: University of California Press, 1994), 54–69.
[61] Jones, *Two Centuries*, 177–80.
[62] Memo by O. M. Poole, Dodwells in the Tea Trade, 1948, Dodwell Archives, MS 27522/2, GHL.

Jardine Matheson also continued its China tea sales through the interwar period. The US sales were handled by the firm's New York office until its closure in 1931, and thereafter by Balfour Guthrie. Its British sales went through the tea wholesaler Thomas Hickling & Co. as well as Matheson's. Tea continued to be important for Jardine Matheson even in the 1930s, and in 1935 it was still described 'as the most consistent and profitable department we have in the firm'.[63] However by then even Jardines was considering diversifying into tea from other areas, notably Java and Ceylon, but also East Africa.[64]

In contrast to China, in India and Ceylon tea trading led into investment in plantations. In India the tea plant was discovered in Assam in the 1820s. The British government was anxious to develop Indian tea production in case Chinese supplies were cut off, and the East India Company started an experimental tea garden in 1835. Five years later this was handed over to a private company, the Assam Company.[65] The development of the industry was slow, however, until the government relaxed restrictions on the granting of land to prospective planters. Thereafter India grew as the largest tea producer in the world, accounting in the interwar years for around 40 per cent of world exports of tea. Indian 'black' teas displaced Chinese 'green' teas, virtually displacing China from the world's export trade in tea.

In India tea developed as plantation crop cultivated with wage labour, and developed almost entirely by European enterprise. Plantations were important in tea production for a number of reasons. Unlike coffee, tea requires immediate processing, because the newly harvested wet leaf loses weight. Only large plantations could afford to have their own processing establishments, while transaction costs could be reduced if these factories had a guaranteed flow of leaves. Moreover as tea developed as an export crop, it required asset-specific marketing and transport costs which again were most efficiently provided by large estates.[66]

Trading companies became involved in tea plantations through a number of different routes. The Calcutta agency houses in the 1860s were trading in the Bengal region and alerted to the opportunities in the plantation industry. Harrisons & Crosfield, and James Finlay were traders in tea who integrated backwards into plantations. There were other instances of unrelated diversification. In 1912 the Bombay Burmah Trading Corporation diversified from its teak business into tea plantations in south India, pioneering in a new area only just opened up to cultivation of tea.[67]

Finlays edged slowly into the tea industry in India and was a follower rather than a first mover. The firm traded in teas in China, and in 1872 shipped

---

[63] W. J. Keswick to D. G. M. Bernard, 12 Dec. 1935, S/O Shanghai to London 1935, JMA, CUL.
[64] Ibid., D. G. M. Bernard to W. J. Keswick, 1 July 1936, S/O London to Shanghai, 1936.
[65] H. A. Antrobus, *A History of the Assam Company, 1839–1953* (Edinburgh: the firm, 1957).
[66] Sarkar, *World Tea Economy*, 709.   [67] Pointon, *Wallace Brothers*, 55.

a small amount of Indian tea from Calcutta to New York. In the following year the Calcutta branch became agents for two small tea estates, and then used a slump in the industry to buy up more tea estates, initially in north India. During the 1880s and 1890s Finlays acquired more estates and these were consolidated into four large Glasgow-registered companies (see Table 6.5). These included the Kanan Devan Hills Produce Co., formed in 1897, which had most of its estates in the High Range, Travancore, south India, an area of virgin high-elevated jungle and forest purchased in 1894 which was cleared for tea plantations. Together these four companies in 1949 had almost 90,000 acres of tea planted plus much smaller areas of rubber, coconuts, tung, coffee, and cardamoms.[68] In addition Finlays had opened its Kenya tea plantation in 1926 with staff transferred from India, and in 1949 its affiliate African Highlands Produce Co. had 5,000 acres under tea.

Harrisons & Crosfield's entry into plantation management was later still than Finlays. In 1895 this tea trading firm opened its first overseas branch in Ceylon. Four years later the partners in Harrisons & Crosfield purchased their first tea estate and this became one of the estates owned by the Lunuva (Ceylon) Tea & Rubber Estates, Ltd., formed in 1907. In the mid-1920s three more tea and rubber companies in Ceylon were taken over and in 1949 the firm had almost 11,000 acres of tea and over 4,800 acres of rubber under cultivation.[69] The firm ranked as the third largest exporter of tea from Ceylon (Sri Lanka) at this time, mostly to North America, Australia, New Zealand, and South Africa. In 1907 Harrisons & Crosfield also purchased its first tea lands in southern India, and in 1921 its tea and rubber plantations were consolidated into one company, Malayalam Plantations. In north India, Harrisons & Crosfield missed out on the development of tea plantations, but in 1927 acquired a Calcutta managing agency—Davenport & Co.—which acted as the managing agent of eleven tea companies with 9,000 acres in the region.[70] In the 1950s Harrisons & Crosfield as a whole had tea plantations in three countries.

The interwar years were a difficult period for the British tea producers. Tea was subject to severe price fluctuations, with very sharp falls in 1920 and again from the late 1920s. The international market for tea was dominated by India, Ceylon, and the Dutch East Indies, and the British trading companies were the largest producers in the first two countries. They were involved in tea restriction schemes, culminating in the International Tea Agreement of 1933 which was enforced by government legislation. Finlays were especially prominent in the negotiation of this agreement.[71] This agreement assigned quotas to all firms based on maximum exports attained

---

[68] J. Brogan, *James Finlay & Co. Limited* (Glasgow: Jackson Sons & Co., 1951), 102–6.
[69] Annual Reports of the Lunuva (Ceylon) Tea & Rubber Estates Ltd., Harrisons & Crosfield Archives, GHL.
[70] Ibid., Accounts of Davenport & Co. Ltd.   [71] Brogan, *James Finlay & Co.*, 109–10.

in any of the years 1929–32, and also regulated expansion in acreage to 0.5 per cent.[72]

The international tea regulation schemes were notably successful, both because of the concentration of ownership in the industry and because of government support for the schemes. Tea prices collapsed between 1927 and 1932, falling by the latter year to just over a quarter of their 1927 prices, but by 1935 tea prices in London had risen to at least three-fourths of the average 1925–9 prices, and remained at that level until 1939. During the same period, the prices of most plantation products remained far lower than their pre-depression levels. The price of coffee averaged only 44 per cent of its 1925–9 level and that of sugar only 36 per cent.[73]

Government-backed international tea control schemes lasted until 1955, and then collapsed on the question of national quotas.[74] Thereafter fluctuating tea prices were a major source of risk for tea producers such as James Finlay. 'My predecessors and I have constantly advocated the revival of the International Tea Agreement', Finlays' chairman told his shareholders.[75] However British firms were no longer in a position to achieve the formation of international cartels for their products, even though they were very large producers. Finlays accounted for around 5 per cent of world tea production in 1960. The cyclical fluctuations in the tea industry caused by variations in yields and exchange problems made the industry a difficult one for publicly quoted firms such as Finlays and stimulated a search for activities beyond tea growing as a 'hedge' should there be a major downturn in the industry.[76]

The tea plantations of the British companies were large-scale enterprises. Finlays' development of the tea estates of Travancore involved extensive infrastructure investment. The population of the area increased from 2,000 in the 1890s to nearer 60,000 in the 1950s, half of which worked on the tea estates, and most of which had originated from the drought areas of Madras. The firm built hundreds of miles of roads, and in 1900 opened a 'ropeway' from the High Range to the plains which over a distance of 2.5 miles rose 6,200 feet in elevation. In the 1900s the Kanan Devan company began generating its own electricity and built the third hydro-electric power plant in India at the time. Later the firm installed its own private telephone system with over 220 miles of lines linking all the tea estates in the region. By the interwar years the company also provided free primary education to the workers' children, and free medical care for its staff in the area and operated a main and subsidiary hospital. Its medical staff finally eradicated malaria in the High

<hr>

[72] Bishnupriya Gupta, 'Collusion in the Indian Tea Industry in the Great Depression: An Analysis of Panel Data', *Explorations in Economic History*, 34 (1997); id., 'The International Tea Cartel in the Great Depression: The Response of Firms in India and Ceylon', *Department of Economics Discussion Papers, University of St. Andrews* (1997).

[73] Sarkar, *World Tea Economy*, 165–6.   [74] Ibid. 163–75.

[75] Annual Report, James Finlay Ltd., 1965.

[76] Interview with Sir Colin Campbell, 16 Apr. 1996.

Range area in the early 1950s. Before the introduction of Indian minimum wage legislation in 1952, the firm also supplied rice at a subsidized rate and also firewood. In order to supply the latter, the company developed a 14,000-acre eucalyptus plantation on the High Range.[77]

From the 1950s the British-owned tea plantations in India experienced growing problems. There were labour disputes in plantations as well as problems paying expatriate staff following the Indian devaluation in the mid-1960s. The Indianization of the Calcutta agency houses had reduced the British presence on Indian tea plantations to a minimal level during the 1970s. In 1976 Finlays sold its plantations to its joint venture with Tata, and then sold its 20 per cent stake in 1981, although it retained its tea plantations in Bangladesh as well as East Africa.

Both Harrisons & Crosfield and Finlays invested in the distribution of tea in the United Kingdom, the United States, Canada, and elsewhere. During the late nineteenth century the marketing of tea in Britain and elsewhere underwent a radical change. Tea was traditionally sold as the product of a specific locality. However when black teas from South Asia first came into the market, both their taste and their cost made them difficult to sell by themselves, and retailers began to blend these teas with Chinese ones. Overtime, the proportion of China tea in these blends fell. Meanwhile wholesale tea merchants or retailers such as Lipton developed brands which guaranteed standardized quality and price, and somewhat later investing in tea plantations.[78] For the most part, the British merchants in the tea trade such as Finlays and Harrisons & Crosfield confined their distribution business to warehousing, blending, and packet labelling for named distributors, and neither of these firms made a sustained attempt to brand their teas, though Harrisons & Crosfield did experiment with a 'Nectar' brand which was mainly exported from Britain before the First World War.

Both British firms opened branches in consuming countries to distribute their teas. This was the original purpose behind Harrisons & Crosfield branches in New York, Montreal, and Melbourne opened in the 1900s. However around the time of the First World War Harrisons & Crosfield opted to merge its operations in consuming countries with local partners. In 1916 its British distribution operation was merged with that of the old-established tea importer Twining as Twining, Crosfield & Co. Ltd., and in the United States there were amalgamations with two leading importers and distributors in 1914 and 1924 to form the partly owned Irwin-Harrisons-Whitney Inc., one of the largest tea importers in the United States in the interwar years.[79]

---

[77] Memo on Indian Tea, n.d. (*c.*1960), Finlays Archives, UGD91/413/10.
[78] Gardella, *Harvesting Mountains*, 134–6; D. Wainwright, *Brooke Bond: A Hundred Years* (London: Newman Neame, n.d.); Peter Matthias, *Retailing Revolution* (London: Longman, 1967).
[79] Harrisons & Crosfield, *One Hundred Years*, 35–6.

Harrisons & Crosfield only held a minority of the equity of Irwin-Harrisons-Whitney—in the 1940s it held about 22 per cent of the shares, with the Irwin family around 35 per cent—but they held half the seats on the board and exercised a considerable influence. Harrisons & Crosfield branches in Colombo, Calcutta, and Batavia bought tea from the estates for which the firm were agents and secretaries, and then sold it on to Irwin-Harrisons-Whitney, for whom they served as buying agents. The situation was ambiguous. At least in the early 1920s, the Harrisons & Crosfield eastern branches, though encouraged to place as much business as possible with the American firm, were also allowed to sell direct to other US tea traders. This was resented by the Irwin family who felt deprived of potential profits.[80]

In Canada, Harrisons & Crosfield's distribution arrangements were initially complex. The Montreal branch distributed tea but the firm also had a number of agents selling to wholesale grocers, but in 1928 a branch was opened in Toronto which replaced the agents. The firm developed a substantial business selling tea (as well as coffee) to wholesalers. Indian and Ceylon teas were imported, but the branch also imported China black and green teas and Japanese teas through Harrisons & Crosfield affiliates in China and Japan. However from the late 1930s this business began to wane with changes as the tea business became concentrated in the hands of the large packers, as wholesale grocers disappeared and supermarkets expanded. Similar developments in the United States also led to falling tea sales in that country.[81]

Harrisons & Crosfield's exporting branches shifted strategy as markets changed. In Sri Lanka, the decline of the US and Canadian markets led to a search for replacements. During the 1970s the firm developed a large business with two British tea buyers, R. Twining (the successor to Twining Crosfield) and the Co-op Tea Society which was so successful that Harrisons & Crosfield became one of the leading exporters of Ceylon tea to Britain, formerly a small market for them. A long-term relationship with a South African firm dating from 1920 was lost in 1977 when it was acquired by Unilever, who switched their tea buying in Sri Lanka to their affiliate Liptons. However in the 1970s and early 1980s new customers were found by the Colombo branch in the shape of the Iraqi and Egyptian state tea buying organizations, who by 1985 accounted for nearly 50 per cent by weight of the firm's tea export trade from Sri Lanka.[82]

Finlays also invested in tea distribution in consuming countries. Before 1914 it took shareholdings in tea blending, tasting, and warehousing com-

---

[80] Irwin-Harrisons-Whitney correspondence files, 1914–27, Harrisons & Crosfield Archives, GHL.

[81] Memorandum on the Harrisons & Crosfield Organization in Canada, c.1961, Harrisons & Crosfield Archives, GHL.

[82] Ibid., Typescript history of Harrisons & Crosfield's Colombo office, 1953–85.

panies in Britain. The firm of P. R. Buchanan, affiliated with Finlays since the 1890s, not only had coffee and tea estates in India, but also owned warehouses for tea in London. After rebuilding, these warehouses could store 120,000 packages of tea by the late 1930s.[83] Around 1900 Finlays also invested in George Payne & Co., distributors of blended tea (and cocoa) both in Britain and overseas. The firm continued through the interwar years and beyond to own substantial blending, packeting, and warehousing businesses in Britain. During the 1960s a large new tea warehouse was built on the River Thames in London, only to be rendered obsolete by the transfer of major tea imports to the new port of Avonmouth near Bristol, where smaller warehousing was then built, before it was sold altogether in the 1970s. Tea blending and packeting continued. Finlays developed a substantial business in 'own brands' for major British supermarket chains, notably Sainsbury's.

The Anglo-American Direct Tea Trading Company was formed in 1898 explicitly to distribute tea and subsequently it established distribution companies in the United States, Canada, and Russia. Initially the North American markets were served by agents, but in 1912 a Toronto branch was opened and in the same year a New York company was formed. A Canadian incorporation followed. During the interwar years the firm opened branches in Chicago, Philadelphia, and San Francisco. As US demand expanded for 'green' tea, Anglo-American expanded into the green tea field and a combined office and plant was opened in Taipei, Taiwan in 1927. In Japan, Anglo-American opened a buying office and plant in Shidzuoka in 1934.[84] In Russia, Finlays and the Anglo-American Direct Trading Company invested in the tea distribution business of M. Rogivue, which in 1906 distributed 3,000 chests of tea per annum through its own retail shops in Moscow and through wholesalers. The tea was initially purchased blended in bulk from Paynes and subsequently—when government regulations favoured imports from Asia—from Finlays in Calcutta.

Finlays' international tea distribution business was not very successful. There were problems with their Russian partner, who was eventually removed from the firm in 1907, and the whole business was lost with the 1917 revolution.[85] Anglo-America's Taiwanese and Japanese operations were closed in 1940, and in 1944 the American firm was sold to the former managing director of the firm. However through the 1960s Finlays continued to supply teas to the now independent successor firm.[86] The Canadian business continued, but experienced the same problems as Harrisons & Crosfield in the post-war period. As a result, the firm diversified out of

[83] Brogan, *James Finlay & Co* , 81–3.

[84] 'The Anglo Story', *Finlays House Magazine*, 1 (1964), Finlays Archives, UGD 91/377.

[85] Ibid., Memorandum Regarding the Business of M. Rogivue, Moscow, Mar. 1906, UGD 91/122; Annual General Meetings of Rogivue & Co., 1902–17, UGD 91/121.

[86] Ibid., 'Transatlantic Tea', *Finlays House Magazine*, 2/6 (1965).

tea into jute importing in 1958, followed by other products such as Indian shrimps by 1970.[87]

There was a revival of Finlays' tea distribution activities in North America in the 1970s. The initial sales of instant tea produced by Tata-Finlay through agents in the USA were not successful, and in 1972 Finlays established a new company—James Finlay & Co. (US)—to take over sales. In 1975 this took over all Finlay tea sales in the United States. The instant tea business was eventually sold to Tatas in 1982, but the US business developed in the 1980s. The Canadian tea distribution company also recovered in the 1980s after incurring losses from a failed diversification into food manufacturing.[88]

A number of British trading companies in South East Asia were also long-term investors in tropical hardwoods, which included a variety of timbers of which the most marketable was Serayah. These investments sometimes, but not always, drew on earlier expertise in teak in Thailand and Burma. The two types of timber extraction were, however, different in important respects, and especially that the pace of extraction was more rapid in hardwoods than in teak because the felling of trees was quickly followed by the shipment of timber. As in the case of tea, the British companies integrated forward from logging to distribution and retail timber sales in consumer countries.

It was Harrisons & Crosfield which made the earliest and ultimately most successful investments in tropical timber extraction and processing. In 1920 Harrisons & Crosfield went into partnership with the British North Borneo Co., the chartered company which was the colonial authority in North Borneo until 1946. A new company, British Borneo Timber Co. Ltd. (BBT), renamed Sabah Timber in 1963, was formed. Harrisons & Crosfield had no prior involvement in timber beyond the making of plywood chests for packing the tea and rubber of its plantation companies. However in 1918 the firm acquired the merchant business of W. G. Darby in North Borneo, which had been in business since the 1890s, and formed a new company, Harrisons & Crosfield (Borneo) Ltd., with Darby as managing director. At that stage there were two main companies involved in logging in North Borneo, and Darby recommended the purchase of one of them—the China-Borneo Co. registered in Hong Kong—which had a well-established logging business as well as sawmills and engineering works at Sandakan, the principal trading centre. Darby had previously served as manager of the China-Borneo Co. The British North Borneo Co. granted BBT the exclusive right to cut timber on any of the 31,000 square miles of its jurisdiction, with an option to terminate the concession after twenty-five years.[89]

[87] 'The Anglo Story', 'The History of James Finlay & Co. (Canada) Ltd.', Finlays House Magazine, Spring 1971.
[88] Annual Reports, James Finlay, 1965–90.
[89] Harrisons & Crosfield, *One Hundred Years*, 46–7; Nickalls, *Great Enterprise*, 78–80.

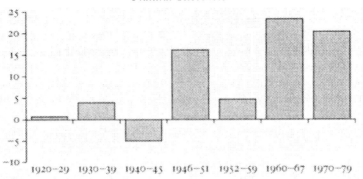

FIG. 9.1 Average post-tax return on net capital employed of the British Borneo Timber Co. (Sabah Timber Co. from 1963), 1920–1979 (%)

British Borneo Timber was established as a British public company in 1920 with Harrisons & Crosfield owning 41.7 per cent of the equity and the British North Borneo Co. 33.3 per cent, and the remainder offered for public subscription. These shareholding patterns fluctuated, with Harrisons & Crosfield's shareholding slipping to 32.7 per cent in 1930, and to just under 32 per cent in 1948. In 1946 the British government took over the administration of North Borneo from the British North Borneo Co., and the latter disposed of its shares in the joint venture. Harrisons & Crosfield's shareholding passed 43 per cent in 1969, and 56 per cent in 1973 when it formally became a subsidiary, and in 1979 full ownership was taken.

Figure 9.1 reviews the financial performance of the timber company from its foundation until 1979. As Figure 9.1 indicates the performance of the company for several decades was far from satisfactory. Between 1920 and 1945 and again in the 1950s its post-tax ROCE was considerably less than that of Harrisons & Crosfield itself. Logging methods were very primitive, and the inherited staff and machinery at the sawmills both proved unsatisfactory.[90] Production of logs, which expanded faster than sawmill output, grew from 1.14 million cubic feet of timber cut in 1920, exceeding 2 million feet for the first time in 1929, and 3 million for the first time in 1933. The pre-war peak of 4.89 million cubic feet was achieved in 1937, after which sales were reduced by declining demand.

China was the main market, largely supplied through Hong Kong and sold by Gibb Livingston, agents of the government of British North Borneo. This market and other Far Eastern markets fell sharply in the late 1930s. Harrisons & Crosfield also tried to develop markets elsewhere, in Britain, Australia, South Africa, and Japan, for the species of timber found in the

[90] Report by W. G. Darby on his visit to Borneo, 1922; directors' file, 1958; file of correspondence with T. G. Bonallo, consultant of TECO, 1957–8. British Borneo Timber Co. records, Harrisons & Crosfield Archives, GHL.

Borneo forest, even managing to sell to the Royal Navy for decking.[91] In part because of market conditions, the firm's profits were modest, and no dividends could be paid between 1923 and 1927, 1929 and 1931, and 1935 to 1940. Harrisons & Crosfield benefited from BBT, however, in other ways. Apart from commission as agents for selling logs and sawn timber, the earnings of Harrisons & Crosfield (Borneo) Ltd. were boosted by income from the shipping, insurance, and stevedorage services provided to BBT.[92]

The post-war years again proved difficult for BBT with the company earning low returns for most of the 1950s. The China market all but disappeared, and the firm's logging concession was revised after North Borneo became a British colony in 1946. Its exclusive forest concession was terminated from 1950 in return for compensation and a non-exclusion concession over 1,000 square miles of Borneo forest. In addition, the British government guaranteed profits for the first three years' working of the new concession. This guarantee had to be implemented and BBT received from the government payments of around £1 million over three years.[93]

In essence until the late 1950s BBT's existence depended heavily on its exclusive concession followed by the subsidy from the British colonial government. The logging methods employed were labour-intensive and inefficient. The removal of the monopoly concession ultimately focused attention on these failings. In the late 1950s a major reorganization began with the introduction of US mechanical logging methods and the acquisition of new heavy duty tractors and log transporters. These new production methods necessitated the building of new infrastructure, including bridges and roads capable of taking trucks loaded with logs and moving at speed. Production increased from 2 million cubic feet in the early 1950s to nearly 19 million in 1969, a peak not again exceeded.

As production increased, new markets were developed. In the post-war period the Japanese market had an insatiable demand for hardwoods and this developed as a major market for BBT. After the Borneo Company purchased Gibb, Livingston & Co. in 1961, BBT replaced their agents and in 1962 a newly formed company, H&C (Hong Kong) Ltd. took over as agents.[94] In 1962 a wholly owned subsidiary of BBT was formed for the purpose of handling BBT timber sales in Europe including Britain: in 1963 it was renamed Sabah Timber Co.

In 1969 the Sabah government confirmed that the (recently renamed) Sabah Timber Company's concession agreement would not be renewed when it

[91] Nickalls, *Great Enterprise*, 117.

[92] Nickalls, Memorandum by W. G. Darby, Nov. 1937, file of correspondence with British North Borneo Co. Ltd., British Borneo Timber Co. records, Harrisons & Crosfield Archives, GHL.

[93] Nickalls, *Great Enterprise*, 161.

[94] Directors' file, 1961–2; file of correspondence with Hong Kong agency, British Borneo Timber Co. records, Harrisons & Crosfield Archives, GHL.

expired in 1962. Earlier in the 1960s it has been acknowledged that North Borneo's incorporation into Malaysia as the state of Malaysia made it likely that the timber concession would not last indefinitely, and the firm had begun to make small investments elsewhere. During the 1960s BBT invested in palm oil plantations in North Borneo, and between 1964 and 1966 it and Harrisons & Crosfield were involved in an unsuccessful investment in a sawmilling company in Barbados. The most significant diversification began in 1960 when BBT began to acquire control of small timber merchanting firms in Britain. This process gathered momentum as the much improved profitability indicated in Figure 9.1 both allowed liquid funds to accumulate and justified the issue of fresh equity, and the announcement of the end of the logging concession accelerated this strategy.

During the late 1960s and 1970s Sabah Timber acquired a series of small timber merchants in Britain aiming to build up a coherent geographical network of distribution outlets. Sabah Timber continued to sell most of their log production in Asia, while the British timber subsidiaries bought their supplies worldwide, and then cut, planed, and graved them for distribution from their depots. Since some of these timber merchants also sold other building materials, BBT came to have a role as a general builders' merchant. From 1971 more than half the total profit after tax always arose in Britain. An internal memorandum two years later described Sabah Timber as one of Harrisons & Crosfield's 'great success stories'.[95] Certainly in the 1960s and 1970s its post-tax ROCE was considerably in excess of that of Harrisons & Crosfield itself.

Tropical timber played an especially important role in the evolution of Harrisons & Crosfield. Its profit contribution in the 1970s was very significant, often contributing 30 per cent of total group profits. Timber provided a 'cash cow' for the firm to expand its presence in developed markets, both in timber merchants and in chemicals. By the early 1980s Harrisons & Crosfield owned the third largest timber group in Britain with just under 10 per cent of the total market. Over that decade the group of timber and builders' merchants, renamed Harcros division, further increased their importance in the turnover and profits of the group as a whole. Timber merchanting ranked beside chemicals in the 1980s as one of the firm's core business areas.

After the Second World War a number of other trading companies invested in tropical hardwoods in South East Asia. Both the Borneo Company and Wallace Brothers became interested in the commodity in response to the loss of their teak concessions in Thailand and Burma, and the attractions of the domestic Japanese market. A timber concession in Rejang, Sarawak, was abandoned in 1954 by the Borneo Company in the 'face of increasing competition from producers in North Borneo and elsewhere'.[96] The Borneo

---

[95] Ibid., Memorandum on Company Position, 1973.
[96] Board Minutes, 11 May 1954, Borneo Company Archives, MS 27178/24, GHL.

Company continued logging in Sarawak, extracting raminwood—used in furniture—through the Austral Timber Company, acquired in 1953.[97] Another timber company, the Borneo Timber Company, jointly owned with a Chinese entrepreneur, was plagued by problems between the partners and was loss-making in the early 1960s.[98] During the 1960s the Borneo Company expanded its timber interests to Australia, beginning in 1961 with the acquisition of control over a Western Australian forest exploitation and sawmilling company, followed by further acquisitions of timber merchants.[99] In 1950 Wallace Brothers and its affiliate the Bombay Burmah Trading Corporation took a half share in a new company, North Borneo Timbers Ltd., which became wholly owned several years later. This venture, like BBT, was primarily concerned to supply the growing demand from Japan, Korea, Hong Kong, and Australia. Its timber leases expired in 1984 and consequently this firm also sought to diversify elsewhere, especially Australia and New Zealand.[100]

9.4 Oil

The emergence and development of the modern petroleum industry coincided with the growth of the British merchant houses as diversified business groups. Following the drilling of the first successful oil well in Pennsylvania in 1859, there was a rapid expansion of oil production which was principally used until the early twentieth century as a lamp oil and lubricant. The principal oil producing nations were the United States and, subsequently Russia, which meant that markets elsewhere had to be supplied by exports. This created a considerable opportunity for merchants in Asia and elsewhere to market the new product.

Once established in oil marketing, the possibility also arose of integrating backwards into production, as the search for new sources of supply intensified. Consequently a number of companies became oil producers, in California, Peru, Ecuador, and Burma and the Dutch East Indies. However petroleum was a capital-intensive industry, involving not only drilling operations, but also dedicated pipelines, refineries, and shipping facilities, all of which also called for growing levels of technical competence. The general pattern, therefore, was either for oil affiliates to outgrow their merchant founders and absorb them, or for the trading company to withdraw from the business, although in a number of cases merchant business groups included small oil companies until after the Second World War. Table 9.2 gives the principal trading company investments in oil production.

---

[97] Henry Longhurst, *The Borneo Story* (London: Newman Neame, 1956), 109–11.
[98] Board Minutes, 11 May 1954, Borneo Company Archives, MS 27178/24, GHL.
[99] P. Griffiths, *A History of the Inchcape Group* (London: the firm, 1977), 143.
[100] Pointon, *Wallace Brothers*, 83–4, 95–6.

TABLE 9.2 Principal trading company investments in oil companies, c.1890–1980

Parent	Oil company	Founded	Region	Fate
M. Samuel & Co.	Shell Transport & Trading Co.	1897	DE Indies	Acquired by Royal Dutch 1907
Finlay Fleming	Burmah Oil	1896	Burma	Burmah Oil autonomous 1928
Steel Brothers	Indo-Burma Petroleum Co.	1908	Burma	Sold 1950s–1970
Steel Brothers	Attock Oil	1913	India	Sold 1970s
Jardine Matheson	London & Pacific Petroleum	1890	Peru	Sold to Standard Oil 1913
Balfour Williamson	Californian Oilfields	1901	California	Sold to Shell Group 1913
Balfour Williamson	Lobitos Oilfields	1908	Peru	Sold to Burmah Oil 1962
Balfour Williamson	Anglo-Ecuadorian Oilfields	1919	Ecuador	Sold to Burmah Oil 1962
James Finlay	North Sea Oil consortia	1970	UK	Sold 1989
	Various	1981	Ohio	Sold 1990s
	Midstates Oil Company	1982	Texas	Sold 1990s

In the Asian market, Wallace Brothers were first movers among the British merchants to become extensively involved in oil distribution. In 1878 they began shipping the lamp oil produced by Standard Oil, the largest American oil company, from New York to the ports of India. 'The oil business', one of the Wallaces wrote in 1880, 'is one of comparatively recent development; it has already assumed large proportions, and promises to be a very large trade indeed with India.'[101] In 1888 Wallace's switched its source of supply when it signed a contract to buy Russian oil from the Bnito oil company, owned by the Rothschilds of Paris, which had begun to export oil packed in cases from the Black Sea port of Batoum. A three-year contract made Wallace's Bnito's sole agents in the Far East.[102]

Wallace Brothers employed merchant firms to sell their Russian oil in Asian markets. Jardine Matheson sold the Russian oil in China and Japan. In 1890 the firm of M. Samuel & Co., which had a profitable trading business with Japan, was granted an option to buy up to one-quarter of Wallace Brothers' oil and to sell it anywhere in Asia except India, Burma, and the Straits Settlements. Wallace Brothers' relationship with Bnito was not smooth, and in 1891 their exclusive contract was replaced with a one-year agreement to sell on commission and hence bore no risk. They continued to sell Standard Oil's products in Asia. In place of Wallace's, Marcus Samuel secured a nine-year contract from Bnito. The arrangement had distinctive features whereby the oil would be supplied in bulk rather than in cases, and transported to Asia via the Suez Canal, hitherto closed to tankers for safety reasons. Samuel's task was to recruit agents in Asian ports to put up tank storage for the oil and in return they received commission on sales of Bnito's oil. Samuel acquired a fleet of tankers, named after shells as a tribute to the business of his father, and in 1893 formed the 'Tank Syndicate' consisting of all the merchants in the Far East through whom the bulk oil, carried in the tankers, was sold as 'Shell' oil. These included the Graham partnerships in India and Boustead in Malaya. This arrangement minimized the capital costs to Samuel of erecting tank installations at Asian ports.

During the 1890s M. Samuel & Co. followed the precedent set by other trading companies and integrated backwards into production. Concerned about the reliability and cost of Russian oil and dependence on the Rothschilds, Samuel searched for, and located, a major oilfield in Borneo in the Dutch East Indies in 1898. In the previous year Samuel merged the Tank Syndicate and the tanker fleet into a new 'free-standing' company, the Shell Transport and Trading Co. This was a public company but, as was often the case, the shareholding was closely held by the Samuels and other former members of the Tank Syndicate.[103]

---

[101] A. F. Wallace to M. Sellem, 25 Aug. 1880, MS 11089, GHL.
[102] Pointon, *Wallace Brothers*, 26–7.
[103] Robert Henriques, *Marcus Samuel* (London: Barrie and Rockliff, 1960), 164.

The Shell Transport and Trading Co. grew rapidly. By the beginning of the twentieth century the company owned oilfields and a refinery in Borneo, thirty ocean-going oil tankers, and storage depots at many ports in Asia. The firm was organized as part of the merchant enterprise with no attempt to develop a managerial hierarchy to match that of Standard Oil in the United States. M. Samuel & Co. were the managing agents of Shell, which had no staff of its own. In the early 1900s M. Samuel & Co. had a staff of around fifty in London, about half of whom worked on Shell business.[104]

It was less this 'lean' management structure per se than a series of misfortunes and poor decisions which damaged the firm. The Borneo oilfield produced 'heavy' fuel oil rather than the kerosene which was the main product for the Asian markets. In 1901 Shell agreed to buy a large amount of oil from a new Texas oil producer, and purchased four new tankers to transport the oil to Europe before the oil supply proved unreliable. In 1903 the Samuels placed their marketing operation in Asia into a new marketing company—the Asiatic Petroleum Company—owned jointly with the Paris Rothschilds and a Dutch oil company, the Royal Dutch Petroleum Co. In 1907 Royal Dutch purchased most of the shares held by the Samuels in Shell Transport, which was effectively acquired by the Dutch company. Under the merger arrangements, the new 'Shell group' was to be organized as two 'holding companies', the Royal Dutch Petroleum Co. and the Shell Transport and Trading Co. The Dutch/British shareholding was fixed in a 60/40 ratio, but initially the purchase of the Samuel shares gave the Dutch a higher shareholding.

A number of other British trading companies in Asia became involved in oil production in the late nineteenth and early twentieth centuries. The Scottish merchant partnership of Finlay Fleming & Co. was behind the formation of the Burmah Oil Company in 1886, which became the largest oil producer in Burma. Finlay Fleming served as the managing agents of Burmah Oil, while after 1891 its marketing in India was held by Shaw Wallace. The managing agencies were very profitable for the firms, but over time Burmah Oil outgrew its parents and developed its own organization. In 1928 the agency agreements of Finlay Fleming and Shaw Wallace were ended.[105]

Among the other trading companies, Wallace Brothers secured an oil concession in the Dutch East Indies in 1892 and formed the Dutch-registered Sumatra Petroleum Company. This searched unsuccessfully for oil for ten years before being closed down. In 1897 the firm also began an unsuccessful three-year search for oil in North Borneo.[106] In Burma, Steel Brothers established jointly with an Indian merchant the Indo-Burma Petroleum

---

[104] Ibid. 437–9; Geoffrey Jones, *The State and the Emergence of the British Oil Industry* (London: Macmillan, 1981), 19–22.

[105] T. A. B. Corley, *A History of the Burmah Oil Company*, vol. i (London: Heineman, 1983), *passim*.

[106] Pointon, *Wallace Brothers*, 42–3.

Company in 1908 and discovered a large oilfield, becoming the second largest
oil company in Burma. Subsequently Steels acquired full control of the
venture. In 1913 they also took shares in the Attock Oil Company which
found oil in the Punjab, 2,000 miles to the west of Burma, in 1915, and by
1922 had constructed refining facilities also. Net capital employed rose from
£1.61 million in 1922 to £1.74 million in 1930, and reached £1.97 million
in 1938.

Unlike M. Samuel & Co. and Finlay Fleming, Steel Brothers maintained
its investment in the oil business without being absorbed by it. During the
interwar years the Indo-Burma Petroleum Company pioneered the drilling
of oil under the Irrawaddy river, a capital-intensive process which involved
building a wall in the river around the drilling sites. This company also had
refineries and oil tankers. The Indo-Burma's installations were virtually
destroyed during the Second World War, and in 1954 the Burmese government merged it into a new Burmah Oil Company, one-third govern-
ment-owned, together with Burmah Oil and a third British oil company.[107]
The Indo-Burma Petroleum Company continued as an oil distributor,
however, until it was sold to the state-owned Indian Oil Corporation in
1970. The Burmese joint venture was nationalized altogether in 1963. The
Attock Oil Company's original oilfield started to decline in 1929, but in 1937
and during the 1940s further oil discoveries were made. In 1968 Attock's
Pakistani subsidiary made a substantial oil discovery also. Although no data
is available on the financial performance of Steels and its affiliates, these oil
ventures assumed a strategic role for Steels in the post-war period, when
many of its assets had disappeared. In the 1950s, the company historian notes,
'the two oil companies virtually kept Steels going'.[108]

British trading companies also became active in oil exploration and production in the United States and Latin America. In 1899 Balfour Williamson,
anticipating that its coal import business would decline as oil production rose
in California, began drilling for oil, but only found dry holes. However
in 1901 it purchased more oil lands and in 1901 organized the California
Oilfields Ltd., which promptly discovered substantial oilfields. Within eight
years of its incorporation, California Oilfields was the largest single producer of oil in California.

Balfour Williamson invested heavily in California Oilfields, but it built
only a small refinery and most of the production went to the predecessor
of Standard Oil of California, which built a 300-mile pipeline to connect
Balfour Williamson's oilfields to their refinery on San Francisco Bay. There
were plans to expand Balfour Williamson's own refinery and to absorb their
Peruvian oil company, Lobitos Oil, but in 1913 the Shell Group offered to
buy California Oilfields for £2.6 million, and the offer was accepted.

---

[107] T. A. B. Corley, A *History of the Burmah Oil Company*, ii: *1924–1965* (London: Heinemann,
1988), 201–3.
[108] Braund, *Calling to Mind*, 59–75.

California Oilfields was the first successful British investment in American oil, and became the basis for Shell's growth in the US market.[109]

Balfour Williamson also invested in Peruvian oil, but in this case it was a follower rather than a first mover. In 1889 a British oil speculator organized the London & Pacific Petroleum Company to develop an oilfield in northern Peru. Raising equity for such a venture from a public share issue was not practical, as the recent War of the Pacific and Peru's financial collapse made the investment too risky. However the speculator was able to attract a group of investors associated with William Keswick of Jardine Matheson, which had trade links with Peru. By these means a private placement of the shares was arranged.[110] Jardine Matheson at the time also marketed oil in China, and later invested in several other oil ventures, including a syndicate to find oil in Borneo.[111]

Despite considerable interest in the potential of oil, neither Keswick nor Jardines was prepared to make a substantial capital investment. The London & Pacific suffered from a lack of technical expertise and capital equipment. It suffered throughout from insufficient capital, lacking liquidity with only one-sixth of the value of its initial flotation actually raised in cash. The venture made heavy losses in the 1890s and 1900s before its sale to Standard Oil in 1913.[112] Jardine Matheson initially retained its own small shareholding.[113]

Balfour Williamson's involvement in Peruvian oil originated with the firm of Milne & Co., which formed a syndicate to prospect for oil in 1901. In 1903 Balfour Williamson joined the syndicate and in 1905 high-grade petroleum was discovered. Balfour Williamson organized the flotation of Lobitos Oilfields Limited in 1908, with its senior partner as chairman, and the firm appointed as its agents Williamson Balfour in Chile and Milne & Co. in Peru. In contrast to London & Pacific, Balfour Williamson drew on their earlier experience in the oil industry, and had their Peruvian property surveyed, their shipping organized properly by C. T. Bowring & Co., the Liverpool specialists in oil-tanker charters, and initially passed dividends in order to preserve capital.[114]

Lobitos's production expanded from around 43,000 metric tons in 1908 to around 105,000 in 1921, and reached almost 350,000 in 1930, by which time it had become the most consistently profitable British company

[109] Hunt, *Heirs*, ii. 28–32, 80–3; Kendall Beaton, *Enterprise in Oil* (New York: Appleton-Century-Crofts, Inc., 1957), 71–6; Mira Wilkins, *The History of Foreign Investment in the United States to 1914* (Cambridge, Mass.: Harvard University Press, 1989), 285, 288–91.

[110] David F. C. Myers, 'The Evolution of the Peruvian Oil Business and its Place in the International Petroleum Industry, 1880–1950' (unpublished Oxford D.Phil., 1993), 173.

[111] W. Keswick to W. J. Greeson, 6 Nov. 1908, S/O London to Hong Kong 1908, 6 Nov. 1908, JMA, CUL.

[112] Myers, 'Evolution', 100–1.

[113] Henry Keswick to David Lansdale, 19 June 1913, S/O London to Hong Kong, 1912/13 JMA, CUL; Rory Miller, 'Small Business in the Peruvian Oil Industry: Lobitos Oilfields Limited before 1934', *Business History Review*, 56 (1982), 402–3; id., 'British Free-Standing Companies', 236.

[114] Miller, 'British Free-Standing Companies', 236–7.

operating in Peru. Before 1914 a series of negotiations were held to sell Lobitos to Standard Oil, but they fell through because of price or other considerations, and by the early 1920s the high level of dividends and share prices deterred buyers. However Lobitos sold most of its oil to Standard Oil for refining, and in return was appointed the sales agent in Chile and Peru for the Standard Oil affiliate, the International Petroleum Company.[115]

Lobitos Oil expanded in a number of directions. Its net capital employed grew rapidly in the 1920s, from £1.44 million in 1922 to reach £3.46 million in 1938. By 1914 it had three oil tankers and it purchased five more ships between 1922 and 1930. These ships both carried its own oil and leased surplus capacity to other oil companies. In 1919 the firm established an Ecuadorian subsidiary, Anglo-Ecuadorian Oilfields, which also grew in the interwar years, with net capital employed rising from £1.10 million in 1925 to £1.81 million in 1938. In 1927 Lobitos was reorganized to become a parent holding company with upstream activities in Peru and Ecuador held by locally registered firms and oil tankers serving both interests.

During the 1920s Lobitos began to invest in Britain. It invested in a British manufacturer of oilfield plant between 1924 and 1927.[116] Most significantly, Lobitos—blocked from Latin American markets by Balfour Williamson's agency agreement with Standard Oil and that firm's competitive strength—entered the British market, opening a refinery at Ellesmere Port in 1934. Another refinery was opened in Ireland later, though closed in 1950. The Ellesmere Port refinery was designed to deal specifically with the low-sulphur and wax-free crudes available from their Peruvian oilfields. Lobitos concentrated on the production of speciality products, such as white oils and cable oils, which could be made more cheaply from its sulphur-free Peruvian crude than by the large oil companies. Distribution interests were acquired through the gradual acquisition of shareholdings in existing concerns, and by 1950 its gas oil, white spirit, and gasoline were marketed by two wholly owned subsidiaries. Between 1946 and 1962 Lobitos also acquired full control of its distributor of cable and other special oils, Dussek Brothers, and through this firm it made its first investment in the Canadian oil industry, beginning with small drilling and servicing companies.[117]

By the 1950s Lobitos Oilfields was one of the few small independent integrated oil companies remaining in Europe. Balfour Williamson and Milne & Co. maintained their agency agreements with Lobitos, and Balfour Williamson provided banking and investment services for the company. Until 1951 all members of the board of the Peruvian company were also members of the board of Milne & Co. However by the 1950s the relationship began to weaken. In 1957 the Peruvian company sold 50 per cent of its concessions

[115] Miller, 'Small Business' 403–12.

[116] Anonymous typescript history of Lobitos Oilfields Ltd., 74; A. Milne, 'Short History of Lobitos Oilfields' (unpublished), box 29, Balfour Williamson Archives, UCL.

[117] History of Lobitos Oilfields Ltd., 74; Milne, 'Short History'.

to the International Petroleum Company, which became operators of the concession. The funds from the sale were used to expand the investments in Canada, the building of a new tanker, and more investments in the refinery. The agreement ended Milne & Co.'s position as managers and agents of the Compañía Petrolera Lobitos.[118] However Milne & Co. continued as sales agents for the firm's products in Peru, where it held 25 per cent of the market. Milne's agency agreement survived the sale of the company to Burmah Oil, but in 1966 it was finally terminated, the new owners considering Milne's services as unsatisfactory.[119]

The end of Milne's agency agreement and the withdrawal of Steel Brothers from most if its South Asian investments in the 1960s represented the end of the remaining pre-1914 trading companies investments in the petroleum industry. However the 1970s saw a brief revival of interest with new entrants into the industry. In 1970 Finlays took a shareholding in a Canadian company exploring for oil in the North Sea, and in the following year a shareholding was taken in an oil company, London & Scottish Marine Oil Company (LASMO) engaged in North Sea oil exploration. The latter's shareholders were mainly Scottish-based companies, and it was this Scottish context which explained the initial diversification into oil, though the underlying rationale rested on the firm's strong belief that they were 'merchant adventurers' who could turn their hands to any industry.[120]

The initial investment in North Sea exploration was followed during the 1970s by investments in North Sea oilfield services leading in 1978 to the acquisition (with the UK construction company Taylor Woodrow) of Seaforth Services, which provided marine, engineering, and logistic services to the offshore oil industry. In 1980 Finlays invested in a syndicate drilling for oil in Ohio in the United States, and this was followed in 1982 by the purchase of 50 per cent of the equity of the Texan oil company Midstates Oil Company. Few of these investments proved worthwhile. The firm experienced acute problems finding reliable US partners in the oil industry.[121] By 1985 Finlays' chairman described the Midstates investment as 'a nightmare'.[122] Two years later Finlays had to buy out their partner because of 'serious philosophical differences'.[123] Jardine Matheson also invested in oil and gas in the United States, even buying part of a small oil refinery in Utah in 1984.[124] By the early 1990s both Jardines and Finlays had divested from US oil. Finlays also suffered from the end of the boom conditions in North Sea oil. Finlays sold all their interests in North Sea oil and gas, including Seaforth in 1989.

[118] Annual General Meeting for 1957, Lobitos Oil.
[119] Milne Agency Agreement, 31 Oct. 1965, Burmah Castrol Archives, 572.
[120] Interview with Sir Colin Campbell, 16 Apr. 1996.   [121] Ibid.
[122] Annual Report, James Finlay plc, 1985.
[123] Annual Report, James Finlay plc, 1987.
[124] Annual Report, Jardine Matheson, 1984.

Swire's, the holder of a substantial share of Finlays equity from 1976, also invested in the North Sea oil industry from the mid-1970s, though in this case the firm stayed out of production and focused on supply services. This formed a natural outgrowth of the group's shipping interests. In 1977 Swire's purchased a company owning an oil platform supply vessel operating in the North Sea and over the following years it invested heavily in support vessels which serviced the offshore oil industry. By 1981 it owned seventy-seven such support vessels, making it one of the world's major operators.[125] Unlike Finlays, the Swire investment in marine offshore services proved a lasting investment. By the 1990s Swire's was the leading provider of transportation equipment to the North Sea oil industry, while a Singapore headquartered subsidiary provided offshore support services, including topside platform maintenance, early production systems, and seismic survey support, to most major oil companies active in the Asia Pacific region.

9.5 Merchants and Resources

During the late nineteenth century British trading companies engaged in large-scale direct investment in natural resources. Asset specificity, uncertainty, and opportunism provided incentives for such backward integration. They favoured commodities such as tea, sugar, and rubber for which the British market was large. Trading companies used region-specific information and contacts to identify profitable opportunities in new commodities. Sometimes trading companies sought to reduce their risks by investing in several commodities. The British merchant houses can be seen as entrepreneurial firms which not only perceived the possibilities of trade in commodities, but knew also how to organize intercontinental movements of those commodities, and were prepared to invest in their production in order to expand and monitor supplies. They were far more cautious about investing in minerals, where the risks were high and sophisticated technical competences were required. A number of companies were drawn into, and successful in, oil exploration and production, where profitable opportunities were especially great in the late nineteenth and early twentieth centuries, but the capital-intensity of the business meant that such investments were seldom sustained in merchant hands.

The trading companies created, managed, and sustained large-scale, vertically integrated enterprises in rubber, tea, sugar, and tropical timber. They opened up new lands, employed large numbers, innovated new and improved crops, and developed marketing outlets. They made and managed substantial infrastructure investments in order to support their operations. They transferred skills and knowledge across continents. These

---

[125] Annual Report, John Swire & Sons Limited, 1981.

businesses called for a wide range of skills, from the management of plantations to knowledge of all stages of distribution and marketing.

During the 1960s and 1970s the trading company investments in commodities were largely swept away by the widespread nationalization of such assets in developing countries, although some resource investments survived. In some cases resource investments were used as 'cash cows' to enable the firms to build up assets in developed markets. Firms reverted to trading and distributing commodities like tea, although plantations were maintained in some countries. A number of firms successfully exploited new opportunities, in agricultural consultancy or offshore oil servicing, but strategies to enter production—for example, in the offshore or US oil industry—did not succeed.

Traders as Manufacturers

10.1 Introduction

This chapter discusses the role of British trading companies in manufacturing. Although the process of 'reinvention' led British traders away from trade into related services, the ownership of shipping lines and even airlines, and the large-scale investments in plantations and mines, their involvement with manufacturing was more hesitant.

There was an ambiguity about the attitude of the British trading companies towards manufacturing. On the one hand, they were merchants whose core ethos was to make profits from the use of other people's capital rather than their own. They made their profits from commissions and fees, and from the movement of goods, rather than from making large capital investments which 'locked-up' capital that might be better employed creating new trading opportunities. The strong preference of most of the trading companies for reliance on reinvested earnings and bank borrowings rather than issuing equity acted as a further constraint on heavy investments in manufacturing.

On the other hand, the trading companies were entrepreneurs, forever seeking opportunities to facilitate new trade flows, or to just make profits. This characteristic led the British traders into making substantial manufacturing investments in some regions in the late nineteenth century. They took advantage of the shortage of entrepreneurship and inadequate access to modern technology in those countries to act as first-movers in a number of industries, mostly related to processing raw materials. Subsequently, they made further manufacturing investments in their traditional host economies after the Second World War, and—often with little success—in Britain and other developed economies from the 1950s.

This chapter begins by outlining the evolving pattern of trading company investment in manufacturing in their overseas host economies. This is followed by case studies of the role of trading companies in two industries: sugar refining and cotton textiles. Section 10.4 examines joint ventures between the traders and manufacturing companies. Finally the post-Second World War investments in manufacturing in developed countries are investigated.

10.2 The Growth of Manufacturing Investment

During the second half of the nineteenth century, the British trading companies were surprisingly active as industrial investors. Table 10.1 summarizes the principal industries and countries in which they invested.

TABLE 10.1 Principal manufacturing investments by British trading companies before 1914

Industry	Country
Cotton textiles	UK, Russia, Portugal, India, China, Brazil, Peru
Leather	UK, USA
Jute	India
Sugar refining	India, China, Peru, Brazil
Flour milling	USA, Chile, Peru, Brazil

Within Europe, British traders had a number of manufacturing activities. Finlays' Scottish textiles mills, founded in the 1800s, stood out as wholly exceptional. Finlays sold one of its three mills in 1845, but its mills at Deanston and Catrine continued to be wholly owned and operated by the firm through the nineteenth century and, indeed, until the 1960s.[1] British merchants in Russia such as the Hubbards also invested in the Russian cotton textile industry. In Portugal, Grahams' spinning and weaving company—the Boa Vista—was initially very profitable after its foundation in Oporto in 1888. It formed part of an integrated enterprise as one of its largest customers was a printing company, also established by Grahams in 1875. However by the early 1920s the operation was affected by the depreciation of the Portuguese currency and needed new plant and machinery.[2] The leather manufacturing business of the Booths was also noteworthy. Beginning in 1877, and developing out of its trade in skins, the firm built a substantial leather manufacturing business in both Britain and the United States. As in the case of the British merchants in Russia, by 1914 Booths more closely resembled a multinational manufacturer than a merchant.[3]

The British firms in India were early investors in manufacturing. During the 1860s the large profits earned from tea and cotton encouraged the agency houses to diversify, especially into the emerging industries of the Calcutta region. The Calcutta agency houses floated numerous jute, tea, and coal companies on the British and local capital markets, retaining a percentage of the equity and a managing agency contract.[4] This became the typical mode used by trading companies to invest in manufacturing. It reflected the concern not to 'lock up' capital in manufacturing, and the interest in deriving income from commission on buying, selling, insurance, and lending rather than through shareholding. It was also a means to develop

---

[1] C. Brogan, *James Finlay & Co. Limited* (Glasgow: Jackson Son & Co., 1951), 54–74.

[2] Memo on Grahams & Co., 7 July 1924, Lloyds TSB Group Archives, file A56c/176; Board Minutes, Grahams Trading Company, 19 Aug. 1926, MS 22465, GHL.

[3] A. H. John, *A Liverpool Merchant House* (London: George Allen & Unwin, 1959), 71–87.

[4] J. Forbes Munro, 'From Regional Trade to Global Shipping', in Geoffrey Jones (ed.), *The Multinational Traders* (London: Routledge, 1998); Andrew Yule & Company, *Andrew Yule & Co. Ltd. 1863–1963* (Edinburgh: T. & A. Constable, 1963).

distinctive managerial competences, as these affiliates had their own staff separate from that of the parent agency house or trading company.

From the 1870s the involvement of the agency houses in manufacturing intensified. Calcutta and its surrounding region of Bengal remained the centre of the activity of the British firms. Although almost all these firms continued to import Lancashire cotton textiles, many firms also took advantage of the new opportunities for commodity exports after the opening of the Suez Canal in 1869. There were extensive investments into jute, as well as coal. According to one estimate, of the companies controlled by seventeen leading British managing agencies, 80 per cent were in jute, coal, and tea in 1911.[5]

The Calcutta jute industry was wholly controlled by the British firms. In the late 1830s India had begun to replace Russia as a source of supply for the factories of Dundee in Scotland, the world's major jute manufacturing centre. By the second half of the 1850s, the availability of the raw material in Bengal, as well as of coal, cheap labour, and a large market, had led to the first production taking place in Calcutta. The Borneo Company built the first successful integrated power spinning and weaving mill in 1859, and from the 1870s the Calcutta industry grew very rapidly on the basis of cheap raw materials and very cheap labour. The export of manufactured products rose sharply and by the end of the century India was the world's leading exporter, driving out the exports of the Dundee mills from many markets. By 1914 India had about 64 jute mills, employing over 200,000 workers, and was one of India's two important factory industries.[6] The British investments were not, however, always profitable. Finlays' mill was plagued by labour problems, and by a high turnover of managers, and its costs were above the industry average. The Champdany Jute Company's profitability and dividend performance compared poorly with its competitors and this was a major factor in the outbreak of shareholder dissent against Finlays in the 1890s mentioned in Chapter 6.[7] As discussed in Section 10.3 below, the British traders were less involved in the cotton textiles industry, although several firms established substantial factories in both Bombay and Madras.

There was little manufacturing investment in South East Asia—the Borneo Company's establishment of a brickworks in South East Asia was a rare exception—but the trading companies on the China coast did venture into manufacturing. Jardine Matheson was the pioneer. Its establishment of a silk filiature in Shanghai in 1870 was followed by a series of other investments. However industrial investment in China was very hazardous as the law did

    [5] B. R. Tomlinson, 'Colonial Firms and the Decline of Colonialism in Eastern India 1914–47', *Modern Asian Studies*, 15 (1981), n. 7.
    [6] M. D. Morris, 'The Growth of Large-Scale Industry to 1947', in D. Kumar (ed.), *The Cambridge Economic History of India* (Cambridge: Cambridge University Press, 1983), 566–72.
    [7] Ross Ernest Stewart, 'Scottish Company Accounting, 1870–1920' (unpublished University of Glasgow Ph.D., 1986), 272–83.

not recognize foreign property rights. This situation only changed with the Treaty of Shimonoseki in 1895 which permitted foreigners to engage in industrial enterprise at the 'Treaty Ports'. Consequently industrial investment was first clustered in the colony of Hong Kong. In 1878 the firm pioneered sugar refining in Hong Kong. In 1879 the Hong Kong Ice Company was founded to manufacture ice in the colony, an operation which was later extended to include insulated cold storage for imported meat. In 1895 the Ewo Cotton & Spinning Company was established with a cotton mill in Shanghai. Two years later the Jardine Spinning & Weaving Company was founded to pioneer spinning and weaving of textiles in Hong Kong.[8] Swire's was less involved in manufacturing but did make a large capital investment in sugar refining with the Taikoo Sugar Refinery Co. founded in Hong Kong in 1881.

The other main area where British traders became involved in manufacturing before 1914 was the Americas. On the Pacific West Coast, trade in primary products led the trading companies into processing raw materials. Balfour Williamson, and, for a time, Dodwells built flour mills in Oregon in the United States. Antony Gibbs, Duncan Fox, and Balfour Williamson were among the firms which began flour milling in Chile and Peru. British merchants manufactured textiles and processed sugar in Peru. On the east coast of Latin America, the British merchants on the River Plate were squeezed between large international grain firms and foreign (mainly British) railroad and utility ventures, but by 1914 a number of merchants had ventured into manufacturing in Argentina, establishing meat-freezing plants and factories making footwear, cement, and paint. In Brazil, the Ashworths manufactured textiles, while Knowles & Foster invested in flour and sugar mills. Edward Johnston & Co., coffee traders, invested in a coffee-processing plant to clean and haul shipments.[9]

By 1914, British trading companies had accumulated quite substantial manufacturing interests. They had invested in the processing of locally produced commodities, as in the case of jute and flour milling, and also moved from traders in skins and sugar into manufacturers or refiners. These firms built on their knowledge gained as importers about local markets and raw material supplies. The diversification into manufacturing was, in other words, a path-dependent process, supporting the predictions of resource-based theory of the firm that firms diversify in directions set by their capabilities.[10] In a number of instances, merchant firms had been virtually

---

[8] Maggie Keswick (ed.), *The Thistle and the Jade* (London. Octopus, 1982); Stanley Chapman, *Merchant Enterprise in Britain* (Cambridge: Cambridge University Press, 1992), 237–241.

[9] Charles Jones, 'Institutional Forms of British Foreign Direct Investment in South America', *Business History*, 39 (1997); Robert G. Greenhill, 'Investment Group, Free-standing Company or Multinational? Brazilian Warrant, 1909–52', *Business History*, 37 (1995); Wallis Hunt, *Heirs of Great Adventure*, 2 vols. (London: the firm, 1951, 1960); R. Graham, 'A British Industry in Brazil: Rio Flour Mills, 1886–1920', *Business History*, 8 (1966).

[10] E. T. Penrose, *The Theory of the Growth of the Firm* (Oxford: Oxford University Press, 1959); G. B. Richardson, 'The Organisation of Industry', *Economic Journal*, 82 (1972), 883–96.

'reinvented' into manufacturers. In other cases the trading companies had remained merchants even when manufacturing investments were made, for their primary concern had remained securing commission rather than dividends.

During the interwar years the conditions seemed ripe for further investments in manufacturing. On the one hand, the spread of protectionism in many countries rendered traditional importing strategies more difficult while making investments in manufacturing in low per capita income markets more attractive. On the other hand, the deteriorating competitiveness of British 'staple' exports—especially cotton textiles—and the penetration of Asian and Latin American markets by competitor products represented a considerable threat. Further threats came from British and other firms wishing to dispose of the services of the trading companies by investing directly in distribution or production overseas.

Although British trading companies continued to 'reinvent' themselves in these circumstances, few chose to invest substantially in manufacturing. An exception was Alfred Booth, which became even more focused on leather manufacture in the United States and Britain in this period.[11] At the other extreme there were also divestments. The British cotton textile investments in Russia were eliminated by the revolution in 1917. The Graham textile investments in Portugal were salvaged from that group's collapse and reconstruction, but in 1930 they were placed in a separate company, West European Industries. Members of the Graham family remained in the management, and made substantial profits after 1945, but there was a need for new capital investment. At the end of the 1950s the business was liquidated, leaving the Grahams active only in the port wine business.[12]

Generally the momentum to invest in new manufacturing ventures slackened. In India, after the brief post-war flurry of investments in engineering and iron and steel, which made huge losses in the post-war slump, the Calcutta managing agencies remained firmly attached to jute manufacture.[13] The industry had been very profitable during the First World War and remained profitable even in the 1920s. However from the late 1920s the British firms ran into growing problems in the jute industry, as Indian entrepreneurs built newer and more efficient mills, and at the same time many of them refused to cooperate with the cartel established by the British mill owners in 1884, the Indian Jute Mills Association.[14] New manufacturing investment was incremental rather than radical. Finlays entered

---

[11] John, *Liverpool Merchant House.*
[12] Annual General Meetings of Grahams Trading Company, 1930–60, MS 22467, GHL.
[13] Maria Misra, 'Entrepreneurial Decline and the End of Empire' (unpublished Oxford D.Phil., 1994), 72–4.
[14] Gordon T. Stewart, *Jute and Empire* (Manchester: Manchester University Press, 1998), ch. 3.

sugar refining, and also upgraded its Indian textile factories in the 1930s in reaction to Japanese competition.

A number of companies continued to diversify in a path-dependent fashion by, for example, developing engineering ventures out of their core activities. Harrisons & Crosfield had opened engineering workshops shortly before the First World War near its tea and rubber estates in southern India, and these facilities grew substantially in the interwar period to include—by the late 1940s—a factory producing structural and sheet metal, a machine shop, a tile works, a sawmill, and a printing works.[15] The same process occurred in South East Asia around the plantations of the agency houses.[16] In India, Binny's engineering business originated in 1926 as a foundry and machine shop erected at Madras port to handle ship repairs. During the Second World War the factory increased its activities by undertaking the manufacture of textile machinery parts and fabricated steelwork. A rare example of diversification from rubber plantations to rubber manufacture occurred in Malaya, where Harrisons & Crosfield manufactured 'Linatex', a new way of processing latex into ribbed sheets, through a partly owned company which erected a factory near Kuala Lumpur in the late 1920s.[17]

In Latin America and Africa there were few new investments in manufacturing. In the former, small investments were made in Brazil in engineering and boat building, and in Chile there were also investments in a number of products in the 1930s, from nails to cigarettes.[18] However no really new investments were made. In West Africa UAC made some modest manufacturing investments in the 1930s in response to import duties and the need to protect an existing market, but it was not until the last two years of the Second World War that the firm began to consider larger schemes, especially in brewing.[19]

There were a number of possible reasons why the trading companies' ventures into manufacturing were rather limited in this period. In the case of the Calcutta firms, Misra argues that it was a characteristic case of British 'entrepreneurial decline'. These firms retained the partnership form and were reluctant to let in the outside capital needed to enter new ventures, but their attitudes also displayed 'deep-rooted caution and conservatism'

[15] H&C Ltd., *Sphere of Operations in 1949*, pp. 8–10; typescript history, *c*.1985, of southern India offices, Harrisons & Crosfield Archives, GHL.

[16] Harrisons & Crosfield, *One Hundred Years as East India Merchants: Harrisons & Crosfield 1844–1943* (London: the firm, 1944), 43–4; Junid Saham, *British Industrial Development in Malaysia, 1963–71* (Kuala Lumpur: Oxford University Press, 1980), 113.

[17] Records of Wilkinson Process Rubber Co. Ltd. and Wilkinson Rubber Linatex Ltd., Harrisons & Crosfield Archives, GHL. D. J. M. Tate, *The RGA History of the Plantation Industry in the Malay Peninsula* (Kuala Lumpur: Oxford University Press, 1996), 411.

[18] Anon., *The History of Knowles & Foster 1828–1948* (London: Ted Kavanagh, 1948); R. Greenhill and R. Miller, 'British Trading Companies in South America after 1914', in Geoffrey Jones (ed.), *The Multinational Traders* (London: Routledge, 1998), 104, 112.

[19] D. K. Fieldhouse, *Merchant Capital and Economic Decolonization* (Oxford: Clarendon Press, 1994), 298–321.

and a pronounced 'ideological hostility to import substitution industries'.[20] However it is not evident that this hypothesis can be generally applied beyond the Calcutta firms, which do seem especially 'conservative' in their attitudes, though the Latin American firms also manifested this characteristic in the interwar years. The scale of the deep post-1919 recession seems to have raised the risk aversion levels of many of these firms and made them reluctant to 'lock up' their capital in manufacturing.

A basic shortage of funds in conditions of increased risk provides a more general explanation of reluctance to make fixed investments. As profitability fell away in the interwar years, with major financial crises in the early 1920s and again in the early 1930s, firms were far from interested in new capital commitments. Indeed, some firms had a clear strategy of reducing fixed investments in order to increase liquidity. In other cases, such as the South East Asian agency houses, they may have made sufficient profits from traditional activities that they had no incentive to take risks in manufacturing.

A further constraint was the competences of the trading companies. The pre-1914 investments in sugar refining, flour milling, and cotton textiles had called for technical skills not possessed by merchants, but these activities were placed in affiliate firms which built up their own staff, often by recruiting from domestic British firms. The most likely manufacturing industries to invest in during the interwar years—engineering, chemicals, brewing—required more and ongoing technical skills. The creation of new 'free-standing' affiliates, with their own staff, declined in this period, while a firm such as UAC basically had an expatriate staff who were generalists specializing in trade. There remained the possibility of forming a joint venture with a manufacturing company, but for reasons discussed in section 10.4 this was often not available.

The British trading companies entered the post-1945 period with considerable franchises and assets in many developing countries, but with growing threats to their traditional trading activities and the ownership of natural resources. However there were also new opportunities through import substitution to expand manufacturing. However, as before the war, the companies were constrained by their own lack of technical expertise and the difficulty of finding suitable joint venture partners. British manufacturers often preferred to invest abroad themselves in larger markets, or avoid the developing world altogether from the 1960s. Capital constraints continued also. While the conversion of most firms to public companies theoretically provided access to the British capital market to fund substantial fixed investments, by the 1960s and 1970s the growing perception of political risk, exchange controls, and currency depreciation in many Latin American, African, and Asian countries made the firms increasingly reluctant to invest large sums in those countries in fixed assets. In addition a number of the

---

[20] Misra, 'Entrepreneurial Decline', 50, 66.

TABLE 10.2 Principal manufacturing investments and divestments by British trading companies in developing countries, 1945–1970s[a]

Industry	Country
New investments	
Cotton textiles	Ghana (1950s), Nigeria (1960s), Rhodesia (1960s), Malawi (1960s), Hong Kong (1960s)
Brewing and alcohol	Ghana (1950s), Nigeria (1950s), India (1950s), Zambia (1960s), Kenya (1960s)
Coca-Cola bottling	Hong Kong (1960s), Zambia (1970s)
Automobile assembly	Nigeria (1950s), Pakistan (1950s), Thailand (1960s)
Engineering	India (1950s), Malaya (1950s), Hong Kong (1960s)
Pharmaceuticals	India (1950s), Nigeria (1960s), Chile (1970s)
Fertilizers	India (1950s), Peru (1960s)
Sugar refining	Malawi (1960s), Swaziland (1970s), Mauritius (1970s)
Divestments	
Cotton textiles	China (1940s), India (1960s/70s)
Jute	India (1960s/70s)
Sugar refining	India (1960s/70s)
Flour milling	Peru (1940s), Chile (1950s/70s)
Brewing	China (1940s)
Fertilizers	India (1960s/70s), Peru (1960s)

[a] This table includes principal industries and countries only and is not comprehensive.

largest British trading companies, among them Jardine Matheson, Swire's, and Inchcape, were extremely cautious about investing in manufacturing.[21]

Table 10.2 lists some of the principal manufacturing investments and divestments between the 1940s and the 1970s. It shows clear industry and geographical patterns. Between the 1940s and the 1970s most of the old-established British manufacturing industries of cotton textiles, jute, sugar refining, and flour milling in India, China, and the Southern Cone of Latin America were eliminated. New manufacturing investment was heavily concentrated in Africa, though India attracted attention in the 1950s and Hong Kong subsequently. Cotton textiles and brewing were especially prominent. In contrast, there was very little investment in consumer goods such as foodstuffs, household products, etc.

In Latin America British trading companies after 1945 were not very active in industrial investments. In 1951 Gibbs sold its flour milling company in Chile.[22] However, Gibbs retained equity shareholding in a number of

[21] Stephanie Jones, *Two Centuries of Overseas Trading* (London: Macmillan, 1986), 277.

[22] Memorandum on the Cía Molinera California de Chile, 1 Nov. 1950; Board Meeting 6 Mar. 1951, Antony Gibbs Archives, MS 16869/1, GHL.

Chilean manufacturing companies, such as a paintwork firm, from many of which it earned commission from acting as distributors and sometimes management fees. Balfour Williamson retained its large flour milling business in Chile longer than Gibbs, finally selling it only in 1967. Balfour Williamson's focus on 'merchanting' resulted in no new industrial investments. In contrast Duncan Fox remained more involved in manufacturing in Chile. Through the 1970s it held the majority of the shares in substantial flour mills and invested in a variety of other industries, from soap and biscuits to pharmaceuticals.

By the 1960s neither Gibbs nor Duncan Fox were prepared to make major new investments in Chile (or elsewhere in Latin America) because of the problems of currency depreciation against sterling and of exchange controls. Local managements were expected to make new investments out of retained profits. However there were other demands on such local funds. Gibbs' Chilean organization had high working capital needs given its large number of branches and the slow payment of debts by Chilean customers. As a result, a series of proposals for new manufacturing investments in Chile by the local management never got under way for lack of funds.[23] Similarly at Duncan Fox by the 1960s new investments in local currency had to be made out of surplus funds in that currency. Thus in 1962 Duncan Fox sold its shares in a Peruvian fish processing company and used them to invest in a Peruvian textile group. In 1968 it sold a fertilizer manufacturer and used the funds for a new company for the production of mushrooms.[24] However, by that date Duncan Fox was preoccupied with the mounting losses of its British printing and engineering subsidiary.

In post-independence India, British manufacturing multinationals took the lead in making substantial direct investments during the 1950s.[25] The British trading companies and managing agencies retained substantial manufacturing investments, but still often focused in the traditional industries of coal, jute, and engineering, and often employing old machines and practices because of under-investment or simple conservatism.[26] However, this was not the entire picture. During the 1950s Shaw Wallace, which had substantial coal and flour milling interests, built factories to produce fertilizers and spraying equipment for crops. In 1940 it purchased a Calcutta firm of alcohol importers and ten years later it purchased a distiller making gin, whisky, brandy, and liqueurs. In 1961 a yeast manufacturing plant was set up next to the distillery in a joint venture with Distillers.[27] Finlays, which

[23] T. Gibbons to D. C. Campbell, 1 July 1963, Antony Gibbs Archives, MS 16876/8, GHL.

[24] Annual Reports, Duncan Fox, 1960–71.

[25] B. R. Tomlinson, 'British Business in India, 1860–1970,' in R. P. T. Davenport-Hines and Geoffrey Jones (eds.), *British Business in Asia since 1860* (Cambridge: Cambridge University Press, 1989).

[26] Stephanie Jones, *Merchants of the Raj* (London: Macmillan, 1992), 180–1.

[27] Sir Harry Townend, *A History of Shaw Wallace & Co. and Shaw Wallace & Co Ltd.* (Calcutta: the firm, 1965), 82–6, 102–3.

already manufactured jute, cotton, and sugar in India, also invested further. In Pakistan, the firm built a plant in association with Leyland and Massey-Ferguson to assemble trucks and tractors.[28] Finlays' three Bombay cotton mills were also re-equipped and their activities expanded. Binny's remained large textile producers in the 1950s though using looms dating from the 1920s, which became progressively obsolete[29]—but also diversified into engineering.

During the 1960s increased taxation, the devaluation of the Indian rupee, and the India government's abolition of the managing agency system provided little incentive for new investments in fixed assets. Andrew Yule did make new acquisitions in engineering and coal, but remained reluctant to invest substantial sums, and Yule Catto sold its shareholding to the government in 1969.[30] In 1968 Finlays sold its long-established Calcutta jute and Bombay textile mills.

In Malaysia and elsewhere in South East Asia, the pattern of investment in manufacturing was almost the opposite of that seen in India. In the 1950s the British traders had only very limited investments in manufacturing.[31] The high perception of political risk meant that the British firms sought to develop manufacturing investments in the developed world, and until the late 1960s they undertook little manufacturing in the region, with the occasional exception such as Anglo-Thai's vehicle assembly plant in Bangkok. By this date the British traders began to reconsider this strategy, as economic growth began to accelerate, and tariff barriers and growing competition threatened established markets.[32] During the 1970s the British companies became quite heavily involved in Malaysian industrialization.[33]

The other region in Asia where British trading companies made some investments in manufacturing was Hong Kong. They played only a modest role in the manufacturing industries—textiles, toys, and electronics—which were to drive that colony's fast economic growth. Although limited investments were made by Jardines—in the 1970s it invested (with no success) in consumer electronics—there was a strong feeling in the company that they were traders and not manufacturers.[34] Swire's regained and rebuilt its Hong Kong sugar refinery. After 1945 Swire's paint factory was transferred from Shanghai to Hong Kong and merged with a local paint company to become Swire Duro. A major development came in 1965 when Swire's were invited by Coca-Cola to acquire the company which held the Hong Kong bottling franchise for that firm. This acquisition led to Swire's

[28] 'People and Events', *Finlays House Magazine*, 1/1 (Spring 1963).

[29] Ibid., Memo on Binny's Engineering Works Private Ltd., 3 Dec. 1949; and Binny & Co. c.1959, Binny Archives, MS 27167, GHL.

[30] Jones, *Merchants of the Raj*, 245.

[31] Geoffrey Jones and Judith Wale, 'Diversification Strategies of British Trading Companies: Harrisons & Crosfield c.1900–c.1980', *Business History*, 41 (1999); Saham, *British Industrial Development*, 113.

[32] Board Minute, 24 Apr. 1968, Anglo-Thai Archives, MS 27008/13, GHL.

[33] Saham, *British Industrial Development*.   [34] Interview with Jeremy Brown, 21 Jan. 1999.

establishing a pre-eminent position in carbonated drinks in Hong Kong. Given that Coca-Cola supplied the concentrate, this was not really as such a large-scale investment in manufacturing as in distribution, an activity where Swire's had considerable expertise.[35] By 1974 Swire's was ranked among the top fifty Coca-Cola bottlers in the world.

In Africa, by comparison, the British trading companies initially increased their manufacturing investments, though from a very low base, but by the 1970s the momentum had largely passed. In West Africa during the 1950s, UAC edged towards a greater involvement in manufacturing in the larger markets, initially Ghana and Nigeria, in response to growing political nationalism, or to protect its trading interests from increased tariffs or foreign competition. Ghana was West Africa's richest state, while Nigeria —although poorer—had a large population of 40 million in 1960. West African incomes at this time compared favourably with those of South East and East Asia and the larger markets seemed full of potential. Projects included an automobile assembly plant, plywood manufacture, and a pig breeding and processing operation.[36] Holts also took shares in a stationer, a canning company, and a metal window manufacturer.

During the 1960s there were more substantial investments, especially in Nigeria. Holts undertook or acquired further investments in—for example —the manufacture of enamelware, perfumes, and agricultural equipment. UAC had large brewing joint ventures with Heineken and Guinness, and also made substantial investments in textiles. By the mid-1970s around 13 per cent of UACs 'capital employed' was in industrial investments, but by then growing political risk, government requirements for local share-holding, and the failure of many ventures meant that UAC made no new investments in West African manufacturing. Even before then UAC's involvement in West African manufacturing had been skewed by its owner-ship by Unilever. It was excluded from manufacturing the consumer goods produced by Unilever itself, which were the responsibility of other parts of the organization.[37] Unilever had manufactured soap in Nigeria since the 1920s, and it was ranked as one of Nigeria's largest industrial enter-prises by the 1960s. The firm also manufactured in Ghana, Kenya, Malawi, Rhodesia, and Zaire.[38]

Lonrho was the most dynamic British group in East African manu-facturing from the mid-1960s. The firm invested in sugar production and refining, textile manufacture, and bottling and breweries. In 1979 Lonrho operated twenty beer breweries in partnership with African companies, while its Zambian Coca-Cola plant was one of the largest in Africa.[39] In this

---

[35] Interview at Swire House, 28 Jan. 1999.
[36] Fieldhouse, *Merchant Capital*, 382–410   [37] Ibid. 495–588.
[38] D. K. Fieldhouse, *Unilever Overseas* (London: Croom Helm, 1978), ch. 6.
[39] Annual Reports, Lonrho, 1965–79. S. Cronjé, M. Ling, and G. Cronjé, *Lonrho, Portrait of a Multinational* (London: Penguin, 1976), 45.

pattern of diversification, the main firm-specific competence lay in Lonrho's strong 'contacts' with the political and business elites of the newly independent countries in Africa.

Through the 1960s and the 1970s there was a perception, not only in Africa but in Asia and even still Latin America, that the trading companies had opportunities to enter manufacturing on a greater scale in their traditional host economies. This perception was usually stronger among the managers in those countries than at the British headquarters. However few firms wanted to invest much capital in a major manufacturing project, and this was a formidable constraint. There was also a perceived recognition inside many companies that their staff lacked the technical competence needed to succeed in manufacturing.[40] Their core or 'House' staff were generalists experienced in trading, not in managing complex manufacturing businesses.

10.3 Sugar Refining and Textiles

This section looks in more detail at two manufacturing industries in which British trading companies invested, sugar refining and textiles.

British trading companies were involved in all stages of the sugar industry. This was appropriate for a country which throughout the nineteenth century had the highest per capita sugar consumption in the world, far exceeding that of other European countries and the negligible consumption in Asia and Africa except for European expatriates. Beet sugar, both raw and refined, became the most important source of British sugar imports in the second half of the nineteenth century—providing 87 per cent of total British sugar imports in 1913. The British did not produce beet sugar themselves and their role in that part of the industry was refining.[41] However they were also owners and/or managers of extensive sugar cane plantations in the West Indies, and also in Peru and Mauritius, where they became active in the processing of sugar. This involved a number of stages. Raw sugar was obtained from the extraction of sucrose from the cane stalks in 'factories' normally located on or near the sugar estates. This raw sugar was sometimes sold for direct consumption, but more often further refining processes were carried out in the consuming countries.

The companies with sugar plantation interests were normally involved in the processing of the cane into raw sugar. In the West Indies, Booker Brothers, McConnell and Henckell Du Buisson processed raw sugar alongside their estates.[42] As the sugar cane industry became concentrated into

---

[40] Board Minute, 26 Oct. 1970, Anglo-Thai Archives, MS 270008/13, GHL.

[41] Philippe Chalmin, *The Making of a Sugar Giant: Tate and Lyle 1858–1989* (Chur: Harwood, 1990), chs. 1–3.

[42] Kathleen M. Stahl, *The Metropolitan Organisation of British Colonial Trade* (London: Faber & Faber, 1951), 36–48.

large estates, mechanized processing facilities were built.[43] The position of the British traders in West Indian sugar was very powerful, even though the arrival of the British refiner Tate & Lyle in the islands in the 1930s produced a strong new competitor. In British Guiana, Booker's not only accounted for 70 per cent of total sugar output in the late 1940s, but also controlled twelve of the sixteen raw sugar factories in the colony.[44] The large West Indian production was then sold to the London-based sugar brokers, of whom the largest was Czarnikow, who sold it on to refiners.[45]

British trading companies also invested in sugar refining in India and China before 1914, without becoming involved in plantations or the manufacture of raw sugar. Both countries were large producers of sugar cane but in both cases sugar refining was very primitive before the British companies made their investments. By the nineteenth century India had largely produced and consumed its own varieties of unrefined sugar, but from the late nineteenth century sugar imports rose as other countries improved their methods of cultivating and refining sugar cane and sugar beet. In contrast most of the Indian sugar cane industry remained very backward.

In south India, Parry's and Binny's were among the pioneers of the refining of white sugar in the early 1840s, a period of booming exports before the adoption of free trade in 1845 decimated the business. Their refineries were the only firms in south India to survive the legislative change, while in north India only one refinery survived. In 1897 Parry's refining interests were consolidated into the East India Distilleries and Sugar Factories Ltd. which sought to develop large-scale refineries using the latest equipment. Binny's also launched a similar company, the Deccan Sugar & Abkhari Company, which refined 'palmyrah jaggery' rather than sugar cane. This venture ran into financial difficulties in the early 1900s and Parry's took over their management, leaving that firm with a monopoly over locally refined sugar, though its markets were open to foreign competition.[46]

In Bihar and the United Provinces, sugar cane was grown outside the tropics which led to lower per acre yields compared to major tropical producers such as Java. In this area the pioneer of white sugar refining was the managing agency of Begg Sutherland, which between 1894 and 1913 established three refineries in Bihar. By the early 1930s this was the largest sugar producing enterprise in India. In addition, some British firms converted their indigo factories into sugar refineries as natural indigo became an unprofitable crop as a result of the growth of the synthetic dye industry

---

[43] Christian Schnakenbourg, 'From Sugar Estate to Central Factory: The Industrial Revolution in the Caribbean (1840–1905)', in Bill Albert and Adrian Graves (eds.), *Crisis and Change in the International Sugar Economy 1860–1914* (Norwich: ISC Press, 1984), 83–94.

[44] Stahl, *Metropolitan Organisation.*

[45] P. Chalmin, 'The Rise of International Commodity Trading Companies in Europe in the Nineteenth Century', in S. Yonekawa and H. Yoshihara (eds.), *Business History of General Trading Companies* (Tokyo: University of Tokyo Press, 1987), 280.

[46] Hilton Brown, *Parry's of Madras* (Madras: the firm, 1954), 83–6, 138–46, 163–4.

at the end of the nineteenth century. Finlays converted its indigo factory in the United Provinces into a sugar refinery in 1913.[47]

During the 1920s the Indian sugar refining industry remained modest in scale and the big change came in the introduction of tariffs on imported sugar in 1932. The sugar refining industry grew very fast in this decade, but the British firms were no longer in the lead. Following the introduction of protection, Indian business groups such as Birla, Thapar, and Narang made large investments in the industry. By the end of the 1930s Narang had outstripped Begg Sutherland in daily crushing capacity. The large Calcutta managing agencies such as Gillanders declined to enter the industry because of their lack of expertise. Birds did set up a factory in 1920, but closed it four years later following technical problems.[48] In Bombay, Shaw Wallace made a large-scale entry into the sugar importing business in 1925 in alliance with a Bombay entrepreneur, but the business collapsed in 1930 when the decline of sugar prices led to their partner's default.[49] In the early 1930s Finlays converted another former indigo factory in Bihar into a refinery, only to have it almost immediately destroyed in an earthquake.[50]

The British trading companies in China made larger investments in sugar refining. Sugar had long been extensively grown in south China, but as in India the refining methods were primitive. Jardine Matheson took the lead and established a small sugar refinery in Hong Kong in 1875, and between 1878 and 1886 also established one in Shantou in China. In 1881 Swire's established the Taikoo Sugar Refining Co. in order to compete with Jardines, primarily in retaliation for their competition on Swire shipping routes. This refinery started production in 1885 with the latest equipment. The venture was capital intensive. The construction of the refinery in the years leading up to its opening in 1885 cost £200,000, while a further £500,000 was spent over the following decade. The strategy was to purchase raw sugar from Java and the Philippines and sell refined products to China and Japan, though initially sales were also made to India, Australia, and California.[51]

The initial competitive struggle between Taikoo Sugar Refinery and Jardines' China Sugar Refinery was won by the former, which by 1900 held around two-thirds of sales on the China market compared to Jardines' one-third.[52] The up-to-date Taikoo refinery produced a range of products, the largest being white refined sugar, but it also made a powdered sugar which enabled Chinese cake makers to store their cakes for longer periods

---

[47] Undated memo, *c*.1945, Finlays Archives, UGD91/413/I; A. K. Bagchi, *Private Investment in India 1900–1939* (Cambridge: Cambridge University Press, 1972), 362–5.

[48] Misra, 'Entrepreneurial Decline', 65.   [49] Townend, *History*, 111.

[50] Undated memo, *c*.1945, Finlay Archives, UGD91/413/I; Rajat K. Ray, *Industrialization in India* (Delhi: Oxford University Press, 1979), 138–44.

[51] S. Marriner and F. E. Hyde, *The Senior, John Samuel Swire, 1825–98* (Liverpool: Liverpool University Press, 1967), ch. 6.

[52] S. Sugiyama, 'A British Trading Firm in the Far East: John Swire & Sons, 1867–1914', in Yonekawa and Yoshihara (eds.), *Business History*, 189.

TABLE 10.3 Average pre-tax return on net capital employed and dividends and commission paid of Taikoo Sugar Refining Co., 1885–1935

	Pre-tax ROCE (%)	Dividends paid (total £)	Commission to Swire's (total £)
1885–94	11.7	203,700	51,633
1895–1904	6.0	160,000	53,233
1905–14	6.0	285,000	186,166
1915–19	12.7	175,000	353,439
1920–29	(3.6)	205,000	506,054
1930–35	4.7	—	—

Source: Taikoo Sugar Refining Co. Ltd., London Sterling Accounts, Swire Archives, JSSV 4/1–5, SOAS

than previously.[53] By 1905 80 per cent of Taikoo's output was sold in China. However during the 1900s both Swire's and Jardines faced serious competition from Japanese refined sugar. Swire's responded by increasing the number of grades and in 1912 by establishing an up-country market-ing system designed to expand markets in inland China.[54] This involved establishing agencies in the interior of China to sell sugar directly to the consumers rather than selling to China sugar dealers in the Treaty Ports who played Swire's off against the Japanese to gain the best advantage for themselves. The up-country agencies were staffed by Chinese, but regularly inspected by Swire's. 'Whatever happens', Swire's in London noted, 'the Japanese must not be allowed to gain any substantial footing in the markets of China'.[55]

Table 10.3 gives the pre-tax ROCE—post-tax data is not available—and other performance indicators for the Taikoo Sugar Refining Co. between 1885 and 1935. No comparable figures are available for Jardines.

In terms of pre-tax ROCE, it is evident that the Taikoo Sugar Refinery was especially successful in its first decade of operation. This reflected in part the fact that it was highly profitable in a couple of years (1889 and 1890) before much of the capital investment had taken place. Thereafter the effects of Japanese competition among other factors became evident. However the evidence on dividends and commission somewhat modify this picture. In particular, commission payments to Swire's and dividends grew in the pre-war period. The First World War was not as profitable for the sugar refineries in Hong Kong as in many other activities, but Taikoo's ROCE

---

[53] Zhang Zhongli, Chen Zengnian, Yao Xinrong, *The Swire Group in Old China* (Shanghai: The Shanghai People's Publishing House, 1995), 45–8.
[54] Sugiyama, 'A British Trading Firm', 189–91.
[55] J. Swire to H. W. Robertson, 2 Dec. 1910, JSSI/1/15, Swire Archives, SOAS.

soared to 35.1 per cent and 48.4 per cent in 1919 and 1920 respectively. Commission payments to Swire's, which only totalled £116,690 between 1914 and 1918, reached almost £600,000 in 1919 and 1920.

The 1920s proved disastrous for British sugar refining interests in China. There were strikes, boycotts, and relentless Japanese competition. By the mid-1920s Jardines' China Sugar Refinery Co. was making heavy losses, which had wiped out the firm's reserves by 1925.[56] Initially Jardine Matheson took the matter philosophically, noting that the venture had 'passed through many bad times and recovered'.[57] However although there was a recognition that the company needed more capital to re-equip itself, Jardines declined to provide it, not wishing to convert themselves 'from the position of creditors into part-proprietors'.[58] By 1928 the refinery had been closed, and a committee of shareholders put the China Sugar Refinery Co. into voluntarily liquidation, a decision not opposed by Jardines.[59]

Swire's also experienced major problems during the 1920s. During the war the Taikoo Sugar Refinery had committed itself to the construction of a new refinery, expenditure on which had exceeded £1 million on its completion in 1925, when it became the largest single unit refinery in the world. Small improvements to the refinery continued up to 1935. At the end of the war Swire's also planned to expand its up-country sales network which—given that it involved high stock levels—obliged the firm to seek substantial overdrafts from the Hongkong Bank.[60] In addition, in 1919 a steamer was purchased by Taikoo Sugar for £147,000.

It was therefore as a substantially stronger and more modern organization than its Jardine twin that Taikoo Sugar encountered the instability of the 1920s. In 1921 the firm made a loss on working of almost £1 million. There was subsequently a recovery and dividends were paid up to 1926, but thereafter there was no dividend again until 1938. The only years between 1920 and 1935 when Swire's earned commission were 1920, 1921, and 1923. There were further substantial losses in 1927 and 1928 by which time the firm's reserves had been almost wiped out. The refinery was closed between 1927 and 1929. A Swire calculation of the 'true' profits of Taikoo Sugar between 1930 and 1935 showed an average ROCE of 2.4 per cent, or even lower than the published figure.[61]

Japanese competition and the growing disorder in the Chinese market lay at the root of Taikoo Sugar's problems. Swire's inspectors could not travel

---

[56] D. Landale to Brook Smith, 29 Jan. 1925, S/O London to Hong Kong 1925, JMA, CUL. The China Sugar Refinery lost $1,732,000 in 1924, $1,504,000 in 1925, and $1,180,000 in 1927.

[57] D. Landale to D. G. M. Bernard, 8 Oct. 1925, S/O London to Hong Kong 1925, JMA, CUL.

[58] Ibid., D. Lansdale to D. G. M. Bernard, 19 Mar. 1926, S/O London to Hong Kong 1926.

[59] Ibid., D. Lansdale to B. D. Beith, 16 Mar. 1928, Telegram from Hong Kong, 27 May 1928, S/O London to Hong Kong 1928. Ibid.

[60] J. S. Swire to N. J. Stabb, 12 July 1918, Swire Archives, JSSI/4/9, Swire Archives SOAS.

[61] Ibid., G. W. Swire to Colin and John Swire, 28 Oct. 1941, Swire ADD 18. The 'true' profits were defined as before depreciation and transfers to or from reserves.

to the up-country agencies, who became progressively indebted to Swire's.[62] Consequently in 1928 Swire's abandoned the system of up-country selling. In 1931 the introduction of a protective tariff by the Chinese was a further blow, as Hong Kong was outside the tariff wall. Swire's reverted to using sugar brokers, appointing Y. K. Mok to this position in 1932. The Moks had 'the best smuggling organisation in the Delta' and for a time smuggled large amounts of Taikoo Sugar into China.[63] The alternative of erecting a refinery in China was considered in the mid-1930s, but not pursued in view of the problems of financing it.[64]

The sugar refining business required a number of skills. Firms such as Taikoo Sugar and the China Sugar Refinery had their own staff who spent their careers with the company and who possessed requisite technical skills, and who accumulated expertise in the key areas such as the buying of raw sugar, which involved estimating future demand and the likely movement of foreign exchange markets. However the senior management of Swire's, for example, were actively involved in such matters and were by no means 'amateurs' in the sugar business. Indeed, the Swire's senior management held informed views on all aspects of Taikoo's business, such as branding strategies.[65]

The most pressing skill needed by Swire's in the 1930s was to locate overseas markets for its products. The deterioration in the China market led to a search for markets in India and South East Asia, and later Africa and elsewhere. 'We have looked into the question of selling to pretty nearly every country in the world', Hong Kong reported to London in April 1931.[66] The firm sold retail and bulk sugar to British trading companies active elsewhere, such as Anglo-Thai in Thailand, Grahams Trading in India and Burma, David Sassoon in Iraq, India, and East Africa, Harrisons & Crosfield in the Dutch East Indies and Guthries in Malaya. The essential problem was that the refinery had to work at 70 per cent capacity in order to make a profit.[67] The strategy was to sell to empire markets to take advantage of imperial preferences.[68] The percentage of Taikoo Sugar's sales there rose from 5 per cent in 1935 to 36 per cent in 1938.[69] Partly as a result of finding these new markets Taikoo Sugar's profits began to improve from 1937 and were substantial by 1940, and dividend payments were resumed in 1938.[70]

[62] J. S. Swire to N. J. Stabb, G. W. Swire to G. A. Mounsey, 3 Jan. 1928, JSSI/4/9 Swire Archives SOAS.

[63] Ibid., J. S. Scott to J. Swire, 4 Nov. 1932, Swire ADD 16.

[64] Ibid., J. S. Swire to Butterfield & Swire, 21 June 1935, JSSV/1/8.

[65] Ibid., J. S. Swire to Butterfield & Swire, 26 Feb. 1922, JSSV/1/1.

[66] Ibid., J. S. Butterfield & Swire to J. Swire, 17 Apr. 1931, JSSV/1/5.

[67] Ibid., J. Swire to Butterfield & Swire, 28 Feb. 1936, JSSV/1/8.

[68] Ibid., J. Swire to Sir Andrew Caldecott, 11 Nov. 1937, JSSV/1/9.

[69] Ibid., J. Swire to Butterfield & Swire, 13 Jan. 1939, JSSV/I/11.

[70] Ibid., Warren Swire to Colin Campbell and John Swire, 6 Oct. 1941 and 28 Oct. 1941, Swire ADD 18.

Sugar refining was not an industry which attracted 'new entrants' from British trading companies after the Second World War, while older investments in Latin America and India passed out of British ownership. Perhaps the only exception was Lonrho in Africa, which became involved in sugar production and refining in Malawi on the basis of an agreement with the Malawi government in 1965 to supply that country with its entire requirements of sugar. By 1979 Lonrho was engaged in sugar growing and processing not only in Malawi, but also in South Africa, Swaziland, and Mauritius. In the West Indies, Bookers remained large processors and shippers of sugar until the 1970s. Perhaps most strikingly, Swire's reacquired its Hong Kong refinery after the end of the Japanese occupation. This was developed into a sugar processing and packaging operation which established a leading position in Hong Kong's retail market, and served as a source of expertise for the firm's entry into beverages from the 1960s. In the 1990s Swire's formed a joint venture with Tate & Lyle to own cane sugar factories in the Guangxi Province of China designed to supply raw sugar to Tai-Koo Sugar (the name by this time) for packaging and to Swire Beverages for the soft drinks industry.

The second manufacturing industry discussed here is cotton textiles. Although the role of the trading companies as traders in British cotton textiles is well established, less attention has been given to their significant role, as cotton textile manufacturers. Cotton textiles was usually the first industry to be modernized in developing economies, given its labour rather than capital-intensive nature, the limited skills required of operatives, and the role of clothing as a basic necessity. Consequently, it was an obvious industry for the British traders to enter if they sought diversification opportunities, especially as they had often acquired knowledge of markets through importing British textiles.

The extent of investment in textiles manufacture varied between countries. In Latin America, only a few substantial investments were made. In Brazil, the Ashworth group had three mills manufacturing canvas shoes, woollens, and cottons, as well as one in Buenos Aires and one in Lancashire. However, this group collapsed in 1930. In Peru, Duncan Fox had cotton gins and textile mills from the late nineteenth century.[71] The Fábrica de Tejidos La Unión, owned by Duncan Fox, had both a spinning and weaving mill in Lima in the interwar years. This was evidently profitable and paid dividends of 8 per cent in the late 1930s.[72] This firm's involvement in Peruvian textiles proved very long-lasting. In the mid-1960s a large proportion of the firm's income was derived from the distribution and sale of textiles produced by its affiliated textile manufacturing company.[73]

---

[71] Rory Miller, *Britain and Latin America in the 19th and 20th Centuries* (London: Longmans, 1993), 101; Jones, 'Institutional Forms', 30.

[72] Head Office, Lancashire Section, General Managers Diaries of Interviews, 25 Apr. 1930, Acc 30/124; 27 Feb. 1934, Acc 30/128, HSBC Group Archives.

[73] Annual Report, Duncan Fox, 1966.

The investments of British traders in India and China reached a much greater significance than in Latin America. In the former country, Indian entrepreneurs took the lead in establishing the modern industry in Bombay in the 1850s, and of the ninety-five cotton textile mills started before the First World War only fifteen were controlled by Europeans. A number of British traders were, however, investors in the Bombay industry. The biggest British managing agency in Bombay was Greaves, Cotton & Co., which controlled seven cotton spinning mills in the city. Most Indian mills did not follow the British practice of specializing in either spinning yarn or weaving cloth, but ended up doing both, but Greaves, Cotton remained specialized on spinning. However this left the firm exposed when the growth of Japanese and Chinese cotton mills displaced Indian yarn exports in the Far East, and in 1915 Greaves, Cotton had to dispose of its mills.[74]

During the early 1900s Finlays began cotton textiles manufacture in Bombay. In 1902 the firm's Bombay branch, which once had a large business importing Lancashire piece-goods, was alerted to the sale of a mill and —according to a later account—persuaded the owner of the Clan Line, Sir Charles Cayzer, to buy it and place it under their management. The mill had obsolete machinery and no weaving. Finlays introduced new machinery—ring spindles—and opened a weaving shed, and in 1908 it was floated as an Indian public company, Swan Mills, under the management of Finlays. Meanwhile a new mill was constructed and floated in 1907 as Finlay Mills. This was the first mill in Bombay to be driven by electricity —using diesel engines—rather than steam. By 1908 the two mills had 60,000 spindles and 1,200 looms in operation. In 1924 Finlays took over the management of a third Bombay mill—Gold Mohar Mills—giving it an overall capacity of 100,000 spindles and more than 2,000 looms.[75] The cotton mills were initially very profitable, especially during the war and immediately afterwards, when Finlay Mills declared dividends of 60 per cent in 1919 and 80 per cent in 1920.

The other major investor in cotton textile manufacture before 1914 was Binny's. In Madras, Binny's invested in two cotton mill companies founded in 1876 and 1881 which constructed mills on adjacent sites. By the end of the 1880s the two factories—which had 31,500 spindles and 129 looms —sold both in the home market and developed an export market to China, and were pioneers in India of the development of mechanized dyeing and finishing, especially of khaki cloth after 1900. The two firms were merged into the Buckingham and Carnatic Spinning and Weaving Company in 1906. In 1884 Binny's also took over a small mill producing woollen yarn and cloth. This became the Bangalore Woollen, Cotton & Silk Mills Company. Cotton spinning was introduced in 1887, and cotton weaving in 1916.

[74] Morris, 'Growth'.
[75] Notes re Bombay Business by Bertram Brown, n.d., Finlays Archives, UGD 91/252.

Several cotton presses were also acquired. The business survived the firm's liquidation and subsequent acquisition by Inchcape in 1906, and was a large manufacturer of textile products in 1914.[76]

The interwar years were a period of substantial growth for cotton textile manufacture in India, though the greatest progress was made in the 1930s when Lancashire imports were largely eliminated from the market, though there was a growing influx of cheap Japanese goods. Unlike the case of sugar refining, the British trading companies did not lose their competitive edge. Binny's has been described as 'the most progressive cotton manufacturing agency in India during the interwar period'. By 1930 the Binny mills employed 2,300 automatic looms—a technology adopted by the Japanese but not by Lancashire firms or the bulk of Indian textile manufacturers. The firm also set up the largest khaki dyeing plant in the world and organized a highly efficient domestic marketing agency for selling their goods in India.[77] During the 1930s the cotton mills around Ahmedabad were far more responsive to market changes than those in Bombay and introduced the spinning of finer yarn and the weaving of finer varieties of cloth. Binny's was aware of, and moved rapidly, to follow the trend set by Ahmedabad.[78] In the late 1930s the Bangalore mill was rebuilt in recognition that its future depended on keeping 'abreast of all modern developments'.[79] With 150,000 spindles and over 3,000 looms by the end of that decade, Binny's was one of the largest and most successful cotton textile manufacturers in India.

The Finlay mills in Bombay, although not as pioneering as those of Binny's, also made substantial new investments in the 1930s which enabled them to change production from coarse to finer grade cottons. In 1933 the Finlay Mills was converted to fine counts followed by the Swan Mills in 1936 and Gold Mohur mills in 1939. This required a radical alteration in the pattern of production at the mills, and to deal with the much finer qualities of cloth woven complete modern plants for bleaching, dyeing, and finishing were imported and put into operation. The move to finer grade cottons also led Finlays to shift from using Indian to Egyptian and Sudanese cotton. In 1940 Swan Mills also began to manufacture tyre cord, initially out of cotton yarn supplied by the American tyre company, Firestone, but in the following year the Mill began to produce itself the fabric used in the manufacture of tyres. This turned into a long-term relationship with Firestone. During the 1950s, as synthetic fibres replaced cotton in the manufacture of tyres, Finlays began producing nylon tyre cord, and at the end of the decade new rayon tyre cord processing machinery was installed.[80]

[76] Jones, *Two Centuries*, 48–52.   [77] Ray, *Industrialization*, 68.

[78] Madras to London, 24 May 1934, Binny Archives, MS 27160/18, GHL.

[79] Ibid., Madras to London, 27 July 1936.

[80] 'The Finlay Group of Mills in Bombay', *Finlays House Magazine*, 2/1 (Autumn 1964), Finlays Archives, UGD 91/377.

These cotton textile businesses required specialist technical skills. A regular pattern would be for managerial staff to be recruited in Britain, sent for some preliminary training for between one and six months in a Lancashire textile firm 'to acquire some little knowledge of their organisation and methods', and then given on-the-job training in the Indian mills.[81] By the interwar years Indian trade unions were active, calling for labour management skills from the British firms. By the 1930s strikes were a regular occurrence in the mills, while local governments dominated by the Indian nationalist Congress Party contemplated or introduced legislation on the rights and privileges of workers.[82] In 1938 Binny's linked the size of the bonus paid to the workforce to the rate of the ordinary dividend in order 'to let the Workpeople, as well as the Shareholders, share in the increased prosperity of the Company', though this was interpreted as more to reduce the bonus than improve it.[83]

In late nineteenth-century China Jardine Matheson was the pioneer of the modern cotton textiles industry. From the 1860s Jardines had quite a large business importing Lancashire piece-goods, though China's low per capita income and the continued resilience of the local handicraft industry kept the size of the trade lower than expected. In the second half of the 1870s the firm also began to plan the establishment of cotton mills in China, despite the acute problems before the Treaty of Shimonoseki in 1895. The initial plan in 1877 involved Jardines in facilitating the creation of a textile mill in Shanghai, but leaving its ownership and management in Chinese hands. Through the next decade, however, Jardines' plans were blocked by the Chinese bureaucracy. Finally in 1894 Jardines began to order cotton spinning machinery from Britain. The outbreak of war between China and Japan, China's defeat, and the subsequent opening of the Treaty Ports to foreign firms finally enabled Jardines to proceed and in 1895 the Ewo Cotton Spinning & Weaving Company opened in Shanghai as the first modern mill.[84] During the 1900s Jardines built a second mill in Shanghai, and although that decade saw Japanese investment as well as Chinese in cotton milling in China, on the eve of the First World War the Ewo mills ranked among the largest in the country. The firm's two Shanghai mills had 100,000 spindles, or around 9 per cent of the 1,200,000 spindles in China at that time. In addition, a further 55,000 spindles were in a mill in Hong Kong under construction.[85]

During the interwar years the Ewo Cotton Mills ranked among the more successful of Jardines' activities, though the Japanese replaced the British as

---

[81] London to Madras, 20 May 1936, MS 27159/9; Memo to Lord Inchcape on Assistants for Madras, 24 Feb. 1930, MS 27163/4, Binny Archives, GHL.

[82] Ibid., Madras to London, 3 Mar. 1938, MS 27160/22.

[83] Ibid., Madras to London, 2 Aug. 1939, MS 27160/23.

[84] Edward Le Fevour, *Western Enterprise in Late Ch'ing China* (Cambridge, Mass.: Harvard University Press, 1968), 31–47.

[85] Memo re Hong Kong mill, 18 July 1911, S/O Shanghai to Hong Kong 1911, JMA, CUL.

the single most important owners of Chinese mills.[86] In 1921 the Shanghai mills were amalgamated into the Ewo Cotton Mills Ltd., which by the end of the 1930s operated 175,000 cotton spindles and 3,200 looms. In addition, the company extended its activities to include the manufacture of waste cotton products, jute materials, and worsted yarns and cloths. The Ewo mills were profitable in the late 1920s and early 1930s.[87] The mills benefited from Chinese tariffs and even flourished in the disturbed conditions of the 1930s. In the late 1930s the mills were reporting 'excellent' profits 'in the midst of the devastation throughout China'.[88]

Like the British companies in India, Jardine Matheson used domestic British firms as a source of recruitment and training for its mill staff. Jardines had a close long-term relationship with the Manchester textile firm Beith Stevenson which extended from 1898 through to the Second World War. Beith Stevenson purchased machinery for the mills on commission, and found staff and arranged training. However a proposal for Jardines to buy a share in Beiths in 1920 met opposition within the trading company and was not pursued.[89] Already by 1914 Jardines' investment in cotton mills was so substantial that plans were made to 'give a specialist training' to juniors joining Jardines 'who may, in the ordinary course of events, be expected to rise to senior positions'.[90]

As in the case of sugar refining, from the 1940s the pre-Second World War investments in cotton textiles were over time divested. Jardine Matheson lost its textile mills in Shanghai in 1949, and did not try to replace them. In India investments were retained longer. After Indian Independence, the Finlay management in Scotland grew steadily more alarmed about fiscal and political trends in India, but they retained their Bombay cotton mills and sought new strategies to develop the business. In the 1950s, in addition to diversifying into nylon tyre cord, Finlays formed a joint venture with the British manufacturer English Sewing Cotton to manufacture cotton sewing thread in India, replacing thread previously imported from Britain. In 1958 Finlays also opened their first retail shop in Bombay to sell cloth, and within six years they had shops in five Indian cities. Automatic looms were also slowly introduced, though even by the mid-1960s the mills were still using much older machines.[91] However by that date the cotton mills

[86] G. C. Allen and A. G. Donnithorne, *Western Enterprise in Far Eastern Economic Development* (London: George Allen & Unwin, 1954), 175–7.

[87] Memo by A. Brooke-Smith, 23 Feb. 1931, S/O London to Hong Kong, Jan.–June 1931, JMA, CUL.

[88] Ibid., A. B. Stewart to W. J. Keswick, 9 Dec. 1938, S/O London to Shanghai. The profit in 1937 was $4.5 million. In 1938 there was another good year with a 'handsome return' of a dividend of $3.59 per share, W. J. Keswick to D. G. M. Bernard, 24 Mar. 1933, S/O Shanghai to London 1939.

[89] Ibid., London to Hong Kong, 14 Oct. 1920, S/O London to Hong Kong, July–Dec. 1920; D. Londale to D. G. M. Bernard, 21 Apr. 1921, S/O London to Hong Kong, Jan.–June 1921.

[90] Ibid., Henry Keswick to D. Landale, 12 June 1914, S/O London to Hong Kong 1914.

[91] 'The Finlay Group of Mills in Bombay', *Finlays House Magazine*, 2/1 (Autumn 1964), Finlays Archives, UGD 91/377.

were running into difficulties caused by foreign exchange shortages which hindered cotton procurement outside India, as did Indian devaluation in 1966, and by strikes. Subsequently the Indian government's decision to end the managing agency system—Finlays continued to control the three mills with around 30 per cent of the equity and an agency contract—was the final straw and the companies shareholding was sold in 1968. At the same time Finlays finally closed its spinning and weaving business in Scotland.

Binny's remained one of India's largest textile manufacturers in the 1950s and early 1960s. The two mill companies employed over 23,000 workers at the end of the 1950s. In 1955 a power station was built to supply the electricity for the Buckingham and Carnatic Co. and in the same period Binny's started to sell its Indian-produced textiles in Britain.[92] In 1960 Binny's responded to the Indian government's policies against managing agents by taking over 50 per cent of the equity of the two mill companies, changing their status to subsidiaries.[93] However by the early 1960s machinery in the mills, mostly automatic looms installed in the 1920s, was out of date and in need of new equipment, which needed to be imported from abroad at great cost.[94] The cost of modernization combined with the deteriorating political environment led in 1969 to a reorganization which placed Binny's south Indian investments, including the two mill companies and its engineering company, into a new Binny Ltd., in which Inchcape held 42 per cent of the equity and Indians the remainder. Subsequently labour disputes and other factors resulted in heavy losses in the early 1970s. Inchcape decided not to divest at that stage, but finally did so in 1983.[95]

There was quite substantial new investment in textiles after the Second World War in West Africa. During the war UAC, a major importer of textiles into West Africa, had put forward to the colonial government a plan to establish a cotton mill in Nigeria. The British authorities, however were not enthusiastic, partly because they wanted to protect Nigeria's hand spinning industry, but mainly because import duties on textile imports were a main source of revenue. Consequently they proposed to levy an excise duty on locally produced cloth in order to compensate for lost revenue. UAC declined to proceed with the project as a result.[96] During the 1950s UAC again considered textile manufacture in Nigeria, but the project foundered when the colonial government declined to allow duty free import of the raw material—unbleached cloth—to be used in the venture.[97]

It was not until 1965 that UAC opened a textiles factory in Nigeria, by which time there was a large local production and growing excess capacity.

---

[92] Memo to Binny & Co., c.1959, Binny Archives, MS 27167, GHL.
[93] Ibid., Memo on South India: The Binny Group, 18 Jan. 1960.
[94] Ibid., Note on a Discussion of South Indian Affairs, 10 July 1963, MS 27164.
[95] Ibid., Notes on a Meeting held on 23 June 1971; Earl of Inchcape to N. S. Bhat, 5 Aug. 1971, MS 27165; Jones, *Two Centuries*, 290.
[96] Fieldhouse, *Merchant Capital*, 315–18.　　　　[97] Ibid. 395–8.

This venture was partly financed by the government, and also came to include a Dutch wax printing firm, Texoprint, later Gamma. UAC had held over 40 per cent of the shares of this firm since 1964, but it was a peculiar arms-length relationship, not emphasized in the Netherlands owing to Dutch sensitivity to 'foreign' control of their firms, and virtually secret in West Africa.[98] The factory was wrecked during the Nigerian civil war and in 1972 it was reconstructed as General Cotton Mills, owned by UAC, a Hong Kong Chinese textiles firm, and Nigerian investors. Localization took UAC's share down to 7 per cent by 1977, and thereafter it experienced growing problems with the collapse of the oil boom.

UAC's other Nigerian textiles venture never made a profit at all. Norspin, a cotton weaving and spinning company, initially involved UAC and two British manufacturers, English Sewing Cotton and Dunlop Rubber, and a Nigerian government agency. However the government did not make the expected reduction in duties on imported yarn, while English Sewing Cotton installed obsolete machinery. After many losses, a Hong Kong company took a shareholding, but it failed to turn the business round and it was liquidated in 1984. Throughout the venture was handicapped by inadequate technical management and demonstrated the limitations, in Fieldhouse's words, 'of an industrialising strategy which depended on technical partners rather than UAC's own skills'.[99]

UAC did, however, build a much more successful textiles business in the former French colony of Ivory Coast. In 1970 UAC opened a factory in Ivory Coast to print wax-block textiles, a venture which emerged out of the large West African trade in Dutch wax prints, itself a product of the old batik prints trade between the Netherlands and the Dutch East Indies which had passed by the West Coast of Africa. Uniwax originated as a venture to protect UAC and Gamma's market for wax prints in the country, potentially threatened by a proposal to create an integrated textile factory by a Japanese textile firm in alliance with the government. This developed as a profitable industrial venture based on Gamma's unique technology and specialized designs combined with the specialist market knowledge of UAC's French arm, Niger France. In 1976 UAC and Gamma controlled 70 per cent of wax print production in West Africa, with additional factories in Ghana and Nigeria, and in 1983 West African textiles contributed 29 per cent of UAC's total trading result.[100]

10.4 Joint Ventures

The use of joint ventures was an obvious strategy for trading companies to diversify into manufacturing. The traders could offer market access, local business, and political contacts, and also distribution facilities to manufacturers

---

[98] Ibid. 687–9.　　[99] Ibid. 512–20.　　[100] Ibid. 582–7.

seeking to undertake local production in their markets. A joint venture with a trading company served as an obvious means to reduce the information costs faced by manufacturers in new markets. The manufacturers could offer the technology and technical skills which the trading companies lacked. When Japanese trading companies in this period invested in manufacturing, they were able to take as partners manufacturing companies who were members of their *zaibatsu* in the interwar years, and *kigyo shudan* subsequently. In contrast, British manufacturers—the obvious candidate as partners for British trading companies—often sought to make direct investments themselves in larger markets. Moreover, the quite different organizational cultures between the trading companies and manufacturers compounded the problems of working together.

The interwar years, when the first joint ventures were made, already demonstrated both the problems of forming joint ventures and of maintaining them. In the former instance, a number of attempts at forming joint ventures with manufacturers were rebuffed. In Chile, Graham Rowe, Duncan Fox, and Antony Gibbs all tried to persuade Lever Brothers and later Unilever into a joint venture in soap manufacturing, but with no success.[101] In the early 1930s Jardine Matheson initially wanted to involve the British brewers McEwan Younger in a Chinese brewing venture, but they did not welcome the threat to their export business.[102] The brewing went ahead, but the beer produced was initially far from successful, partly because of the 'antiquated brewing practice' used.[103] In other instances the trading companies were more of a 'problem' than the manufacturers. The conservative Calcutta managing agency of Gillanders pulled out of a joint venture engineering firm with Armstrongs in 1919 because they thought they could not secure the kind of agency agreement they desired, which would allow them commission on output rather than profit. A similar proposal from another British engineering firm later in the 1920s was rejected for the same reason.[104]

Joint ventures which were formed had a tendency to run into difficulties. Jardine Matheson's investments in Chinese egg exports were in association with the firm of Goldrei Foucard under an agreement originally signed in 1916. This firm imported eggs into Britain from the rest of Europe and, especially, from Poland, and also sold the frozen and shell eggs of Jardine Matheson. In 1929 Goldrei Foucard was hit by a collapse in egg prices and Jardine Matheson agreed to finance the firm.[105] Matheson's in London

[101] Greenhill and Miller, 'British Trading Companies', 112.
[102] D. Beith to D. G. M. Bernard, 18 Aug. 1933, D. Beith to D. G. M. Bernard, 22 Sept. 1933, S/O London, Shanghai, Hong Kong, July–Nov. 1933, JMA, CUL.
[103] W. J. Keswick to D. Beith, 26 Oct. 1940, S/O Shanghai to London 1940, JMA, CUL.
[104] Misra, 'Entrepreneurial Decline', 57–8.
[105] D. G. M. Bernard to J. J. Paterson, 20 Oct. 1920, P&C Letters London to Hong Kong, Aug. 1929–Dec. 1930, JMA, CUL.

ended up committing large sums to the Foucard business—over £200,000 in 1934[106]—and through the 1930s there were bad feelings and distrust inside Jardines and between them and Foucard.[107]

Swire's began manufacturing paint in Shanghai in 1934 in a 50/50 joint venture with the British paint manufacturers Pinchin, Johnson & Co. The joint venture was based on the principle, as Swire's London office observed, 'that they will readily bow to us on all things Chinese and expect us to bow to them on technical matters'.[108] There was considerable synergy between the two partners, in that Swire's affiliates in shipping and other activities offered a large 'in-house' market for paint. In practice there were considerable initial problems getting the joint venture to work, especially because of organizational differences. 'One of the things that has struck me most', a member of the Swire family noted in 1936, 'is the tremendous difference between P.J.s system of organisation and our own'.[109] Swire's was a firm which put an especially heavy influence on socialization, and it was not surprising that it responded to the problems of integrating Pinchin, Johnson staff by encouraging them to take lunch every day with Swire staff.[110] After initial difficulties, this joint venture proved highly durable. Swire's recovered its paint factory after the end of the Pacific War, and moved it to Hong Kong. Over time its British partner became ICI and through to the 1990s Swire Paints remained one of the group's larger industrial investments.

In the post-war decades the trading companies continued to employ joint ventures when they diversified into manufacturing. Trading companies diversifying into engineering often employed a joint venture. A pioneer was Harrisons & Crosfield. Harrisons & Crosfield was an accomplished user of joint ventures to develop new business streams. Already in the interwar years it had developed a substantial business in tropical timber using the British Borneo Timber Company. The following section will document how in the late 1940s the firm also expanded into chemical manufacturing in Britain and other developed markets using a joint venture. In 1945 Harrisons & Crosfield also entered into joint venture to expand the engineering business which had developed in the interwar years in a small way out of its plantation interests.

Harrisons Lister Engineering was formed in 1946 as a 50/50 joint venture with the British firm of R. A. Lister & Co. Ltd. Both the choice of partner and the management of the joint venture help to explain the durability and relative success of this joint venture. Listers manufactured a range of diesel engines for use on plantations and elsewhere and from around 1920

[106] Ibid., D. G. M. Bernard to D. Beith, 13 Sept. 1934, P&C Letters London, Hong Kong, Shanghai 1935–7.

[107] Ibid., W. J. Keswick to D. G. M. Bernard, 13 Feb. 1936, S/O Shanghai to London 1936.

[108] J. Swire & Sons to Warren Swire, 15 May 1934, Swire ADD 16, SOAS.

[109] Ibid., John Swire to Jack Swire, 24 Apr. 1936, JSS I/3/9.

[110] Ibid., J. Scott to J. Swire & Sons, 21 Apr. 1936, JSSI/3/9.

Harrisons & Crosfield had acted as sales and service agents in Ceylon, Malaya, and North Borneo for the firm. The joint venture was initiated by Harrisons & Crosfield and reflected the belief that a more robust form of business organization was preferable to the relationship of principal and agent. In particular there was a recognition that Harrisons & Crosfield lacked the engineering expertise to provide a competitive selling and after sales service.[111]

The new subsidiary was initially almost entirely integrated into the Harrisons & Crosfield organization. It shared Harrisons & Crosfield's head office in London. The trading company was appointed secretary and given responsibility for all the London administration. Harrisons & Crosfield's export department bought supplies for Harrisons Lister in Asia and provided shipping and financial services, for which they received commission. Harrisons Lister branches were effectively administered as branches of the company. Not surprisingly the new company had problems establishing its own identity in such circumstances, and there were serious culture clash problems between traders and engineers.[112]

During the 1950s and 1960s Harrisons Lister established a more discrete identity. Its branches in Colombo and Kuala Lumpur gained agencies for firms other than Listers, not only mechanical but also electrical engineering firms, although selling Lister equipment remained the largest single source of income through the 1950s and 1960s. In Malaya the most important agency was that of the large British electrical firm English Electric. This business included refrigerators, but was mainly concerned with large government contracts for power generation equipment. English Electric came to play a role in the recruitment and training of engineers to provide after sales service.

After Malaysian independence Harrisons Lister, which had also acquired Whyte & Co. (owned by James Whyte who joined the board), diversified further in engineering, encompassing sales not only of tin mining and logging plant, but also of equipment for the armed forces and lifts for office blocks. The less profitable branch in Sri Lanka saw among other activities the development of a yard for ship repair work and fishing boat construction. The joint venture survived the acquisition of Listers by the Hawker Siddeley group in 1965 and an amicable relationship continued between the two operators, which alternated in providing the chairman of the affiliate. By around 1969 local manufacture of mining equipment had begun in Malaysia under Harrisons Lister. In 1972 it started local manufacture of diesel engines in Malaysia through a new Malaysian-registered company which was a joint venture undertaken with local shareholders. Throughout the 1970s

---

[111] Correspondence files, Harrisons Lister Engineering (HLE) London and R. A. Lister & Co. Ltd., Harrisons & Crosfield Archives, GHL.

[112] Report of 1 Dec. 1950 by Frank Blackstone to the directors of HLE and Listers, Correspondence File, HLE Colombo and HLE department London, July 1950 to Dec. 1952 Harrisons & Crosfield Archives, GHL.

it continued to engage in manufacturing in both Malaysia and Sri Lanka, expanding in the middle of the decade into production in a Malaysian-registered company of fuses used in electric power distribution. During the early 1970s trading activities had also increased, generating significant profits which could be used in manufacturing ventures. In 1982 Harrisons & Crosfield finally took full control of the venture.[113]

During the 1960s other trading companies investing in engineering also made joint ventures with manufacturing firms. Booker McConnell formed a number of joint ventures in engineering in the 1960s including a firm making sugar machinery and turbines in India in a joint venture with an Indian group, and the manufacture of central heating equipment and electronic components in Britain with British and US manufacturers respectively. In India, Binny's formed a 60/40 joint venture with the Swiss company of Giovanda Freres to manufacture 'penstock' equipment used in hydroelectric plants. This came after a search for a collaborator, 'either British, American, Indian or even possibly of other nationality', who could reinvigorate Binny's under-capitalized and unsuccessful engineering affiliate by launching a new manufacturing activity.[114] However by 1972 relations between the Swiss and Binny's had reached a very low point, with the former complaining bitterly of 'bad planning, operational inefficiency . . . and lack of decision-making' on the part of the Binny management.[115]

By the 1960s some trading companies were also entering joint ventures with powerful local business groups. Finlays—for example—formed a joint venture with India's Tata group to develop packaging of tea and the manufacture and sale of instant tea. This was a difficult technology involving freeze-drying from green leaf which Finlays began to develop in the mid-1950s, but it took a long time to perfect, as did the marketing strategy for the initial target market of the United States, and as a result the joint venture was initially loss-making.[116] Just as the instant tea business seemed to be coming right, Finlays took the decision to divest from its Indian tea plantations by selling them to its joint venture, in which Finlays initially retained a 20 per cent shareholding. In 1981 Finlays disposed of its shareholding in Tata-Finlay, even though Tatas wished them to continue their association.[117]

The British trading companies in West Africa also employed joint ventures when they began to develop manufacturing schemes in the 1940s and 1950s. Holts entered a number of joint venture manufacturing projects,[118] and UAC also sought joint venture partners. UAC was in a curious position

[113] Harrisons & Crosfield annual reports; Harrisons & Crosfield branches department, London, files on HLE, Harrisons & Crosfield Archives, GHL.

[114] BEW, Note on the Discussion held in London on 14 Jan. 1964, Binny Archives, MS 27164, GHL.

[115] Ibid., Lord Inchcape to N. S. Bhat, 25 May 1972.

[116] Annual Report, James Finlay & Co. Ltd., 1974.

[117] Interview with Sir Colin Campbell, 16 Apr. 1996.

[118] Annual Reports, John Holt & Co. (Liverpool) Ltd., 1950–70.

of being wholly owned by one of the world's leading consumer goods manufacturers, but because of the internal organizational arrangements of the firm it was virtually excluded from Unilever's industrial activities. On occasion UAC drew on Unilever expertise—for example a venture into Nigerian pig farming in the 1970s was assisted by staff from Unilever's Walls division, which manufactured sausages—but in general there was little contact between the trading company and its parent.[119] Consequently UAC was as much in need of manufacturing expertise as any other of the British trading companies. In some ways the firm was disadvantaged because the same internal organizational arrangements ruled out joint ventures between UAC and the core Unilever manufacturing concern.

UAC's most successful joint ventures were in brewing. In 1945 UAC approached the Dutch brewer Heineken about a project to establish a brewery in Nigeria. UAC undertook this venture in response to a perceived threat to its markets by another company which was about to start production there. Heineken was a major supplier of the beer which UAC exported to West Africa. UAC and Heineken took one-third of the equity each of Nigerian Breweries Ltd. with the remainder going to other beer-importing companies as compensation for loss of business. Production started in 1949 and the main product became an established market leader. Two additional breweries were built in 1957 and 1963.[120] Meanwhile in 1958 UAC and Heineken built a brewery in Ghana.[121]

In 1961 UAC also entered a joint venture with the British brewing firm of Guinness to brew Guinness stout. In the post-war period Nigeria had become Guinness's largest overseas market, the firm selling the products of its British and Irish breweries through UAC. However the firm had no experience of manufacturing in foreign countries and no direct knowledge of the West African market. Eventually Guinness decided to build its first brewery outside the British Isles in Nigeria in association with UAC. The shareholding in Guinness (Nigeria) Ltd. was Guinness 57.4 per cent and UAC 32.6 per cent, and Nigerian local government the remainder. By the mid-1960s this venture was also a considerable success as Guinness stout gained a reputation in Nigeria for enhancing virility and for curing various diseases. By 1970 the brewery had a capacity of 750 hectolitres. In 1975 UAC opened a joint venture brewery in Ghana also.[122] Fieldhouse calculates that in 1972/3 Nigerian Breweries had a pre-tax ROCE of 41.6 per cent and Guinness (Nigeria) Ltd. of 50 per cent.[123] These figures are almost certainly not comparable to the pre-tax ROCE calculations in this book, but in terms of order of magnitude they give a fair impression of the financial success of the joint ventures, at least until the introduction of price controls in Nigeria and elsewhere in the late 1970s.

---

[119] Fieldhouse, *Merchant Capital*, 539–43.   [120] Ibid. 384–5.
[121] Ibid. 403–4.   [122] Ibid. 558–9.   [123] Ibid. 511.

The financially successful joint venture strategy in brewing, however, had drawbacks. UAC contributed market knowledge, and marketing and commercial management to the joint ventures, but remained dependent on Heineken and Guinness for their technical expertise, and as a result it was dependent on their strategies concerning investment locations. In the mid-1960s Heineken proposed and UAC agreed to a badly planned project to brew beer in Burgos, Spain. This operation was undertaken entirely separately from Unilever's Spanish organization, and by the time it was sold in 1968 UAC/Unilever were estimated to have lost £900,000.[124]

The wider problem was that UAC's two brewing partners did not need UAC's skills outside West Africa. By the late 1960s Heineken was declining to enter into new projects with UAC.[125] Guinness was slightly more flexible—at one stage it sought to entice UAC into a joint venture in Brazil—but effectively UAC remained in a strategic straight-jacket. The possibility of acquiring their own brewer was considered, but rejected, and through the 1980s UAC attempts to extend their relationships to other countries met no response. By then the brewing companies had themselves acquired considerable knowledge of West Africa themselves and had begun to question the value of UAC's contribution.

While Heineken and Guinness were, in technical terms at least, very satisfactory joint venture partners for UAC, some of their other manufacturing partners proved less than ideal, at least in West Africa. UAC's problems with its British partner in the textile company Norspin were discussed earlier. There were other problems of this nature. In 1963 UAC agreed to a joint venture with its long-standing supplier of 'crocodile matchets' to start local manufacture in Nigeria. However the venture was on too small a scale, there was insufficient tariff protection, and UAC's British partner persisted in importing matchets, leaving the local factory with little work.[126] In other cases UAC could not persuade partners to enter ventures they considered would be successful. In the 1960s UAC tried to persuade Wander, the Swiss manufacturer of the hot milk drink Ovaltine, to enter a joint venture to manufacture in Nigeria, but terms could not be agreed.[127]

A final point is that in considering UAC's problems with joint ventures it is important to remember that its Unilever parent—like most large Britain and US multinational manufacturers—had little desire to enter into, or expertise in managing, joint ventures at least until the 1970s. Within the Unilever organization, UAC was regarded as possessing considerable competences in this area. The main problem was that UAC's key contribution to such joint ventures—market access and knowledge—was both vulnerable to manufacturers' accumulating such information themselves, and locked the firm into a region whose locational advantages were in decline.

---

[124] Ibid. 694–700.   [125] Ibid. 510–11.   [126] Ibid. 527–9.   [127] Ibid. 540–1.

10.5 Developed Markets

From the late 1940s the trading companies began to invest in manufacturing in developed markets, largely in the British Commonwealth until the end of the 1970s. In quite a number of cases firms sought to manufacture in new markets products in which they already had expertise, but in other cases their investments took the form of unrelated diversifications. In such instances firms had to learn about new processes and new markets, and the results were usually especially unsuccessful. Table 10.4 lists some of the principal investments and activities in developed Commonwealth markets between the late 1940s and the 1970s.

The flurry of small investments in manufacturing in Canada in the decade after 1945 made little lasting impact. Most of the investments were made by acquisition and often these did not work out well, leading to divestments within a few years. This was the fate of the Borneo Company's attempts to transfer its brick-making expertise in Singapore to Canada. This was done through the purchase of a firm in Alberta and was motivated in part by a belief that bricks would be 'required in very large quantities by the Alberta Government for their defence plans'.[128] The venture did not flourish—and was sold in 1957. The Borneo Company persisted in Canada with the purchase of concrete block and oil tool companies, but these and other acquisitions by British trading companies also ran into difficulties.[129] Guthries' acquisition in 1975 of a US manufacturer of induction heating and melting equipment—Ajax—with manufacturing operations also in Canada and Britain was partial exception, and this proved a successful venture which was initially retained by the new Malaysian management of Guthries in the 1980s.

In contrast to Canada, the British traders made only limited manufacturing investments in Australia. Harrisons & Crosfield made its first venture into manufacturing in Australia in 1947 when it established a zinc oxide plant, the outcome of the firm's joint venture with a British chemicals company. The plant was soon closed, and there were no further manufacturing investments until 1957, when a joint venture was formed with Pyrene (UK) to manufacture fire extinguishers, which arose out of a sales agency which Harrisons & Crosfield had held for Pyrene since the late 1920s. This was sold in 1969. A sheet manufacturer was acquired in 1970, but the firm retreated from textiles in Australia in the late 1970s. At the end of the 1970s the firm's timber interests led to the establishment of a timber processing operation in Queensland, though this was ended three years later, and in the 1980s Harrisons & Crosfield began to develop chemicals manufacturing in Australia. Among the other investors in Australia, Jardine Matheson

---

[128] Board Minutes, 5 Dec. 1951, Borneo Company Archives, MS 27178/24, GHL.

[129] H. E. W. Braund, *Calling to Mind* (Oxford: Pergamon Press, 1975), 103; Anglo-Thai Board Minutes, 25 Feb. 1964, 7 Apr. 1964, 19 May 1964, 19 Jan. 1965, 21 Apr. 1965, 17 May 1965, Anglo-Thai Archives, MS 27008/13, GHL.

TABLE 10.4 Trading company investments in manufacturing in Canada, Australia, and Britain, 1946–1970s

Firm	Date	Activities	Fate by 1980s
Canada			
Harrisons & Crosfield	1946	Zinc oxide manufacture	Sold before 1960
	1951	Fine chemicals	Sold 1960
Borneo Company	1952	Brick making	Sold 1957
	1955	Concrete blocks	Acquired by Inchcape
	1958	Oil tools	Sold
Steel Brothers	1952	Lime kilns	
	1954	Building blocks	Sold 1967
Anglo-Thai	1954	Cold roll manufacture	
Guthries	1972	Light engineering	Sold post-1986
	1972	Carpets	Sold early 1980s
	1975	Induction heating	Sold post-1986
Australia			
Harrisons & Crosfield	1947	Zinc oxide	Closed early 1950s
	1957	Fire extinguishers	Sold 1969
	1970	Sheets	Sold by 1982
	1979	Timber processing	Sold 1982
Borneo Company	1961	Sawmills	
Antony Gibbs	c.1960	Timber mouldings	Sold early 1980s
Jardine Matheson	1968	Textile machinery	Sold 1978
	c.1970	Sugar harvesting machinery	Sold 1979
Guthries	1970	Carpets/towels	Sold 1988
United Kingdom			
James Finlay	pre-1946	Textile mills	Closed 1971
	pre-1946	Confectionery	Sold 1998
	1965	Whisky distillers	Closed 1972
Harrisons & Crosfield	pre-1946	'Linatex' rubber	Continued
	1950s	Chemicals	Continued
	1960	Glass manufacture	Sold 1982
	1973	Chrome chemicals	Continued
Balfour Williamson	pre-1946	Oil refining	Sold 1962
Dodwells	1946	Hot water bottles	Liquidated 1949
Steels	1956	Glass	
Duncan Fox	1959	Light engineering	Sold 1973
Booker McConnell	1960	Engineering	Sold early 1980s
	1970	Health foods	Continued
Guthries	1966	Rubber/carpets	Sold early 1980s
	1973	Vacuum forming of plastics	Sold post-1986
John Holt	1968	'British wine'	Sold 1984
Lonrho	1970s	Engineering	Sold early 1990s
	1970s	Textiles	Sold early 1990s
UAC	1964	Office copying machines	Closed 1967
	1976	Automobile body building	Sold 1986
	1973	Pharmaceuticals	Closed 1982

acquired a textile manufacturer in Victoria in the 1960s followed by a manufacturer of sugar harvesting equipment. Both were sold at the end of the
decade, the latter described as 'loss-making'.[130]

Before 1945 Finlays provided a rare case of a firm with a manufacturing
presence in Britain. Finlays' Deanston Mill remained active until 1965,
when it was converted to a whisky distillery, while the Catrine Mill only
closed in 1972. The distillery was subsequently abandoned after making losses.
In addition, its George Payne affiliate, originally tea blenders and later pack-
agers of tea and coffee, which began manufacturing confectionery near London
in 1921, continued in operation throughout the post-war decades. The other
noteworthy pre-war investments were the oil refining operation of Lobitos
Oil, managed by Balfour Williamson before its sale to Burmah Oil in 1962,
and Harrisons & Crosfield, which incorporated Linatex into manufactured
products near London from the late 1930s.

After 1945 various companies made small investments in manufacturing
which were not sustained. Dodwells' venture into hot water bottles arose
from the financial problems of the supplier with whom it had placed an
order for 250,000 such items. Dodwells ended up owning the company,
but there were endless problems with the factory and the product.[131] Many
subsequent investments in Britain were equally problematic. In 1959 Duncan
Fox acquired a British company engaged in printing on metal, Reginald
Corfield Ltd. This and a further purchase of a light engineering company
became a serious source of losses and was sold in 1971.[132] Among other investments in Britain were Guthries' initial investments in Scottish carpets,
which incurred heavy losses in the late 1960s, partly because the company
which was acquired was almost moribund and had to be re-equipped.
After some recovery, Guthries' carpet division encountered major problems
in the mid-1970s as its focus on woven carpets rendered its products too
expensive compared to the competing 'tufted' carpets.[133]

UAC also made some investments in British manufacturing from the
1960s as part of its strategy of 'redeployment' of some of its capital and skills
outside Africa. In 1964 UAC invested in a firm intended to develop and
market a new type of office copying machine. The inventor had originally
approached Unilever, who referred the project to UAC, because it was
looking for business to develop in Britain and because it marketed office
equipment overseas. The product, however, needed further development
and UAC lacked any technical skills, and in 1967 the project was ended with
heavy losses.[134] From the basis of its motor distribution business in West

---

[130] Annual Report, Jardine Matheson & Co. Ltd., 1979.
[131] Board Minutes, 1 Sept. 1948, 14 Dec. 1948, Dodwell Archives, MS 27498/6, GHL.
[132] Annual Reports, Duncan Fox Ltd., 1959–71.
[133] Chairman's Statement of 1974, Guthrie Corporation.
[134] Fieldhouse, *Merchant Capital*, 690–4. UAC's losses totalled £400,000 and Unilever's
£150,000.

Africa, UAC tried to develop a motor business in Britain, but one focused on body-building and motor parts rather than distribution and service. Between 1976 and 1980 UAC purchased a number of small body-building and component manufacturers. These were badly affected by the problems of the British motor industry in the 1979–82 recession and sold at a loss in the mid-1980s. UAC's ventures into British manufacturing suffered from the same defects of its diversification strategy in general. By acquiring multiple small companies in a variety of industrial activities, it compounded the management tasks while failing to achieve any scale. In British manufacturing, UAC lacked any technical skills to add to the companies it bought.[135]

Harrisons & Crosfield and Booker McConnell made successful ventures into manufacturing in Britain. The former was noteworthy for its incremental and path-dependent diversification into chemicals manufacture. Harrisons & Crosfield's first involvement in chemicals came in Canada in the 1930s when the firm's branches began to import various commodities indigenous to Asia which were used to manufacture chemicals. This led after 1935 to a number of acquisitions of Canadian chemical distribution firms.[136] In 1951 Harrisons & Crosfield's Dillon's subsidiary invested in a small Canadian pharmaceutical manufacturer, Fine Chemicals of Canada Ltd., and by 1954 it had joint control of this firm together with the British chemicals manufacturer Fisons. However there were constant tensions between Harrisons & Crosfield and Fisons and in 1961 the two British companies sold their shares.[137]

In the late 1940s Harrisons & Crosfield entered the chemicals business in Britain by forming a joint venture called Durham Raw Materials with Durham Chemicals. One of Durham Chemicals' main products was zinc oxide, used as a paint pigment but also as an accelerator in the curing of rubber, especially synthetic rubber. This investment enabled Harrisons & Crosfield to extend its involvement in the rubber business in Britain, and to become involved in synthetic as well as natural rubber,[138] and in the late 1940s and early 1950s Harrisons & Crosfield and Durham Chemicals attempted unsuccessfully to manufacture this product in both Canada and Australia. In Britain the joint venture was concerned with distribution, selling in Britain and overseas the products of Durham Chemicals, and imported chemical products in Britain. Over time and slowly Harrisons & Crosfield built up a shareholding in Durham Chemicals itself, and in 1967 the shareholding was increased to 90 per cent. In 1971 a Dutch chemicals company was purchased, followed in 1973 by the purchase of a British manufacturer of

[135] Ibid. 743, 758–61.   [136] Jones and Wale, 'Diversification Strategies'.
[137] Memo on the Harrisons & Crosfield Organization in Canada by H. J. Williams, Oct. 1961, Harrisons & Crosfield Archives, GHL.
[138] G. Nickalls, *Great Enterprise: A History of Harrisons & Crosfield* (London: the firm, 1990), 152–4.

chrome chemicals for use in jet engines.[139] Harrisons & Crosfield made
its large investments in chemicals manufacture just as the industry entered
a major downturn in the 1970s, but the firm persisted in the industry,
emerging as the largest producer of chrome chemicals in the world.

Another ultimately successful UK manufacturing enterprise on the part
of Harrisons & Crosfield was the Wilkinson Rubber Linatex company, a
wholly owned subsidiary. Though first of significance during the early years
of the Second World War, it did not re-establish profitability until the
mid-1950s. The rubber-based product Linatex, manufactured from latex in
Malaysia, came eventually to be incorporated into a widening range of products, notably pumps. Manufacture was gradually extended from the UK to
a number of locations worldwide during the 1970s. Overseas manufacture
was often undertaken initially by concessionnaires who had received training from WRL in the UK, but the plants of the important concessionnaires
in the USA and Canada became wholly owned subsidiaries of Harrisons &
Crosfield in the early 1980s. Products incorporating Linatex remained
important to Harrisons & Crosfield in the 1990s.[140]

Booker McConnell also established a viable manufacturing business
in Britain from the 1960s, initially building on expertise from its sugar
plantation and other businesses in British Guinea. It began by acquiring
engineering firms making pumps and subsequently acquired firms making
sugar machinery, hydraulic mining equipment, and domestic and industrial
central heating equipment. On a smaller scale, in 1970 Bookers bought
a health food manufacturer, as well as a retail chemist and a supermarket
chain, and over the next decade acquisitions were made in health food and
pharmaceuticals.

Also striking was the 'reinvention'of Dalgety from an Australian-centred
wood and refrigerated food merchant in the 1960s to an agricultural and
food manufacturer and distributor in Britain and North America two
decades later. During the late 1960s Dalgety began acquiring British feed
companies, followed in 1972 by that country's largest malting firm, while
in 1979 Spillers, one of Britain's largest flour milling and grocery companies, was acquired. The following decade saw the firm acquire a series
of potato chip, frozen pizza, and other snack food manufacturers.

The British traders showed little interest in the United States as a
location for manufacturing until the mid-1970s. An early investor at that
stage was the Guthrie Corporation. In 1974 its Canadian affiliate made the
group's first US takeover when it acquired an Ohio manufacturer of water
treatment equipment, and this was followed by acquisitions of several
other US engineering firms. In 1978 Bookers made its first significant

---

[139] Details sent to shareholders of the acquisition of the chrome chemicals business of
Albright & Wilson Ltd., 31 Oct. 1973, Harrisons & Crosfield Archives, GHL.
[140] Files on Wilkinson Rubber Linatex. Harrisons & Crosfield Annual Reports, Harrisons
& Crosfield Archives, GHL.

investment in US manufacturers when it acquired one-third of the equity of a Chicago-based mining engineering company, and much larger investments in US agribusiness followed. In 1979 Harrisons & Crosfield acquired its first US chrome chemicals manufacturer. In the same year Dalgety purchased Martin-Brower, a large distributor of fast food and supplier to McDonald's restaurants in the United States and Canada. Finally between 1977 and 1981 UAC attempted to buy a US manufacturing company to produce the laboratory equipment which it had developed, but no suitable candidate could be found.[141]

The interest in investing in the United States in the late 1970s was part of a much wider trend in British business, which saw many companies acquire US businesses, often with disappointing outcomes. The key challenges were to invest in businesses in which the British firm had real competences, and to identify the right acquisition target or US partner, which many firms found difficult.[142] In this context the strategy of Swire's in the United States was instructive. In 1978 Swire's invested in a Coca-Cola bottling company in Salt Lake City. This was a business in which the firm had built up knowledge and expertise since it had entered the industry in 1965 in Hong Kong. Coca-Cola encouraged Swire's to invest in the United States, while Swire's chose as their first US partner a firm owned by Mormons, who they considered possessed the characteristics of stability and honesty lacking in parts of American business.[143] The upshot was a successful entry strategy which laid the basis for Swire's to become one of the leading US Coca-Cola bottlers by the 1990s.

10.6 Merchants and Manufacturing

The creation and ownership of large manufacturing complexes was not the main concern of British trading companies. Nevertheless the search for profitable opportunities and the exploitation of scope economies led the trading companies in the late nineteenth century into investments in manufacturing jute and cotton textiles, and processing raw materials. The traders counted among the pioneer industrial enterprises in their host economies at that time. However for the most part they remained merchants in orientation, more interested in commission than dividends. During the interwar years the trading companies were more cautious towards manufacturing, apart from the surge of investments after the end of the First World War. After 1945 the new political and economic conditions in Asia and Latin America led to the loss of many earlier manufacturing investments. There were new manufacturing ventures especially but not only in West Africa, but by

[141] Fieldhouse, *Merchant Capital*, 747–8.
[142] Interview with Sir Colin Campbell, 16 Apr. 1996.
[143] Interview with Sir John and Sir Adrian Swire, 30 July 1996.

the 1960s the momentum had come to a standstill. Instead, many traders attempted to establish a manufacturing presence in the United Kingdom, Canada, or Australia, and from the mid-1970s the United States.

It has been the deficiencies rather than the achievements of these manufacturing investments which have tended to be stressed. The conservatism of many of the Calcutta agency houses in the interwar years which resulted in their being replaced by local firms in the jute industry and failing to take advantage of import substitution opportunities in India stands out. From the interwar years onwards too a common theme in many regions was a reluctance of the British firms to invest in new equipment and plant, initially because of financial difficulties, and from the 1950s because of perceived political and other risks. Yet the British trading companies also built and controlled over successive generations substantial manufacturing businesses, in sugar refining, textiles, flour milling, and breweries. All these businesses required considerable organizational, technical, and marketing skills.

The general competences of the trading companies lay in knowledge and information about their regions, in the commercial skills of their staff, and in the robustness of their organizational forms. However their senior managements had sufficient knowledge and competence to preside over manufacturing businesses also. The business group system enabled the recruitment of more specialist and technically qualified staff for affiliates. There was more of a problem after 1945 when the trading companies sought to enter new industries often in joint ventures with manufacturing firms. The trading companies encountered problems identifying suitable partners, or making the joint ventures work, while market access was a dwindling asset. The trading companies were rarely able to acquire or learn key technologies from their joint ventures, and consequently could not evolve independent strategies.

The limitations on the manufacturing capabilities of the traders became evident in their strategies to invest in manufacturing in developed markets as they sought to diversify from their developing host economies. A number of the larger firms learned painful lessons that skills in their traditional host regions were not easily transferable elsewhere. Too many firms acquired small companies in industries about which they knew little. Consequently, many of the investments 'failed' or else proved very time consuming, and many were unwound subsequently. In general, related and path-dependent diversification strategies had the most positive outcomes.

II

End Game

11.1 Introduction

The trading companies founded in the nineteenth century, together with their more recent emulators such as Lonrho, remained important elements of British multinational enterprise at the beginning of the 1980s. The surviving firms were substantial in terms of capital employed and employment, and they were significant in their regional context. UAC in West Africa, Lonrho in Central and East Africa, Harrisons & Crosfield and Guthries in South East Asia, Jardine Matheson and Swire's in Hong Kong and other Asia Pacific countries were among the largest firms in their regions.

The external environment faced by these firms showed a marked improvement over recent decades. From the interwar years they had faced increasingly hostile conditions as restrictions on trade and capital flows, state intervention in the marketing of commodities, and legislation against foreign ownership of resources and services had restricted or eliminated their businesses in developing countries. During the 1980s many of these policies were reversed. The governments of developing countries switched from restricting to attracting foreign multinationals. Foreign ownership of resources and services again became possible. The huge economies of China and, after 1989, Russia were again opened for foreign direct investment. In some respects at least, the 'global' economy which had prevailed in the decades before the 1920s and in which the trading companies had flourished was restored in the last two decades of the twentieth century.

It therefore represents a paradox that it was precisely these decades which witnessed the demise of most of the remaining British trading companies. Guthries became a Malaysian-owned company in the early 1980s. UAC disappeared altogether after having been merged into its Unilever parent in 1987. Ocean Wilsons became a Bermuda-registered firm in 1992, though continuing in business thereafter as a supplier of maritime services in Brazil and an international portfolio investor. Other firms had 'reinvented' themselves and were no longer trading companies. Booker McConnell had become a food distributor by the end of the 1980s. Harrisons & Crosfield—renamed Elementis in 1997—became a speciality chemicals group. Yule Catto acquired Revertex Chemicals in 1980 and thereafter evolved as a speciality chemicals and building products manufacturer. Boustead became a speciality engineering manufacturer. This was also the strategy of Mitchell Cotts. In the early 1980s it still operated a diversified trading, transport, consulting,

TABLE 11.1 Net capital employed of British
trading companies, 1997 (£ million)

John Swire & Sons	8,262
Jardine Matheson	4,291
Inchcape	923
Lonrho Africa[a]	182
James Finlay	132

[a] In 1997 Lonrho Africa was still part of Lonrho,
which had a total net capital employed of £1,185
million in that year.

and plantations business in Africa, but almost three-quarters of pre-tax profits
came from engineering, mostly in Britain. In 1987 the firm was acquired by
the British industrial conglomerate Suter, itself acquired nine years later.

Lonrho and Inchcape, which employed nearly 190,000 and 50,000 persons respectively in the mid-1990s, broke themselves up. In 1998 Lonrho
demerged its African trading business into a separate company, Lonrho
Africa, sold off other assets, and became a mining company renamed
Lonmia. In the same year Inchcape began disposing of its general trading
and all other businesses and by the following year had become a focused international motor distributor. By 1998 Lonrho Africa and Inchcape employed
25,000 and 12,000 persons respectively.

By the end of the twentieth century, therefore, there were few British
survivors of this genre of international business. Table 11.1 gives the net
capital employed of the remaining firms in 1997. UAC and Guthries had
wholly disappeared. Booker McConnell was still in existence but not as a
trading company. It was acquired by the retailer Iceland in 2000. Inchcape
was about to break itself up, while Lonrho Africa was about to be divested
from Lonrho. James Finlay, 30 per cent owned by Swire's, continued in
independent existence as a tea trader and plantations company, having shed
almost all of its non-tea interests. The two really substantial survivors from
the nineteenth century to enter the twenty-first century were John Swire &
Sons and Jardine Matheson. At the beginning of the new century these groups
employed 120,000 and 170,000 persons respectively.

11.2 From Diversity to Focus

For much of the twentieth century a striking feature of the British trading
companies was their durability and their ability to survive external shocks,
such as world wars, depressions, and the end of empire. They were rarely
found at the frontiers of innovation, and in some times and places they were
notably conservative, but their ability to manage diverse and risky businesses

was considerable. During the 1980s and 1990s, however, there appeared a number of challenges to these firms.

The first challenge arose from further changes in the economic and political environment of important host economies. The trading companies, as regional specialists, were always vulnerable to adverse changes in their host economies. In the post-war period the demise of most British traders in Latin America and South Asia reflected the difficult economic, fiscal, and political environment faced by all foreign firms—especially ones involved in services and resources—in those areas. It has been suggested earlier that the decline of the British merchants in these regions was not necessarily 'inevitable', but reflected in part their inability or unwillingness to adjust to new conditions. Certainly Inchcape's history demonstrated that it was possible to 'escape' to a more hospitable environment given the resources of capital and management ability. However Inchcape was fortunate that it was able to shift sideways from South to South East and East Asia rather than across whole continents, and that a number of leading British firms in those regions were available for merger or acquisition.

The new policy environment of the 1980s appeared to offer new opportunities for the trading companies, as countries reopened their borders to foreign multinationals. In Latin America, Inchcape built on the Balfour Williamson inheritance to expand its trading and automobile distribution activities, and to invest in bottling. A director of Inchcape joined the board of Ocean Wilsons in 1981 and the two firms had a number of joint ventures until 1986. Swire's and Jardine Matheson resumed their historic role as direct investors in China, starting dozens of joint ventures in that country in the 1980s. In the early 1990s Inchcape and Lonrho began investing in Russia.

However there were specific problems for the British trading companies. Booker McConnell's withdrawal from trading stemmed from the earlier age of governmental hostility to foreign companies. During the 1970s Booker McConnell had encountered the same problems in its Caribbean host region that had previously adversely affected British trading companies elsewhere. As late as 1970 this firm's chairman emphasized that the firm's 'main overseas operations will still be concentrated in the Commonwealth, particularly in the Caribbean and in Africa, where our long experience has given us a fund of special knowledge'.[1] However the nationalization of the group's core business in Guyana in 1976 shattered this strategy. Like Inchcape, Booker McConnell was able to 'escape' from its past heritage. By 1982 the firm had decisively shifted its business from the developing world to the United Kingdom and North America. It had greatly reduced its agricultural business, sold all its former overseas trading interests, and the long-established Booker Line sailing between Britain and the Caribbean.[2]

[1] Annual Report, Booker McConnell, 1970.
[2] Annual Report, Booker McConnell, 1982.

TABLE 11.2 Post-tax return on net capital employed of selected British trading companies by decade, 1980–1998 (%)

	Swire's	Jardine Matheson	H&C	Finlays	Ocean Wilson	UAC	Booker	Inchcape	Lonrho	Average
1980–9	12.7	10.0	10.2	7 4	14 7	9.8[b]	21.3	12.9	9.2	12.2
1990–8	8.8	10.4	11 7[a]	4.8				6.7[c]	8.4[d]	8.3

[a] 1990–6 only.
[b] 1980–3 only.
[c] The ROCE for 1990–97 was 14.0.
[d] 1990–7 only

By the end of the 1980s 90 per cent of the firm's pre-tax profits originated from Britain and the United States, though a residual business continued in selling some West Indian sugar crops and in agricultural consultancy.[3]

Table 11.2 demonstrates the comparative success of Booker's strategy as measured by post-tax ROCE in the 1980s.

Booker emerges as by far the most profitable of the trading companies in the 1980s. Ocean Wilson, Swire's, and Inchcape were the better performers of the remaining firms. The decadal averages, however, underplay the achievements of certain firms. Inchcape's post-tax ROCE, for example, was in excess of 26 per cent in 1988 and 1989. In comparison, BP's post-tax ROCE was 12.1 per cent and Unilever's 10.7 per cent between 1980 and 1989. The figures for the following decade are heavily influenced by exceptional events, such as Inchcape's large loss in 1998 through restructuring costs, and—more generally—the negative impact of the Asian financial crisis in 1997 and 1998.

The situation faced by the large British trading companies in sub-Saharan Africa was different again. As elsewhere, by the 1980s many governments began to slowly dismantle the bureaucratic controls and anti-foreign restrictions which had spread over the continent. However the economic conditions of most countries deteriorated. Sub-Saharan Africa did not experience the 'economic miracles' seen in South East Asia or parts of Latin America, and instead real incomes declined in many countries. Exchange controls, shortages of foreign currencies, widespread corruption, and deteriorating economic conditions became the main threats to foreign firms rather than nationalization.

The deteriorating economic and political conditions in West Africa undermined UAC's position as an independent entity within Unilever. The Nigerian oil boom of the 1970s had been a remarkable period for UAC, enabling it to contribute upwards of one-third of Unilever's total profits despite the dilution of its shareholding through local equity participation. However in 1978 Nigeria—which accounted for almost three-fifths of

[3] Annual Report, Booker McConnell, 1989.

UAC's total turnover—entered a major recession. A brief recovery in 1980 was followed by a further downturn which continued for the rest of the decade. UAC's other significant host region was the Gulf, where its business was also not without risks, given that around one-third profits came from sales of alcohol.

In 1984 Unilever ordered a major review of the UAC because of its enormous dependence on Nigeria. The issue was especially sensitive because Unilever itself had other substantial investments in sub-Saharan Africa, especially Nigeria. In the mid-1980s Nigeria was Unilever's third largest market outside Europe and the United States in terms of sales after India and Australia. Unilever's review of UAC supported the firm's continued existence, but with a resolute strategy to focus on 'core activities'. However the Nigerian devaluation of 1985/6, which drastically reduced the sterling value of profits made in that country, further highlighted the political and economic risks of Nigeria, and the need to reduce UAC's large head office. This led to the decision to end the independent existence of UAC and, in effect, to dispose of many of its assets.[4] Employment in UAC shrank from 71,000 in 1979 to 15,000 a decade later. Unilever retained a 20 per cent shareholding in UAC Nigeria until 1994, but the combination of an inflation rate of 100 per cent and foreign exchange controls and bureaucracy which made it difficult for legitimate businesses to engage in international trade prompted Unilever to dispose of its remaining equity, though Unilever remained in Nigeria as a manufacturer of detergents, margarines, and personal products.[5]

In contrast to West Africa, the economy of Hong Kong continued to grow very fast in the 1980s and the 1990s, and a radical policy shift in China opened new opportunities for the trading companies. From the beginning of the 1980s the Chinese government radically revised its economic policies by introducing market reforms and beginning again to permit inward FDI. This policy shift led by the late 1980s and early 1990s to fast economic growth in China's coastal regions, sometimes approaching 25 per cent per annum. For the first time since the 1920s, the British trading companies in Hong Kong could contemplate large-scale investment in the China market. The problem for the British companies was not economic opportunities, but changing political circumstances. In 1984 the British government agreed to return the colony to China in 1997. The post-war growth of Swire's and Jardine Matheson had rested heavily on the political stability, laissez-faire policies and fast economic growth of the British colony, which continued to provide a large proportion of their profits. Consequently the 1984 Sino-British agreement raised the prospect of a radical change in the environment of their main host economy.

[4] D. K. Fieldhouse, *Merchant Capital and Economic Decolonization* (Oxford. Clarendon Press, 1994), 763–810.
[5] 'UAC Nigeria begins a new chapter', *Financial Times*, 8 Nov. 1994.

Jardine Matheson and Swire's responded to the new situation with different strategies. The former, which was legally domiciled in Hong Kong despite its ultimate control by the Keswick family in Britain, took the view that the risks of asset appropriation through arbitrary decision-making by regulators were considerable. Giving evidence to a British House of Commons committee in 1989, Henry Keswick—himself born in Shanghai in 1938—described China's regime as 'Marxist-Leninist, thuggish, oppressive'.[6] In 1984 Jardine Matheson moved its domicile to Bermuda, causing a large temporary fall in the Hong Kong stock market. In 1991 it moved its primary stock exchange listing to London, and in 1994 Jardine Matheson and Jardine Strategic ceased trading of their shares on the Hong Kong stock exchange, with Singapore becoming the primary trading market. These moves led to a considerable deterioration in Jardine Matheson's relationships with the Chinese government which passed through a number of low points, as in 1992 when a Jardine-led consortium's application to develop Hong Kong's ninth container terminal was blocked by the Chinese.

In terms of business strategy, Jardine Matheson continued to have a substantial proportion of its business in Hong Kong, but there were also asset sales, especially in the late 1980s and early 1990s, the proceeds of which were used to diversify elsewhere. Jardines developed its food retailing affiliate Dairy Farm, which included a British discount supermarket chain 'Kwik Save', while in 1992 it took a 25 per cent shareholding and took effective management control over the British construction and shipping group Trafalgar House. The latter attempted but failed to buy a British electricity utility two years later,[7] but in 1996 large losses led to Jardine Matheson selling its shareholding. Nevertheless, despite this determined but often problematic strategy to diversify out of Hong Kong, and the firm's sometimes tense relations with the Chinese government, Jardine Matheson invested in China through joint ventures on a large scale. By 1996 Jardine Matheson had around 70 joint ventures in China with a turnover of almost £700 million. These included all the main industries in which Jardines was active in Hong Kong itself, such as automobile distribution, retailing, shipping, insurance, and property development.[8]

The strategy of Swire's differed markedly. Although in the 1970s, in the aftermath of the 'cultural revolution' in China, the firm had used resources generated in Hong Kong to diversify geographically, in the following decade the firm sought to develop a partnership with the Chinese. John Swire & Sons (China) Ltd. was incorporated in 1983. Sir Adrian Swire, the

    [6] 'Taipans who missed the boat', *Financial Times*, 2–3 Mar. 1996.
    [7] 'Suspicions on both sides about the motives of Hongkong Land', *Financial Times*, 15 Dec. 1994.
    [8] 'The end of a chapter at Jardine Matheson', *Financial Times*, 21 Dec. 1994; 'British hongs facing fresh strategy challenges', *Financial Times*, 2 Apr. 1996; *Jardine Matheson Facts and Figures 1996*.

chairman of John Swire & Sons after 1985, became a regular visitor to Beijing.[9] In part, the search for an accommodation with China reflected a traditional Swire strategy of adaption to political realities in China, but it also reflected the importance to the group of their Cathay Pacific affiliate, whose future as Hong Kong's de facto flag carrier airline self-evidently rested in the hands of the Chinese government.

The Swire strategy centred on partnerships with mainland Chinese interests, both for its Hong Kong affiliates and for new ventures in Hong Kong. The firm developed in the 1980s an especially close relationship with the China International Trust & Investment Corporation (Citic), the largest Chinese investment group. In 1987 this relationship was cemented by selling a 12.5 per cent stake in Cathay Pacific to Citic. Three years later they jointly took control of Dragonair, an entrepreneurial Hong Kong airline established in 1985 which had encountered managerial difficulties. The impending end of British colonial rule led, in 1996, to a further reorganization whereby Citic increased its shareholding in Cathay Pacific from 10 to 25 per cent, and CNAC, the commercial arm of China's aviation regulator, acquired 36 per cent of Dragonair. This left Swire's with less than 50 per cent of the shares of Cathay Pacific, but the retention of management control.[10]

During the 1980s Swire's built on its relationship with Citic to develop joint ventures in China in some of its main activities, such as bottling, where it became a leading Coca-Cola franchisee. By 1998 Swire Beverages had ten Coca-Cola production factories in China, and held the Coca-Cola franchise for seven provinces in China, as well as Hong Kong and Taiwan. During the 1990s Swire's also made joint venture agreements with European manufacturers such as ICI, Carlsberg, and Tate & Lyle to establish paint manufacturing, brewing, and sugar refining activities in China.

A second challenge to the trading companies from the 1980s arose from the management costs of running their diversified businesses. In one sense, this was a general problem faced by many British and US firms, which had diversified with abandon during the 1960s and 1970s only to encounter severe managerial constraints. In the case of the trading companies, however, the 'merchant adventurer' ethos and the desire to escape from their traditional developing country hosts had led firms in some cases far away from core competences, however widely defined. During the 1980s many of these diversification strategies ran into great difficulties. Dutch trading companies went through a similar experience, and like their British counterparts, there was a general return to 'core business'.[11]

The consequences of failed diversification strategies were the most fatal for UAC. During the 1970s 'redeployment' had been a central strategy of

---

[9] 'Attitude the key to colony's destiny', *Financial Times*, 4–5 Sept. 1993.
[10] 'Chinese to take large stakes in HK airlines', *Financial Times*, 30 Apr. 1996.
[11] Keetie E. Sluyterman, 'Dutch Multinational Trading Companies in the Twentieth Century', in Geoffrey Jones (ed.), *The Multinational Traders* (London: Routledge, 1998), 95–8.

the firm to protect itself should its traditional African business collapse. This strategy had rested on an underlying assumption that UAC's skills were transferable elsewhere. However this largely proved not to be the case, while the process of diversification by division led to the acquisition of numerous small businesses, mainly in Britain and France, which were difficult to manage, as well as having little or no synergy with UAC's overseas business. By the early 1980s it was evident that many of the acquisitions were either commercial failures or at the very least not the basis for dynamic growth. It was the combination of the collapsing Nigerian economy with the failed diversification outside Africa which effectively ended UAC's existence.

The UAC initially responded to the failure of its diversification policy by seeking to return to its 'core' activities. By the mid-1980s it had been decided to focus on its 'core' regions, tropical Africa and the Middle East, and its 'core' activities. These were changed over time but were by 1985 reduced to nine, of which five—breweries, foods, textiles, agriculture and forestry, and trading—had some relation to activities conducted by Unilever, and four—air-conditioning, electrical materials, motors, and power applications—which had virtually no connection at all with anything else within Unilever. However even this range of activities was far too wide for Unilever, which by this period had decided to concentrate worldwide on the four key businesses of personal products, food and drink, detergents, and speciality chemicals. The integration of UAC into Unilever became the next logical step.

UAC was far from the only firm to reverse its past diversification strategies. During the 1980s Ocean Wilsons, though primarily a provider of shipping services in Brazil and a portfolio investor, continued its tradition of searching for new opportunities. The firm had begun to diversify from shipping and towage in the mid-1970s, 'in order that the companies should not be reliant on such a limited number of activities'.[12] Trading and other opportunities were pursued with Inchcape. In 1981 it acquired a distributorship franchise for Mercedes for a city in the state of São Paulo. This company, which was jointly owned with Inchcape, had a difficult start, with Ocean Wilsons buying Inchcape out in 1986, and after the shift of domicile to Bermuda in 1992 the new Ocean Wilson Holdings withdrew from the motor sector to focus on its shipping and port business.[13]

The problems faced by James Finlay in its diversification strategies were more serious. Finlays, which had diversified extensively and largely opportunistically as a 'hedge' if tea prices collapsed, experienced severe problems in almost all the US acquisitions which had led it into the oil industry, fruit

[12] Annual Report, Ocean Wilsons Holdings Ltd., 1973.
[13] Annual Reports, Ocean Wilsons Holdings Ltd., 1993–8.

farming, and other diverse activities. Finlays sold its North Sea oil and gas investments in the late 1980s, and its US energy interests in 1994. It ran into especially difficult problems in financial services, especially from the Lock group, an international confirming and finance house active in Australasia, which was acquired in 1968. In 1986 Finlays made a post-tax loss, after 'disastrous' losses by Lock arising from foreign exchange dealing in Australia and bad debts in Britain.[14] By the early 1990s the firm's banking business was also in difficulties. Its ROCE was low or even negative between the mid-1980s and the mid-1990s, and this provided the background for the renewed focus on tea in the second half of that decade, when virtually all of its non-tea businesses were wound up and sold.

By the end of the 1990s Finlays had reverted to being a tea trading and distribution company, and owner of large tea plantations in Bangladesh and Kenya. The firm also took the opportunity of changed governmental policies towards foreign companies to expand its plantations. In 1992 it began managing a group of tea estates in Sri Lanka on behalf of the government, and in 1995 it took over a group of dilapidated tea estates in Uganda together with the Commonwealth Development Corporation and the government of Uganda. By 1998 the only remaining non-tea business was a general trading and agency business in Sri Lanka, Pakistan, and Bangladesh, and Finlay Industries in Wisconsin, providing inventory management to original equipment manufacturers and dealers.[15]

Finlays' return to its 'core' tea business in the 1990s reflected the strategies of its main shareholder, Swire's, whose own strategies had been based firmly on the premiss that the group should stick to its core business and only enter a new market when it had established and proven expertise.[16] Swire's continued to build on its core competences in transportation and distribution. It strictly avoided financial services and on the whole avoided the unrelated diversifications of Finlays. Thus Swire's entry into Coca-Cola bottling in the United States in 1978 built on its earlier experience in Hong Kong, while its investment in cold storage in the United States dating from 1979 (fully owned from 1982) grew out of its earlier interests in this industry in Australia. Both ventures were sustained and successful. Swire's trading, agricultural, and transport interests in this industry in Australia similarly formed the basis for the group's investments from the mid-1980s in two of Papua New Guinea's largest trading companies, both of which also had substantial interests in agriculture and transport.

A noteworthy feature of Swire's business strategy was a reluctance to divest businesses,[17] and it was consequently fortunate that the firm made few really poorly performing diversifications which needed to be sold. Its attempts to

---

[14] Annual Report, James Finlay plc., 1986
[15] Annual Report, James Finlay plc., 1998.
[16] Interview with Sir John and Sir Adrian Swire, 30 July 1996.
[17] Interview at Swire House, 28 Jan. 1999.

invest in manufacturing were one exception, where the firm found it hard to build successful businesses.[18] An example was Swire Technologies, founded in the 1980s to provide semiconductor assembly and test services to the electronics industry in Hong Kong, which made substantial losses before being sold in 1996.[19]

In contrast to Swire's, Jardine Matheson—as well as a number of other firms such Harrisons & Crosfield, Inchcape, and Lonrho—continued to maintain or even extend their diversified business in the 1980s. Although the group withdrew from shipowning in the mid-1980s, it continued in a formidable range of activities, including trading, property, hotels, engineering and construction, and retailing. It operated pizza restaurant franchises in Australia, Hong Kong, Taiwan, and Canada, and distributed Mercedes cars in Australia, Hawaii, Britain, and elsewhere. The main thrust of Jardines, strategy remained to reduce its exposure to Hong Kong, a strategy which involved buying companies in 'safer' countries. Its acquisitions, of the British discount grocer Kwik Save in the late 1980s and, especially, Trafalgar House in 1992 failed to deliver the expected results. By the time of the sale of its shareholding in the latter firm, Jardine Matheson was estimated to have lost most of its original £350 million investment.[20] Among other 'failures', in 1991 Jardine Matheson had to pay almost £40 million compensation to the shareholders of Bear Stearns, a US investment bank, after pulling out of buying a shareholding after the 1987 crash of world stock exchanges. In 1996 Hong Kong and China produced 64 per cent of the group's profits (and Hong Kong alone over 50 per cent) and Asia Pacific a further 14 per cent, and the group again emphasized that its focus of activity was the Asia-Pacific region.[21]

Harrisons & Crosfield continued through the 1980s to be a highly diversified trading company. The sale of its Malaysian plantations and the end of its timber concession in Sabah changed the balance of the company, increasing the importance of its chemicals and timber merchant businesses. It continued to buy British timber merchants.[22] The firm also continued to operate an extensive network of general trading offices which operated from India and throughout the Pacific Basin to Australia, where its branches acted as import and export agents, shipping and insurance agents, and traders and distributors of a wide range of commodities and industrial raw materials.

In the mid-1980s Harrisons & Crosfield, in pursuit of a policy called 'highly selective diversity', undertook a major new diversification when cash from the sale of its Malaysian plantations and profits from its remaining

---

[18] Interview at Swire House, 28 Jan. 1999.
[19] Annual Reports 1990–6, John Swire & Sons, Limited, 1990–6.
[20] 'A moment of danger', *Financial Times*, 20 Oct. 1995; 'Trafalgar faces its Waterloo', *Financial Times*, 28 Feb. 1996.
[21] Annual Report, Jardine Matheson, 1996.
[22] Guy Nickalls, *Great Enterprise* (London: the firm, 1990), 235.

plantations due to high world palm oil prices were used to acquire the food and agriculture business of Pauls plc, a specialist in malts, cereals, and animal foodstuffs.[23] Two years later George Paul, the former chief executive of Pauls plc, became chief executive of Harrisons & Crosfield. Subsequently three core businesses were identified—chemicals, timber and building materials, and food. In 1990 the general trading business was sold, mostly to local interests in the country where it operated.[24] In 1994 its Indonesian plantations were sold, followed in 1996 by its last plantations, those in Papua New Guinea.[25]

During the early 1990s Harrisons & Crosfield continued to make acquisitions in its 'core' businesses. It acquired the large British builders' merchant Crossley in 1990, just as an exceptionally severe British recession got under way. In 1992 it acquired BOCM-Silcock, an animal feeds business, shortly before 'mad cow' disease (BSE) began to seriously impact British cattle feed sales. Following a further strategic review, the timber merchant businesses in Britain and the United States were sold in 1997, followed by the various foodstuffs businesses in 1998.[26] The company renamed itself Elementis, a speciality chemicals company.

Inchcape also continued through the 1980s as a highly diversified general trading company, even though in 1986 ten businesses were identified as 'core' to the firm. Its principal sources of profit in the mid-1980s were derived from motor vehicle distribution and general trading—both of which accounted for more than 20 per cent of group profits—but it was also engaged in shipping and marine services, tea estates, insurance, and many other activities in over eighty countries. Inchcape represented thirty motor manufacturers, and maintained its especially long-term relationship with Toyota Motors, whose vehicles it distributed exclusively in such markets as Hong Kong, Singapore, Belgium, and Britain. In 1993 Inchcape sold nearly 400,000 new and used vehicles, making it the world's largest independent importer and distributor of motor vehicles. It was the firm's motor distribution business, and its growth in the dynamic markets of the Far East and South East Asia, which accounted for the sharp increase in its ROCE in the second half of the 1980s and the early 1990s.

During the 1980s Inchcape's general trading business was remarkable. It marketed the products of over 700 manufacturers in Asia, the Middle East, and Latin America. It held the agencies for leading brands in some of the world's fast-growing markets. In Hong Kong, it distributed among other things pharmaceuticals, refrigerators from General Electric, Heinz baked beans, Kellogg's corn flakes, Timberland shoes, Ricoh office equipment, and Hi-Tec sports shoes, as well as controlling 40 per cent of the car market.

[23] Ibid., 244.   [24] Annual Report, Harrisons & Crosfield plc., 1990.
[25] 'Harrisons to pull out of plantations', *Financial Times*, 3/4 Aug. 1996.
[26] 'Elementis off 20% as UK groups warn over trading', *Financial Times*, 1 Dec. 1998.

It sold Nestlé coffee and chocolate and Heineken beer in the Middle East, and Durex condoms in China. In Malaysia, it manufactured under contract for companies ranging from Unilever, SmithKline Beecham, and Quaker Oats to the bed maker Slumberland. Inchcape's Massey Ferguson tractor distributor led the Thai tractor market, but Inchcape also supplied Thais with Fuji X-ray film, Chubb locks, and Ovaltine drinks from Nestlé. In 1983 Inchcape also became a Coca-Cola bottler in Chile. Subsequently Inchcape began bottling in Russia in 1994 and Peru in 1996, when it acquired a 25 per cent share in that country's largest bottler. [27]

During the early 1990s Inchcape continued to diversify. It expanded its business in China through joint ventures. In 1994 it purchased the Hogg insurance group, which it merged with its existing broker to form Bain Hogg, which became Britain's largest retail insurance broker. However by this period the firm's pre-tax ROCE had collapsed from over 30 per cent in 1994 to under 3 per cent in 1995, and 10 per cent in 1996. In 1996 its chief executive was forced to resign, and a programme of divestment began with the sale of Bain Hogg. Five businesses, all within the sphere of international distribution, were identified as 'core'. These included bottling, where the firm made further acquisitions in Peru in early 1997, and trading, where the firm was engaged in opening shops in Japan to sell Timberland shoes and clothes. However the economic crisis in South East Asia—beginning in autumn 1997—prompted a more radical strategy, and in 1998 the firm decided that its 'core' business was motor distribution. [28]

Over the next two years Inchcape was dismantled. Its Russian bottling business was sold to Coca-Cola in 1998 and its Latin American bottling business sold to a Chilean company in the following year. [29] In 1999 its Asia-Pacific marketing division was sold to a private Asian investment group. The remaining major assets—Middle Eastern marketing, shipping services, and an Asia-Pacific office automation affiliate—were disposed of over the following twelve months, leaving Inchcape transformed into a motor distribution company.

Lonrho also remained an extremely diversified multinational trading company in the 1980s. The firm's portfolio continued to include mining—55 per cent of operating profits in 1994; hotels in Africa, Britain, the United States, and elsewhere; farming and ranching activities in eleven African countries, of which sugar plantations were the largest element; and general trading. It was also involved in engineering, printing, insurance, property, and finance. Lonrho also undertook automobile distribution and textiles manufacture. John Holt & Co. which retained its identity within Lonrho,

---

[27] Inchcape, Annual Review 1993; 'Inchcape invests in Coca-Cola's push into Russia', *Financial Times*, 22 July 1994.

[28] Charlotte Butler and John Keary, *Managers and Mantras* (Singapore: John Wiley, 2000) provides a detailed study of Inchcape's strategy between the 1970s and the end of the 1990s.

[29] 'Inchcape disposes of Chilean bottling side', *Financial Times*, 2 Feb. 1999.

continued to invest in Nigeria, engaging in a joint venture to assemble motor-cycles in the country, as well as extending its trading business to Oman and especially South Africa.[30]

By the 1990s Lonrho's 'hybrid' character was in considerable difficulty. It owned more than 600 subsidiaries in nearly fifty countries. Acquired companies were seldom reorganized or given central direction. Lonrho's main host region, Africa, provided more than 75 per cent of the group's profits but was the poorest performing area of the developing world. Lonrho's constant acquisitions produced a vast growth in turnover but little growth in earnings and assets per share. The firm's weakening financial performance was not reflected in its generous dividend policy, which benefited its largest single shareholder, 'Tiny' Rowland. Rowland's 'personal' style of management did not suit a large international group, especially as he displayed increasingly erratic behaviour. During the 1980s he diverted Lonrho funds to support a personal vendetta against the Fayed family which defeated him in a takeover bid for House of Fraser stores, owner of Harrods, the upscale London department store long sought after by Rowland. Rowland also used company funds to maintain a lavish lifestyle and to spend on entertaining African leaders and their relatives.[31]

As in the case of Inchcape, the mid-1990s proved the decisive turning point for Lonrho. In 1993 Rowland sold most of his shareholding to a German property dealer, Dieter Bock, and in 1995 Rowland relinquished his executive position. Bock began a process of divesting 'non-core' activities and in 1996 launched a strategy to demerge Lonrho into three components, hotels, trading, and mining, while selling his own 18 per cent shareholding in Lonrho to the Anglo-American Corporation of South Africa.[32] Following a decision by EU regulators to order Anglo-American to reduce its shareholding on competition grounds, the new management launched a strategy to make Lonrho a specialist mining company. Its residual hotel investments were sold, as were its African sugar cane plantations and factories, and in 1998 the African trading business was demerged into a separate company, Lonrho Africa.

Lonrho Africa inherited a diversified regional trading company active in fourteen sub-Saharan countries. Its largest turnover arose from automobile distribution, and it held African franchises for Ford, Toyota, and Massey Ferguson among others. It also undertook cotton growing and ginning in Mozambique, South Africa, Uganda, and Zambia, meat processing in Kenya, brewing in Malawi and Zambia, and farming and ranching in Kenya, Malawi, and Zimbabwe. It had hotels in three countries, while its

[30] Annual Reports, Lonrho plc, 1980–96; Annual Reports, John Holt & Co. (Liverpool) Ltd., 1980–96.
[31] 'Tiny Rowland faces his day of reckoning', *Financial Times*, 31 Aug. 1994; 'The talented but ultimately unacceptable face of capitalism', *Financial Times*, 27 July 1998.
[32] 'Rowland to quit Lonrho board', *Financial Times*, 4 Nov. 1994.

general trading business included John Holt in Nigeria.[33] By 1999, however, Lonrho Africa had identified its 'core' as wholesale distribution, motor dealerships, and food processing, and its hotel, cotton, timber, and other businesses began to be sold or else floated on local stock exchanges.

A third challenge to the trading companies arose from the nature of the British capital markets. In the late nineteenth century the British trading companies had been able to utilize Britain's position as the world's largest capital exporter and London's position as the world's largest international financial centre to finance their diversification strategies. They had enabled the thousands of individual investors to invest in overseas plantations, mines, and other ventures by their reputations as a guarantee of honesty and responsible management. In turn the ability to use other people's money had enabled the trading companies to build diversified business groups.

In some respects the pre-1914 conditions of the capital markets were restored in the last decades of the twentieth century. Despite the relative decline of the British economy, London was reborn as the world's largest international financial centre following the development of the Euro markets in the 1960s. The British equity market was by far the largest in Europe. The remaining British exchange controls were abolished in 1979 to restore again the free movement of capital in and out of London. However the nature of shareholding was different from before 1914 as individuals had been largely replaced by financial institutions. While in 1957 British insurance companies and pension funds held 22 per cent of the shares of British firms and individuals held around two-thirds, by 1998 institutional investors owned 75 per cent of the British stock market by value.

The changed nature of British equity holders held considerable implications for the trading companies. While the individual shareholders before 1914—and indeed much later—were passive and often long-term holders of stock, the financial institutions viewed shares as short-term investment vehicles. They were responsible to the owners of the funds that they invested, and as such had a duty to maximize investment returns. Consequently the main preoccupation of the institutions was short-term financial performance and share prices. British firms were expected to provide much higher returns on capital employed over shorter periods than those of other European countries, and their dividend payout rates were among the highest. The nature of British capital markets meant that British firms in large, capital-intensive, cyclical, and risky businesses had considerable problems, and during the 1980s and 1990s British firms in industries such as automobiles, consumer electronics, and investment banking were largely eliminated.[34]

[33] 'Liberation from the shackles of a corporate parent', *Financial Times*, 27 Apr. 1998; Annual Report, Lonrho plc., 1997.

[34] Geoffrey Jones, 'Corporate Governance and British Industry', *Entreprises et histoire*, 21 (1999), 29–42.

Diversified conglomerates were not favoured by institutional investors in Britain, who held diversified portfolios themselves and preferred individual firms to focus on their 'core' areas enabling their performance and prospects to be more efficiently monitored. Firms such as Dalgety, which had become a diversified agriculture and foodstuffs company by the 1980s, came under pressure to focus on core businesses to 'create value' for shareholders. The firm began disposing of most of its operations in 1997 and in the following year was renamed PIC International Group, focused entirely on pig breeding and genetic improvement. During the second half of the 1990s Britain's once large industrial conglomerates—Hanson Trust, BTR, Tomkins, and Suter—were dismantled, focused on a 'core' business, or acquired by other firms. Diversified trading companies were especially unfashionable in such a context, as the evident difficulties of many diversification strategies only reinforced the poor reputation of diversified conglomerates.

The influence of the capital markets on the trading companies was evident in their strategies in these decades. Unilever had been a firm where market share rather than profitability had been the major concern. From the 1970s, and especially in the 1980s, financial performance and return on capital had grown in importance. This both encouraged Unilever's focus on 'core' products—highlighting the anomaly of a large consumer goods multinational owning UAC—and made the UAC's deteriorating financial performance in the 1980s a matter of immediate concern.[35]

Capital market pressures were evident in the last years of Harrisons & Crosfield, Inchcape, and Lonrho as diversified trading companies. All three firms experienced falling share prices and poor dividend performance immediately prior to the reviews which ended their diversified structures. In the case of Harrisons & Crosfield, the firm's share price fell from 215p in January 1994 to 102p in May 1997 prompting the strategic review which led to the focus on speciality chemicals.[36] It was reported in September 1997 that the firm had had 'rocky' relations with institutional investors 'after disappointing results, a plummeting share price', and the incoming chairman identified ensuing 'proper communications between the company and the City' as a key priority.[37] Inchcape also experienced a declining share price from 600p per share in 1993 to around 250p for most of 1996. The firm dropped out of the FT-SE 100 index in 1995. The Inchcape family shareholding, still substantial in 1979, was no longer significant by this period. The decision to demerge Inchcape in 1998 was justified by its chief executive on the grounds that 'Inchcape's share price (had) been undermined because investors (had) not been able to appreciate the true value of such a complex business'.[38] It remained to be seen whether a specialist automobile distributor could deliver the high profits expected by the capital markets.

---

[35] Fieldhouse, *Merchant Capital*.
[36] 'Farewell to a conglomerate', *Financial Times*, 25/26 Oct. 1997.
[37] 'H&C appoints Fry new Chairman', *Financial Times*, 3 Sept. 1997.
[38] 'The best part of breaking up is when it takes you up', *Financial Times*, 7/8 Mar. 1998.

Lonrho's last decade as a diversified trading company was also characterized by a falling share price, from 300p at the beginning of 1989 to almost
50p in the middle of 1992, and just over 100p in the autumn of 1997. Until
1992 Rowland's personal shareholding and the unusually large number of
private shareholders enabled him to effectively manage the company as he
wished. Rowland's sale of most of his shareholding in 1993 ended any protection from capital market pressures. The large institutional shareholders
supported the subsequent removal of Rowland's executive authority.[39]
Subsequently the split of Lonrho's mining and trading operations was
justified as grounds of 'delivering maximum value to shareholders'; divid-
ing them, it was argued, would 'allow each to be accorded an appropriate
rating by the market'.[40] The subsequent purchase of 10 per cent of the equity
of Lonrho Africa by an emerging markets fund manager concerned to break
up the company stimulated the radical restructuring into a focused distribution business during 1999, as well as suggesting that the new trading company's life might be short.[41]

Another way of conceptualizing the end of most of the old British trading companies in the 1980s and 1990s was that control of their assets was
transferred from a corporate governance system which placed little value
on them to corporate governance systems closer to their business operations and better able to value them. Harrisons & Crosfield's general trading
and plantations, Inchcape's Latin American bottling and Middle Eastern and
Asian marketing business, and most of UAC's and parts of Lonrho's business in Africa all passed into the hands of investors in their host economies.

Leaving aside the special case of Lonrho Africa, the trading companies
which survived into the twenty-first century were those immune from the
British capital markets. The Keswick family continued to control the Jardine
Matheson group with around 10 per cent of the equity. Another abortive
takeover bid in 1987 led to the adoption of a complex cross-shareholding
structure. New holding companies—Jardine Matheson Holdings and Jardine
Strategic—were incorporated in Bermuda. Jardine Matheson owned 57 per
cent of Jardine Strategic Holdings which in turn owned 38.5 per cent
of Jardine Matheson and 32 per cent of Hongkong Land. In addition the
Bermuda takeover code had a number of further obstacles to takeovers,
including a regulation requiring investors to reveal their identities if they
accumulated more than 3 per cent of a company.[42]

The Swire group was even more closely controlled by the founding families. John Swire & Sons, the parent company, remained a private company

[39] 'A friendship splits over the way forward', *Financial Times*, 18 Oct. 1993.
[40] 'Lonrho does the splits', *Financial Times*, 18/19 Jan. 1997.
[41] 'Blakeney offers concessions', *Financial Times*, 2 Dec. 1998; 'Lonrho Africa hit by currency
devaluations', *Financial Times*, 21 Jan. 1999.
[42] 'Defences activated by stake building moves', *Financial Times*, 7 Aug. 1997; 'Taipans who
missed the boat', *Financial Times*, 2/3 Mar. 1996.

owned two-thirds by the Swire family and one-third by the Scott family. The shareholding structure of the group gave Swire's ultimate control over its affiliates, while the system whereby all the senior management of affiliates were employed by John Swire & Sons further cemented the control. Swire's control of its major affiliate, Swire Pacific, through a substantial but minority shareholding, was not unusual in Hong Kong, where listing on the local stock exchange remained dominated by family-controlled groups exercising control through minority equity states in their primary companies. Finlays was also protected from takeover before 2000, when Swire's acquired full ownership. Swire's' senior management emphasized the importance of insulation from capital market pressures in their continued existence as a diversified business group.[43]

Curiously, therefore, whilst family ownership and management is sometimes used to explain the conservatism of earlier generations of British trading company, in the final years of the twentieth century it was only to be the family owned firms that survived.

11.3 Conclusion

At the beginning of the 1980s the successors to the British trading companies originating in the eighteenth and nineteenth centuries were alive and active as large and complex multinational business enterprises. Two decades later some had disappeared altogether, while others had focused on becoming food companies, automobile distributors, or chemical companies. In other cases, substantial and successful businesses continued but were no longer British-owned. Of the surviving British trading companies, Lonrho Africa remained as a residual of the great merchant empires in Africa, while in Asia Pacific Swire's and Jardine Matheson continued in business as large and ultimately British-controlled multinational enterprises.

The demise of so many of the old British trading companies was curious given that the world political economy appeared once again to offer prospects for their skills, as economies were liberalized and opened to foreign trade and investment. In part the firms fell victim to their failed attempts to diversify into regions and industries where they lacked expertise. The fate of particular firms rested in part on their main host regions. Jardine Matheson and Swire's, most obviously, continued to draw enormous advantage from their position in Hong Kong, while—conversely—UAC's fate was all but sealed by the decline of the West African, and especially the Nigerian, economies from the 1970s.

However the ultimate arbiter of the fate of the diversified trading companies in the late twentieth century was the British capital markets. The capital markets which had made the creation of the diversified business

---

[43] Interview at Swire House, 28 Jan. 1999.

groups possible before 1914 were to prove their nemesis in the 1990s. It was the declining share price of the publicly quoted firms which led to their ultimate demise as diversified trading companies, while it was the family control of Swire's and Jardine Matheson which ensured their survival.

Although most of the old-established British trading companies had gone by the new century, 'trading companies' as such did not disappear. In the emerging markets of Eastern Europe, Latin America, and Africa, there were new opportunities for trade intermediaries, paralleling to some extent the opportunities of their predecessors in the nineteenth century. Trading houses which initially traded with Communist Eastern Europe used their contacts to trade with their successors in the 1990s. The internet and the worldwide web provided new challenges for such traders, as it was never easier for buyers to contact sellers directly rather than using intermediaries.[44] However there remained large transactions and information costs trading with countries such as Russia which provided opportunities for intermediaries. Fund managers became interested in trading opportunities in emerging markets also. In 1997 a group of fund managers, including the Quantum Emerging Growth fund of George Soros, the US investor, acquired African Lakes, a British firm founded in the late nineteenth century by missionaries, which had trading activities in Ethiopia, Zimbabwe, and elsewhere, and had more recently made losses through dealing in motors in Britain. The firm was recapitalized and used as a vehicle for trading and other acquisitions in East and Southern Africa.[45] It seemed unlikely that the twenty-first century would dispose of the services of trading companies, though it remained to be seen whether these new British-based trading firms would grow to the size of their predecessors.

[44] Interview with Robert Brouwer and Ingrid Hoffmann, directors of Arcon Overseas Ltd., 21 Mar. 1999.

[45] 'African Lakes seeks fund raising', *Financial Times*, 27 July 1998; 'Groups linked to Soros eye Lonrho Africa', *Financial Times*, 8 June 1998.

12

Conclusion

12.1 Merchants to Multinationals

This book has examined the evolution of multinational trading companies from the late eighteenth century to the start of the twenty-first century. It has shown how individual British merchants or merchant partnerships evolved into trading companies, and how trade intermediaries became foreign direct investors on a large scale. It has examined how these merchant intermediaries retained a substantial role in the world economy in the 'era of industrial capitalism' in the twentieth century despite the pressures for internalization of many markets.

From the eighteenth century merchants began to set up business in overseas ports to sell British textiles and to take advantage of new opportunities for trade as state monopolies and chartered companies crumbled. Once established in ports, they began to export local products as well as import manufactured goods. Trading companies economized on information costs in a world characterized by uncertainty and risk due to distance and poor communications. These high levels of uncertainty and risk meant that merchant firms, even the largest ones, regularly failed, while the financial performance of individual firms fluctuated alongside the progress of the commodities in which they dealt, and with their own capacity to avoid ill-judged speculations or defalcations by their staffs.

In India, and later elsewhere, British merchants diversified into non-trading activities such as plantations, mining, and textile manufacture, often preferring others to invest most of the capital, leaving them to manage the ventures. This trend increased between 1870 and 1914. As a result, merchants came to form an important component of British FDI. By using limited liability legislation to form 'free-standing' companies registered both in Britain and overseas, they encouraged individuals to invest in overseas plantations, mines, and other 'risky' activities by providing a badge of respectability, not always justified given the conflict of interest inherent within the business group system.

There are major implications for understanding the size and composition of British FDI before the First World War. The governance structures of the business groups organized around trading companies were more robust than suggested in earlier descriptions of 'investment groups'. Real management control from Britain was exercised over the free-standing companies in these groups. However the evidence presented here highlights the danger of using the issued capital of such British-registered free-standing firms as a proxy for FDI, as in the Dunning estimates. The use of the partnership form and of local registration of many affiliates mean that much overseas business ultimately controlled by British trading companies is excluded from such a calculation. From the First World War the country of registration of free-standing companies within business groups was sometimes shifted out of Britain for fiscal reasons. Most importantly, large business groups were often 'controlled' by contracts, cross-directorships, and debt rather than by equity. In this respect, the Dunning estimates probably underestimate the scale of British FDI before 1914. This book has not presented new quantitative estimates, but when such estimates are made they will need to incorporate long-term debt and to recognize that 'control' can be exercised with little or no equity.

The trading companies before 1914 were very heterogeneous. They differed greatly in size, their activities, and their performance. Most firms undertook insurance and shipping agency work alongside trading, but the other activities in which they invested varied widely between regions and firms, and included the control of plantations, mines, and processing facilities. British merchants, like British overseas banks and the trading companies based in other European countries, specialized in particular regions, where they acquired and then exploited local knowledge. The bilateral nature of trade between Britain and developing countries and the wide inter-country and inter-regional differences in markets and political situations, made such specialization the only viable strategy in the nineteenth century. Yet by 1914 a number of embryonic multi-regional business groups had emerged which can be regarded as being amongst the most extensive multinational businesses in the world at the time. Although there were many similarities between the British and Dutch, Danish, French, and other European companies of this era, the scale and the scope of some British firms was distinctive.

During the interwar years tariffs, declining world trade, the loss of competitiveness of British exports, and falling commodity prices provided a more difficult environment than before 1914. There was a deterioration in the financial performance of many companies, especially in the 1930s, with firms encountering grave problems in the two severe recessions of the era. Not surprisingly, risk-aversion rather than risk-taking was more characteristic of the interwar years, and the momentum to create multi-regional business groups notably slackened.

The interwar years saw few heroic business strategies, but firms continued to evolve and change. They handled more complex goods, including motor distribution. They withdrew from some loss-making commodities, and invested in others with more economic potential. Sometimes they integrated forwards into distribution and pursued branding strategies for their products. In general, the British merchants in India and in Latin America appear especially risk averse by this period, while the British traders became active promoters of commodity cartels.

The British trading companies entered the post-war economy with considerable advantages. The British Empire persisted in much of Asia and Africa, and the firms themselves possessed excellent franchises based on long-established positions in host economies. However there were also many factors working against them. British manufacturing exports were losing competitiveness, or else manufacturers wanted to internalize their overseas business, while the structure of British foreign trade was shifting towards developed markets in which they had no representation and no role as trade intermediaries. Their traditional business in the sale of commodities was challenged by increased governmental intervention. The relative decline of London-based commodity markets helped weaken the rationale for London headquarters of the firms. Although the trading companies possessed considerable knowledge of their host economies, the political and other risks of doing business in many developing countries increased.

In the circumstances, the resilience of many merchant firms was striking. Although the family and other shareholders of the British trading companies and agency houses in Latin America and India mostly preferred to sell out their investments, either to other British firms or to local businesses, elsewhere they responded to the changing political and economic conditions by identifying new business opportunities. As in earlier periods, some firms were more successful than others and there continued to be substantial inter-firm differences in financial performance, while the fortunes of individual firms fluctuated in response to changing conditions and the outcome of particular strategies. However taken as a group the post-war decades saw the businesses of many surviving firms radically transformed and renewed, with the result that by the 1970s firms such as UAC, Inchcape, or Swire's bore little resemblance to their predecessors three decades earlier.

During the post-war decades these firms were not relics of empire, but formed a cluster of substantial general and regional trading companies, whose financial performance was comparable at times to or exceeded that of 'modern' multinationals. They continued to benefit from asymmetries of information and access in their host economies. They were often first-movers as modern business enterprises, and long-established contacts and relationships continued to function despite a quite different political and economic environment than in the nineteenth century. This powerful historical inheritance, reinforced by flexible business strategies, was only overcome by radical exogenous shocks such as nationalization, massive tax hikes, or economic collapse.

Contrary to some theoretical predictions that the use of trade intermediaries was most likely in standardized products and bulk commodities, trading companies were able to establish strong positions in automobile distribution and consumer goods distribution in some developing economies in the post-war decades. In these markets, trading volumes were sometimes too low to encourage Western manufacturers to invest in distribution or manufacturing, while the 'psychic distance' between them and developing economies only narrowed slowly. In motor distribution, the British trading companies possessed considerable advantages in the form of real estate to build showrooms and the capacity to provide after sales service facilities. The British firms were able to adjust to the declining competitiveness of British goods by distributing US, Japanese, and other European products.

Given the differences the business systems of their home economies, it would be facile to suggest that the British trading firms 'failed' after the Second World War because they failed to develop on the scale of the Japanese *sogo shosha*. They had no potential to develop as the trading arms of groups of British manufacturers, nor did the British government support them as tools of industrial policy as in Japan. There did seem more potential for the British firms to have expanded in commodity trading, activities in which US and Swiss companies in particular grew rapidly after 1945. However the firms with potential to evolve in this direction were too small or risk averse, or else fell victim to the vagaries of the British capital markets.

Over the last two decades of the twentieth century most of the surviving British trading companies were finally swept away, their assets in Latin America, Africa, and Asia sold to local firms and investors. By 2000 there were only a handful of 'survivors' although a number of other long-established firms continued in existence, albeit sometimes with different names and no longer trading companies. Ironically, firms which survived radical political and economic upheavals in their traditional host regions finally succumbed to the pressures of the British capital markets for focus and short-term financial performance. The two largest survivors, Swire's and Jardine Matheson, were protected from the logic of the capital markets. Their fate would depend on the continuation of family ownership, and their success in dealing with the succession to the next generation.

12.2 Diversification and Reinvention

A central theme of this book has been diversification and the process of 'reinvention'. The general pattern of diversification before 1914 was from trade to related services such as insurance and shipping agencies, to FDI in resources, and processing in developing host economies. The British trading companies made the largest investments in tea, rubber and sugar plantations, and teak. Chilean nitrates, Indian coal, and petroleum were also the recipients of considerable investment. As merchants, they were less interested in 'locking up' capital in manufacturing, but during the second half of the nineteenth century and later they did make substantial investments in cotton textile and jute manufacture, sugar refining, and flour milling. Unlike Danish and Swedish trading companies, they seldom sought to integrate backwards in their own home economy before the Second World War.

During the interwar years diversification by function or geography was more constrained, or at least it had an evolutionary rather than a radical nature. While some firms extended their range of activities conducted in particular countries, others transferred their established expertise in one product to other countries. There was an evident financial constraint on diversification. The shock of the post-1919 recession and the continuing liquidity problems of many firms exercised a strong dampening effect on firms that relied heavily on reinvested earnings. In other cases, firms may have been performing sufficiently well from their traditional activities as to reduce enthusiasm for new departures.

After 1945 the British trading companies continued to diversify and 'reinvent' themselves. There were new investments in tropical hardwoods in Borneo and oil palm in Papua New Guinea, and in textiles and brewing in Africa. General and produce trading gave way to more specialized trading and sales agencies. Firms diversified geographically, while the Inchcape group relocated itself out of India towards the faster-growing and more open economies further east. In the post-war decades, constraints were often more political than financial. Leaving aside such 'havens' as Hong Kong, the general thrust of public policy in most developing host economies was to restrict or prohibit FDI, especially in natural resources and services. Among the most successful trading companies were firms which had suffered traumatic 'shocks' as a result of the Pacific War and the Chinese revolution. The British merchants in the Far East and South East Asia acquired new premises and facilities which probably improved their efficiency compared with the pre-war period, but more importantly their losses seem to have stimulated an entrepreneurial urge to rebuild and renew their businesses. Motivation of this type was lacking perhaps among the British firms active in India and South America, whose owners and managers often seemed resigned to slow decline.

Against this background, diversification strategies between the 1960s and 1980s were heavily focused on 'redeployment' from high-risk developing to developed countries. This often meant a functional redeployment also as firms pursued opportunities in manufacturing and financial services. Dutch and other European trading companies pursued similar strategies in response to political risk. The British firms encountered major difficulties as a result of their encounters with British carpet, shipbuilding and engineering firms, Spanish breweries, Californian fruit farms, and Texan oilmen. In retrospect, it is apparent that British firms exaggerated the risks caused by political change in the developing world, while firms also misjudged their core competences by acquiring firms in industries and countries where they had no advantage and could add no value. However in the case of some firms, successful transitions were made from traders and plantation owners in developing economies to manufacturers or distributors in developed countries.

Diversification strategies were conditioned by the historical environment. In the nineteenth century, the lack of infrastructure and local entrepreneurship in developing countries meant, first, that trading companies had to invest themselves rather than rely on others to create complementary businesses, and second that there were numerous profitable opportunities which could be exploited as the borders of the international economy and of empires advanced. In particular they perceived and could exploit the large profits to be earned from the exploitation of, and trade in, natural resources.

From the interwar years there were fewer 'opportunities' for the trading companies, at least on a grand scale. Concessions and the best land were already allocated in many regions creating formidable barriers to entry. Surplus capacity and falling prices in the interwar years did not encourage new investments on marginal lands. However the trading companies could and did still exploit 'virgin' territories and take advantage of burgeoning markets for crops such as palm oil. There remained opportunities in import substitution manufacturing in many developing countries, but financial problems in the interwar years, the nature of their capabilities and conservative risk-assessment constrained their willingness and capacity to invest in such activities.

There were systematic influences on diversification strategies. In the nineteenth century there were strong internalization incentives for integration arising especially from asset-specificity, uncertainty, frequency of transactions, and opportunism. Quality control was an important element behind vertical integration strategies. In many cases the trading companies often sought access rather than full internalization. They made money through commissions on the sale of commodities and these profits were linked to the volume of business they undertook. As a result, they sought trading rights and control over quantity and quality of the trade flow rather than ownership per se.

Risk sharing was a major determinant of diversification. The business of intermediaries between buyers and sellers was always under threat. The trading companies were exposed to multiple risks from fluctuations in exchange rates, commodity prices, and shipping rates, as well as from the risks of operating in different political jurisdictions. The traders often sought to diversify risk by adding to their business portfolios. Given the regional-specificity of the trading companies, political risk or instability was a major factor behind geographical diversification.

Although the strategy of diversification to reduce risk is thoroughly unfashionable in a climate in which focus on 'core' products is regarded as the optimal business strategy, it made more sense for trading companies dependent—for example—on the prices of primary commodities. In an evolutionary perspective, these companies were often adept at using income streams from one business activity or country whose future seemed in doubt to develop new businesses which over time became important sources of profit. There were also examples of the reverse outcome, when profits from, say, tea trading were used to finance unsuccessful strategies to reduce risk.

The trading companies exploited economies of scope. Their region-specific information and expertise represented indivisible assets that reduced the set-up costs of forming entirely new businesses. Acquisition of knowledge about regions, marketing channels, or products involved experience, know-how, and search—all of which were costly—but once in possession of these factors, the trading companies were well positioned to diversify their activities. Knowledge and know-how had a semi-public goods characteristic and the marginal cost of employing it in a new venture was often low. The 'business group' structure often provided the organizational mode which permitted scope economies to be obtained. However region-specific knowledge and know-how was both a competitive advantage and a competitive disadvantage, in that it provided a constraint on diversification options outside the host region.

Diversification strategies were heavily influenced by time, host economy, and firm-specific factors. The late nineteenth century was an era of frantic diversification into non-trade activities, when large fixed-investments were made. Thereafter there was consolidation until, from the 1960s, there was a renewed period of diversification associated with the attempts of firms to relocate to developed countries, and the use of acquisition strategies to reposition assets functionally and geographically. The direction of diversification was influenced heavily by the resource endowments of host regions. In West Africa, the diversification was mainly horizontal, reflecting the fact that the production of export crops such as palm oil was in the hands of peasant cultivators. In nineteenth-century China, the prohibition of foreign ownership of factories or plantations ruled out the kind of strategies undertaken by the British agency houses in India.

The strategies of individual firms were the outcome of the opportunities and threats which they faced, their entrepreneurial skills and competences, and their corporate cultures, which differed substantially even between firms in the same region. In East Asia, Swire's diversified incrementally mainly in the areas of transport and distribution, though in shipping and airlines the firm took some substantial risks. Jardine Matheson had more of a risk-taking trader mentality, searching for new opportunities in diverse areas. In many instances firms responded opportunistically to unexpected offers or openings in the tradition of 'merchant adventurers'. However, such 'opportunistic' strategies were rarely sustained unless the firm had competences which added value to the new opportunity.

The case studies in this book lend general support to the conventional wisdom concerning the superiority of related diversification over unrelated diversification. There were successful outcomes for firms that moved from rubber to oil palm plantations, from general trading to automobile distribution, from growing tea and bottling Coca-Cola in one continent to undertaking the same task on another continent, and from chemicals distribution to chemicals manufacture. In contrast, the great era of unrelated diversifications in the 1960s and the 1970s produced a series of mishaps.

However in the case of firms such as trading companies care has to be taken regarding the appropriate definition of 'related' and 'unrelated'. The trading companies 'knew' about their regions, and in that respect diversification from (say) opium trading to textiles manufacture, or guano trading to mining nitrates, in nineteenth-century China and Chile respectively, is better regarded as related than unrelated diversification. From another perspective, the transition from owning the land on which dockyards and sugar refineries were located to real estate development on such land, or from timber logging in the tropics to owning timber merchants in Britain, might be considered as 'related' diversification, but this would underestimate the wholly different skills involved in these activities, as well as the scale of the entrepreneurial risk-taking involved in such diversification.

Finally, the outcomes of diversification strategies were contingent on time and place. Unrelated diversification in a nineteenth-century developing economy devoid of capital markets and entrepreneurs was far from risk free, but considerably different from unrelated diversification in a late twentieth-century developed economy. Insofar as a systematic observation about diversification strategies can be proffered from this study, it is that it was when firms invested in both activities and countries about which they knew little that the most serious problems arose, regardless of time period.

12.3 Competences

British trading companies created and sustained complex diversified businesses using managerial methods and organizational forms radically different from textbook models. It is the robustness of the traders and their ability to sustain 'reinvention' strategies which is so striking.

The competences of the trading companies rested on the locational advantages of their home economy. They developed at a time when Britain dominated world trade flows and, by the late nineteenth century, world capital flows. They were able to access the world's largest equity markets. Many of their investments were located within the British Empire or parts of Latin America under British informal influence. In the interwar years the merchant firms were able to protect their business through extensive collusive cartels supported by the colonial authorities. Although Britain's relative importance in the world economy began to decline from the late nineteenth century, the British trading companies in Asia, and Africa continued to benefit from the umbrella of British colonial rule through until the 1950s and even later. The continued colonial status of Hong Kong until 1997 forms one of the central explanations for the growth and survival of Swire's and Jardine Matheson compared to the firms whose business was centred on Latin America.

The historical longevity of the trading companies in their host regions and the colonial status of many of these countries resulted in multiple 'contacts' which provided a major competitive advantage. British colonial officials were frequently critical of the merchant firms, and certainly did not protect them against competitors. The interwar decline of the Calcutta agency houses, or the failure of the West African traders to prevent the creation of marketing boards after the Second World War, illustrate this point. But if colonial administrations had their own agendas, they were still sufficiently close to the merchant firms in their ideological and cultural outlook to provide an immensely supportive context. However the trading companies also established long-standing 'contacts' with local business elites in Asia, Africa, and Latin America which gave them a 'quasi-local' status, akin to indigenous business groups today. Such 'contacts' were renewed in successive generations and provided the basis for a sustained competitive advantage in these host economies.

The importance of the British economy and Empire in some respects makes the role and longevity of British trading companies more understandable than, say, Swiss or Danish trading companies. However this book has argued that the British firms were not simply 'free-riders' on the British economy or Empire. There were core competences centred around the areas of knowledge, information, and external relationships. Management systems which involved staff and directors spending their entire careers abroad generated extensive tacit knowledge about regions, products, and marketing channels. The upshot was the creation of a generalist managerial cadre able to provide senior management that could control a surprisingly wide range of businesses. Site-specific learning was enhanced by systems and routines to control flows of information. The requirements for motivating staff while preventing opportunism were dealt with by remuneration systems combining commission payments with strong 'moral' cultures.

Writers on twentieth-century British business have often characterized British managers as amateurs lacking in formal educational qualifications compared to their other European or US counterparts. To some extent the recruitment patterns of the British merchant houses conform to this picture, with their emphasis on 'character' and social and sporting skills. However selection on the basis of character or personality is more appropriate for a trading firm than, for example, a chemicals manufacturer, given the risky and non-routine nature of parts of the business. Moreover, some of the trading companies were among the earliest British firms to recruit university graduates as potential managers. Similarly the attention given to learning local languages belied stereotyped images of managers as amateurs.

These managers had sufficient skills to undertake all sorts of trading and distribution, run shipping companies and dockyards, manage large plantation companies and eventually in one case, a major airline. They were able to sustain long-term investments in processing of locally produced commodities. The sustained investments in tea plantations and tropical timber, textile manufacture and sugar refining, have been used as case studies in this book. There were more problems for the firms from the interwar years when they might have invested further in manufacturing if they had possessed the skills. The use of joint ventures was an obvious answer, and employed successfully in the 1960s and 1970s, in West African brewing and textiles, and in Malaysia. However the opportunities for the trading companies to pursue this strategy more extensively, even if they had wished to do so, was constrained by the desire of British manufacturing firms to integrate forwards themselves if market volumes justified it.

The persistence of family ownership and control was a striking feature in the management of the trading companies, although some of the largest had no family influence. There is little evidence that family control was of necessity a disadvantage for a trading company, provided it could be combined with allowing sufficient 'outside' capital into the business to permit growth. It could provide an element of continuity to firms that engaged in risky businesses and 'reinvented' themselves. Reputations for probity, competence, and durability are major assets for trading companies, which sustained ownership by a family could enhance. Especially after 1945, continuing family ownership was an important key to the continued independence of firms. Few firms made a successful transition from a family to a managerial business. The sale of family shareholdings usually triggered a period of shareholder instability followed by acquisition or dissolution.

The internal architecture of the trading companies was more robust than has been described in the literature. The activities of the diversified trading companies are not adequately captured by the term 'investment group' which suggests that their purpose was primarily financial. In fact, the constellation of firms around the trading companies need to be seen as complex 'business groups' employing multiple institutional and contractual modes, and inside which there existed flows of managerial, financial, and trading relationships. They possessed real advantages related to imperfections in capital, labour, and product markets and in the area of property rights enforcement. These groups resembled the universal banks seen on the Continent in their combination of financial and entrepreneurial roles, and in their ongoing managerial involvement in the enterprises they promoted. There were numerous conflicts of interest and potential for opportunist behaviour, but in practice rent-seeking was restrained.

The external relationships surrounding the trading companies were also important elements of their architecture. These networks often relied on trust rather than contracts and were extremely durable. British merchants emerged from hubs such as London, Liverpool, and Glasgow and clustered in hubs overseas, and this provided one support for the high trust levels which facilitated such networks. Long-term relationships with banks provided a source of credit for routine operations. At times of crisis, banks supported trading companies that experienced serious financial problems, occasionally becoming involved in the reconstruction of firms. Long-term relationships with shipping and insurance companies, and even some manufacturers, provided important elements in the business of the trading companies.

The British trading companies as a group were significant agents of economic growth before 1914. While not the creators of major technological breakthroughs through innovation or the application of science to manufacturing, they played an innovative role in developing new sources of supply of resources and opening new markets. They not only intermediated trade, but mobilized capital flows and directed them towards expanding supplies and markets in the emerging global economy. They were entrepreneurial firms which pioneered new industries, from jute manufacture in India and cotton textile manufacture in China, to the oil industry in California. They were not portfolio investors in these activities, but employed and transferred specific organizational and technological skills and competences. In the twentieth century their roles as agents of economic growth look less heroic. They were supplanted over time by locally owned firms or other types of multinational enterprise. However they continued to innovate in the production of commodities such as tea, rubber, and palm oil, and during the 1950s and 1960s were significant in the industrialization of a range of developing countries. In some countries they remained large-scale business enterprises which continued to innovate, to open new marketing and distribution channels, and to offer employment well into the 1970s and in some cases until today.

A major contribution of business history to the study of international business is to demonstrate the diversity and complexity of institutions and organizations which have engaged in multinational investment in the past, and to challenge theories and models based on contemporary experience to explain such diversity. In a literature in which multinational investment in high-tech manufacturing industry remains a central preoccupation, this study has focused instead on a group of service sector firms which were largely involved in developing economies. It has identified competitive advantages and management skills residing in contacts, knowledge, information, and relationships, and shown how 'network' forms of organization were employed over long time periods to control large and diversified multinational groups. By examining trading companies over two centuries, this study has also demonstrated how international business activity is shaped by historical circumstances, and how advantages and competences develop in a cumulative and evolutionary fashion. A historical perspective makes international business activity less analytically tractable, insofar as it demonstrates the complexity of the real world, but it also opens the way to a wider and deeper understanding of the behaviour and performance of firms.

APPENDIX I

Post-tax return on net capital employed of selected British trading companies, 1895–1998

	Borneo Co.	Swire's	Dodwells	H&C	Finlays	Brazilian Warrant	Wilson, Sons	Niger Co/UAC	Booker McConnell	Anglo-Thai
1895	4.4	11.3	—	—	—	n/a	3.9	6 7	n/a	—
1896	6.1	(4.4)	—	—	—	n/a	15 7	7.7	n/a	—
1897	10 4	7.9	—	—	—	n/a	6.7	9 5	n/a	—
1898	13.2	10.7	—	—	—	n/a	9 0	12 0	n/a	—
1899	7.7	8 3	31 9	—	—	n/a	8 8	14 5	n/a	—
1900	14 5	18 5	29 5	—	—	n/a	15 8	9 8	n/a	—
1901	15 0	4 8	23 5	—	—	n/a	14 5	9.4	—	—
1902	17 4	4 3	4 1	—	—	n/a	1 5	14.2	—	—
1903	20 0	7 0	8 4	—	—	n/a	8.9	14.0	—	—
1904	21 3	9.0	17.5	—	—	n/a	11.7	10.2	—	—
1905	18 1	8.2	10.2	—	—	n/a	11.5	7 4	—	—
1906	20.2	4.8	6 4	—	—	n/a	15.0	8 3	—	—
1907	16.1	2 9	7 1	—	—	n/a	21 2	6 8	—	—
1908	15 8	2 3	2.9	—	—	n/a	15 7	5.8	—	—
1909	13.4	3.9	1 0	11 0	—	n/a	11.8	7 1	—	—
1910	11.5	5 9	2 3	23 0	10 2	5.3	9 0	19 2	—	—
1911	10 8	6 1	(32 0)	19.4	9.6	9 4	15.1	9 2	—	—
1912	19 1	8.7	4.5	16.1	—	14 7	18 0	8.1	—	—
1913	12.1	10.3	8 9	10 2	14 7	14.6	16 4	6 2	—	—
1914	22 7	8 2	7 8	10 0	10.7	9 8	8 5	(1.9)	—	—
1915	16.4	15 2	18 8	10 6	14 7	7.7	20 5	8 3	—	—
1916	16.1	19.3	32 6	10.9	17.8	5.3	24 9	8 7	—	—
1917	27.3	18.2	22 2	12.7	17 5	6.8	25 4	12 0	—	—
1918	10 3	26.2	16 0	14 1	19 2	11 0	26.0	14 7	—	—
1919	25 2	32.1	24.3	10 5	23 4	8 1	21.2	—	—	—
1920	5 5	32.0	(30 8)	9 8	8.3	2 1	3 4	—	—	—
1921	(6.7)	12.3	(50.9)	6 6	—	0.1	(0 3)	—	(13.7)	—
1922	1 6	13 3	9 6	6.0	—	14.0	4 7	—	(8 1)	—
1923	1 8	22 5	5 6	7.6	10 9	11 9	5 1	—	14 6	—
1924	3 3	14 3	(8 1)	9.3	12 6	9 4	9 5	—	14 9	—
1925	3 9	6 9	(6.4)	10.4	12 5	4 6	9.1	—	7 4	—
1926	6 0	6 5	(5.6)	12 3	11 6	(1 1)	12.9	—	4 3	—
1927	7 1	6 2	1 3	12.8	11 6	3 1	14 0	—	4 9	—
1928	7 2	13 5	0 2	11 8	11.4	5.9	7 3	—	9 3	—
1929	8 5	7 7	(1 2)	13 4	9 5	2.1	4.4	—	6 5	—
1930	6 3	3 0	(3 2)	12.0	5 2	2 4	1.7	0.2	2.6	—
1931	1 1	4 6	(8 9)	8.3	3 5	3 0	0 0	(8 7)	3 4	—
1932	(3 0)	7 5	(9 1)	6 4	3.3	2 3	1 9	0.9	3 8	—
1933	(5.1)	5.7	(4 7)	7.5	3.6	(2.3)	1 3	3 7	6.6	—
1934	0 3	4 9	(10 5)	8 9	5 0	3.5	1.9	4 9	5 9	—
1935	0 4	1.3	(14 4)	9 1	4.1	(2.8)	2 9	9.0	5.1	—
1936	0 8	3.8	0 7	9 1	4.0	4.0	5 5	11 0	6.7	—
1937	5 1	11.2	9 9	10.7	5.0	(2 8)	8.8	13.0	7 8	—
1938	6 4	3.2	12 8	10 7	5.1	6 3	3 3	5.2	8 3	—
1939	2.0	3 6	7 1	10 9	9.8	6 8	5 0	8.1	8 4	—

Gray Mackenzie	Smith Mackenzie	Inchcape	Guthries	John Holt	Lonrho	Antony Gibbs	Duncan Fox	Balfour Williamson	Jardine Matheson	Average
—	—	n/a	—	—	n/a	—	—	—	—	6 6
—	—	n/a	—	—	n/a	—	—	—	—	6 3
—	—	n/a	—	—	n/a	—	—	—	—	8.6
—	—	n/a	—	—	n/a	—	—	—	—	11.2
—	—	n/a	—	—	n/a	—	—	—	—	14.2
—	—	n/a	—	—	n/a	—	—	—	—	17 6
—	—	n/a	—	—	n/a	—	—	—	—	13 4
—	—	n/a	—	—	n/a	—	—	—	—	8 3
—	—	n/a	—	—	n/a	—	—	—	—	11 6
—	—	n/a	—	—	n/a	—	—	—	—	13 9
—	—	n/a	—	—	n/a	—	—	—	—	11 1
—	—	n/a	—	—	n/a	—	—	—	—	10 9
—	—	n/a	—	—	n/a	—	—	—	—	10 8
—	—	n/a	—	—	n/a	—	—	—	—	8.5
—	—	n/a	—	—	n/a	—	—	—	—	8.0
—	—	n/a	—	—	n/a	—	—	—	—	10 8
—	—	n/a	—	—	n/a	—	—	—	—	5 9
—	—	n/a	—	—	n/a	—	—	—	—	12.7
—	—	n/a	—	—	n/a	—	—	—	—	11 7
—	—	n/a	—	—	n/a	—	—	—	—	9 5
—	—	n/a	—	—	n/a	—	—	—	—	14 0
—	—	n/a	—	—	n/a	—	—	—	—	17.0
—	—	n/a	—	—	n/a	—	—	—	—	17 8
—	—	n/a	—	—	n/a	—	—	—	—	17 2
—	—	n/a	—	—	n/a	—	—	—	—	20 7
—	—	n/a	—	—	n/a	—	—	—	—	4 3
—	—	n/a	—	—	n/a	—	—	—	—	(7.5)
—	—	n/a	—	—	n/a	—	—	—	—	5 9
—	—	n/a	—	—	n/a	—	—	—	—	10 0
—	—	n/a	—	—	n/a	—	—	—	—	8 2
—	—	n/a	—	—	n/a	—	—	—	—	6 1
—	—	n/a	—	—	n/a	—	—	—	—	5 9
—	—	n/a	—	—	n/a	—	—	—	—	7 6
—	—	n/a	—	—	n/a	—	—	—	—	8 3
—	—	n/a	—	—	n/a	—	—	—	—	6 4
—	—	n/a	—	—	n/a	—	—	—	—	3 4
—	—	n/a	—	—	n/a	—	—	—	—	0 7
—	—	n/a	—	—	n/a	—	—	—	—	1 6
—	—	n/a	—	—	n/a	—	—	—	—	1 8
—	—	n/a	—	—	n/a	—	—	—	—	2 8
—	—	n/a	—	—	n/a	—	—	—	—	1 6
—	—	n/a	—	—	n/a	—	—	—	—	5 1
—	—	n/a	—	—	n/a	—	—	—	—	7 6
—	—	n/a	—	—	n/a	—	—	—	—	6 8
—	—	n/a	—	—	n/a	—	—	—	—	6 9

	Borneo Co	Swire's	Dodwells	H&C	Finlays	Brazilian Warrant	Wilson, Sons	Niger Co/UAC	Booker McConnell	Anglo-Thai
1940	6 2	5 5	4 1	10.6	5 0	6 1	6 6	6 3	7.2	—
1941	2.3	3 6	0 4	10 9	5.1	11 3	9 7	8 6	7 2	—
1942	0.9	0 9	4 1	12 5	1 9	5 1	7 0	13 7	7 8	—
1943	(3 1)	0 8	5.4	7 2	4 7	2 5	4.3	15.6	6 9	—
1944	(2 1)	0 2	(0 5)	7.7	4 8	5 5	3 5	15.2	6.6	—
1945	—	(3 2)	2 2	8.8	5.9	9 6	3 4	15 1	4 9	—
1946	0.1	1 4	4.0	5 3	8.4	7.8	7 0	13 8	5 2	—
1947	3 5	1 9	21 4	6 1	9.2	4.8	5 2	14 4	12 3	—
1948	16 7	2.3	15 0	23 5	8 5	7.1	5.8	7.5	8 6	15 0
1949	15 1	0 2	8.9	8 2	6 1	35 0	6 3	10.7	12.0	10.8
1950	15 6	2 3	11.6	20.2	3.8	n/a	7 1	7 1	9 3	16.9
1951	23 9	4.5	19 8	19 0	3 9	n/a	5 1	6.8	12.1	17.6
1952	28 1	2.4	3.7	17 4	2 4	n/a	(10 1)	6.5	10.0	19.7
1953	16 5	8 3	10.6	4 8	2 7	n/a	(8 2)	8 7	7.7	15.2
1954	6 7	5 3	7.3	11 3	4 1	n/a	4 7	7 8	10.7	6.9
1955	4 5	5 1	11 6	6.8	7.4	n/a	—	5 9	8.4	8 6
1956	9 5	6 3	11 2	13.3	5.0	n/a	—	5 7	8 5	3 7
1957	8 1	7 4	6.1	9 4	4 9	n/a	—	5.5	10.8	8 3
1958	6.2	7 3	(5 7)	4 1	3.9	n/a	—	7 9	8 9	2 7
1959	1 8	34.4	3 9	6 9	4 6	n/a	—	7 5	10.4	3 7
1960	6 2	10.7	3 7	12 4	3 9	n/a	—	2.8	9 9	5 8
1961	9 1	14 2	6.0	6 6	4 8	n/a	—	3.1	7.9	8.9
1962	8 6	9 6	8 4	8.7	3 6	n/a	—	2 9	7 6	9 4
1963	10 2	4 6	15 8	6.4	5 5	n/a	—	1 2	9 0	10 7
1964	8.5	4 8	19 6	10 4	4 2	n/a	—	1 4	7 2	10 9
1965	7.9	—	20 5	13 8	4.1	n/a	—	3 1	6 1	10 2
1966	9.4	—	13 3	10 2	6.3	n/a	—	2 7	6 9	9 3
1967	7 3	6.3	15.2	11 8	6 7	n/a	—	4.4	7.4	10.5
1968	n/a	9 3	15 2	16 0	6 8	n/a	7 3	7 4	6.6	11.0
1969	n/a	9 7	15.3	13 2	7 4	n/a	5 7	4 1	5.1	12.0
1970	n/a	12.8	20 8	14 6	5.8	n/a	8 3	3 5	6 7	13 9
1971	n/a	6.1	5 7	15 2	2 4	n/a	8.4	6.5	8 1	15 4
1972	n/a	6.8	6.9	16 4	2 2	n/a	13.7	7.1	10.2	11.6
1973	n/a	8 2	12.0	31.0	6 3	n/a	24 4	8 5	9 2	18.2
1974	n/a	10 1	n/a	17 1	6 4	n/a	21 4	9 0	11 9	22 7
1975	n/a	11 4	n/a	9 9	6 6	n/a	19 2	15 5	11 3	18.6
1976	n/a	13 8	n/a	14 9	16.4	n/a	19 1	19 4	12 9	n/a
1977	n/a	13.8	n/a	15 1	12 8	n/a	16.2	18 9	17.8	n/a
1978	n/a	15.2	n/a	16 7	7 0	n/a	16 0	14 9	20 2	n/a
1979	n/a	8.8	n/a	14 7	8 1	n/a	12 3	13 3	20.2	n/a
1980	n/a	8 9	n/a	11 5	9 4	n/a	8 9	10 8	11 9	n/a
1981	n/a	11 4	n/a	7.6	10 3	n/a	12 0	12 6	12 3	n/a
1982	n/a	8 8	n/a	6.0	10 0	n/a	17 4	9 6	11 8	n/a
1983	n/a	12 9	n/a	6.4	14 4	n/a	8 1	6 3	12 8	n/a
1984	n/a	13 3	n/a	8 8	15.1	n/a	13 5	—	20 4	n/a
1985	n/a	12 9	n/a	7.8	3.7	n/a	13.7	—	25 8	n/a
1986	n/a	14.1	n/a	9 2	0.2	n/a	12.3	—	24.7	n/a
1987	n/a	16 6	n/a	13 9	1 6	n/a	12.2	n/a	27 6	n/a
1988	n/a	13.3	n/a	16 2	3 5	n/a	22 5	n/a	31 1	n/a
1989	n/a	15 3	n/a	15.1	5 6	n/a	26 1	n/a	34 6	n/a
1990	n/a	12 0	n/a	11 6	5 2	n/a	10 1	n/a	n/a	n/a
1991	n/a	10 2	n/a	7 4	5 7	n/a	6.5	n/a	n/a	n/a
1992	n/a	9 2	n/a	7.0	3 8	n/a	n/a	n/a	n/a	n/a
1993	n/a	7.8	n/a	8 2	4 2	n/a	n/a	n/a	n/a	n/a
1994	n/a	8.8	n/a	22 4	3 1	n/a	n/a	n/a	n/a	n/a
1995	n/a	9 9	n/a	12 1	(0 1)	n/a	n/a	n/a	n/a	n/a
1996	n/a	10 0	n/a	13 2	5 5	n/a	n/a	n/a	n/a	n/a
1997	n/a	8 6	n/a	n/a	8 0	n/a	n/a	n/a	n/a	n/a
1998	n/a	3 0	n/a	n/a	8 0	n/a	n/a	n/a	n/a	n/a

n/a not applicable

Gray Mackenzie	Smith Mackenzie	Inchcape	Guthries	John Holt	Lonrho	Antony Gibbs	Duncan Fox	Balfour Williamson	Jardine Matheson	Average
—	—	—	—	—	n/a	—	—	—	—	6.4
—	—	—	—	—	n/a	—	—	—	—	6 6
—	—	—	—	—	n/a	—	—	—	—	6 0
—	—	—	—	—	n/a	—	—	—	—	4 9
—	—	—	—	—	n/a	—	—	—	—	4 5
—	—	—	—	—	n/a	—	—	—	—	5 8
2 5	5 3	—	—	—	n/a	—	—	—	—	5 5
8.0	12.0	—	—	—	n/a	—	—	—	—	9 0
18 0	14 6	—	—	—	n/a	—	—	—	—	11.9
5 9	16 2	—	—	—	n/a	—	—	3 0	—	10 6
1 0	16 2	—	—	8.2	n/a	—	—	2 3	—	9 3
12 4	9 6	—	—	7 5	n/a	—	—	7.3	—	11 5
10.2	11 3	—	—	1 9	n/a	—	—	5 3	—	8 4
8.4	—	—	—	9 6	n/a	—	—	4 7	—	7 4
5 6	—	—	—	5.0	n/a	—	11 1	6 4	—	7 1
11 2	—	—	—	2 5	n/a	—	6 4	7 3	—	7 1
9.1	—	—	—	4 6	n/a	—	6 5	7 2	—	7.5
20.2	—	—	—	6 6	n/a	—	6 8	6 4	7.1	8 3
15 6	—	—	—	2 4	n/a	—	5 6	9.2	6 4	5.7
16 0	6 7	7 5	—	11 1	n/a	—	7 4	6.8	8.4	9 1
17 4	5 1	9 1	—	7 4	n/a	—	6.7	6.5	7.3	7.7
n/a	8 4	7 3	—	5 3	4 4	—	3 3	1 6	8 5	6 6
n/a	8.1	7 0	—	2.5	5 9	—	5 1	(1 2)	7.6	6 2
n/a	10.3	7.2	—	2 3	6 0	—	5 5	0 6	10 7	7 1
n/a	5 0	7.3	—	2.7	2.5	—	5 1	6 0	10 5	7 1
n/a	n/a	6 7	—	10 6	4 6	—	4 8	6.4	11 0	8 4
n/a	n/a	5 8	14 9	3 7	7 7	—	7.0	9.9	11 5	8.5
n/a	n/a	7 3	11 9	(6 2)	7 3	—	8.7	1 2	12 3	7.5
n/a	n/a	6 9	9 6	5 1	4 2	—	8.4	5.3	15.0	8.9
n/a	n/a	9 3	10 1	12 1	3 8	—	6 5	5 1	13.2	8.8
n/a	n/a	9 6	12 3	n/a	5.2	—	8 1	6 5	14 7	10 2
n/a	n/a	9 7	12 6	n/a	5 4	—	(32 3)	8 0	14 9	6 1
n/a	n/a	11 4	11 0	n/a	6 3	—	11.4	8 2	10 1	9 5
n/a	n/a	11.8	5 2	n/a	8 5	5 2	0 3	1 7	6 3	10.5
n/a	n/a	14 1	2 2	n/a	11 4	(3 7)	8 4	2 7	8 4	10 1
n/a	n/a	11 3	1 5	n/a	11 8	3.2	5.8	14 6	9 6	10 7
n/a	n/a	10 4	2 9	n/a	12 0	3 5	8 5	n/a	10 2	12 0
n/a	n/a	15 6	6 7	n/a	12 4	2 9	0 4	n/a	10.8	12.0
n/a	n/a	13 7	4 4	n/a	12 1	2 8	7 2	n/a	11 7	11 8
n/a	n/a	6 0	5 0	n/a	8 6	0 3	2 0	n/a	12.6	9.3
n/a	n/a	13 4	3 8	n/a	8 2	n/a	n/a	n/a	11.4	9 8
n/a	n/a	8 2	4 0	n/a	6.3	n/a	n/a	n/a	11 8	9 6
n/a	n/a	3 1	n/a	n/a	3 4	n/a	n/a	n/a	12.6	9 2
n/a	n/a	3 6	n/a	n/a	8 7	n/a	n/a	n/a	4 0	8.6
n/a	n/a	6 5	n/a	n/a	8.8	n/a	n/a	n/a	3 1	11 2
n/a	n/a	3 5	n/a	n/a	10.4	n/a	n/a	n/a	4 8	10 3
n/a	n/a	15 4	n/a	n/a	11 2	n/a	n/a	n/a	10 5	12 2
n/a	n/a	22 8	n/a	n/a	11 4	n/a	n/a	n/a	13 8	15 0
n/a	n/a	26 6	n/a	n/a	11.8	n/a	n/a	n/a	12 7	17.2
n/a	n/a	26.4	n/a	n/a	12 2	n/a	n/a	n/a	15.3	18.8
n/a	n/a	23.3	n/a	n/a	12 0	n/a	n/a	n/a	14 8	12 7
n/a	n/a	22 0	n/a	n/a	10.0	n/a	n/a	n/a	13 9	10 8
n/a	n/a	23 0	n/a	n/a	2 8	n/a	n/a	n/a	13 8	9 9
n/a	n/a	21 9	n/a	n/a	9 6	n/a	n/a	n/a	12 0	10 6
n/a	n/a	20 7	n/a	n/a	6.0	n/a	n/a	n/a	12 2	12 2
n/a	n/a	(4.9)	n/a	n/a	8 3	n/a	n/a	n/a	10 6	6 0
n/a	n/a	3 6	n/a	n/a	4 1	n/a	n/a	n/a	6 9	7 2
n/a	n/a	2 7	n/a	n/a	14.3	n/a	n/a	n/a	6 8	8.1
n/a	n/a	(52.0)	n/a	n/a	n/a	n/a	n/a	n/a	2.3	(9 7)

APPENDIX 2

Pre-tax return on net capital employed of selected British trading companies, 1948–1998

	Borneo Co.	Swire's	Dodwells	H&C	Finlays	Brazilian Warrant	Wilson, Sons	UAC	Booker McConnell	Anglo-Thai
1948	36.3	2.1	33 0	18 7	12.3	15.2	13.3	18 3	18 8	30 1
1949	24.6	3.0	36.3	21.4	8.2	52.9	17 1	21.4	19.5	26.3
1950	28 5	2.7	37.3	22.0	9.7	n/a	14.9	17 4	17.6	36.1
1951	44.4	6.0	38.9	30 2	11 7	n/a	13.2	—	24.3	38 3
1952	55.9	3.0	8.8	28.3	7 8	n/a	(9.7)	12.2	18.9	35.1
1953	32.2	7.6	19 6	22.2	1.4	n/a	(6 3)	—	19 8	25.4
1954	14.5	5.9	11.9	20.1	9.2	n/a	6.2	14.3	20.7	14.6
1955	11.4	5.9	21.0	19.9	17 2	n/a	—	12.1	20 3	16 6
1956	19.2	7.8	31 0	22.0	11.6	n/a	—	12.3	22.5	7.8
1957	18.2	9 0	20.6	19.7	11.0	n/a	—	10.5	28.9	13.5
1958	12 9	8.2	0.3	16.5	8.3	n/a	—	8.0	22.2	10.6
1959	5.5	34.7	14 3	16 1	9.7	n/a	4 6	11.7	23.3	10.6
1960	11.8	12 1	18.1	19.2	9.1	n/a	14.7	7.1	20.8	12.6
1961	16.6	15.1	16.4	18 7	9.6	n/a	9.2	7 2	17.1	17.9
1962	15.9	11.1	21.4	17.7	8.4	n/a	8.1	5 0	16.9	15 4
1963	19 2	6.4	33.6	17.7	13.7	n/a	11.1	2 3	20 6	15 8
1964	14 9	7.5	41.0	18.5	10.5	n/a	4.4	3 2	14 7	18.3
1965	14 5	—	34.6	20.8	7.8	n/a	7.7	5.2	11.6	18.0
1966	15 5	—	23.9	19.5	12.8	n/a	11.1	4.7	12 3	18.9
1967	10.4	8.9	29 1	19.2	11 1	n/a	5.6	8.2	13.8	19.8
1968	n/a	11.9	27.9	20 6	8.3	n/a	10.8	11.3	11.3	18.4
1969	n/a	11.9	31.0	21 3	10.8	n/a	7.7	8.1	9.9	20.7
1970	n/a	16 8	34.3	22.4	9.1	n/a	10.7	6.9	12 6	21.1
1971	n/a	9.8	14 5	24.0	6.7	n/a	11.1	11.1	15.6	24.7
1972	n/a	9.3	10 3	27.7	4.8	n/a	21.6	11.5	18 9	18 9
1973	n/a	12 6	22.8	34.5	10.1	n/a	38.8	12.2	18.2	28.1
1974	n/a	16.6	n/a	37 6	16.0	n/a	31.1	—	25.1	44.5
1975	n/a	16.5	n/a	20.9	14 4	n/a	31.2	—	26.7	36.9
1976	n/a	21.6	n/a	30.6	32.6	n/a	33.8	—	24.3	n/a
1977	n/a	22.0	n/a	27.3	31.4	n/a	28.2	—	36 8	n/a
1978	n/a	22.0	n/a	30.6	16.9	n/a	28 9	—	26.4	n/a
1979	n/a	13 4	n/a	27.0	14.5	n/a	24.5	—	23 9	n/a
1980	n/a	14.0	n/a	19.8	14.1	n/a	23.0	—	13.7	n/a
1981	n/a	18.4	n/a	13.6	15.1	n/a	24.6	—	15.4	n/a
1982	n/a	13 6	n/a	8.9	16.2	n/a	32.2	—	16.8	n/a
1983	n/a	17.1	n/a	11.6	26.6	n/a	22.6	—	19.5	n/a
1984	n/a	18.5	n/a	15 5	30.6	n/a	29.9	—	28.3	n/a
1985	n/a	18.5	n/a	12 3	6.4	n/a	29.7	—	36.3	n/a
1986	n/a	19 8	n/a	13 9	4 4	n/a	29.7	—	35.4	n/a
1987	n/a	22.4	n/a	20.2	2.8	n/a	26.8	n/a	39.7	n/a
1988	n/a	16.6	n/a	22.6	6.3	n/a	44.5	n/a	42 8	n/a
1989	n/a	17.8	n/a	21 4	10 9	n/a	48.2	n/a	45 9	n/a

Gray Mackenzie	Smith Mackenzie	Inchcape	Guthries	John Holt	Lonrho	Duncan Fox	Balfour Williamson	Jardine Matheson	Average
41 1	25.6	n/a	—	—	n/a	—	—	—	22 1
17.2	29 1	n/a	—	—	n/a	—	8.4	—	21 9
6.9	26.0	n/a	—	8.2	n/a	—	7 2	—	18.0
15.2	15 8	n/a	—	8 3	n/a	—	11.2	—	21.5
35.8	16 3	n/a	—	1 9	n/a	—	11.5	—	17.4
25 5	—	n/a	—	14 1	n/a	—	9 9	—	15.6
16.2	—	n/a	—	10.8	n/a	16 3	10.3	—	13.2
24.4	—	n/a	—	2 3	n/a	17 3	9.9	—	14 9
22.4	—	n/a	—	10 6	n/a	18 0	12.2	—	16.4
21.6	—	n/a	—	10 7	n/a	15.8	12.0	8 9	15.4
16.7	—	n/a	—	3 8	n/a	14.0	12.7	8.0	10.9
16.9	8.8	12 3	—	15.5	n/a	16 1	10 4	12.4	13 9
18.1	7.3	14 5	—	10.5	n/a	15 1	10 2	11.6	13 3
n/a	12.0	10 7	—	7.7	6 4	9 4	6.0	14.1	12 1
n/a	13 2	11.5	—	5 4	12 8	11.8	(0.8)	13 0	11 7
n/a	17.0	11 7	—	5.1	12.6	10.7	6.4	15.3	13.7
n/a	9.1	11 0	—	6.2	10.0	11.3	14 4	14.2	13 1
n/a	—	9.9	—	14 5	13 8	13.1	13.9	15 4	14.3
n/a	—	7.4	26.3	6.9	19.3	11.5	16 0	16 4	14 8
n/a	n/a	10 0	22.2	(4 9)	18 1	13.5	1.8	16 9	12 7
n/a	n/a	9 1	19.9	10.6	13.6	11.3	8.6	19 1	14.2
n/a	n/a	13 6	19.0	24.8	12.2	11.1	8.7	22 0	15.5
n/a	n/a	14.8	18.8	n/a	12.4	15.1	11 4	21 6	16.3
n/a	n/a	15.4	20.1	n/a	11.5	(22.8)	12 5	23.4	12 7
n/a	n/a	17 6	14.9	n/a	12 8	20.5	13 2	20.4	15 9
n/a	n/a	19 4	4.2	n/a	16 2	0.7	5.1	12.6	16 8
n/a	n/a	24 5	8.1	n/a	23 0	8.4	8 5	29.3	22 7
n/a	n/a	22 3	6.3	n/a	19 8	11.1	30.0	17.8	21 2
n/a	n/a	20.9	8 7	n/a	21 7	3.3	n/a	17 8	21.5
n/a	n/a	30 2	13 0	n/a	19.4	0.6	n/a	17 2	22.6
n/a	n/a	24 7	9 3	n/a	18.8	7.4	n/a	17 7	20.3
n/a	n/a	13.7	10 4	n/a	13.9	1.0	n/a	19.0	16.1
n/a	n/a	21.6	9.1	n/a	14.0	n/a	n/a	15.3	16 1
n/a	n/a	18 1	7.6	n/a	11 5	n/a	n/a	15.7	15 6
n/a	n/a	9.3	n/a	n/a	7.1	n/a	n/a	16 3	15 0
n/a	n/a	11 8	n/a	n/a	17.2	n/a	n/a	9.3	17 0
n/a	n/a	16 5	n/a	n/a	17.2	n/a	n/a	8.6	20.6
n/a	n/a	13.1	n/a	n/a	19.9	n/a	n/a	10.0	18 3
n/a	n/a	27 9	n/a	n/a	19.8	n/a	n/a	17.0	21.0
n/a	n/a	37 0	n/a	n/a	19.4	n/a	n/a	19 0	23.4
n/a	n/a	41.8	n/a	n/a	17.8	n/a	n/a	15.8	26.0
n/a	n/a	40.6	n/a	n/a	18.4	n/a	n/a	19.6	27.8

	Borneo Co	Swire's	Dodwells	H&C	Finlays	Brazilian Warrant	Wilson, Sons	UAC	Booker McConnell	Anglo-Thai
1990	n/a	14.6	n/a	16.5	8.3	n/a	22.9	n/a	n/a	n/a
1991	n/a	12.4	n/a	10.9	9.1	n/a	14.8	n/a	n/a	n/a
1992	n/a	11.3	n/a	11 0	8.1	n/a	n/a	n/a	n/a	n/a
1993	n/a	9.3	n/a	13.0	11 0	n/a	n/a	n/a	n/a	n/a
1994	n/a	11 0	n/a	27.1	5 8	n/a	n/a	n/a	n/a	n/a
1995	n/a	12 1	n/a	17 2	2.8	n/a	n/a	n/a	n/a	n/a
1996	n/a	11 7	n/a	18 2	9.5	n/a	n/a	n/a	n/a	n/a
1997	n/a	10.3	n/a	n/a	10.8	n/a	n/a	n/a	n/a	n/a
1998	n/a	4.0	n/a	n/a	11.4	n/a	n/a	n/a	n/a	n/a

n/a not applicable

Gray Mackenzie	Smith Mackenzie	Inchcape	Guthries	John Holt	Lonrho	Duncan Fox	Balfour Williamson	Jardine Matheson	Average
n/a	n/a	35.2	n/a	n/a	17.0	n/a	n/a	19 2	19 1
n/a	n/a	33.5	n/a	n/a	14.3	n/a	n/a	18 5	16.2
n/a	n/a	34 0	n/a	n/a	5 3	n/a	n/a	17 0	14 4
n/a	n/a	31 0	n/a	n/a	12 1	n/a	n/a	14 9	15 2
n/a	n/a	30 5	n/a	n/a	8 1	n/a	n/a	15 3	16 3
n/a	n/a	2 6	n/a	n/a	11 1	n/a	n/a	12.9	9 8
n/a	n/a	10.5	n/a	n/a	7.4	n/a	n/a	9.0	11.0
n/a	n/a	9 7	n/a	n/a	16 7	n/a	n/a	8 9	11 3
n/a	n/a	(43.1)	n/a	n/a	n/a	n/a	n/a	4.6	(5 8)

APPENDIX 3

Sources for calculations on capital employed of British trading companies

This Appendix gives the sources used to calculate net capital employed and return on net capital employed of individual firms. Data are based on published reports and accounts except when indicated.

Anglo-Thai Corporation · 1913 capital employed: capital employed was £300,822 in 1918, while issued capital was £85,000 in 1913. Profits were around £300,000 for 1913–18, while dividends were £94,800. A figure of £100,000 for 1913 appears reasonable. 1938 capital employed: estimated from 1923 figure of £601,452. Request for quotation files, Anglo-Siam Corporation, MS 18000, GHL. Company annual reports, MS 27013, GHL.

Balfour Williamson · 1913 capital employed: based on Wallis Hunt, *Heirs*, ii. 92. 1938 capital employed: based on Wallis Hunt, *Heirs*, ii. 205, 217, and 1949 actual figure. Company annual reports, Companies House.

Booker Brothers, McConnell & Co. · 1913 capital employed: estimated, based on actual capital employed in 1921 of £545,145. Company annual reports held by the company.

Borneo Co. · Company annual reports, MS 27200, 27185 GHL.

Brazilian Warrant · Greenhill, 'Investment Group', 103. Annual accounts, Stock Exchange series, GHL.

Dodwell & Co. · Company annual reports, MS 27501–2, GHL.

James Finlay · 1913 capital employed: the earliest available figure in the accounts is £3.9 million for 1923. The 1913 figure is estimated on the basis of a 1920 report by Alexander Sloan & Co. giving net value of assets of the partnership handed over to the company in 1908 at £1,341,647 and capital and reserves in 1920 at £2,101,299. Data in the 1924 prospectus gives average profits back to 1914. Company annual reports held by the company, Glasgow University archives, Companies House (Edinburgh).

Duncan Fox · 1913 capital employed: records of London & River Plate Bank, BOLSA archives, D40/1, UCL, give total for partners' capital (apparently excluding the firm's investments) in 1909 as £930,000 representing both capital in the firm and capital privately held. This is too high because of the inclusion of private funds, but has been used because another four years' profits would have accumulated by 1913. 1938 capital employed: estimated from data for 1928 and 1954. Company annual reports, Companies House.

Antony Gibbs — 1913 capital employed: based on company archives, GHL. Chapman, *Merchant Enterprise*, 255, gives a figure of £2 million, but this appears too high. 1938 capital employed: estimated from data for constituent partnerships. 1978 capital employed: company annual reports, Bodleian Library.

Gray Mackenzie — 1913 and 1938 capital employed: crude estimates from 1940 annual report. Company annual reports, MS 27698, 27701, GHL.

Guthrie & Co. — 1913 capital employed: the company was established in 1903 with a share capital of $1 million Straits dollars. Archives in SOAS show that profits outweighed losses in the following decade. 1938 and 1954 capital employed: estimated from records of Mercantile Bank, HSBC Group Archives. Company annual reports, Companies House.

Harrisons & Crosfield — Company annual reports, GHL, Companies House.

John Holt — 1913 and 1938 capital employed: estimated from records of District Bank, 11025, 11041, NatWest Group Archives. Company annual reports, Companies House.

Inchcape — Company annual reports, Companies House.

Jardine Matheson — 1913 capital employed: Chapman, *Merchant Enterprise*, 282–3. Company annual reports held by the company.

Lonrho — Company annual reports, Bodleian Library, Companies House.

Niger Company — Company annual reports, Unilever Archives, UAD/4/1.

Smith McKenzie — 1913 capital employed: crude estimate from 1937 annual report. Company annual reports, MS 28126–8, GHL.

John Swire & Son — JSS I 7/26; balance sheet book (166), Swire ADD, box 3, SOAS. Company annual reports held by the company.

United Africa Company   Unilever Archives;
                         1978 capital employed estimate: Fieldhouse, *Merchant
                         Capital*, 497, gives 'average gross capital employed' for
                         1975/6 as £506.7 million. McKinsey (1984) gives
                         'consolidated historic cost total assets less current
                         liabilities' for 1982/3 as £462 million.

Wilson, Sons & Co.   Minute books, MS 20186/1–10, MS 20189/30, GHL.
                         Company annual reports, Companies House. The data
                         used for 1895 to 1954 is for Wilson, Sons & Co. and
                         not for Ocean Coal & Wilsons, the holding company
                         of which it formed a part after 1908. The data after
                         1955 is for Ocean Wilsons (Holdings) Ltd.

Select Bibliography

This book has drawn extensively on the confidential records of British trading companies and books. However the records of many firms have been lost, and in most cases confidentiality considerations mean that archives are not available from the 1970s or even after 1945.

Guildhall Library, London (GHL), is a major repository for the archives of British trading companies. The major collections are those of the Inchcape predecessor firms (the Anglo-Thai Corporation, Assam Company, Binny's, Borneo Company, Dodwells, and Gray Mackenzie), Harrisons & Crosfield (now Elementis), and Antony Gibbs. These three archives are used extensively in this book. In addition, the Guildhall Library holds smaller archival collections of Brazilian Warrant, Grahams, Ralli, Steel Brothers, and Wilson, Sons & Co. The huge archival records of Wallace Brothers, deposited at Guildhall Library over twenty years ago, are still not catalogued and remain unavailable for research.

The School of Oriental and African Studies, London (SOAS), holds the archives of John Swire & Sons and their associated firms from the nineteenth century until the 1940s, and these have been consulted in depth. The surviving archives of Guthries are also held at SOAS and were researched. University College, London (UCL), D. M. S. Watson Library holds the archives of Balfour Williamson and its associated firms, notably the Santa Rosa Milling Co. Ltd., as well as the Bank of London and South America and its predecessors.

Cambridge University Library (CUL) contains the archives of Jardine Matheson and Jardine Skinner. The nineteenth century records of the former are enormous and have been extensively consulted by other scholars. As a result, the research for this book was largely based on the recently available archives covering the twentieth century before 1945.

The University of Glasgow, Business Records Centre (UGD), holds the archives of James Finlay plc which were extensively researched. In addition the records of the Arracan Rice & Trading Co. were consulted.

The archives of John Holt & Co. (Liverpool) Ltd. are held at Rhodes House, Oxford, and the Liverpool Record Office (collection 380 HOL 1). The Oxford collection is the more extensive and covers material between 1863 and 1961. Both archives have been researched.

A number of archival collections retained by companies were consulted. The main records of Lobitos Oilfields, some of which are included in the Balfour Williamson archive, are held in the Burmah Castrol Archives, Swindon. Surviving archives of Booker Brothers, McConnell & Co. were consulted at Booker plc, London. The annual reports of James Finlay plc were consulted at that company's head office in Glasgow. The annual reports of John Swire & Sons between 1935 and the early 1970s were consulted at that company's head office in London. The vast archives of the United Africa Company are held by Unilever Historical Archives at their Port Sunlight depository. They are not catalogued. Very limited access was provided to the collection for this project. D. K. Fieldhouse's study of UAC, *Merchant Capital and Economic*

Decolonization (Oxford: Clarendon Press, 1994) provides a comprehensive history of the firm from its creation in 1929.

This book has utilized the archives of four leading British banks. Lloyds TSB Group Archives, London, contain the records of Lloyds Bank. HSBC Group Archives, London, has the archives of the Midland Bank, and the North and South Wales Bank, the Mercantile Bank of India and the Hongkong Bank, National Westminster Group Archives, London, has the records of the National Provincial Bank and the District Bank. Barclays Bank Group Archives has the records of Barclays Bank and Martins Bank. In addition, some material from the archives of Standard Chartered plc, which were researched for the author's earlier project on British multinational banks, have been utilized. The trading companies made extensive use of banking facilities and as a result a great deal of information about them can be found in banking records, including about firms which left no records.

The statutory company information deposited at Companies House was used extensively and it proved especially valuable for firms such as Duncan Fox whose records are no longer extant.

Interviews were held between 1996 and 1999 with Robert Brouwer and Ingrid Hoffman (Arcon Overseas Ltd.), Mr Jeremy Brown (Matheson and Co.), the late Sir Colin Campbell (James Finlay), and Sir John and Sir Adrian Swire, Edward Scott, and other members of J. Swire & Co.

Secondary Sources

This bibliography is a guide to the most relevant literature on the evolution of British trading companies, and the wider theoretical and historical literature utilized in this book. It does not list all the sources cited in the text.

ALLEN, G. C., and DONNITHORNE, AUDREY G., *Western Enterprise in Far Eastern Economic Development* (London: George Allen & Unwin, 1954).
—— *Western Enterprise in Indonesia and Malaya* (London: George Allen & Unwin, 1957).
ANON., *History and Activities of the Ralli Trading Group* (London: the firm, 1979).
—— *The House of Binny* (London: the firm, 1969).
—— *The History of Knowles & Foster 1828–1948* (London: Ted Kavanagh, 1948).
ANTROBUS, H. A., *A History of the Assam Company, 1839–1953* (Edinburgh: the firm, 1957).
ARNOLD, A. J., 'Profitability and Capital Accumulation in British Industry during the Transwar Period, 1913–1924', *Economic History Review*, 52 (1999).
—— '"Publishing Your Private Affairs to the World": Corporate Financial Disclosures in the U.K. 1900–24', *Accounting, Business and Financial History*, 7 (1997).
BAGCHI, A. K., *Private Investment in India 1900–1939* (Cambridge: Cambridge University Press, 1972).
BAUER, P. T., *The Rubber Industry* (London: Longmans, 1948).
BEACHY, R. W., *The British West Indian Sugar Industry in the Late Nineteenth Century* (Cambridge: Cambridge University Press, 1957).
BLAKE, GEORGE, *Gellatly's 1862–1962* (London: Blackies & Son, 1962).
BLAKE, ROBERT, *Jardine Matheson. Traders of the Far East* (London: Weidenfeld & Nicolson, 1999).
BONIN, HUBERT, *C.F.A.O. Cent Ans de Compétition* (Paris: Economica, 1987).

BOYCE, GORDON, *Information, Mediation and Institutional Development* (Manchester: Manchester University Press, 1995).

BRAUND, H. E. W., *Calling to Mind* (Oxford: Pergamon Press, 1975).

BROEHL, WAYNE G. Jnr., *Cargill: Going Global* (Hanover, NJ: University Press of New England, 1998).

BROGAN, J., *James Finlay & Co. Limited* (Glasgow: Jackson Sons & Co., 1951).

BROWN, HILTON, *Parry's of Madras: A Story of British Enterprise in India* (Madras: the firm, 1954).

BROWN, R. A., *Capital and Entrepreneurship in Southeast Asia* (London: Macmillan, 1994).

BUCKLEY, PETER J., and CASSON, MARK, *The Future of the Multinational Enterprise* (London: Macmillan, 1976).

BUTLER, CHARLOTTE, and KEARY, JOHN, *Managers and Mantras* (Singapore: John Wiley, 2000).

CAIN, P. J., and HOPKINS, A. G., *British Imperialism: Crisis and Deconstruction 1914–1990* (London: Longman, 1993).

—— *British Imperialism: Innovation and Expansion 1688–1914* (London: Longman, 1993).

CARLOS, A. M., and NICHOLAS, S., '"Giants of an Earlier Capitalism": The Chartered Trading Companies as Modern Multinationals', *Business History Review*, 62 (1988), 398–419.

CASSON, MARK, 'Institutional Diversity in Overseas Enterprise: Explaining the Free-Standing Company', *Business History*, 36 (1994), 95–108.

—— 'The Economic Analysis of Multinational Trading Companies', in Geoffrey Jones (ed.), *The Multinational Traders*.

CHALMIN, PHILLIPE, *The Making of a Sugar Giant: Tate and Lyle 1859–1989* (Chur: Harwood, 1990).

—— 'The Rise of International Commodity Trading Companies in Europe in the Nineteenth Century', in S. Yonekawa and H. Yoshihara (eds.), *Business History of General Trading Companies* (Tokyo: University of Tokyo Press, 1987).

CHANDLER, ALFRED D. Jnr, *Scale and Scope* (Cambridge, Mass.: Harvard University Press, 1990).

—— *Strategy and Structure* (Cambridge, Mass.: MIT Press, 1962).

—— *The Visible Hand* (Cambridge, Mass.: Harvard University Press, 1977).

CHAPMAN, STANLEY, 'British-Based Investment Groups before 1914', *Economic History Review*, 38 (1985), 230–51.

—— 'Investment groups in India and South Africa', *Economic History Review*, 40 (1987), 275–80.

—— *Merchant Enterprise in Britain* (Cambridge: Cambridge University Press, 1992).

—— 'The Commercial Sector', in Mary B. Rose (ed.), *The Lancashire Cotton Industry* (Preston: Lancashire County Books, 1996).

—— *The Rise of Merchant Banking* (London: George Allen & Unwin, 1984).

CHAUDHURI, K. N., *The Trading World of Asia and the English East India Company 1660–1760* (Cambridge: Cambridge University Press, 1978).

CHEONG, W. E., *Mandarins and Merchants* (London: Curzon Press, 1979).

COASE, R. H., 'The Nature of the Firm', *Economica*, 4 (1937), 386–405.

CORLEY, T. A. B., 'Britain's Overseas Investments in 1914 Revisited', *Business History*, 36 (1994), 71–88.

COTTRELL, P. L., *British Overseas Investment in the Nineteenth Century* (London: Macmillan, 1975).

CRISSWELL, COLIN N., *The Taipans: Hong Kong's Merchant Princes* (Hong Kong: Oxford University Press, 1981).

CRONJÉ, S., LING, M., and CRONJÉ, G., *Lonrho: Portrait of a Multinational* (London: Penguin, 1976).

CUNYNGHAM-BROWN, S., *The Traders* (London: Newman Neame, 1970).

DAUNTON, M. J. 'Firm and Family in the City of London in the Nineteenth Century: The Case of F. G. Dalgety', *English Historical Review*, 60/11 (1989), 154–77.

DAVENPORT-HINES, R. P. T., and JONES, GEOFFREY (eds.), *British Business in Asia since 1860* (Cambridge: Cambridge University Press, 1989).

—— 'British Business in Japan Since 1868', in R. P. T. Davenport-Hines and Geoffrey Jones (eds.), *British Business in Asia since 1860.*

DAVIES, PETER, 'Nineteenth-Century Ocean Trade and Transport', in Peter Matthias and John A. Davis (eds.), *The Nature of Industrialisation* (Oxford: Blackwell, 1996).

DAVIES, P. N., *Fyffes and the Banana* (London: Athlone Press, 1990).

—— 'The Impact of the Expatriate Shipping Lines on the Economic Development of British West Africa', *Business History*, 17 (1977), 3–17.

—— *The Trade Makers: Elder Dempster in West Africa 1852–1972* (London: George Allen & Unwin, 1973).

DAVIS, RALPH, *The Industrial Revolution in British Overseas Trade* (Leicester: Leicester University Press, 1979).

DRABBLE, JOHN H., *Malayan Rubber: The Interwar Years* (London: Macmillan, 1991).

—— and DRAKE, P. J., 'The British Agency Houses in Malaysia: Survival in a Changing World', *Journal of Southeast Asian Studies*, 12 (1981), 297–328.

DUGUID, PAUL, and LOPES, TERESA DA SILVA, 'Ambiguous Companies: Institutions and Organisations in the Port Wine Trade, 1814–1854', *Scandinavian Economic History Review*, 47 (1999), 84–102.

—— 'The Company You Keep: The Port Trade in the Declining Years of the Wine Companies, 1812–1840', in *Os Vinhos Licorosos e a História* (Centro de Estudos de História do Atlântico, 1998).

DUNNING, JOHN H., *The Globalisation of Business* (London: Routledge, 1993).

FALKUS, MALCOLM, *The Blue Funnel Legend* (London: Macmillan, 1990).

—— 'Early British Business in Thailand', in R. P. T. Davenport-Hines and Geoffrey Jones (eds.) *British Business in Asia since 1860.*

FEINSTEIN, CHARLES, 'Britain's Overseas Investments in 1913', *Economic History Review*, 43 (1990), 280–95.

FERGUSON, NIALL, *The World's Banker: The History of the House of Rothschild* (London: Weidenfeld & Nicolson, 1998).

FERNÁNDEZ, MANUEL A., 'Merchants and Bankers: British Direct and Portfolio Investment in Chile during the Nineteenth Century', *Ibero-Amerikanisches Archiv* (1983).

FFORDE, J. S., *An International Trade in Managerial Skills* (Oxford: Basil Blackwell, 1957).

FIELDHOUSE, D. K., *Merchant Capital and Economic Decolonization* (Oxford: Clarendon Press, 1994).

—— *Unilever Overseas* (London: Croom Helm, 1978).

GEER, HANS DE, 'Trading Companies in Twentieth-Century Sweden', in Geoffrey Jones (ed.), *The Multinational Traders.*

GERTZEL, CHERYL, 'John Holt: A British Merchant in West Africa in the Age of Imperialism' (Oxford D. Phil., 1959).

GIBBS, ANTONY, & SONS, *Merchants and Bankers 1808–1958* (London: the firm, 1958).

GRAHAM, R., 'A British Industry in Brazil: Rio Flour Mills, 1886–1920', *Business History*, 8 (1966).

GREENBERG, M., *British Trade and the Opening of China 1800–1842* (Cambridge: Cambridge University Press, 1951).

GREENHILL, ROBERT G., 'Investment Group, Free-Standing Company or Multinational? Brazilian Warrant, 1909–52', *Business History*, 37 (1995), 86–111.

—— 'The Brazilian Coffee Trade', in D. C. M. Platt (ed.), *Business Imperialism 1840–1930* (Oxford: Clarendon Press, 1977).

—— 'The Nitrate and Iodine Trades 1880–1914', in D. C. M. Platt (ed.), *Business Imperialism 1840–1930* (Oxford: Clarendon Press, 1977).

—— and MILLER, RORY, 'British Trading Companies in South America after 1914', in Geoffrey Jones (ed.), *The Multinational Traders*.

GRIFFITHS, PERCIVAL, *A History of the Inchcape Group* (London: the firm, 1977).

GROSSE, ROBERT, 'International Technology Transfer in Services', *Journal of International Business Studies*, 27 (1996), 781–800.

GUEX, SÉBASTIEN, 'The Development of Swiss Trading Companies in the Twentieth Century', in Geoffrey Jones (ed.), *The Multinational Traders*.

GUPTA, BISHNUPRIYA, 'Collusion in the Indian Tea Industry in the Great Depression: An Analysis of Panel Data', *Explorations in Economic History*, 34 (1997), 55–73.

—— 'The International Tea Cartel in the Great Depression: The Response of Firms in India and Ceylon', *Department of Economics Discussion Papers, University of St. Andrews* (1997).

GURUSHINA, NATALIA, 'Free-Standing Companies in Tsarist Russia', in Mira Wilkins and Harm Schröter (eds.), *The Free-Standing Companies in the World Economy 1830–1996*.

HARCOURT, FREDA, 'The P&O Company: Flagships of Imperialism', in Sarah Palmer and G. Williams (eds.), *Chartered and Unchartered Waters* (London: National Maritime Museum, 1981).

HARRISONS & CROSFIELD, *One Hundred Years as East India Merchants: Harrisons & Crosfield 1844–1943* (London: the firm, 1944).

HARVEY, CHARLES, and PRESS, JON, 'The City and International Mining, 1870–1914', *Business History*, 32 (1990).

HENNART, JEAN-FRANÇOIS, *A Theory of Multinational Enterprise* (Ann Arbor: University of Michigan Press, 1982).

—— 'The Transactions Cost Theory of the Multinational Enterprise', in Christos N. Pitelis and Roger Sugden (eds.), *The Nature of the Transnational Firm* (London: Routledge, 1991).

—— and KRYDA, GEORGINE M., 'Why do Traders Invest in Manufacturing?', in Geoffrey Jones (ed.), *The Multinational Traders*.

HENRIQUES, ROBERT, *Marcus Samuel* (London: Barrie and Rockliff, 1960).

HERTNER, PETER, and JONES, GEOFFREY (eds.), *Multinationals: Theory and History* (Aldershot: Gower, 1986).

HOLLANDER, STANLEY C., *Multinational Retailing* (East Lansing: Michigan State University, 1970).

HOPKINS, A. G., 'Imperial Business in Africa Part 2: Interpretations', *Journal of African History*, 17 (1976), 267–90.

HUFF, W. G., *The Economic Growth of Singapore* (Cambridge: Cambridge University Press, 1994).

HUI, LIM MAH, *Ownership and Control of the One Hundred Largest Corporations in Malaysia* (Kuala Lumpur: Oxford University Press, 1981).

HUNT, WALLIS, *Heirs of Great Adventure*, vols. i and ii (London: the firm, 1951, 1960).

HYDE, FRANCIS E., *Far Eastern Trade 1860–1914* (London: Adam & Charles Black, 1973).

—— and HARRIS, JOHN R., *Blue Funnel: A History of Alfred Holt and Company of Liverpool from 1865 to 1914* (Liverpool: Liverpool University Press, 1956).

JOHN, A. H., *A Liverpool Merchant House* (London: George Allen & Unwin, 1959).

JONES, CHARLES, *International Business in the Nineteenth Century* (Brighton: Wheatsheaf, 1987).

—— 'Institutional Forms of British Foreign Direct Investment in South America', *Business History*, 39 (1997), 21–41.

JONES, GEOFFREY, *Banking and Empire in Iran* (Cambridge: Cambridge University Press, 1986).

—— *Banking and Oil* (Cambridge: Cambridge University Press, 1987).

—— *British Multinational Banking 1830–1990* (Oxford: Clarendon Press, 1993).

—— 'British Multinationals and British Business since 1850', in Maurice W. Kirby and Mary B. Rose (eds.), *Business Enterprise in Modern Britain from the Eighteenth to the Twentieth Centuries* (London: Routledge, 1994).

—— (ed.), *British Multinationals: Origins, Management and Performance* (Aldershot: Gower, 1986).

—— 'British Overseas Banks as Free-Standing Companies, 1830–1996', in Mira Wilkins and Harm Schröter (eds.), *The Free-Standing Company in the World Economy, 1830–1996*.

—— 'Corporate Governance and British Industry', *Enterprises et histoire*, 21 (1999), 29–43.

—— 'Great Britain: Big Business, Management, and Competitiveness in Twentieth Century Britain', in A. D. Chandler Jnr, Franco Amatori, and Takashi Hikino (eds.), *Big Business and the Wealth of Nations* (Cambridge: Cambridge University Press, 1997).

—— 'Multinational Trading Companies in History and Theory', in Geoffrey Jones (ed.), *The Multinational Traders*.

—— *The Evolution of International Business* (London: Routledge, 1996).

—— (ed.), *The Multinational Traders* (London: Routledge, 1998).

—— and WALE, JUDITH, 'Diversification Strategies of British Trading Companies: Harrisons & Crosfield c.1900–c.1980', *Business History*, 41 (1999), 69–101.

—— —— 'Merchants as Business Groups: British Trading Companies in Asia before 1945', *Business History Review*, 72 (1998), 367–408.

JONES, STEPHANIE, *Merchants of the Raj* (London: Macmillan, 1992).

—— *Trade and Shipping: Lord Inchcape 1852–1932* (Manchester: Manchester University Press, 1989).

—— *Two Centuries of Overseas Trading* (London: Macmillan, 1986).

JONES, S. R. H., and VILLE, S. P., 'Efficient Transactions or Rent-Seeking Monopolists? The Rationale for Early Chartered Trading Companies', *Journal of Economic History*, 56 (1996), 818–915.

KAY, JOHN, *Foundations of Corporate Success* (Oxford: Oxford University Press, 1993).

KENWOOD, A. G., and LOUGHEED, A. L., *The Growth of the International Economy 1820–1990* (London: Routledge, 1992).

KESWICK, M. (ed.), *The Thistle and the Jade* (London: Octopus, 1982).

KING, F. H. H., *The Hongkong Bank in Late Imperial China 1864–1902* (Cambridge: Cambridge University Press, 1987).

KOCK, CARL, and GUILLÉN, MAURO F., 'Strategy and Structure in Developing Countries: Business Groups as an Evolutionary Response to Opportunities for Unrelated Diversification', *Industrial and Corporate Change*, 10/1 (2001), 77–113.

KYNASTON, DAVID, *The City of London*, i: *A World of its Own 1815–1890* (London: Chatto & Windus, 1994).

LANGE, OLE, *Den hvide elefant: H. N. Andersens eventyr og ØK 1852–1914* (Copenhagen: Gyldendal, 1986).

—— 'Denmark in China 1830–65: A Pawn in a British Game', *Scandinavian Economic History Review*, 19 (1971), 71–112.

LANGLOIS, RICHARD N., and ROBERTSON, PAUL L., *Firms, Markets, and Economic Chance* (London: Routledge, 1995).

LE FEVOUR, EDWARD, *Western Enterprise in Late Ch'ing China* (Cambridge, Mass.: Harvard University Press, 1968).

LOKANATHANI, P. S., *Industrial Organisation in India* (London: George Allen & Unwin, 1935).

LONGHURST, HENRY, *The Borneo Story* (London: Newman Neame, 1956).

LYNN, MARTIN, *Commerce and Economic Change in West Africa* (Cambridge: Cambridge University Press, 1997).

—— 'From Sail to Steam: The Impact of the Steamship Services on the British Palm Oil Trade with West Africa, 1850–1890', *Journal of African History*, 30 (1989), 227–45.

MACAULAY, R. H., *History of the Bombay Burmah Trading Corporation Ltd., 1864–1910* (London: Spottiswoode Ballantyne, 1934).

McCRAE, A. G. *Pioneers in Burma*, Occasional Papers in Economic and Social History No. 2, University of Glasgow, 1986.

McMANUS, J. C., 'The Theory of the Multinational Firm', in G. Paquet (ed.), *The Multinational Firm and the Nation State* (Don Mills, Ont.: Collier-Macmillan, 1972).

MASS, WILLIAM, and LAZONICK, WILLIAM, 'The British Cotton Industry and International Competitive Advantage: The State of the Debates', *Business History*, 32 (1990).

MATHEW, WILLIAM M., 'Antony Gibbs & Sons, the Guano Trade and the Peruvian Government, 1842–1861', in D. C. M. Platt (ed.), *Business Imperialism 1840–1930* (Oxford: Clarendon Press, 1977).

—— *The House of Gibbs and the Peruvian Guano Monopoly* (London: Royal Historical Society, 1981).

MARRINER, SHEILA, *Rathbones of Liverpool 1845–73* (Liverpool: Liverpool University Press, 1961).

—— and HYDE, FRANCIS E., *The Senior: John Samuel Swire 1825–1898* (Liverpool: Liverpool University Press, 1967).

MATTHIAS, PETER, and DAVIS, JOHN A. (eds.), *The Nature of Industrialisation* (Oxford: Blackwell, 1996).

MAUDE, W., *Antony Gibbs & Sons Ltd., Merchants and Bankers, 1808–1958* (London: the firm, 1958).

MAYO, JOHN, *British Merchants and Chilean Development 1851–1886* (Boulder, Colo.: Westview, 1987).

MICHIE, RANALD C., *The City of London* (London: Macmillan, 1992).

MILLER, RORY, *Britain and Latin America in the 19th and 20th Centuries* (London: Longman, 1993).

—— 'British Free-Standing Companies on the West Coast of South America', in Mira Wilkins and Harm Schröter (eds.), *The Free-Standing Companies in the World Economy, 1830–1996* (Oxford: Oxford University Press, 1998).

—— 'Small Business in the Peruvian Oil Industry: Lobitos Oilfields Limited before 1934', *Business History Review*, 56 (1982), 400–23.

MINOGLOU, IOANNA PEPELASIS, 'The Greek Merchant House of the Russian Black Sea: A Nineteenth Century Example of a Traders' Coalition', *International Journal of Maritime History*, 10 (1998), 61–104.

—— and LOURI, HELEN, 'Diaspora Entrepreneurial Networks in the Black Sea and Greece, 1870–1914', *Journal of European Economic History*, 26 (1997), 69–104.

MISRA, MARIA, 'Entrepreneurial Decline and the End of Empire' (Oxford D. Phil., 1994).

MONTEITH, KATHLEEN E. A., 'Barclays Bank (DCO) in the West Indies, 1926–1962' (University of Reading Ph.D., 1997).

MORRIS, M. D., 'The Growth of Large-Scale Industry to 1947', in D. Kumar (ed.), *The Cambridge Economic History of India* (Cambridge: Cambridge University Press, 1983).

MUIR, AUGUSTUS, *Blyth, Greene, Jourdain & Co. Ltd. 1810–1960* (London: the firm, 1961).

MUNRO, J. FORBES, 'British Rubber Companies in East Africa before the First World War', *Journal of African History*, 24 (1983), 369–79.

—— 'From Regional Trade to Global Shipping: Mackinnon Mackenzie & Co. within the Mackinnon Enterprise Network', in Geoffrey Jones (ed.), *The Multinational Traders*.

—— 'Scottish Overseas Enterprise and the Lure of London: The Mackinnon Shipping Group, 1847–1893', *Scottish Economic and Social History*, 8 (1988), 73–87.

—— '"The Gilt of Illusion": The Mackinnon Group's Entry into Queensland Shipping, 1880–1895', *International Journal of Maritime History*, 3 (1991), 1–37.

MYERS, DAVID F. C., 'The Evolution of the Peruvian Oil Business and its Place in the International Petroleum Industry, 1880–1950' (University of Oxford D.Phil., 1993).

MYNORS, SIR HUMPHREY BASKERVILLE, *Thomas Sivewright Catto* (Edinburgh: T. & A. Constable, 1962).

NAPIER, CHRISTOPHER J., 'Allies or Subsidiaries? Inter-Company Relations in the P&O Group, 1914–39', *Business History*, 39 (1997).

NELSON, RICHARD R., 'Why do firms differ, and how does it matter?', *Strategic Management Journal*, 14 (1991), 61–74.

NEWBURY, COLIN, 'Trade and Technology in West Africa: The Case of the Niger Company, 1900–1920', *Journal of African History*, 19 (1978).

NICHOLAS, S., 'Agency Contracts, Institutional Modes, and the Transition to Foreign Direct Investment by British Manufacturing Multinationals before 1939', *Journal of Economic History*, 43 (1983), 675–86.

—— 'British Multinational Investment before 1939', *Journal of European Economic History*, 11 (1982), 605–30.

NICKALLS, G. (ed.), *Great Enterprise: A History of Harrisons & Crosfield* (London: the firm, 1990).

NOTTINGHAM, LUCIE, *Rathbone Brothers: From Merchant to Banker 1742–1992* (London: the firm, 1992).

ORBELL, JOHN, *Baring Brothers & Co Limited: A History to 1939* (London: the firm, 1985).

OSTERHAMMEL, JÜRGEN, 'British Business in China, 1860s–1950s', in R. P. T. Davenport-Hines and Geoffrey Jones (eds.), *British Business in Asia since 1860*.

PEARSON, SCOTT R., 'The Economic Imperialism of the Royal Niger Company', *Food Research Institute Studies in Agricultural Economics, Trade, and Development*, 10/1 (1971), 69–88.

PEDLER, FREDERICK, *The Lion and the Unicorn in Africa* (London: Heinemann, 1974).

PENROSE, EDITH T., *The Theory of the Growth of the Firm* (Oxford: Oxford University Press, 1959).

PERRY, ANNE C., *The Evolution of U.S. Trade Intermediaries* (Westport, Conn.: Quorum Books, 1992).

PLATT, D. C. M., *Latin America and British Trade 1806–1914* (London: Adam & Charles Black, 1972).

POINTON, A. C., *Wallace Brothers* (Oxford: the firm, 1974).

POLLARD, SIDNEY, 'Capital Exports, 1870–1914: Harmful or Beneficial?', *Economic History Review*, 38 (1985), 489–514.

PRAHALAD, C. K., and HAMEL, GARY, 'The Core Competence of the Corporation', *Harvard Business Review*, 66 (1990), 79–91.

PRAKASH, O. M., *European Commercial Enterprise in Pre-Colonial India* (Cambridge: Cambridge University Press, 1998).

PUTHUCHEARY, J. J., *Ownership and Control in the Malayan Economy* (Singapore: Eastern Universities Press, 1960).

RAY, RAJAT K., *Industrialisation in India* (Delhi: Oxford University Press, 1979).

REBER, VERA BLINN, *British Mercantile Houses in Buenos Aires 1810–1880* (Cambridge, Mass.: Cambridge University Press, 1979).

ROBERTS, RICHARD, *Schroders* (London: Macmillan, 1992).

ROEHL, THOMAS, 'A Transactions Cost Approach to International Trading Structures: The Case of the Japanese General Trading Companies', *Hitotsubashi Journal of Economics*, 24 (1983), 119–35.

ROSE, MARY B., *Firms, Networks and Business Values: The British and American Cotton Industries since 1750* (Cambridge: Cambridge University Press, forthcoming).

—— (ed.), *International Competition and Strategic Response in the Textiles Industry Since 1870* (London: Frank Cass, 1991).

—— 'The Family Firm in British Business, 1780–1914', in M. W. Kirby and Mary B. Rose (eds.), *Business Enterprise in Modern Britain from the Eighteenth to the Twentieth Centuries* (London: Routledge, 1994).

SAHAM, JUNID, *British Industrial Development in Malaysia, 1963–71* (Kuala Lumpur: Oxford University Press, 1980).

SARKAR, GUITAM, *The World Tea Economy* (Delhi: Oxford University Press, 1972).

SLUYTERMAN, KEETIE E., 'Dutch Multinational Trading Companies in the Twentieth Century', in Geoffrey Jones (ed.), *The Multinational Traders*.

STAHL, KATHLEEN M., *The Metropolitan Organisation of British Colonial Trade* (London: Faber & Faber, 1951).

STEWART, ROSS E., 'Scottish Company Accounting, 1870–1920: Selected Case Studies of Accounting in its Historical Context' (University of Glasgow Ph.D., 1986).

STONE, I., 'British Direct and Portfolio Investment in Latin America before 1914', *Journal of Economic History*, 37 (1977), 690–722.

STOPFORD, J. M. 'The Origins of British-Based Multinational Manufacturing Enterprises', *Business History Review*, 48 (1974), 303–45.

SUGIYAMA, S., 'A British Trading Firm in the Far East: John Swire & Sons, 1867–1914', in S. Yonekawa and H. Yoshihara (eds.), *Business History of General Trading Companies* (Tokyo: University of Tokyo Press, 1987).

Swire Group, *180 Years* (Hong Kong: the firm, 1996).

TATE, D. J. M., *The RGA History of the Plantation Industry in the Malay Peninsula* (Kuala Lumpur: Oxford University Press, 1996).

THOMPSTONE, STUART, 'British Merchant Houses in Russia before 1914', in L. Edmondson and P. Waldron (eds.), *Economy and Society in Russia and the Soviet Union, 1860–1930* (London: Macmillan, 1992).

TIGNOR, ROBERT L., *Capitalism and Nationalism at the end of the Empire* (Princeton: Princeton University Press, 1998).

TOMLINSON, B. R., 'British Business in India, 1860–1970', in R. P. T. Davenport-Hines and Geoffrey Jones (eds.), *British Business in Asia since 1860*.

—— 'Colonial Firms and the Decline of Colonialism in Eastern India 1914–1947', *Modern Asian Studies*, 15 (1981), 455–86.

TOWNEND, SIR HARRY, *A History of Shaw Wallace & Co. and Shaw Wallace & Co. Ltd.* (Calcutta: the firm, 1965).

TURRELL, ROBERT, and VAN HELTEN, JEAN JACQUES, 'The Investment Group: The Missing Link in British Overseas Expansion before 1914', *Economic History Review*, 40 (1987), 267–74.

TYSON, GEOFFREY, *Managing Agency: A System of Business Organisation* (Calcutta: Houghty Printing Co., *c*.1960).

UNITED NATIONS, *World Investment Report: Transnational Corporations, Employment and the Workplace* (New York: UNCTC, 1994).

VAN HELTEN, JEAN-Jacques, and JONES, GEOFFREY, 'British Business in Malaysia and Singapore Since the 1870s', in R. P. T. Davenport-Hines and Geoffrey Jones (eds.), *British Business in Asia since 1860*.

VAUGHAN-THOMAS, WYNFORD, *Dalgety: The Romance of a Business* (London: Henry Melland, 1984).

VILLE, SIMON, *The Rural Entrepreneurs* (Cambridge: Cambridge University Press, 2000).

WARDE, EDMUND, *The House of Dodwell: A Century of Achievement 1858–1958* (London: the firm, 1958).

WERNERFELT, BIRGER, 'A Resource-Based View of the Firm', *Strategic Management Journal*, 5 (1984), 171–80.

WHITE, NICHOLAS, J., *Business, Government and the End of Empire* (Kuala Lumpur: Oxford University Press, 1996).

WICKIZER, V. D., *Coffee, Tea and Cocoa* (Stanford, Calif.: Stanford University Press, 1951).

WILKINS, MIRA, 'Defining a Firm: History and Theory', in Peter Hertner and Geoffrey Jones (eds.), *Multinationals: Theory and History*.

—— 'The Free-Standing Company, 1870–1914: An Important Type of British Foreign Direct Investment', *Economic History Review*, 41 (1988), 259–85.

—— 'The Free-Standing Company Revisited', in Mira Wilkins and Harm Schröter (eds.), *The Free-Standing Company in the World Economy, 1830–1996.*

—— *The History of Foreign Investment in the United States to 1914* (Cambridge, Mass.: Harvard University Press, 1989).

—— 'The Significance of the Concept and a Future Agenda', in Mira Wilkins and Harm Schröter (eds.), *The Free-Standing Company in the World Economy, 1830–1996.*

—— and SCHRÖTER, HARM (eds.), *The Free-Standing Company in the World Economy, 1830–1996* (Oxford: Oxford University Press, 1998).

WILLIAMS, D. M., 'Liverpool Merchants and the Cotton Trade 1820–1850', in J. R. Harris (ed.), *Liverpool and Merseyside* (London: Macmillan, 1992).

WILLIAMSON, OLIVER, *Markets and Hierarchies* (New York: Free Press, 1975).

—— 'The Modern Corporation: Origins, Evolution, Attributes', *Journal of Economic Literature*, 19 (1981).

—— *The Economic Institutions of Capitalism* (New York: Free Press, 1985).

WILSON, CHARLES, *The History of Unilever*, vol. i (London: Cassell, 1954).

—— *Unilever 1945–1965* (London: Cassell, 1968).

YOSHINO, M. Y., and THOMAS, B. L., *The Invisible Link: Japan's Sogo Shosha and the Organisation of Trade* (Cambridge, Mass.: MIT Press, 1986).

YOUNG, GAVIN, *Beyond Lion Rock* (London: Hutchinson, 1988).

YULE, ANDREW & CO., *Andrew Yule & Co. Ltd. 1863–1963* (Edinburgh: T. & A. Constable, 1963).

ZHONGLI, ZHANG, ZENGNIAN, CHEN, and XINRONG, YAO, *The Swire Group in Old China* (Shanghai: Shanghai People's Publishing House, 1995).

Index

Printed in the United Kingdom
by Lightning Source UK Ltd.
104991UKS00002B/8